CW00916920

Companion to Briti
Road Haulage History

Companion to British Road Haulage History

Edited by

John Armstrong
John M Aldridge
Grahame Boyes
Gordon Mustoe
Richard A Storey

Science Museum

Published 2003 by NMSI Trading Ltd,
Science Museum, Exhibition Road, London SW7 2DD

All rights reserved. No part of this publication may be reproduced, stored in a retrieval system, or transmitted in any form or by any means, electronic, mechanical, photocopying or otherwise, without prior permission in writing from the publisher.

British Library Cataloguing-in-Publication Data
A catalogue record for this publication is available from the British Library

Printed in England by the Cromwell Press

Cover and illustrated sections designed by Jerry Fowler

© 2003 Board of Trustees of the Science Museum

ISBN 1 900747 46 4

Website: http://www.nmsi.ac.uk

Contents

Tables and graphs

/

Contributors

JMA	John M Aldridge
JA	Professor John Armstrong
SB	Sarah Bailey
MB	Mike Baines
JB	John Barraclough
RFdeB	Roger de Boer
GAB	Grahame Boyes
NC	Nigel Cook
RC	Roger Cragg
PJD	Peter J Davies
MD	Maurice Doggett
JF	Judy Faraday
AJH	Alan J Halfpenny
JH	Professor John Hibbs OBE
DMH	David M Holding
DJJ	Professor David J Jeremy
SJ	Stephen Joseph
RWK	Roger W Kidner
GK	Gordon Knowles
RL	Roy Larkin
JL	Jeff Lemon
DL	David Lowe
GMcB	Glen McBirnie
AM	Dr Andrew Millward
AMo	Alan Moss
GM	Gordon Mustoe
AGN	Tony Newman
DJO	Professor Derek Oddy
ADO	A David Owen
CRP	Colin R Parrott
JP	John Pearson
ARP	Ron Phillips
TP	the late Tony Pomeroy
CS	Chris Salaman
PLS	Philip Scowcroft
JS	Professor John Sheail
PS	Dr Paul Smith
RAS	Richard A Storey
EWPT	Edward Paget-Tomlinson
GT	Garry Turvey CBE
BV	Brian Veale
NW	Nigel Watson
SW	Steve Wimbush
IAY	Ian Yearsley

Preface

Origins

This volume has been compiled under the general guidance and encouragement of the Roads & Road Transport History Association (R&RTHA), a not-for-profit body set up in 1992 (as the Roads & Road Transport History Conference; its name changed in 2002) to promote the study of road transport history in all its manifestations. The book has its origins back in June 1996 at a colloquium held in Chorley, Lancashire, when gaps in the literature were discussed. There seemed to be no text or monograph which analysed the history of goods haulage by motor lorry in the twentieth century.

Accordingly, at its autumn 1996 meeting, the R&RTHC set up a working party to investigate the possibility of putting together a text book or monograph on the history of road haulage. The members of the working party were the compilers of this volume, plus Arthur Ingram for a few meetings, until pressure of work caused him to drop out. Given the dearth of existing material, and being aware of the problems of writing a comprehensive history of road haulage with so little foundation, the working party decided against building a cathedral. Instead we thought we could put together some of the bricks from which a latter-day cathedral might rise. This would also allow us to draw on the wide range of expertise within and outside the R&RTHC where many individuals had in-depth knowledge on a limited range of topics. Our decision to put together a Companion, rather than a narrative account, was inspired by our knowledge of, and in several cases contributions to, the highly successful *Oxford Companion to British Railway History* edited by the late Jack Simmons and Gordon Biddle. We are grateful to the two editors for their inspired idea. Their volume has been our constant touchstone. We trust they would agree that imitation is a very sincere form of flattery.

Coverage

The central focus of this volume is the carriage of goods by motor vehicle in the twentieth century. Although we have occasionally strayed into the nineteenth century it is only to trace the roots of an essentially twentieth century phenomenon. Since all cut-off dates are arbitrary, we have chosen 2000 as at least the last year of the century and apposite for this topic. Thus developments which occurred after 2000 have not been detailed, though we have used post-2000 sources to illuminate twentieth century issues. We have mentioned non-motor delivery methods, such as horse-drawn transport, bicycles and hand-carts, but only to point up the transition from horse to motor and to illustrate those niches where motor vehicles were slow to get a foothold. We have emphasised movement of goods by road and ignored totally passenger traffic. We have also not tried to cover other motor conveyances for people, such as ambulances and hearses. Nor have we concerned ourselves in detail with motor transport which did not carry goods such as local authority vehicles like dustcarts, road sweepers and tower wagons.

We have concentrated on goods traffic and the operators that carried out this work rather more than the companies which built the lorries. That said, there was no way in which we could have an entry on all the firms that ever carried out road haulage activities. At various dates when we get a snapshot of the industry, we know the number of road haulage firms was in the thousands – perhaps in excess of 20,000 around 1939 and about the same number in 1947, of which some 3600 were acquired by the British Transport Commission for British Road Services – and of course many of these left no records and any entry would have been brief in the extreme. Although we have entries on haulage firms these are only a fraction of those that ever existed. The basis of our choice may need some explaining. Firstly we included those for which there was plenty of information such as a book already written about them, a living descendant with a good memory, records and artefacts, or articles in one of the commercial vehicle magazines. We decided we must include all those firms currently in the road haulage industry which are quoted on the stock exchange, especially as these had often grown in part by acquisition of others. Otherwise we have tried to provide a geographical spread of haulage firms, a range of specialist traffics and a representative range of company sizes. In one regard at least we are aware of a bias. There have always been a large number of small-scale firms operating anything between one and a handful of lorries. These are under-represented in our sample because they were the least likely to leave any records.

Corrections

Inevitably in a work of this sort errors, mistakes and omissions occur. We accept responsibility and would be pleased to have details in the hope that we may be able to correct them if there is ever a second or revised edition.

Lorry weights

The ways in which lorry weights were expressed has changed over time. In the text we have used the convention which was in force at the time we are discussing in the entry. We summarise, below, a rather complex subject. Although there was much confusion, before 1920 lorries were largely described in terms of the weight of cargo they were capable of carrying, as declared by the manufacturer. There was often an element of pious hope here more than actuality. Many lorries were overloaded compared to the manufacturer's recommendation, while others were not capable of carrying the amount claimed. From the 1920s to the 1960s the convention was for lorries to be classified by their unladen weight, that is their tare weight, being that of the lorry without the cargo. From the 1960s the convention has been to cite the gross vehicle weight, that is the weight of the lorry plus the weight of the cargo it is carrying. This was subject to legal maxima which increased over time.

Lorry weights when cited for military vehicles do not equate to those of civilian vehicles. The army consistently under-rated what an individual lorry could carry because they wished to specify the maximum load in the worst conditions, such as cross-country, uphill on churned-up fields. So army lorry capacities are usually about half of the same lorry's peace-time load.

Cross-references

We have used two forms of cross-reference in this volume. Within the text after some words '(q.v.)' will be seen. This means there is an entry on that topic under that heading in the volume. It also means that the entry referred to, in our opinion, adds something to the topic being discussed in the original entry. The exceptions to this q.v. rule are two-fold. British commercial vehicle manufacturers, where they appear in the text, have no q.v., because we have entries on all major British manufacturers and virtually all of those producing only small numbers of units. Thus when readers see the name of a commercial vehicle builder in the text, they can assume there is an entry on that business. The other exception is for widely used terms like 'nationalisation', 'de-nationalisation', and 'BRS'. They are used so often in the text that cross-referencing them would break up the flow.

The other form of cross-reference we have used is at the end of some entries where we have appended "see also ....." This signifies that the topic being discussed is related to another entry in this volume in some way, for example, where an entry can be contextualised by another entry.

Sources

After most entries we have listed some relevant sources. They comprise the articles used to compile the entry and also material that could be followed up by the reader wishing to go into greater depth. For those books that appear in the bibliography we have used a short form of citation at the end of the entry, namely the author's surname, the date of publication, and page numbers, where relevant. This allows the reader to ascertain the full publication details from the Bibliography. Where the source is an article in a journal or magazine and that periodical is frequently cited we have abbreviated the title to save space. A full listing is given on page 13. In some cases entries are heavily based on the personal experience and knowledge of the author who worked (or is still working) in the industry. We have not referenced this, which explains why some entries have no sources cited. Some volumes are so fundamental to a study of this industry that they would have been cited after almost every entry. We thought this might be tedious for the reader. Instead we are happy to acknowledge here the centrality of the following works which have <u>not</u> been cited each time they are relevant.

Peter J Davies, *The World Encyclopedia of Trucks* (Lorenz, 2000), which covers virtually all lorry and van manufacturers mentioned in this volume. Nick Georgano, *The Complete Encyclopedia of Commercial Vehicles* (Motorbooks, 1979) which covers similar ground to Davies but at an earlier date and which has been used for almost every chassis entry in this volume. Thomas Gibson, *Road Haulage by Motor in Britain* (Ashgate, 2001) which deals in detail with the main issues, trends and developments in the industry up to 1939.

Acknowledgements

As with any such long-term, multi-author enterprise we have drawn on help and advice from an enormously wide range of sources. Here we can acknowledge only the most outstanding. Firstly we are intellectually indebted to those academics who pioneered study of the road haulage industry, particularly Theo Barker, Bill Reader and Gerard Turnbull. Then there are the aficionados and professional writers of road haulage who have written books and articles for the enthusiast market, such as Bill Aldridge, Nick Baldwin, Robert Coates, Peter Davies, Graham Edge, Nick Georgano, Arthur Ingram, Pat Kennett, Denis Miller, S W Stevens-Stratten, Alan Townsin, Bob Tuck, Mike Wells, R A Whitehead and Mike Worthington-Williams. Special thanks are due to Nick Baldwin, who read through the typescript and made many helpful suggestions as well as offering much help with illustrations, and to Bob Rust who also ploughed through the whole draft and much improved it. More prosaically but no less essential were those who gave us meeting places and word processing expertise. In the former category, the Institute of Historical Research in London, and the Modern Records Centre at the University of Warwick provided venues, as did the café in Coventry bus station, the last at unearthly hours on Saturday mornings, and one of our members' family home in Kenilworth High Street. For help with illustrations we are grateful to Barry Collins at the Museum of British Road Transport at Coventry, John Edsor, Colin Parrott, the Words & Machines Collection, Ian Carter at the Science Museum Library. Ela Ginalska and Lawrence Ahlmeyer chivvied and encouraged in equal parts. For the word processing we are indebted to Ms Giuliana Taborelli and her team at Thames Valley University, London, and for photocopying to Patrick Flannery of the same institution. Their patience, speed and accuracy made our job so much easier. Finally we wish to thank our families for their support, forbearance and encouragement.

Abbreviations used in the text

AA	Automobile Association
am	ante meridian (before noon)
bhp	brake horse power
BP	British Petroleum
BRS	British Road Services
c.	about
ch.	chapter
cm	centimetres
cu.	cubic
cwt	hundredweight (approx. 50 kilos)
EC	European Community
EEC	European Economic Community
ft	foot/feet (approx. 30 cm)
GLC	Greater London Council
GWR	Great Western Railway
hp	horse power
IAE	Institution of Automobile Engineers
in.	inches (approx. 2.5 cm)
ISO	International Standards Organisation
kg	kilogram(s)
km	kilometre(s)
LMSR	London Midland & Scottish Railway
LNER	London & North Eastern Railway
LNWR	London & North Western Railway
LSWR	London & South Western Railway
m	metres
MoD	Ministry of Defence
MoT	Ministry of Transport
mm	millimetres
mpg	miles per gallon
mph	miles per hour
NATO	North Atlantic Treaty Organisation
NFC	National Freight Corporation (later Consortium)
nhp	net horse power
ohv	overhead valve
p (pp)	page(s)
pm	post meridian (afternoon)
q.v.	*quod vide* (which see)
RAC	Royal Automobile Club
RFC	Royal Flying Corps
rpm	revolutions per minute
SMMT	Society of Motor Manufacturers & Traders
SR	Southern Railway
T&GWU	Transport & General Workers Union
UN	United Nations
WD	War Department

Abbreviations used in source references

CECV	G N Georgano, *The Complete Encyclopedia of Commercial Vehicles* (Osceola, Wis: Motorbooks, 1979)
CM	*Commercial Motor*
CVC	*Classic and Vintage Commercials*
CVRTC News	*Commercial Vehicle and Road Transport Club News*
DBB	David J Jeremy (ed.), *Dictionary of Business Biography*, vols. 1 to 5 (London: Butterworths, 1984–6)
DNB	*Dictionary of National Biography*
IDCH	Various editors, *The International Directory of Company Histories*, vols. 1 to 42 (St James Press, 1991–)
JTH	*The Journal of Transport History*
ModT	*Modern Transport*
MT	*Motor Traction*, later *Motor Transport*
OCBRH	Jack Simmons and Gordon Biddle (eds), *Oxford Companion to British Railway History* (Oxford: Oxford University Press, 1997)
OED	*Oxford English Dictionary*
OM	*Old Motor*
PRO	Public Record Office, Kew. The records referred to are in classes RAIL (railway company records prior to the 1948 nationalisation), AN (post-nationalisation records of the British Transport Commission and the British Railways Board) and MT (Ministry of Transport records)
R&RTHA	Roads & Road Transport History Association
VCV	*Vintage Commercial Vehicles*
VCVM	*Vintage Commercial Vehicle Magazine*
VRS	*Vintage Roadscene*
WWW	*Who Was Who* 1897–1980, 7 Vols (Adam & Charles Black, 1920–1981)

Introduction

All of the volumes mentioned here are included in the Bibliography which follows the entries and where full details can be found.

That road haulage in the twentieth century became increasingly crucial to normal economic life is undeniable. In 1918 there may have been about 40,000 goods motor vehicles registered. By 1938 this had risen to 500,000. This growth continued after the Second World War and by 1950 about 840,000 goods vehicles were registered, rising to 1.5 million in 1965, 1.7 million in 1979 and 2.6 million in 1995.[1] At the same time as numbers grew so did the maximum capacity of the lorry so that the quantity of goods being moved rose much more steeply than the simple numbers of lorries. With the improvements in road networks, such as bypasses, arterial roads and motorways, and advances in technology, speeds rose and turnaround times fell, so increasing the amount of work performed in any given period of time. At the beginning of the twenty first century road haulage is an integral part of any country's economy.

Despite the centrality of road haulage in sustaining modern life, its rise and role have been poorly served by academic historians. This was especially true when the working party began its deliberations in 1996. Since then a number of relevant publications have appeared. There were available in 1996 a quartet of excellent books on transport history. (Dyos and Aldcroft, 1969; Barker and Savage, 1974; Bagwell, 1974; and Aldcroft 1975). Three of them had a wide time span, at least from the early-eighteenth century, and thus could only devote at best a chapter or two on road transport in the twentieth century. There was much more emphasis on the railways than on road transport, perhaps because there had been much greater detailed research on and a large enthusiast following for the railway network than on road transport. Also those pages devoted to motor transport had to cover more than merely goods traffic. There was the rise of the private motor car, the growth of motor bus routes and the evolution of long-distance coach travel, and these attracted much more attention than did the lorry and van. Another drawback of these texts was that some of them were looking rather dated by 1996. Dyos and Aldcroft only produced one edition, in 1969, and the Pelican edition of 1974 contained no major revisions. Barker's revision of Savage was published in 1974 and there were no later editions. Bagwell's book was the most recent, as he brought out a second edition in 1988, which brought the story more closely up-to-date, but did not revise the earlier chapters. The fourth of these studies of transport history, that by Aldcroft on his own, was also looking rather dated, but, as it claimed to cover the period only since 1914, had the potential for greater depth of analysis of road haulage. Thus there was available a number of brief overviews, but no in-depth, definitive studies of motorised road haulage in the twentieth century.

There were some books on the history of road haulage available in 1996, but the sole academic one was brief and the others, though commendable, were not scholarly. The earliest needing note was Robert Allan's *Royal Road* published in 1946. It was a good attempt at a history of the industry but is frustrating to the scholar as it has no bibliography, index or list of sources, so it is difficult to follow up some of the incidents. Also the book had an objective, namely to demonstrate the value of private enterprise and the foolishness of nationalisation, and to press the need for significant improvements in the road network, including motorway construction. By virtue of its early date of publication, though a pioneer, it could only cover the first half of the century. The volume by Seth-Smith had an index and a select bibiography, so it was easier to follow up particular points. It was sponsored by Foden, so might have a bias in that direction, but endeavoured to put the firm in the context of the industry, and the industry in its wider economic and social setting. It was an honest attempt by a non-specialist and largely successful. Because of its date of publication it left the last quarter of the century uncovered.

Dunbar's volume was even more restrictive in its coverage, only dealing with the twenty years between the two world wars. It was well illustrated, had a good index and useful glossary of terms used in the trade. Its main drawback was the briefness of the period covered. For that twenty years it was informative, clear and contained good insights from someone who had been deeply involved in the industry, as a journalist and in the express parcels business.

The most recent, and also the most authoritative, book on road transport was that by Barker and Gerhold.[2] It was, however, a thin book, less than 90 pages of text, and covered three centuries and all forms of road transport, goods and passenger, so that the amount devoted to motorised goods traffic was quite brief, about 14 pages. It is a masterly summary of the main trends in the period, but there is little detail and at many points one wants examples and amplification. It is among the best treatments available, but in no way a full story.

In addition to the books on road transport in general there were a number of case studies of individual firms available in 1996. Some were in the business history mould, others were company histories. There were a few company histories, looking rather old-fashioned by the later standards of business history, and often with no specific author. The volumes on McNamara of 1937 and Hay's Wharf of 1947 are good examples. They are hagiographic, anecdotal, and lack analysis, but give a general and rather uncritical picture of the growth of the firm. Obviously, one major weakness is that they cover less than half of the century, for example McNamara was nationalised in 1948 as part of BRS and ceased to have a separate existence.

There were three modern analytical business histories on transport companies available in 1996. The oldest was by one of the founders of business history as an academic discipline, Bill Reader. Having helped Charles Wilson write the pioneering volumes on the history of Unilever, Bill then wrote the history of Unilever's transport subsidiary, SPD, standing for Speedy Prompt Delivery. It has all the strengths of that school of history – it is good on strategic direction, the directors and top level personnel, and marketing policy – and the weaknesses – little on the labour force, thin on the financial side and rather uncritical. The second scholarly treatment was that by Gerard Turnbull on Pickfords. It was very strong on the early history of the firm in the horse-drawn road and canal era. This is not surprising given that Turnbull was known for his pioneering work on horse-drawn road transport in the early modern period. The book is also good on Pickfords' complex relationship with the railways but when it comes to the twentieth century there is less detail, especially of the motor transport activities, and more concentration upon the internal structures and external relationships. It is an excellent business history but not so strong on motor traffic. The third business history available in 1996 was that by Theo Barker on Jempsons of Rye. This was ebullient and upbeat, well illustrated and put the story of the individual firm in its wider context. It was also a thin volume, no doubt reflecting the paucity of sources, and in many places the reader wishes for more detail or coverage of certain aspects. The book was an excellent vignette, but not a full picture. There was another business history available, this time of a carting firm, doing mostly short-distance work. This was Edward Paget-Tomlinson's study of Wordies. The author was related to the family and it was a labour of love, as is shown by the beautiful presentation, numerous illustrations, many of them drawings made by the author. Although not an academic himself, this volume combines a scholarly text with the excellent illustrations, though there is more space and sympathy devoted to the horse than the motor lorry.

There were also two biographies available in 1996 which shed light on the road haulage industry. One was the autobiography of Sir Peter Thompson, who made a career in transport management, rising via SPD to become chief executive of NFC. He took the company from being a nationalised corporation into privatisation, but a company wholly owned by the workers and pensioners. Inevitably, most of the book dealt with the intricate negotiations needed to achieve the consortium, and as this was one of the earliest privatisations many of the problems encountered were novel and needed innovatory solutions. There were insights into the transport business but they are incidental to the main story of the privatisation of NFC. The other relevant biography is that of Lord Hanson.

This deals with both the man and the eponymous firm and is written by a pair of financial journalists. As such it concentrates on outlining and explaining the rise of the business from its earliest days as a removers and furniture warehouse to one of the largest UK multinationals. The transport business, however, only occupies one of the eleven chapters and the authors concentrate on the rise of the firm in the nineteenth century and the traumatic fire of 1919. There is a little on the complex relationship between the Hanson and Holdsworth families and firms but only at a superficial level.

Of course there were many other books on lorry transport, of which the predominant type was highly illustrated, with pictures taking precedence over the text and concentrating on the vehicles rather than the traffic.[3] These were aimed at the enthusiast for the marque or the mode of transport and helped them to distinguish between model types and manufacturers, and were strong on technical peculiarities and innovations but they rarely explained for what sort of good or traffic the particular lorry was used. Some were poorly written and produced but most were informative given their self-imposed limitations. In addition to the enthusiast works on lorries in general, there was available in 1996 a host of volumes on one particular make.[4] Many aficionados feel particular affinity for a particular marque, such as Scammell, and these one-marque people were well catered for by a range of histories on individual manufacturers. These were usually lavishly illustrated, dealt with mergers and takeovers, were strong on technical changes embodied in the vehicles and the development of engine types. They were, however, not always good on the social and economic changes which led to the alterations in lorry size or type, or the consequences of these developments, and of course they tended to see developments of the one make in isolation and not the more integrated transport picture.

Another rich vein of information on road haulage was from the memoirs or reminiscences written by those who had had a career in the industry, either on the management or, later, the driving side. This tradition started early with Walter Gammons' book pioneering in this field, and others followed such as Rees Jeffreys and later Nancollis, Bridges, Sanders and Wynn. These tended not to be self-critical and in retrospect nearly all decisions were correct, and luck or being in the right place at the right time were never elements. Another complication is knowing how accurate are their memories, often over long periods of time and how far the original incidents have grown in the telling. Additionally there is the problem of how representative are those few who did put their memories to paper. Can we generalise from their experience or were they atypical? We know they were unusual in actually having their reminiscences published, but have to assume they are typical until the contrary is demonstrated. Similarly, although we can check their facts against other sources, we have to assume only a low level of embroidery and reasonable accuracy. The same applies to the growing numbers of lorry driver reminiscences (Murphy, 1963; Downs 1983; McTaggart 1985, 1986 and 1989; Coster, 1995; Farnsworth 1996). They are often more colourful than the managers — though Walker's is the exception there, containing details of the sharp practices and frankly illegal activities he felt he had to indulge in, in order to build up his firm — and stress the culture, informal habits and short cuts carried out by the drivers. They demonstrate very clearly how hard a life it was, with physical exertion, exposure to all weathers, dirt, danger, long hours, and poor overnight accommodation. Their reflections certainly counterpoint some of the more managerial ideas and shed light on the actual practices as distinct from how it was claimed to be done.

Having briefly surveyed the literature available in 1996, the conclusion was drawn that there was a dearth of coverage of the history of motor road vehicles when it came to goods transport. The vehicles themselves were well served but the hauliers and the traffics were largely ignored. There were some exceptions. Brewery traffic was quite well covered by Ingram and by Coates. A useful series of brief histories of some hauliers were published from the late 1980s to the early 1990s. These broadened out the coverage of individual firms but still left significant gaps.

The working party having decided by about 1998 that there was a gap in the coverage, inevitably a number of volumes appeared between then and the completion of this volume. On the transport history front a new appearance was Bagwell and Lyth which covered all modes and a long period. It devotes a chapter to motor transport but relatively little of it to goods transport by motor. There are some other references to the impact of the lorry but it is by no means an extensive treatment. A major step in filling the literature gap was the appearance of Gibson's book. It only covers the first forty years, up to the Second World War, which means less than half of the total period, and it is not very well contextualised into the existing secondary literature, but it is well written, draws extensively on primary sources, especially the *Commercial Motor*, and narrates the most important developments very cogently. It is a significant step forward.

There has been a plethora of histories of individual haulage firms since 1996. Although variable in quality, they add greatly to our stock of case studies of businesses in the industry. They range from the very large and well known firms which are still active today, includinge Christian Salvesen (Watson, 1996), Eddie Stobart (H Davies, 2001) to the less well known, such as Bassetts of Tittensor (Phillips and Baron, 1997). Some were of firms now deceased, such as Fisher Renwick (Mustoe, 1997) and BRS (Ingram and Mustoe, 1999). Both of these volumes were full of detail of working practices, the vehicles employed and, most importantly, the routes served and goods carried. They in no way fill the need for an overarching history of motor road haulage, but they do widen the evidential base on which such a work must rest. There have also been a few additions to the memoirs (Moye, 1996; Grieves, 1997), and a useful volume on the developments in petroleum transport by Eaton but otherwise the same gap that was identified in 1996 still exists in this century. There is a crying need for a monograph dealing with the whole topic of motor goods traffic for the last 100-odd years. This current volume in no way fills that gap, but we hope it will indicate some of the relevant literature, outline some of the debates and discussions, and suggest some of the trends. If it were to stimulate others to take up this challenge, we should be delighted.

REFERENCES

[1]   Barker and Gerhold (1993), pp. 85 and 92; Dept of Transport, *Transport Statistics Great Britain* HMSO, (1995), pp.53 and 55.

[2]   Barker and Gerhold (1993), pp.81-8 and 92-5.

[3]   Cornwell (1960); Geary (1979); Georgano (1979); Klapper (1973); Ingram (1975 and 1990); Stevens-Stratten (1978, 1988, 1991 and 1992).

[4]   Baldwin (1986, 1987, 1988, 1989, 1990); Davies (1994); Edge (1994 and 1998); Geary (1976, 1991 and 1993); Kennett (1978 and 1978 to 1983).

A

A licence, see LICENSING

Aberdeen Shore Porters' Society, see SHORE
PORTERS' SOCIETY

Abnormal or indivisible loads (Figures 1,
165 and 166) are single items which are very
heavy, very long, very wide or any
combination of these attributes. The term was
only applied when these were first transported
mechanically using steam traction. Probably
the first such load which was well documented
was the movement of Big Ben from
Whitechapel to Westminster pulled by sixteen
horses. There have been changes in methods
of moving such loads and in the regulations
affecting the operation and type of vehicles
used. Road locomotives were finally able to
move loads of around 100 tons. An early
alternative to the road locomotive was the
Thomson Road Steamer. Thomson's design
was produced by Burrell, Ransome and
Robey, besides Scottish makers. A number
were used in India under the control of Col
Crompton (q.v.). The early death of Thomson
in 1873 and the transfer of Crompton ended
this use and further development of the design.
They were used in the USA and continued to
be used in Glasgow until the 1920s.

The trailers or trolleys originally used in
heavy haulage were unbraked, but had drag
shoes on chains similar to those used on carts,
using steel unsprung wheels, often lacking
steering. Transport of abnormal loads always
required specialist skills and management.
Each job was different. The route had to be
planned and checked. Common problems were
narrow roads, tight bends, low or weak
bridges, obstructions from street furniture and
steep hills. Before movement occurred there
was the loading and, on arrival, there might be
unloading and sometimes precise location of
the item. After 1904 faster steam road tractors
eased the movement of abnormal loads.

The 1931 Authorisation of Special Types
order and the 1934 Road Traffic Act

introduced national regulation, replacing the
varying requirements of local authorities. Until
then there were few firms undertaking regular
long distance movement of abnormal loads.
Notable were Norman E Box (q.v.), Marston
Road Services (q.v.) and Pickfords (q.v.). The
introduction of the Scammell articulated low
loaders in 1922, later developed to carry up to
45 tons, gave firms which had confined
themselves to local or regional heavy moves
the capability regularly to carry out long
distance moves. These included Robert Wynn
(q.v.), Currie of Newcastle and E W Rudd
(q.v.). Rudd introduced the Scammell 80-ton
Pioneer tractor and, with design aid from
Scammell, built their own two-bogie trailer,
with interchangeable girder or drop frame
carriers.

The development of the national electric grid
and the growth of light industry in the
Midlands and the South changed the pattern of
movements. Boiler movement and setting
decreased, to be replaced by power-generation
equipment and to some extent by machine
tools, partly associated with the growth of the
motor industry. These required millwright
skills for positioning. The development of the
Ransome mobile crane (q.v.) in the 1920s
eased the physical effort required, even with
the use of monkey winches. The development
of fork-lifts (q.v.) and the Iron Fairy cranes
eased the physical effort. The abnormal load
operators were the earliest hirers of mobile
cranes. The introduction of hydraulic Mega-
Lifts from the USA in the late 1970s made the
erection or dismantling of heavy machinery
easier and less hazardous. The movement of
construction plant remained an awkward load,
the increase in size and weight required care in
securing the load, including jibs etc. and
ensuring everything came within a height or
width limit. One difference between a haulage
contractor and an own-account operator was
that the former's driver did not operate any of
the plant that was loaded, whereas the latter's
driver did, as he was fully qualified.

The growth in size and weight of electrical
plant, refinery and other machinery meant the
carrying ability of existing equipment had to
be increased. The weights and dimensions

became beyond the limits of British Railways. John Crane comments on the effect of the post-war power station programme on heavy haulage and the manufacture of road trailers. Ironically, in the year before Hixon (q.v.) the CEGB published a monograph on abnormal load transport for transformers and similar equipment. The solid-tyred 100-ton low-loading transporters were replaced by trailers running on pneumatic-tyred four-axle eight-wheel bogies, with detachable side girders and hydraulic adjustment for height. By 1966 300-ton trailers were in use with 12 axles, using air-cushioning adapted from hovercraft, thus reducing the load stress on roads and bridges.

The next advance was the introduction of modular hydraulically-suspended multi-axle systems able to be built up as required to 20 axles, with steering ability. These could be adjusted for height and load equalisation. Load security was important from the earliest days. Chains and cable were used as needed. The objective was to ensure that if an accident occurred the load remained attached and on the trailer.

The regulations for a load that is over-long, too wide or of excess weight to be carried on vehicles under the Construction & Use Regulations 1986, come under the Motor Vehicles (Authorisation of Special Types) General Order 1979 (STGO) Section 18. This defined an abnormal load as one that cannot without undue expense or risk of damage be divided into two or more loads for the purpose of transport, or owing to its dimensions cannot be carried by a vehicle complying with the C & U Regulations, or owing to its weight cannot be carried on a vehicle having a total laden weight of less than 44,000 kg. The use of vehicles which did not comply with the 1986 regulations was allowed when used for moving abnormal loads. The width of STGO vehicles could not normally exceed 2.9 metres. If the load could not be safely carried on such a vehicle, this width might be increased to 6.1 metres, but if the width of the vehicle and load exceeded 5 metres, prior permission had to be obtained from the Department of Transport for a Movement Order (VR1). STGO1 vehicles came within the C & U limits, but might operate at up to 46 tonnes. STGO2 vehicles having at least five axles might operate up to 80 tons. STGO3 vehicles having at least six axles operated up to 150 tonnes, with a limit of 100 tonnes on any group of axles. An identification plate with the STGO letters in white on a black background had to be carried on the front of all ST vehicles to show in which category the vehicle was operating. All STGO 2 and 3 vehicles also had to have a Special Type Use plate showing the manufacturer's design gross vehicle weight, gross tare weight, and individual axle weights when travelling at speeds between 12 and 40 mph. Statutory attendants had to be carried on ST vehicles when the vehicle or load was more than 3.5 metres wide or more than 18.3 metres long (excluding the tractive unit); and when the total length of vehicle and trailer exceeded 25.9 metres. When three or more vehicles requiring attendants moved in convoy only the first and last vehicle needed attendants. All movements of abnormal loads had to be notified by giving at least two working days notice to each police authority through which an STGO vehicle would pass. Each highway and bridge authority through which the vehicle passed had to have at least five clear days notice if the vehicle and load weighed more than 80 tonnes. If the C&U axle weight was not exceeded, only two days' notice was required. The operator had to indemnify each authority against road or bridge damage. All abnormal loads passing over rail bridges had to be notified to Railtrack, and all high loads had to be notified to the relevant electricity companies. Late-twentieth century abnormal load hauliers used multi-axle tractors which might be converted to run in articulated or drawbar form as required. The use of a dolly was legal and was often used to keep articulated vehicles within the axle loading limit. **GM**

Crane (1991); CEGB, *Transport for Power* (1967); *CM* (26 January 1980), p. 52 and (23 February 1980), p. 56

Accidents. (Figure 65) Generalising about accidents involving commercial vehicles is difficult as there is a paucity of statistics.

There are a number of problems. One is separating out commercial vehicles from the private motor car, the other is that the statistics on the causes of lorry accidents were never kept systematically. As a result, although the general trends in road accidents in the twentieth century are clear, the part played by commercial vehicles is obscure before the 1960s. In the absence of statistics we have to rely on anecdotal evidence such as the memoirs of lorry drivers and others in the industry. Although before the 1960s commercial vehicle accidents cannot be disaggregated from car or bus accidents, the overall trend of all motor vehicle road accidents from the mid-1920s to 1960 is clear. It is a rise of threefold over the whole period, with the growth interrupted in the late 1940s and early 1950s, only to resume rapid growth in the late 1950s and early 1960s.

Since the early 1960s fairly reliable statistics have been kept on some aspects of motor vehicle accidents. They show a number of trends of importance to commercial vehicles. The first is that the accident rate for commercial vehicles was lower than for all other motor vehicles (predominantly the motor car). In 1962, commercial vehicles had three quarters the number of accidents of all motor vehicles, per road mile. This relationship continued to hold in the early 1970s, and by the early 1980s commercials had about two thirds of the accident rate of all vehicles. A second trend was that light commercials (vans under 1½ tons unladen weight) were more accident-prone than heavy commercials. In 1962 vans had 1½ times as many accidents as lorries. By 1972 the figure was more like 1.3 and this relationship held in the early 1980s, though by the mid-1990s the accident rate had evened out a little more and vans were only having 1.2 as many accidents as lorries.

Throughout the period 1960 to 2000 heavy goods vehicles had the lowest accident rate of all motor vehicles when account was taken of mileage travelled. In 1962, for example, their accident rate was 60 per cent of all motor vehicles, in 1974 about 63 per cent, and 50 per cent in 1982.

The third startling but pleasing trend is that the accident rate for both light and heavy commercials has dropped steadily from the early 1960s to the mid-1990s. From 1962 to 1974 (when there was a change in the basis on which the figures were collected) accident rates of all commercials nearly halved. From 1974 to 1982 the van and lorry accident rate fell by one third and between 1985 and 1995 the van accident rate fell by a third again and the lorry accident rate fell by nearly one quarter. As a result the accident rate of commercial vehicles in the closing years of the twentieth century was about one quarter of what it had been in the early 1960s. This can be explained by the continual improvement in road and vehicle safety, such as the growth of the motorway network, by-passes, speed limits, dual carriageways, improved braking systems, side and rear under-run barriers.

Road goods vehicles were subject to the same types of accidents as any other road traffic. Some were caused by human error, such as driving too fast, falling asleep at the wheel, or going through traffic lights at red, and some resulted from mechanical breakdown, such as brakes failing or steering becoming erratic. These will not be discussed here. Rather we will look at accidents peculiar to commercial vehicles, and those factors which increased the likelihood of a commercial vehicle having an accident.

There are a number of types of accident that are peculiar to lorry traffic. The most obvious is losing all or part of the load. In the interwar period this appeared to be a normal hazard of the job and was reported quite regularly. It was more common when much traffic was carried on flat-bed trucks, where the efficiency of the sheeting and roping was crucial to retaining a load, and when negotiating roundabouts. Any deficiency in this regard might cause it to shift. It was aggravated when lorries were overloaded and their loads made more precarious. Murphy mentions an incident in which he was carrying a large stack of square cardboard packages of soap flakes. The load moved and many packages burst. In some cases a load spillage led to partial loss of cargo by pilferage, especially where it was an easily transportable consumer good such as oranges.

Another fairly commonly mentioned incident in the 1920s and 1930s was that the driver was killed by the load. This occurred where the load was heavy and then moved, perhaps because the wagon braked sharply or came to a sudden halt. This was such a problem with iron or steel girders and ingots that flat-bed lorries specialising in such traffic often had steel plates installed behind the cab to protect the driver if the load did move forward (see STEEL TRAFFIC). Tankers carrying liquids in bulk were subject to accidents caused by a less-than-full load and the liquid moving and making the lorry deviate. Movement of liquids also meant wear on the drive shaft. The solution to this surge problem was to put in baffle plates to break up movement, or to use separate tanks.

Lorries also hit bridges (q.v.) too frequently. This might be because the lorry was overloaded and the height of the load was greater than the driver anticipated or simply the driver forgetting or not knowing there was a low height restriction on the road. In the luckier cases some of the load might be lost, in the more serious, damage to the lorry and the bridge occurred. Such accidents became less common as bypasses skirted city centres, signs became more obvious and common, and motorways were built with 16 foot height clearances. On the other hand accidents involving lorries hitting bridges were more likely when lorry drivers moved out of the area they knew and lacked local knowledge of low-height hazards. Thus container lorries or double-deck car transporters were vulnerable.

Large loads of any sort presented particular hazards. At the least a large load caused some cracking of kerbs or pavements, or perhaps demolished the odd lamp post or telegraph pole. More seriously, because it moved slowly and awkwardly it held up other traffic and caused frustration and foolish manoeuvres on their part. Crossing railway lines was another point of danger as demonstrated so tragically by the Hixon disaster (q.v.) of 1968. Large loads could also run away with the traction engines or tractors pulling the trailer, causing

them to topple or end in a ditch with danger for the driver and damage to the vehicle.

Brakes on early vehicles were poor and skidding common. This was made worse by the lack of adhesion of solid tyres on wood-block or granite-sett roads, particularly in the wet. A widely-held opinion that brakes on the front wheels increased skidding meant that, until the mid-1920s at least, only rear wheels were braked. Dennis was one of the first makes to fit front-wheel brakes. Similar fears in the 1930s when the eight-wheeler was introduced meant that often only one of the two front axles was braked. Not until well after the end of the Second World War did Leyland's Octopus gain brakes on both front axles.

Articulated vehicles, though a great boon in terms of capital utilisation, were subject to particular accidents. They were prone to jackknifing and skidding. Murphy, writing of the 1930s and 1940s, thought that articulated vehicles which got into a skid could seldom be brought back under control, whereas a rigid lorry could often be brought out of a skid. The tendency to uncontrollable skids in articulated vehicles was partially a function of limitations on current brake technology but also some wrong thinking. Until the mid-1960s it was thought that the maximum braking effort should be put on the trailer and after that on the rear wheels of the tractor. In braking weight is transferred forward and so the rear wheels of the tractor and those of the trailer lose adhesion as weight is thrown onto the front wheels. Thus the rear wheels skid more easily under braking. When this was realised, the solution from the mid-1960s was to put most of the braking effort on the front wheels. Because weight was thrown forward they skidded less easily and if they did skid the rig stayed in a straight line. A further breakthrough in preventing jack-knifing was the development of anti-lock braking systems, introduced from the late 1970s. The Armitage (q.v.) Report of 1980 commented on the reduction in the number of lorries which jackknifed.

Some accidents were aggravated because the lorries and their drivers were working under commercial imperatives. For instance, accidents might occur more frequently as a result of mechanical failure if routine maintenance and inspection were skimped. This arose from a short-sighted attempt to cut the cost of running a fleet and also to minimise the time a lorry was not in service. If drivers complained about mechanical defects or deficient maintenance some employers sacked them, so discouraging complaints. Another vice of the hard-pressed haulier was to overload the lorry, with the deleterious effects discussed above. The incentives to maximise revenue and so load were often difficult to resist and many firms fell foul of the law on this. Another fault was for drivers to exceed the maximum permitted number of hours. This was understandable with tight delivery schedules, but could lead to over-tired drivers more likely to make a mistake or doze off at the wheel. Similar pressure encouraged drivers to exceed speed limits to ensure delivery in time or to maximise their income if paid piece rates or on a bonus. This was at one time particularly prevalent in aggregates transport.

Although compared to other road users lorry drivers generally had fewer accidents, as confirmed by the Armitage Report, when they were involved the effects were proportionately worse because of the size and weight of a laden lorry. So as early as 1964 the phrase 'motorway madness' was applied to horrific multiple vehicle accidents on the M1 in which lorry drivers as well as other road users were accused of excessive speed in foggy conditions. Generally motorways had much lower accident rates than other roads and the rate on the M1 and M6 in the mid-1960s was less than 10 per cent of the rate on urban roads. When lorries were involved in accidents with other road users or pedestrians the results could be horrendous and gave rise to pressure groups such as Brake (q.v.). One cause of grisly accidents was when cars ran under lorries; this could apply to cyclists as well. To correct this, the law was changed in 1984 to require lorries to have side guards and low rear bumpers. Despite these measures there were, in the late 1990s, examples of brake failure and driver inattention, but they were less frequent. **JA**

Dickson-Simpson (1968); Hollowell (1968), pp. 18–24; Murphy (1963); Michael Austin, *Accident Black Spot* (Penguin, 1966); *Road Accidents*, 1956–1980 (HMSO); *Transport Statistics*, 1992– (HMSO); Armitage (1980); *Independent* (5 June 2001); *Guardian* (15 June 2001), PRO, MT 102/24

ACV, see ASSOCIATED EQUIPMENT CO. LTD

ADC, see ASSOCIATED DAIMLER CO.LTD

ADR is the abbreviation for the *European Agreement concerning the International Carriage of Dangerous Goods by Road* (the letters are taken from the French version of the title), which was signed in 1957 but did not come into force until 1968. Most of the detail is in two complex technical annexes: Annex A dealing with packaging and labelling of dangerous goods and Annex B with the vehicles in which they are carried. These were based on an equivalent set of regulations for international carriage of dangerous goods by rail (RID) first published in the UK in 1957, but which had their origins in agreements dating back to the 1890s. Over the years the regulations governing road transport of dangerous goods within the UK have been progressively brought into line with ADR.

Since 1990 all new editions of the Agreement have been published by the United Nations on behalf of the Inland Transport Committee of the Economic Commission for Europe. The 2001 edition was titled *Restructured ADR*, having been re-written to be more user-friendly and, for the first time, fully consistent with the international codes for carriage of dangerous goods by sea, air and rail. By then the Agreement had grown to 1150 pages and been accepted by all the countries of Europe except Albania, Slovenia and Turkey and also, beyond Europe, by Azerbaijan. **GAB**

CM (2 February 1980), pp. 70–2

AEC, see ASSOCIATED EQUIPMENT CO.LTD

Aggregates (Figure 67) covers a wide range of materials from quarried sand, ballast and various types of stone, to recycled crushed concrete, brick and tarmac. Fifty per cent goes to road building and repair, the other fifty per cent to the construction industry, not only for building, but for the manufacture of sewer pipes, kerbs, slabs and various pre-cast concrete units (such as beams), and to the do-it-yourself industry. The demands of the aggregate industry had a major part in the design and development of tipping vehicles.

Until the 1920s most aggregate transport was done with a horse-drawn tipcart. Pulling a lever undid a latch that allowed the body to tip by overbalancing. Early mechanisation came with the advent of Atkinson, Foden, Fowler, Garrett, Leyland, Mann, Sentinel and Thornycroft steam wagons. Mostly these were three-way tippers. By dropping the appropriate sideboards and removing two pins the body could be tipped in the required direction by a ram powered by water pumped by the steam engine. Some of these steamers were powerful enough to pull a trailer.

Many early motor tippers were imported from America, as there were few small British lorries. Examples are Reo Speed Wagon, Diamond T, Chevrolet and Dodge, 2-, 3-, 4- and 5-tonners. Eventually the British manufacturers produced suitable chassis, notably Bedford with its WTH model, built with a hydraulically tipped body in the mid-1930s, and the OST built from 1945 to 1956, Ford and the British-built Kew Dodge. In the 1960s Foden and Scammell 8-wheelers were well-favoured and some of the latter were surprisingly long-lived. That decade saw the beginning of the articulated tipper, aided by the change in law of 1964 which raised the maximum capacity of an artic to 32 tons. Originally lorries were hand-tipped, either with rack and pinion or screw and nut. With the advent of the gearbox power take-off and from the swash plate hydraulic pump developed by Edbro (q.v.) in 1936 it was possible to return to power-tipping even for large vehicles, with a great deal of engineering expertise going into ram design.

As roads got bigger and demand grew after the Second World War, tippers quickly went from the 4-wheeler carrying 4 tons or 5 cubic yards, operating at 6¾ tons, through 6-wheelers, 8-wheelers (notably Scammell and Foden) to the 6-axle artic carrying 24 tonnes or 40 cubic metres operating at 44 tons. At one time tipper bodies had to be fitted with a calibration scale that was certified and sealed by the local authority.

Up to the 1940s hand-loading with shovels and forks was commonplace. As late as 1964 an Essex tipping contractor advertised for drivers 'All hand loading, bring your own shovel.' With growing mechanisation, quarries which had had steam shovels for many years introduced narrow gauge railways, power screens (for sizing), conveyors and hoppers where lorries could be backed under a chute for loading, although there had always been loading straight off the face by the 'face shovel.' Wooden bodies were no longer adequate for loads being dropped into them, although they were lined with metal plates. By the mid-1950s the all-steel body was becoming the norm, both bolted and welded. In the mid-1960s the bolted aluminium body was introduced, followed in the 1970s by the innovative all-welded, weight-saving aluminium construction.

This industry was and is dominated by small operators although some quarrying firms ran their own fleets. Yeoman and ARC are good examples. Rationalisation in the roadstone industry began with the work of Sir Henry Maybury (q.v.), and in the 1980s the Ready-Mixed Concrete Group (q.v.) acquired a number of aggregate suppliers.　　**JP**

Earle (1974), pp. 125–7

Agricultural transport, (Figure 68) as used by a farm or estate to transport its crops or livestock, was commonplace before 1914 for most arable crops, livestock, flowers, fruit and vegetables, meat and milk. They were either delivered to the nearest railway station for transport to the buyer or taken to his premises which were usually within ten miles, a horse's working distance in one day. The farmer was responsible for delivery to the buyer. With grain the change from country mills to large port-based mills in the early-twentieth century was helped by the railway-served country depots. The railways had a considerable trade in sack hire and warehousing for grain and, in the largest centres, provided facilities for storage. The availability of motor transport after 1918 saw a gradual change. Haulage firms using motor vehicles replaced the farms' own horse-drawn carriage. This change was for a variety of reasons. They included mergers between suppliers requiring deliveries to more distant points, changes in farming methods including the new marketing boards, particularly the Milk Marketing Board which took over responsibility for milk transport. Improvements in livestock, including tuberculin-tested attested cattle, created a demand for livestock transport and reduced the number of markets, increasing the distances to be travelled. After the introduction of licencing in 1933 the F or Farmers Licence enabled farmers to carry for neighbours.

Whereas in 1924 the railways carried three quarters of the agricultural produce of the country, by 1938 it was below one half as road vehicles made inroads into longer distance traffic. The Second World War saw increased outputs and changes in marketing with more traffic being delivered by road partly because of the rise of the grower merchant lorries. The need for buffer stocks or storage away from ports or other likely targets for enemy action was directed by the Ministry of Food. It also introduced zoning for supplies from growing areas, for example potatoes, or in the case of milk, rationalised collections. From 1942 the presence of American forces in this country saw meat and dairy products supplied to American bases, much as a part of Lease-Lend. The post-war development of the frozen food industry created demanding requirements for transport from field to freezing plant when crops such as peas were harvested. Mechanisation meant changes to bulk-handling, by the late 1970s. The last milk churn collections in England and Wales were in 1979. Similarly the use of grain sacks ended, bulk tippers and central storage taking over. The seasonal use of farmers' F-licenced vehicles also affected demand for the haulier. Outbreaks of foot-and-mouth disease and BSE affected every section of the industry, reducing the traffic. New, possibly over-zealously applied,

hygiene regulations caused abattoirs to close. Butchers too were affected by this, compounded by customers choosing to buy from supermarkets and the decline in meat consumption. Among hauliers handling agricultural traffic were Routh & Stevens, Davies & Brownlow and Robert Sinclair, who tended to favour standard vehicles, generally by the mass producers. These were fitted with flat, drop-sided, sometimes with added slatted sides or if engaged in livestock, container or convertible bodies. The changes in regulations, with the changes in distribution led to specialist undertakings for example Christian Salvesen (q.v.), Wincanton (q.v.), NFT (Northern Food Transport) operating articulated van or curtain-sided trailers, designed for temperature-controlled transport. Livestock transport has also changed to the use of specialist articulated vehicles. Sugar beet haulage remains a considerable, seasonal traffic. The use of fast haulage tractors and farmers' own vehicles remains a contention between the farmer and the haulier. The British Sugar Corporation, the only buyer, is also responsible for allocating growers' deliveries to the processing factories, and has considerable influence on the prices paid and the acreage grown. It also dictates delivery date and time at the processing plants. The agricultural traffic background of such major haulage concerns as Langdons (q.v.) and Stobart (q.v.) is worth remembering: egg and poultry collection and agricultural contracting respectively. The development of large agricultural tractors, allowed to use red lower-taxed diesel fuel, and the farmers' lower road tax, with a relatively high top speed and their increasing use by farmers, has led to concerns by hauliers that some farmers are carrying produce for payment, rather than for moving their own crops. **GM/JMA**

Ailsa Trucks Ltd was established in 1967 as the sole Volvo (q.v.) truck and bus concessionaire in the UK. It took over a former military depot site of 75 acres (30 hectares) at Redburn, Irvine in 1972. The plant received built-up vehicles from Gothenburg and assembled chassis peculiar to the UK market. Jim McKelvie was a successful haulier from

Barrhead, near Paisley, who had sold his business for a substantial sum to the Transport Development Group (q.v.). He wanted to start a Leyland commercial vehicle dealership, but was rebuffed. Volvo was not represented in the UK, though the maker had very briefly tested the market with a left-hand drive 8-ton lorry. McKelvie persuaded Volvo to let him set up as its importer. The success of the venture was aided by the higher standard of equipment in the cabs, coupled with the availability of parts from dealerships on Sundays. These features were of a considerable attraction for owner-drivers, who formed a large proportion of the early buyers.

Two gaps in the UK market were soon identified, for 8×4 and 6×4 chassis, and it was agreed to build these at Irvine, thus changing Ailsa Trucks in 1975 from an importer to an assembler. A separate bus-building operation had also been set up in 1974. Ailsa Trucks Ltd was renamed Volvo Trucks (Great Britain) Ltd in 1978. By that time production was running at 1,000 vehicles annually, with over 400 UK parts suppliers. Two wholly-owned distributor-ships (Northern and Heathrow) retained the Ailsa Trucks title.

A Volvo Truck Distributors' Association was founded in 1971, which had 23 distributor members by 1978. The distribution of Volvo truck parts was moved from Irvine in 1986, to the Wedgnock Industrial Estate, Warwick which was close to the M40, and so geographically ideal for Volvo's 48-hour guaranteed service. In June 2000 Volvo closed the Irvine plant. **RAS**

CM, Volvo Trucks supp. (6 October 1978); Volvo Parts Divn leaflet (March 1986); Jack (2001)

Air freight was initially limited by the capacity and capabilities of the planes available. The categories of traffic suitable for transport by air were items of high value-to-weight ratio, and those requiring rapid transit. Bullion, newspapers, mail, perishables such as out-of-season fruit and flowers, bloodstock, racehorses and urgently needed spare parts for machinery all benefited from transport by air. Between the wars air freight was limited, but

the Second World War stimulated the development of aircraft and left a surplus of military planes, some of which could be converted for commercial use, and a pool of experienced air- and ground-crew. This led to a plethora of small, often under-financed concerns, operating such aircraft as the Avro Lancastrian, Handley Page Halton, Douglas DC-3 and Avro York. The Berlin Air Lift, 1948–9, gave such businesses an opportunity, or at least staved off collapse, and helped to show the potential of air freight, albeit in an untypical situation. The Bristol Freighter operated especially by Silver City Airways Ltd of Lympne, demonstrated the usefulness of the aeroplane for carrying MG cars, and some Rootes Group products to the Continent.

The spread of large jet aircraft from the 1960s led to the major expansion of air-freight world-wide, some operators having associated road fleets to do the collection and delivery. This included, from the 1980s, the transport of fresh produce on an unprecedented scale. Air freight (almost all international) handled at UK airports rose from 31,000 tonnes in 1950 to 2.3 million tonnes in 2000. Although some haulage firms developed a specialism in air freight, such as Roy Bowles and C Claridge Ltd (q.v.), existing hauliers and customers' own vehicles sufficed to service the new traffic before the advent of the cargo airlines. Specialised handling equipment was developed for air-side transfer, such as the scissors-lift, and the igloo pallet maximised the use of aircraft cargo space. Major new traffic centres, such as the Parcelforce hub at Baginton Airport, Coventry, developed in 1998, required substantial road transport support. Much airfreight traffic from London and the South-west for non-European destinations is in fact trunked by road (and sea or tunnel) to near-Continental airports such as Schipol (Amsterdam). The same applies to incoming traffic. **RAS**

A C Merton-Jones, *British Independent Airlines since 1946* (Liverpool/Uxbridge: Merseyside Aviation Society/LAAS International, 4 vols., 1976–7); John Stroud, *Railway Air Services* (Ian Allan, 1987); *Birmingham Post* (8 July 1998); *Independent* (16 November 1991)

Air-management is the term for bodywork developments that seek to improve airflow around a moving vehicle, reducing aerodynamic drag and hence fuel consumption. Forerunners may be seen in the 1930s vogue for streamlining under the influence of Raymond Loewy, the American pioneer of industrial design. Carried to extremes this could produce striking but not always highly practical designs, e.g. Duple's (q.v.) van for the GPO air-mail service and Holland Coachcraft (q.v.) vans. For goods vehicles this was really no more than styling, since there was little economy to be gained until sustained speeds of over 60 mph became possible on the new motorways and trunk roads.

There is an inherent conflict between the need to retain an optimum load-carrying body-cube and aerodynamic improvement of its shape within the legal length limit; there is even less scope on open vehicles, such as machinery carriers and those with lorry-mounted cranes or ramps. Nevertheless, cabs were given cleaner lines and the front bumper took on an aerodynamic role. The rapid rise in container haulage in the late 1960s led to the introduction of the cab-top deflector. This was followed by the introduction of side body-skirts on rigid vehicles and then on both tractors and semi-trailers of artics. These are particularly effective in cross-winds. The use of sleeper cabs with their extra height reduced the need for deflectors.   **RAS/GAB**

J Phillips, 'A breath of fresh air', *Truck* (April 2000), pp. 60–2.

Albion Automotive was created by a management buy-in team after the bankruptcy of Leyland DAF in 1993. It manufactured axles and other vehicle components at part of a former Albion (later Leyland) factory in Glasgow and at the former Leyland components plant in Leyland. It was American owned by 2000.   **JMA**

Albion Motors Ltd (Figures 2, 7 and 107) was founded in 1899 in Glasgow by two engineers who had previously worked for the Mo-Car Syndicate, Thomas Blackwood Murray (1871–1929) and Norman O Fulton

(1872–1935). They were joined in 1902 by James F Henderson (1875–1941), an engineering graduate of Glasgow University, and these three families remained major shareholders until the 1950s, as well as holding top managerial positions. The atmosphere was of a family firm but with judicious employment of professional managers.

Initially Albion made cars, its first commercial vehicle not coming until 1902. This was a 10-cwt van on a motor car chassis with an 8 hp motor. Lacre was the agent for the south. By 1903 the firm needed larger premises and moved to Scotstoun. Among the customers were Harrods (q.v.), the London store, which by 1917 had 103 Albion vans for deliveries. The A3 model was produced in sizes up to 2 tons and the A10 for 3-ton loads. So successful were commercial vehicle sales that the firm abandoned car production in 1913 to concentrate on lorries. The A10 model was much used by the armed forces in the First World War, with over 6000 being produced.

After the war Albion concentrated on two models: a 25-cwt van and a 3-ton lorry. They were simple and straightforward designs but rugged and durable. In 1927 they expanded the model range with a 4- to 6-ton lorry. Output in the 1920s averaged about 1500 chassis per year. The range was further extended in 1936 with a 7- to 8-ton chassis, the introduction of the firm's own direct injection diesel engines, (it had previously used proprietary diesels including Beardmore) and some 10-ton chassis. Output rose in the 1930s to reach nearly 4000 vehicles in 1938. In 1937 a large repair centre was built in London at Brentfield Road, Harlesden, with some of the staff being brought from Scotland. The Scots foreman and his wife bought a café on the parade of shops where Brentfield Road joined the North Circular, called the Highland Glen, to cater for the workforce's needs. It is now the site of a Hindu temple. In the mid-thirties the Halley factory at Yoker in Glasgow was acquired to provide expansion space.

After producing various lorries and tank transporters in the Second World War, Albion introduced a range of models with names associated with Scotland, such as Clansman and Clydesdale. In 1951 Leyland made a successful bid for Albion. The latter's board accepted because it was worried about sustaining sales in a near monopsonistic market, namely where much goods haulage was in the hands of the nationalised BRS (q.v.). Albion slowly lost its separate identity. Initially it concentrated on the lighter end of the market and Leyland on the heavier, but by the 1960s there was little real distinction.

Albion was the longest-lived and most-successful of Scottish commercial vehicle manufacturers. The design was technically conservative but the product was high quality and reliable. Many of the components were manufactured in-house and Albion stuck to batch production. Exports were important to the firm with between 40 and 60 per cent of output going abroad. Among the best customers in Scotland was the co-operative movement (q.v.). The Scottish Co-operative Wholesale Society's transport department in Glasgow held the concession to supply Albions to co-operative societies throughout Scotland. Much of the bodywork was built at the SCWS coachworks in Rutherglen. Co-operative societies in both Scotland and England favoured Albions. Other customers included Express Dairy and London Brick (q.v.) in the 1950s, Smiths Crisps, J Lyons (q.v.), breweries and Post Office Engineering. Part of one Albion factory was still used in 2000 for manufacturing vehicle components by Albion Automotive (q.v.). **JA**

Sam McKinstry, 'The Albion Motor Company: growth and specialisation, 1899–1918', *Scottish Economic and Social History,* 18 (1991), pp. 36–51; Michael French, 'Manufacturing and models in the commercial vehicle industry: the Albion Motor Company, 1920–1956', *JTH,* 15, 1 (1994), pp. 59–77; Anthony Slaven and Sydney Checkland (eds), *Dictionary of Scottish Business Biography 1860–1960, I: The staple industries* (Aberdeen University Press, 1986), pp. 258–9, 261 and 263–5; Stevens-Stratten (1988), (1983) and (1991); Baldwin (1988); McKinstry (1997); McKinstry (1997); Grieves (1999), pp. 27 and 52

Allchin steam wagons were made by a long-established (1847) Northampton firm of agricultural engineers, which in 1906 added undertype steam wagons to its production of traction engines. Its first steam wagons had side-fired boilers. In all, 256 overtype wagons were built, before the firm petered out in 1931. Allchin supplied local breweries and midlands co-operative societies and 22 wagons to Hall & Co. Ltd, the builders' merchants and aggregate suppliers. **RWK/RAS**

'Allchin of Northampton', *VCVM,* 2, 7, p. 86; Middlemiss and Sawford (1990)

The **Alldays & Onions Pneumatic Engineering Co. Ltd** was a Birmingham engineering firm, dating from the seventeenth century, which produced commercial vehicles from 1906 to 1918. A light 10-hp van was followed by a three-wheeled van similar to the Autocarrier and a 5-cwt van on Alldays' Midget cyclecar chassis. A range of heavier vehicles was also produced from 1912, some of which served as lorries and ambulances in the First World War. Weekly commercial vehicle production in 1913 amounted to thirty, of which two-thirds were Midget vans. National customers included the GPO Stores Department (six vans) and Shell (several 2½-ton lorries). The Midget light delivery van was promoted on the grounds of economy. With a standard finish of dark carriage green or red, its horizontally-panelled body lent itself well to signwriting. After the war Alldays merged vehicle production with its subsidiary, the Enfield Autocar Co. Ltd, as Enfield-Alldays Motors Ltd; only one commercial model, a 2-ton chassis, was then offered to 1923. **RAS**

Vintage Commercial, 1, 7 (March 1963), p. 222; Wright (1986), p. 6; Norman Painting, *Alldays & Onions: a brief history* (Landmark, 2002)

Allen, William Gilbert (1892–1970) was chairman of Atkinson Vehicles (1933) Ltd from his acquisition of the ailing steam wagon manufacturers in 1933 to his retirement in 1966. The connection of his family business, Nightingale Engineering Co. Ltd, London, with Atkinson led to his involvement in the commercial vehicle industry.

Educated at Haileybury, with distinguished service in the Royal Artillery in the First

World War, Allen, who was a chartered accountant, established his own accountancy firm in the City in 1932. He retained close City connections despite his chairmanship of a northern firm. He was Sheriff of the City of London in 1955–6 and also served on motor industry bodies, including the council of the Society of Motor Manufacturers & Traders (q.v.) and the British Transport Vehicle Manufacturers' Association of which he was chairman. He had two sons, one of whom, Antony W Allen, succeeded him as chairman of Atkinson. **RAS**

Rangeability, 1 (Summer 1963); obituary issued by Atkinson; *WWW*, 6

Alternative fuels. There have been three reasons for development of alternative fuels. Lower running costs were the main impetus for the development of the diesel engine, with a benefit also for the oil companies of being able to extract more usable product from each gallon of crude oil. Creosote (also called tar oil) was tried in the early 1930s and was an unwanted by-product from the carbonisation of coal. Experiments by Edinburgh Corporation with five Leyland 4-ton lorries cut operating costs per mile by 20 per cent but there were engine lubrication and other problems.

The threat, and later onset, of the Second World War increased interest in home-produced alternatives to conventionally-sourced petrol and diesel fuel. The alternatives included petrol derived from coal (for which, the government guaranteed a lower level of tax) and producer gas (q.v.) in which coal, coke or anthracite was burned on the vehicle or on a trailer behind to produce a gas which fuelled petrol engines. Town gas was used in the First World War, and occasionally again in the Second World War, but required a large gas bag or other storage method that was difficult to accommodate on a lorry. Producer gas was only produced when required, and various makes of apparatus were available and fitted immediately behind the cab on a platform or dropside lorry. Government interest and some sponsored research into producer gas took place after the end of the Second World War.

The third and most recent reason for interest in alternative fuels is environmental with concerns about harmful health effects from vehicle exhausts and the threat from global warming. Lower taxation and subsidies to meet part of the cost of vehicles powered by alternative fuel became available through the government-funded Energy Saving Trust, formed in 1992. Its Powershift programme was for use of 'clean fuel vehicles'. Vehicles eligible included battery-electrics.

Liquefied petroleum gas (lpg) is the best-known alternative fuel, commonly used in the Netherlands and by some London taxis since the late 1960s. Lpg is a mixture of propane with low percentages of butane and other gases. It is stored in liquid form at low temperatures but becomes a gas at atmospheric temperature. It is heavier than air and care has to be taken to avoid leakage, particularly into pits in depots. Lpg tanks on vehicles take up about one-and-a-half times as much space as a diesel tank giving the same energy content. There were 1000 public filling stations in the UK offering lpg by 2002. Securicor began using a trial fleet of 17 converted petrol-powered Ford Transits in 1998, while Vauxhall offers lpg-powered vans.

Compressed natural gas (cng) is mainly methane, which occurs naturally, and is distributed by pipeline as domestic gas throughout the UK. It has a low energy density, so has to be stored at very high pressure to overcome this. Gas containers on vehicles are heavy and usually of thick steel, They take up considerable space, making them used mainly on medium or large commercial vehicles, to which they add about 800 kg in weight. Refuelling is quick but the cost of providing a filling station at least £200,000 at 2002 prices. At that date there were under a dozen publicly-accessible cng filling stations in the UK, with about another 100 in operators premises. Safeway Supermarkets was an early user of cng, in 1988, through transport contractor TDG Harris, with ten Perkins-engined ERFs. By 2002 Safeway was running 27 gas-powered trucks within the M25. Scania instituted a major conversion programme in 2001 on used Scanias it acquired on buy-back deals from supermarkets. Duel-fuel variants, that is, trucks able to run on cng or petrol, were also available in 2002 but there was no tax advantage when petrol was used. Engines of cng-powered trucks are quieter than diesel-powered examples.

Over the years the Post Office (q.v.) ran various trials of battery-electrics, the most recent with three Peugeot 106 car-derived electric vans in 1997 in the Coventry area. A more ambitious project the same year saw a four-way comparison with 27 Ford Transit vans based in Croydon and used on mail collection work: 12 ran on cng, nine on lpg, and the rest on petrol or diesel. Three of the vans were run on each of four different cng conversion systems, and three on each of three different lpg systems.

Hybrids represent another possible alternative, with vehicles conventionally powered, but also with electric motors and a battery pack for operation in environmentally sensitive areas, but battery weight and cost are added drawbacks.

Other simpler alternatives include using 95 per cent conventional diesel (derv) fuel and five per cent biodiesel, produced from home-grown oil seed rape. In 2002 Asda supermarkets began using a diesel-biodiesel mix. Its biodiesel came from processing waste fat from its in-store cafés with methanol. **JMA**

Ancillary user denotes a business employing road vehicles for the purposes of its own manufacturing or trading, rather than operating them for hire or reward as a public carrier. This was also known as own-account operations. Under the Road & Rail Traffic Act 1933 ancillary users operated under a C licence as private carriers. The nationalisation of road haulage after the Second World War led to a huge growth in C-licence operation by businesses which were either dissatisfied with the service they received from BRS or British Railways, or which felt they could respond more cheaply or more quickly to their customers' requirements. **RAS/JMA**

Annis & Co. Ltd, heavy haulage contractors, operated from Hayes, Middlesex, from the late 1930s into the 1960s. It worked for civil engineering contractors, and was also a pioneer in bulk cement carriage for the Cement Marketing Board. Many Annis vehicles were Scammells, but the firm built, by conversion, two 6×4 Diamond T tractors and a number of trailers, installed Gardner engines in all its vehicles and operated such uncommon machines as two cancelled-export order AEC Moguls. On the death of Frank Annis, the firm passed to nearby haulier Joe Moore and many Annis vehicles went for scrap. **RAS**

D Miller, 'Hauling the Annis way', *Classic Commercials* (undated: 1981?), pp. 16–19

Anti-jack-knife device, see HOPE

Appeal Tribunals. The Road & Rail Traffic Act 1933, under which the licensing (q.v.) of goods vehicle operators was established, required the Minister of Transport to appoint an appeal tribunal to hear appeals against decisions of the Licensing Authorities (q.v.). The Road & Rail Traffic Appeal Tribunal, comprising a chairman with legal experience and two other members, came into being in 1934. E S Shrapnell-Smith (q.v.) was one of the members throughout its existence. Hearings on Scottish appeals had to be held in Scotland.

The functions of the Tribunal were suspended, along with the licensing system, at the outbreak of war and re-established in 1946. As provided in the Transport Act 1947, this Tribunal was combined in 1951 with the Railway Rates Tribunal to form the Transport Tribunal. A Road Haulage Appeals Division was set up within the Tribunal under the terms of the Transport Act 1962, but abolished again by the Transport Act 1985. In 1988 the Lord Chancellor assumed responsibility for the Tribunal. **GAB**

The Public Record Office holds the files of a small number of specimen cases heard by both Tribunals (class MT 69) and the registers of the Transport Tribunal's decisions (class MT 145). Significant cases were reported in *Traffic Cases*, published until 1976.

The **Argyle Motor Manufacturing Co. Ltd** was formed by Argyle Diesel Electronics of East Kilbride to build 16-ton gross vehicle weight 4-wheel lorries using bought-in components. The Christina had a Motor Panels cab and Perkins 6.354 diesel engine. Production lasted only from 1970 to 1973. A 24-ton 6-wheel lorry and 32-ton tractor, though designed, were never built, although there was also the Trilby, a heavy tractive unit built in some numbers for use within a large steel works, Colvilles of Coatbridge, near Glasgow.   **JMA**

Argyll commercials, 1902–14, were initially car-derived light vans. The parent company was originally the Hozier Engineering Co. Ltd, so named from its location in a former cycle component factory in Hozier Street, Bridgeton, Glasgow. Argyll Motors Ltd was registered in 1905 and a grandiose factory built on an 11-acre site at Alexandria, twenty miles north west of Glasgow. Alex Govan, the firm's founder, died in 1907 and a year later the firm went into voluntary liquidation. The re-formed company produced a range of commercials from 30-cwt to 3-ton lorries. A second liquidation occurred in 1914, following the development, production and litigation costs incurred by the Burt McCollum single sleeve-valve engine, which other sleeve-valve makers alleged infringed their patents, but also attributable to the extravagant production facilities built at Alexandria.   **RAS**

G Oliver, *Motor Trials and Tribulations* (1993); Grieves (1997); Sam McKinstry, 'Argyll Motors Ltd: a corporate post-mortem', *Business History,* 37, 4 (1995), pp. 64–84

The **Armitage Report** was written in 1980 at the behest of the then minister of transport, Norman Fowler. The terms of reference were to enquire into the causes and consequences of the growth of road freight traffic, its impact on people and the environment and whether there should be any changes in the maximum weight limits on lorries. The committee was chaired by Sir Arthur Armitage and had four other members, three academics and a county planning officer. The background to their appointment was growing pressure from the Freight Transport Association (q.v.) and other members of the road lobby for the 32 tonne weight limit on lorries to be raised. At the same time there were expressions of disquiet from environmentalists about the effect of these so-called juggernauts (q.v.) in terms of vibration, noise, fumes and safety.

The committee produced a report of 424 clauses over 159 pages, having taken oral evidence from 34 organisations and received written submissions from hundreds of individuals and organisations. It was an informative and scholarly report with much incidental detail on the trends in road haulage since the Second World War. It decided in favour of raising the maximum weight limit from 32 tonnes on four axles to 44 tonnes on six axles, with various intermediate combinations. It recommended higher taxes on large lorries to take account of their effect on road wear, and more by-passes and trunk roads. The committee also recommended more stringent braking standards on lorries, that there should be guards against under-running (when cars or motor cycles collided with the rear of lorries or trailers), and that spray suppression was needed, while noting the steep fall already achieved in the accident rates of commercial vehicles. Most of these suggestions were implemented. The government was more cautious on weight limits and in 1982 gave the go-ahead to 38-tonne lorries on five axles. Then in 1983, by allowing a five per cent margin of overloading before prosecution was activated, government effectively allowed the 40-tonne lorry. The Armitage report thought that 44 tonnes was the maximum that could ever be allowed, as Britain's bridges would stand nothing larger, but it was not until 2001 that 44 tonnes became generally legal, though they had been allowed for intermodal operations since 1994. This was twenty one years after the original recommendation.   **JA**

Armitage (1980); Hamer (1987), pp. 96–9; *CM* (12 January 1980), p. 4 and (8 March 1980), p. 22

Armstrong-Saurer Commercial Vehicles Ltd. Diesel-engined lorries were built at

Scotswood from 1931 to 1937 after Sir W G Armstrong-Whitworth & Co. acquired the British manufacturing rights to the Swiss Saurer diesel engine. For a time Armstrong-Saurer held an important position in heavy diesel transport in Britain. Shell Mex & BP was one of its customers; other well-known names operating Armstrong-Saurers included Fairclough Brothers, the meat hauliers, and Tarmac Ltd. Joseph Rank's British Imperial Transport employed 50. Models included the 4-wheel Defiant, Dauntless and Active/Effective, the 6-wheel Dominant, replaced by the Dynamic, and the 8-wheel Samson, introduced in 1935. About 40 of the latter were built, and operated by firms such as Pickfords, Beckett Brothers of Fenton, Stoke-on-Trent and the Scottish Co-operative Wholesale Society, before Armstrong concentrated on re-armament, the Saurer rights subsequently going to Morris Commercial.

RAS

Klapper (1973); Stevens-Stratten (1988); Edge, *A Century of Petroleum Transport* (1998)

Arran Motors Ltd of Welwyn Garden City, Hertfordshire, although short-lived, was of significance in that it produced, between 1934 and 1937, one of the first series of medium-weight diesel-engined lorries in the UK, the Dieselet. The first model had normal control, but this was complemented by a forward-control version. Perkins or Gardner engines were installed. In 1937 Arran Motors went into liquidation and was acquired by William Hurlock (q.v.) Junior Ltd. Compulsory purchase of one of its premises meant that only three lorries designated HAC were produced by the new owner. **RAS**

MT, 'Fifty years ago' series; N Baldwin and W D Hurlock, 'The Hurlock Family', *OM*, 11, 4 (1971), pp. 326–7

Articulated vehicles (Figure 3) give better labour productivity by enabling the tractor to be disconnected from the trailer, so allowing the load to be packed or unpacked while the tractor is employed in other haulage activities. They also have greater manoeuvrability. In the 1898 Lancashire Heavy Motor Vehicle Trials

(q.v.), one of the four vehicles competing was a 5-ton, 6-wheel, steam-driven articulated Thornycroft which had troubles throughout the trial and was judged last. Not surprisingly Thornycroft did not pursue this design. In the First World War some American manufacturers sent tractors and trailers, but they were not a great success with the notable exception of Knox.

The post-war fear that heavy lorries damaged the highway and needed to spread the load over a number of axles gave articulated vehicles a boost. In 1920 Scammell launched an articulated 6-wheel petrol lorry which was the first successful 'artic'. Soon larger versions, up to 15 tons, were available. At first there was some concern that articulated lorries would be restricted to 5 mph under the Heavy Motor Car Order of 1904 if the semi-trailer was considered a 'trailer.' In 1922 an amendment which provided that if at least 15 per cent of the weight of the trailer was superimposed on the towing vehicle it counted as a single unit, ended this worry and gave artics the green light.

Scammell's success led to several other makers offering what were called matched trailers. Leyland made an arrangement with trailer builder Carrimore, while AEC produced a single 8/10-ton vehicle in 1923, but did not manage to sell it until 1926, and then with a different trailer. The main disadvantage was lack of any easy or quick method of coupling and uncoupling the trailer. Eventually two types of coupling came into use generally, the automatic coupling for lighter outfits and, for heavier loads, the fifth wheel (q.v.). The latter is in general use today.

Development of a suitable automatic coupling was slowed down by the railways' attempt to use former horse-drawn carts with little modification. Experience subsequently proved that most carts were unsuitable for mechanical haulage. The Karrier Cob and the Scammell Mechanical Horse (q.v.) more than maintained the manoeuvrability of the horse-drawn vehicle. Just how big the gains that could be achieved was demonstrated at the Farringdon, London, goods depot of the LNER. It became entirely mechanised in 1933 with a fleet of 60 Scammells and 92 semi-trailers able to handle 85,844 tons of goods in the year. Previously a similar tonnage needed 87 horse teams and 134 drays.

Artics became more common from the late 1930s when Scammell produced a range of articulated vehicles from 16 to 22 tons for everyday transport rather than for specialist applications. At this time Bedford produced the WSS which had an 8-ton carrying capacity. Light artics were few and far between, probably the biggest user being Hellmuth's Haulage on its *Radio Times* contract which employed Flexion trailers.

After new legislation allowing higher weights (32 tons instead of 24 tons) was introduced in 1964 use of heavier articulated vehicles became widespread. This legislation saddled the rigid eight, previously the heaviest vehicle permitted, with a 28 ton maximum and required a long wheelbase. Although the 1970s saw more favourable legislation allowing eight-wheelers to run at 30 tons, with more sensible axle spreads, development of the artic never looked back. With yet more axles and an increase in overall length from 13 metres to 15 metres in 1999 it could carry up to 44 tonnes.

The oil companies were early users of articulated tankers, in some cases from the late 1920s, but exploited them for the benefits of added manoeuvrability and not for any ability to swap trailers. Indeed virtually all used semi-trailers which were not fitted with landing legs (which saved weight), a practice still followed by some companies today. **JMA**

Dickson-Simpson (1968); Robert Coates, 'Bedford practically started the artic business,' *CVC*, 114 (June 1999), pp. 22–5; Carverhill (2002), pp. 50–1; Mike Wells, 'The history of articulated vehicles in Great Britain' *VRS*, 11, 42 (1995), pp.77–81

The **Artillery Transport Co.** was started in the mid-1920s by Captain T S Riley. He had seen the difficulties experienced by the army's artillery units through the lack of suitable mechanical vehicles for training. He obtained a Karrier 6×4 WD type army lorry to hire out for training. This was so successful that he rapidly acquired a large fleet of Karrier WD vehicles. The earlier ones had Tylor petrol engines, later versions used Dorman engines. This led to the creation of the Artillery Transport Co., described as military mechanisation contractors, with its base at Copmanthorpe, York. Besides use in annual training and manoeuvres, they were used to train recruits as drivers. ATC provided the vehicles and the training and the Territorial Army conducted the tests. The regular army was also a customer, augmenting its own fleet for its manoeuvres.

A subsidiary company, Mechanisation (York) Ltd, was formed to operate a large fleet of Morris Commercial D light 6×4 military lorries. It also operated six small and 12 medium Citroen-Kegresse half-track tractors and three Armstrong-Siddeley of Pavesi artillery tractors. The title was changed to Military Tractors Ltd about two years later and it was finally absorbed into the ATC.

Other types of vehicles were added to the ATC fleet to meet the requirements of the Army. These included a fleet of Fordson tractors, at least two Clayton caterpillar tractors, Manchester 35-cwt lorries, Thornycroft 6×4 WD lorries, and Morris cars and vans. ATC also had a modified Leyland Lion bus as a mobile HQ. When not on hire to the army, some haulage was undertaken, notably in steel and timber transport, while sugar beet was moved in conjunction with the LNER. Pylons were carried for an electricity supplier. The ATC fleet was taken over at the outbreak of war in 1939. Another company, also hiring vehicles to the army was Mechanisation Ltd of Cheltenham, but no connection between this and ATC has been found. **GM**

Ashworth, James C, haulier of Allerton, Bradford, is an example of a firm which became so closely associated with a single, large customer that the closure of one of its plants contributed to the haulier's demise. The firm was founded by James Clifford Ashworth (1901–67), who set up as a coal merchant, diversifying into a night soil contract with Bradford Corporation. His first mechanical load carrier was a Dennis in about 1921. The fleet grew before the Second World War with

ERFs and a Thornycroft cattle carrier; the firm specialised in livestock haulage, ensuring wartime work and exemption from nationalisation.

Following partial denationalisation of the haulage industry, Ashworths acquired vehicles and licences from small firms and BRS (q.v.). In addition to its base at Allerton, Ashworths had main workshops in Bradford and a sub-depot in Liverpool for dock traffic. The takeover of the former Jowett works at Idle in 1954 by the International Harvester Co. gave Ashworths significant traffic opportunities for the movement of tractors and machinery. Transverse loading of tractors gave way to two double-deck AEC eight-wheel-plus-trailer units, devised by John (Jack) Ashworth, James's son, and built in-house. A smaller, reinforced ten-baler-capacity, double-deck trailer was also produced. Baled wool was an important traffic for Ashworths, giving rise to the fitting of a cab-over platform (q.v.). Following James's death, his sons, Jack and Richard, took over, beginning continental work to Dunkirk and then further afield. Livestock traffic was phased out, but further machinery trailer development took place. The fleet rose to about 80, but the closure of the Idle, Bradford, IH works and Dick's ill-health led to Ashworth's closure in 1981.   **RAS**

B Tuck, 'The innovative Ashworths', *Truck* (May 2001), pp. 86–9

Associated Commercial Vehicles Ltd, see ASSOCIATED EQUIPMENT COMPANY

Associated Daimler Co. Ltd. (Figure 69) Daimler was first involved with AEC in 1912 as sole selling agent for AEC products outside London. Under a further agreement in 1913 Daimler phased out production of its own heavy commercial chassis (those above 2 ton), with AEC building Daimler-badged 3-, 4- and 5-ton chassis with Daimler engines. AEC came under direct government control in 1916 with the result that supply of any chassis to Daimler ceased: the agreement was terminated in 1917. An anticipated reduction in AEC's order book and an approach from the Daimler Co.

reviving the idea of co-operation over commercial vehicle sales, combined to bring about the formation of Associated Daimler in 1926. AEC's new works at Southall (commenced in 1926) housed ADC's administration and produced chassis, for which Daimler provided the engines. ADC models were predominantly for passenger work, although the 418 3½-ton goods vehicle was added to the range in 1927. It continued in production until 1931, when 375 had been built. Problems with the Daimler CV25 sleeve-valve engine and the inherent dissimilarity of the two partners brought ADC to an end in 1928 after only two years.   **RAS**

Townsin (1998); Thackray (2001)

Associated Deliveries Ltd was established in 1946 by Sir Eric Palmer as a successor to the wartime Biscuit Delivery Pool, which had been set up by Huntley & Palmers of Reading (already involved in a joint distribution system with Peek Frean of Bermondsey). In the wartime scheme various biscuit manufacturers pooled storage and distribution resources and delivered each other's products in their allocated areas to reduce running costs. As Associated Deliveries, the scheme was extended to other food manufacturers with a large customer-base liable to receive small orders. There were forty depots and 300 vehicles with a large overhaul and bodybuilding works at Theale Road, Reading. The operation was taken over by BRS in the mid-1960s.   **RAS**

T A B Corley, *Quaker Enterprise in Biscuits: Huntley and Palmers of Reading 1822–1972* (Hutchinson, 1972); R C Haughey, 'Chivers from jam busters to jam carriers', *Classic Bus*, 26 (December 1996/January 1997), p. 33

The Associated Equipment Company Ltd (Figures 66, 77, 78, 82, 87, 97, 122, 127–9, 142, 147, 150, 155, 164, 170, and 185), normally refered to as AEC, was formed in 1912 from the vehicle manufacturing arm of the London General Omnibus Company with a factory at Walthamstow. Three years later the company ceased building bus chassis in favour of a War Office subsidy (q.v.) goods chassis, the Y type, which became the most numerous British Forces vehicle of the First World War with over 10,000 produced, powered by Daimler or Tylor engines. The Y's frame was all metal. Factory expansion during the First World War included installation in 1917 of a 265 ft long 'endless chassis assembly platform,' the first British (or European) example of a moving track assembly line.

After the war, AEC returned to bus manufacture, while large numbers of ex-WD Y-type vehicles were placed in service with hauliers throughout Britain.

AEC continued to build the Y type (formerly of 3- or 4-ton capacity) as a 5-ton model 501 with its own engine and introduced a lighter chassis, the first specifically designed civilian goods model, in 1923. In 1926 AEC and the Daimler Motor Company of Coventry formed the short-lived Associated Daimler Co. In 1927 the AEC factory at Walthamstow closed and production was moved to a new factory at Southall, Middlesex.

In July 1928 AEC engaged a new chief engineer, G J Rackham, appointed after two years with Leyland. From 1930 AEC introduced modern custom-made haulage chassis (Mercury, Monarch, Majestic and Mammoth) and in 1931 introduced its own diesel engine. Innovation flourished, spurred on by an intense rivalry with Leyland Motors. A rigid eight-wheel lorry, the Mammoth Major, joined the well-received commercial vehicle range. The 7.7 litre and 8.8 litre petrol and diesel engines produced by AEC were employed in vehicles of other makes, including FWD/Hardy (which AEC acquired) Daimler and Bristol.

Not until 1933, when the London Passenger Transport Board was formed, did AEC gain a separate, fully-independent existence. There had been unsuccessful negotiations for a merger with Leyland from 1926, and they were followed by a proposal in 1929 for creation of a holding company, British Vehicles, to acquire AEC and Leyland. During the Second World War AEC built large numbers of the Matador 4×4 military tractor lorries (model 0853) and 6×6 version known as

the 0854. The 7.7 litre diesel engine continued in production throughout the war and appeared in a great range of other manufacturer's products such as Maudslay, Atkinson and Coles Cranes. Many of the military vehicles continued in service as breakdown lorries, forestry tractors and crane chassis up to the 1980s and 1990s.

AEC took over in 1948 the Maudslay Motor Co. whose range included a single bus and numerous lorry models. Many employed AEC diesel engines. After a period during which the Maudslay name survived as a badge on AEC-designed products, vehicle production ceased.

The purchase of Crossley and Maudslay, together with the body-building plants of Park Royal Vehicles Ltd and Charles H Roe Ltd saw the creation of a new holding company, Associated Commercial Vehicles Ltd. Post-war production of AEC vehicles at Southall followed on from the pre-war pattern, but a 9.6 litre diesel engine was introduced. New models and cabs were launched in the mid-1950s for the goods range (by this time, bus chassis had diverged from lorry production). Heavy earth-moving trucks were added to the range, the 6×4 AEC 690 Dumptruk later being manufactured by Thornycroft, Aveling-Barford then Scammell.

The mid-1950s models were powered by a new range of diesel engines, the AV410 (later the AV470) derived from the old 7.7 litre engine and the AV590 (later to develop into the AV690 and AV760) derived from the 9.6 litre engine. AEC continued to supply engines to other manufacturers of road and rail vehicles. A final acquisition by AEC was specialist vehicle manufacturer Transport Equipment (Thornycroft) Ltd in 1961. From 1961 to 1968 the Thornycroft factory continued to manufacture a series of off-road vehicles, the Mighty Antar and the final version of the mechanical horse (q.v.), the Townsman, for use by British Railways. Like its rival Leyland, AEC had overseas branches for the assembly and marketing of its vehicles. These existed in South Africa and Australia, and in collaborative ventures with UTIC in Portugal, Willème in France, and Barreiros in Spain. One curiosity was that in Spanish-speaking countries, AEC traded as ACLO, to avoid confusion with the German firm AEG.

In 1962, the ACV group was purchased by Leyland Motors Ltd. At first AEC continued with the marketing and development of its own models. A new V8 diesel engine, the 800, was developed to power the Mandator tractor for heavy haulage, but was dropped because of its unreliability and high noise levels. Rationalisation of Leyland Group production caused the Ergomatic cab to be fitted to AEC lorries in common with those built at Leyland, and the replacement of the AEC truck models by vehicles built at other group factories.

In 1968 the formation of the British Leyland Motor Corporation brought Guy Motors into the fold. Guy built a haulage chassis (Big J) which was widely used and often powered by AEC engines. BLMC replaced the Guy Big J and similar AEC chassis in the early 1970s by a new 'interim' model called Marathon, which was built at Southall but badged Leyland. Production at the Southall factory ended in early 1979.   **ARP**

Nick Baldwin, 'AEC – the Great War and after', *VCV*, 3, 10 (1987), pp.49-53; Townsin and Goulding (1992); Edge (1994); Townsin (1998)

Associated Road Operators was formed in 1935 by the merger of the Motor Hirers' & Coach Services' Association with the first Road Haulage Association (q.v.). It thus included both hauliers and coach operators among its first members. R W Sewill, who had been joint managing director of London & Southern Counties Transport Co. Ltd, was appointed national director. In 1936 merger negotiations took place with the Commercial Motor Users' Association (q.v.), but the only outcome was some local action, which resulted in the ARO losing members to the CMUA in a few centres. The ARO continued in existence, representing hauliers as the RHA had done, until it became a principal constituent of the re-formed RHA in 1944.   **RAS**

CM (28 August 1936), p. 69; (8 January 1937), pp. 714-15; (22 January 1937), pp. 783, 788-9; Dunbar (1981)

Atkinson & Co. Ltd (Figures 70 and 177) was a latecomer to steam wagon manufacture, its first wagon being built in 1916. In 1907 Edward Atkinson (1875-1932), who had been an apprentice at the Coulthard steam lorry factory, joined his brother Harry and established Atkinson in Preston, as millwrights and engineers. Servicing the locally-built Pullcar van (with which Edward had been involved as an employee) was followed by work on steam wagons and an agency for Alley & McLellan's Sentinel wagons. The agency was given up when Atkinson began manufacture in 1916 of a 6-ton undertype lorry, similar to the Sentinel, of which 335 had been sold by 1929.

In the First World War and immediately after the firm thrived briefly, building a new factory but producing only three wagons a week. Despite the advantages of Atkinson's 'Uniflow' engine and the introduction of an articulated wagon in 1922, Atkinson felt the effects of the early-1920s depression. In 1926 Atkinson took over spares and completion of Leyland steam lorries after that maker concentrated on internal-combustion-engined vehicles. In 1929 Atkinson took over the spares of the Mann's Patent Steam Cart & Wagon Co. of Leeds. Activity dwindled to repair and modification work and receivers were appointed in 1930. The business continued under H B Fielding, with trailer production and third-axle conversions. W G Allen (q.v.) bought the business and revived it as Atkinson Lorries (1933) Ltd. Lorry production on a small scale got under way in 1935, about fifty being completed before the outbreak of war. The company's growth was strengthened by large orders for heavy lorries for essential civilian users, including the Petroleum Board (q.v.).

On the strength of this wartime experience premises capable of producing 300 chassis a year and a new factory were opened at Walton-le-Dale, Lancashire in 1947. The company went public in 1948. The mid-1950s to the end of the 1960s was a period of expansion under production controller, later managing director, Peter Yates. Between 1955 and 1960 output increased more than three-fold, though this included small chassis and tractors. To offset the problems of the heavy lorry market in the wake of nationalisation came innovation in the lorry range. Innovations included a bonneted tractive unit for Pickfords (q.v.), a new cab design in 1958, the introduction of the ZF gearbox and power-steering, and a major switch to tractive unit production following the weight changes of the 1964 Construction & Use Regulations (q.v.), as well as semi-autonomous production in Australia.

The cumulative success of all this activity made Atkinson an attractive takeover target. In 1970 ERF made the first bid, followed by Foden and then Seddon, whose bid was supported by Leyland, which had a 20 per cent shareholding in Atkinson. Seddon's range fitted neatly with Atkinson's, but its management did not and Tony Allen, W G's son, resigned as chairman, Peter Yates staying on for one year to assist in unification. There was a strong rearguard action by a shareholders' committee, organised by A G and P M Horsnail and supported by committed Atkinson operators. The late Alan Horsnail recorded the episode in a 1978 article and his files have been preserved in the Modern Records Centre, University of Warwick Library. See also SEDDON ATKINSON.

RAS

Kennett (1978); articles in *Business Archives*, 44 (1978), pp. 7–20 and 56 (1988), pp. 39–40; *Atkinson* (priv. pub., 1967); Edge (1998)

Atlas Express commenced business in 1863 as a 'packed parcels carrier'. It was a partnership between William Taylor, who had been employed by Globe Express Parcels Delivery Ltd and William Manson. Its first depots served London and Glasgow, and by 1877 there were branches at Liverpool, Manchester and Dublin. Taylor's three surviving daughters became co-partners with Manson on Taylor's death in 1895. James Stewart, who had been at Glasgow, became the London manager. The company prospered, becoming a private limited company in 1908 based in Glasgow. Taylor's two sons-in-law, John H Farmer and James Turner and their wives became directors. Atlas opened branches in Birmingham, Leeds, Nottingham, Sheffield, and Belfast. Atlas used horse vans (q.v.), carrier cycles (q.v.) and handcarts (q.v.) for local deliveries, relying upon the railways for trunking its parcels to branches and a growing number of agents.

At the Armistice the business was reduced to branches at London, Nottingham, Aberdeen and Glasgow. Agents replaced the closed branches. The business began to recover, branches re-opened and a Leicester carrier, City Parcels Delivery, was acquired in 1923. By 1927 Atlas was again profitable. A move to a new London depot at Little Britain, near Smithfield market, was made in 1938, replacing the Whitecross Street depot, used since 1901.

Atlas had experimented unsuccessfully with motor vehicles during the war but it was 1936 before it again began replacing horses or using motors on trunk routes. By 1940 40 motors were operated. Carter Paterson (q.v.) considered acquiring Atlas. These talks ended with the outbreak of the Second World War. Atlas, with other carriers, operated profitably, despite the destruction of its London depot in the Blitz of 1941. Carter Paterson loaned depot space and horse vans until Atlas could return to Little Britain. Also in 1941 Arthur Packham became a director, leading Atlas to negotiate with the railways to divert some inter-depot traffic to road. A former garage was purchased in Nottingham to replace the depot, which had been requisitioned by the army. The election of the Labour government meant Atlas decided in 1950 that it would not seek nationalisation despite being limited to the 25-mile radius of operation from any depot. It continued using railway and now BRS (q.v.) services for trunk routes and parcels deliveries to agents. It was allowed permits for Scottish services and used local interworking arrangements and could claim to be the only independent carrier providing a national service.

The growth in London traffic meant a move to a more extensive depot at Barnham Street, SE1. Denationalisation saw Richard Farmer, managing director, appointed to the Road Haulage Disposal Board (q.v.). A consequence was that BRS Parcels vehicles were included in the offer for sale, though there were few bidders. Atlas later successfully tendered for 23 Special A-licensed vehicles, operating some of their own trunk services. Atlas began to expand, opening new depots, appointing agents, for Tyneside, or acquiring agents if the opportunity arose. Atlas had a subsidiary, Atexco, providing a forwarding and shipping service. For many years, it had problems and made losses. In 1954 John Ambler suggested using Atexco to start an air freight service and this grew to provide airport cargo services. A new depot at Wakefield opened in 1955, a new depot for Manchester and the acquisition of agents at Luton and Liverpool followed in 1956. This rapid expansion created problems, with delays in handling the increased traffic. Late trunk deliveries to Collins, the Birmingham agent, caused them to end their agency. Atlas then had to acquire a Birmingham operator, fortuitously available. A new depot was constructed for Birmingham, and an ex-BRS depot at Rotherhithe was purchased in 1958. By 1962, the Edinburgh agent and carriers at Bradford and Coalville had been acquired and new depots opened at Bristol, Cardiff, Nottingham and Oxford. The acquisition of Essex Carriers was completed in 1962. Atlas became Atlas Express Ltd. A century after foundation Atlas still used railway services and road transport sub-contractors for depot trunk traffic. Between 1963 and 1983 Atlas continued to expand, suffered management problems in handling traffic, and reduced reliance on British Rail for trunking and agents for local work, and used sub-contractors essentially for trunking only. Management problems and limited finances continued, also affecting maintenance and replacement of vehicles, not least to meet the requirements of the 1968 Transport Act. In 1971 the thirty-first depot opened, at Warrington, conforming to a new policy to site depots near the motorway network. A reorganisation in 1974 had Atlas Express Group as the holding company, Atlas Express, Atexco and the new Eurofreight as subsidiaries. A new office in Leicester housed a new computer department. A change to articulation for all trunk lorries created further problems, but by 1975 Atlas again claimed to be the largest independent carrier, operating 1200 vehicles and trailers. Atlas Express

suffered computer failures (affecting cash flow), poor traffic and inflation. A new managing director designate was unable to reverse management failings. The firm was saved from receivership by its acquisition by United Carriers Ltd (q.v.). **GM**

ATP is the official abbreviation, taken from the French version of the title, of the *Agreement on the International Carriage of Perishable Foodstuffs and on the Special Equipment to be used for such Carriage*, the standard for insulated and refrigerated bodies on vehicles used for international transport, published by the UN Economic Commission for Europe. Signatory states now extend beyond Europe to central Asia, Morocco and the USA. The agreement dates from 1970, but did not come into force in the UK until 1980. Though not legally needed for transport within the UK, most vehicles are built to an ATP standard.

Six classes of mechanically-refrigerated body are specified. The most common is Class C, which has heavy insulation and can be adjusted to any temperature between +12 and –20 °C; it is thus suitable for all perishable foodstuffs and is virtually standard for trailers in the UK. Class A is more common on smaller, rigid vehicles; this has less insulation and a temperature range of +12 to 0 °C, suitable for non-frozen foods.

ATP certification can apply to an individual body with its fridge unit or for type-approved production runs. Certification lasts for six years, after which a body must be resubmitted for a test, as thermal efficiency can deteriorate through damage of panels or by water seepage at joints. At one time riveted exterior panels were said to be prone to long-term ingress through the rivet holes. **JMA**
See also BODYWORK, DOORS AND ROLLER SHUTTERS

CM (24 Jan 2002)

The Austin Motor Co. Ltd (Figures 71, 115, 144 153 and 189) is best known as a car maker but it also made light commercial vehicles. It produced its first commercial vehicle in 1908, a 15-cwt chassis for use as a van or taxi, the driver sitting above the engine. In 1909 a normal-control version was produced. The first lorry was introduced in 1913; this was unconventional in having a radiator at the rear of the bonnet and a central change, four-speed gearbox with two propeller shafts, one to each rear wheel. Using an unusual pressed and pierced sideframe instead of the usual channel-section chassis and a 20-hp 4-cylinder petrol engine, a 2- or 3-ton lorry was produced. The unusual design meant it did not meet War Department requirements, so civilian buyers were still able to buy new vehicles which remained in production until 1919, the major customer being the Russian army. A smaller 30-cwt chassis, now driven through a worm-drive rear axle, was built in limited numbers for a few years from 1920.

From 1923 to 1939 Austin built only car-derived vans. In 1939 the K-series commercial vehicle range was introduced, initially as 30-cwt and 3-ton K2 chassis. The K series, it was claimed, was designed by Stepney Acres who had joined Austin from Bedford. The specification was advanced for that date, with a six-cylinder ohv engine, a 4-speed constant-mesh gearbox and Lockheed hydraulic brakes. The overall appearance and some individual parts were said to be similar to those of contemporary Bedfords, which led to the range being referred to as 'Birmingham Bedfords'. A 5-ton K4 chassis was introduced shortly after. During the Second World War civilian sales were restricted, whereas over 115,000 chassis were produced for military use. These included the 6×4 K6, which was popular as a nominal 8-ton chassis in civilian use though with single tyres it was more realistically 5-6 tons. A 4×4 K5 chassis was also produced from 1943.

After the war the K series continued until 1950, with the K3 also being marketed with a works-supplied Luton (q.v.) van body and the addition of the 25-cwt K8 forward-control chassis, sold mainly as a 'Three Way' van with side- and rear-loading. A redesigned cab and bonnet were introduced in 1950 and marketed as the Loadstar, the merging of wings and bonnet into one doing little for visibility and increasing the likelihood of dents. In 1949 the Perkins P6 diesel engine became an option.

Between the wars Austin had concentrated on car-derived light vans, built only in modest numbers. Post-war car-based vans included the A30/A35 5-6 cwt models, of which Great Universal Stores ran a huge fleet, painted green but unlettered, for mail order deliveries. A50/A55 10 cwt models followed from 1957 and 1960 saw the introduction of the transverse-engined front-wheel-drive Mini, produced in van and pick-up versions.

The merger between Austin and the Nuffield Group to form the British Motor Corporation in 1952 did not affect the Austin contract awarded in the same year for a new 4×4 K9 1-ton army chassis. From then on integration of the two makes, designs, and component parts gradually took place, the Austin ohv engine replacing the Morris Commercial side valve design. The normal-control chassis were based on the Loadstar range, but the forward-control models were largely those developed by Morris Commercial. In 1953 BMC's (q.v.) own diesel engine was introduced. Austin commercials were well received but never achieved the mass market penetration of Bedford. Following the 1952 merger, production was moved from Longbridge to Adderley Park. **GM**

Roy Church, *Herbert Austin: the British motor car industry to 1941* (Europa, 1979); Arthur Ingram, 'Austin, a pictorial survey', *Vintage Lorry Album* (1980), pp. 36–49

The **automatic coupling** (Figure 72) was originally developed for the mechanical horse (q.v.) to allow the driver to couple up to, and uncouple from, semi-trailers rapidly and without assistance. The first was the Wolverton coupling, developed in 1930 for the Karrier Cob three-wheeled tractor and patented by John Shearman, road motor engineer of the LMSR, and later developed by Karrier Motors as its BK coupling. The trailers were fitted with rollers under the turntable and with a pair of small jockey wheels on legs that supported the trailer when it was uncoupled. As the tractor reversed onto the trailer, a pair of inclined ramps on the rear of the tractor chassis engaged with the rollers, raising the jockey wheels (which were outside the tractor's rear wheels) off the ground and guiding the two halves together.

The Scammell patent coupling gear, which appeared in 1933 on Scammell's Mechanical Horse, was a more sophisticated design that had been originated by D Napier & Son Ltd, but acquired by Scammell Lorries Ltd in 1932 and refined by its chief designer, O D North (q.v.). The jockey wheels were on a central leg that automatically folded-up backwards as the coupling engaged. This allowed a full-width back axle on the tractor, giving it greater stability than the Cob tractor, whose rear wheels had to fit inside the trailer's jockey wheels. The Scammell coupling also automatically connected the trailer-brake rod and rear-light cable. Because Scammell made it available to other manufacturers, it quickly became the most commonly-used form of automatic coupling and Karrier had to bring out a compatible design: its J-type coupling.

The automatic coupling was not confined to 3-wheel mechanical horses and Karrier's 4-wheel equivalent, the Bantam. In 1939 Bedford and Scammell jointly produced an 8-ton payload 4×2 articulated tractor unit with the Scammell coupling, which remained in production for the services and essential users during the Second World War. During the war years Blands of Leicester was one of the first long-distance hauliers to use such tractors for the trunk haul, swapping trailers at the destination with a mechanical horse kept there for the town delivery and collection round. After the war the fifth wheel coupling (q.v.) became increasingly popular because it was suitable for heavier weights, and the preferred articulation system for BRS. While BRS standardised on fifth-wheel coupling, BRS Parcels used the Scammell coupling as its operations necessitated many trailer changes and movements within depots, and its loads generally cubed out (q.v.). By the late 1950s almost all lorry makers were offering 8- to 12-ton payload tractors with Scammell couplings. J Brockhouse & Co. (q.v.), Taskers of Andover (q.v.) and Hands (Letchworth) Ltd, the last in conjunction with Commer, developed their own Scammell-compatible variants of the coupling. However, two events

in the 1960s marked the beginning of the end of the automatic coupling: the introduction in 1964 of the 32-ton gross weight limit, which was beyond the practical limit of its development, and the demise soon afterwards of the mechanical horse. **GAB**

J Shearman, 'Commercial motor vehicles for short-mileage work', Proc. IAE, 33 (1938–9); Twells and Bourne (1983); Aldridge (2000)

The **Automobile Association** was founded in 1905. Although not usually associated with commercial vehicles, it had an involvement with commercial operators for many years. The AA's Industrial Vehicle Section can be traced from 1911 (and may have been inherited from the Motor Union which joined the AA in 1909). A version of the familiar AA badge, but with a red background, was provided for commercial members. A rather unexpected benefit of Industrial Vehicle Section membership after 1918 was the maintenance by agents of registers to bring loads and carriers together in a form of clearing house scheme (q.v.). During the 1919 railway strike and the General Strike (q.v.) in 1926 the AA, although professing a neutral stance, organised volunteer members to provide essential transport services, for example assisting with the carriage of mail, and, in the case of AA scouts, escorting milk supply convoys. **RAS**

H Barty-King, *The AA: a history of the first 75 years of the Automobile Association, 1905–1980* (Basingstoke, 1980)

Aveling & Porter. Thomas Aveling set up a workshop in Rochester in 1850 and in 1858 began altering some local 'portable' steam engines to make them self-moving. He then designed a complete engine, which he had built by Clayton & Shuttleworth of Lincoln. By 1861 a new works made it possible to make his own engines with two-speed gears from 1863. Aveling was also very interested in road-rollers and, from his first in 1867, they became a major product. Steam traction engines for road use were manufactured from about 1871.

Originally his traction engines were designed mainly for threshing, but after 1904 some 4-nhp engines running on solid rubber tyres took advantage of the new road speed limit. Some overtype steam lorries were also produced, similar in appearance to the Foden, but with the white horse of Kent on the smokebox door or chimney. Between 1909 and 1925 about 290 compound overtype steam wagons were built, twelve under licence by Garrett (q.v.). From 1913 to 1916 a number of petrol-engined lorries were built as well as Steam Sappers for the War Office. In 1919 it joined Agricultural and General Engineers (AGE), a gathering of steam engineers and vehicle makers.

In 1930, following a financial crisis at AGE, the firm joined Barford Perkins of Peterborough, makers of internal-combustion-engined rollers, as Aveling-Barford. Aveling moved out of its factory on the banks of the Medway relinquishing it to Winget Ltd which made cement mixers and dumper trucks. The last Aveling steam engine, made in the group's Grantham factory in 1938, was a convertible either for traction or rolling. Aveling-Barford made dumpers from the late 1930s and dumptrucks from 1947 till the present. **RWK**

Edward Barford, *Reminiscences of a Lance-Corporal of Industry* (Elm Tree, 1972)

AWD Ltd was set up in 1987 by the highly successful engineer David J B Brown, manufacturer of Artix articulated dump trucks, when he purchased the former Bedford commercial vehicle plant at Dunstable from General Motors. AWD was the acronym for 'all-wheel drive', a feature associated with Brown's products. He was denied the use of the Bedford name, which some considered was a handicap. From a dominant position in the UK truck market in the 1960s with its TK range, Bedford had lost ground to rivals such as Ford and Leyland. AWD's initial aim was to build improved TL and TM trucks from the former Bedford range standardising on Perkins (q.v.) engines. The 7.5 litre TL sold to a variety of mainly own-account operators. It

also produced the normal-control TJ model, first introduced in 1958 with a cab based on a 1947 GM design, mainly as chassis or in completely-knocked-down form for export. AWD got off to a good start with a £50 million Ministry of Defence order for 2000 army trucks in March 1988 and in September of the same year introduced an updated 7½-tonne TL and announced plans to raise output by 50 per cent. The UK market was targeted at this time, with a 47-distributor network. A number of breweries bought AWDs, including the TL-based 'urban articulated'. Swift (q.v.) Transport Services acquired 12 AWDs in late 1990; other customers included Cheshire Highways department and own-account users, but AWD remained over-dependent on overseas and military orders. Overseas orders were forthcoming, but in June 1989 AWD was an unsuccessful bidder for the crucial Ministry of Defence £500 million contract for 20,000 army trucks which went to Leyland-DAF. Attempts to sell off part of the site for residential use failed on planning grounds and the company was faced with an unprecedented slump in domestic commercial vehicle sales, which was not compensated for by sufficient overseas orders. The result was that in June 1992 the company's bankers called in the receivers, after only 22 trucks had been built in the first quarter. In October 1992 AWD was sold to Marshalls SPV (q.v.), which moved design and production to its Cambridge site. Some production continued, but in 1999 the Bedford parts business and some designs were sold to Western Star's ERF (q.v.). Brown's other business concerns were not directly affected by AWD's downfall.

In the 1950s another AWD business, initially at Camberley, made specialist vehicles, primarily for off-road use. It became crane chassis makers, Vickers-AWD at South Marston, Swindon in the 1970s. **RAS**

Modern Records Centre, University of Warwick Library: MSS.226X/IND/60; Broatch and Townsin (1996); *VCV*, 115, (July 1999), p. 6; Coates (1993), p. 128; Nick Baldwin, *CVC* (1996)

B

B licence, see LICENSING

Back-loading, see RETURN LOADS

Baico Patents Ltd is often associated with chassis extension, but the firm began in 1914 as the British & American Import Co., selling US chassis in the UK. After the war Baico specialised in extending and strengthening the Ford T chassis to provide up to 2½-ton capacity. Such vehicles formed the basis of many country carriers' business. Baico later concentrated on normal- to forward-control conversion, chassis extension and third-axle addition. Baico became part of the Ryland Group in 1975. **RAS**

N Baldwin, 'A to Z of world buses', *Bus & Coach Preservation*, 2, 2, (1999), p. 43; P R Daniels, *Vintage Lorry Album* (1983)

Bank (Figure 73) was the term applied to the raised platform at a parcel or goods depot used for the loading and unloading of goods carried by cart or lorry. Its height accommodated that of the average vehicle floor. The term came into use on the railways, where even a modest goods shed had a bank for the transhipment of goods under cover from railway wagons to road vehicles. 'Across the bank' was a common expression for the movement of goods from vehicle to vehicle on this loading platform or 'deck'. **RAS**

Dunbar (1981), p. 132; J Simmons, *The Victorian Railway* (1991), p. 185; *OCBRH* (1997), p. 183

Barrington, Claud, MIMechE, MInstT (1893–1960) was badly wounded at the Battle of the Somme in August 1916. After recovery from his wounds he was appointed 'Royal Engineers, Docks & Inland Waterways, Chief Road Inspector, Scotland'. During his service, he also met Lt Col Alfred Scammell and by 1922 became an agent for Scammell Lorries. He saw the opportunities in road transport and

was involved in the setting up of the National Road Transport Clearing House (q.v.), which operated 20 Scammell 6-wheel lorries. The NRTCH was placed into receivership in 1923, the 20 Scammells being resold. Barrington then became an executive director of a London clearing house, Carey, Davis & Thomas Ltd. From this he created a haulage subsidiary, General Roadways (q.v.), again operating Scammells. This became the basis for the formation of a publicly-quoted company, Transport Services Ltd (q.v.), in 1936 of which he was managing director. It expanded to some 26 subsidiaries, covering all types of traffic. In 1941 he was appointed chief road officer of the Road Haulage Organisation (q.v.), and then Director of Road Haulage. With the voluntary acquisition of Transport Services by the British Transport Commission in 1948, he was appointed a member of the Road Transport Executive, later the Road Haulage Executive, with responsibility for mechanical and civil engineering, and for freight traffic, operations, commercial rates and claims. He became managing director of BRS (Parcels) in 1956. He was also chairman of the Atlantic Steam Navigation Co. Ltd and BRS (Pickfords) Ltd. **GM**

The Times (1 November 1960)

Bassetts. The family-owned general haulage firm L J Bassett, based at Tittensor, Staffordshire, grew out of an agricultural and road-building contracting business founded by Leonard John Bassett's father, Joseph, in 1897. Its first petrol lorry was bought in 1915 to join a fleet of steam wagons that had been built up primarily for moving road stone. Initially the firm operated locally within the Potteries, but in the mid-1930s, after it had been renamed L J Bassett & Son Ltd and the son, Reginald Guy Bassett, had taken over its management, trunk services to Liverpool and Birmingham were introduced. It had 22 vehicles when nationalised in 1949.

In 1945 the family established Grayswood Transport Ltd, to operate B-licensed (q.v.) lorries on local work, leaving the original firm to operate the A-licensed (q.v.) vehicles. Thus it remained in local haulage when the trunking firm was nationalised. In 1951 the area of operation was expanded by partial acquisition of another local haulage firm, H Mason Transport (Stafford) Ltd.

Bassett Roadways Ltd was created in 1954 to purchase de-nationalised A-licensed vehicles from BRS and to re-establish the Liverpool and Birmingham services. By 1958 it had a fleet of 34, while Grayswood Transport had 30. The 1960s saw expansion into warehousing. Because the family firms were controlled by his mother, Reg Bassett registered some vehicles in his own company which became R G Bassett & Sons Ltd in 1964. In 1968–9, following the Transport Act this company absorbed the fleets of the other three. It is now managed by the fourth generation of Bassetts, Reg's sons, Ashley and Leonard. In 1996 it entered the international haulage business by purchasing Beresford Transport Ltd of Tunstall, Stoke-on-Trent, which had been operating European routes since 1965. In 1997 Bassetts operated a fleet of 55 heavy goods vehicles. **GAB**

Phillips and Baron (1997)

Baxendale, Lloyd Henry (1858–1937) was always known as Harry. His grandfather, Joseph, had acquired ownership in 1850 of the road haulage firm of Pickfords from the family. After education at Eton and Christ Church College, Oxford, Harry went into Pickfords in 1879. By 1894 he was one of the partners and in 1901, when Pickfords became a private limited company, he was allotted about one third of the capital and became a director. The major part of Pickfords business at this time was collecting and delivering for the railways but, strangely, in 1901 it was decided to break with the LNWR, which precipitated a crisis as Pickfords revenue plunged and the directors fell out. The senior partner withdrew, taking his capital with him and leaving the firm hard pressed to finance the change from horse to motor transport. As a result in 1912 Pickfords merged with Carter Paterson & Co., until then its main rival.

Harry Baxendale became chairman of the joint company, the largest in the road haulage industry. To reap the benefits of the merger significant rationalisation was needed. In London Carter Paterson took over virtually all the parcels work while Pickfords was dominant in the provinces. As these changes were being implemented, the firm was hit by competition in London from W&G Express Carriers (q.v.) which was well financed and by 1913 had over 100 light motor vans. This forced the amalgamated company to buy even more motor vehicles to compete. In 1914 the firm carried over 28 million parcels.

In 1920 Pickfords was sold to the Hay's Wharf Cartage Co. (q.v.) and Baxendale, who had been chairman of Pickfords as well as the joint company, stood down to allow Major O C Magniac of Hay's Wharf to take it over. Baxendale remained a director of Pickfords as well as joining the Hay's Wharf Cartage board. After the four mainline railway companies jointly bought the Hay's Wharf Cartage Co. and Pickfords in 1933, Baxendale resigned from his directorships, ending the family's connexion with the firm.

Baxendale oversaw the shift from horse to motor transport by Pickfords, but with little enthusiasm and a strong emotional attachment to the horse, as demonstrated by his long involvement in Newbury racecourse. Given that he was one of those responsible for the break with the LNWR in 1901, which seems akin to corporate suicide, there must be some doubt as to his judgement. He seemed to believe that the firm could pick up work from the Great Central and Lancashire & Yorkshire Railways, which proved illusory. After the merger of 1912 it is difficult to discern his hand on the tiller and Pickfords appear to have been subject to impersonal economic forces and much larger scale players. It lacked dynamic leadership until the 1930s when W J Elliott became general manager. **JA**

DBB, I, pp. 218–19; Turnbull (1979)

Bean Cars Ltd of Dudley, Worcestershire, in 1926 succeeded A Harper Sons & Bean Ltd, founded in 1907, becoming a parts supplier to the motor industry. Its roots went back to the Harper family foundry set up in 1826. In 1919 car production began and, despite financial crises arising from the ill-advised Harper Bean consortium, which included Vulcan, a 20/25-cwt lorry was introduced in 1924. The Hadfield steel company took over Beans in 1926, a 30-cwt lorry was introduced in 1927, the 50-cwt Empire chassis in 1929 and the 20/25-cwt New Era in 1931. A substantial order for can-carrying trucks was received from BP in 1927. Profit margins were negligible and the company could not compete with the larger manufacturers and went into liquidation in 1931. It was re-formed as Beans Industries and once more supplied components to the motor industry. In 1968 it became part of British Leyland. Between 1924 and 1931 Beans built over 6000 lorries. **GK/RAS**

J Boulton and H Parsons, *Powered Vehicles in the Black Country* (Black Country Society, 1990); Wood (2001); Geoffrey Tweedale, 'Business and investment strategies in the inter-war British steel industry: a case study of Hadfield Ltd and Bean Cars', *Business History*, 29, 1 (1987), pp. 47–72

Beardmore, William, & Co. Ltd was best known as heavy engineers and shipbuilders on Clydeside. It had a somewhat unfocussed involvement with the commercial vehicle industry, principally between the two world wars. Sir John I Thornycroft was chairman from 1901 to 1907 and Thornycroft steam vehicles were made under licence by Beardmore's Stewart subsidiary to 1911. Despite its purchase in 1919 of J H Kelly's commercial vehicle works in the appropriately named Van Street, Glasgow, it was best known and most successful at building taxicabs, from 1919 in Paisley. The chassis provided the basis for a rather expensive van for a few years in the 1920s.

Beardmore's involvement in heavy commercial vehicles was short-lived. In 1930 it acquired the patent of the French Chenard-Walcker tractor (q.v.) which enabled part of the drawbar trailer weight to be taken on the tractor. Production started in Clapham, London, of normal-control tractor vehicles: the Cobra, for 10-ton loads; the Python for 10- to

15-ton loads; and the Anaconda, a 15-ton tractor. All used Meadows engines. Customers included George Cohen, Watneys the brewers and Manbré & Garton. In 1932 the business was sold to Multiwheelers of Harrow which continued production of the tractors until 1937 but using AEC or Gardner engines.

Subsequently Beardmores itself produced a new rigid maximum-load (12 tons gross) forward-control, 4-wheel lorry which was built in limited numbers on Clydeside until the Second World War intervened. In the mid-1930s there was also a new Beardmore diesel engine which proved embarassingly unsuccessful. **GK/RAS**

Hume and Moss (1979); Baldwin and Ingram (1977); Stevens-Stratten (1992); Townsin (2001)

Beck & Pollitzer (Figure 74) was started in the 1850s by John Beck and Sigismund Pollitzer as warehouse keepers, wharfingers and carmen, expanding into shipping and forwarding agents, export packers, specialist haulage contractors, machinery removal and installation and exhibition contractors. B&P worked mostly in London and the Home Counties. Among services provided were groupage of export traffic to Port of London Authority docks, a parcels delivery service in London for own-account operators and provincial carriers, and stand-fitting and lifting services at the Earls Court and Olympia exhibition halls.

In 1961 B&P became publicly-quoted and later was acquired by the Transport Development Group (q.v.). Subsequently there were various re-structurings. The exhibition work and forwarding division became a separate subsidiary within TDG Southern Ltd, as did distribution and warehousing. Lorry types favoured included Albion, ERF and Scammell. Later the exhibition stand contracting and the machinery and installation division became subsidiaries within TDG Contract Holdings Ltd. Further reorganisation resulted in mergers of other TDG subsidiaries form TDG Beck & Pollitzer, specialising in industrial logistics contracts. The machinery installation and transport business was the subject of a management buy-out. **GM**

Bedford. (Figures 3, 11, 36, 75, 156 and 171) Chevrolet trucks were imported completely-knocked-down from Detroit and assembled at Hendon from 1929 to 1931 under the management of Vauxhall Motors. A full dealer network was established so that in 1931, when Vauxhall opened its new truck-building facility at Luton, the new product, called 'Bedford', was able to replace the Chevrolet seamlessly. The Bedford had been designed in Britain for American-style mass production and, although similar to the Chevrolet, had nothing in common with the imported product, only that General Motors had provided the expertise and finance.

Within six years Bedford could claim 25 per cent of the British commercial vehicle market, despite having a payload range confined to the 3-ton or less sector. In addition, Vauxhall claimed that 60 per cent of exported British commercial vehicles were Bedfords. The success was due to rigid adherence to standardisation, which kept prices low and volume high. Any variations from the standard were done by authorised outside contractors, who provided such things as extra axles, extended chassis and specialised bodies. Only one petrol engine, built by the company, was offered for heavy vehicles and this continued in production for more than twenty years, although its capacity was increased (to 3.5 litres) in the mid-thirties. There were some cosmetic changes to the exterior of the vehicles. The first range was upgraded twice with first a new cab and radiator shell, and then a new cab and bonnet with the well known O-series 'bull nose' radiator. No sooner had this appeared in 1939 than the Second World War interrupted production.

The Ministry of War Transport valued the mass production facility at Luton. Indeed the British government had earlier asked Bedford if it could produce 20,000 light to medium trucks a year if war should break out. Thus production of road vehicles for military and later, limited civilian use, continued. A revised utility cab structure replaced the rounded O-series cab, to produce the OW series. Further military lorries were provided, including 4-wheel-drive (Q series), small-capacity trucks (MW series) and high-set trucks for rough terrain (OY series). The diversity avoided by Bedford in the pre-war years was thus brought to the factory in wartime.

The civilian demands of peacetime brought a return to the Bedford catalogue of 1939, reintroducing the O series, but with some military production retained and a slightly larger range. In 1950, a new 7-ton Big Bedford was launched, introducing the first normal-control model designed for civilian use. Known as the S series, this had an American-inspired curvaceous pressed metal cab and grille; for greater payloads it was powered by a new Bedford 4.9 litre petrol engine. Pressure for diesel engines resulted in such units being offered from 1953, with Perkins (q.v.) and Leyland engines made available in new machines. From 1957, a diesel version of the 4.9 litre Bedford engine became available. Many older Bedfords were fitted with Perkins engines by their owners. Also in 1953, the O series was superseded by the A series with pressed metal cab/bonnet of American appearance, although the engine remained the 3.5 litre petrol unit first built in the 1930s.

In 1954, a new truck factory was established at Dunstable and the number of models increased. Many were passenger chassis, but the most significant new truck was the forward-control 3- to 4-ton T series, with engine set well back in the frame. First produced in 1960, the initial TK model went through a number of developments over the years and became a best-seller with more than half a million sold worldwide by 1980, making it the UK's all-time best-selling lorry. Market pressure for a bigger-capacity truck led to the introduction in 1964 of the KM, powered by a new Bedford 7.6 litre engine. This was followed by the first factory-made 3-axle Bedford trucks. The post-war military truck (R series) was replaced by a new model (M series) in 1970.

Bedford produced one million vehicles between 1958 and 1968, but the best days were over. Foreign imports into Britain, increased competition in overseas markets, particularly from Japanese and German products in the medium capacity (2- to 5-ton) range, and increased sophistication of motor vehicles, did not favour the Bedford ethic of simple and cheap. The heavy vehicles failed to impress, the medium weight market was subjected to intense competition, and the coach market was in severe decline. The T series was improved by the introduction of a turbo-charged engine in 1976 (TM) and a tilt-cab in 1980 (TL) and it remained popular in Britain. The ranges suffered from a lack of funding for development and improvement and in the mid-1980s the parent General Motors decided to cease manufacture of buses and trucks, and to continue only with light vans and pick-ups.

Initially, Vauxhall car chassis provided the basis for small 5-cwt to 1-ton capacity vans and pick-ups. In conjunction with Martin Walter, a low-cost glazed van/personnel carrier was marketed as 'Utilecon' (Ford also used this name, combining utility and economy). The vehicles carried Bedford badges. This procedure continued until, in 1952, a purpose-built semi-forward-control van called the CA was introduced. This was modified too by Martin Walter as the 'Dormobile'. Alongside this model, car derivatives continued, notably the HA series based on the Viva (1964), the Chevanne based on the Chevette car, and Astravan based on the Astra. In 1968, the long running CF van was produced to compete with the Ford Transit.

Vauxhall entered into a contract to build Suzuki small-capacity forward-control vans to attract those wanting a small-size, easy-to-manoeuvre 5-cwt type vehicle, although the model declared itself to be a full half-tonner. The vehicle was marketed as the Bedford Rascal, although examples have been seen outside Britain carrying GMC badges. Larger vans were Isuzu-based and badged Bedford. When Vauxhall pulled out of commercial vehicle manufacture, the TL and military M series trucks continued to be made by AWD, but when this entity went bankrupt, the military design was taken over by Marshall (q.v.) SPV of Cambridge. While car manufacture ceased at Luton in 2002, a joint project between General Motors and Renault built increasing numbers of large vans for sale with Nissan, Opel, Renault and Vauxhall badges. **ARP**

Broatch and Townsin (1995 and 1996); *CM* (1 March 1980), p. 39

Belhaven Engineering & Motors Ltd was founded in 1910 by Robert Morton & Son Ltd, metal founders of Wishaw, Morton continuing in being as the Morton Machine Co. Ltd after vehicle production ceased in 1924. Before the Belhaven company was established, Morton produced steam vehicles under licence from Lifu, badged as either Morton or Belhaven. Petrol-engined taxis and light vans were produced from 1908, being replaced from 1910 by heavier commercial vehicles, buses and charabancs. Some lorries were supplied to the War Department; steam vehicle production was phased out during the First World War. After the war, chassis were supplied to the Scottish Co-operative Wholesale Society as the basis of its Unitas marque and the United Co-operative Baking Society also operated Belhaven/Unitas vehicles. **RAS**

Anon, *Scottish Cars: their history and a descriptive Guide to a few of those which survive* (Glasgow: Art Gallery & Museum, 1962); G Oliver, *Motor Trials and Tribulations* (Edinburgh: HMSO for Glasgow Museums, 1993); Grieves (1997)

Belsize Motors Ltd of Clayton, Manchester, cycle-makers, began to build French Hurtu cars in 1897. It was re-formed in 1906 to add commercial vehicles to its motor car and taxi range. By 1911 it had a workforce of 1200 in a 7-acre works, producing 1300 vehicles a year. During the First World War output peaked at fifty per week. After the war the firm concentrated on 12-cwt vans and light cars. It collapsed in 1925 with £500,000 of debts. **RAS**
N Baldwin, 'A to Z of world buses', *Bus & Coach Preservation*, 2, 6 (October 1999), pp. 43–4

Berliet, Automobiles M, based in Lyon, produced both cars and commercial vehicles, the latter from 1902. Despite going into receivership in 1921, Berliet opened a UK plant on a 2-acre site at Richmond Bridge Works, Twickenham, in 1925. The general manager was an English production engineer, S J Egerton Banks, who had organised Berliet's wartime production and taken charge of Berliet's English subsidiary in 1921. The

Twickenham works held a vast spares stock and also supplied new vehicles, mostly of 3- to 5-ton capacity, apparently imported both complete and part-assembled. Banks pursued a vigorous publicity campaign, for example producing the *Berliet Times* between 1924 and 1927, and developed a colonial sales network. However, sales dwindled and he left in 1927. A new subsidiary, the Berliet Motor & Engineering Co. Ltd, was set up in July 1927, but went into liquidation in 1932. The French parent company continued in existence, producing a range from vans to 12/15-ton lorries in the 1930s. Berliet concentrated after the war on vehicles above four tons. It was taken over by Citroen in 1967, but passed to Renault in 1974. **RAS**

Kennett (1981); information kindly supplied by the Fondation de l'Automobile Marius Berliet, Lyon; Twickenham Urban District Council minutes

Berna. This Swiss marque, established in 1905, was for a few years (1908–12) British-owned, in the hands of the financial group Hudson Consolidated, with vehicles for the UK market assembled in Kensington. Berna vehicles were of robust construction and nearly 600 Swiss Berna lorries were supplied to the British army in the First World War and to civilian customers in the 1920s, including 45 6-ton models to the Union Cartage Co. Ltd for meat transport in 1928. They were considered more capable of hauling a trailer than UCC's Pierce-Arrows and their compression braking system was also regarded as a point in their favour. After Saurer (q.v.) and Berna merged in 1929, the Saurer marque took precedence in exports to the UK.

British Berna Motor Lorries Ltd (1914–18) marketed a lorry closely related to the Swiss version, but manufactured by Henry Watson & Sons Ltd, Newcastle upon Tyne, producers of metal castings. More than three hundred of the British Berna were supplied to the Army. Watson continued as lorry manufacturers under its own name after the First World War, adding a 6-ton model in 1922 to the original 3½- and 4½-ton models announced in 1920. The firm was listed until 1929, but Georgano

doubts that they manufactured for the whole of this period. **RAS**

Lorries, Trucks and Vans since 1928; CVC (January 1999), p. 16; K C Blacker, 'Moving meat', *Vintage Commercial*, 1, 8 (April 1963), pp. 251–7; Ingram (1975)

BETAC was formed in 1972 as the Brewery Transport Advisory Committee but in 2001 changed its name to the British Transport Advisory Committee. It holds regular meetings, an annual conference and a fuel efficiency and technical evaluation event. The latter includes comparative fuel consumption tests between a range of vehicle configurations, different makes or the same-sized vehicles with engines of various outputs. Stability trials of tractor-trailer combinations have been another feature. The change of name resulted from decisions by some major breweries to outsource all their transport operations or to obtain vehicles on financial arrangements in which the manufacturer or its dealers were responsible for all maintenance and repair. Membership in 2002 included transport managers from distribution companies, supermarket chains and other major commercial vehicle users with fleets totalling over 100,000 vehicles. **JMA**

Betz, Willi, international haulier, had no vehicles registered in the UK at the beginning of the twenty-first century, but had been working into the country for a quarter of a century, and had an office in Felixstowe and a terminal in Dover. In recent years the higher profile here of the blue-liveried Betz lorries with bright yellow tilt, often crewed by two central-European drivers, led to questions in the UK about the use of non-EU nationals by the firm. Founded in Undingen, West Germany, in 1951 by Willi Betz, who still headed the business in 2000, with his son Thomas, the firm, later based in Reutlingen, had deep penetration into eastern Europe, resulting originally from its working agreement with the Bulgarian enterprise Somat in 1968, which became a 55 per cent holding on privatisation of Somat in 1994. Betz had

4000 vehicles, with an equivalent Somat fleet. The very large percentage of Mercedes-Benz Actros tractors in the Betz fleet has given rise to questions about the relationship between manufacturer and operator and the fleet, by virtue of its size and scope of operations, was clearly a subject of interest to the trade press. A wide variety of bodies was employed for the range of traffic, including refrigerated and vehicle transporter trailers. Logistics services are a significant element in Betz's current business. **RAS**

Truck (March 1999), p. 37, (December 2000), pp. 40–5; *transporte mundial*, 153 (March 2000), pp. 50–2; *Sistema Globale*, supplement to *Tuttotransporti*, 222 (October 2000), pp. 8–11

Birmingham Bedfords was the name by which the Austin K series was colloquially known.

Biscuit Delivery Pool, see ASSOCIATED DELIVERIES LTD

The **Bishop's Move Group,** (Figure 76) now owned and run by the fifth and sixth generations of the Bishop family, is surely the oldest family transport business in Britain. It was established in Pimlico, London, in 1854 by Joseph James Bishop, who originated in Norfolk as a greengrocer's business, but by 1861 the focus of activity had shifted to furniture storage and removals (q.v.). In 1878 the company became Joseph James Bishop & Sons and in 1927 it was incorporated as Bishop & Sons' Depositories Ltd. Bishop's Move Ltd was formed in 1955 as an associate company to protect the familiar trade name. The headquarters remained in Pimlico, where extensive depositories were established, until 1988 when its London operations moved to new premises near Nine Elms, Battersea.

At the peak of horse operation 24 horses, mainly Suffolk Punches, were in use. Mechanisation began in 1910 with the purchase of a Foden 5-ton steam lorry, followed by a Foden 3-tonner in 1912 and Bishop's first motor lorry in about 1913, but horses were retained for local use until 1948/9. From 1920 onwards Bishops grew by the purchase of existing removal firms, especially in the south and south-west and in Scotland. More recently it turned to franchising, through which it has extended its coverage throughout Britain. By the end of the century the Bishop's Move Group had 11 branches and 11 franchisees in provincial centres, as well as the London branch.

At Nine Elms there were also two specialised branches. The first was the overseas branch set up in 1974. Bishops had arranged overseas removals using lift vans (see CONTAINERISATION) since at least the early 1900s, but the introduction of roll-on/roll-off ferries meant that Bishop's vehicles and drivers were now travelling through to the continent. This was followed by a corporate relocations branch for handling staff relocation removals, a market that had developed largely since the Second World War. A major operation in 1953 was the removal of the offices of the British American Tobacco Co. Ltd from Egham to Millbank: a convoy of 23 vehicles was employed, which transferred 100 loads in under two days. At least two Fordson Thames articulated pantechnicons were involved in this operation.

Bishops have bought and taken over a great variety of vehicles at different times, but Morris Commercials predominated from the 1930s to 1960, then Bedfords into the 1970s, and Mercedes-Benz since then. It also used several body-builders, particularly Sparshatts and the North British Coach Works which it acquired in 1950 and renamed Edinburgh Coachworks Ltd. At the end of the century Bishops itself operated some 120 vehicles and its franchisees another 24, carrying the distinctive Bishop's move logo on a pale yellow livery. Justly proud of its history, the company has restored in its livery a Purdey-built horse-drawn pantechnicon of 1900 and a Foden 5-ton steam lorry and lift van. **RAS/GAB**

Bishop's Move Group, *On the Move for over 125 years* (1979); Robert Coates, 'Bishop's Moves', *VCVM*, 76 (April 1996), pp. 6–9, 77 (May 1996), pp. 12–17; *Old Glory*, 122 (April 2000), pp. 42–4; information supplied by Roger J Bishop

Blue Band Motors Ltd, express parcels carriers of Lockerbie, began in 1928 as a bus service which also carried parcels. It was acquired by Matthew Turnbull in 1951, expanding into haulage in 1955 following a successful tender for Special A-licensed vehicles delivering hanging meat to London, returning with fruit. A rail strike led to the provision of a parcels service between Glasgow and the south of Scotland, augmenting the bus parcels service. By 1971, when Matthew's son Michael joined, Blue Band comprised coaches, haulage and parcels, and operated some 30 vehicles.

The decision to expand the parcels operation led to the acquisition of some small carriers, at first in the north west. Acquisitions in 1981 included Sunray Transport of Leicester and Turnbulls of Airth, Falkirk, each with 15 vehicles. The other parts of Blue Band were sold and the now-titled Blue Band Express became purely a parcels carrier. Other Scottish carriers were acquired. Blue Band used some inter-working and was a member of the short-lived ten-member Proprietor Express Parcels Services started in 1984. After a period of consolidation, the acquisition of Ailey Transport Ltd of Raunds, operating over 100 vehicles from six depots, gave a virtually nationwide service. Two later acquisitions improved the service to the south west, that of Contraflow of Ilkeston in 1996 introducing hanging garment deliveries.

In 2000 Blue Band remained a family business operating some 300 vehicles and 160 trailers from 15 depots, and also handling palletised distribution. It acquired the Focus parcels division of Pall-Ex in 2000 then was subject to a management buy-in in 2001 but went into liquidation and ceased to operate in 2002. The livery was dark and light blue with red lettering. **GM**

BMC, see BRITISH MOTOR CORPORATION

Boalloy Industries Ltd, (Figures 4 and 57) bodybuilders, was founded as Bowyer Brothers (Congleton) Ltd in 1947, the founding directors including two staff from Jennings of Sandbach (q.v.), Harold Lea and R Fletcher. The business developed as producers of alloy cabs for most forward-control chassis and a wide range of alloy lorry bodies. By 1958 there was a workforce of forty. Bowyers came up against unfamiliar body-construction problems, posed by palletisation, problems solved relatively easily by the fitting of extra cross-members to the alloy sub-frame. Cabs were produced for major manufacturers, such as ERF, Foden, Guy, Leyland, Seddon and Thornycroft and such minor producers as Rutland and TVW. Alloy flat and tipper bodies were produced for direct sales by ERF and Foden. Box, Luton and pantechnicon bodies were also an important part of Boalloy output, which moved to semi-mass production following successful co-operation with Syd Abrams, Bedford dealers of Manchester, to produce an integrated pantechnicon (q.v.). This line conveniently replaced cab production, after ERF bought Jennings, Guy had moved to supply by Motor Panels, and some smaller customers had disappeared.

Boalloy's greatest claim to fame was from the late 1960s when under the enthusiastic guidance of Gerald Broadbent it pioneered development of curtain-sided bodywork (q.v.) named the Tautliner for both rigid vehicles and semi-trailers, creating a market that it dominated for a time.

Ownership of the company passed in 1988 to Marling Industries, which bought it from Gerald Broadbent, Jeff Browning and Brian Abrams. In 1992 the management team at Boalloy bought the company from Marling. In 1994 it developed the 'one-stop shopping' (q.v.) concept for larger vehicles, initially with Leyland DAF. It established a small, satellite body-assembly plant adjacent to that maker's truck-building plant in Lancashire. The chassis-cab was delivered to Boalloy, which fitted a body in accordance with the customer's order, and the complete vehicle then underwent its pre-delivery inspection by the maker, and was ready for the customer to put straight into service. Until then it was normal — and is still common — for chassis-cabs to be delivered to bodybuilders situated perhaps hundreds of miles away from the chassis-builders, a process that takes time and costs money. In 2000 Boalloy Industries included M&G Trailers of Lye, Stourbridge, and works at Bellshill, Cumbernauld, Newcastle-under-Lyme, Purfleet and Avonmouth, as well as the original Congleton location.   **RAS/JMA**

G Broadbent, 'A life in the world of transport', *VCVM*, 5, 24–5, (1990), pp. 148–52, 166–9; Boalloy advertisement, January 1997

Bodybuilders The number of bodybuilders has always been far higher than the number of builders of chassis, and they have always ranged in size from the smallest (employing just one or two people) to large well-known names with several hundred staff. Traditionally the smallest have operated from premises situated under railway arches (or from small yards). Some were in business building (or bodying) horse-drawn carts before the motor era, and other bodied cars as well as lorries, but such diversity gradually waned as the larger car makers adopted production-line techniques and pressed metal panels from the late 1920s onwards. Another change that took away the skills and added value of bodybuilding was the development of new paints and cellulose, initially for the car market, that gave better coverage and dried quickly: no longer did a well-finished body need 22 coats of paint and varnish.

Competition for bodybuilders came from several sources, obviously from other nearby bodybuilders, but also from chassis makers and from the workshops of many large operators such as McNamara (q.v.) or Pickfords (q.v.). Even today there are a few operators still building their own bodies. Until the end of the 1930s most chassis builders offered a comprehensive range of relatively simple body types, partly because they already had a body shop for building cabs. A few, such as AEC, did not build cabs, merely providing designs or dimensional drawings for others: even here AEC produced literature illustrating specific body types such as tippers though none had AEC-built bodies. The major volume producers of the mid- and late-1930s, such as Ford and Bedford, soon distanced themselves from bodybuilding and after the end of the

Second World War other manufacturers too generally limited themselves to building their own cabs but little else.

Operators with their own body shops generally had more than enough work after 1945 in patching and mending their existing worn fleets, but some resumed bodybuilding. Accounting was fairly rudimentary then and few operators had much idea of what the real costs were. In any event, the urgent need for new vehicles was probably more important than their actual cost. The backlog of orders and deliveries meant that many new bodybuilders set up, producing new bodies to go on new chassis, or on older overhauled chassis, or just undertaking rebuilds.

By about the early 1950s the backlog had been overcome and the number of bodybuilders began to drop. Pricing became more competitive and the number of operators building for their own use declined. By the 1970s those that remained were a mixture, with some of those tied bodybuilders producing only a proportion of the requirements of their associated fleet. A small number of them had to tender for the work in the same way as outside bodybuilders. Earlier, nationalisation of most hire and reward road haulage had meant more standardisation with relatively few being selected to build in quantity for BRS or for the then large fleets of British Railways.

Even so the bodybuilding industry continued to be made up of numerous firms of varying size. A 1971 estimate put the total number of UK bodybuilders at around 550 of which about one hundred were fairly well-known with production facilities of some substance. The remainder were either relatively small or very specialised, the latter usually offering only a few specific types or alternatively producing custom designs for an individual operator.

The larger, better-known bodybuilders over the years have proved almost as likely to fade away as small firms. Since the 1980s the position has probably worsened. Larger operators generally buy from larger bodybuilders, as they alone can supply the quantities required within a relatively tight timescale. Recessions or potential recessions can quickly lead to decisions to cut back orders, or perhaps stop buying new vehicles for, say, a year, a decision that is relatively easy to make. It is much harder for an individual bodybuilder to replace the large volume of work that such a customer represented. In addition, repeat business for larger customers has sometimes only been obtained at the expense of lower profit margins, a process that ultimately drove a bodybuilder out of business.

Outside influences can work the other way and bring in work almost undreamt of. Tighter legislation and new trends in food-buying habits led to a boost in refrigerated vehicles and trailers from about the late 1970s and a need for multi-temperature bodywork, with separate — and usually moveable — compartments for goods at ambient, chilled and frozen temperatures led to enormous growth in this area. By early in the 21st century this demand had been virtually satisfied with future orders likely to continue at a much lower level.

Difficult times can also bring added competition from unlikely sources. For example coach and bus bodybuilder Plaxtons of Scarborough produced small quantities of commercial vehicle bodies from time to time, including cattle floats in the 1930s and vans for the US Air Force and bakery vans in the 1950s. Then, during a downturn in the coach market, a short period in the late 1960s saw well over 600 bodies built for Post Office Telephones: all were 1- or 1½-ton utility vehicles on Morris chassis. **JMA**

Bodywork (Figure 22). Often those who built horse-drawn drays used the same skills and materials for bodying the first commercial vehicles. The relative speed of the motor vehicle and its vibration soon pointed to the need for greater strength and durability, when still using timber as the main material. The point was demonstrated dramatically in the early 1930s when the railways experimented with the first mechanical horses (q.v.) hauling former horse-drawn drays: the drays almost literally fell apart.

Woodworking was widely practised and timber was reasonably priced and widely available, if not home-grown then imported mainly from the British Empire. The timber was usually of high quality and seasoned, with oak or ash used for framing, while mahogany was popular for panelling. In contrast, three-ply birch might be used for panelling less expensive bodies. Teak was also used for framing and was still being advertised for use in the mid-1950s. The merits of different timbers were taken seriously by some bodybuilders. Ash is lighter than oak, stronger and more elastic but very susceptible to worm, whereas oak is immune. In the 1930s the move to curved bodywork favoured ash, or American oak. Often quite a senior employee visited the supplier to select or approve the timber before it was delivered.

Bodies on early commercial vehicles were generally of just two types, either a simple open platform, with or without low sides — dropsides — to help retain the load, or an enclosed van. Early van bodies often had a low capacity as they were built inside the width of the rear axle track: boxed-in wheelarches as part of a wider body came a little later. Access was usually through a single rear door. The poor reliability of early commercials meant their operators paid scant attention to their bodywork: they were too busy trying to get the mechanicals to work.

After the First World War vehicles became more reliable and there were plenty of people to drive and maintain them. More thought was given to making better use of bodywork designed for specific purposes. Most manufacturers of vehicles offered a wide choice of body types in the 1920s and 1930s, built in their own workshops. They needed a bodybuilding section to build cabs (q.v.) anyway, and there was a fair degree of standardisation such as widths and lengths. In the mid-1930s Bedford, building a standardised range of chassis in quantity, offered 50 standard bodies for a chassis range of five different models, from an 8-cwt van to a 3-ton lorry. They were all available through 400 Bedford dealers. Most of the bodies were approved by the company but made by outside suppliers.

As early as 1921 an Albion tipper exhibited at that year's Commercial Vehicle Show (q.v.)

was fitted with a U-shaped steel body, the panels being riveted to a heavy-steel-angle frame. In contrast at the same show Bromilow & Edwards had a three-way tipper with twin under-body rams but the body itself was of timber construction with one-piece sides. Three-way tippers were popular, particularly with local authorities, in the 1920s and 1930s, and are still widely used in Continental Europe today, but not common in the UK.

Aluminium came into use surprisingly early. J Lyons & Co Ltd (q.v.) in the early 1920s ran a van bodied by the Dartford Engineering & Carriage Co with a duralumin frame and aluminium panelling. That was a huge contrast to the lead-coated iron used by some builders for panels. Duralumin was a brand of aluminium offered for bodybuilding for many years by among others Duramin (q.v.). Short Brothers of Rochester was a big user of aluminium by the early 1920s and was unusual in building bodies at the same factory for cars, commercial vehicles and buses.

Another example of relatively modern technology was the frameless tanker (q.v.) first produced by Scammell in 1924. Steel or aluminium for panelling became more generally used in the 1930s, though many tipper builders continued to offer all-timber or all-metal bodies, with tipping gear either hand or hydraulically operated.

Legislation on vehicle weights helped heighten interest in the 1930s in lighter bodies, particularly when vehicles with an unladen weight of 2½ tons were allowed to run at 30 mph, while heavier ones were limited to 20 mph. Leyland's Cub range, built at the Kingston factory, was offered for this market. Leyland also offered lighter bodies for heavier vehicles. In 1932 its goods body (as it was named) — actually a platform body — of steel-framed construction was 'considerably lighter than the better-known type of wood construction'. It was still floored with tongued and grooved oak boards, Phillipine teak being used for the other timber parts.

Use of aluminium grew considerably in the 1930s with a number of producers plugging the merits of the material. It gained increasing popularity immediately after the Second World War, initially because it was easy to obtain (as a result of the run-down of the aircraft-building industry), whereas timber and steel were scarce. At first materials were government-controlled, with priority being given for exports. Such timber as was available was often of poor quality — and hastily kiln-dried rather than seasoned — and steel supplies remained inadequate for several years. The situation gradually improved, and properly kiln-dried timber became the acceptable norm. On relatively standard bodywork metal framing gradually became favoured.

The 1950s saw a new material quickly come into widespread use: glass fibre. It could be easily moulded into curved or complex shapes. Such shapes no longer had to be hand-beaten out of sheet metal by a panel beater. Just one example was made in metal, or even plywood, and then used as a mould for unlimited numbers of identical repeats, albeit one-at-a-time, but using unskilled labour. The material was also used in unpainted translucent form for the roofs of vans, when it allowed daylight into the interior.

Another material enjoyed a brief vogue: stainless steel, usually in ribbed form, when it looked attractive and eye-catching and needed no painting. To get the cost down to a reasonable level meant using a thin gauge, which proved unable to take the stresses and strains and was easily damaged.

Plywood was available in the 1930s in sheets with a thin aluminium facing bonded to one side to provide a good waterproof finish. A big jump forward was the introduction of glass-reinforced plastic/ply panels. Factory-produced in lengths up to 40 ft, much of their considerable strength derived from the reinforced plastic coating in which they were enclosed. Demonstrations of panel strength included hitting panels with a sledgehammer; the merits of the material were not just its strength but also the cleanliness and gloss finish of both sides. As important, suitable top, bottom and end framing was all that was required with no need for intermediate pillars on a van body. The ply itself was usually ½ in thick Douglas Fir or Finnish Birch for a panel 5/8 in thick. Insulated panels were also available, consisting of two thinner panels, joined at intervals, with a foam insulant between. Panel thickness depended on the level of insulation required. London bodybuilder H Tidd & Sons was one of the first to make quantity use of standard grp/ply panels for bodies, while Crane Fruehauf built 40 ft containers with one-piece sides in the material. They did not need subsequent painting, and were available in a wide range of British Standard colours.

In the early 1970s timber framing was still being specified by some operators. For example, in 1972 a Post Office contract for 80 mobile workshops on Bedford chassis were timber-framed. Paradoxically, most of the interior workshop fittings including benches, drawers and ladder racks were in aluminium.

The standard rear opening on van bodywork for many years has been hinged doors or a roller shutter (q.v.), with the doorway as wide as possible. Rear door framing is usually of steel because of its superior strength, even on bodies otherwise framed in aluminium.

Ease of loading and unloading became increasingly important to operators and time taken in sheeting and unsheeting became critical as limits on drivers' hours tightened. This led to the ever-increasing popularity of curtain-sided (q.v.) bodies, or alternatives such as sliding doors. Conventional sliding doors suffered from obstruction or damage to their lower tracks and also posed problems if pallets were placed side by side. Curtain-siders, originally developed mainly by Boalloy (q.v.), gave access to the whole of the side of a vehicle or trailer at once, a particular advantage if loading was by fork-lift truck. On van bodywork without side access, loading by fork-lift brought the need for heavy-duty floors as the point loading imposed by the small wheels is high. Alternatives to curtain-sides include linked narrow panels and, more recently, cantilevered up-and-over doors which rise above roof height when open.

Changes in body design since the 1970s have not been dramatic, but customers' specifications have often become more precise and challenging. Despite the wide availability and use of computer-aided-design (cad) systems, larger bodybuilders now need more design staff than used to be the case.

Something that has not changed materially is the use of timber and plywood. Timber is still generally preferred for floors on semi-trailers, perhaps covered by a sheet of non-slip aluminium: the barleyseed pattern is much used. Special plywoods such as Wisa-Truck or Wisa-Trans are offered for truck and trailer floors and are lighter than conventional timber. Some breweries, for example, still prefer conventional timber floors for their vehicles and trailers but with a 2 mm plywood overlay. This is removed and replaced by an identical overlay after a couple of years. Another approach to floor covering is a polyester overlay with heavy-duty carborundum granules in its top surface to give non-slip properties.

Standard factory-built vans are usually sold without interior lining panels, but the inevitable dents from loads carried soon detract from the exterior appearance and the residual value. This has led to a side industry growing up offering plywood sides and floor lining panels for virtually every make and size of van. An extension of this concept of adding an interior is the use of standard factory van bodywork as the basis for a small refrigerated delivery vehicle, insulation and lining panels being added inside, with the fridge unit mounted externally, above the cab.

Rising standards in food hygiene and quality and the growth of supermarket sales of food have brought an enormous increase in the production of insulated and refrigerated bodywork, with a few builders such as Gray & Adams specialising in this work. Glass-reinforced-plastic-exterior panels have been generally preferred by operators, though metal faced panels are used by some builders. In all cases, insulation of different thicknesses is incorporated between interior and exterior surfaces. The need for sufficient insulation together with the ability to carry Continental-standard pallets side-by-side led to a legislative change in the later 1990s, allowing a small increase in overall width specifically for insulated or refrigerated vehicles and trailers.

Sales of frozen foods have remained relatively static, while those of chilled food have increased dramatically, giving rise to a requirement for multi-temperature semi-trailers and, to a lesser extent, rigid vehicles. Most designs incorporate movable bulkheads, so that varying proportions of a load can be carried at ambient, chilled and frozen temperatures, in the same body. Carrying three different types of produce in the same vehicle offers efficiency gains, and reflects a general wish by supermarkets to have fewer (albeit larger) vehicles delivering to them.

For ordinary boxvan bodies a number of designs of lightweight panel are now available, incorporating a honeycomb or other interior for strength. The inside components of some such panels are fusion-bonded together rather than glued. Some bodybuilders have designs in which advanced adhesives, originally developed for the aerospace industry, are used instead of conventional fastenings. On larger bodies and semi-trailers there have been moves towards bolted assembly rather than welding, since the former is easier to repair in the event of accident. Welding is regarded as stronger and usually retained for the front bulkheads of semi-trailers. Bolted van bodies are also available, and are quicker to assemble.

Perhaps the biggest change in bodybuilding is in its complexity. Even a relatively simple boxvan body may have a tail-lift and perhaps a second deck. There may well be an interior load-restraint system and often one or more side doors. Add to this an air dam at the front and aerodynamic sideguards, plus a heavy-duty floor, and you have a vehicle that is much more highly specified than its counterpart twenty years ago. Many designs are even more complicated than that. There is also increasing ingenuity with bodies intended for carrying specific loads. For example, semi-trailers for British Vita could traditionally carry 12 blocks of foam. By fitting a compression roof the number is doubled: the roof is raised for loading (or unloading) and then lowered to compress the load.

Stricter controls on paint, solvent emissions and isocyanites from spray guns have led to installation of new spray booths or changes in paint finishes. One or two companies have built bodies that do not require painting, the necessary colour being impregnated in the glass fibre panels during manufacture, with alloy cappings or powder-coated or stove-enamelled metal used for corners and joints. This did not significantly reduce build time since the panels needed considerable buffing.

Another change in bodybuilding is the increasing availability of kit bodies from specialist suppliers: the bodybuilder has merely to assemble. Take-up does not appear to be high, perhaps because they only suit relatively standard specifications and the kit supplier's profit margin also has to be taken into account. **JMA**

A **bolster** is an extended headboard with a cross-bar above cab height to support and restrain lengthy loads, commonly used in the building and construction industries; or alternatively, a timber baulk placed laterally across the bed of a flat lorry or trailer used both to spread the weight and to allow crane slings to be passed underneath loads such as steel girders and plates. **GM**

Bonallack & Sons Ltd, coachbuilders, began in east London in 1825, to serve horse-drawn dock traffic and the East Anglian coach services terminating at Aldgate. It expanded and moved during the nineteenth century, having premises at Cable Street and Forest Gate by 1904. In the 1920s it imported the Canadian Gotfredson lorry chassis and planned to sell the Kerr Stuart diesel lorry. As work on motor bodies grew, Bonallack made increasing use of aluminium panelling, developing its first all-aluminium body in 1928, at the request of John Knight, soap manufacturer. It required a body weighing less than 7½ cwt to allow a 3-ton payload on a 42½-cwt Thornycroft van chassis. In collaboration with James Booth & Co. Ltd a body framed and panelled in duralumin was designed and six vans were built, remaining in service after the Second World War. Bonallack went on to develop 'Bonallumin' Luton bodies, exhibiting one at the 1935 Commercial Motor Show and supplying more than 30 to a single customer, although the bulk of its production retained conventional timber-framing. Demand for aluminium bodies grew after the war and Bonallack, on the strength of its export output, built a new factory at Basildon New Town, opened in 1953 and soon extended. In the mid-1950s output included some 500 cabs for forward-control Leyland Comets. Product developments included aluminium tankers and pressure vessels for pneumatic discharge, the Pneumajector, for such materials as cement, flour, sugar, lime and chemicals. Later Bonallack became Freight Bonallack within the Alcan Booth group based at Norwich. **RAS**

R Bonallack, 'The Bonallack Story', *Light Metals* (November 1962); Edge, *The Leyland Comet* (1998), p. 24; *CM* (17 September 1976), p. 77

Boughton International was founded in 1897 as T T Boughton & Sons, hauliers and agricultural contractors, by Thomas T Boughton. It was a round timber haulage specialist until the 1970s and then carried abnormal-length concrete beams for motorway bridge construction. TTB Haulage was sold to Allison, a Dundee-based haulier, in the 1980s. From the 1930s it met the specialised engineering needs of the timber-producing Chilterns around Amersham, such as winches for timber extraction and loading.

After the Second World War it undertook a variety of special body and equipment production, especially for overseas and military use, and 6-wheel and 4×4 conversion of Bedford chassis kept the firm going, latterly as Reynolds Boughton Ltd. Short-run manufacture and building for stock brought it to the brink of receivership in 1997. Manrow Venture Partners rescued Boughton, rationalising its product range and moving production to Winkleigh airfield, Devon and Barton-under-Needwood, Staffs. From the road haulage aspect, its most important product is the hook-loader for container handling. From the late 1980s Boughton produced some 1000 military cross-country vehicles, based on Dodge Renault chassis but problems with the design of the vehicle led to an unprecedented House of Commons enquiry. **RAS**

Manwaring, (1971); *CM* (13 September 1974), p. 28, (16 December 1999), p.14; Boughton (1990) and (1992)

Bouts-Tillotson Ltd (Figure 77) was originally registered as Bouts Brothers in the early 1920s to carry parcels and 'smalls' between Manchester and London — though 'smalls' included 4-cwt gas cookers. Its founder was Ernest Leslie Bouts (d. 1996) who turned to road haulage when his trade in ex-WD vehicles declined. In the early years the firm, based at Bow, London E3 (later at Stratford, London E15) tried a variety of marques, in what was then an unusual white livery, before settling on Leylands from 1928. Part of its success was because its trunk vehicles kept to a fixed route and ran at the same times whether fully laden or not. The haulage fleet reached 50 in 1928. In addition, lighter parcel collection lorries, including Albions, Chevrolets and Vulcans, were operated on feeder services. During this period Bouts made a name for himself racing at Brooklands. The capital was increased in 1931, with J Oswald Tillotson becoming a director. The business expanded rapidly, with Oswald Tillotson, as AEC dealer and bodybuilder, supplying the new trunk vehicles. In 1933 a further increase in capital took place and the title changed to Bouts-Tillotson Transport Ltd, J Oswald Tillotson acquiring a large personal interest. Oswald Tillotson Ltd (q.v.) received shares for the transfer of its carrier subsidiaries, W V Greenwood and City Express Motors.

The additional capital and the ability to issue shares as part of the purchase price was used by Bouts-Tillotson to make further acquisitions enabling it to serve most of the country. First, in 1934, was R V Morris of Norwich operating a London to East Anglia service with 17 vehicles, followed by Mac Carriers of Bournemouth, with 70 vehicles serving London and the South West.

Both Bouts-Tillotson and Oswald Tillotson Ltd were acquired by Holdsworth & Hanson Ltd in 1935 but continued as separate trading subsidiaries. Oliver Holdsworth became chairman, and Charles Holdsworth and Robert

Hanson directors of both companies, E L and Cyril Bouts resigned. Edgar R Bouts continued as a representative at the Bouts London depot. H&H replaced Bouts' original Bow depot with the Waterden Road depot. The two businesses continued as separate trading subsidiaries, but with close liaison through their common directors. Bouts switched from Leyland to AEC following G J Rackham's move to AEC. From the late 1930s until its nationalisation Bouts was involved in the direction of British Amalgamated Transport Ltd. It then comprised C & L Transport Ltd, J T Elwell, Oxley & Shergold, and T S Sharnell & Sons. He returned to the motor trade after the Second World War, when he handled thousands of ex-WD vehicles.

Bouts-Tillotson was known for its licence renewal appeal before the Transport Tribunal in 1936. The railways objected to the renewal of Bouts' licence on the grounds that they had sufficient available capacity and the vehicles were therefore unnecessary. The Tribunal refused the railways' appeal, setting the precedent for future decisions by licensing authorities. A later decision, also in their favour, allowed operators of regular trunk services to have a reasonable number of collection and delivery vehicles at depots.

In 1933 the takeover of Ryburn United Transport was completed. Started in Halifax as the Ryburn Transport & Garage Co. in 1919, it was acquired in 1930 by E B Hutchinson (q.v.). After moving to a new depot at Bradford, Hutchinson merged it with Transport Services of Leeds to form Ryburn United Transport. The fleet now comprised 125 vehicles. Then Dawson Transport of Manchester and Aire & Tyne Parcels services were acquired. These operated services to the Tyne and Teeside region.

Ryburn United was under-capitalised and its mixed fleet in poor condition. Bouts-Tillotson was unable to give the management needed to merge successfully the separate businesses and a heavy loss resulted. Also to fail through lack of interest was Bouts Air Services, pioneering an air freight service between London and Manchester using an Airspeed aircraft.

H&H introduced a twice-weekly Liverpool–Belfast liner service in association with W G James & Son Ltd. The H&H group continued its expansion. Wylie & Lochead of Glasgow was acquired, to become Holdsworth & Hanson (Glasgow), followed by J W Poulter Ltd, in 1936. The service to Birmingham and the West Midlands followed the takeover of J W Warrington, its sub-contractor, which became Hanson & Holdsworth (Birmingham) Ltd. with a 12-vehicle fleet. H&H was now the largest independent carrier, with Bouts-Tillotson, the largest subsidiary, operating some 370 vehicles. They shared a common red and yellow livery.

During the Second World War, the H&H Group and its directors were again engaged on government work, many depots becoming Road Haulage Organisation (q.v.) units.

At nationalisation the Group became a voluntary acquisition by the British Transport Commission, but before this made further acquisitions. Bouts-Tillotson acquired Packard's Transport of Welwyn Garden City, F & H Croft (Yeadon) Ltd, S L Whiteley Transport and Chelmsford Transport.

The Hanson family, now under the control of James and William Hanson, retained Oswald Tillotson Ltd, the Hanson bus operation and formed Hanson Haulage Ltd, which took over the James Hanson contract with ICI. Tillotson in 2000 were Lex-Tillotson, part of the Lex Group, and Hanson Haulage still operated and included a home delivery service. **GM/RAS**

Nick Baldwin, 'E L Bouts, pioneer hauler', *OM*, 8, 1 (January/February 1974), pp. 75–80; N Baldwin, 'Farewell to E L Bouts', *Automobile,* 14, 11, (January 1997), p. 62; Dunbar (1981); Brummer and Cowe (1994); Ingram and Mustoe (1999)

Bowker, W H, Transport Ltd was founded by William Henry Bowker (d. 1955) in 1919, supplying transport to carry produce to a fruit and vegetable business in Blackburn market. He soon became a full-time haulier, with a dozen vehicles, mostly Leyland, by 1926. At nationalisation the company remained in business as a warehousing firm, moving back into road haulage in 1953. Textiles, cotton machinery and Covent Garden fruit traffic were significant areas of Bowker's activity. International traffic began in 1961 and in 1972, after using Scanias, Volvos were acquired for this purpose. In 1989 the firm relocated to Preston, which had a private rail-head facility and warehousing. The fleet in 1999 comprised 150 vehicles and 350 trailers, some on dedicated contracts. **RAS**

C Gardner and A Kermotschuk, 'Bowker's 80th', *CVC*, 5, 5 (January 2000), pp. 28–30

Box, Edward, & Co. William Box senior, a brickmaker of Market Lavington, Wilts, developed and patented a jack-shaft drive as an alternative to the chain or gear drive, for use on his traction engine in 1851. His sons, William junior, Edward and Herbert established a brickworks at Aintree in 1884 employing various makes of traction engine. In 1885 Edward moved into his own depot at Brazenose Street in Bootle, trading as Edward Box & Co. and developing a business mainly hauling bricks. By 1894 Fowler, McLaren and Marshall traction engines were in service and Edward was increasingly moving boilers and heavy machinery.

In 1903 Edward's son, Norman, joined John Fowler & Co. as its South African representative, returning to England in 1906. Edward had hoped his son would join him as a partner, and had changed the company's name to Edward Box & Son Ltd, opening a further depot at Ardwick, Manchester. Norman chose to start his own business, Norman E Box (q.v.), so Edward transferred the Manchester depot to him. Edward continued his business in Liverpool moving and installing boilers and machinery. He also supplied traction within the shipyard for Harland & Wolff.

When Edward died in 1926 Norman declined to help his stepmother with the sale of the business, for there was no love lost between them. This resulted in the majority of the business being purchased by Edward Charles Marston, also engaged in heavy haulage as Marston Road Services (q.v.). In 1930, when Marston severed his connections with the business and MRS was taken over by Col Hudson, the name Edward Box & Co. was revived and used until nationalisation, despite a challenge from Pickfords. In 1939 Box was part of the attempt to form a freight haulage company, Hauliers Ltd (q.v.), which was stopped by the outbreak of war. **GM**

PRO: AN files; Road Locomotive Society, Journal and Portfolios

Box, Norman E, Ltd was established in 1907 when Norman, a prickly and opinionated character who resented his father's re-marriage, declined to join his father's business, Edward Box & Co. (q.v.). He began by delivering lime by traction engine to a Wellington tannery. The business, and his fleet of traction engines, expanded with an increasing range of customers. The First World War created a considerable demand for his services, both in moving loads and in the erection and installation of machinery. He moved to bigger premises, opened a depot at Birmingham and became a limited company. Box's operations frequently brought him into conflict with the police and local authorities: in heavy haulage large and unwieldy loads often caused damage to pavements or road surfaces and the odd lamp post was knocked awry. Box established a close working relationship with William Joynson-Hicks (q.v.), who became a leading advocate, almost always defeating any summons issued to Box.

Some twenty new and second-hand engines were bought and then sold between 1914 and 1925, when the engine total stabilised at five Fowler B and one D road locomotives with a wide variety of heavy-haulage trailers, varying from iron-wheeled trolleys to an 85-ton well trailer on solid-tyred bogies. Three Scammell 25-ton and a 45-ton low loaders were added between 1925 and 1929.

In 1930 Box sold his heavy haulage business to the Hay's Wharf Cartage Co. (q.v.), with a five-year consultancy contract. The business was run by Pickfords, by then a subsidiary of Hays Wharf Cartage. Surprisingly, the Box family retained preference shares in the business until the 1960s when the arrangement was terminated. Box started a new business,

57

Box Spraying & Grouting Co. Ltd. He died in Canada in 1957. **GM**

Lane (1980); Ingram (1993); McTaggart (1986)

Boys, Henry, & Son of Oxford Road, Walsall, trailer makers and vehicle converters, was an example of commercial evolution, from milling, through haulage, to transport equipment manufacture. Henry Boys, who ran the New Mills, Walsall, died in 1897. His son, Sidney went into haulage with traction engines and turned to making his own trailers. In 1931 the business moved to Oxford Street, Pleck, Walsall. Boys & Son was noted for chassis conversion and extension into six-wheel lorries, on a variety of chassis. Its range of trailers, as advertised in *World's Carriers* in 1949, included standard platform, lowloader, timber drug, articulated and tipper models. On the proprietor's retirement in 1999 the business became dormant. **RAS**

N Baldwin, 'Wrecks to riches', *CVC*, 6, 3 (November 2000), pp. 44–5; there are some records, including photographs, in Walsall Local History Centre (Acc. 926)

Bradford light commercials, see JOWETT CARS LTD

Brady, T, & Sons Ltd, hauliers of Barrow-in-Furness from 1921 to 1999, is an example of a firm largely dependent on traffic from heavy industrial concerns, such as Barrow Steelworks and Vickers-Armstrong, which suffered from the decline in UK manufacturing from the 1970s. Latterly, transporting and storing paper products formed an important part of the business. Haulage operations ceased in 1999, the firm then concentrating on warehousing. Brady was unusual in that it began with a horse and cart in 1921 and remained a horse-drawn operation, concentrating on local delivery of coal, beer and other traffic, until 1945, when the first motor lorries were acquired. The business expanded to about 160 vehicles by the late 1960s, with Leylands predominating. **RAS**

P Davies, 'Authentic Octopus', *CVC*, 6, 4 (December 2000), pp. 4–8

Brake is 'an independent, national research and education organisation working to eliminate death and injury caused by unsafe operation of commercial vehicles and offering support to accident victims'. It was set up in 1995 by Mary Williams, a former transport journalist, whose mother had died in 1992 in an accident involving a laden powder tanker with defective brakes. Its patron, the Hon. Gwyneth Dunwoody MP, chaired a Brake all-party Parliamentary group. Corporate supporters include both manufacturers and operators. Research was undertaken on its behalf by the University of Huddersfield and in 1996 Brake issued two reports on the nature and extent of dangerous operation of commercial vehicles and commercial vehicle wheel loss. It also campaigned successfully for a manslaughter charge to be brought against the transport manager of the firm whose vehicle caused the Sowerby Bridge crash of 1993, which resulted in six fatalities. Mary Williams was awarded the OBE in 2000 for herroad safety work. **RAS**

M Williams, 'Viewpoint', *MT* (29 October 1998); *idem.*, 'Sound off', *CM* (6 May 1999); Volvo, *Trucksense*, 1 (1996)

Brakes. In the 1900s commercial vehicle braking systems were very basic. Increases in weight, speed and traffic volume necessitated progressive development, culminating in the sophisticated systems found on current heavy goods vehicles. Some early lorries relied on a simple mechanically-applied shoe or 'brake block' pressing against the rear tyre, rather like the brake on a horse-drawn cart. In the early 1900s external contracting band brakes acting on the transmission or on the rear wheels represented some technical advance. Brakes were not commonly fitted to the front wheels until the 1920s. Up to this time technology had not progressed very far.

Transmission brakes operated by a foot pedal were quite common in the early 1920s and internal expanding drum brakes were taking over from band brakes. Often these were operated by a hand lever, sometimes referred to as a 'side' brake, and relied on metal-to-metal contact between the shoe and drum.

Overheating was a serious problem. Significant advances took place in the late 1920s with the introduction of hydraulic systems providing greater efficiency with reduced driver effort. Shoes with friction linings also came into widespread use. Initially hydraulic pressure was used to operate a slave cylinder connected to a mechanical linkage until individual cylinders for each wheel were introduced.

On steam lorries, steam pressure was utilised to assist braking performance. From about 1929 air pressure braking began to appear, based on the Westinghouse principle developed for railways during the nineteenth century. Some manufacturers opted for vacuum brakes. By the 1930s vacuum-assisted hydraulic brakes were in wide use and all-wheel braking had become the norm. The leading supplier of vacuum servos was Clayton Dewandre. On heavy vehicles cam expanders were the most effective and they required little maintenance. The alternative wedge type expanders, though lighter and more compact, needed more attention to maintain efficiency.

As speeds and weights rose, friction-lining areas increased to provide adequate retardation. In the late 1940s most systems lacked protection in the event of sudden loss of hydraulic fluid or air pressure. Split circuits, which maintained some braking capability in such failures, appeared in the 1950s.

Braking technology developed rapidly during the 1960s with the arrival of fail-safe spring parking brakes and independent secondary circuits to protect against brake failure. The old-fashioned ratchet handbrake lever gave way to a small air valve control when spring brakes were introduced. Supplementary braking in the form of exhaust brakes, engine brakes and, in some cases, electric retarders also appeared during the 1950s and 1960s.

Experiments with disc brakes were taking place as early as the 1950s but brake pad life and heat generation were major obstacles to overcome. It was not until the 1990s that disc brakes were sufficiently advanced for use on heavy trucks. Today's lorries have anti-lock braking systems (ABS) and load-sensing valves to adjust the braking effort automatically according to axle loadings. **PJD**

Breakdown lorries, see RECOVERY SERVICES

The **Bressey report** was drawn up between 1935 and 1938 by Col Charles Herbert Bressey (1874–1951), principal technical officer of the roads division of the Ministry of Transport, and Sir Edwin Lutyens (1864–1944), architect and town planner. Commissioned by the Minister of Transport, Leslie Hore-Belisha, it reported on the need for improved roads in Greater London. It made 66 recommendations for new and improved roads, and roundabouts for traffic in general, not specifically for commercial vehicles. The only feature directly relevant to goods transport was that on one day in June 1936 a census was taken of the origins and destinations of all vehicles exiting from the 79 gates of London docks. 7614 cards were handed out, indicating the scale of the traffic, but less than a quarter were returned. Not surprisingly the destinations of these lorries were in east and south-east London with Canon Street as the furthest west destination. The war intervened before any real implementation occurred. **JA**

Charles Bressey, *Highway Development Survey 1937 (Greater London)* (HMSO, 1938); *WWW*, 5, p. 133

Brewery transport. (Figures 6, 78, 99 and 162) Breweries were among the first industries to make considerable use of motor vehicles, just as earlier they were big rail users, which led to the concentration of much of the industry on Burton-on-Trent. Bass and Guinness in particular developed as national suppliers through rail usage.

Originally virtually every public house brewed its own beer, but soon arrangements were made for one pub to brew for another in a neighbouring village. A multiplicity of small brewers emerged, but the ability of motor vehicles to reach further afield than horse-drawn transport soon encouraged mergers or take-overs, a process still continuing in the present century. Initially some brewers retained their fleets of horses and drays but used outside contractors to run the steam vehicles that delivered further afield. The dray was a heavy, 4-wheeled flat wagon pulled by draught horses and driven from a raised central position. The drayman's assistant, the trouncer, normally stood behind the drayman to his left. As petrol-engined motor vehicles came into more general use some brewers continued to employ outside contractors while others built up their own fleets. Since the 1970s cost pressures led to more breweries outsourcing their transport operations, and the same pressures led to development of vehicles with lower deck heights and other aids to improve efficiency. Interest in lower deck levels began soon after the Second World War and more recently received further boosts in the light of Health & Safety Executive guidelines on maximum weights to be lifted or handled manually. The traditional delivery crew of three (allegedly one to drive, one to drink and one to unload) came down to a crew of two, with coffee or soft drinks offered by more hospitable publicans.

In the early days some breweries built up considerable fleets of steam wagons, sometimes with close links with their makers, such as between Fremlins Brewery and Jesse Ellis & Co. Ltd (q.v.), the Maidstone wagon builders. By 1912 Isleworth Brewery had at least 12 Foden steamers, each able to take a four-ton load. By the early 1920s the motor lorry was in the ascendancy, AECs and Leylands being particularly popular. Heavy battery electrics had some following between the wars. Whitbread ran 15 GV Electrics from the early 1920s until after the Second World War, when many were sold to other smaller brewers. Meux & Co was another user of GV Electrics. In a dense city network where the mileage of a delivery round was low, the horse dray remained economic until the 1950s, and also had publicity value, which led to its continuance by Whitbread and Youngs of Wandsworth, among others.

The typical horse dray had side and end load restraining devices, usually the boxing ring system of stanchions and chains or slatted timber sides which hinged down, designs that often carried over to the early motor age. The loads carried were low in value in relation to their weight and bulk, both barrels and bottles being heavy. Modern developments such as cans and aluminium kegs have reduced weights and permitted use of lighter (and often longer) delivery vehicles. The traditional 'barrel skid', a concave slide for lowering barrels to the ground, was replaced by 'bump bags' in the 1960s, on to which the lighter kegs were bounced.

Interest in lower platform heights has steadily grown since the 1950s, though some smaller breweries have not followed the trend. Larger breweries were still highly profitable and keen to reduce unladen weights, so often bought quite expensive vehicles. In the late 1950s Mackeson and Whitbread bought the Dennis Pax NC low-loader with 17 in wheels and in the late 1960s at least a dozen breweries operated the Dennis Pax V six-wheel low-loader. Most makers sold to breweries and the breweries were one of the largest groups of C-licensed operators in the 1950s.

From the 1960s interest in height and weight reduction grew, Bass and Whitbread probably working hardest and spending the most. Whitbread's ideal dray had a platform height of 3ft 6in and a low unladen weight. At about the same time bottles began to be shrink-wrapped and carried on pallets instead of in wooden boxes, while smaller containers and casks were sometimes loaded on pallets – three to a pallet. Obtaining low platform height with higher capacity vehicles was more of a problem, and one experiment by Mitchells & Butlers used 16 in wheels and an extra axle to produce an Albion Reiver eight-wheeler with long, low body able to carry a ten-ton load. Later urban artics became popular for brewery and other work. Brickwoods of Portsmouth bought a batch of BMC Laird six-wheelers in 1970 and in 1973 Bedford introduced a twin-steer version of its TK for brewers and soft drink suppliers.

By the 1980s there was yet another approach to the problem, with special drop-frame chassis, produced either by the chassis manufacturers or by converters. These either had a single centre chassis member extending from behind the cab to the back axle or there was a drop frame with two parallel chassis members running at a low height before rising to support the back axle. Some operators built up quite considerable fleets of such vehicles, Whitbread, for example, having 220 of the type by 1990, on Ford Cargo and Volvo FL6 chassis. Based on a seven-year life it put their initial cost at about ten per cent above that of conventional trucks.

Not all deliveries to pubs or off-licences were made in the fashion so far described. Particularly in the north of England larger pubs and clubs from the 1960s (or even earlier) installed bulk beer tanks in their cellars and these were served by specially-equipped vehicles. At their simplest they are articulated units pulling platform trailers on which are mounted demountable tanks with a delivery pipe connected to a meter. Rigid vehicles may also be employed on this work, and some artics and rigids had neatly enclosed or curtain-sided bodies covering or shrouding the tanks (which might be fewer but larger) with the metering, pump and hoses contained in a separate cabinet.

Another type of brewery vehicle is the bulk tanker, which became more common as smaller breweries closed and brewing concentrated on larger centres which sent bulk supplies to local bottling plants. Some bulk traffic of this nature was handled by rail, continuing into the Freightliner (q.v.) era, but changes in rail freight policy, brewery mergers, the motorways and the greater efficiency of the modern lorry ended the use of railways. Road tankers were used to bring beer from the Continent for bottling in the UK. The reverse has also applied. A different kind of rail usage began in the early 1930s with specially-built tank trailers which were carried aboard rail flat wagons for the trunk journey but delivered by road for the first and last parts of the trip. Some were fitted with steel wheels inside their rubber tyres so they could run on rail in sidings. Substantial lashing rings were provided to anchor them firmly for the rail journey. Guinness for many years brought in its brew from Dublin by rail and sea in such trailers and its 1930s Park Royal, London, bottling plant had rail sidings. Whitbread was another user of the system, but the original concept was developed by the railways, tank and trailer builders R A Dyson (q.v.) and the

Co-operative (q.v.) Dairies for carrying milk. In the early 1950s to cope with escalating demand in Belgium, Whitbread used the road-rail tankers. They were filled at the Chiswell Street brewery, taken by road to British Railways at Mile End, then carried to Harwich by train, put on the ferry to Zeebrugge, and then onward to Brussels. The Tilbury–Antwerp rival service with ex-tank landing craft was also used. By the mid-1950s direct road journeys with conventional eight-wheel tankers using the Dover–Dunkirk ferries took over.

Since the 1980s several of the largest breweries as well as some of the remaining smaller ones have contracted out their road transport operations, but in one sense this only represents a trend that began some 150 years ago, if not earlier. In 1854 Thomas Allen began a contract with Guinness and when the Park Royal Guinness depot opened in 1936 Thomas Allen built a new garage alongside. Beer brought in by rail to St Pancras, mentioned earlier, was carried from the large warehouse there (complete with conditioning cellars) by United Service Transport (q.v.), whose fleet ran in Bass Worthington colours. The Thomas Allen operation at Park Royal was acquired by Guinness in 1955 as the basis of an in-house transport department.

In 1982 Whitbread set up a joint operation with the National Freight Corporation (q.v.). Named Bar Delivery Services, it covered London and the northern Home Counties, and followed an earlier and smaller contracting-out exercise for serving the 'take-home trade' of off-licences and supermarkets, a trade in which there are no returnable empties. Subsequently other work has been taken on by TNT (q.v.) Contract Distribution and by Tibbett & Britten (q.v.), while Exel Logistics (q.v.) has replaced Bar Delivery Services in London and the Home Counties.

Some other major breweries also contracted out, with Bass and Exel setting up Tradeteam as a joint venture in 1995. That company in 2002 made over 29,000 deliveries a week and claimed to account for one-quarter of all beer served in UK pubs. The same year it won a contract to take over distribution for

InterBrew, the Belgian group owning Stella Artois and Boddingtons.

Four brewers now account for some 75 per cent of the UK market, while 130 national or regional beer brands disappeared in the last 12 years. Wine consumption grew. While contracting out has increased, some major contractors now make considerable use of sub-contractors, and there are a few examples of smaller breweries taking back delivery work previously contracted out.

Urban artics or 6×2s usually with curtain-sided bodies are the most common, with maximum length artics for bigger loads. Most of the 6×2s have a third steered axle, with Iveco Ford and Volvo both offering this layout as a standard option. Drop-frame vehicles are still used but are less popular than previously. One reason for the popularity of 6×2s in various forms is the leeway it gives on axle loadings, which is important on multi-drops.

Publicity vehicles, bodied in the shape of bottles or barrels, were a minor aspect of brewery traffic: both Bass (on a Daimler car chassis) and Burtonwood (on a Bedford W) featured bottles, and Watneys commissioned tankers imitating barrels (including an Orwell electric). Some breweries were large enough to employ their own vehicles in the collection of raw materials, such as hops, with their low weight-to-volume ratio, carried in large sacks or pockets, and malting grains in bulk. The collection of spent grains also gave rise to businesses such as James & Son (Grain Merchants) Ltd, of Olmar Wharf, London SE1, employing distinctively bodied lorries including Reo Speed Wagons and later Fords for their trade in brewers' wet and dried grains. **RAS/JMA**

T R Gourvish and R G Wilson, *The British Brewing Industry 1830–1980* (Cambridge: CUP, 1994), esp. pp. 548–57; Wright (1986); Ingram (1991) and (1992); Coates (1993); *OCBRH*; *CM* (7 February 2002), pp.32–7

Brick traffic, see LONDON BRICK CO.

Bridges. Until 1760 nearly all highway bridges were over waterways. Starting to a limited extent with the building of canals, and developing rapidly with the coming of railways, bridges *over* the highway became common. Often, where the roadway crossed over or under the line of the canal or railway at a skew angle, right angle bends were introduced into the highway in order to secure a square crossing. Many examples of this still exist and often present difficulties for the passage of large commercial vehicles. One example is found on the A458 Shrewsbury to Welshpool road where the crossing of the ex-Cambrian Railway line east of Buttington involves two sharp right angle bends.

Highway bridges have had an important bearing on the development of commercial vehicles. Firstly, the maximum gross weight of the vehicles must be related to the load-bearing capacity of bridges which they will use. This was a significant factor in commercial vehicle design and for many years increases in the maximum gross weight of commercial vehicles were inhibited because of weak highway bridges. Recently there has been a major programme to upgrade bridges to take heavier vehicles and to allow maximum permitted gross vehicle weights to come into line with our European neighbours.

Secondly, for bridges over the road, the height of the bridge soffit above the carriageway is an overriding factor in determining the maximum height to which commercial vehicles can be constructed. For many years a standard bridge height of 16 ft 6 in (5.03m) has been adopted. There are, however, many bridges over the highway which are less than this height and the problem of collisions between high vehicles and low bridges is a serious one. In extreme cases, over-height warning systems can be installed to reduce the likelihood of bridge strikes.

In 1961, with the opening of the 1100 ft (335 m) span Tamar suspension bridge, an extensive programme of construction of large estuarial bridges was begun. Estuaries spanned included Milford Haven, Forth, Severn (twice), Tay, Thames and Orwell and culminated with the opening in 1981 of the 4624 ft (1410 m) span Humber suspension bridge, at the time the world's longest suspension span. (See CARGO FLOW PATTERNS). **RC**

Bridges Transport Ltd of Preston, the well-known north-western parcels business, and its predecessor, Harold Bridges Ltd, owed much of their success to the strategic choice of depots and to the acquisition and profitable development of operating sites. Harold Bridges began as a carrier at Lytham in 1921 with a Ford 1-ton lorry, having identified a potential market on the Fylde coast. By 1924 a new Vulcan and Bean had been acquired; the fleet comprised six vehicles, including three new Bean 35-cwt lorries, by 1927, and in 1935 the ten vehicle fleet was replaced by a bulk order for twelve Dodge lorries. In 1936 relocation in Preston, provided a larger and more central operating base. After the move the Dodge 2-ton lorries were replaced with ten new 3-ton vehicles. By 1938 the fleet numbered 18, the depot had been adapted to provide storage with mechanical handling and a maintenance workshop and Bridges served the whole of Lancashire, delivering goods brought from elsewhere by numerous other carriers, and operating an egg-delivery service to Maypole Dairy shops.

Wartime operations included the servicing of buffer depots of foodstuffs, for which a 6-ton Dodge was acquired, bringing the fleet to 21. Bridges established a separate company, Walton Vale Storage Ltd, which handled this side of its business until nationalisation. After the war two small operators in the locality were acquired to provide extra fleet capacity and the Bridges and related Transport Factors Ltd fleet together numbered 36 as nationalisation threatened. Bridges played a waiting game in the hope of increasing compensation and recommenced, in the name of Harold's elder son, Charles, and within the permitted 25-mile radius.

The new operation began with the purchase of a small concern, based at Farington, and thus providing a viable operating area. Growth occurred by the purchase of other small businesses, and was stimulated by the removal of the 25 mile radius restriction by the Transport Act 1953. To cope with expansion a new depot was developed in Preston. By the early 1960s the fleet had grown to 70 vehicles on regular daily services, including 40 low-cab

Albion Claymores. A significant contract was secured with Shell for lubricant storage and distribution and the fleet grew to 90 vehicles, and two garage and transport firms in financial difficulties were acquired to provide more depot space and maintenance facilities. In 1964 a surprise offer from Tayforth Ltd (q.v.) led to protracted negotiations, in the course of which Bridges further enlarged its property holdings. The end result was the sale of Bridges Transport for £1.3 million in March 1966; Harold Bridges stayed on as depot manager for two years. Tayforth moved the Bridges operation to a new depot at Leyland, where a sorting system installed on the loading deck proved a failure. Profitability declined and the operation was closed down by BRS (Parcels), by then its owner, in 1988.   **RAS**

Bridges (1992)

Bristol Industries Ltd, an enterprise of the Wills tobacco family, was founded as the Bristol Haulage Co. Ltd in 1919, to operate a London trunk service. It grew with the acquisition of other businesses, which retained their separate identities. These included the parcels carriers, Henry Russett & Sons Ltd, Wild & White, Premier Transport Ltd, and L H Dimond & Co. Ltd, general haulier and remover. By 1946 Bristol Industries had a fleet of 300 vehicles and its activities included cold stores and ice factories. It was nationalised in 1948.   **RAS**

Dunbar (1981); Labour Research Department, *Why Haulage must be Nationalised* (1946); MT (6 December 1947), p. 15

The **Bristol Tramways & Carriage Co.** (Figure 80) was a bus operating company that from 1908 manufactured buses. It also made lorries in two distinct phases: in the 1920s, when the main purchasers of the 4-ton chassis were oil companies; and from 1952 to 1964 for BRS (including some of its contract operations). In the 1920s the design of many chassis, including those built by Bristol, was identical, whether sold for fitment of bus or lorry bodywork. While its 4-ton chassis and its lighter 2-ton counterpart (the latter unusual for that time in being forward control (q.v.), met Bristol's own bus-operating needs, they also proved popular as lorries. Later large numbers of the buses built on this chassis were rebodied as lorries, including over 50 from the Bristol fleet sold to Pointers of Norwich.

The company was nationalised with the rest of the Tilling Group in 1948 and its vehicle-building subsidiary became Bristol Commercial Vehicles Ltd in 1955. Bristol resumed lorry production, exclusively for the Road Haulage Executive, in 1952 with the HG (heavy goods) 8-wheeler and later the HA articulated tractor unit. The RHE at nationalisation had acquired too many medium-weight vehicles, hence the heavier specification of the models ordered from Bristol. 517 of the HG6 type were made by 1958 and 653 HA tractor units by early 1964, as well as 946 twin-axle semi-trailers, mostly bodied by Longwell Green Coachworks. The Transport Act 1947 did not permit nationalised companies to supply private operators. Bristol could not, therefore, compete on equal terms with private industry and lorry production ceased in 1964, even though the HG and HA models had been by no means unsuccessful. A heavier articulated tractor unit of 30 tons gross vehicle weight, designated HD, was under development for BRS when lorry production ceased. The last HG was withdrawn from service by BRS in 1969; some went on to serve in independent fleets. More recently, and after legislative changes permitting outside sales, 15 LH bus chassis were given pantechnicon bodies and operated by Lawrence Wilson & Son Ltd, pram makers. **RAS**

Baldwin (1982); Charles Harvey and Jon Press, 'Sir George White and the urban transport revolution in Bristol, 1875–1916', in Charles Harvey and Jon Press (eds), *Studies in the Business History of Bristol* (Bristol, 1988), pp. 146–59; Janes and Sposito (1989); Ingram and Mustoe (1999)

Bristow, Frederick George (1885–1945) was a barrister who advocated the use of motor transport, served on many committees and associations, and wrote a number of books explaining motor vehicle law. As such he advanced the cause of motoring and highway

improvement. His reputation rests mainly on the quiet committee work which he pursued assiduously. He was secretary and chief executive officer of the Commercial Motor Users Association (q.v.) throughout its existence from 1906 to 1944 and also general secretary of its offshoot, the Motor Transport Employers' Federation, from 1918 to 1942. He was the honorary secretary of the Standing Joint Committee of Mechanical Road Transport Associations (q.v.) from 1912 to 1934 and at times chairman of the Royal Society for the Prevention of Accidents (q.v.), and honorary secretary of the British Road Federation from 1933 to 1936 and 1939 to 1943. He served on more than a dozen government committees on various aspects of transport between 1920 and 1944. He was awarded the CBE in 1932. His publications over more than two decades were mainly to explain the law to the lorry builder and user, especially the complex requirements on 'construction and use' (q.v.).   **JA**

WWW, 4; Birch and Harper (1995), p. 11; Allan (1946), p. 42

Brit European Transport, (Figures 5 and 27) previously Carman's Transport Ltd, in 2000 operated 270 vehicles in four divisions: automotive, bulk liquids, carpets (q.v.) and contract distribution. It was founded in 1928 by the grandfather of the present managing director and operated 45 vehicles by 1964. It ventured unsuccessfully into carpet transport in 1997 with a division based in Zeebrugge, in view of Belgium's pre-eminence in the trade; UK loads were accumulated there with 70 Belgian-registered vehicles. The operation was shut down within six months and taken over by Carpet Express. Automotive work, which is focussed on commercials, began with a single contract in 1988, but developed significantly. JCB products are carried on Andover trailers, and trailers to carry three MAN rigid cab-chassis have been jointly developed with the Swiss trailer-builder Lohr. A joint venture with Auto Carriers resulted in the formation of Silver Arrow to handle a DaimlerChrysler contract for transporting cars, MPVs and commercial vehicles. The composition of Brit European's fleet reflects its biggest customers,

MAN, Mercedes-Benz and Renault. A seven-acre site in Middlewich is being developed as the headquarters, to replace its Stoke-on-Trent base. **RAS**

A Salter, 'Brainpower', *Truck* (August 2001), pp. 50–5

British Association of International Furniture Removers, see BRITISH ASSOCIATION OF REMOVERS

British Association of Overseas Furniture Removers, see BRITISH ASSOCIATION OF REMOVERS

The **British Association of Owner Drivers,** linking at its inception ten regional and local associations, was founded in 1978, at the third of a series of national conferences of representatives of owner-drivers' associations. The initiative came from the North Humberside ODA, which was the first to establish a freight office for its 80 members. Known as Owner Drivers' Freight Services (Hull) Ltd, it was financed by members' shareholding and by a 10 per cent charge for each load arranged and could call on 140 vehicles. Among bodies represented at the conferences was the National Owner Drivers' Association. This was founded *c.*1960 and had 4500 members. It represented primarily drivers in the construction industry, plus some coal tippers. Whilst advocating co-operation, it had different objectives from the BAOD. Although not affiliated to the TUC, the National Association was registered as a trade union, which gave its members the benefit of a card to produce in certain industrial relations situations. Mention was made at the second conference of the Allied Independent Hauliers, which had been formed to back up international owner drivers. The chief concerns of the three conferences were the attitude of the trade unions and existing clearing houses to owner drivers' associations. On a practical level the possibility of discounted insurance, printing, fuel, batteries and tyres was aired. **RAS**

Reports of national conferences of haulage owner drivers' associations, 1977–8: Modern Records Centre, University of Warwick Library: MSS.21/1862/1–3

The **British Association of Removers** became the sole national organistion for the removals (q.v.) industry in 1972, when the hitherto separate associations for national and international furniture removers merged.

The Furniture Warehousemen & Removers' Association was founded in 1900, became incorporated in 1914 and changed its name to the National Association of Furniture Warehousemen & Removers Ltd in 1935. As furniture removal work is essentially a tramping (q.v.) operation and needs a national network of contacts for assistance at remote destinations and for arranging return loads, the Association played a more central role in its members' businesses than did the other road haulage trade associations. This was aided by early adoption of standard conditions for carriage and warehousing (before 1916) and by the issue of recommended rates.

In 1924 the British Association of International Furniture Removers was set up under the auspices of the FWRA to extend these benefits to overseas removal work. Fortnightly lists were issued of British lift vans abroad and foreign lift vans in the British Isles available for return loads and of lift vans required for loading abroad. Members offered each other 'most favoured trade terms' for work done on the other's behalf. It was renamed the British Association of Overseas Furniture Removers in 1954.

At the end of the century the BAR had 650 UK members and 250 overseas. It published the members' journal, *Removals & Storage*, begun by the FWRA in 1925. In 1990/1 a Commercial Moving Group was established to cater for members that specialised in office removals. The BAR's role as an industry lobby group extends to the European Parliament and Commission through membership of FEDEMAC, the Federation of European Moving Associations; it is also a member of FIDI, the Fédération Internationale des Déménageurs Internationaux.

Like its predecessors the BAR is more than a trade association; it is also a professional body requiring members to meet prescribed standards. A firm's membership of the BAR is thus an assurance for customers of its professional status. In 1937 the NAFWR established the Institute of the Furniture Warehousing & Removing Industry, later renamed the Movers Institute, which is the professional education and accrediting body for individuals employed in the industry and has 1800 individual members. **GAB**

World's Carriers Year Book, various editions; information supplied by the BAR

British Berna, see BERNA

British Hauliers Unite, see PROTEST MOVEMENTS

The **British International Freight Association** was established in 1944 as a trade association for the freight forwarding industry in the UK. Based in Feltham, it has groups for air cargo and couriers, for short-sea road and rail, for deep-sea and intermodal traffic, and for customs affairs. It also runs the Institute of Freight Professionals and publishes the *Freight Services Directory*. In 2000 it had some 1250 members, ranging from small haulage firms to major logistics operators such as Danzas and MacGregor Swire Air Services. **RAS**

Information supplied by BIFA

British Leyland Motor Corporation was formed in 1968 as a merger between British Motor Holdings (which comprised Austin, Morris, BMC plus Jaguar Group which included Daimler and Guy) and the Leyland Motor Corporation (AEC, Albion, Rover, Scammell, Thornycroft and Triumph). It has been described as the defining moment in the history of the British motor industry. It has also been heavily criticised. The request for the merger came from Prime Minister Harold Wilson, and the Industry Secretary and was endorsed by the government-sponsored Industrial Reorganisation Corporation. Speaking in retirement in 2001 Lord Stokes, former managing director and later chairman of the new organisation, thought there was no other option, though Leyland had almost walked away from the deal when it discovered BMH's financial position. There was 'tremendous government pressure'. On balance the board thought there was a chance of making the merger a success. In another interview Stokes said it might have been more sensible to let BMH go broke, and then buy some of the pieces.

The merger gave BLMC 60 sites and 180,000 employees at a time when considerable militancy was developing within the labour force in the car industry. It was already too late to create 'a cohesive manufacturing group with factories scattered all over the place'. Continuing problems at the car plants and their lack of profit saw the truck and bus operations deprived of funds for improvements and development of new models, ultimately resulting in a serious loss of business, though it was not until 1976 that Leyland's truck and bus section failed to make a profit. Undoubtedly there were some bad decisions, for example in favouring former Leyland plants for overseas expansion instead of former AEC ones. Lack of good quality middle and higher management also played its part after many existing staff were moved to sort out the car plants.

The merger left the new group with a host of duplicated models and 219 sales and service locations for one or more of the truck makes in the UK. Bristol took the prize with all marques represented, but at five different locations. The ingenious solution was to colour code the marques and dealers and depots handling them. All BMCs were now built at Bathgate, and became Leyland Redline. Guy had green on its signing, AEC orange, and Leyland and Albion blue. The range of models was rationalised, but far too slowly.

The process of building one chassis range at one factory took a long time to implement, and resulted in the closure of the AEC factory at Southall in 1979, Guy at Wolverhampton the same year, with Albion chassis production moving to Bathgate in 1980: but Bathgate itself closed in 1984. Part of Albion in Glasgow continued to build components such as axles for the group and under new ownership continued in business. The new range built at Bathgate after Albion's closure still used mainly Albion frames and other components, but with a better version of the Bathgate-built former BMC cab, and other upgrades.

The first model changes announced in the late 1960s had been of improvements and changes already under way before the merger. There was the new AEC V8 engine, initially in the maximum weight Mandator tractor, but rushed into production before adequately proved, and an announcement of the new 500 fixed-head engine, that was later to power Leyland Buffalo, Lynx and Bison trucks, but which had considerable problems. When finally solved, the engine's reputation was so poor it was decided to discontinue production. The biggest new step, so far, was Marathon, a new maximum weight tractor with a 'new' engine, the TL12, actually a heavily-reworked existing engine. The success of the TL12, with its adaptation of the existing cab and other compromises, convinced Leyland to build a completely new heavyweight range. That was the T45 or Roadtrain, built in a highly automated assembly plant at Leyland. Not long after the Albion assembly plant and AEC and Guy closures, Leyland's North and South works were also closed. Marathon continued in production until T45 arrived, but from 1981 had Cummins or Rolls-Royce engines, production of the TL12 being too small to be economic.

Early expansion at Bathgate in 1969 had seen the introduction of Mastiff and Boxer medium-weight trucks, followed in 1970 by the Terrier, a 6.5 to 9.5 ton gross vehicle aimed at the delivery market. It proved to be remarkably successful with a direct lineage to the DAF 45, still built, at that new Leyland assembly plant.

Difficult circumstances at home and abroad in 1974 resulted in Leyland turning to the government for help, and ultimately its nationalisation. The subsequent plant closures already mentioned and other events made the late 1970s and most of the 1980s such turbulent years. Even so there were successes: for example, in 1985 Leyland was second only to Ford in truck sales. The Conservative government decided to sell off Leyland as part of a move to reduce government involvement in industry. General Motors almost became its buyer, and apparently was impressed by the quality of the product, but a backlash by Conservative MPs about Land-Rover and Range-Rover becoming US-owned caused a change of heart, and Leyland was sold in 1987 (albeit with a range of financial inducements) to Dutch maker DAF, a company whose success in entering the truck making industry after the Second World War was based on Leyland technology, such as its 600 engine, built (and improved) by DAF under licence for many years. A third suitor that was prepared to buy Leyland, but was ignored in the government-led negotiations was Paccar, which – ironically – now owns DAF. **JMA**

Turner (1971)

The **British Motor Corporation Ltd** was the title of the new company incorporated in 1952 following the merger of the Austin Motor Co. Ltd and Morris Motors Ltd, which included Morris Commercial Cars Ltd among its subsidiaries. Both Longbridge and Cowley continued as production centres, Austin and Morris identities were retained and it was recognised that rationalisation would take time. In 1954 the Austin and Morris-Commercial lorry ranges were rationalised with some competing models dropped. The Morris-Commercial FV and FVO four-wheelers were among those discontinued. In 1966, following the acquisition of Jaguar Cars Ltd and its Guy and Coventry Climax subsidiaries, the title of the parent company was changed to British Motor Holdings Ltd, subsidiary companies becoming divisions of the British Motor Corporation. In 1968 the merger of BMH and the Leyland Motor Corporation resulted in the formation of the British Leyland Motor Corporation.

Although a measure of badge engineering was introduced during the period 1952–8, the promotion of BMC as a marque occurred only during two short periods, 1955–6 and 1968–70. The mid-1950s BMC badging was applied to the heaviest of the forward-control Austin/

Morris range; between 1968 and 1970 it was applied to all models other than car-derived vans, thus including the EA350 forward-control van built at Birmingham and FG, FJ and WF types built at the new Bathgate truck factory, opened in 1961, including Boxer, Laird and Mastiff ranges. The famous VA 'Noddy' van was developed on an Austin chassis by BRS Parcels. It offered cross-cab access with sliding doors on each side of the cab to ease delivery. It usually carried the BMC badge. After August 1970 lighter vehicles were again badged as Austin or Morris and the heavier trucks produced at Bathgate became the Leyland Redline series. **RAS**

Stevens-Stratten (1978); Edwards (1992); M Wells, 'The BMC Models', *VCVM*, 29 (November/December 1990), pp. 86–91; 'BMC en Angleterre: Une nouvelle marque, mais pas un nouveau nom', *Homme et Camion*, 12 (December 1998), pp. 74–5; the TM.135 featured in a BMC advertisement in the UK press (1 November 1967)

The **British Road Federation** was founded in 1932 by the Commercial Motor Users' Association (q.v.), the Omnibus Owners' Association, the Petroleum Distributors' Committee, the Road Haulage Association (q.v.) and the Society of Motor Manufacturers & Traders (q.v.), which had come together in reaction to the Salter Enquiry (q.v.). Its objective was 'to develop in a more constructive form a progressive transport policy in the interest of the community as a whole'. This early policy statement suggests that the BRF was always more than the uncritical voice of the road lobby, as some commentators tend to depict it. The BRF was a federation (in 1958) of 110 national organisations representing most aspects of the many-sided road transport industry. Private motorists were not directly represented, the AA and RAC only joining in 1963 and 1973 respectively. Finer noted the work undertaken by the BRF in its early years for the road haulage industry, although he seems to overlook its post-war role in the campaign against nationalisation of road haulage of 1946–7. The BRF also acted on behalf of ancillary users or C licence holders (q.v.),

through its Associates Committee, set up in 1934. This defended them vigorously in the anti-nationalisation campaign and again in 1952–3, when the transport levy was proposed by the Conservative government, and in its evidence to the Geddes Committee (q.v.) of 1963, when it urged the continuation of the freedom of manufacturers and traders to carry their own goods in their own vehicles.

The Roads Improvement Association (q.v.) long preceded the BRF, but, perhaps with the tacit connivance of the SMMT, the BRF rapidly reduced the influence of the RIA, whose income declined during the 1930s. Although the BRF, in Hamer's words, 'hibernated during the war' (its involvement in the German Roads Delegation to examine the *Autobahn* system in 1937 was something of an embarrassment), it rapidly resumed energetic activity after the war. Throughout its existence well-produced publications played an important part in the BRF's work, including such series as *Basic Road Statistics*, *Britain's Road Progress*, *Monthly Bulletin of Road Information*, *Road Fact* and the BRF's annual report, and numerous other titles.

During the 1990s the administrative structure of the BRF was made flatter and leaner. It was 'a business organisation representing users and providers of the road network in the United Kingdom' (BRF *Annual Report* 1997). Its mission statement was 'To be the single most influential campaigning organisation in the UK for a safe and efficient road system as part of a coherent transport strategy', but the BRF recognised the need for a multi-modal and integrated approach to solving transport problems. As well as direct company membership, for example, vehicle manufacturers, road builders and material suppliers, and several major hauliers, the presence of numerous trade associations in its membership, including the FTA and RHA, ensured that the BRF had contacts with many companies across a wide sectoral span. It ceased activity in 2001 when its archive was transfered to the Institution of Civil Engineers. **RAS**

Hamer (1987); S E Finer, 'Transport interests and the road lobby', *Political Quarterly,* 29, 1 (1958)

British Road Services (Figures 7, 80 and 81) was the trading name adopted in 1948 for the newly-nationalised goods road transport services, although the statutory name of the owning organisation was the Road Transport Executive (from 20 June 1949 the Road Haulage Executive), one of the subsidiary executives of the British Transport Commission.

As nationalisation (q.v.) proceeded, BRS grew to a peak level of activity in 1951, when it carried 47 million tons of traffic, with a staff of 80,000 and a fleet of more than 41,000 lorries and 3000 trailers. It had also inherited 2750 horse-drawn vehicles and 1400 horses from the railway-owned carriers, but their numbers were fast diminishing and the last were taken out of service in 1955. With no precedent in the goods road transport industry to serve as a model for organising a business on this scale, it is not surprising that the RHE chairman, Major-General G N Russell (q.v.), adopted a military-style solution. The general haulage depots were organised into a hierarchy of eight geographical divisions, each of which was divided into 3–5 districts and 5–10 groups. At the end of 1950 there was a total of 871 depots and 157 sub-depots in 225 groups and 29 districts. A separate nationwide Special Traffics (Pickfords) Division was established for furniture removals, meat traffic and abnormal loads.

The new organisation and its pattern of services were very fluid during the early months as the multiplicity of companies was forged into national services for general haulage, parcels and special traffics. Duplicate facilities and services were rationalised and, quite soon, the management structure was simplified by abolishing the groups. A new national general haulage trunk network was developed, with an increasing proportion of scheduled services and less tramping; by 1953 next-day delivery was normal over most of the country. Conditions of carriage (q.v.) and documentation (q.v.) were standardised and rates harmonised. Standard vehicle liveries were adopted: 'Ayres red' for general haulage, 'Carter Paterson green' with red wheels for parcels, and dark blue with red wheels for specialised services.

Before nationalisation was completed, a Conservative government, intent on reversing it, was elected. The article on denationalisation (q.v.) describes the way in which this was carried out between 1953 and 1956. The first step was the abolition of the Road Haulage Executive, BRS now being managed directly by the BTC through a British Road Services Board of Management. In 1955 the parcels services were split from the Divisions and brought together into a separate company, BRS (Parcels) Ltd (q.v.). In 1956 the other activities that had not been disposed of were also formed into companies: British Road Services Ltd (for general haulage), BRS (Contracts) Ltd, BRS (Pickfords) Ltd and BRS (Meat Haulage) Ltd. It turned out to be only a partial denationalisation, as the sale of assets was less successful than the government hoped. When the process was brought to a halt, BRS was still by far the largest public carrier. During the years 1957–62, its motor vehicle fleet remained almost constant at around 16,000, although its tonnage capacity increased by 25 per cent through investment in larger vehicles; traffic carryings fluctuated at around 16–17 million tons annually; while the number of employees fell from 40,000 to 35,000, still many times the size of any of its privatised competitors.

BRS began operating services to and from Northern Ireland in 1951, using the pioneering Preston–Larne/Belfast Ro-Ro ferry services of the Atlantic Steam Navigation Company, which was acquired by the BTC in 1954. ASN's Tilbury–Antwerp service, inaugurated in 1955, allowed BRS to extend its services into mainland Europe. Seeking to expand these trades, BRS Ltd acquired specialised operators of through services for trailers and containers: Irish Ferryways Ltd and Ferry Trailers Ltd in 1957; and Anglo-Continental Container Services Ltd, an early operator of container ships on the Preston–Larne and Ardrossan–Larne routes, in 1958. The ACCS ships were transferred to ASN management in 1960.

When the BTC was abolished in 1963 the BRS companies were vested in the new Transport Holding Company (q.v.). They owned 16 per cent of all A and Contract-A licensed vehicles. The THC divided BRS into three groups, each with a chief executive: general haulage, including contract hire; parcels; and specialised traffic (the Pickfords and meat haulage companies). All the companies were members of a new BRS Federation Ltd which formulated common policies and provided common services. They became members of the Road Haulage Association (q.v.). During 1963–5 the organisational structure of BRS Ltd was further simplified by abolishing the divisions; there were now about 100 local branches administered by 13 districts.

Meanwhile the BRS companies were quietly making a few further acquisitions of specialised hauliers in areas where they were seeking to consolidate or expand their businesses. For example, in 1964 BRS Ltd acquired Furness & Parker Ltd, a specialist car-transporting business, and consolidated into it its own car-transport operations that it had been developing since 1958; in 1968 this became Cartransport (BRS) Ltd.

In 1964 BRS (Pickfords) Ltd reverted to its pre-nationalisation name, Pickfords Ltd, presumably because it was felt that the association with the BRS name did not help its marketing. From this time the BRS name was gradually dropped. When Tayforth Ltd (q.v.) and Lawther & Harvey Ltd (q.v.) were acquired in 1965–6 to enhance the THC's presence in Scotland and Ireland, they were kept separate from the BRS companies. Then in 1967 BRS's Irish and Continental ferry and container services were merged into Containerway & Roadferry Ltd and also made independent.

BRS (Meat Haulage), which had operated as part of the meat haulage co-operatives, the Meat Transport Organisation Ltd (q.v.) (1948–54) and United Carriers Ltd (1954–60), consistently failed to make a profit after it began trading independently. In 1966 it was sold to its biggest competitor, the Union Cartage Co. Ltd owned by Vestey International.

In 1969 the THC's freight interests were taken over by the National Freight Corporation (q.v.). BRS (Contracts) Ltd had been the most successful BRS company, growing from 900 lorries in 1956 to 4200 in 1970. From 1971 BRS began to withdraw from its declining and less-profitable general haulage business and to expand its profitable contract work. To further this policy, in 1973 British Road Services Ltd and BRS (Contracts) Ltd were combined under the former name, and reorganised into a group of seven regional companies (Eastern British Road Services Ltd, etc.), each with its own new livery. They diversified into truck rental in 1974 and trailer rental in 1979 and set up BRS Rescue, a breakdown and recovery (q.v) service for hauliers, in 1977.

In 1984/5 BRS generated more than half the profits of the now-privatised National Freight Consortium. However, following the NFC's acquisition of the SPD Group Ltd (q.v.), BRS concentrated on straightforward contract hire, leaving NFC's new Distribution Group to develop the physical distribution opportunities. In 1994/5 the BRS name was extinguished when it was amalgamated with Exel Logistics Ltd (the re-named SPD) and the logistics arm of National Carriers Ltd (q.v.) to form NFC UK Ltd, operating as Exel Logistics (q.v.)

At nationalisation BRS acquired an incredibly mixed fleet at a time when new vehicles were in short supply. When nationalisation had seemed inevitable, some operators spent a minimum on maintenance while others ran smart, well-kept fleets to the very end. Initial orders for new vehicles favoured not only the better-known makers but others too: the new Proctor was an unusual choice, though its major components were also used in Seddons and Vulcans.

A standardisation policy was developed, covering items such as brake systems, electrics, injectors, wheels, tyres and cabs. Wherever possible maximum-capacity eight-wheelers were to be used, from just four makers. By the mid 1950s these were coming from Bristol and Leyland, both using Leyland engines. In the late 1950s load-carrying capacities were narrowed with, for example, all 2-, 3- and 5-ton vehicles having to weigh under 3 tons unladen and therefore able to run at 30 mph. The AEC Mercury was particularly favoured in this size range.

Artics gradually increased in numbers, Austin/Morris/BMC prime movers being very popular. Once a model had proved itself, it generally featured in further orders over the years. AECs were being bought at a rate of 60 a month in the mid 1960s, with annual orders placed in November and BRS allowed to 'call them off' the production line as required. Over 12 years more than 1,000 Guy Big Js were bought. The Ergomatic-cabbed Leyland was later regarded as the best 32-tonner, BRS considering it of better durability than those built by the mass-producers, but also cheaper than those from the so-called quality makers.

From 1971 the Scammell Crusader, usually with Rolls-Royce Eagle engine, became the standard artic. It continued to be bought until 1978. BRS and its executive director, Walter Batstone, were closely involved in its development and it became the most cost-effective vehicle in the fleet. It was the last example of a vehicle developed specifically for one operator. **GAB/JMA**

Annual Reports & Accounts of the BTC (1948–62), THC (1963–8) and NFC (1969–99); Ingram and Mustoe (1999)

British Telecom. At its formation in 1981 British Telecom was the UK's largest operator of commercial vehicles, with a fleet of 53,970 (including a few cars). Since then the total has continued to grow, mainly as the result of the boom in phone, fax and internet usage. Traditionally the fleet was a mix of small vans, medium-sized vans, and a miscellaneous selection of larger and more specialised vehicles, for example, telephone pole carriers and erectors. Some of the fleet were direct descendants of the former stores department of the GPO, from which fleet BT was separated in 1981. By far the largest proportion of vehicles consisted of Ford Transit vans, bought by the thousand almost every year. BT is the Transit's biggest buyer: in the four years from 1987 it took over 12,000 Transits.

In the early 1990s BT became by a large margin the greatest user of demountable bodies (q.v.) when it adopted the concept for 15 cwt

and 1 ton vans. The original aim was also to change bodies when a van underwent maintenance, to avoid the need for its driver to have to transfer all his tools and equipment to another van, and then have to move them back afterwards. The idea lapsed after a few years. BT also pioneered the use of all glass reinforced plastic bodies on vans.

The fleet has seen changes of livery. When still part of the GPO vehicles changed from the traditional dark green to yellow, to make vehicles parked in country areas stand out more. The new BT changed the colour to grey, but with a large light-reflective logo. More recently, white has been adopted, but with a red and blue logo. **JMA**

British Transport Commission, see NATIONALISATION

Brockhouse, J, & Co. Ltd, trailer makers of West Bromwich, was established as spring and axle makers by John Brockhouse in 1886. A small works was built a few years later and extended in 1897. The company floated in 1898 and a cycle department was in operation for a time before the First World War. Road axles and springs became the chief business.

As producers of road springs, axles, metal sections and vehicle fittings, the move to trailer manufacture in the inter-war period was a logical step. Under the slogan 'Brockhouse, the name that carries weight' a wide range of trailers was produced, including Gibson light trailers in the 1930s. The company history lists the product range as articulated, agricultural, cable drum, 4-wheel commercial vehicle and farmers' trailers, light, medium and heavy types, pantechnicon drop-frame trailers, pole, telescopic timber and tipping trailers. In addition to the West Bromwich site, trailers were made at the Clydebank works, established in 1934, which also produced commercial bodywork.

The founder was succeeded by his son, John T Brockhouse, in 1922 and the latter's son, John L Brockhouse joined the board in 1936. 1937 saw notable expansion, including purchase of the Vulcan works at Southport. The Vulcan plant was needed for military trailer production, followed by aircraft turrets. After the Second World War, Brockhouse pioneered in the production of vehicle-carrying semi-trailers, but eventually withdrew, leaving the field to Carrimore (q.v.). Brockhouse ceased trailer manufacture in 1974, to concentrate on its forge work.   **RAS**

C Mackenzie, *Brockhouse: a study in industrial evolution* (West Bromwich: the firm, 1945)

BRS Parcels. At nationalisation in 1948 the Road Transport Executive (later the Road Haulage Executive) acquired the recently-formed joint parcels service of Carter Paterson & Co. (q.v.) and Pickfords Ltd (q.v.), by virtue of their previous ownership by the main line railways. Various other acquisitions also had substantial parcels businesses, including Bouts-Tillotson (q.v.), Fisher Renwick (q.v.), Holdsworth & Hanson (q.v.), Sutton & Co. (q.v.) and Scottish-based Youngs' Express Deliveries Ltd. McNamara & Co. (q.v.) continued to operate a major contract it had with the General Post Office for a year or two after acquisition. Over a period of about four years all the parcels operations were welded into a national service by amalgamating them into parcels groups within each of the geographical divisions into which British Road Services (q.v.) was divided. One change begun in 1949 was to replace van boys (q.v.) with trained dogs (q.v.), many being recruited from Battersea Dogs Home.

During the process of denationalisation, all the parcels groups were put into a new company, BRS (Parcels) Ltd, in 1955 with the aim of selling it as a single unit. It attracted little interest, however, and remained with BRS. Mechanisation of depots began and the first VA or Noddy van appeared in 1957. Based on the Austin 3-ton chassis, it was developed by the BRS Engineering Group to give the driver cross-cab access as well as easy access to the load compartment from the cab. Production ran on into the mid-1970s with the fleet of these distinctive vehicles peaking at 2700.

The Transport Act 1963 put the remaining state-owned goods transport operations under the new Transport Holding Company (q.v.), which completely separated the parcels operations from the mainstream BRS. In 1965 it became BRS Parcels Ltd — the brackets in the title had gone. From 1955 through to 1969, when it became a constituent of the newly-formed National Freight Corporation (q.v.), its business remained remarkably steady: employing 4100 vehicles and about 11,000 staff, its carryings varied only 5 per cent either side of 95 million parcels per year. Profits were more variable, the best being £2.9m on a turnover of £19.1m in 1964.

The delivery times at this period were generally 2–4 days, but BRS Parcels was starting to face challenging competition. In the early 1970s it brought delivery times between main centres down to 48 and then 24 hours and in 1975 it was re-launched as Roadline UK Ltd, but this did not stop it sinking into unprofitability. In 1981 its Scottish parcels services were brought together, and subsequently integrated, with those of National Carriers Ltd (q.v.) under the name of Scottish Parcel Services Ltd. Merger with NCL's parcels division in England and Wales followed in 1986. Despite opposition from the Transport & General Workers Union, which proposed closure of NCL (whose members were represented by the National Union of Railwaymen), it was Roadline's operations that were largely closed, because it was decided to abandon home deliveries. Its name was preserved in the new, but short-lived, National Carriers-Roadline.

Several small-to-medium sized parcels carriers were acquired, including N Francis & Co. Ltd (q.v.) in 1960, the Tayforth (q.v.) parcel companies in 1965 and Bridges Transport Ltd of Preston in 1966. They were never absorbed into BRS Parcels, but kept separate in a small holding company, British Express Carriers Ltd, and held up by the NFC as an example of how small units providing selective services were able to withstand economic stringencies better than large companies providing general services. In the 1970s they became regional distribution operators.   **JMA/GAB**

Annual Reports & Accounts of the BTC (1948–62), THC (1963–8) and NFC (1969–99); Baldwin (1982); Thompson (1990); Ingram and Mustoe (1999)

The **Bulkmobile** bulk feed transporter body was designed by Edward Baker Ltd of Cornard Mills, Suffolk, which set up a subsidiary to market it, although F G Smith (Motors) Ltd of Goodmayes appear in advertising as patentees and selling agents. Production of the tipping body with pneumatic discharge facilities began in 1956 by Duramin Engineering (q.v.). The design was promoted by a film, 'A day with Bulkmobile'. Although a technical success, with good European sales and UK fleet sales (such as 15 to J Bibby & Sons Ltd by 1960), in the longer term Bulkmobile apparently did not live up to its commercial promise and production ended by 1989.   **RAS**

C Clark and R Munting, *Suffolk Enterprise* (Norwich: UEA, [2000]), p. 53; *CM* (23 September 1960), Supp. p. 187; Some records are held in the Bury St Edmunds branch of Suffolk Record Office (HC 545).

Burford lorries (1914–1930s) were of American origin: Buda-engined, Fremont-Mais vehicles, sold in the UK by H G Burford & Co. Ltd of North Kensington. This firm was set up by Henry George Burford (1867–1943), a time-served engineer with a long and complex involvement with the motor industry, including founder and managing director of Milnes-Daimler. The Burford came to have an increasing British content and a forward-control model was introduced in 1923.

The GWR was a substantial customer, employing 200 Burfords as lorries and buses. The British & Argentine Meat Co. Ltd replaced Milnes-Daimlers acquired from one of its constituents with eight 2- and 4-ton Burfords. The larger of these vehicles were significant for their high-roofed bodies by Liversidge, which lessened dockers' objections to lorries, by facilitating the loading of sides of beef. By 1924 twenty Burford lorries were operated by Industrial Transport of Whitechapel on contract hire to the grocery trade. Having imported the Cletrac crawler

tractor in the First World War, Burford marketed the Burford-Kegresse half-track in 1924. In 1926 Burford went into liquidation, but was acquired as a going concern by its former general manager and some production continued, moving from Kensington to Teddington in 1931, three years before Lacre took over. Burford spent his later years in consultancy. He held office in the Society of Motor Manufacturers & Traders (q.v.) and the Institution of Automobile Engineers (q.v.).

RAS

K C Blacker, 'Moving meat', *Vintage Commercial*, 1, 8 (April 1963), pp. 251–7; Kelley, (1982); Stevens-Stratten and Aldridge (1987); N Baldwin, 'The Burford Story', *VCVM*, 29 (1990) and 30 (1991), pp. 103–5 and 126–8

Bus carriage of goods and parcels. As the motor bus industry expanded after 1919 the majority of rural operators, and some of the newer 'territorial' companies, offered to carry parcels, which had long been the practice in a number of municipal tramway (q.v.) and bus undertakings, particularly in the north of England, which in turn had inherited the practice from the country carrier (q.v.). Some bus companies developed van fleets in the process. Newspapers were a standard cargo. For instance, D C Thomson, and George Outram, periodical publishers, had contracts with the Scottish Bus Group to deliver packages of their papers, just after the Second World War. Such facilities have largely disappeared today but, during the post-1945 years of scarcity, chain stores such as Woolworths situated in neighbouring towns used the bus company's parcel service to balance stocks. Sometimes buses even carried livestock.

In 1924 Percy Steer began operations from Bow, Devon, with a Chevrolet lorry which could be fitted with bench seats. On market days he carried produce and passengers to Exeter with return loads of goods from wholesalers to village stores. Passengers were sometimes accompanied by small livestock on the way to or from market. This writer observed in 1943 a bus operator with a licensed route into Ipswich running a 14-seat vehicle with the back seats removed for parcels and on at least one occasion the space was occupied by a live goat. That the facility was not universal is illustrated by the public outcry when in the late 1960s the Bristol Tramways & Carriage Co. acquired a Gloucestershire bus operator, and terminated the carriage of parcels along the interurban route that he had served.

The link with the GPO seems to have reappeared in the 1930s. Prior to the outbreak of war in 1939 the head post office at Colchester had an arrangement with the Eastern National Omnibus Co., which provided a late postal collection for towns within a range of twenty miles and villages en route. The local post office padlocked a metal container to the rear platform of the bus on the last journey into Colchester, and the public could post their letters in it during the layover period of some fifteen minutes, usually just before ten pm. At Colchester, postmen waited with sack-barrows to unlock and remove the containers and wheel them into the Post Office. Some David MacBrayne (q.v.) buses in Scotland also carried mail, while a network of once-a-day rural services operated by Sutherland Transport & Trading Co. survived until the mid-1980s. They were based on Lairg railway station and Lairg Post Office and used buses with special goods compartments at the rear. Mail, milk, newspapers and other goods were carried on routes to Bettyhill, Durness, Kinlockberrie, Lochinver, Scourie and Tongue.

Rail replacement service was another way in which buses carried parcels, once the railways began shutting rural branch lines. For instance, following the closure of the Lynton to Barnstaple railway in 1935, Southern National introduced AEC single-deck buses with large rear luggage compartments to carry mail, milk churns and other goods. They remained in use into the 1950s. In 2000 a few bus operators serving remote areas still carried parcels. **JH**

R Grimley, *Bow Belle: the story of Steers Bus and Parcel Service* (Bigbury: Grimley, 1993); A T

Condie, *Alexanders Buses Remembered, I: 1945–1961* (Nuneaton: Condie, 1996), pp. 93–4; R C Anderson, *A History of the Midland Red* (Newton Abbot: David & Charles, 1984), p. 12; M Hawkins and R Grimley, *A Century of Coaching on Exmoor* (Dulverton: Exmoor Books, 1998), pp. 88–9

Bus chassis conversion into lorries. (Figure 82) As early as 1912 the London General Omnibus Co. used lorries based on B-type bus chassis to ferry items from its central Walthamstow works to operational garages. At that time chassis designs for carrying passengers or goods were virtually identical. Many major bus operators such as London Transport and Birmingham Corporation made use of chassis taken out of passenger service for conversion into service vehicles for use as breakdown vehicles, staff canteens or cash transit vans. It was not uncommon, especially between the wars, for the chassis of time-expired or accident-damaged buses and coaches from a variety of operators to be rebodied as lorries. Post-war single-deckers have on occasion had their bodies converted to serve as mobile shops or racing car transporters. The building of specialised commercial bodywork, such as horse-boxes, on to new passenger chassis was not restricted to longer, high-specification chassis such as Daimler: Woodhams records several coach builders producing horse-boxes on Bedford OB chassis, also mobile libraries, a mobile bank (for the Clydesdale Bank) and specially-cabbed pantechnicons. Arlington Bodybuilders Ltd of Enfield introduced the Coronet pantechnicon on the Bedford SB chasssis in 1953. **RAS**

J Bowden-Green, *London Transport Service Vehicles (November 1939–May 1978)* London Omnibus Traction Society); A Townsin, *75 years of AEC* (1987); J Woodhams, *The Bedford OB and OWB* (Twickenham: DPR Marketing & Sales, 1986); R M Warwick, *An illustrated History of United Counties, Part 2* (Northampton: the author, 1978), pp. 56–63; *CM* (3 July 1953), p. 634

C

C licence, see LICENSING

Cab-forward layout is a variant of forward-control (q.v.). The whole or a greater part of the cab is located forward of the front axle, giving greater ease of access, a three-person capacity cab and improved manoeuvrability. Such a layout was advocated by John Shearman (q.v.) for short mileage work in his 1938 IAE paper; examples of such vehicles include the Karrier CK and Bantam series, the Albion Claymore and Dennis Stork. **RAS**

The **cab-over platform** (Figure 83) was typically associated with the carriage of hay and straw and is still to be seen on vehicles engaged in that trade. It has also served for the carriage of other goods with a high volume-to-weight ratio, including hops in pockets and wool in bales, cut flowers in boxes, chairs and brooms. As an extension to the vehicle's load-carrying area, it is a permanent fixture of solid construction, attached to a vertical back-board behind the cab, usually with metal bracing stays from each front corner of the platform to the front bumper. It should not be confused with the sheet platform or open box, also fixed on the cab roof, on which folded tarpaulins were carried when not in use. The operator's name-board was often attached to the front of the sheet platform. **RAS**

Sedgwick (1980); G Edge, 'Flower drop men', *CVC*, 6, 6 (February 2001), pp. 18–21

Cabs. (Figures 8, 13, 171 and 181) Over a century the lorry cab progressed from a primitive, almost non-existent after-thought to one of the most recognisable and arguably most important parts of a vehicle. The first motor lorries provided nearly no weather protection for the driver, just as the horse-drawn goods dray had offered no shelter, but the early petrol engine provided a modicum of winter warmth. On small vans the driver was usually luckier, perhaps because they were directly derived from the car. Often there were at least half-height side doors too.

In contrast a retractable canvas awning was all that was found on most large vehicles, often until well into the 1920s. Provision of windscreens followed the general availability and reasonable reliability of windscreen wipers, and it soon became a legal requirement for windscreens to be openable, to provide slightly better visibility in the winter fogs common in urban areas. Before windscreen wipers came into use in the late 1920s if a windscreen was fitted, when it rained a driver either opened the screen fully or rubbed half of a cut raw potato on it. For a time hand-operated windscreen wipers were also available. Some operators were reluctant to fit windscreens fearing the warmth and enclosed atmosphere might make drivers drowsy. Some vehicle makers, notably Ford, fitted wipers worked by vacuum from the inlet manifold: these raced when the engine was idling, but slowed or even stopped when it was accelerating hard. Compulsory fitment of wipers was slow to come. Even new legislation in 1937 only made 'an efficient automatic windscreen wiper' a requirement on vehicles in which the 'windscreen cannot be opened.' Doors to cabs were generally provided in the 1930s, though some operators preferred half-height versions, or sometimes just a near-side door so that a spare wheel could be mounted on the offside. Many vehicles used on local collection and delivery work, particularly those railway-owned, usually still had no door, just a piece of canvas that could be unfurled on a wet day.

Makers such as Bedford, at the light-to-medium end of the market, in the early 1930s provided a cab as an integral part of the vehicle. While a cab became an essential part of the appearance of individual makes or models, it was not infrequently a 'bought in' component. For example, from its start in 1933 until well after the Second World War ERF's cabs were built by the firm next door, old-established bodybuilders, J H Jennings. Ultimately ERF bought the company. Among the larger and heavier truck makers, AEC from the 1930s had a common appearance to its models, but, while AEC provided general arrangement drawings and dimensions, the cabs were built by a large number of different companies.

Almost universally cabs were constructed of timber framing clad with metal panels, the curved ones being individually hand-beaten to shape. Again it was the volume producers such as Bedford and Ford (the latter as Fordson or Thames) that pioneered the use of styling, to produce more modern and attractive-looking vehicles with cabs whose shape identified the make. Later it was these higher-volume makers who first utilised steel pressings for cabs.

In 1947 Leyland's new medium-weight Comet chassis, with its American-style Briggs-built bonneted cab (used also by Ford and Dodge), took modernity and styling a stage further. It was manufactured as a complete unit and if damaged operators could buy a new cab. New cabs were still being sold to operators by Leyland well into the 1960s. In contrast, cabs from some makers were still coach-built affairs, built up on the chassis frame and partly depending on it for structural rigidity.

Another early example of a cab with a clean, modern external appearance was Foden's S18 cab on its new goods range designed in 1946. This had a flush-fronted cab with a distinctive grille panel with (as on the Leyland Comet) the real radiator hidden behind. The cab was still built with an ash frame and aluminium panels, but the wooden door and corner pillars were now covered with an aluminium skin.

The next real step forward in cab design came in 1960 with the Bedford TK, for it was designed to be driver-friendly. All-round visibility was good and entry and exit were easier, aided by small wheels. The engine was set back in the frame and protruded through the back of the cab, which enabled the cab to be lower than usual and also to seat three. Lorry cabs were now moving from being a necessary component perched on top of the mechanical parts to becoming an integral part of the design considered at an early stage.

Leyland took cab design forward again with its tilting Ergomatic cab announced in 1964, though the first European production tilt-cab had been Foden's some two years earlier. Before then Neville (q.v.) had produced a tilt-cab as part of his forward-control conversions. Tilt-cabs had been common in America for some years and Leyland bought and ran a White truck from the US while developing its own design. The tilt-cab has become standard on virtually all trucks. It provides good access to all engine and chassis components, so that even fairly major work on an engine can be undertaken without its removal or without having to remove part of the cab to get at the engine. Providing access in this way, the engine can be more effectively sealed off from the driver, thus reducing noise levels.

More important than tilting, the Leyland cab was the first to make use of human factors engineering or ergonomics. Leyland studied the weight, height and reach of the human body and then used a '95 percentile dummy' to produce an internal layout which in terms of seat adjustment, angles of vision, reach to controls, and steering wheel rake would be comfortable for 95 per cent of drivers. The cab was also relatively low, with entry and exit eased by putting steps and handles in the right places. Previous cab design had usually put them where they were cheapest to fit, the bottom step into a cab often being an inadequate metal ring mounted on the front wheel, while hand grips, if any, were fitted haphazardly so that a driver might really need two left hands to reach the cab interior safely.

An earlier successful attempt to provide a safer and more comfortable working environment, albeit from a less-scientific basis, was made by Austin with its so-called threepenny-bit cab, introduced on its Series Four range in 1959. The resulting cab had a unique appearance. It had angled sides and relatively narrow doors, so that an open door projected little beyond the full width of the vehicle. Visibility was excellent, with extra sighting windows below the windscreen on either side of the radiator. Proper steps and grab rails made entry and exit easy and Austin commissioned comparative tests on drivers analysing the amount of energy and driver fatigue (or lack of it). The new cab came out the clear winner. It was only suitable for designs with a modest payload, unfortunately, and rear-hinged doors would not be acceptable today. At the lighter end of the market the BMC FJ was the first to be fitted with a tilt cab.

The growing number of imports from Volvo and Scania focussed on driver amenities with attention to details such as provision of an electric razor socket. Sweden already had legislation on cab strength, including dramatic tests to prove crash worthiness. The Swedes led European thinking, but cab strength and safety have subsequently become important issues. As a result almost all recent cabs were metal-framed, the only exception being ERF's composite plastics cab which is based on a steel tubular frame clad in sheet modular compound (SMC).

Probably the most striking glass-fibre cab design was by Michelotti, an Italian car stylist, for Scammell. It was particularly popular on the Routeman tipper chassis, as it was easy to repair, while the interiors could be hosed out without fear of corrosion. Routeman tippers lasted far beyond their expected lifespan with small operators and owner-drivers.

Earlier ERF, like other makers, had made extensive use of glass-fibre as a cladding on what was otherwise a conventional timber framing. Glass-reinforced plastic is easily moulded into curved or other shapes, whereas metal-shaping is far slower and labour-intensive.

Not all operators in the 1950s and 1960s were happy with factory-designed or standard cabs, particularly timber-framed ones, and this led to the emergence of a few specialised cab builders who generally used aluminium, such as Boalloy (q.v.) and Holmes of Preston. Alloy cabs were lighter and did not rust or rot. The oil companies were quite large customers of the specialised cab builders for a time, no doubt partly because they could specify design features such as sliding doors.

For many years the traditional truck was bonneted, with the cab behind the engine. This normal-control layout persisted with some makes or models into the 1950s or even later,

but was ultimately almost entirely replaced by the forward-control (q.v.).

Great ingenuity in cab design has been exercised in the lighter end of the market, with attempts to provide vehicles suitable for multi-drop operation. They need cross-cab access and a low floor. There have been uncommon models such as Albion's Claymore, which achieved this by mounting a relatively conventional cab far forward, ahead of the front axle, with the horizontal underfloor engine behind it. The Sentinel diesel had a horizontal engine under the frame. The BMC 'Noddy van' for BRS Parcels was more conventional and bonneted, while the Commer Walk-Thru van was also aimed particularly at the collection and delivery market. Specialised adaptions of conventional van chassis are currently used by Parcelforce, among others, while United Parcel Service (q.v.) operates a large European fleet of vans built by several makers to its unique design.

There were some ingenious ideas on accessibility, such as an Albion design in which the cab could be craned or lifted upwards in order to reach the engine. From 1926 Garner was building forward-control chassis with wings and a cab floor which hinged out to provide engine access.

There have been fashions in cab design too. There was a period when big, bluff, almost aggressive and angular cabs were favoured by some makers, but less brutish and more rounded designs, led by Leyland's T45 series, subsequently became the norm. The rising cost of fuel contributed to modest changes in cab shape, since more aerodynamic designs reduced fuel consumption (see AIR MANAGEMENT).

Sleeper cabs were once merely an add-on extra, built or provided by outsiders rather than mainstream makers. One of the earliest was built for the Midlands Transport & Trading Co. in 1928 on a Foden rigid six-wheel steamer. It had hinged double bunks and an auxiliary tank which boiled water to make a cup of tea. But it was not until the 1960s that sleeper cabs started to become popular. Now they are widely available as an option from most makers. The poor quality of many overnight lodgings, improved heating and ventilation (or even air conditioning) of cabs, and the availability of equipment to permit the use of kettles, microwaves and even refrigerators contributed to the popularity of sleeper cabs. Sleeper-cabbed vehicles are popular on driver-accompanied operations to and from the Continent, but are also quite widely used on vehicles running only in the UK. Secondhand values of vehicles with sleeper cabs are usually high, which prompted some operators to specify them, as residual values were disproportionately higher.

Cab makers tried to produce designs that provided relatively low floor height for use on vehicles for local delivery work, with the driver frequently leaving and entering his cab. The same shell also had to provide a vehicle suitable for long-distance operation with a higher driving position and a greater degree of amenity. This was achieved by mounting the cab higher, to accommodate the larger engine with higher output which was usually specified for such work.

Renault's Magnum was launched in 1991 and featured an exceedingly high and spacious cab designed exclusively for long-haul work. Steps were needed to reach the cab but once inside the tallest driver could walk about without stooping. It was seen as a prestige vehicle likely to appeal to a small number of owner-drivers, but sales vastly exceeded expectations, with some purchases by fleets keen on the image presented or anxious to attract the best drivers.

Cabs have become an expensive part of the modern vehicle, particularly the press tools needed to shape the panels. As a result cabs are often out-sourced from an independent supplier, even if designed by the truck manufacturer. Such arrangements help reduce the initial costs of a new model, with the capital costs of development being effectively paid for over a period. Cabs may also be shared with another manufacturer, with minor cosmetic features suitably disguising the common ancestry.   **JMA**

The **Caledon lorry** (1915–27) originated with Scottish Commercial Cars Ltd of Glasgow, Commer distributors who found themselves without a vehicle to market in the First World War. Former Argyll motor designers came up with a 4-ton chassis, Dorman-powered. About 400 were made during the war, mainly for civilian use, but 50 were supplied to Russia. In the marque's best year, 1919, some 170 Caledons were produced, but development costs and the post-war slump resulted in the goodwill and stock being sold after a total production of only some 700 vehicles, to Garrett (q.v.) of Leiston in 1926, which made no progress beyond the assembly of three further vehicles. The Caledon was distinguished by a saltire badge on a fluted radiator.   **RAS**

N Baldwin, 'Caledon of Scotland', *VCVM*, 15 (July/August 1988), pp. 16–19

Car, an abbreviation of the legal term 'motor car', was used by some operators from the 1920s to denote a light motor lorry or van. Paterson refers to Carter Paterson having '30-cwt, 2-ton, and 3-ton cars, which are most generally used to make deliveries from warehouses to shops'. It survived in use in some quarters for many years, with BRS and Pickfords, for example, referring to their vehicles as 'cars' into the 1960s.   **RAS**

Paterson (1927), p. 98

Car delivery. (Figures 9 and 84) The earliest deliveries of cars involved movement to the owner by rail and horse. As car driving skills increased vehicles were sent by rail to the nearest station, then driven to their destination. In the 1920s the growth of larger dealerships led to the entry of specialist firms capable of delivering numbers of vehicles. The motor trade operated on an ex-works basis, being responsible for collection once the car had left the assembly line. Delivery drivers used the 'limited' category 'trade plates', identified by their red registration on a white background and the details on a triangular label. Hence the term 'platers' was used to describe them. Rail continued to play a part in car distribution, providing special vans for this traffic. After the Second World War the emphasis on exports required large numbers of cars to be delivered at the same time to catch sailing dates. This led to new entrants using a convoy system. The plater drivers delivering to docks required more than rail passes or hitch-hiking, as normally used for their return journey. The large number of drivers, plus the batteries removed from the export vehicles, were returned to the assembly plant by bus.

Platers were a mixed bag, with evidence of some new cars being driven at excessive speeds and of accidents. The use of car transporters had long been part of the USA motor industry and these began to appear in this country in the late 1940s, despite the high capital investment involved. A pioneer builder of the semi-trailers was J Brockhouse Ltd (q.v.), which had subsidiaries in the USA. The earliest had a fixed top deck, and was based on American practice. Loading and unloading was lengthy and hazardous. Despite this, the advantages saw new manufacturers enter the market and improvements soon followed, notably a fold-down top deck. Brockhouse developed its version, just as demand was taking off, but then decided, not for the first time, to cease production, leaving the market open for Carrimore Ltd (q.v.), which became market leader. Taskers produced a two-deck design, using a Burtonwood tail-lift, which folded up against the rear when travelling. The length of the lift platform could give an unsettling sag in use and was awkward for access when placing the vehicle on the lift. Taskers claimed its use of the Scammell-type automatic coupling was a benefit. In practice it was rarely used. The Carrimore trailer with its retracting turntable had a longer deck, without the danger of catching a car against the cab.

The Austin Motor Company, with large export sales to the USA, chose to build its own fixed-deck trailers. These remained in use for some ten years to 1958, when Austin discontinued operating its own transporters partly because the pay rates and conditions of outside drivers were lower than internal drivers. Car delivery was becoming more segmented: a number of firms still used platers; a group of large distributors found it economical to operate their own transporters;

and the specialist operators who, while introducing transporters, continued to use platers for some jobs, notably commercial vehicles. They became adept at taking advantage of the Construction & Use Regulations to increase the capacity of the trailers by extending the decks to carry an extra car or cope with new longer models.

The casual treatment by many operators of their plater drivers and then their introduction of transporters led to the T&GWU (q.v.) organising drivers. This made them among the highest paid in transport. Without a recognised union card, cars could not be collected from the plant or unloaded at the docks. Cars were usually collected from the assembly plant by platers and driven a short distance to a compound to be sorted for onward delivery. The power of the T&GWU in the Midlands was shown in the late 1950s with transporter deliveries to Humberside docks. The driver invariably ran out of hours on the return leg around Leicester, but was unwilling to park for the rest period so near home. The union secured an understanding with the authorities that the driver could continue to base, the next day working on local or transfers to make up the missing rest period. Longer term storage was dealt with by use of airfields or, more recently, redundant industrial sites, for example part of Corby Steel works. British Railways competed by using flat decks based on obsolete carriage underframes, but their charges became uncompetitive. The use of rail for European exports was more successful as imports grew and it became a two-way traffic. The specialist was Mechanical & Transport (MAT) who introduced two-deck articulated sets, able to carry 4×4 and light vans. MAT also continued to use the BR car flats. Since the acquisition of this operation by Société de Transport de Véhicules Automobiles (STVA), part of French Railways, some of their wagons are now used. Where there is no rail access at the assembly plant, STVA use car transporters to transfer cars to the rail head.

Although Carrimore remained market leader, Hoynor and Carter had considerable success with their versions of transporters. Carter, developed his two-deck articulated or rigid-and-drawbar transporters. These used an electric drive screw to raise the lift deck. The Carter design had longer deck space than the Carrimore, because Carter was talented in interpreting the Construction & Use Regulations to his customers' advantage. The rules were amended in 1965. Carrimore was acquired by York Trailers (q.v.) in 1976 and Carter by Crane Fruehauf (q.v.).

Carter also built a limited number of transporters based on underfloor-engined bus chassis. These carried up to 12 cars. The larger versions had the second man seated behind the driver. Their success was limited by a disagreement with the T&GWU on the rate for the driver. A limit of 9 larger and 10 mini cars was imposed, affecting the economics resulting ultimately in the acquisition of BTC by Maurice James Industries (MJI). The earliest transporters were operated on 'general' trade plates then costing £25 per annum, with white registration details on a red background. This was recognised as abuse of their purpose and also raised the question of operating licences, so they were taxed as commercial vehicles by unladen weight and operated on B licences. There were many lengthy appearances before licensing authorities for additional vehicles or increased weights and objections, not only from operators but also from BR. In the mid-1960s a change in the manufacturers' pricing policy saw the delivery charge included in the price. This meant that the maker rather than the dealer employed the car delivery agent, with new contracts on a regional basis. This favoured the largest operators, but also made it less attractive for dealers to use their own transporters. A number of mergers, particularly affecting smaller operators, took place, encouraged by the need for holding compounds for storage before delivery. The introduction of operator licensing in 1968 allowed considerable expansion in both operators and the number of vehicles in use. In 1964 BRS acquired Furness & Parker, based at Coventry Airport, and in 1974 took over Lathams and Auto Clearances, creating Cartransport (BRS) Ltd. One of the largest was Autocar & Transporters of Wythall,

Birmingham, which started in 1946, acquired B J Henry, the main delivery operator for Morris in 1962, followed by Dealers Deliveries. They later became a subsidiary of Western Motor Holdings and then part of Autologic Holdings. A new entrant was Maurice James, which had a considerable involvement in the distribution of coal. It acquired the closed Griff Clara Colliery, at Nuneaton, with ample space for car storage and acquired Canley Car Deliveries, which had lost a planning appeal to continue using its Coventry depot. It went on to acquire Avon Car Transporters, started by Major Lea (referred to as 'the Mad Major' for the risk he took with heavy loads on light transporters) handling Rover and Land Rover deliveries. BTC (Barnett) also became part of James Car Deliveries. When James acquired Progressive Deliveries, whose principal was known as 'Trader Horn', it was the largest operator. Maurice James hoped to group or merge with other operators to overcome the increasing power of the manufacturers and the restrictions imposed by unions. An attempt to reach agreement with BRS Car Transport failed and James suffered illness, which with some less successful ventures led to the sale of James Car Deliveries to Tolemans of Dagenham. Later new entrants included Richard Lawson and Roger Bastable, whose main base was Yeovil, trading as Abbey Hill. Bastable still appears with his own group at the Glastonbury Festival. Having built up a large business, he lost a major contract with Fiat and was forced to sell out. TNT was among those interested, but it was purchased by Walon Auto Transport, now part of Autologic. Bastable re-entered the industry with a smaller operation, Sensible Transport.

A major problem for operators is manufacturers that want reductions in the contract price for deliveries, with little regard for years of excellent service. With the growth of exports, just-in-time deliveries, and with cars built to order, a pre-delivery inspection service was one way to develop the relationship with manufacturers and increase turnover and profit. Other add-on services included minor remedial work, particularly with cars manufactured abroad. Tolemans of Dagenham was acquired in 1994 by Tibbett & Britten, who found car deliveries required different skills, and suffered losses. They re-organised this subsidiary as Axial. Recently the long-standing Ford contract was terminated and they changed the pattern of the business, expanding into Europe with the acquisition of Causse-Walon.

The latest transporters are built by Lohr and Transporter Engineering Ltd, the successor to Hoynor Trailers, usually with a tractor and drawbar configuration. Capable of carrying up to 11 cars, the complicated loading sequence is computerised, and can be a lengthy process to ensure the cars are in the right order for off-loading. A recent development at the other end of the scale was the use of small vehicles with enclosed bodywork to deliver expensive new and classic cars direct to the home of the purchaser. Apart from the major operators, a number of smaller operators act as sub-contractors to these or specialise in movement of auction, leased or second-hand cars. Even smaller businesses move new cars between dealers, sometimes using plates. Tibbett & Britten decided to leave the industry and to sell their Axial subsidiary in 2001.   **GM**

Car industry traffic (Figure 85), as distinct from car delivery (q.v.), resulted from the geography of the motor industry with related plants (for engines, body pressings, sub-assemblies and numerous components) often widely separated. These locational factors gave rise to considerable road haulage activity, much of it, especially in recent years, on a 'just-in-time' (q.v.) basis. An excellent introduction to the location of the industry is given in Turner's book on car manufacturing. It captured the industry at the peak of its post-war activity. From Coventry, as one of the main centres there was a long-standing Morris Engines link to Cowley, a Rootes link with its British Light Steel Pressings subsidiary at Acton and, in the post-war period, government-created links with Speke (Standard-Triumph) and Linwood (Rootes). Pressed Steel, Swindon to Cowley and Ford's Dagenham–Halewood axis were other

examples of long-distance links. The trunk roads between these locations became in effect part of the production line. In addition to the manufacturers' own transport, which, as in the case of Rubery Owen, only operated within a limited radius, there developed specialists, such as Crinage & Son of Coventry working exclusively for Morris Engines since 1919. Its mixed post-war fleet included Scammell rigid-six units and Macks.   **RAS**

Graham Turner, *The Car Makers* (Harmondsworth: Penguin, rev. edn 1964); *CM* (24 September 1954), advertisement

Carbodies, coachbuilders of Coventry, was associated between the wars with stylish car bodies. Wartime production included lorry, ambulance and specialised bodies for the armed services. After the war the firm became the producer of the standard London taxi and in 1997 the business was renamed London Taxis International. For several years after the end of the Second World War commercial body production helped the business survive. This work included milk-float bodies for Morrison Electricar and bodies for the Austin K8 3-Way van and the Commer N-type 30-cwt van. Carbodies' pre-war links with Rootes and wartime work on Austin chassis provided the contacts for this post-war work. Commercial vehicle work on a small scale was carried out in the 1960s, including cab panels for assembly by AEC, bodies for the Leyland 15 and 20 van derived from the Standard Atlas and some Commer lorry crew-cab conversions. A unitized box-body for the Bedford TK was not taken up by the chassis makers, for fear of harming independent bodybuilders.   **RAS**

Bill Munro, *Carbodies: the complete story* (Ramsbury: Crowood Press, 1998), ch. 3–4

Cargo flow patterns are determined in the first place by the location of centres of production and consumption. Manufactured consumer products flow from factories to retail outlets, both chiefly within the major urban conurbations, but the patterns have changed as new products have come onto the market, often produced away from the traditional manufacturing districts. Raw materials and semi-finished industrial products generally have quite different flow patterns, some of which may only be of a short-term nature, such as deliveries of aggregates, cement and steel to a major civil engineering construction site. Where raw materials were not processed locally, for instance china clay or metalliferous ores, this gave rise to significant cargo flows, but these being high bulk and low value were more suited to transport by rail or coaster. Agricultural products likewise have their own flow patterns and are usually seasonal, with a clear difference between those going directly to the market and those such as grain and sugar beet that go for industrial processing. Imports and exports have yet another very distinct pattern, channelled through the ports and other entry/exit points. There have been major changes here too, with the rise of Felixstowe (q.v.) as the principal container port, although the opening of the Channel Tunnel (q.v.) has consolidated Kent's position as the principal route to the Continent.

The number and location of storage and distribution depots between the points of production and consumption also determine cargo flow patterns, particularly in the case of consumer products. Faster average speeds allowing nation-wide coverage from fewer depots (but often with a substantial increase in vehicle mileage), the growth of superstores and the development of logistics (q.v.) have contributed to considerable changes in flow patterns. Faster speeds, with advances in mechanical handling and sorting techniques, have brought great changes to the pattern of parcels services (q.v.) by reducing the numbers of depots required and by allowing some operators to replace complex networks of direct depot-to-depot trunk services by the 'hub-and-spoke' systems, with 'spoke' services radiating from a central sorting 'hub' located in the Midlands. The growth of air parcels services with related road servicing is another relevant trend (see AIR FREIGHT).

At a more micro level, vehicle routing is continually changing in response to road congestion on the one hand and road improvements on the other. The Severn and Humber bridges, of 1966 and 1981, are notable examples of more direct routes, but journey time and reliability are more important than distance as evidenced by the density of lorry traffic going around London on the M25.
RAS/GAB

'Shops want full loads', *MT* (29 October 1998), p. 1; A J Wright, *abc Cargo Airlines* (Shepperton: Ian Allan, 2000)

Carman's Transport Ltd, SEE BRIT EUROPEAN TRANSPORT

Carmen, The Worshipful Company of, was founded in 1668 to 'improve the occupation of carmen in the City of London' but did not receive its Royal Charter as a livery company until 1948. The first by-laws affecting London's carters were in 1277. The first trade guild for carmen was the St Katherine's Fraternity, formed in 1517. This was soon controlled by the Company of Woodmongers, which also organised the stands where carmen waited to be hired.

After bitter disputes, control of the carmen passed to Christ's Hospital as a means of obtaining an income for its work with poor children. To identify licensed cars, a number was branded on the underframe, then costing 1d. There was an additional charge for the new 'chip and brass' identifying the purposes that the car could be used for. Carmen and Woodmongers also paid Christ's hospital 6s.8d. quarterly. The Woodmongers regained control of the Carmen between 1605 and 1665. Despite the best efforts of the Carmen to remain independent, Christ's Hospital again had control of their conduct. This continued until 1868. Today it is a ceremonial, charitable organisation, part of the tradition of London. Admission is by patrimony, apprenticeship and redemption. Branding is still carried out as an annual ceremony on invited commercial vehicles at London's Guildhall.   **GM**

Carpet traffic recently became a specialised operation with dedicated vehicles. For many years it was one of the wide range of commodities routinely handled by carriers.

Carpets were originally high-value imports from the Orient or Asia, and later from France, their high value meaning that transport costs were not an issue. English manufacture began in about 1740 at Wilton, 1745 at Kidderminster and 1750 at Axminster, and was taken to merchants by carriers using stage wagons. Introduction of power looms in the early nineteenth century and other improvements led John Crossley of Halifax to become the largest producer. Linoleum (using a cork and linseed oil base) later became a lower-cost alternative and was made in Scotland (mainly around Dundee) and Staines, with delivery of its raw materials also providing a valuable traffic.

Rail's virtual monopoly of this traffic ended in the 1920s, when the boom in housebuilding saw greater demand for linoleum and carpets, with road services being widely used. Local carmen were sometimes used for break-bulk deliveries. Loading bank staff did not welcome the work as the rolls were usually heavy and awkward to handle. Carpets had not to be bent, while linoleum rolls were carried vertically to avoid "flats".

Demand took off when furniture rationing finished after the Second World War, though linoleum sales were hit hard by the development of thermoplastic floor tiles, particularly Marley tiles. In the 1990s there was an increase in linoleum sales as a more upmarket product. Carpet sales steadily increased, with the establishment of a number of retail carpet chains, with direct selling by mail order. Cheaper carpets of man-made fibre and rubber backing were first developed by a short-lived newcomer, Cyril Lord Carpets, based in Northern Ireland, which often made direct delivery to customers' homes using British Railways' container service from the factory.

In the late 1960s dedicated services began, with Lex Wilkinson introducing its Carpet Express service. It was acquired by United Carriers (q.v.) in 1993 and merged with its Carpet Care subsidiary. The Carpet Express name was retained, the total fleet growing to 140 vehicles. Encouraged by some Carpet Express customers Carmen Brit European (q.v.) started its Carpet Express Logistics

subsidiary in 1997, but it closed within a year after incurring substantial losses. Following the acquisition of United Carriers by GEODIS in 1999, the Carpet Express operation was bought out by its management.

Some carpet wholesalers still used their own transport in the twenty-first century while the large chains used own-account or contract transport for full-load service. Loading and unloading at warehouses was usually by fork-lift truck with an extending boom which fits inside carpet rolls. Deliveries to smaller specialist retailers are often problems for regional carriers because of the unavailability of help in unloading, but a newer niche traffic in higher-value carpets offers next-day or regular deliveries of short lengths.   **GM/JMA**

Carrier cycles, see CYCLE DELIVERY

Carrimore commenced as a British business in 1914, having left France because of the war. It produced trailers and bodies, but still traded under its French name as Carrosserie Latymer, from Notting Hill in 1915. About 1925 it moved to new premises on the A1 at Finchley and became heavily involved with articulation, building trailers and modifying lorry chassis for use as tractor units. A subsidiary company, Worthmore Motors, fitted more-powerful engines in tractors, partly to compete with Scammell. The title was changed to Carrimore Six Wheelers Ltd. About 1930 it assembled articulated lorries with official factory approval from Leyland and Thornycroft. The Carrimore-Leyland sold as the Lynx (not to be confused with a lightweight Leyland model of the same name of the late 1930s) and was available until 1936. In 1928, inspired by the success of Shelvoke & Drewry, it produced a low-loading chassis, the Lowtruck, based on Ford T components. It did not sell and was soon discontinued. More successful was the conversion of agricultural tractors for road haulage. The cabs had rubber mountings and a form of weight transfer from the front axle of the drawbar trailer to the tractor's driving axle. From then it concentrated on articulated trailers (at first referring to them as 'attachments'), although also producing drawbar trailers and bodies for trailers and rigids. Its patented automatic retracting coupling was a feature of its earlier car transporters and it was market leader in these for a period. Carrimore acquired Anthony Hoists Ltd in the late 1950s, its expertise in hydraulic lifting being of particular value in the development of car transporter bodies. Anthony had supplied tipping bodies for Fords starting with its 7V range in the late 1930s. It became part of the Steel Barrel, Scammell group, which was acquired by the York Trailer Co. (q.v.) in 1976. **GM**

Carryfast Ltd, a nationwide parcels service, was set up in 1971 by Miles Druce, and later sold to GKN, then acquired by SPD (q.v.) in 1976. It carried little Unilever product, but had major contracts with stores such as Argos, B&Q and Debenhams. In 1983, when it operated some 250 vehicles, it was the subject of a management buy-out, supported by Industrial and Commercial Finance Corporation and a major bank. It then had eleven depots and was able to continue using SPD and Tibbett & Britten depots. Its general haulage and contract fleet operated as Haulfast from its Birmingham and Dewsbury depots. It was acquired by United Parcel Service (q.v.) as a British subsidiary in 1992. **RAS**

MT (30 November 1983)

Carter, Paterson & Co (Figure 86). Prior to the nationalisation of road transport in 1948 one of the best-known names for the carriage of parcels and sundries was that of Carter Paterson. The name was familiar and their green vans with the red stripe and poster advertisements on their sides were as well known as the London bus.

James Paterson was one of Pickfords' (q.v.) drivers in the border regions in the early 1840s, but in 1847, when a Berwick to Newcastle railway line was built, the rail route to Scotland from London was complete and his employment ceased. He moved to London and with financial support from Walter Carter, a Manchester-based carrier, started his own

business, known as Carter, Paterson & Co. It is part of the folklore of the industry that originally Walter Carter did not want his involvement with an evolving firm to be known. He had a successful business which became the removals division of Harrods. He suggested that the firm's name include a comma giving the impression that Paterson's trade was a carter. The comma was gradually dropped, in vehicle liveries, for example, and the version of the name without a comma has been used throughout this text. By the 1860s the firm was known for express parcels carriage, using the railways for the trunk stage, and with fourteen receiving offices in London. It became a limited company in 1887 with James Paterson as its chairman. Two years later, on Paterson's death, Walter Carter became chairman by then happy to be known, as the parcels business was a success.

CP had its first motor van in 1897 a 10-cwt chain-drive Daimler. In 1902 a Straker steam wagon was purchased for transfer work between depots, this sometimes pulled a horse van converted to trailer. In 1908 CP began using the Leyland XT in large numbers. This was a 35-hp, 3-ton van. After a flirtation with steam, CP switched entirely to petrol vehicles in 1911, as they were best suited to the lighter, parcel delivery activity.

It introduced its Home Counties Express service to serve the suburbs, which were developing, but not always with good rail links. Competition with Pickfords and other parcel carriers such as Globe Parcels Express, McNamara (q.v.) and Suttons (q.v.) led to a fall in profitability and so CP entered into a rate-fixing agreement in 1907 with Pickfords and Beans Express. This was not successful, so a formal amalgamation took place quietly in 1912 although CP and Pickfords Ltd maintained their separate identities. The chairman of the combined boards was Harry Lloyd Baxendale (q.v.) a Pickfords' man. CP's dominance meant that it absorbed the other three firms and its share capital rose threefold from £250,000 to £750,000. To eliminate competition, in 1915 CP bought W&G Express Carriers (q.v.).

During the First World War CP lost men and machines to the military and several depots were closed. After the war Pickfords and CP drifted apart and in 1920 the Baxendale family sold Pickfords to Hay's Wharf Cartage Co. Ltd (q.v.). As a result of the brief amalgamation CP acquired the ex-Pickfords City Road Basin premises which became Macclesfield Road depot. A proposed large central depot was never built but Express Body Building (a wholly-owned subsidiary, which later became Express Motor & Body Works Ltd (q.v.) and moved to Enfield) moved in there.

In 1925 CP's building department was the basis for Tersons Ltd, a wholly-owned company until nationalisation. Its name derived from the last syllable of each name. This company built many of the new depots. In 1930 the London–Manchester service was moved from rail to road to compete with Fisher Renwick (q.v.) and Bouts Tillotson (q.v.) who had both started long distance services.

An Act of 1928 empowered the railway companies to undertake road transport. This resulted in joint negotiations by all four companies with CP and Hay's Cartage Co. As a result of this the purchase of both companies became effective in 1933, to reduce competition and ensure they controlled this new alarming rival. James Milne, general manager of the GWR, became chairman and James Paterson became managing director of CP. Under railway ownership aggressive searching for traffic was discouraged and especially if it impinged on railway revenue. In 1934 CP bought its last major competitor, City and Suburban Carriers Ltd, a company set up in 1918.

The Second World War brought a slump in parcels traffic, as had occurred in the First, which led to drastic reorganisation, causing James Paterson to resign the board. Thus ended the family involvement in the firm. By 1944 CP was operating a fleet of over 1000 motor vans. This reorganisation involved greater integration of the parcels services, with a co-ordinated central management. In 1946 Carter Paterson and Pickfords Joint Parcels Services was formed. In its first year it carried 34 million packages. Its joint fleet consisted of 1150 vehicles and 300 horses.

Besides the dairies, CP was the last firm to use horses in large numbers. It was noted for its well-treated and well-turned out horses and vans. From its earliest days it employed lads to ride on the back of its vans to watch the load and deliver the parcels. As they swung themselves back onto the high floor with a thick rope they were known as 'monkey boys.'

In 1948 when the railways were nationalised CP went too, becoming a constituent of the Road Transport Executive. In 1953 it became part of BRS (Parcels) (q.v.). For its trunk work in the early years of nationalisation it used a mix of ERF wartime 7-ton lorries with a drawbar trailer, post-war AECs with drawbars and Dennis Max wartime rigids without trailers.

Turnbull (1979); Allan (1946), pp. 177–9; Hay's Wharf Cartage Co. (1947); notes by the late Philip Hine

Castle, Barbara (1910–2002) was minister of transport from December 1965 to April 1968 in Harold Wilson's Labour government. She was responsible for the introduction of, and thinking behind, the 1968 Transport Act, which was of great importance to the government. It was a well-considered response to six white papers issued between 1966 and 1968 and the report of the Geddes Committee (q.v.). It was a massive piece of legislation, of over 160 clauses and 18 schedules. Although introduced by Castle, it took nearly a year to pass through parliament and much of this work was undertaken by Castle's successor, Richard Marsh. The Act was the longest and most important piece of post-war legislation affecting transport. It was wide ranging and aimed at greater integration of transport, more emphasis on service, and a larger role for the railways and a reversal of the Beeching philosophy. In road haulage it created the National Freight Corporation (q.v.), to include Freightliner (q.v.) services, abolished the A, B and C licences and replaced them with quality licences, and wound up the Transport Holding Co. (q.v.). It also led to the introduction of the tachograph (q.v.).

Castle was remembered for her enthusiasm and energy and her determination to have her own way. She went on to other distinguished positions, including campaigning on behalf of old age pensioners, and was created a baroness. Her diaries demonstrate that road haulage absorbed a very small proportion of her time as minister and much of it was taken up with wider Cabinet issues. **JA**

Bagwell (1988), pp. 338–46; Barbara Castle, *The Castle Diaries, 1964–70* (Weidenfeld & Nicolson, 1974); T R Gourvish, *British Railways, 1948–73: a business history* (Cambridge University Press, 1986), pp. 362

C B radio, see CITIZENS' BAND RADIO

Cement traffic (Figure 87) by road developed greatly from the 1920s onwards, having previously relied on rail or water carriage. The industry itself had slowly grown during the nineteenth century in numerous localities where the necessary raw materials (chalk and clay or lias) were available. The principal cement-making areas were the Medway, Humberside, and parts of Cambridgeshire, Bedfordshire and Warwickshire and in the 1920s many private companies were involved in cement production. From these evolved major concerns, including Castle (which had absorbed Clyde, Tunnel, Ribblesdale, and Ketton), Blue Circle Cement, and Rugby Portland Cement (RPC), which included Kaye & Co., George Nelson, William Batchelor, Chinnor and Eastwoods. In 1999 vertical integration occurred with the acquisition of RPC by the RMC Group, producers of ready-mixed concrete (q.v.).

Until after the Second World War cement was normally delivered in hundredweight bags on flat lorries regardless of quantity. Some hauliers utilised the moving floor (q.v.) to assist handling. Post-war reconstruction on a massive scale, followed by an increase in road-building, forced a partial changeover to bulk traffic, with box-tipper lorries delivering to building sites and underground storage areas. In the mid-1950s pressure vehicles were introduced, both tipping and non-tipping, mainly on rigid chassis; these evolved into the familiar bulk tanker lorries. As an example of the early tankers, Eastwoods in the 1950s used '3 pot' Klinger tank vehicles on Foden 8-wheel chassis, each tank having a capacity of 5 tons.

Both bulk and bagged cement has to be kept dry during transit, handling and storage. This, is achieved today by curtain-sided trailers for the delivery of bagged cement shrink-wrapped onto pallets, and articulated bulk tankers, fitted with turbine blowers capable of discharging 25 tonnes of bulk cement within 40 minutes. In the early 1980s RPC devised a loading system using spaced blocks fixed on a platform lorry, on to which packs of bagged cement were placed by overhead crane. The spaces between the blocks permitted unloading by fork-lift truck. There were drawbacks to the method. It was sometimes difficult to extract the forks once the load had been deposited and it denied the vehicle any flexibility of load as it could only be used for that traffic. Some independent hauliers specialising in cement have developed an appropriately equipped fleet: for example, W H Higgins & Sons of South Luffenham, Rutland (founded in 1962) owned eight tractive units and eight bulk powder tanker-trailers for the carriage of Castle cement, also fly-ash and sand. 1990s tanker suppliers to RPC included Thompson Carmichael, Metalair, Spitzer Silo-Fahrzeugwerke and Feldbinder Fzw. In the post-war period Thornycrofts (to the 1960s), Commers and ERFs had been the mainstay of the RPC fleet.

To illustrate the scale of traffic, the central garage of RPC's Rugby Works operated 550 vehicles at its peak (with haulage contractors also operating into the works), before the company abolished its own fleet between 1988 and 1991, changing the status of those drivers who stayed to owner-drivers. Their vehicles remained in RPC livery and the trailer units were owned, but not maintained, by RPC. All RPC garages closed in 1998. Tractors and drivers were also supplied by contract hauliers, examples in 1995 being M&B Hauliers (Basildon) and Turners Transport. In 2001 Rugby Cement reverted to own-account operation, managed by TNT (q.v.). It acquired a fleet of 42 Renault Premium tractor units on a five-year contract and nine Foden Alphas with a trailer fleet of 120. **GMcB/RAS**

A J Francis, *The Cement Industry 1796–1914* (Newton Abbot: David & Charles, 1977); Tuck (1991), ch. 8; *International Cement Review* (January 1995), pp. 40–1; 'Profile: W H Higgins & Son', *CM* (4 November 1999), pp. 37–8; *Truck* (November 2001), p. 24; McBirnie (2002)

The **Channel Tunnel** was opened in 1994, 192 years after the idea was first promoted, by the twin British and French Eurotunnel companies, which together form, with their subsidiaries, the Eurotunnel Group. It comprises two 7.6 metre diameter rail tunnels and a central service tunnel, each 49.4 km long between Cheriton, near Folkestone, and Sangatte, near Calais. The project was approved by the Anglo-French treaty of 1986, rival bridge, tunnel and part-bridge-part tunnel road schemes having been rejected on a mixture of financial, feasibility and safety grounds.

Road vehicles are conveyed through the Channel Tunnel on Eurotunnel's shuttle trains, the journey time being 35 minutes. The single-deck freight shuttles carry heavy goods vehicles; their capacity was initially 25 heavy goods, but has been progressively increased to 32. The wagons are only partially-enclosed to save weight and the drivers travel in a club car at the front. The number of lorries conveyed increased from 390,000 in 1995 to 1,198,000 in 2001, the latter being a 48 per cent share of the Dover/Folkestone–Calais trade. Light vans are carried on the passenger trains, in double- or single-deck wagons depending on height.

The emergency plan, which uses the service tunnel as an escape route, proved effective when a major fire occurred on a freight train in 1996. The damage to the tunnel was such that the freight shuttle service was closed for seven months, yet there was no loss of life. **GAB**

Peter Semmens and Yves Machefert-Tassin, *Channel Tunnel Trains: Channel Tunnel rolling stock and the Eurotunnel system* (Folkestone: Channel Tunnel Group, 1994); Eurotunnel Group, *Annual Reports; IDCH*, 37 (2001), pp. 134–8.

Chaplin & Co., (Figure 88) founded in the 1760s, became London's biggest proprietor of stage- and mail-coach services. In 1837 William James Chaplin, grandson of the founder, decided to sell the coaching business and to throw in his lot with the new railway companies. Together with B W Horne, who had been London's second-biggest stagecoach proprietor, he formed the partnership of Chaplin & Horne which became goods and parcels agent for several railway companies. Most contracts were eventually cancelled as the railways took over the work themselves and the partnership was dissolved in 1879. One exception was the LSWR, which retained Chaplin & Co. as its goods and parcels cartage agent at many of its principal stations outside London. At some places this involved handling, clerical and accountancy work as well as provision of road collection and delivery services. Chaplins now concentrated in this region, adding a furniture removal and storage service in 1883. It established a network of offices and warehouses in 26 towns from Wokingham and Guildford to Plymouth and Barnstaple. Five were in the Isle of Wight linked to Gosport, Portsmouth and Southampton by Chaplins's four sailing vessels, later replaced by steam and then by motor vessels.

The firm, though still family-owned, was incorporated in 1926 as Chaplins Ltd, with its famous City headquarters address dating back to its coaching days: *The Swan with Two Necks*. Its assets then included 406 horse-drawn vehicles, 210 horses, 23 motor vehicles and 3 steam wagons. By then the LSWR had become part of the SR. Over the next decade its dividends increased from 10 to 16 per cent.

In 1933 the four main-line railway companies became joint owners of Pickfords Ltd (q.v.), which also operated in the same territory. Chaplins, now led by William Hugh Chaplin, great-great-great-grandson of the founder, saw this as a threat to its railway contract, which accounted for 60 per cent of turnover, and agreed to sell-out to the SR. In the event Chaplins was acquired in 1936 by the Hay's Wharf Cartage Co. on behalf of all four railway companies for £140,000. It continued as a separate company, though now as a subsidiary of Pickfords, with the four railway general managers replacing the family shareholders as its directors. During 1926–35 the family firm had invested in its road fleet much more slowly than the railway companies, having increased its motor fleet by only 21, with a reduction in horses and horse-drawn vehicles of 50. The new owners immediately put this right by purchasing eleven 3- and 6-ton Scammell mechanical horses, eleven 2- and 3-ton Bedfords and a secondhand 5-ton Bedford in their first year, but how much further mechanisation had been advanced before war intervened is not recorded.

Chaplins continued to act as cartage agent for the SR and Southern Region of British Railways until 1949, when BR took over this function. The residue of Chaplins' assets and work was absorbed into the South-Western Division of BRS and the company was formally dissolved in 1960.   **GAB**

Chaplins Ltd, *Our eventful history* [c.1930]; Chaplins Ltd, minutes of directors' and shareholders' meetings, 1926–60: PRO, AN 68/356, 406–8; LNER file on purchase of Chaplins Ltd: PRO, RAIL 390/1004; *OCBRH*

Chartered Institute of Transport, see INSTITUTE OF LOGISTICS & TRANSPORT

Chemical traffic (Figures 89 and 90). The first commercial movements of chemicals by road were recorded in the early 1900s, primarily commodity chemicals and petroleum spirit, and carried in relatively small quantities, packed in containers for use at the point of delivery. They included tallow, ammonia, paints and paint components, varnishes, bitumen, tar derivatives, soda ash, dyes, caustic soda, soap oils, petrol, lubricating oils and a wide variety of acids. Containers were generally cans, drums, glass carboys protected by straw, barrels, casks and a range of specially designed packages to suit the ultimate use of the product. Initially these were carried by the railways to goods yards with final delivery to the customer by horse-drawn carts (still common until the 1940s) or by petrol-engined vans and 2–3 ton lorries. Some steam-driven commercial vehicles were still in use but in relatively small numbers lingering on into the mid 1930s.

Petroleum and chemical transport, whilst having many distinct features, developed together with much cross-fertilisation of technical design and operating systems.

The 1920s saw a proliferation of suppliers and hauliers. With chemical transport most manufacturers ran their own fleets for delivery to other production sites and customers. Private hauliers were not totally excluded, especially if extra short term capacity was needed, but the specialised and hazardous nature of many chemicals prompted companies to keep direct control of operations. This practice declined slowly and major changes came about only in the 1970s and 1980s.

The chemical driver fast became a specialist receiving basic training over and above that of his general haulage colleague. This ensured the safety of the load and the public and has been a marked characteristic of the industry. He was also required to understand the optimum weight distribution when loading, how the vehicle handled when carrying large liquid loads, the avoidance of contamination, the compatibility or otherwise of loads with the material of construction of the barrel and loads previously carried. He also had to be aware of load measurement when filling and emptying tanks and passing over weighbridges.

Manufacturers and private hauliers became innovative in the design and use of road tankers and other specialised vehicles which might carry powders, polymer chips, fibres, molten products, cylinders, hoppers and intermediate bulk containers (q.v.). Lighter materials, alloys and composites gave opportunities for bigger payloads. The true general purpose tanker with its stainless or coated barrel, capable of carrying a different product every day, did not emerge until the late-1950s.

By the 1930s the railways faced increasing road transport competition. It initially affected merchandise mainly over short and medium distance cross-country routes. As commercial road vehicles became larger and more reliable longer distance destinations became the daily routine. Competition was fierce in service and cost, with motor transport providing a more flexible and convenient service.

This is a typical programme of routes used during a 6-month operating period by a manufacturer employing his own fleet and private haulage in the early 1950s. On grounds of safety and traffic density, operators were encouraged to keep to trunk routes in the days before motorways.

Region	Access Routes
North East Stockton, Billingham, Newcastle	A1, A67, A66
Hull	A63
North West Leeds Manchester Liverpool St. Helens	A64, A62, A653 A6, A62, A572 A41, A57 A58
West Midlands Birmingham Black Country	A38, A435, A34 A41, A5, A454
South Wales Cardiff/Swansea	A48, A470
Glasgow & Mid. Valley	A77, A736, A737, A71, A721
London & South East East North West South	A12, A13 A1, A6, A5, A10 A4, A40, A41, A30, A3 A23, A20, A21

By 1953 the political situation began to change and a new Transport Act sold off 35,000 vehicles, many back to their former owners. Included in BRS was Pickfords Tank Haulage, Harold Wood and Caledonian Bulk Liquids. These companies were the basis of a new grouping, the National Freight Corporation (q.v.).

Companies needing chemical transport in the 1950s included Armour Hess, Associated Octel, British Oxygen Chemicals, British Steel Chemicals, Carless Capel & Leonard, Durham Chemicals, CIBA, Esso, Dow Chemicals, Fisons, Glaxo, Imperial Chemical Industries, Laporte, Monsanto, Reckitt & Colman, Shell Chemicals, Union Carbide, and Yorkshire Chemicals.

By the early 1970s serving these manu-facturers was an array of chemical transport companies, small and large, and often with specialised niche activities based on the chemicals they carried. These included Sutton and Sons, Harold Wood, Smith and Robinson (once the largest European tanker owner), Rankin and Sons, Stockton Haulage, Youngs of Stokesley, P&O Group, Hanson, Tankfreight, Calor Transport, Liquids Powders and Gases, F & F Robinson, Bulwark United Carriers, Burn Bros, Bulk Haulage, Queensgate Motors [J Riding], Buckley Transport, Freighthire, Hoyer Transport with German headquarters, Fearns Transport, Cleveland Tankers, Hargreaves, Prestons of Potto, Wincanton, Hemphill, R Durham, Reliance Tankers, Ancliff, Meeks, Crow Carrying and a host of small concerns, some running fewer than six vehicles.

Tanker barrels and specialised bodies were built by a relatively small engineering industry, major contsructors including W & P Butterfield, Charles Roberts, John Thompson, Carmichaels, Crane Fruehauf (q.v.) and Yorkshire Engineering. All had catalogue designs for everyday requirements but could produce highly sophisticated equipment in conjunction with chemical manufacturers and hauliers and occasionally with input from the Ministry of Transport. Typical of this co-operation was production of a fleet of liquefied ethylene carriers for Imperial Chemical Industries in the early 1950s. These tankers ran from ICI's works at Wilton near Middlesbrough, day and night via Leeds and Lancashire, to the company's plant at Winnington in Cheshire. The great weight of the barrel and fittings of these 22 ton gross vehicles meant the payload was only 7.8 tons of ethylene.

From the 1970s a steady reduction took place in the number of manufacturers' own fleets, driven by a spate of industrial relations problems. The unions realised an effective method of disrupting production was to prevent movement of raw materials and finished goods, especially since this could be achieved legally by stopping drivers outside the factory gate. These tactics rapidly brought plants to a halt and since the cost of transport was seen as a relatively small proportion of the product value, managements took the easy way out and made major concessions. As militancy increased so much was conceded that business began to be lost to overseas competitors, inevitably company attitudes hardened and it was resolved to change the situation.

Own fleet drivers who might be expected to remain loyal during strikes became, often unwillingly, involved in sympathetic action or intimidated into withdrawing their labour. It was the efforts of private hauliers in defying picket lines which kept some production going. The outcome was for manufacturers to reduce their reliance on own fleets, contracting the work out to private haulage which achieved higher productivity and significantly reduced costs. These firms needed training and auditing on their ability to handle large volumes of hazardous chemicals. This was achieved relatively quickly and led to the establishment of an effective and independent chemical transport industry.

Surprisingly rail did not benefit from the changes, even with the most hazardous of products, and detailed safety studies confirmed that it was safer to carry the most hazardous chemicals by road rather than by rail. Hazard analysis demonstrated that rail had the disadvantage of moving a large volume in a single train load. It was under the control of staff trained in only basic chemical handling procedures, and furthermore, since most main lines ran through the centres of towns, major populations would be exposed to spillages. Road held the advantage with relatively small quantities on a single vehicle, using mainly motorway routes which avoided town centres. Most important was a skilled driver at the wheel trained to handle the product concerned.

The advantages of road did not end there, because the chemical producers had operated for many years, in conjunction with police and fire services, a nationwide assistance service for all chemical vehicle incidents irrespective of vehicle ownership. Safety came before commercial interest. This service was available for rail incidents but was more difficult to apply because of the inaccessibility of rail lines to emergency road vehicles.

The chemical transport industry, although having an excellent safety record, suffered at the hands of sensationalised reporting. Alarmist headlines such as, 'bombs on wheels' and, 'Juggernauts (q.v.) of Death' were common even when reporting minor incidents. Managements set out to demonstrate that the industry did care by placing great store on publicising its response systems.

Introduced formally in 1974 at a conference on Teesside which included the chemical producers and transporters, police, fire, ambulance, and Ministry of Transport officials, the 'Hazchem' load labelling and emergency recovery system set out to influence public opinion through its labelling and emergency recovery systems. 'Hazchem' is totally self-regulated and based on coded labels giving details of the load carried, a direct telephone number to an emergency centre which will give appropriate advice and if necessary despatch specialist teams to the site of the incident. The label also carries the name of the chemical manufacturer and coded advice on the safe handling of the chemical for the benefit of the emergency services. Additionally the driver carries a card with full details of the load. Driver training has been improved over the past 30 years and it is mandatory for drivers to possess a certificate of competence for loads in their care.

Innovation maintains the competitive position of chemical road haulage and its customers. This is apparent in the now widespread use of transportable tank containers in place of conventional road tankers for deliveries in domestic markets, into Europe on ferry and via deep sea shipping services to export destinations around the world.

Introduction of the 'quality' philosophy into the industry came in the 1980s. Management was concerned that customer service and general operating standards were not as effective as might be desired. The 'quality' process then being applied to industry in America and Japan was analysed for its benefits. The quality programme was taken up by the chemical industry, particularly by ICI, the first application being made in its distribution function in the north-east. This encompassed all the contractors used by ICI and the first accreditation to British Standards Institute requirements soon followed. It soon moved into the rest of the distribution industry. Performance was measured, valued, and used as an operating standard for the prime benefit of the customer.

Road transport has no monopoly of chemical traffic since chemical manufacturers have strategically tried to keep a balance between the modes of transport at their disposal. It was the political skewing of rail charges in the 1990s which led companies to expand road transport usage. The chemical business looks to continuing improvement in safety and cost. An example is the increased use of long distance high pressure pipelines for movement of the most hazardous products which has taken millions of tons of material from UK roads. A philosophy of good distribution being perhaps no distribution is being actively pursued, driven by the evils of congestion and environmental pollution. This necessitates a complete examination of plant location and is influenced by the increase in global sourcing which is a major feature of the modern chemical industry.   **AJH**

Commercial Motor, *The British Commercial Vehicle Industry* (1951 & 1953 eds.); Assocn of British Chemical Manufacturers, *British Chemicals and their Manufacturers* (1961 ed.); Walker, *The Hazardous Goods Handbook* (1987)

Chenard-Walcker road tractor. Between the wars this road tractor of French design occupied a niche position in the UK market, partly as a result of its pulling power-to-weight ratio and its patent weight-transferring drawbar, whereby several tons of a laden trailer's weight could be put on the driving axle of the road tractor. UK marketing was initially by a firm of waste paper merchants in Peckham impressed by its performance, then by Archie Simons & Co. of Great Portland Street, and subsequently by CW's own concessionaires. They were assembled by Hall, Lewis & Co. Ltd, rolling stock manufacturers of Cardiff and Park Royal. Fleet customers included the LMSR and

George Cohen, the scrap metal merchants. In 1930 the Scottish engineering firm Beardmore (q.v.) acquired British manufacturing rights, but assembly took place not at Parkhead or Paisley, but at Clapham and in 1932 Beardmore sold the business to Multiwheelers of Harrow. It produced a few road tractors during the 1930s, but changed to trailer manufacture entirely during the war. Chenard-Walcker principles were embodied in the Karrier TT drawbar tractor of 1930, for which customers included the LMSR. Eagle Engineering of Warwick (q.v.) was involved in trailer production for Chenard-Walcker and Beardmore. There was a reverse link between Chenard-Walcker and the UK commercial vehicle industry: a C-W subsidiary, Tracteurs FAR of Gennevilliers, made the Scammell mechanical horse (q.v.) under licence from 1937 to 1970.   **RAS**

Hume and Moss (1979); Stevens-Stratten and Aldridge (1987); Georgano (1997); *CVC* (February 1998), pp. 30–1; C Rouxel, J Dorizon, M Clouet and F Vauvillier, *Chenard & Walcker-FAR. L'Empire disparu de Gennevilliers* (Paris: Histoire & Collections, 2000); M Wells, 'Multi-wheelers of a different kind', *VRS*, 67 (June–August 2001), pp. 108–11

Chevrolet light trucks first entered the UK market in 1923 and were the direct forebears of the Bedford marque (q.v.), with a common General Motors parentage. In the later 1920s Chevrolet commercials were assembled in Hendon, chassis were converted to articulated use or extended, and Chevrolet box vans and 25-cwt trucks were introduced to a wider public by such marketing ploys as inclusion in the General Motors Convoy which visited dealers in 1928. Vauxhall Motors, the car manufacturers, had been acquired by General Motors in 1925 and it was logical to move UK commercial production to Luton under Vauxhall direction. Hence the 'British Bedford', which appeared in 1931 initially using some Chevrolet parts. The Hendon works were used in the 1930s for the assembly of imported GMC lorries.   **RAS**

Sedgwick (1980); A Burman, *Joseph Grose and the Motor Car* (Chichester: Phillimore, 1998), p. 70; Broatch and Townsin (1995)

Chinese six (Figure 91) was the nickname for a six-wheel lorry with twin steerable axles at the front. It was able to carry the payload allowed for a six-wheel vehicle, but avoided the heavy tyre wear experienced on the twin rear axles of a conventional 6-wheeler. ERF claimed to have built the first such model in 1936 and other manufacturers followed suit. Although still offered in the 1960s, the use of this configuration was largely superseded as the law on axle loading changed. It was also known as a twin-steer, or four in hand, with overtones of horse-drawn transport. Between 1962 and 1973 Bedford produced VAL twin-steer coach chassis of which three received horse-box bodies, six became pigeon (q.v.) transporters and nine pantechnicons.

Paget-Tomlinson (1990), p. 117; D Kaye and A Witton, *Twin Steer* (Manchester: Fleetbooks, 1983)

Christian Salvesen. The emergence of Christian Salvesen as a major force in logistics and distribution came comparatively recently in relation to the firm's long history. The founder came to Scotland from Norway in 1851 and established the business which bears his name in the port of Leith in 1872. Until the 1890s the fortunes of the business were based principally on coal-carrying tramp steamers and cargo liners plying between the Scottish coast and Norway and the Mediterranean.

Christian's son, Theodore, took the business into the rapidly growing whaling industry in 1891. By 1914 Christian Salvesen & Co had become the world's largest whaling concern. Thanks to a prudent policy of retaining most of its profits each year, Salvesen survived the slump in shipping between the wars. This was accompanied by a fall in the price of whale oil as a result of unrestricted whaling. The first voluntary whaling quotas were introduced in the early 1930s and Salvesen's whaling empire began to shrink before 1939.

The Second World War almost wiped out both the whaling and shipping fleets through losses and requisitions. Under Harold Salvesen, who recruited professional managers for the first time, Salvesen embarked on a largely unsuccessful attempt to rebuild its shipping and whaling operations. Whaling operations were wound up in 1963.

During the 1950s Salvesen experimented with the processing and freezing of fish at sea. To meet the needs of its small fleet of trawlers at a time when the frozen food market was developing rapidly, Salvesen acquired a cold store in Grimsby in 1958. The company was soon renting out the surplus space to other businesses involved in frozen food and went on to acquire further cold stores.

From this diversification Salvesen's road transport operations began. Its cold store customers persuaded the firm to transport their frozen produce. Since there was very little competition and rivals were providing a less efficient service, Salvesen expanded this side of the business with the acquisition of Daniel Stewart Transport Ltd in 1969. By 1973 the transport fleet numbered 170 vehicles, many operating third party distribution contracts, and the newly formed Food Services division accounted for a quarter of the company's sales and profits. Under the direction of Barry Sealey, the expansion of the cold storage and distribution businesses drove Salvesen's growth over the next 25 years.

Left with heavy debts from its involvement in the housing market which collapsed in the early 1970s, the Salvesen board retrenched. Salvesen's intention was to reduce borrowings substantially, releasing any available capital for investment in areas of potential growth. Of these, the two most important were cold storage and distribution for which there was a rapidly rising demand within the UK and Europe. During the 1970s and early 1980s the Food Services division grew steadily. Within the division, the most striking development was in the growth of distribution. Third party distribution services, based on contracts with specific customers, took over from general food haulage. One of the most significant was a frozen food distribution contract for Marks & Spencer in the mid-1970s which eventually became Salserve and attracted the custom of several other major national multiples. Such specialist distribution contracts enabled Salvesen to outperform most of its rivals.

Salvesen's distribution ambitions were international. As well as a fledgling European business based on the company's network of Continental cold stores, a cold storage business in the United States, Merchants Refrigerating Company, was taken over in 1981.

The flotation of Christian Salvesen in 1985 reinforced concentration on its core interests. Although the generator rental business, Aggreko, had been acquired in 1984, other businesses, including the company's port and shipping operations, were sold off in the late 1980s and early 1990s. During this period the last members of the Salvesen family relinquished their executive responsibilities.

By the late 1980s Salvesen operated a fleet of 600 vehicles in the UK and Europe and was expanding its US operations. Industrial distribution in Europe and the UK started in 1986 with a spare parts contract for Mercedes-Benz while Salstream, involving general merchandise for Marks & Spencer, marked a move into consumer goods. By the early 1990s, Christian Salvesen Distribution, given renewed impetus under newly decentralised management, was operating throughout the European Union and concentrating its US operations on the East Coast and Central regions. Having withdrawn entirely from the hire and reward business, Salvesen's distribution business grew on the basis of long term contracts providing dedicated distribution services and centres.

In 1993 the distribution businesses with 7800 employees accounted for £276 million of Salvesen's £491 million turnover and £35 million of its £78 million pre-tax profits. In that year a major boost was given to Salvesen's non-food distribution business when Swift Transport Services (q.v.), with 22 depots, 750 vehicles and 1500 employees, was acquired. With customers such as Ford, Mobil and Unipart, Swift's strength lay in the industrial distribution sector where Salvesen was weak. Swift's Continental links led to Salvesen taking a substantial stake in a leading German industrial distribution firm, Wohlfahrt, in 1995. Elsewhere in Europe Salvesen pursued a path of developing both the food and non-food distribution businesses. In 1994, for example, Salvesen acquired Gel Service, a major distributor of frozen foods in France and the creation of a pan-European distribution service was strengthened by integrating the European business with Salvesen's UK distribution operations.

In the late 1990s financial considerations changed the complexion of the whole group in reponse to shareholder pressure after a failed bid for the company from Hays (q.v.), in 1996. In the following year, the Aggreko generator rental business was demerged and Christian Salvesen moved its corporate headquarters from Edinburgh to Northampton, where Swift was located. The USA business was sold so that Salvesen could concentrate upon its European interests where growth potential was stronger. At the time of this break-up, the logistics operations accounted for sales of £478 million out of total turnover of £700 million and profits of £38 out of £83 million. The most important part of the logistics business remained food which accounted for 60 per cent, followed by industrial with 25 per cent.

As Salvesen approached 2000, this major logistics operator was developing into a pan-European business, acquiring a leading Portugese and Spanish business, Transportes Gerposa, in 1999. The company was investing heavily in the sophisticated IT systems which were now an integral part of increasingly complex supply chain management. Salvesen was benefiting from the continuing trend for manufacturers to rely on specialists to provide their distribution services while at the same time ensuring the optimum use of its fleet through shared-user operations, which in 2000 accounted for 60 per cent of all the company's business. A new single brand identity was developed to replace subsidiary and acquired brands. With the reorganisation of the business into two divisions, Food & Consumer, and Industrial, Salvesen's turnover in 1999–2000 reached £666 million with operating profits of £46 million. Food & Consumer accounted for nearly two-thirds of turnover and 60 per cent of profits. The business employed 14,000 people with 140 sites in eight countries. **NW**

Wray Vamplew, *Salvesen of Leith* (Edinburgh, 1975); Watson (1996); Christian Salvesen plc, *Annual Report & Accounts*, 1997–2000; *IDCH*, 45 (2002), pp. 100–3

Cifco, see GAMMONS, WALTER

Citizens' Band (CB) radio came to Britain in the mid-1970s, having been developed in the USA from 1958. It was taken up by long-distance drivers, particularly owner-drivers, who used it to warn each other of police patrols and road conditions. It acquired an anarchic cult status, partly through its popularisation by American films such as *Convoy* (Sam Peckinpah, 1978) and partly because both the import of the 'rigs' and their use were initially illegal and risked prosecution. It had its own slang language, sprinkled with profanities. So even after CB radio was legalised in November 1981, it was not favoured by the larger operators. By then mobile phone systems covering a limited radius and, from the mid-1980s, cellular phone systems, which were expanding towards national coverage, provided a better means of maintaining contact with their drivers without the same risk of being used in ways that they might disapprove of. **GM/GAB**

The **City Group,** founded in 1979 and based in Milton Keynes, was wound up in 2002 after two months in administration failed to secure the sale or restructuring of the business, which included the City Truck Group, City Logistics, City Coolkit, City Trucks and City Group Services. At its collapse it was a major operator in UK road haulage, with more than 2500 trucks and trailers in the City Truck Group and 1500 refrigerated units in the Coolkit operation. City's white-liveried vehicles carried its name in a large, blue-bordered red oval and the group's slogan, 'driven by our customers'. In 2001 City had acquired the business of John Bridge, former director of the RHA, who became City's strategic development director. Most of City's trucks were Renaults and its 600 leased tractive units were reclaimed after its collapse. **RAS**

Truck (May 2002), p. 18

Claridge, C, Ltd of Manchester was founded as shipping and forwarding agents at Hull by Cecil Claridge in the 1930s. The business developed into haulage and was joined by the founder's sons, Alan and Keith (d.2000). Much activity centred on textile packing for export. Nationalised in 1949, it resumed in 1960, building up an AEC, Commer, Ford and Leyland fleet and developing air freight collection, with offices at Liverpool and Manchester airports. Commer TS3 and Thames Trader box vans and Morris LD and Commer Walk-Thru vans were used on the air freight work. In the early 1970s for general haulage AEC Mercury platform lorries were the mainstay of the fleet, which rose to some 40 vehicles. After its acquisition by the Constantine Group in 1977, the Claridge business soon lost its separate identity and the family left the industry. **RAS**

'Claridge's carriages', *CVC*, 6, 2 (October 2000), pp. 24–5

Clearing houses were introduced in the First World War as a means of making motor transport more efficient, by reducing empty running through the provision of back loads. In July 1917 Manchester Chamber of Commerce started a clearing house at Parr's Bank Buildings in York Street with Nathan Fine as manager. In July 1919 the Chamber broke its connection but Fine continued. Nottingham Chamber of Commerce also started a clearing house in 1919 with W Donaldson Wright as manager. This continued until the mid-1930s when the Chamber withdrew. Some clearing houses were operated by commercial firms, one scheme was sponsored briefly by the trade paper, *Commercial Motor*, one by the Automobile Association (q.v.) and others were encouraged by the Road Transport Board. Many were set up in the early 1920s, often under the aegis of the local chamber of commerce. A number of names were used, including 'freight exchange' and 'return loads bureaux', but 'clearing house' became most common. The national body established in 1920 to represent them was the Association of Road Transport Clearing

Houses, which was chaired by J F Shaw. Its aim was to co-ordinate every clearing house and road transport agency in the country, estimated at over 600 in 1920.

There was considerable controversy over the role of clearing houses. A ten per cent commission, deducted from the freight rate paid to the haulier to cover the cost of operating the clearing house, was seen as fair, but some charged more. There were complaints that the clearing houses acted more in the interests of the trader needing lorry space than the haulier, pushing down the rate for a job to an unprofitable level. There was concern that the clearing houses invoiced their customers rapidly but were very slow to pay the haulage firms. Worst of all was the belief that some clearing houses encouraged the establishment of new firms by offering lorries on hire purchase and requiring operators to buy tyres, batteries and other running necessities from them at inflated prices. These hauliers were tied in to the clearing house, which protected its position by having the right to reclaim the lorry if the payments were not kept up, then re-hiring it to another hopeful new entrant. This situation was aggravated in 1919–20 when a large number of ex-army lorries were bought by men who had learnt to drive in the forces, and were keen to set up their own firms. This led to large numbers of owner-drivers (q.v.), desperate to make a living, becoming dependent on the clearing houses. To make ends meet they were accused by the Long Distance Road Haulage Committee (q.v.) of working over-long hours and failing to maintain their vehicles, thus endangering other road users. These adverse effects of the clearing house system did occur, but were the worst end of the spectrum. Most operated fairly and many were exemplary, such as those in Nottingham and the Lancashire textile trade.

Walter Gammons (q.v.) and J F Shaw, who both operated clearing houses, put up a spirited defence of them in the trade press. The latter became managing director of National Road Transport Clearing Houses Ltd (q.v.), active 1921–2 but in receivership by 1923, finding it impossible to make a profit. Some large transport operators acted as clearing houses when they had too much work, effectively sub-contracting to independent drivers. Many large groups operated their own internal clearing houses and so did not need outside agencies.

In theory nationalisation ended the need for clearing houses, as planning should eliminate empty trips. To aid this the Road Haulage Executive (q.v.) set up 'traffic report centres', later 'traffic exchange centres', to organise return loads for its newly acquired companies. From late 1949 this work was absorbed into the new BRS (q.v.). But empty running continued in BRS, mainly because depots tended to favour their own vehicles for loads, rather than back-loading vehicles from other depots. This approach benefited the workload and financial statistics for their own depot, though not BRS as a whole.

Clearing houses survived into the post-nationalisation period. Some were less formal than others. For instance in the 1960s lorry drivers in London, seeking a return load, congregated around Tower Hill where there was a line of phone boxes. Their numbers were known to merchants seeking haulage and an informal co-operative allocation based on destination and price took place. A number of trends killed them off in the 1970s. They included the decline of independent drivers as firms were absorbed into ever larger groupings; contract hire which reduced the number of loads seeking haulage; changes in the nature of industrial structure which reduced bulk movement of raw and semi-processed materials. The essential function of the clearing house continued into the twenty first century in the guise of publications such as *Return Loads* which advertised for owner-drivers (q.v.) and back-load availability.   **JA/GM**

P E Hart, 'The restriction of road haulage', *The Scottish Journal of Political Economy*, 6 (1959), pp. 119–128; Hollowell (1968), pp. 52–3; Walker (1942), pp. 99–101; Brunner (1928), p. 43; Dunbar (1981), pp. 130–1; Fenelon (1925), pp. 40–4; Peter Scott and Chris Reid, 'The white slavery of the motor world: opportunism in the interwar road haulage industry', *Social History*, 25, 3 (2000), pp. 300–15; *Railway Gazette* (28 January 1921), p. 91

The **clerestory roof** (Figure 92) consists of a relatively low and narrow raised section of a vehicle roof, normally longitudinal, vertically glazed along all or part of its length. It was a popular feature of mobile shop (q.v.) bodywork, especially for co-operative societies between the wars, giving extra headroom and light to a central gangway for customer access to the stock shelves. It is also known to coach-builders as a lantern roof. **RAS**

The **Club of Four** was formed by four Continental manufacturers – DAF, Magirus-Deutz, Saviem and Volvo – in 1971 to develop a range of trucks with payloads between 3½ and 8½ tons using many common components, including cabs. It was an early and dramatic example of the direction the world's truck industry was destined to take. Actual production began in 1975, with Magirus-Deutz being the only one to offer an air-cooled diesel engine. The other three were builders of heavier vehicles but hahad little or no previous models at the lighter end of the market. The official name was the Euro Truck Development Group. **JMA**

Coachfreight, marketed as 'a fast, flexible small parcels service', was begun in 1982, utilising National Express coach routes, serviced at each end by motor cycle courier. It was a short-lived operation. **RAS**

Coal traffic (Figure 93) until the late twentieth century was supremely the business of the railways, but this should not obscure the growing role of road haulage after the Second World War. The National Coal Board had a substantial fleet of lorries, also specialist vehicles, such as Sentinel ballast tractors and Thornycroft dump trucks, the latter used in opencast mining, which by its temporary nature was unlikely to develop rail links. Other specialist vehicles included sludge tankers and tipping/blower discharge tankers for its Coal Tanker Service to bulk users. Brick production was an important subsidiary activity for the NCB, which required significant transport provision. In areas near coal mines there was also substantial delivery work by NCB or by contractors supplying miners and retired miners with their free allocation of coal. The Speedway Group (q.v.) was primarily engaged in long distance coal haulage, sending nearly one hundred lorries a night to London at the height of its operations. During the 1980s a considerable tonnage of coal was road-borne, including to power stations, and the patterns of movement changed with pit closures and the concentration of electricity generation. Domestic consumption declined with the implementation of clean air legislation; coal had traditionally been delivered to households in 1-cwt sacks carried on small to medium capacity platform lorries. A post-war development was the bagging delivery truck, with a hopper-type body by Charrold-Neville (a subsidiary of Charringtons, the coal merchants) combined with weighing and sack-filling apparatus; at least one example is preserved, by Botts Fuels of Staffordshire, which used it from 1967 until 1999. A notable feature of the road haulage industry was the coal merchant-turned haulier, making use of under-used carrying capacity in the summer months; occasionally this worked in the opposite direction, with a haulier developing coal trade to assure vehicle use. **RAS**

CM (19 March 1965), p. 40; *OCBRH;* Wright (1994), pp. 28–9; Matlock (1987); Townsin (2001), p. 111; *CVC* (February 2002), pp. 43, 44

Coastal traffic. The impact of road haulage on coastal traffic might be thought to be minimal, given that coasters usually carried large loads (100 tons plus) long distances, say about 250 miles, just before the First World War, whereas the average load of a lorry was a few tons and the average distance perhaps 20 miles. By the 1920s the relationship had become much less unequal. For a start there was the coastal liner sector, which had existed since the earliest days of steam navigation, carrying mixed loads of higher-value goods such as soap or meat extract in sometimes small consign-ments. This was the soft underbelly of the coastal trade and road haulage targeted it. Their advantage was not so much price as speed. For instance, Liverpool to London took the coaster about two and a half to three days, depending on the number of intermediate stops. By comparison, by the mid-1930s a lorry could do the same journey, probably by bending the rules about maximum speeds or drivers' hours or both, in 28 hours. Fisher Renwick (q.v.), for example, ran Scammell lorries between London and Manchester carrying high-value goods like chests of tea and boxes of margarine. As a result of technical and organisational improvements in road haulage their steamers were discontinued by the Second World War.

Similar incursions occurred on other routes. Dunbar cites the example of the hoy traffic from north Kent which had been taking place for several hundred years, mostly bringing agricultural commodities into the metropolis. After the First World War this traffic declined as hauliers like Jempson (q.v.) began bringing the goods by road. Similarly the barge traffic to London from the small Essex and East Anglian ports bringing their agricultural goods was taken over by road haulage firms such as Eastern Roadways of Norwich. Michael Bouquet suggests that after 1918 sailing ships in particular could not compete with the economics of road transport and some schooner owners shifted into the road haulage business. An intermediate step was for sailing ship owners to install auxiliary oil engines to use when contrary tides or winds precluded a pure sailing ship making any progress. Ships need harbours and ports and their associated infrastructure and this added to the costs of the coastal trade, whereas lorry traffic needed no special terminal facilities. Above all, commercial vehicles provided a seamless journey with only one loading and unloading for large loads carried long distances, whereas the coaster almost certainly needed a road or rail journey at each end of the sea voyage and hence incurred much greater handling costs. As real labour costs rose this extra handling put coasters at a disadvantage. The lorry's low costs and flexibility gave it an edge.

The coaster retained a competitive advantage in moving large quantities of low value goods, like coal, iron ore and china clay, long distances until after the Second World War.

Even here, the rapid strides made in reducing road haulage costs and the declining demand for heavy bulky raw materials, as the economy restructured in the last third of the twentieth century, made this of declining importance. **JA**

Dunbar (1981); Mustoe (1997); Michael Bouquet, *No Gallant Ship* (Hollis & Carter, 1959), p. 104; Robin Craig, *Steam Tramps and Cargo Liners* (HMSO, 1980), pp. 49–50; 'Coastwise shipping and road transport', *Syren & Shipping* (8 July 1931), pp. 60–1; L T C Rolt, *The Potters' Field: a history of the South Devon ball clay industry* (Newton Abbot: David & Charles, 1974), pp. 135, 146–150; H J Trump, *West Country Harbour: the Port of Teignmouth 1690–1975* (Teignmouth: Brunswick, 1976), ch. 10

Collier, R H, & Co. Ltd, 'The Spares Specialists' of Birmingham and Wolverhampton, was significant in the inter-war period as the bulk purchaser of spares which enabled owners of defunct marques to keep their vehicles on the road after the demise of the manufacturer. Colonel Collier (b.1887) had a background in motor engineering, the Royal Flying Corps, bodybuilding and the motor trade. He set up in business in Birmingham in 1925, becoming R H Collier & Co. Ltd in 1926. Convinced of a niche in the market, Collier bought up the spares of a number of failed marques. Commercial spares handled included those for pre-1919 Vulcan lorries, Manchester and Overland lorries, the stock of Reo and BAT spare parts formerly held by Harris & Hassell (1931) Ltd of Bristol and those of Halley Industrial Motors, acquired in 1935. **RAS**

Nick Baldwin, 'R H Colliers', *OM*, 8, 1 (January/February 1974), pp. 20–3

Combination vehicle was a term used in the inter-war period to describe a tractive unit with a non-detachable, articulated trailer, for example, a Garner-Brockhouse combination of the late 1920s. **RAS**

Combined transport is the direct translation of the French term for inter-modal transport, *transport combiné*, and is the term used in EC legislation. It appeared in UK legislation in the

1990s in connection with the government's policy to encourage road/rail combined transport movements (see WEIGHT LIMITS).

GAB

Commer Cars Ltd (Figures 48, 74, 84–5, 93–5, 104, 110, 112–3, 118, 124, 126, 138, 146, 152, 157, 167, 173, 183 and 188) was established as Commercial Cars Ltd at Lavender Hill, London, in 1905 to manufacture a 4-ton lorry. It moved to larger premises in Luton in 1906, where the 3-ton SC model in 1907 and the HC and LC models in 1908 were produced. Its customers included Pickfords, which bought six 5-ton Commer cars in 1908, and Dove & Dove, furniture removers and haulage contractors of Nottingham, which included 3-ton Commer lorries in its fleet in 1914.

A particular attraction of its vehicles from the beginning was fitment of the Linley constant mesh gearbox instead of the almost universal crash gearbox. Gear changes with the Linley were made by dog clutches that pre-selected the gears. Although not to be confused with the true pre-selector gearbox that came into use on buses and some cars in the 1930s, engagement of gears with the Linley was much easier and quieter, a valuable feature when most drivers had no previous experience and little mechanical sympathy. Charles M Linley became works manager of the Commercial Car factory.

During the First World War, Commercar produced over 3000 4-ton lorries for the War Department. After the war it abbreviated its name to Commer and produced a full range of commercial vehicles from two to ten tons. In 1926 Humber bought the business to give itself an alternative to car production. Two years later the Rootes brothers bought Humber to form the Rootes Group, which from the mid-1930s included Karrier and Commer, as well as several car marques. Commer was the first maker of popular light trucks to offer diesel engines. From 1933 it fitted the Perkins Leopard engine, gradually increasing sales of such vehicles. In the late 1930s Commer introduced the Superpoise range, with models from 8 cwt to 7 tons. They were well designed and popular.

In the Second World War Commer made over 20,000 vehicles for the War Office including the Q2 tractive units for the Queen Mary (q.v.) trailers, used for moving aircraft fuselages. In 1954, a new engine, the TS3, was introduced of unusual Tilling-Stevens design, a 3-cylinder, 2-stroke diesel with horizontally-opposed pistons. It needed to be driven hard and had the disconcerting habit of decarbonising itself as it went along, creating a shower of sparks which many other road users, and some drivers, took to indicate the engine was on fire. Commer used this type of engine for many years, although a more conventional Perkins diesel engine was also available. The two-stroke developed 105 bhp from an engine capacity of 3261 cc and had a high pitched whine. The diesel option became increasingly popular in the QX forward-control range and, like the petrol engine, which continued to be available, was mounted beneath the floor. Commer moved to a larger plant at Dunstable in 1953. In 1955 a new range was announced from 2- to 5-ton payload using a 6-cylinder petrol engine. In 1958 a 6-wheel vehicle was added to the range. In 1961 the popular Walk-Thru range of vans was introduced, for which Commer became famous and which set an industry standard that many other makers tried to imitate. The driver could move right across the cab, which was particularly useful when making door-to-door deliveries. In 1964 Rootes became part of Chrysler Corporation of America and commercial vehicle production was concentrated in Dunstable, the Commer name disappearing in the mid-1970s in favour of Dodge. See also MOTH, J COVENTON; SHEFFLEX MOTOR CO.

JA

Stevens-Stratten (1983, 1988 and 1991); Carverhill (2002); Nick Baldwin, 'Commer through the years', *CVC,* 3, 10 (1987), pp. 62–6. Commer archives are held by the Museum of British Road Transport, Coventry

The Commercial Motor Users' Association was founded by the RAC in 1904 as the Motor Van & Wagon Users' Association, changing its name to CMUA in 1907. It had some haulier members, but mainly represented ancillary users (q.v.). In 1928 it claimed about 4500 haulage members of which over 70 per cent were ancilliary users. George Monro, for example, a fruit and vegetable wholesaler, was a prominent CMUA member. The secretary of the MVWUA was W Rees Jeffreys (q.v.); the CMUA's secretary throughout its existence was Frederick George Bristow. He was also secretary of its offshoot, the Motor Transport Employers' Federation (q.v.), which was intended to keep the CMUA at arm's length from wage negotiations. In 1929 Walter Gammons proposed that the CMUA act as an independent assessor of freight clearing houses, inspecting them and issuing certificates to those judged to reach the required standard. Although the suggestion was never implemented, it shows the standing the CMUA had attained by then. The CMUA was dissolved at the end of 1944, when its members joined the re-formed Road Haulage Association (q.v.) or the Traders' Road Transport Association (q.v.), as appropriate, and the CMUA's function was taken over by the National Road Transport Federation (q.v.). The *CMUA Journal* was first published in 1927 and circulated only to members. It went on general sale in 1941 as the *Commercial Vehicle Users' Journal*, retitled again in 1955 as *Commercial Vehicles*. It was absorbed into *Commercial Motor* in 1972. **RAS**

Jeffreys (1949); Plowden (1973); Dunbar (1981); Birch and Harper (1995); *CM* (26 June 1928), p. 647; *Vintage Lorry Album* (1980), p. 32

The **Commercial Vehicle Show** (Figure 95) also known as the Commercial Motor Show and more formally as the International Commercial Motor Transport Exhibition, was a combination of two elements: the trade fair, where exhibits were displayed, customers examined them, and deals were begun and concluded; and a publicity event where enthusiasts could keep up to date and important people could be impressed by the technological modernity of the product.

The first Commercial Motor Show took place in autumn 1907 at Olympia. It was organised by the SMMT. There were 167 exhibitors and 21,000 visitors and it was considered so successful that another was organised for 1908. The next was not held until 1913, as the years in between were somewhat depressed. The First World War caused this activity to cease and the next was arranged for 1920. After that they were held on average biennially, though the Second World War saw an interruption and they were not resumed until 1948. All the shows were held in Olympia till 1935, but in 1937 their allegiance switched to the newly-opened Earls Court, which remained their venue until 1976 after which it moved to the National Exhibition Centre at Birmingham. They grew in popularity: the 1937 show was visited by over 60,000 people and the 1948 show attracted over 130,000 visitors.

As well as the move to the larger NEC halls, the show was for the first time combined with the car show, following a trend that began on the Continent. Gross overcrowding resulted and this, together with the longer duration of the show, led to the creation of other, initially minor, shows. The most important of these was organised by the Institute of Road Transport Engineers, and ran in conjunction with its annual conference, and ultimately was so successful that it outgrew its venue at Telford.

For some years there was also a separate event, Tipcon, organised by the Road Haulage Association and aimed at tipper operators. It began in a quarry near Buxton, but soon moved to Harrogate, until in the late 1990s non-availability of its venue forced a further move. Meanwhile the Society of Motor Manufacturers and Traders had begun its own truck show at the Agricultural Showground at Stoneleigh, but subsequently also moved to the NEC. Ultimately the IRTE and the RHA joined up with the SMMT, and a large commercial vehicle show is held annually in March.

Two other regular shows are for specialised sections of the industry. The RHA holds its Tankcon show for tanker operators every two years at Donington, while the Association of Vehicle Recovery Operators has an annual show at Stoneleigh.

The largest attendances are achieved by a few annual truck shows aimed mainly at drivers, other personnel and the general public: Truckfest (q.v.) at Peterborough is the biggest. These truck shows are a modern-day version of the annual van parades and similar events held in the 1930s, though these were relatively local affairs, often held in town or city squares.

Manufacturers tried to have something novel to display at the shows, whether it was a restyling or a technological innovation. Thus at the 1920 show Scammell displayed their 7½-ton articulated vehicle which was the first successful artic to be produced. In 1927 at Olympia, Mercedes-Benz pointed the way to the future by displaying a 6-cylinder diesel engine which gave superb fuel economy, and by the 1931 show fourteen exhibitors had oil engines on display, whereas in 1929 there had been only three. The 1964 show saw Leyland introduce their 'Ergomatic' cab which could be tilted forward to allow easy access to the power unit and was claimed to be much more driver-friendly. Thus a study of the special motor show editions of the trade press gives a good idea of the trends in the industry.　**JA/JMA**

Common carrier is a term used in common law since at least 1485 to denote a person or firm that offers to carry goods for anyone, though the service may be confined to certain types of goods and the places served may be restricted. The significance of the distinction between private and common carriers was that the former were only liable for damage or loss caused by their own negligence or that of their employees, whereas common carriers were deemed in common law to be insurers of the goods in their charge and liable for damage or loss regardless of cause (but with four exceptions: act of God, hostile action of enemy forces, 'inherent vice' within the goods, and the consignor's own fault). This onerous additional risk dated back to the seventeenth century and was imposed by the courts to ensure the honesty of the proprietors of stage coaches and wagons.

The railways had a statutory obligation to carry and were thus common carriers until 1962. Although there was no such statutory duty on road carriers, parcels and express carriers were generally considered to be common carriers. Conversely, general hauliers and furniture removers, who could pick and choose which consignors they offered to serve, were, in common law, private carriers (even though after 1933 they might hold a public carrier's, or A, licence). By the twentieth century, this difference was no longer so significant, since it had long been the accepted practice for common carriers to limit their liability by applying conditions of carriage (q.v.). By the 1990s legal opinion was that few, if any, carriers would now be regarded as common carriers. The law relating to common carriers is rarely invoked, although it is not obsolete.　**GAB**

OED; Kahn-Freund (1956), pp. 187–98; *Halsbury's Laws of England*, 4th edn, vol 5(1) (1993) p. 314; *CM* (3 July 1928), pp. 680–1; John R Pagan, 'English carriers' common-law right to reject undeclared cargo: the myth of the closed-container conundrum', *William & Mary Law Review*, 23 (1982), pp. 791–833

Computer transport. The growth of the computer industry in the 1960s, and the enormous size of the earliest for commercial use, led to a number of transport operators specialising in delivering this equipment. One such was Vanguard of Perivale. In parallel with the transport of specialised plant and machinery, the work often developed into providing an installation service. For computers, vehicles were equipped with air suspension and tail-lifts as an almost universal fitment, at a time when use of these components was not widespread. In the 1980s as computer size decreased, a number of operators diversified into next-day or even same-day delivery of computer spares and consumables, sometimes also operating warehousing on behalf of the mainly international computer makers.　**JMA**

Conditions of Carriage. From the seventeenth century common carriers (q.v.) were deemed in common law to be insurers of the goods they carried and to be liable for their loss or damage regardless of cause (with some exceptions). The carriers were able to compensate themselves for this onerous risk by requiring consignors to declare goods above a specified value and to pay an insurance premium in addition to the basic transport charge; the law allowed them to disclaim liability if the value was not disclosed and the additional fee not paid. This was the substance of the early conditions of carriage. However, a carrier needed to be able to prove that the consignor had been made aware of them when he handed over his goods. A landmark court case of 1796 decided that it was sufficient for a carrier to display or publish his general conditions and unnecessary to bring them verbally to the notice of consignors at the time of the transaction. Posting conditions of carriage in parcels and goods receiving offices was therefore a normal practice from this date.

The Carriers' Act 1839 embodied this principle in statute law, relieving common carriers of liability for loss or damage of goods worth more than £10 per package, unless the value was declared and the insurance paid. The Act allowed common carriers to limit their common-law liabilities further by entering into an agreement with each consignor. As far as railway and canal companies were concerned, however, an Act of 1854 invalidated agreements containing special exclusionary clauses unless they were signed by the consignor. The practice was therefore adopted of printing the conditions of carriage on consignment notes, which the consignor was required to sign.

The long-established carriers of parcels and smalls, many of whom had acted as railway collection and delivery agents, had no doubt adopted conditions of carriage similar to those developed by the railway companies even before the motor transport era. Before the Second World War, however, the most that general hauliers might have was a vague reference to limitation of liability on their notepaper or consignment notes. The Furniture Warehousemen & Removers' Association (see BRITISH ASSOCIATION OF REMOVERS) was very early (before 1916) in issuing standard conditions of carriage to its members, partly to help them protect their interests, but also to promote fair competition between them. Other trade associations did not begin work on standard conditions until 1938, when it was

seen as a preliminary to the establishment of standard rates (q.v.). The parcels carriers soon reached agreement, but the war halted the work of the committee representing general hauliers. However, this groundwork no doubt helped the Road Haulage Executive to issue standard conditions of carriage for all its subsidiaries in 1951 and also the Road Haulage Association when, later in the 1950s, it produced recommended conditions for its members to use either unchanged or adapted to suit to their particular businesses. The RHE conditions extended to 37 clauses, covering such details as the consignee's failure to take delivery, consequential loss, perishable traffic, dangerous goods, warehousing while waiting collection, and the application of tonnage rates to low density traffics.

The original £10 per package limit of liability continued to be applied by the railways until it was increased to £25 in 1922. Road hauliers usually set a limit per ton or per load. The limit in the RHE's 1951 conditions was £400 per ton. By 2000 road hauliers were quoting limits of £1100–1300 per tonne.

DL/GAB

World's Carriers Year Book 1916; Dunbar (1953); Dunbar (1981) pp. 81, 94, 109; John R Pagan, 'English carriers' common law right to reject undeclared cargo: the myth of the closed-container conundrum', *William & Mary Law Review,* 23 (1982), pp. 791–833; Birch and Harper (1995), p. 20

Consignia, see POST OFFICE

Consortia occur where a number of firms join together, often for a specific purpose, without the formality of a merger or takeover. They can involve written contractual agreements or be more informal. A few consortia existed before the Second World War and one of the first formal ones was Covent Garden Haulage Ltd established in 1967. They remained uncommon.

A modern example of a consortium of independent haulage companies joining forces to gain a major contract, without losing their individual identities, is Wisbech Roadways, set up mid-1998 by Garn Transport of Spalding,

Knowles Transport of Wisbech and Jack Richards & Son of Fakenham and Warrington. The contract, for £7 million per annum, was with HL Foods, a subsidiary of Hillsdown Holdings, for the distribution of canned foods throughout the country. A Wisbech site owned by Knowles became the hub of the new business, for which 60 new tractive units and 83 trailers were acquired. The directors of the haulage companies were known to each other through membership of the Transport Association (q.v.) and the consortium operated on a handshake basis, rather than a formal contract. Similarly, board meetings of four, including the general manager who acted as contract overseer, operated on a consensus basis. **RAS**

Truck (July 1999), pp. 52–4

Construction & Use Regulations. Regulations governing the construction and use of road vehicles can be traced back to a proclamation of James I in 1621 which limited the weight that could be carried on a 4-wheeled waggon to one ton. The regulations for locomotives were in the Locomotives Act 1861 and subsequent amending Acts. The Locomotives on Highways Act 1896 established the principle that detailed regulations should be delegated to the responsible government department (the Local Government Board and later the Ministry of Transport) and issued as secondary legislation. The initial Light Locomotives on Highways Order 1896 was superseded by the Motor Cars (Use and Construction) Order 1904 and Heavy Motor Car Order 1904, which contained regulations on weight limits (q.v.), speed limits (q.v.), overall width, steel tyres, brakes, application of trailer brakes, lights, legal lettering (q.v.), wheels and springs. The ideas that lay behind the heavy motor car regulations can be found in the report and minutes of evidence of the LGB's Departmental Committee on Motor Cars. Later, additional regulations were introduced on silencers (1912), overall length (1922), overhang and brakes (1927), rear view mirrors (1928), tyres and variation of wheel load (1929).

The regulations for locomotives, heavy motor cars, motor cars and showmen's engines (for which separate regulations had been issued in 1927) were all brought together in 1931 into a single set of Motor Vehicles (Construction and Use) Regulations, which covered all types of vehicle except tracked vehicles (which were subject to separate C&U Regulations from 1941 to 1986) and special type vehicles (q.v.). This first edition of 1931 added regulations on parking brakes, safety glass, audible warning instruments, silencers, emission of smoke, vapour, sparks or grit, maintenance and loading so as not to be a danger, excessive noise, use of warning instruments, duties of driver, application of brakes on trailers, length of tow rope, restrictions on drawing trailers, and attendants on trailers. From this date speed limits were not part of these regulations.

Since then the C&U Regulations have been subject to frequent amendments, which have been consolidated into new editions on eleven occasions, the most recent being in 1986. By then the 19 pages of the 1931 regulations had grown to 162. The 1937 edition added regulations on servo braking systems, speed indicators, reversing, view to front, windscreen wipers, speed limit discs, trailer plates, maintenance of critical components, condition and maintenance of tyres, stopping engine when stationary and testing of brakes. Later editions covered: direction indicators, stop lights, and gas containers (1951); width of loads (1955); lighting equipment and reflectors (1959); distance between motor vehicle and trailer, and wide or long loads (1962); seat belts (1966); windscreen washers, measurement of noise, and plating (1969); strength of side door latches and hinges, protective steering mechanism (1969); radio interference suppression, minimum power to weight ratio (1972).

Although a start was made in 1964 in quoting maximum vehicle lengths and widths in metres, with the corresponding imperial dimensions in brackets, the full changeover to metric units for all dimensions except speed did not take effect until the 1973 edition of the C&U Regulations came into force a few weeks after the UK's accession to the European Communities.

Subsequent changes to the regulations were for the purpose of harmonising UK practice with that in the rest of the EC, or in response to new EC Directives.

Table 1: Maximum Vehicle Widths

	Motor car	Heavy motor car	Motor tractor	Loco-motive	Trailer
1861				7ft 0in	
1865				9ft 0in	
1896	6ft 6in			9ft 0in	
1904/5	7ft 2in	7ft 2in		9ft 0in	7ft 6in
1931	7ft 2in	7ft 6in[1]	7ft 6in	9ft 0in	7ft 6in[1]
1941	7ft 6in	7ft 6in[1]	7ft 6in	9ft 0in	7ft 6in[1]
1955	7ft 6in	8ft 0in	7ft 6in	9ft 0in	8ft 0in
1964	2.5m 8ft 2½in	2.5m 8ft 2½in	2.5m 8ft 2½in	2.75m 9ft 0¼in	2.5m 8ft 2½in
1986	2.5m[2]	2.5m[2]	2.5m	2.75m	2.5m[2]
1996	2.5m[2]	2.55m[2]	2.55m	2.75m	2.55m[2]

1   extra width allowed over wheels and tyres in certain circumstances to allow for conversion to pneumatic tyres and for steam vehicles
2   increased to 2.58m in 1986 and 2.6m in 1989 for refrigerated vehicles

Table 2: Maximum Vehicle Lengths

	Rigid vehicle 4-wheels	Rigid vehicle 6/8 wheels	Drawbar trailer[1]	Rigid+ trailer	Artic	Semi-trailer
1922						33ft 0in
1927	27ft 6in[2]	30ft 0in[2]				33ft 0in
1930	27ft 6in[2]	30ft 0in[2]				33ft 0in[3]
1931	27ft 6in[2]	30ft 0in[2]	22ft 0in			33ft 0in[4]
1947	27ft 6in	30ft 0in	22ft 0in	60ft 0in		33ft 0in[4]
1954	27ft 6in	30ft 0in	22ft 0in	–		33ft 0in[4]
1955	30ft 0in.		22ft 0in	–		35ft 0in[4]
1964	11m 36ft 1in		7m 22ft 11in	18m 59ft 0in	13m 42ft 7in	
1968	11m		12m 39ft 4½in	18m	15m 49ft 2½in	
1983	11m		12m	18m	15.5m	12.2m[5]
1986	12m		12m	18m	15.5m	12.2m[5,6]
1990	12m		12m	18m	16.5m[7]	14.04m[8]
1991	12m		12m	18.35m[9]	16.5m[7]	14.04m[8]
1998	12m		12m	18.75m[9]	16.5m[7]	14.04m[8]

1   Excluding drawbar
2   26ft 0in. if drawing trailer
3   36ft 0in. for 8-wheel articulated vehicle registered before 2 July 1930
4   36ft 0in. for 8-wheel articulated vehicle registered before 1 January 1931
5   Length available for load carrying
6   Semi-trailers used on international journeys exempted from this length limit
7   18m for articulated tractor with a low-loader (but not a step-frame low-loader) semi-trailer
8   16.69m for car transporters
9   Subject to 15.65m maximum length of the load-carrying space

The difficulty of ensuring that the increasing numbers of visiting Continental lorries conformed to the types and components that met the EC Directives was overcome by issue of a type approval certificate; the manufacturer could then issue a certificate of conformity, valid throughout the EC, with each vehicle or component of that type.

Since 1973 the C&U Regulations have been further enlarged to include: indication of overall travelling height (1979); height of semi-trailers, rear under-run protection, sideguards, and use of bridging plates between motor vehicles and trailers (1983); minimum ground clearance (1984); spray suppression devices (1985); turning circle for articulated vehicles (1990); speed limiters for goods vehicles (1992)

The width and length limits allowed by the regulations (ignoring the dispensations for vehicles designed for carrying abnormal indivisible loads) are summarised in the tables. After taking account of the space occupied by the cab, the floor area available for load carrying on the largest articulated vehicles has more than doubled, mostly since 1955, and on rigid vehicles and drawbar outfits to a lesser extent. This is one of the factors that led to a progressive reduction in the real costs of road haulage. Generally there has been no specific height limit for goods vehicles or their loads within the UK, except between 1983 and 1995 when the height of 5- and 6-axle vehicles, including any container being carried, was limited to 4.2m. Since 1996 the height of vehicles on international journeys has been restricted to 4.0m **GAB**

Containerisation (Figure 10) is the loading of goods that are to be carried on journeys involving more than one mode of transport into standard-sized re-useable containers for the throughout journey; at the inter-modal changeover point only the container has to be transferred, considerably reducing the costs, delays, damage and loss that would be incurred if the goods themselves were unloaded and re-loaded. The inter-modal transfer is usually achieved by means of a crane or other lifting device, compared to demountable bodies (q.v.) which are usually transferred horizontally.

Because the concept is simple, it is not surprising that it has a long history. Open-topped boxes or removable wagon bodies were used at several locations for inter-modal transport (q.v.) of coal and minerals by rail and canal from the 1770s and by rail and road from 1830. In the 1830s they were also used by Pickfords for general merchandise. The next phase began around the 1890s with various rail/road applications. The most significant was the lift-van or sling-van, which began as a transferable body of a horse-drawn furniture van for long-distance furniture removals (q.v.) by road, rail and occasionally ship. This was a development of the earlier practice of transporting the complete vehicles on railway wagons (see PIGGYBACK TRANSPORT). The Great Central Railway introduced container tanks for carrying live fish from Grimsby to Marylebone and thence by road to London's Billingsgate market and the railway companies that served the cotton industry developed the Lancashire flat (q.v.).

By 1916 lift-vans were being adopted by manufacturers, particularly for more-vulnerable goods, and by 1921 they were also being called containers. The use of containers grew rapidly from 1926 after the railway companies recognised that they could use them to offer a door-to-door service in competition with road. Through the Railway Clearing House they agreed a range of standard designs: types B and D were full-size containers, covered and open respectively; types A and C were half-size, two of which fitted onto a wagon or lorry. These were followed by a quarter-size open container (type H) and a covered equivalent with small wheels (type SW). The large covered containers were 16 ft 5 in × 7 ft 5 in × 8 ft high and had a capacity of 4 tons. Some had doors in one end only; the BD type had doors in both sides too. Most were constructed of tongue-and-groove boards, but later builds had pressed steel ends and some had plywood panels. Like the original lift-vans, they had four lifting shackles at roof level connected by inclined steel straps to the main frame at the base. Some were fitted out

for specialised use, notably type BK for furniture removals (q.v.). Other variants included ventilated containers (BM) for fresh produce and meat and insulated containers (FM), which could be refrigerated with ice or dry-ice, for chilled or frozen meat. The main railway goods depots were generally equipped with mobile cranes of 5–8 tons capacity for handling them.

Railway containers were also shipped, not only within the British Isles, but also, from 1928, to the Continent. The various Continental railways had their own designs, but attempts through the International Railway Congress Association to agree international standard designs or dimensions had made no progress by the Second World War.

The use of containers continued to grow after the Second World War and British Railways reached a peak of over 50,000 in 1960. These included new designs of hopper containers for limestone and other bulk materials and highly-insulated containers for frozen foods and ice-cream. As lorries increased in size, however, the maximum capacity of this generation of containers ceased to be competitive and they disappeared in the 1970s.

After the war, the application of containerisation to shipping led container design in a new direction. From 1947 the US Army used its own steel containers, 8 ft 6 in long × 6 ft 3 in wide × 6 ft 10½ in. high, in large numbers for supplying its overseas troops, but they were carried on conventional ships. The modern container revolution is credited to Malcolm McLean, an American truck operator, who developed the concept, and first demonstrated the benefits, of standard-sized containers, strong enough to be stacked on top of each other in cellular ships designed specially to accommodate them. From the start his containers were of 8 ft × 8 ft cross-section, but for his first shipping service in 1956, working down the US west coast, their length was only 33 ft, the longest then permissible on US highways.

Thereafter the idea spread with increasing momentum around America and then to the rest of the world. In Britain severe industrial relations problems were caused in the docks by the introduction of containers and the question of who filled them. The first transatlantic container ship crossed to Europe in 1966, by which date British Railways had already launched its first Freightliner (q.v.) services. The process was helped by early agreement on standard dimensions, approved by the American Standards Association in 1961 and subsequently accepted by the International Standards Organisation (ISO) in 1968. Initially McLean's 8 ft × 8 ft in cross-section was retained, but over the years 8 ft wide × 8 ft 6 in high containers became the norm and 9 ft 6 in high containers also came into international circulation. The standard lengths were 10, 20, 30 and 40 ft and the corresponding maximum gross weights were 10, 20 (later increased to 24), 25 and 30 tons. For statistical purposes containers are measured in twenty-foot-equivalent units (TEUs), that is a 30-ft container is 1.5 TEUs. The most common form of ISO container is a steel box strengthened by corner posts that carry the weight of other containers stacked on top and take the load when lifting from the top. In the search for lighter forms of construction to allow increased payload, aluminium, all-welded pressed steel and GRP-covered plywood have been widely used with varying degrees of success. The standard corner fittings have pockets to allow the container to be lifted from either the top or bottom; the bottom corner fittings also have slots for twist-locks to secure the container during road or rail transits. Many containers also have pockets in the base for lifting by a large fork truck. Specialised types include open top, open sided, tank, insulated, refrigerated and car-carrier containers, but together they form only a small percentage of the total. Major UK manufacturers of containers included Crane Fruehauf (q.v.) and Central Containers Ltd of Wigan.

By fixing a minimum range of sizes that have to be catered for in the design of container ships and port facilities, the ISO standards have successfully enabled the development of a truly world-wide network of inter-modal transport. However, they do not exploit the maximum dimensions of road vehicles and, ironically, they are incompatible with the ISO standard

sizes for pallets (q.v.). In Europe this led to the development of swap-bodies, designed solely as a rail/road module to fit within the road vehicle dimensions allowed by EC legislation. They are of lighter construction, not being designed to stack on top of each other, and can be lifted only from the bottom. Their length has increased to 13.6m and their width has increased to 2.5 m as the maximum vehicle dimensions have been relaxed (see CONSTRUCTION & USE REGULATIONS). They were first developed on the Continent in the 1980s and little known in Britain until they began to arrive on Channel Tunnel freight trains in 1994, but are now commonly seen on British roads.

The air-freight (q.v.) industry has different requirements. Although wide-bodied freight aircraft can carry containers of ISO standard dimensions (for example, the freight version of the Boeing 747 can accommodate twelve 20-ft containers), they are not required to be stacked or lifted by crane and are therefore much lighter. Unique to this industry is the igloo, a solid-walled, covered large pallet (q.v.), shaped to fit the aircraft contours.

In Britain containers were at first often carried on flat lorries or trailers, secured by ropes or chains. This was neither very efficient nor safe. Articulated lorries with skeletal trailers (q.v.), to which the containers are secured by twist-locks, became the norm, although rigid vehicles are also used for heavy 20 ft containers.

The early terminals for handling ISO containers were equipped with travelling portal cranes, with or without cantilever extensions on one or both sides; they were generally rail-mounted although some smaller ones ran on pneumatic tyres. They had lifting frames that engaged the container's lifting pockets either at the top or, by means of retractable legs, at the bottom. Although such machines were necessary for the high throughput at large terminals, they were very expensive. Cheaper alternatives — side-loaders, straddle-carriers, large fork-lift trucks and reach-stackers — were developed for subsidiary work at the large terminals and to allow the establishment of smaller depots. **GAB**

Railway Clearing House, *Use of Mechanical Appliances and Labour Saving Devices in connection with Goods Train Traffic: [first] report of Sub-Committee* (1918) p. 4; 'Lift vans for road transport', *Transport & Travel Monthly* 23 (1921) pp. 38–9; Thompson (1980), pp. 29–32; Gordon Jackson, *The History and Archaeology of Ports* (1983) pp. 154–6; Don Rowland, *British Railways Wagons: the first half million* (1985); Ignarski (1996)

Contract hire of horse-drawn goods vehicles to customers for their exclusive use for an agreed period of time, either with or without a driver, goes back at least to the first main line railways in the 1830s and contract hire of motor vehicles was well established before the First World War. The benefit to the customer was that he was relieved of both the capital investment and the responsibility for maintenance and providing replacements in the event of breakdowns. The vehicles were usually painted in the customer's livery and might be specially designed to meet his requirements.

During the period that such vehicles were given Contract A licences they increased from 5200 to 9500 before the Second World War and then to 38,000 (16 per cent of all public haulage vehicles) in 1968. Although there are no later figures, contract hire has continued to grow in importance as part of a wider trend for companies to buy-in all kinds of services from specialist contractors that were previously undertaken in-house. Contract-hire companies often also offered warehousing services, which later developed into physical distribution and logistics (q.v.) services. **GAB**

Convertible (or interchangeable) bodies. Bodies for early petrol vehicles were often built as separate units and could be transferred from one vehicle to another, allowing buses and charabancs to become flat lorries or vans and vice versa, according to need. Before 1914 the North Eastern Railway, for example, registered several of its motor vehicles as 'omnibus/char-a-banc/lorry' and no doubt took advantage of this versatility to supplement its summer season charabanc fleet. During the summers of 1921–7 the Great Western Railway regularly converted some of its ex-War Department AEC London cartage motors for tourist services in the West Country.

It was not uncommon for country carriers and small haulage contractors to make use of their lorry at weekends for the conveyance of people. A rudimentary passenger-carrying body was fitted on to a platform lorry for the occasion, or benches were installed in a tilt lorry, to form what was sometimes known as a lorry-bus, for Saturday shopping and cinema runs or football team away fixtures or Sunday trips to the country or seaside. Since some of the businesses concerned later moved to bus operation only, rather than to road haulage, details may sometimes be found in bus historical literature. A removable two- or three-deck cattle-carrying body mounted on a conventional flat platform-bodied lorry made a similarly versatile vehicle for farmers and others involved in animal transport.

At least one model was placed on the market to meet the joint requirements of goods and passenger-carrying, the Busvan of 1921, produced by Henry Garner Ltd. At the same period W Shepherd of Market Bosworth produced a range of seven demountable (q.v.) Dixie Patent Convertible Bodies, enabling the same chassis to serve serially for example as bus, delivery van, 'pig-dray' or ambulance. A version was built on a Ford model T chassis by Gray-Podmore of Manchester in 1921. Convertibles and lorry-buses persisted into the 1930s in such areas as rural Gloucestershire, where they were used for miners' transport in the Forest of Dean. **RAS/GAB**

Joan Thornton (ed), *Turton's Omnibus Service: Pontefract to Ackworth, 1922–1962* (Castleford, 1996); Hoole (1969); John Cummings, *Railway Motor Buses and Bus Services in the British Isles, 1902–1933,* 2 (1980), pp. 110–11, 171–2; Colin Martin, *Gloucestershire's Independent Buses and Coaches: the years to 1945* (Brimscombe Port: Tempus, 2000), ch. 3

Cook, Siddle C, Ltd see ELDDIS TRANSPORT

Co-operative movement. (Figures 11 and 96). The Co-operative Wholesale Society and Scottish Co-operative Wholesale Society began as bulk purchasers for the Co-operative retail societies, but steadily progressed into warehousing, packaging and manufacture, the CWS becoming the country's biggest trading and manufacturing conglomerate. In 1938 it had 182 factories and production units in 55 categories from aerated water manufacture to wool-weaving, including eight flour mills, ten clothing factories, ten boot and shoe factories, 14 creameries and a colliery.

Through a process of amalgamation the number of retail societies steadily declined from around 1350 in 1914, but their combined membership expanded massively from 1.8 million in 1901 to over 10 million in 1950. Over the same period their overall share of the domestic retail trades that they engaged in rose from about 6 to 11 per cent. Many bought their first petrol lorry before 1914, but most still employed mixed fleets of motor, horse-drawn and pedal-powered vehicles for their regular delivery rounds of milk, bread and confectionery, meat, groceries, coal and laundry and for delivery of household goods from their multiple-stores until after the Second World War. The traffic department assets of some representative retail societies in the 1930s were: Birmingham 105 motor vehicles and 438 horses; Walsall 60 motors and 102 horses; Cambridge 60 motors, 40 horses and 70 cycles; Liverpool 100 motors and 90 horses; Bath 38 petrol, 12 electric, 20 dairy dandies and one surviving horse-drawn coal lorry.

The wholesale societies were early users of motor lorries, the CWS participating in the government's subsidy schemes (q.v.). After the First World War they began to divert from rail to road some of their longer-distance deliveries from factories and depots to retail societies, especially of perishable goods on cross-country routes. By 1920 48 per cent of the SCWS's delivery work was already being undertaken by its 70 motor lorries and 52 per cent by its 200+ horses (implying that each lorry was about equivalent to 3 horses). In 1938 the CWS motor vehicles were 'counted in hundreds'. The Co-operative movement employed several thousand motor vehicles at the start of the Second World War, ranking alongside the railways as the biggest owners of goods road

vehicles. Both the CWS and SCWS had regional motor repair and bodybuilding works, where they undertook work for themselves and for retail societies. The movement also built its own CWS-Bell lorries from 1919 to 1930, having bought the business of Bell Bros of Ravensthorpe.

Although closely allied to the labour movement, the Co-operative societies had a record of putting their retail members' interests before those of organised labour. In 1911 the Clydebank Co-operative Society sacked those of its carters who refused to resume work after their strike had been settled unless paid for the time they had been on strike. During both the 1919 railway strike and the 1926 General Strike the CWS took the line that 'the co-operative movement must feed its people at all costs' and used its road fleet to supply 'essential foodstuffs' to the retail societies. As a development of its door-to-door delivery rounds for single commodities, such as milk and bread, Co-operative societies were among the early providers of mobile shops (q.v.).

The Co-operative movement was already starting to show signs of decline in the 1950s. Indeed the CWS Retail Co-operative Society, renamed Co-operative Retail Services Ltd, had been established in 1934 to take over failing retail societies. The Co-operative movement was left behind by the changes in manufacturing and retail trading, its coal business disappeared as users turned to cleaner fuels, and further consolidation followed. The SCWS and Scottish retail societies were merged into the Scottish Co-operative Society, which in 1973 was absorbed by the CWS. As in the grocery trade generally, home deliveries largely ceased, except for a declining market for home-delivered milk. In 1977 the CWS still operated a fleet of 4000 vehicles, but only 700 (which would have included funeral cars) were allocated to the Retail & Services Division. In 1967 a standard house style in 'Co-operative blue' was introduced for CWS shop fronts and vehicles.   **RAS/GAB**

The People's Year Book and Annual of the English & Scottish Wholesale Societies (1918–1950); P. Redfern, *The New History of the CWS* (1938); Sir W. Richardson, *The CWS in War and Peace 1938–*

1976 (1977); various histories of individual Co-operative retail societies

Cost-insurance-freight, see GAMMONS, WALTER

Coulthard, T, & Co., of Preston, steam road vehicle manufacturers, began experimenting *c.* 1895, before going into production with steam wagons in 1899. These had a vertical boiler behind the driver and an underfloor engine halfway along the frame. They were especially popular in the Manchester area. Customers included E W Rudd Ltd (q.v.) of London, who acted as Coulthard's London agents. Coulthard with its spares stock was taken over by Leyland in 1907. **RAS/RWK**

Stevens-Stratten and Aldridge (1987); R A Whitehead, 'Coulthards of Preston', *VCVM*, 34, 5 (1991)

The **country carrier** played an important part in the life of small villages and hamlets up to about 1930. He linked them with towns, carrying almost anything that could be fitted into his vehicle — people, goods, animals. Before car ownership became widespread he provided the only means (other than walking or riding) of getting to market and back afterwards. The 1930 Road Traffic Act with its specific requirements for licensing of bus routes and for the design of buses effectively killed off this kind of 'on demand' operation with its ability to carry a varying mix of humans and goods. **JMA**

A Everitt, 'Country carriers in the nineteenth century', *JTH*, 2nd series, 3, 3 (1976), pp. 179–202; Nicholas Herbert, *Road Travel and Transport in Gloucestershire* (Gloucester: Alan Sutton, 1985), ch. 4; Sprake (1993)

Country Lorry Services: all four mainline railway companies obtained an Act of Parliament on the same day in 1928 which allowed them to operate passenger and goods road transport services that were not simply rail feeders. They issued joint promotional material for this activity. As Twells describes it, the idea was to use the surplus capacity of railway road vehicles which were already delivering seed, fertilisers and animal feed to rural areas. To this end, delivery services on particular routes and specified days were advertised; on the outward journey farm and grocery supplies and miscellaneous parcels from normal railway traffic were carried, but en route (usually within a 30-mile radius) the railway lorry would call as requested to pick up other traffic. It was felt to be a practical way of meeting road competition. The SR used it to reduce its dependence on contractors.

Within the limitations of the railways' legal powers, the GWR had begun Country Lorry Services between two pairs of Welsh towns in 1912, primarily to relieve GWR bus services in the areas concerned of excessive goods traffic. In the 1920s the operation was changed from a bus-type pattern, with a timetable, to a locally-based, on-demand service. By 1928 the GWR had 65 Country Lorry Services, operated by 3–4 ton lorries, a size dictated by rural goods yard layouts and perhaps to some extent by the nature of rural roads. These services were killed off by a combination of the Beeching cuts and the 1968 Road Traffic Act. For Beeching cut many of the branches which they were meant to bolster, and then the 1968 Act did away with the need for restrictive licences and opened up the market. **RAS**

Stevens-Stratten and Aldridge (1987), ch. 2; Aldridge and Earnshaw (2000), pp. 28–33; Twells and Bourne (1983)

County Commercial Cars Ltd of Fleet, Hants (1929–83) began as converters of light lorries (mainly Fordsons) into larger capacity vehicles. The founders were the brothers Ernest and Percy Tapp; Ernest was an engineer who with R E B Crompton (q.v.) had designed the three-axle road roller and Percy was in business. They built up the Market Transport Co. after the First World War for the carriage of meat to Smithfield and general food transport. The company, which bodied its own vehicles, remained in existence until 1984 under Tapp family control. It was their transport experience which led the brothers to devise and introduce conversion equipment for the Ford AA lorry (a third axle and chassis extension were fitted) to enable it to carry three tons at the permitted speed of 30 mph, providing sufficiently light bodywork was fitted.

County's unwritten agreement with the Ford Motor Co. lasted from 1933 until Ford introduced its own four-wheel-drive tractor conversions. County's two best-known models were the Surrey (6×2) and the Sussex (6×4) with County-patented double spiral-bevel drive). County also devised a three-wheel version of the Ford Y car as a mechanical horse (q.v.); built by Ford, it was introduced in 1935 as the Fordson Tug, with municipal as well as industrial and dock-work applications. A year later County produced a van version as the Devon Distributor. Also in the 1930s County designed a hydraulically telescoping scupper body for bulk discharge; this 'Jekta' system was the responsibility of a subsidiary, Walkers & County Cars Ltd, and was produced from 1946 to 1960. There was substantial wartime production of Sussex conversion kits for assembly by Fords.

After the war most County conversions were of Fordson tractors, for agricultural and special purposes, including tracked versions and a forward-control version from 1965, with some road-going examples. Ford produced County six-wheel conversions on 7V and ET6 chassis and County carried out its own conversion and marketing of the Thames Trader range from 1957. Ford D-series received County conversions, including a specially-bodied low-loader version for soft drink distribution, and some four-wheel-drive conversions of Transit vans were produced. From the D-1000 series of the mid-1970s, Ford produced its own six-wheeler.

Decline of export and home markets in the early 1980s forced County into receivership in 1983 (when it had 200 employees). It was bought by one of its former dealers, resold within a few years and relocated, tractor production coming to an end in the 1990s.

RAS

Gibbard (1997); N Baldwin 'A to Z of classic commercials' pt 45, *CVC*, 4, 9 (May 1999), pp. 37–8; *Task Force: a history of Ford commercial Vehicles* (1976); Meadows (1997)

Cousins, Frank (1904–84), General Secretary of the Transport & General Workers' Union (q.v.) 1956–69, at fourteen years of age followed his father into coal mining at the Brodsworth colliery, Doncaster. After five years he left to join a former colleague in his coal delivery business. Following the General Strike (q.v.), in which he was co-opted by the local strike committee to deliver relief supplies, he had various jobs in transport before becoming a long-distance driver with Spans-the-South (q.v.) in 1931, when he joined the TGWU. After a few years he took a job with Faircloughs, driving meat lorries, principally between Yorkshire and London.

He had married, in 1930, Anne (Nance) Judd, daughter of a future Labour mayor of Doncaster, a woman of 'remarkable perception and political intelligence' according to Goodman. Cousins now made a reputation as a union activist in the Doncaster area. In 1938, at first on a temporary basis, he became a full-time TGWU official, as South Yorkshire district organiser for the road haulage section, in Bevin's campaign to recruit road transport workers. During the Second World War he took the opportunity to recruit among the influx of new workers into wartime production, then in February 1944 moved onto the national labour scene on his appointment as National Officer in the union's Road Transport Group. Four years later he succeeded to the post of National Secretary of the Group. His work on union organisation contributed to a 50 per cent increase in road haulage membership in the immediate post-war years.

Cousins' relationship with the then General Secretary, Arthur Deakin, was politically and personally difficult; in mid-January 1947 Cousins succeeded where Deakin had failed to settle an unofficial strike which threatened to lead to government intervention with troops to maintain essential supplies and Cousins became joint secretary of the resulting National Joint Industrial Council. The immediate result was Deakin's accusation of Cousins 'seeking personal favour' by his conduct during the strike negotiations. However, following Deakin's death and the selection of 'Jock' Tiffin to succeed him, Cousins in 1955 swung the union Executive to elect him as assistant general secretary. Tiffin's sudden death by the end of the year found Cousins as Acting General Secretary and in the spring of 1956 he received an overwhelming vote in the election for Tiffin's successor.

The TGWU, as bequeathed by Deakin, was in crisis and Cousins as general secretary could do little immediately to ameliorate this. But over time, by careful appointment of new officers to key positions (exemplified by his support for Jack Jones), the TGWU adapted to the growth of workplace trade union organisation. In 1968, on the eve of his retirement, Cousins persuaded the Union's Biennial Delegate Conference to rescind the ban on members of the Communist Party from becoming TGWU office-holders.

His union career was interrupted by a less than successful period in national politics, as Minister of Technology in the Wilson government from October 1964 to July 1966, when he resigned over differences on incomes policy, and as MP for Nuneaton from January 1965 to November 1966. Not long after he resumed the full-time general secretaryship, he was faced by the major problem posed by Section 97 of the Transport Act 1968: the proposed introduction of the tachograph (q.v.). Cousins accepted it in principle, on the grounds that it could improve the driver's lot, but it was rejected by the Trade Group and a two-day strike ensued in 1968, although the union did not give official support. It began on Teesside and was most strongly supported by the key 5/35 branch in the West Midlands and its secretary, Alan Law (q.v.). In the event, however, the tachograph remained a dead issue until the government was pressed by the European Commission to implement Section 97. In 1969 Cousins retired from the general secretaryship on reaching 65, after strongly endorsing the controversial Alan Law at the union's 1969 Biennial Delegate Conference. He then served a 5-year term as one of the first board members of the National Freight Corporation (q.v.).   **RAS/PS**

Geoffrey Goodman, *Brother Frank: the man and the union* (1969); Corfield (1982); Goodman (1979 and 1984)

Covent Garden Haulage Ltd (1967–79) was a consortium of thirteen London market hauliers, established by Ralph Cropper (q.v.). He had previously opposed imposed consortia when the topic arose at a RHA conference, but in 1967 he stressed the voluntary nature of CGH. Its objects were to enable its members to handle imported fruit more efficiently and to feed traffic into member firms. The background to its foundation was the changing pattern of fruit imports into London over the previous decade: hitherto imported fruit had largely come into the middle (Royal) group of docks or to the inner railheads of Bishopsgate, King's Cross and Nine Elms. Bishopsgate had been devastated by fire, King's Cross traffic declined, Nine Elms had been replaced by Hither Green and the docks were hampered by strikes and labour inflexibility. Hence alternative ports around the south coast, from Rochester to Shoreham, were being brought into play, introducing difficulties of control of the traffic by London fruit hauliers, necessitating the sending down of a foreman, and creating problems with part loads and split deliveries. The consortium, described as 'absolutely new and unprecedented', set up an office at Sheerness, followed by one at Newhaven, and could call on a pool of 400 vehicles to meet the seasonal and to some extent unpredictable demands of the traffic. It was an interesting experiment, but seems to have been too dependent on a few major traders; when one of these, the New Zealand Apple & Pear Marketing Board, changed its arrangements for the 1978 season and required a 600-pallet pool the voluntary winding-up of the consortium followed within a year.   **RAS**

CGH records: Modern Records Centre, University of Warwick Library (MSS.331/C); *Fruit Trades Journal* (30 September 1967), p. 9; *CM* (29 December 1967), pp. 26–7

Crane Fruehauf Trailers Ltd (Figure 12) was the name used from 1978, when Fruehauf of America absorbed Crane of Dereham, until the 1990s when the Crane prefix was dropped. William Crane began as a blacksmith in 1865, expanding to make implements, cart wheels and wagons. His sons developed the business, which moved to Dereham in Norfolk in 1913. After a short association with Dyson of Liverpool in the 1920s, Cranes decided to go it alone and produced its first 100-ton capacity trailer in 1929. Useful orders were received in the 1930s from the railway companies, especially the LNER and LMSR, for trailers for both Karrier and Scammell mechanical horses, a source of orders which was renewed after the war. Pressed steel wheels and axles were produced for other trailer manufacturers, notably Alexander Laurie of Falkirk. East Anglian customers were scarce, but Harry Pointer of Norwich, demolition contractor and haulier, was an exception. Wartime production, largely an assembly process, resulted in over 3200 units, of which more than half were tank recovery trailers. Two 120-ton trailers were sanctioned in 1942, for Pickfords and E Box; the Pickfords trailer, which broke through the A1 bridge over the Ure at Boroughbridge in 1945, was subsequently rebuilt by Cranes. Another order for a 120-ton trailer was received from Isaac Barrie & Co. of Glasgow before the end of the war. Significant overseas business was secured over a decade after the war from the Iraq Petroleum Co. In the UK the development of the electricity generating industry created new demand for heavy, hydraulic suspension trailers for the road movement of equipment from manufacturer to power station. To secure the future of the firm, in view of the advancing age of W F ('Pop') Crane, the business was converted to a public company in 1950. It remained a major heavy trailer producer until 1972, when it was decided that the investment necessary to develop the next generation of such trailers could not be justified.

An interest in Crane was acquired by the American Fruehauf Corporation in the post-war period. Expansion followed with the containerisation-related growth in the semi-trailer market, and an additional large new production facility was opened at North Walsham, also in Norfolk, in 1964. Initial experience with Fruehauf designs was not good, as early semi-trailer chassis frames tended to lozenge because of stresses imposed by the greater number of corners on the

average UK road compared to the US. Bodens Ltd was acquired and its Oldham factory produced Highway trailers under the 1971 agreement between Highway Trailers and CF, following Highway Trailers' loss of its Southampton Airport manufacturing site. Bodens, like Crane, had foreseen the huge growth likely in the semi-trailer market. Trailers of the Multiwheeler and D H Morgan (Engineers) ranges were produced by CF at Dereham under the same agreement. Also in 1971, CF acquired Imperial Coachbuilders Ltd of Basildon, a commercial vehicle body builder, and in the same year began to make shipping containers.

Fruehauf acquired complete control of Cranes in 1978 and by the late 1970s CF was offering a wide product range, including TIR, partial-skeletal trailers, skeletal trailers, dry freight and refrigerated vans, bulk hoppers, tippers, tankers, low-loaders (for which Cranes had been noted), flat semi-trailers, and such non-standard types as coil carriers, vehicle transporters and extendibles. In 1977 CF claimed to offer 'Europe's biggest range' of semi-trailers, rigid bodies and de-mountable systems (Pengco) and to be 'the largest manufacturers of containers'. Pengco was the trade name of the Peterborough Engineering Co. Ltd, later Pengco Transport Systems Ltd, which also produced pneumatic discharge systems for grain, feedstuffs and other flowing materials. Facilities provided included renting (Rentco), leasing and financing, as well as servicing and major modifications, with a network of UK depots.

The effects of subsequent industrial recession on the UK road haulage industry were keenly felt by CF, with serious fluctuations of employment at the North Walsham plant. In 1998 Fruehauf, Trailor and Benalu, two French acquisitions of Fruehauf, were joined under the General Trailers marque and in 1999 UK production was concentrated at Dereham and the North Walsham plant closed. General Trailers is owned by an American investment bank and has no connection with the American Fruehauf company. Trailer chassis were subsequently built in France and bodied at Dereham, but this brought delays and higher costs. From mid-2002 chassis were again built in the UK, in a four-line assembly plant at Dereham. Complete curtainsiders, box vans and tippers were built there, at a rate of some 50 trailers a week. **RAS**

See also DENNISON TRUCK MANUFACTURING

B Tuck, 'Hauf measures', *Truck* (July 2000), pp. 78–80; *Commercial Vehicles*, 45, 7 (July 1971), p. 47; Crane (1991); Crane Fruehauf product brochure, 1977; information supplied by General Trailers United Kingdom Ltd. There is a Crane photographic archive in the library of the National Motor Museum, Beaulieu

Crime.   One of the oldest lorry crimes, and one still a concern at the end of the twentieth century, was stealing a loaded lorry for the value of its cargo. This was usually targeted against high value commodities, which in the 1920s might be cigarettes or alcoholic drinks, and in the 1990s the same commodities were joined by personal computers and designer clothing. To dispose quickly of large quantities of such products suggests a well-developed criminal distribution infrastructure with large-scale fences. The pinpointing of which lorries were carrying particularly valuable consignments in some cases suggested inside information on the part of drivers, loaders or security staff. The two most common points to hijack a lorry were at the depot or on the road. All sorts of ruses were used to bring a lorry to a stop, from apparent accidents to blocking the road. These incidents presented very real dangers to the lorry drivers who might be beaten, threatened or, on some occasions, killed. Another ploy was for robbers to dress up as bogus policemen and flag the lorry down. This caused sufficient concern in the early 1960s that the Metropolitan Police were advising lorry drivers flagged down by an apparent policemen to stay locked in the cab and drive to the nearest police station. Before proper lorry parks and secure depots in the 1960s, lorries parked in the street overnight were also vulnerable to stealing, especially given the low level of security measures then available.

Lorry stealing reached such a level that in 1959 the Road Haulage Association established a Vehicles Security Committee to investigate the problem. In 1962 this committee set up an observer corps to search for goods vehicles reported to be stolen in London. This was enthusiastically supported by the Metropolitan Police and, encouraged by finding some stolen lorries, 34 in the first two years, it was expanded and in 1968 strengthened. This apparent success should be contextualised by the number of lorry thefts in the Metropolitan Police area, which in the early 1960s were running at over 4000 per year. Those recovered by the corps were a small fraction of the total.

The other main crime against the haulier was to steal the lorry in order to dismantle the vehicle and sell the parts for spares. Given the increasing size and sophistication of lorry specifications, this could be a lucrative trade, provided the thieves had large covered spaces, such as disused aircraft hangars. Some criminals specialised in this type of crime and apparently respectable parts suppliers were occasionally convicted of being involved in it.

In the last decade of the twentieth century another crime for which the lorry firm suffered, even when unaware of the situation, was the smuggling of illegal immigrants into the country in the backs of lorries whether by ferry or through the Channel Tunnel. In order to encourage lorry drivers to check more carefully, the British government imposed a £2000 fine per immigrant, levied on the haulage firm. The apparent attractiveness of the British way of life motivated significant numbers to pay organisers large sums to get a place on such a vehicle, despite the occasional case of deaths in transit and the likelihood of being returned if discovered. Many operators felt victimized, as they argued that migrants smuggled themselves aboard the lorry unbeknown to the driver, and hence the haulier was more sinned against than sinning, and the fine unfair. **JA**

Hollowell (1968), pp 21–2 and 26; *Evening Standard* (19 June 2001); *Independent* (14 June 2001); P S Wodehouse, 'Parking loaded lorries overnight', *Road Way* (February 1958), p. 36; Birch and Harper (1995), pp. 60, 71 and 86; *CM* (29

October 1998), p. 8; *idem* (2 March 2000), p. 10; *Daily Telegraph* (6 April 2002), supplement, pp. 39–42

Crompton, Rookes Evelyn Bell (1845–1940), electrical equipment manufacturer and consulting engineer, showed aptitude for engineering while at Harrow in 1858–60, making a steam road engine during school holidays in a workshop on his father's estate. Commissioned in the Rifle Brigade in 1864, he spent four years in India, where he was responsible for initiating a government road steam train service (of which he was appointed superintendent) to replace the conventional bullock train. Crompton was impressed by the 'Thomson system' (R W Thomson, 1822–73), which involved 'pot-boilered' tractors running on solid rubber tyres, although only one of the tractors ordered by the Indian government was Thomson-boilered. Demonstrations of the Thomson system given in Britain by Crompton in 1871 were only a partial success, but the Indian experiment was significant in pointing up road haulage possibilities which were hindered by restrictions in the UK.

When Crompton returned to civilian life in 1875, he bought a share in a Chelmsford engineering firm, but his attention was taken by developments in electric lighting and it was in this direction that his business interests developed, co-founding the firm of Crompton Parkinson. However, he kept his interest in road transport, and in 1900 was retained as consultant to the War Office on mechanical transport. This followed active service in South Africa with the Volunteer Corps of Electrical Engineers, as a result of which he was promoted to Lt Colonel. Leslie Hounsfield, the Trojan designer, served with Crompton and, although non-commissioned and much younger, their friendship and mutual respect were further strengthened. Crompton judged the first motor show in 1903, becoming a founder member of the Royal Automobile Club (q.v.), chairman of the Motor Van & Wagon Users' Association (q.v.) in 1906, and first president of the Institution of Automobile Engineers (q.v.). Crompton advised the National Physical Laboratory on testing methods of road construction and surfacing and was appointed engineer to the newly-created Road Board in 1910. He jointly designed a rotary machine for testing road crusts and was considered by Rees Jeffreys (q.v.) to be one of the pioneers in the UK of bituminous carpeting for roads. He was elected FRS in 1933. **RAS**

DBB, 1 (1984); T R Nicholson, *The Birth of the British Motor Car 1769–1897*, 2 (Macmillan, 1982), especially pp. 241–9; A Bird, *Roads and Vehicles* (Longmans, 1969), p. 61; Jeffreys (1949); *DNB*; Eric Rance and Don Williams, *Can you Afford to Walk?: the history of the Hounsfield Trojan motor car* (Minster Lovell: Bookmarque, 1999)

Cropper, Ralph Charles Frederick (1913–1992), transport manager and consultant, held degrees from the London School of Economics (BA, MSc) and was a significant figure in road transport administration throughout his working life. He was assistant to Quick-Smith (q.v.) as the secretary of the National Conference of Express Carriers (q.v.) and was a senior executive officer of the Road Haulage Association (q.v.) to 1949. From 1952 to 1982 he was managing director of his own haulage firm, Conquers Transport Ltd, and from 1956 to 1980 of Transport Counsellors Ltd, a consultancy business. He was secretary to the Wholesale Meat & Provisions Transport Association and its successors from the 1940s to the 1970s. Although these bodies were at times almost moribund, Cropper described his work for a trade association, Meat Carriers Association (Southern) Ltd, in 1974 as 'a half-time job of a pretty skilled kind', for which his lifetime's experience of road haulage admirably fitted him. In 1967 he established Covent Garden Haulage Ltd, (q.v.). In retirement Cropper was chairman of Movement for London from 1982, a pressure group to oppose restrictions on lorry traffic, and an active member of the British Road Federation council. He served on industrial tribunals, was a freeman of the City of London, liveryman of the Worshipful Company of Carmen and Fellow of the Chartered Institute of Transport. **RAS**

Debrett's Distinguished People of Today (1989); BRF, *Report 1991*, p. 2; Modern Records Centre, University of Warwick Library, MSS.331/C&M

Crossley Motors Ltd of Gorton, Manchester, was separated from Crossley Brothers' stationary engine manufacture in 1910, cars having been produced from 1904. Commercial variants of the Crossley 25/30 hp car were introduced in 1912 and achieved fame and quantity production as Royal Flying Corps tenders in the First World War. They subsequently appeared in civilian guise, as light commercials and small public service vehicles, the type being available until 1926, in addition to the release of ex-WD vehicles. As well as the Manchester, Crossley produced a variety of military types. Between 1936 and 1945 over 12,000 military vehicles were built. In addition, civilian goods models, including the Delta, Beta and Atlas, respectively two 4-wheel and a 6-wheel lorry, were offered in the 1930s and sold in small numbers and, as with other quality marques, bus chassis were utilised for goods vehicles such as livestock carriers. A major post-war order from the Netherlands State Railways included 250 normal-control tractive units which were used with bus semi-trailers. In 1948 Crossley was acquired by AEC and with Maudslay formed a constituent of Associated Commercial Vehicles (q.v.).

RAS

N Baldwin, 'A to Z of classic commercials, pt 47: Crossley', *CVC*, 4, 11 (July 1999), pp. 39–41; *A Short History of Crossley Motors Ltd* (ACV Sales, 1950). There are a few business records in the Modern Records Centre, University of Warwick Library, MSS.226/CR; S J Brown, *Albion and Crossley Buses in Camera* (Shepperton: Ian Allan, 1982), p. 92; Eyre (2002)

The **Crow Carrying Company Ltd** (Figure 97) was started in 1920, by Latimer Crow, following his retirement from Thomas Crow & Sons Ltd, tar distillers of Barking and West Ham. The first three vehicles, two an ex-WD Thornycroft JS and an ex-WD AEC Y type, were used for distributing petrol in 2-gallon cans. The first tanker was placed in service in 1920 when a depot was rented adjacent to the Barking tar distillery. By 1926 25 vehicles were operated and a parcels service began between Northampton and London, concentrating on boot and shoe traffic. This was discontinued in the late 1930s. The logo 'As the Crow Flies' was prominent on the cab doors and the rear of tanks. The first Scammell tanker joined the fleet in 1925. Thereafter Crow became associated with Scammell for their articulated bulk liquid carriers. The heavier rigids were mostly AEC, with Albion and Bedford for the smaller tankers. In 1931 it first used an aluminium alloy frameless articulated tanker to keep down weight and in 1939 a stainless steel 3000 gallon tanker. The range of liquids carried, particularly chemicals and edible oils, increased to include vinegar, ammonia, tar and naptha. Gradually Crow covered much of Britain. The Second World War saw vehicles parked at Manchester. The success of a new spot hire tanker trunk service between London and the north-west, with drivers changing over at Coventry, led to a depot being opened in 1949. Loads were collected by shunters (q.v.). The first depot was replaced by a purpose built base, at Greengate, Middleton, in 1959 which included a Crow petrol filling station. The growth in business also resulted in new covered accommodation for the fleet, new offices and the first Crow petrol filling station being completed between 1951 and 1956 at Barking. Stainless steel tanks were standardised to allow maximum flexibility in operating the bulk liquid tanker fleet. Crow provided up-to-date steam tank-cleaning facilities from the earliest years. Bulk powder tankers were introduced in the 1960s. Both depots in Barking always had private rail facilities, and latterly were increasingly used for imports carried in continental rail tankers via the Harwich–Zeebrugge train ferry. Crow was more successful than any other entrants in the Lorry Driver of the Year (q.v.) award section for vehicle maintenance. They fitted special bonnet sides with a perspex panel to show the high state of cleanliness of the Gardner engine, on such occasions. These were replaced by the steel bonnet sides in normal use. Gardner engines were known for their seepage and dribbling. Crow had a tradition of having one of their latest Scammell tankers exhibited at the Commercial Motor Shows (q.v.). After Scammell's takeover by Leyland, and the new chassis having a Leyland drive-line replacing the Scammell Gardner drive line, and dissatisfaction with reliability, outstanding orders were cancelled and Scandinavian tractors chosen for future replacements. In 1926 Crow's fleet was 26 strong and by 1946 it owned 57 vehicles. By 1970 some 250 vehicles were operated. Crow were taken over by Transport Development Group (q.v.) in 1965 with some 200 vehicles, and merged into Reliance Tankers in 1986. The bulk liquids then transferred into TDG's new Linkman and the powder tankers into Nexus in 1991. **GM**

Allan (1946), pp. 170–2

Crowfoots Carriers Ltd, Leicestershire express parcels operator, formerly of Earl Shilton, later of Barwell (also Derby and Stalybridge), was established in 1912 as a carrier for the local shoe trade and became a limited, though still family, firm in 1955. By the 1980s it had grown from nine vehicles in 1964 to fifty vehicles, mainly Bedford and Dodge 7½- to 10-ton lorries, acquiring a number of small firms, for example in Derby and Loughborough, as well as ZS Bodies of Barwell. Its range then was between Grimsby and Shrewsbury, east–west, and Sheffield and Milton Keynes, north–south. By the later 1990s, the fleet had grown to seventy, almost all of which were Leyland-DAF, the first having been bought in 1988. The firm's livery is dark brown and cream. In the 1990s it ran Volvo drawbar units for trunk traffic and Renaults for collection and delivery. **RAS**

To **cube out** or cubing out, describes the position where a vehicle is fully loaded, yet in terms of weight is well below its legal maximum payload. The term is particularly common in parcels, because the weight of an average parcel is not high but its bulk is often disproportionately large. 'Bulk out' is another phrase sometimes used to describe the same situation. 'Weigh out' describes the opposite, where a vehicle is laden to its maximum permitted weight, although there is still space available. **JMA**

The **culture of the road haulage industry** exhibits three major defining values. These were well in place by the 1920s and persisted into the 1960s and 1970s but have lost a little force since then. The first defining value is to be individualistic. There has always been a large number of small operators. These were much reinforced after the First World War when many ex-servicemen used their gratuity to buy ex-army lorries and start their own business. These symbolised the value of private enterprise and individualism. This attitude was reinforced in the railway strike of 1919 and General Strike (q.v.) of 1926 when lorry drivers refused to stop work and ran convoys to help break the strike. Before the Second World War lorry drivers became synonymous with anti-union activity and the refusal to act en masse symbolised by the railway and dock workers. This emphasis on individual decision-making was reinforced by the nature of the work. Once in the cab, even the employed driver was free of immediate supervision. He was out of touch of the base and the boss and appeared to be able to determine the pattern of his day. In this sense he was independent. This individualism was reinforced by comparison with the railway or tram worker: their routine was constrained by the tracks and timetables, and points and signals determined their route, whereas the lorry driver appeared to have a multitude of choices on the 'open road'. On the road there was considerable camaraderie engendered by the nature of the traffic and the frequent meeting of drivers on well-used routes. If a vehicle broke down the next commercial vehicle along would invariably stop to assist or pass on a message to owner, breakdown service or customer. It did not matter if their respective companies were in competition with one another, this unwritten code of mutual assistance typified the industry until well into the 1960s and the advent of the motorway.

The downside of these individualistic values was less celebrated. Intense competition, the need to cut rates below those of rival carriers or the railways, and consequent pressure on wage rates, hours of work and vehicle maintenance costs resulted.

The second enduring value is that the industry contained significant numbers of hauliers who existed on the margins of legality. The main misdemeanours included: over-loading of lorries beyond the manufacturers' recommendations and legal limits; lorries running at illegal speeds; drivers exceeding their legal hours of work and failing to take required rest and meal breaks; owners failing to maintain their vehicles adequately and sending them out with defects which could prove dangerous. Thus a combination of these minor transgressions could turn the lorry into a lethal weapon and the lorry driver into an outlaw. This cloak of semi-legality was reinforced by the dubious reputation of lorry drivers for honesty. The phrase 'fell off the back of a lorry' became synonymous with illegal acquisition of products and the belief was widespread that boxes and crates were deliberately broken in order to be undeliverable and so retained by the drivers. In an odd way this image of outlaw or pirate reinforced the idea of individualistic behaviour.

The third value to be emphasised is a macho, hard masculine image. Lorry driving was not for women or wimps. The long hours, regular night work, the need to help load and unload, and the physical exertion of driving heavy vehicles before power steering, automatic gearboxes and air brakes, made lorry driving physically demanding. It was reinforced by drivers' self-perception and the 'masculinity' was given a hard edge by girlie pictures in the cab or even transfers on the outside of the cab and women's names for lorries. Some of the adverts appearing in the trade press, such as *Commercial Motor* or the Freight Transport Association's *Yearbook,* employing images of scantily-clad ladies reinforced this, as did some 'models' at commercial vehicle shows (q.v.). This could become more active participation, as many regular overnight stops and transport cafés were associated with easily-available women or prostitutes. The concept, borrowed from sea-faring, grew up of lorry drivers having a different 'girl' in every town on their route. To provide the raw energy needed for this physically demanding job, the stereotypical truckers' greasy breakfast developed. It was all carbohydrate and cholesterol washed down by strong, dark tea, taken in none too salubrious surroundings. This resulted in the obligatory 'beer gut' which in the lorry driver's case was more likely to be caused by chips and beans.

This concept of lorry drivers as 'real men' was played on by Rowntrees in their advertising for the chocolate Yorkie Bar of the 1970s, when much play was made of the chunkiness of the bar compared with the flimsy rivals, and the lorry driver of the advertisement chomped noisily onto this solid piece of confectionery.

These three attributes were quite different from those in either the railway or bus industry, where the culture was much more corporate rather than individualistic, ordered and legal and not renowned for any macho image. Railway workers obeyed rules and regulations which were required for safety reasons. **JA**

Hollowell (1968); Gordon Baron and Ron Phillips, *The Shap Story* (Gingerfold, 1998); Barker (1982); Murphy (1963); Anne Barrowclough, 'Addicted to life on the road', *The Times* (18 May 1999), p. 19

Cummins Engine Co. Ltd. This American diesel engine manufacturer began production in the UK in 1957, in a disused textile mill at Shotts in Lanarkshire, Scotland, to tackle the 'loose engine' market already occupied by Gardner and Perkins and to gain access to the European market. Early customers included ERF, Atkinson and Foden. Take-up of the NH engine by UK truck operators was slow because outputs of 180+ bhp seemed excessive and thirsty. Euclid, making earth-moving plant nearby at Newhouse, was a steady customer, but the Shotts operation was unprofitable before 1964, when Cummins entered a joint venture with Chrysler UK to build a diesel engine factory and a components plant at Darlington. The early V6 and V8 engines were a disaster. They overheated, broke down, had valve problems and high fuel consumption. The Cummins engine in Chrysler's heavy-weight

Dodge commercials and Dennis Max trucks proved unpopular: drivers were not used to the different techniques required by a high-revving engine, and additional noise, cost and poor fuel efficiency were associated with Cummins. In 1968 Cummins bought out Chrysler from Chrysler-Cummins Ltd. The Darlington-built V8 was re-engineered as the 504, latterly gaining a 'big cam'. In this form as an option in Ford D series and Cargo trucks it proved successful with operators willing to satisfy its demand for clean air, fuel and oil and regular coolant change. The Shotts-built NH engine was increased to 14 litres (855 cu. in) and was widely used by ERF, Foden, Guy and Seddon Atkinson, where power in excess of that offered by Gardner was required. Cummins managed to combine power and economy with the 1978 Big Cam E 290 and its derivatives, which established the company as the UK's leading engine supplier with Ford, Leyland and Bedford becoming customers. Following the success of the Cummins E series engine of 1978/9, the Shotts factory was totally rebuilt. The Darlington plant was re-equipped to produce the B and C series engines introduced in the early 1980s. These 3.9 litre, 5.9 litre and 8.3 litre engines put Cummins into contention in the light and medium truck sectors, with thousands being sold to Leyland DAF, Ford and others. **RAS/JMA**

S Young and N Hood, *Chrysler UK: a corporation in transition* (New York, 1977); *Truck* (June 1986); Jeffrey L Cruickshank and David B Sicilia, *The Engine that Could: 75 years of the Cummins Engine Co* (Harvard University Press, 1997)

Curtain-side (Figure 14) is a term usually used to describe a form of bodywork which has become one of the most popular designs. It describes bodies with or without conventional rear opening doors which have curtains on each side. Initially these curtains were not load-bearing but now are, so that in the event of an accident the load will probably still be retained within the bodywork. Often too, the bodies will be equipped internally with load control straps, using similar but much stronger webbing and buckles to those used for seat belts in cars.

Having curtains running the length of each side makes loading and unloading much simpler and quicker than if a body has fixed sides. The idea was pioneered by Boalloy (q.v.) in the UK in the late 1960s but can now be found in most parts of the world. Before its advent, tilts or TIR tilts were the nearest equivalent. Removing and then refitting these for loading and unloading was a time-consuming job and the desire for greater productivity, more stringent limits on drivers' hours and the requirement for speed limiters to be fitted to larger vehicles have all brought about greater use of curtain-sided lorries.

Over the years curtain design has improved and now usually curtains incorporate strips of strong webbing in both horizontal and vertical planes. Buckles and runners have also improved and modern methods of silk screen and other printing have allowed curtains to carry striking and dramatic advertising logos and lettering. Don-Bur (q.v.) pioneered buckle-less load-bearing curtains. **JMA**

Cycle delivery (Figure 15) was a widespread method of delivering goods from the 1900s to the 1960s. Carrier cycles, the pedestrian-controlled electric vehicle and the pedestrian-powered handcart (q.v.), barrow, and dairy pram, are the end of the wheeled delivery chain. 'Carrier cycles' includes errand boys' bicycles, box tricycles, quadricycles and such exotica as the Horsham Pentacycle. The errand boys' bicycle (still made in 1999 by Pashleys of Stratford-upon-Avon) is characterised by a basket-carrying cage fixed to the frame, typically over a smaller front wheel and with an advertising panel for the trader's name fitted to the frame tubes. The carrier tricycle has a load-box, basket, or other form of load-carrier (such as a churn carrier), located behind or in front of the rider.

The heyday of tricycling was the 1880s, but its significance persisted beyond that decade: the Coventry firm of Triumph was producing carrier tricycles in the early years of the twentieth century with a payload of 2 cwt; lighter basket-carriers were produced by them for the General Post Office. In 1927 there were 68 manufacturers of delivery tricycles in the

UK. Between the wars tricycles with insulated box containers were common for retailing ice cream. T Wall & Sons Ltd of Acton had over 1,500 'Stop me and buy one' tricycles in use. Motorisation of the delivery tricycle resulted in such vehicles as the Autocarrier. In 2000 Lynx Express, the parcels carrier, used six Brox quadricycles with a rear loadbox to deal with traffic congestion in London. Bicycles are again widely used by the Post Office (q.v.) for Royal Mail deliveries.   **RAS/AM**

J Pinkerton, *At Your Service: a look at carrier cycles* (Birmingham, 1983); A Ritchie, *King of the Road* (1975); *Motor Cycle & Cycle Trader* (25 November 1927), pp. 228–30; *MT* (4 May 2000), p. 1

D

Daewoo, the Korean vehicle manufacturer, in 2000 granted sole UK and Ireland import rights for its heavy truck range to Sheridan Commercials of Tullamore, Co. Offaly. Daewoo had already been involved in the UK, working with LDV on the Gemini joint venture for a replacement LDV van, the BD 100, but Daewoo operations worldwide were put in jeopardy by its bankruptcy in 2000. LDV bought out Daewoo's stake in the BD100 project in August 2001.

A separate business, Daewoo Trucks UK, reached agreement in 2001 to market in the UK the Czech-built Daewoo-Avia D range of light-to middle-weight trucks. General Motors took effective control of Daewoo in 2002. **RAS**

Transporte mundial Catalogo 2000, p.66; *Truck* (September 2000), pp. 7, 8, (November 2000), pp. 48–51; (September 2001), pp. 16–17; (December 2001), p. 14; Daewoo Avia Supplement (February 2002); *Freight* (November 2000), p. [27]; *Independent* (9 November 2000)

DAF (Figures 16, 37, 43 and 98) was set up by the Van Doorne family at Eindhoven, Netherlands as a trailer manufacturer in 1938, developing from a small metal fabrication business which had begun in 1928. The acronym in Dutch represents (Van) Doornes' trailer, later automobile, factory. Some vehicle work began with all-wheel-drive conversions from 1936, but lorry production on a commercial scale did not commence until 1950. Leyland engine manufacture under licence was agreed in 1955. Penetration of the UK market on any scale dates from the establishment of a DAF UK sales company in 1973, at the same time as the sale of DAF's car business to Volvo and the acquisition of a sizeable share in DAF by International Harvester (q.v.). Two years later Dutch state and business interests stepped in with a rescue package when factory expansion coincided with a sales slump. Recovery enabled DAF to take a 60 per cent interest in Leyland in 1986, but another crisis led to DAF being acquired by Paccar in 1993. The subsequent history of DAF is dealt with as part of that of Leyland-DAF (q.v.). **RAS**

Millar (1997)

Daimler (Figure 99) commercial vehicles were produced over a much shorter period of the company's existence than either cars or public service vehicle chassis, although as many as 4000 lorries were manufactured during the First World War and 1000 ambulances. As well as 3- and 5-ton lorries, military orders included utilities and wagonettes based on 20-hp car chassis. The foundation of the Daimler Motor Co. at Coventry in 1896 as part of H J Lawson's precarious motor empire effectively marked the beginning of the UK motor industry and there seems to have been from the outset an awareness of the potential of the commercial motor as well as the private car. An order from the London Motor Van & Waggon Co. in 1897 for 100 chassis proved to be an expensive exercise in troubleshooting for Daimler.

The company was reconstituted in 1904 after financial difficulties and was taken over by BSA in 1910. In the interim Daimler had taken up the Renard Road Train. This was more suited to the colonial outback than British roads, although one was operated by Daimler between Coventry and Birmingham. The Knight sleeve-valve engine which powered Daimler commercial vehicles from 1910 won a high reputation for reliability in the First World War, but post-war lorries presented an outmoded image. After the end of Associated Daimler, Daimler's large vehicle production concentrated on bus and coach chassis, with the occasional horsebox. **RAS**

Lord Montagu and D Burgess-Wise, *Daimler Century* (Sparkford: Patrick Stephens, 1995) especially chaps 4 and 5

Davis Brothers (Haulage) Ltd. The firm's origins are obscure, but R. Davis (haulage) began in about 1935 in Vallance Road, London E1, and at one stage the 'R' stood for Rebecca. The family business of R Davis (Haulage) Ltd and its subsidiary companies were compulsory acquisitions at nationalisation (q.v.) in June 1949, when they comprised about fourteen subsidiaries and some 300 vehicles, mostly Leylands. After appeals the compensation was reputed to total some £450,000. The Davis brothers re-entered transport in 1954 after denationalisation (q.v.) by successfully bidding for units and a considerable number of special A-licenced vehicles. By mid-1956 they were operating 208 vehicles and 16 trailers. Davis Brothers and its subsidiaries, C Bristow Ltd, A May, W D Monger and Tozer were the specific responsibility of Harry, Sammy and Ubby Davis. By 1965 they were operating 342 vehicles and 215 trailers from premises in London, Airdrie, Brentwood, Cardiff, Moxley, Newcastle, Norwich and Warrington. The growth continued through further acquisitions with considerable purchases of new vehicles including Mercedes-Benz LP1418 units, AECs, Leylands and Thames Traders, bringing the total fleet at peak to 480 vehicles and 300 trailers. The financial burden, together with a slow-down in the economy, saw receivers being appointed in 1968. With no acceptable offers for the group or any of its subsidiaries, the formal arrangements for compulsory winding-up were made. The creditors' meeting was held in April, the business and its six remaining depots closed in May. Norwich had closed the previous week and Newcastle in mid-March. Many newer vehicles were re-possessed, a few sold with their licences, others (300 lots) sold at auction at Catfield Airfield and the remainder (223 lots) at Farnborough and Measham in June. Attempts were made to sell the remaining licenced vehicles, subject to licensing approval. Larrow Transport (Northern) Ltd applied for the transfer of 185 former group vehicles and Charles Poulter Ltd for 43 vehicles. The applications met with strong objections and were unsuccessful.

Frank and Solly Davis were not then affected, having operated their companies independently. Frank's business comprised E Goldsmid, carrying mainly fruit, produce and fish from London's markets. Some trunk services were done by English Express Ltd, trading from 1966. The two between them operated some 90 vehicles. These were placed in receivership in 1968. In the same month Frank led the purchase of Larrow Transport (Metropolitan) Ltd with 44 vehicles from the receiver. This was renamed Bow Bells Transport. In June Larrow Transport (London) with 12 vehicles was acquired. This became St Mary le Bow Transport Ltd.

Solly Davis operated as Charles Poulter Ltd, the Highway, E1, running some 89 A- and B-licensed vehicles. This firm too had problems and in June 1969 Chesford Haulage Ltd applied for transfer of the licences. The hearing was adjourned and then refused in December 1969, with the claim that there had been intent to deceive. This was confirmed when Solly and Poulter were fined £82,000 in January 1970. Charles Poulter was placed in voluntary receivership and ceased trading. In March 1970 an application for a new operator's licence was refused, although they were granted an interim licence pending an appeal against the fines imposed. This was dismissed in May 1970 but a further appeal led to the fines being reduced, but not the suspended prison sentences. In mid-July a new company with no members of the Davis family as directors re-applied for an interim licence. This was granted until a re-hearing set for August. This was adjourned. In late August Poulter's bank petitioned for the compulsory winding-up of the company. In December further time was granted for finance to be raised to end the petition. This was not possible and Poulter was wound up in February 1971, with 78 vehicles laid up by 1 May. The other brothers made a comeback, with Harry leading, to acquire Larrow Transport (Northern) Ltd, operating 10 vehicles from Birtley. These Larrow companies were part of the nine companies created by the receivers for Tower Hill Transport Co. operating 148 vehicles from nine depots, the road transport operation of Boston Stevedores Ltd, placed into receivership in November 1965. It had proved impossible to sell it as a going business and they formed nine companies, based on the nine depots, applying for transfer of the appropriate licences, to sell these as operating businesses. Larrow Transport (East Midlands) Ltd at Boston with 43 vehicles was purchased by Grounds Transport of Spalding. Larrow Transport (Grimsby) Ltd with nine vehicles was acquired by Morrison's Transport of Aberdeen. Larrow Transport (Yorkshire) Ltd became Rother Transport. Larrow (London), (Metropolitan), and (Northern) were purchased by Davis Brothers. Larrow (Hull), (North Western), and (West Midlands) do not appear to have been sold. By July 1968 the operating base for Larrow (Northern) moved to London, with applications being made for the transfer of licences of the Northern companies as possessed to Davis for 65 vehicles including bulk liquids, for Bristow for 32 vehicles, and Ewer for 12 vehicles, with a further application for 37 vehicles for general goods, fruit and vegetables. There were objections, not least because Larrow (Northern) appeared to be operating 125 vehicles and 94 trailers on the original ten vehicle licence margin. The applications for 108 vehicles and 69 trailers were refused. This meant 65 of the former Davis group vehicles, purchased by Harry for use by Larrow were again auctioned at Farnborough in July 1969. A reorganisation of Larrow took place in April 1970, with no members of the Davis family said to be involved. No application had been made for the carriers licences to be changed to an operators licence, losing the transitional grant. An application for nine vehicles and nine trailers with a margin of 25 vehicles and 25 trailers was duly made. Objectors included the Road Haulage Association which thought Davis Bros was sailing too close to the wind. A licence for six vehicles and nine trailers, without any margin, was granted in September 1970 with the requirement that directors of the operating company had no connection with the Davis family. In 1971, an enquiry was held by the Metropolitan Licencing Authority into Plaistow Transport, reputedly owned by H Brown. The allegation was made that he also acted for Larrow Transport (Northern) who operated from the same base and shared the facilities, and Mr Brown was operating 12 vehicles previously operated by Larrow. The enquiry, opened, was adjourned when witnesses failed to appear, and reopened in October when licences were refused. So ended the Davis brothers' operations in haulage. They disregarded maintenance, and the law, but paid their drivers well, though driving them hard. Their alleged insensitivity in buying Mercedes-Benz lorries when many of their customers were Jewish helped their downfall.　　**GM**

'Bigger than ever', *Leyland Journal* (September 1957), pp. 20-2

Dealers. Initially makers of most larger trucks, such as Leyland, sold vehicles — or rather, chassis-cabs — direct to customers, whereas the quantity producers at the lighter end of the market such as Ford sold through dealerships and distributorships, as did Bedford (q.v.). In the 1960s selling through such agents became the norm for every maker, though the largest users such as the Post Office might still negotiate direct. There is just one exception. Since 1996 Isuzu trucks have been sold only direct, but with dealers handling after-sales service and maintenance.

A function of the proliferation of outlets was the growth of distributors' associations, and today there is one association for each make. An association will liaise with the maker and vice versa, over matters of policy, new models and problems such as disputed warranty claims.

A further twist to changes in this area as makers demand higher standards of equipment for workshops and better showrooms was for the makers themselves to own dealerships. For example, Seddon bought Halls Finchley Ltd in 1957. The trend in the late 1980s was originally most noticeable in the London area, where the high costs of land and property made it increasingly difficult for an independent dealer to be profitable. Increasingly makers had to take over, or set up their own, dealerships.　　**JMA**

Deck, see BANK

Demountable bodies (Figure 100) of varying designs have been a feature of the road transport industry for more than 80 years, but only relatively recently has the concept become more widely used.

The earliest demountable bodies predate the First World War. The Enfield Autocar Co. built light vans with removable bodies: the van part could be removed to allow use as a private car at weekends. After the First World War larger vehicles could be bought with simple platform or sided bodies which were removable: at weekends they could be easily replaced with charabanc bodies. This dual-purpose use was effectively killed off by new legislation in the early 1930s prescribing much stricter standards for public service vehicles.

The railways were among the earliest users of demountable bodies in their search for quicker and more economic handling of goods transfer from rail to road, though later they embraced the mechanical horse (q.v.) and semi-trailer as a better option. A system with 'stand lurries and trays' was already in operation in 1919 on the LNWR for horse-drawn cartage. The tray was placed on the stand lurry for loading and then transferred to the cartage lurry when it returned for its next load. The method of transfer is not clear, but did not require a crane. In 1920 when ordering its first 'steam motors' for delivery work it considered whether they should be fitted with trays, which added about 8 in to the height. It was decided that the extra height made it difficult to unload at firms' premises. In 1921 consideration was given to the wider use of flatbottoms or flats – presumably Lancashire flats (q.v.) – which were already in use in the Warrington district for carrying cloth traffic. Experiments with flats on 'ordinary fixed top motors' were unsuccessful, probably because of the height problem. At about the same time the Midland Railway had some electric trucks fitted with a cantilever frame that permitted the body to be dismounted and stood on its own legs.

The GWR tried two methods. One was the Rendell demountable body system, which used former horse drays fitted with guide wheels, and an AEC lorry with similar guide wheels. A loaded body was rolled or slid forward from the dray on to the lorry, which was parked in line directly ahead of the dray. A more successful system was adopted at its South Lambeth (London) goods depot, which was said to be the first to be fully mechanised. It used roller conveyors fitted at intervals in front of the loading bank. Bodies were mounted on a frame that was wheeled but was anchored when

being loaded. Each conveyor accommodated two bodies side by side. Goods were loaded on to the body or bodies and when ready for delivery were moved sideways on to a lorry backed up alongside a conveyor and whose previous body had already been demounted. The snag was that space had to be kept vacant between each conveyor, and if there were two bodies on a conveyor they could only be released in order.

Shelvoke & Drewry of Letchworth, Herts, patented a demountable system in 1922. Initially the body rolled on pulleys on the chassis frame as the vehicle reversed under the body. In 1928 a hydraulically raised sub-frame was introduced. In the 1930s when most municipalities were replacing horses and trying to modernise door-to-door refuse collection, the Pagefield (q.v.) System, introduced and made by Walker Brothers of Wigan in 1922, had become remarkably successful. Purpose-built 200 cu ft wheeled containers drawn by horses were collected by Pagefield trucks and winched on to the collecting lorry, an empty container being dropped so that the street collection work could continue uninterrupted.

A common use of the demountable body was carrying cattle. Farmers and those specialising in animal transport often bought a conventional flat platform-bodied vehicle, with in addition a two- or three-deck cattle-carrying body which fitted on to the platform but could be lifted off, usually with a fairly primitive hoist or with a ramp, as in the Penman (q.v.) system. They thus had a vehicle that could be utilised for a wide variety of jobs. They had a particular advantage in that the weight of the removable body did not count as unladen weight for taxation purposes. Demountable bodies with small metal wheels running on a substantial track on a heavy sub-frame mounted on a rigid vehicle (usually an eight-wheeler) have also been widely used for removal of refuse in bulk from depots or transfer stations to tipping sites.

Use of demountable bodies became wide-spread within the last decades of the twentieth century, following the development and widespread adoption of air suspension on vehicles. Initially hydraulic systems were used to raise the body slightly, before driving out the chassis from underneath but air suspension later became the preferred option. For demounting a body a vehicle's air suspension system can be used to lower the vehicle, temporarily exhausting the air supply so that the vehicle can be driven away from under the body: landing legs on the body must first have been positioned to take its weight. To load a body, a vehicle's air supply is again dumped and the vehicle is then reversed under the body. When correctly positioned the air suspension is raised to normal height, thus engaging with the body: the landing legs are then stowed. Among the earliest producers of demountable equipment was Dobson Park Holdings of Nottingham, which also made hydraulic pit props.

Demountable bodies tend to be used today for specific operations rather than for general haulage. They are particularly suited for products that are difficult to load, such as furniture, or for work where turnaround time is at a premium. Operation normally uses more bodies (which are relatively cheap) than vehicles or trailers (which are relatively expensive). A vehicle can come to a factory, warehouse or distribution depot with its demountable box or body, drop it, and pick up another already-loaded box within a few minutes. Such speed of operation has become more important as drivers' hours and rest period legislation has become more onerous. Demountables are frequently used in conjunction with overnight trunking systems. Typically a rigid vehicle and trailer each carrying demountable boxes will run from warehouse to sub-depot or redistribution point. From there daytime deliveries – for example to shops – will be made by smaller vehicles each picking up one body, or perhaps with the rigid making one delivery without its trailer.

A solitary attempt to revive the 1920s idea of a chassis able to carry a passenger or goods-carrying body occurred in 1984 when Strathclyde Passenger Transport Executive sponsored the building of a bus body seating 20 by Marshalls (q.v.) of Cambridge and a van body by Aitken Coachbuilders of Linlithgow, on a Dodge forward-control GO8 midibus chassis. It was operated by the Arran Transport and Trading Co. on the Isle of Arran on a trial basis, the vehicle being used to carry children to and from school, and (with van body) to deliver parcels, bags and boxes after the morning school run was over.

Most demountable applications have used boxvan bodies of reasonable size or capacity, but a number have involved smaller boxes that can be mounted on a 3.5 tonne chassis/cab for the final part of a delivery run. Ray Smith's Metro Swap system is an example of this. By far the largest operator of demountables was British Telecom (q.v.) which for a time standardised on 15 cwt and 1 tonne demountable bodies for its Telecom engineers' fleet. Between 1987 and 1989 it bought over 3500 such bodies from five bodybuilders – Anglian GRP, Coachwork Conversions, Coachwork Walker, Lynton Industries and Papworth Industries. Suitable lifting pockets to take the forks of a fork-lift truck were fitted beneath the bodies, together with a securing mechanism. All were mounted on Ford Transit chassis/cabs, but the scheme was discontinued after a few years.

A different demountable system came into use in 2001 with Waitrose, the supermarket. Its home delivery service, Ocado, used interchangeable boxes, called Pods, manufactured by Paneltex, which were loaded at the distribution centre and then lifted on to 3.5 tonne chassis/cabs by fork-lift trucks and held in place by a mini fifth-wheel system. The pods were quite short, but 2.4 m high, giving the vehicles a distinctive appearance. **JMA**

Denationalisation. Less than four years after nationalisation of road haulage began, a Conservative government returned to power in 1951 with a manifesto commitment to reverse the process for that part of the industry that had not been railway-owned. The Transport Act 1953 duly provided for the sale of most of the British Transport Commission's road haulage interests, which were now registered in the name of BRS (q.v.), the Road Haulage Executive being abolished in 1953.

The Act allowed BRS to retain vehicles with an aggregate unladen weight not exceeding 1¼ times the unladen weight of the vehicles that had been taken over from the railway-owned road haulage companies at nationalisation. It decided to retain the Pickfords heavy-haulage, tanker and furniture-removal fleets, plus a general-haulage fleet — altogether about one-tenth of the total. The BTC was responsible for disposing of the rest under the supervision of the Road Haulage Disposal Board (q.v.)

Its first problem was how to divide up the assets in a way that would meet the government's twin aims of maximising the total sum realised from sales of vehicles, property and other assets, while affording small operators full opportunity to enter or re-enter the haulage industry. It decided to offer for sale two types of 'transport unit': small vehicle-only units (the average size of those sold was 1.9 vehicles per unit) and larger units that included depot premises (average 17.3 vehicles per unit). A third formula was to transfer assets into a new company which was then immediately offered for sale. The Road Haulage Association (q.v.) suggested that companies should be operated for some months before being advertised, so that they could be offered for sale as a going concern with a financial record, but this was deemed to be outside the scope of the Act. All the units and companies came with operating licences and with immediate powers to operate outside the 25-mile limit, so that the new owners could get established before the general abolition of the limit at the end of 1954.

There was strong demand for the small vehicle-only units, but the level of interest in the larger transport units and the companies was disappointing. Many pre-nationalisation operators were able to buy back their businesses for less than the compensation they had received, but even this was not tempting enough for many. By mid-1955 some of the vehicles were being put up for sale for the third time and it was apparent that many, particularly the large trunking vehicles, were going to remain unsold. The government therefore announced on 21 July that it was allowing BRS to retain the vehicles required for continuance of its trunk network.

Most parcels services had been split from general haulage into separate groups within each BRS division since 1952, but on 1

January 1955 their assets were transferred to BRS (Parcels) Ltd in preparation for sale as a single national company. Meat haulage was also offered as a single unit. Both failed to attract any bidders. By now the denationalisation process had been running for three years, twice the time originally expected by the government. It was decided to bring it to an end in August 1956, with these two businesses still in BTC ownership. This was sanctioned by the Transport (Disposal of Road Haulage Property) Act 1956 which also allowed BRS to retain its contract-hire vehicles as long as the contracts on which they were employed continued.

The final tally of vehicle disposals was as follows, with the BTC retaining 41 per cent of the total:

retained under the 'x 1¼' rule	3,559	
additional trunk vehicles retained	5,311	
retained contract hire vehicles	908	
unsold Parcels company	4,109	
unsold Meat Haulage transport unit	491	14,378
sold in vehicle-only transport units	14,171	
sold in units with premises	5,132	
sold as 'chattels', without licences	1,337	20,640
total available for disposal		35,018

On 9 September 1956 the retained assets (other than those of BRS (Parcels) Ltd) were vested in one of four companies: British Road Services Ltd. (for general haulage), BRS (Contracts) Ltd, BRS (Pickfords) Ltd, and BRS (Meat Haulage) Ltd.

The total sum realised from the sale was £26.2 million, which was £7.8 million less than the associated 'goodwill' that had been the current book value of the disposed assets (including the associated 'goodwill' that had been paid by the BTC at nationalisation). When the expenses of acquisition and disposal were added, the overall loss was calculated as £12.4 million, which was reimbursed to the BTC from the Transport Fund. **GAB**

British Transport Commission, *Annual Reports and Accounts*, 1948–1962; Road Haulage Disposal Board, *Reports*, 1953–6; Bonavia (1987)

Dennis Bros Ltd (Figure 101) of Guildford, Surrey, was formed in 1901 when John and

Raymond Dennis moved their business to a new multi-storey factory, the 'Rodboro' building, which still stands and is considered to be the oldest purpose-built motor factory in the world. The brothers started to manufacture cycles in 1895 progressing to motor tricycles (1899–1902), cars (1901–1913), buses (1903 onwards), fire engines (from 1908) and refuse vehicles (from 1921). Output of commercial vehicles was generally below that of fire engines and buses, but during their peak production years, in the First World War and the mid-1920s to the early 1930s, there was little to choose in output.

The first commercial vehicle was made in 1904 and sold to Harrods. It was a 15-cwt van with a two-cylinder De Dion engine and the Dennis patent worm final drive. This was a key feature of subsequent vehicles at a time when most rivals had chain drive. It featured a separate sub-frame carrying the engine, transmission and auxiliaries to minimise the stress from torque. By 1907 the range comprised 15- and 30-cwt, 2-, 3-, 4- and 5-ton models, the latter being one of the largest on the market.

During the First World War over 7000 WD 3- to 3½-ton subvention lorries were produced and in 1919 White & Poppe of Coventry, their engine manufacturers, was bought. 2000 heavy chassis were made in 1923 and this level of production was achieved annually until the depression in the early 1930s. In 1925 a new 30-cwt model was introduced with either normal- or forward-control. It proved to be very popular. Further forward-control models were introduced in 1927 including the M-type 12-ton six-wheel lorry which was not a success. It was under-powered and over-priced. In 1934 the company produced its own diesel engine.

One of the undoubted successes was the 40/45-cwt chassis of 1935, which had the engine ahead of the front axle resulting in the nickname 'flying pig'. In 1937 the Max 12-ton 4-wheel chassis and a 5-ton four-wheeler were introduced. During the Second World War over 3000 WD Max 6- to 8-ton lorries, tanks, and light infantry carriers were made.

Lightweight Stork and Heron trucks were built in the 1950s as well as the very successful Pax with an ohv 4-cylinder 80-bhp petrol engine developed from the pre-war 5-ton wagon. The Jubilant 15-ton 6-wheel lorry was introduced soon after the end of the war as a successful development of the Max. It was popular in the produce trade and with brewers. The 22-ton Pax V trucks with Perkins engines in the mid-1960s developed into the less successful Maxim 30-ton tractor in 1968. In 1969 the successful DB 15½-ton tipper truck had an edge over other 16-ton gross laden weight competitors by saving on excise duty. In the 1970s the 24-ton Defiant tractor, powered by a Perkins T6.354 turbo-charged engine, proved to be both economical and rugged. Regular customers for Dennis commercial vehicles were breweries, the railways, furniture removers and retail delivery.

Both Dennis brothers died in 1939 and family control ceased. Post-war business was good but Dennis Motors Ltd went through difficult years, and a succession of managing directors in the 1960s and since then has had several different owners. In spite of undertaking a massive modernisation programme in 1965 a substantial trading loss was made. The order book was thin and productivity was still not as good as that of competitors. A potential merger with Seddon Lorries Ltd (q.v.) in 1969 did not materialise and in 1972 Hestair plc, a financial group, bought the business and rationalised the products. Hestair already owned Yorkshire Vehicles, makers of tankers and road sweeper bodies. Then Hestair bought Eagle Engineering of Warwick, also a maker of tankers and road sweeper bodies and moved refuse vehicle production to Warwick under the Dennis-Eagle name. Dennis-Mercury, makers of airfield tugs, was sold while lawnmowers, a post-First World War introduction, went to Hestair's equipment division. Hestair-Dennis, as it was now named, reduced commercial vehicle manufacture to a single model, the Delta with a 16-ton payload and a Gardner or Perkins engine. In 1989 the business was sold to Trinity Holdings, a buy-out group, which renamed the Guildford operation Dennis Specialist Vehicles and in 1990 moved to a new factory and dropped commercial vehicle production. The name Dennis was perpetuated in specialised commercial vehicles built by Dennis Eagle at Warwick (see Eagle Engineering Co. Ltd). **GK**

Dennis archives in the Surrey History Centre, Woking; Kennett (1979); Stevens-Stratten (1993); Baldwin (1987); Brown (1995)

Dennison Truck Manufacturing Ltd of Rathcoole, County Dublin, began truck building in 1977 with a range of 4×2 tractor units and 6×4 and 8×4 lorries. It used a wide range of British and American proprietary parts including cabs from Motor Panels (later replaced by the Finnish Sisu cab), Gardner or Rolls-Royce diesel engines, Eaton axles and Fuller gearboxes. The company was founded in 1964 by George and James Senior Dennison, who had earlier begun Dennison Trailers, which he sold to Crane Fruehauf (q.v.). Dennison obtained its first UK customers in 1979 and a UK service agent was appointed. It failed to break into the British market with its tipper in 1980 and it ceased manufacturing in May 1981, except for special orders, and moved to share a site with Irish Commercials, the Volvo distributor, to continue spares and service operations. All told it built some 250 trucks. **RAS/JMA**

CM (6 June 1981); N Baldwin, 'A to Z of classic commercials', *CVC*, 6, 2 (October 2000), p. 37

Dentressangle, Norbert, see NORBERT DENTRESSANGLE

Depots (Figures 17 and 19) All carriers or hauliers have needed a base or depot, if only to receive customers' messages. When horses provided the motive power dry stabling was needed, with a form of drainage, storage for food, a supply of pure water and, depending on the number of horses, room for the harness to dry overnight. When stage wagons were used for long distance journeys, this might be provided by inn-keepers. Rudimentary shelter might be provided for some types of vehicle, e.g. vans. Even the small country carrier(q.v.) required an area to sort or hold consignments. They often used a convenient hostelry or

carriers' quarters for a base. Carriers serving cities or towns needed premises with adequate deck or bank (q.v.) space for sorting into rounds and later, as rail trunks became used, for organising bagged or container traffic. The general haulier, carman or tip cart operator while needing stabling for the horses, might park his vehicles separately. Those serving docks frequently were able to arrange for some parking within the dock area.

As mechanised transport was introduced, space was needed for parking and servicing vehicles. Steam-powered vehicles needed coal, water and provision for ashes and boiler washouts. Their garaging also needed flues above the funnels. The early petrol vehicles were a large capital investment and had covered shelter as a minimum. The increase in road transport from 1920 and the experiences of many new entrants under battle conditions, saw their lorries being parked outside their homes or wherever convenient at their destination, until the next load. Larger firms, particularly those in the increasing specialist traffics, parcels carriers, bulk liquids and powders, meat and removals, needed adequate depots with a fuel supply, offices and sometimes facilities for drivers. Tanker depots also need tank-cleaning facilities, which require arrangements for handling the residue. General haulage depots sometimes included drivers' accommodation. The largest might have storage or depositories and garages near the depot or a principal customer. The modern articulated vehicle needs adequate turning and parking areas.

The overnight courier-type carrier uses a central hub or sortation station with sophisticated information technology-based mechanised sorting. Despite the capital investment these are idle for much of the day, and limited to the size, weight and shape of the items they can handle. Some found it useful to introduce regional hubs. The traditional regional parcels carrier remains, able to deal with awkward non-compatible traffic. The most recent developments are the ever-increasing pallet (q.v.) networks. These use hangar-type buildings or suitable adapted premises such as a former bus repair centre, with a large level floor area able to accommodate up to 60 maximum-length vehicles, with the pallets exchanged and loaded by forklift trucks. Abnormal load operators need space for spare vehicles and trailers, sometimes standing loaded, and for the equipment or tackle until needed. Livestock transport may need washing facilities and depending on the operation, lairage. In recent times many machinery removal specialists have warehousing with overhead lifting capacity, for storage and for container packing for exports. Since 1968 even the owner driver (q.v.) had to have an approved operating centre (q.v.) with a need to satisfy environmental standards, including hours and noise. Many, particularly those contracted to ready-mix, tipping or container traction, are able to use the quarry, plant or container base as the specified operating centre. With servicing now frequently included as part of a vehicle lease or out-sourced, workshop facilities may not form part of a depot. Some larger operators rent their workshops to a distributor as part of the servicing contract, with some outside servicing being carried out within the agreement. Some operators have either introduced premises with existing rail facilities in place or have opened depots in new purpose-built international rail distribution centres, such as Daventry. Changes in retailing with the growth of supermarkets and national chains of specialist stores, have led to outsourcing, with contracts for logistics being placed for building and operating regional distribution centres (rdcs), with every aspect of the supply to stores being carried out by their operators. This allowed retailers to concentrate on serving customers and reduced capital investment and responsibilities under the legislative requirements now involved with logistics. These specialists now serve food industries, supermarkets, fashion chains, DIY and the electronics and technology consumer products. Recent developments involve collecting items from manufacturers as a return load, saving costs and limiting the vehicles dealt with at the rdc. Most supermarket chains continue to operate an rdc to enable them to assess costs or possible developments. Fewer still keep the distribution 'in-house'. A recent development,

on owners' retiring is that their most valuable asset is their property being bought for development. **GM**

See also SUB-DEPOTS

DHL Worldwide Express was founded in 1969 in California by three entrepreneurs, Adrian Dalsey, Larry Hillblom and Robert Lynn, who combined the initial letters of their surnames for the company name. They worked in shipping and wished to expedite the turnaround of ships in port. The method they hit upon was to send the shipping documents by air to be processed while the ship was en route, and were ready to begin unloading as soon as it arrived, thus saving port costs. From this beginning the firm developed into an express delivery service for priority documents, especially those from the banking sector between California and Hawaii and then to other far eastern destinations.

In 1972 the company established a subsidiary, DHL International Ltd with headquarters in Brussels which began to build a global network. In 1973 it extended its international service into Western Europe, including the UK, and in 1985 opened its European hub in Brussels by when it had a virtual global network. By 2000 it was serving over 225 countries.

Until 1985 DHL was unchallenged as an international express carrier of documents, computer tapes and spare parts. It remains the market leader for small parcels. In 1983 it began to build market share at home but found it hard. In 1985 it experienced fierce competition on international routes from FedEx (q.v.) and UPS (q.v.), perhaps inspired by DHL's incursion into 'their' domestic market. Outside the USA DHL is essentially an international carrier. In 2000 it had UK hubs at London (Heathrow) and East Midlands airports.

It entered the freight services market in 1990, removing the 70 lb limit previously imposed. In 1990 it sold both Japan Air Lines and Lufthansa a small shareholding which by 1992 had been raised to 25 per cent each. In 1998 Deutsche Post took a 22½ per cent holding in DHL. **JA**

IDCH, 6 (1992), pp. 385–7 and 24 (1999), pp. 133–6; A J Wright, *abc Cargo Airlines* (Shepperton: Ian Allan, 2000)

Diamond-T trucks (Figure 18) were manufactured in Chicago, USA, from 1911 to 1961, then for five years in Lansing, Michigan, until the White Motor Co. merged the Diamond-T and Reo marques. From 1934 Diamond-T made a determined attack on the UK market with its handsomely-styled trucks, embellished with chromium. They were imported completely knocked down via Diamond-T Motors of Isleworth, Middlesex. Their impressive appearance and high power-to-weight ratio were features of the 1935 range. Diamond-T were particularly famed for their 980/981 tractors used for British army tank transport in the Second World War and also allocated to Pickfords. After the war ex-army units were used by heavy hauliers, Wynn operating the largest fleet, and recovery operators.   **RAS**

CM (8 November 1935), advert. p. 42, p 478; *VCV* 102 (June 1998), p. 14; Les Freathy and Robin Pearson, (2001)

Direct action, see PROTEST MOVEMENTS

Disposal Board, see SLOUGH

Dock traffic (Figures 102 and 164) The twentieth century saw huge changes in the pattern of Britain's overseas trade and the ways in which it was handled. One constant throughout the period has been that a large proportion of Britain's national income has been made up by overseas trade and hence dock work, collecting imports from the ship or delivering exports to the quay, has been a significant part of road haulage.

Before the First World War loading and unloading ships was labour intensive and time consuming as cargoes were contained in a wide variety of sacks, crates and barrels needing much manhandling. The goods were often initially moved from the ship's hold to a nearby warehouse, and only later from the sheds to be delivered to the owner, hence requiring double handling. Pilferage was endemic, as it was too easy to 'accidentally' break a box or burst a sack or to miscount. For road haulage firms, whether using horse-drawn or motor vehicles, there was much waiting to be loaded or unloaded and congestion was a common complaint. The need for railway lines and sidings for long-distance traffic, plus warehousing space left little room for lorries and vans, initially for short-haul work. The proliferation of level crossings and swing bridges in London docks so impeded road traffic that in the 1930s the elevated Silvertown Way was built to by-pass some hold-ups. One attempt to resolve the lack of space and long standing times was the mechanical horse (q.v.), which could service a number of trailers, each of which was loaded while the tractive unit could be elsewhere. It was widely used in Liverpool docks from 1935 to 1960. Another ploy to overcome the problem was the use of Lancashire flats (q.v.), which could be stacked on one another when returned empty.

After the Second World War a number of inter-related changes took place. In 1948 the Atlantic Steam Navigation Co. introduced a drive-on, drive-off Preston–Larne service, with three ex-army landing ships. Atlantic Steam Navigation's developing Irish sea services received the first purpose-built roll-on/roll-off ship the *Bardic Ferry* in 1957. The same year saw the company begin the first commercial roll on/ roll off service to the continent, from Tilbury to Antwerp. The system was quite cheap in capital requirements, it allowed a very quick turnaround and the same berth could be used by several ships per day. The advantage to the haulier was a seamless journey with no need to disturb the load and thus less opportunity for losses. Because costs by road were less than by sea and speeds higher, the haulier chose the short-sea crossing and thus some ports, such as those nearest the continent, grew in importance. For instance Dover, Harwich, Felixstowe (q.v.) and Southampton all increased their share of total UK foreign trade in the 1960s and 1970s. This was emphasised by the increasing orientation towards Europe of the UK's overseas trade. As a result of the wide spread of ro-ro ferries the amount of international traffic increased

Figure 1 Abnormal loads were denoted by the STGO sign, as seen on this 1999 Foden 405/3000 tractor unit with sleeper cab, used for heavy haulage and owned by Frizell of Crewe. (J H Edser Collection)

Figure 2 Albion A10 chain-driven lorry of 1915 presented to the Science Museum by, and in the livery of, L D & J Cole, tipper operators of Leeds. In its original form it would not have had a roof over the cab or a nearside mirror. The lack of doors and windscreen was typical of the period. (Science & Society Picture Library)

Figure 3 Articulated vehicle: Bedford O-type articulated tractor made *c*. 1939 with Tasker 8- to 10-ton low-load trailer. (Science & Society Picture Library)

Figure 4 Boalloy's Linkliner body offers full side access for loading and unloading by fork-lift truck. Based on a Leyland Boxer 16-tonne chassis, this one was operated by Lever Brothers. (J H Edser Collection, reproduced by permission of Boalloy)

Figure 5 Brit European were quick to take advantage of the relaxed legislation on drawbar outfits. This left-hand-drive MAN 19-291 four-wheeler is hauling a close-coupled three-axle drawbar trailer and is engaged in Continental work. The combined guard and storage box below chassis level obviates the requirement for sideguards. (J H Edser Collection)

Figure 6 Brewery traffic: 1981 Dodge Commando G16 16-ton drop-side brewery dray using a fork-lift truck to unload the kegs, which are pallet-mounted and of two different sizes. Note the skeletal form of the drop-sides. (Reproduced by permission of Renault UK Ltd)

Figure 7 British Road Services was the umbrella group for the nationalised road transport industry. It soon standardised on a small number of makes, types and sizes of vehicle. This Albion two-axle rigid, seen in London in 1968, carries the LAD cab also used by Dodge and Leyland. BRS ran all three types. (John M Aldridge Collection)

Figure 8 Cabs: this S21 Foden was introduced in 1957 and was colloquially known as a 'Mickey Mouse' cab. It caused some comment because of its shape and styling. The cab was of glass fibre. (John Armstrong Collection)

Figure 9 Car delivery: 1982 Mercedes Benz 1617 16-ton double-deck car transporter in use to deliver Porsches. Two-axle car transporters are relatively uncommon, but the value of this load would have been high. (Reproduced by permission of Mercedes-Benz UK Ltd)

Figure 10 Containerisation led to the development of skeletal semi-trailers able to carry a variety of ISO sizes. This example is designed to carry a maximum gross vehicle weight 20-ft box mounted at the rear to meet axle-loading needs. Lack of outriggers limits its use for other sizes of box. It is hauled by a Volvo F12 three-axle unit of Liverpool Warehousing Co. Ltd. (J H Edser Collection)

Figure 11 Co-operative colours feature on many units. This milk tank trailer was used by Associated Co-operative Creameries and was hauled by a Bedford TM 32-ton tractor provided by Gullivers Hire of Bristol. TMs were relatively uncommon, particularly in hire fleets. (J H Edser Collection, reproduced by permission of Bedford Trucks)

Figure 12 Crane Fruehauf made this curtain-sided three-axle trailer for *Commercial Motor* to use in their road tests of articulated outfits, thus ensuring one variable was held constant. (J H Edser Collection)

Figure 13 Crew cab: Mercedes Benz LP 809, built 1980, 7½-ton box van in Milelink livery. (Reproduced by permission of Mercedes-Benz UK Ltd)

Figure 14 Curtain-sided: 1976 Dodge 100 16-ton curtain-sided van used for distributing breakfast oats, seen in Crewe in 1984. (J H Edser Collection)

Figure 15 Cycle delivery: this Raleigh of Nottingham tradesman's cycle dates from 1935, when cycle deliveries were still commonly used by local traders. The load was clipped or tied to the flat carrier over the small front wheel, which gave a lower centre of gravity for large baskets. (Science & Society Picture Library)

Figure 16 DAF: this 32-ton sleeper cab with a wide-spaced two-axle tilt trailer, in the livery of Redcliffe Roadways of Bristol, was used for international haulage to the Middle East, a type of business that has now ceased. (J H Edser Collection)

Figure 17 Depot: these ERFs and Fodens of the late 1970s are 32-ton tractors with bulk powder, sugar and milk trailers, one at least in stainless steel. This view was taken outside Wincanton's workshops at Barlaston depot in 1981. (J H Edser Collection)

Figure 18 Diamond T 6×4 980 tractor of the Second World War, with a Rolls-Royce engine replacing the original Hercules, in the livery of George Sanders of Davyhulme, Manchester. It was built for the British Army as a tank transporter and converted to a recovery vehicle. Controls for the winch can be seen behind the cab. (J H Edser Collection)

Figure 19 Distribution centre: a number of MAN 16.170 16-ton curtain-sided bodies are being loaded by fork-lift truck, *c*. 1985. Some pallets are being stacked two high, others to a greater height. (Reproduced by permission of MAN-VW Ltd)

Figure 20 Doors: while curtain-sided bodywork gives easy access for loading and unloading, opening and closing is not particularly fast and security less than 100 per cent. The SafeSide, built by Cartwright Group, is an alternative. Its gull-wing doors are electrically operated and the metal leaves fold concertina style as they open. (Reproduced by permission of Cartwright Group/TNT)

Figure 21 ERF: 1987 ERF E14 38-ton 4×2 tractor, with three-axle bulk-powder trailer, on the M6 near Sandbach services in 1990, in Harris Powderline livery. Harris was part of the Transport Development Group. (J H Edser Collection)

Figure 22 Flatbed: this preserved 1951 AEC Mammoth Major in the livery of R C Cresswell of Hilderstone is pulling a Dyson drawbar trailer. Note the safety chain between the lorry and the trailer. (J H Edser Collection)

Figure 23 Foden: this 17-ton Alpha 2 of 2000 in the livery of Massey Feeds of Holmes Chapel, Cheshire, has Tautliner bodywork. It has a Spanish-built cab of a design also used by Pegaso and DAF. (J H Edser Collection)

Figure 24 Ford Model A: this example has had its chassis extended to accommodate a Curtis two-horse body of about 1929. There is a groom's compartment at the rear. Curtis were based on the Park Royal industrial estate in west London. A hinged ramp on the offside gave access for the horses. (Science & Society Picture Library)

Figure 25 Gardner's L2 marine engine, a Daimler gearbox and a Kirkstall back axle powered this 6-ton Foden of 1931. It was the maker's first diesel-powered model and served with its original purchaser for many years. (Science & Society Picture Library)

Figure 26 Garner type WDL6 6×4 lorry of 1929 with canvas tilt, built to a military specification and designed for the Indian army. It is fitted with a winch to the rear. (Science & Society Picture Library)

Figure 27 Glass carriage is the intended load of this specialised tri-axle trailer operated by Brit European. It carried plate glass mounted on A frames and was designed to permit easy and safe loading. (J H Edser Collection)

Figure 28 Harrods, the famous department store in Knightsbridge, London, used battery-electric delivery vans like this for many years for household deliveries, as they were quiet. This 1930s version was rebuilt by Harrods and later presented to the Science Museum. There is no door on the driver's side and the small battery on the running board is for the lights. (Science & Society Picture Library)

Figure 29 Heavy haulage: this 1980 Scammell Contractor 85- to 240-ton heavy haulage tractor has a GEC generator on its multi-wheeled trailers. There is a push tractor at the rear. (J H Edser Collection)

Figure 30 Horse-drawn goods vehicles: this single-horse delivery van has had the canvas tilt removed to show its basic timber framing. It delivered Brooke Bond tea from about 1900. The front axle swivels for steering and a pedal below the driver's position operates the brakes. (Science & Society Picture Library)

Figure 31 Igloo container: a Scandinavian Airways igloo container being loaded at Manchester Airport using a scissors lift. The container is shaped to maximise the load within the aircraft fuselage. (Reproduced by permission of Manchester Airport)

Figure 32 Leyland: the operator of this early postwar Leyland Beaver was so pleased with it that, despite its age, it bought a new Boalloy glass-fibre cab with wrap-round windscreens for the vehicle in 1965. The traditional radiator was, however, retained. (John M Aldridge Collection)

Figure 33 Lorry-mounted crane: 1989 Leyland DAF 17.16 Freighter 16-ton drop-sided body with integral Atlas crane to lift pallets of bricks, in the livery of Johnstons & Paton of Glenrothes. Extendible stabilisers have been positioned on both sides to ensure the vehicle's steadiness. (Reproduced by permission of Leyland-DAF)

Figure 34 Lynx came into being in 1986 when National Carriers Roadline, previously BRS (Parcels), was renamed. Here we see a Leyland DAF Roadrunner with a beaver tail carrying a Ford Transit used by the Lynx engineering department. (John Armstrong Collection)

Figure 35 MacBrayne operated this Guy Big J four-axle articulated outfit. It dates from about 1969, but the photograph was taken in the 1980s. The flatbed is carrying steel fabrication. (John M Aldridge Collection)

Figure 36 Machinery traffic: this four-axle Foden 4380 from the mid-1990s is hauling a five-axle trailer for moving heavy machinery. The eight-wheel configuration is ideal for a heavy lorry-mounted crane. Note the RHA badge on the front bumper. The shape of the load makes it awkward to sheet. (John Armstrong Collection)

Figure 37 Meat traffic: DAF FT2800 DKS sleeper-cab tractor with refrigerated meat trailer entering Smithfield Market before dawn, having left Aberdeen the previous day. (Reproduced by permission of Leyland-DAF Ltd)

Figure 38 Mercedes-Benz vans have been a popular choice with parcels and courier firms. Panic Transport of Rugby put this 307D into service in 1982. It has an unusually tall box body and air dam above the cab to reduce fuel consumption. (J H Edser Collection, reproduced by permission of Mercedes-Benz GB)

Figure 39 Milk delivery: this is a Purley-type pony-drawn milk delivery float of the mid-1930s in the livery of United Diaries. It was used up to the 1950s. This illustrates the final development of the animal-drawn cart with pneumatic tyres. (Science & Society Picture Library)

Figure 40 Mini-vans like this Morris of 1961 were among the smallest vehicles available for local deliveries. Service engineers making house calls also used them. They were economical, but the very low loading height was not universally popular. (Science & Society Picture Library)

Figure 41 Newspaper traffic moved to road transport in the 1980s, often under contract. This Volvo FH12 of the late 1990s was contracted to carry *Daily Mirror* newspapers but was operated by Eddie Stobart Ltd. Loading at the printing plant and unloading at the wholesalers was through the side doors. (John Armstrong Collection)

Figure 42 Norbert Dentressangle employing a Renault Major tractor in 1995 to haul a tri-axle tipping powder tanker. The firm has considerable import and export traffic and uses UK drivers on vehicles based in Britain. (J H Edser Collection)

Figure 43 Pallets: this 1978 DAF F2100 16-ton lorry with flat-bed body is carrying a palletised, partly-sheeted and roped load. (Reproduced by permission of Leyland-DAF)

Figure 44 Petroleum tanker design has evolved in recent years. This Australian-concept Lowmax tanker semi-trailer has a low centre of gravity aided by small wheels to improve stability. It is a five-tank 36,000-litre unit with bottom loading and is coupled to an ERF E14 6×2 tractor. (Brian Veale Collection)

Figure 45 Powder traffic: 1970 Foden S39 28-ton tractor with bulk powder trailer in the livery of Walker Bros. Unusually, unloading is powered by the compressor mounted on the trailer, rather than by a power-taker-off on the tractor. (J H Edser Collection)

Figure 46 Racing pigeon transport: 1982 Scania P82M with two-axle drawbar trailer, both bodied to carry racing pigeons. A quick-release mechanism frees all the pigeons at once. There is a sleeping compartment for the driver above the cab. (Reproduced by permission of Scania-Vabis)

Figure 47 Recovery services: this 1979 Foden S95 24-ton, heavy-duty recovery vehicle with crew cab was used by the Road Transport Industry Training Board for several years to train recovery crews. It has a Dial-Holmes crane, stabilisers and an Eminex vertical exhaust. (Reproduced by permission of Fodens Ltd)

Figure 48 Refrigerated bodies: 1977 and 1979 Commer Dodge 16-ton 4×2 lorries with insulated and refrigerated bodies for carrying dairy products. They were photographed in 1983 at a Milk Marketing Board depot run by Dairy Crest in Crewe. Fixed ladders are provided at the front of the bodies to give access to the fridge units. (J H Edser Collection)

Figure 49 Roping and sheeting: this Foden DG 15-6, made shortly after the Second World War, represents an early move to hide the radiator behind an ornamental grille. It is a rigid-eight with flat-bed body and was restored and preserved by John Pearson. The 'load' hides sleeping quarters for the preservationist when attending rallies. (John Armstrong Collection)

Figure 50 Rotinoff: this GR7 Atlantic road tractor of 1957 was bought new by heavy haulage contractors Sunter Brothers of Northallerton, for their demanding Bradwell nuclear power station contract. A surprising proportion of the small number of Rotinoffs built have survived. (Science & Society Picture Library)

Figure 51 Sentinel Standard steam wagons like this restored 1917 model continued to be important into the 1930s. It is a 6-tonner, single geared, with chain drive and is a typical heavyweight from the days before the internal combustion engine became dominant. (Science & Society Picture Library)

Figure 52 Sentinel Super steam tractor of 1924, drawing a drawbar trailer and in the livery of Criddle & Co. of Liverpool. It is a Liverpool conversion of a four-wheel rigid for running between docks and warehouses. The short, lightweight trailer is not typical, but is of a type sometimes seen with preserved examples. (J H Edser Collection)

Figure 53 Steam wagons: a close-up of the smoke door of the Foden 5-ton steam wagon of 1916. This example was immaculately restored as part of the maker's commercial vehicle collection and was presented to the Science Museum following Foden's acquisition by Paccar. (Science & Society Picture Library)

Figure 54 Stobart: this picture shows the bold colour scheme of Stobart's vehicles in the late 1990s, in this case a Volvo FH12 with sleeper cab. Airflow management is achieved with a dam above the cab roof and with sloped sideguards. Like the rest of the fleet, the Volvo carries a female name. (John Armstrong Collection)

Figure 55 Sugar tankers: this 1970 eight-wheeled Foden was designed by and built for Tate & Lyle and was one of the first vehicles to be used for bulk sugar deliveries. The short wheelbase would be unacceptable on a modern equivalent. (Science & Society Picture Library)

Figure 56 Tail lift: VW cooperated with MAN in the 1970s to produce the MT range, which used VW's LT cab, as seen on this 1990 MAN 8.150 8-ton box van. It has a tail-lift and air-dam deflector on the cab roof, and is seen here delivering in Stafford. (J H Edser Collection)

Figure 57 Tautliner trailers were employed by Robsons of Carlisle to carry glass bottles on pallets from maker United Glass to drinks manufacturers. Boalloy pioneered the curtain-sided design. This example, mounted on a Fromant chassis, is unusual in having no rear doors. (J H Edser Collection, reproduced by permission of Boalloy Ltd)

Figure 58 Temperature-controlled traffic: this box-type delivery tricycle represents the simplest form of temperature control, using a cork-insulated box. It was made in 1938 for T Wall & Sons Ltd of Acton, London, and known by its logo as a 'stop me and buy one'. Dry ice helped keep the contents frozen. (Science & Society Picture Library)

Figure 59 Timber traffic: a 1988 Foden 4200 rigid-eight with a lorry-mounted crane to load and unload its cargo of timber trimmings. The substantial and removable upright pins are designed to retain the load. (John Armstrong Collection)

Figure 60 TIR covers haulage across more than one country without intermediate customs examination. The tilt cover on this semi-trailer had seams and joints all double-stitched to eliminate the possibility of tampering en route. It is hauled by an MAN 20,321 twin-steer 6×2 tractive unit with sleeper cab. (J H Edser Collection, reproduced by permission of MAN/VW UK)

Figure 61 TNT, after acquiring Inter County Express, introduced a guaranteed next-day parcels service, the forerunner of its Overnite guaranteed service. This box van is suitably lettered and is hauled by a Mercedes-Benz 1625S tractive unit rated at 37.5 tons gross. (J H Edser Collection, reproduced by permission of TNT)

Figure 62 Volvo F86 model of 1977, a 32-ton tractor with a flat-bed trailer loaded with steel pipes, caught in a traffic jam on the M6 in 1990. This was the model that established Volvo in the UK, and the one against which drivers judged British vehicles. This one is in good condition for its age and sports a sun visor. (J H Edser Collection)

Figure 63 Vulcan VSD 2-ton lorry of 1926, as restored. This flat-bed is in the livery of Isaac Arnold of Oswestry in Wales, a scrap metal dealer. Vulcan was one of the smallest makers of commercial vehicles and was often in financial difficulties. (Science & Society Picture Library)

Figure 64 Wincanton operated this Scania 124L in the late 1990s, with its Euro 2 low-emission engine. The tanker trailer was on hire from TIP, and is a stainless steel unit for carrying foodstuffs. It has a guard and ladder by its top-loading hatch. The Scania cab carries twin nearside rear-view mirrors and a low mounted offside one. (John Armstrong Collection)

drastically and in the 1990s firms such as Willi Betz (q.v.) and Norbert Dentressangle (q.v.) became common liveries on Britain's motorways.

The value of goods carried rose, as bulk trades gave way to manufactured goods, coal and grain being replaced by cars and televisions, white and brown goods. The higher intrinsic value of lorry loads encouraged changes in body type, so that flat beds were replaced by box-van bodies and curtain-siders, so protecting the load, without the need for time-consuming sheeting and roping. Ro-ro traffic was also much easier to track and monitor as, later on, were containers, by using electronic data interchange, which was important as consignment values rose and consignors expected to be kept informed of progress.

A similar trend in sea traffic was the introduction of containerisation (q.v.) from the 1960s in Europe. Its main advantage was that very little labour was needed to load or unload boxes. They were weatherproof and so did not require warehousing but could be stacked in the open. Pilferage was almost eliminated, as they were sealed throughout the journey, though it was not unknown for whole containers to go missing. Also container berths were more productive, handling perhaps ten times the tonnage of a conventional berth, because they speeded up turnaround, reducing average time at the berths from a couple of weeks to two days and later, as little as 12 hours. There were disadvantages. Initially considerable opposition by dockers, who demanded the right to load and unload containers, meant that most containers were handled at berths not covered by the Dock Labour Board, such as Felixstowe or Tilbury. The equipment for handling containers was large and expensive. There needed to be simultaneous investment in at least four sectors – the ships, the docks, the railways and road transport – to ensure through traffic. Also the dock facilities required large quantities of land on which to park containers awaiting collection or delivery. Thus existing city centre docks, where space was at a premium, were not suitable or too expensive, and often new terminals further down-stream

were developed, such as Tilbury for London, the Seaforth Dock at Liverpool and Portbury, Avonmouth for Bristol. This tendency for ports to move out of the city centres was reinforced by the growth in size of ships. By the 1980s a 30,000 ton container ship was not unusual. The large, deep docks required were only economically possible where land values were low. The effect of containerisation on road transport can be found in the entry on that topic.   **JA**

Gordon Jackson, *The History and Archaeology of Ports* (Tadworth: Worlds Work, 1983), pp. 153–6; Charles V Waine, *Coastal and Short Sea Liners* (Wolverhampton, 1999), p. 57; Ronald Hope, *A New History of British Shipping* (John Murray, 1990), pp. 404–16; Frank Broeze, 'Containerisation and the globalisation of liner shipping', in David J Starkey and Gelina Harlaftis (eds), *Global Markets: the internationalisation of the sea transport industries since 1850* (St Johns, Nfd, 1998), pp. 385–423; E Williamson and Nikolaus Pevsner with Malcolm Tucker, *London: Docklands* (Penguin, 1998)

A **dockspotter** is a specially-built or adapted tractor with reversible or other suitable driving position and with a height-adjustable fifth wheel (q.v.) for moving trailers within a depot, rail terminal or port. Major suppliers included Douglas (q.v.) and the Finnish manufacturer Sisu.   **GM**

Documentation. A transport company documents the traffic that it carries for four main reasons: to record its contractual transactions with its customers (the details of each consignment, its hand-over by the consignor and its delivery to the consignee); to provide drivers and depot handling staff with the information they need to route the traffic correctly; to maintain an audit trail for each consignment in case of the need to trace responsibility for loss or damage; and, for certain traffics, to satisfy statutory requirements. The format of the documents has evolved over time and varied according to the size and type of transport company.

The most complex documentation was that of the parcels carriers, who typically used three basic documents: the consignment note; the waybill; and the delivery sheet. The waybill was of some antiquity, probably going back to the beginnings of long-distance carrying in the 14th or 15th centuries. Pads of consignment notes were issued to regular consignors, on which they entered the description, weight and delivery address of the goods, together with a signature to indicate acceptance of the carrier's conditions of carriage (q.v.) that were printed on the form. The consignor retained a copy as a receipt, signed by the collection driver or, if the consignment was handed in at a parcels office, by the counter clerk. The consignment note was the basis for calculating the charge. At the forwarding depot the goods were sorted and loaded onto the appropriate trunk vehicle and their details listed on a waybill, which was taken by the driver to the receiving depot. Here the goods were checked off the trunk vehicle, sorted onto the delivery vehicles and their details transferred to the delivery sheet of the relevant delivery round (sometimes also called a waybill). This had spaces for the consignees to sign for receipt and provided proof of delivery (POD) in case of a query or dispute.

If the carrier sub-contracted part of the operation to another carrier (the delivery round, for example) or was part of a consortium (q.v.), the documentation also had to provide for recording the hand-over from one carrier to the other. Conversely the documentation could be simplified for general hauliers collecting and delivering from a single depot. For bulk loads, a combined consignment/delivery note would suffice, with multiple copies for the consignor, haulier and consignee.

In some types of operation, for example bulk loads or contract haulage, the documentation was often provided by the customer. In the major logistics (q.v.) contracts that were set up from the 1970s, the documentation was designed to be part of the customer's overall information system and catered for other details required by the customer, such as instructions on the timing of deliveries. By this time new telecommunications techniques — first telex and then facsimile transmission — were coming into widespread use and provided the means to transmit consignment data to receiving depots or customers ahead of the

vehicle's arrival, thereby allowing the next stage in the delivery chain to be expedited. (BRS had been using teleprinter links since 1949.) The whole process was eminently suitable for computerisation and from the mid-1980s documentation was increasingly computer-generated.

Various types of traffic movement that present a health or safety risk are governed by statutory regulations that require special documentation to be issued to the driver: the authorised route for an abnormal load (q.v.); a movement authority for toxic waste and restricted livestock movements; and, for a consignment of dangerous goods, details of the action to be taken in the event of an emergency. The movement of international traffic has been facilitated by the introduction of internationally-agreed documentation.

Other records that goods transport operators are required to maintain are concerned with licensing of goods vehicle operators (q.v.), drivers' hours (q.v.), vehicle maintenance and plating and testing (q.v.), as well as the requirements that are common to all businesses in respect of company law, taxation, insurance, employment law, road vehicles, health and safety legislation, etc.   **MB/DL/GAB**

Dorian Gerhold, *Road Transport before the Railways: Russell's London Flying Wagons* (Cambridge Univ. Press, 1993) pp. 5–6, 76–8; Dunbar (1953); Dunbar (1981); Lowe (2002)

Dodge commercial vehicles (Figures 6, 14, 68, 103, 106, 154, 162, 178 and 181) originated in the USA, the first UK imports being made in the early 1920s. Dodge Brothers (Britain) Ltd, was an importer/assembler at Fulham from 1922/3, moving to larger works at Park Royal in 1926. Dodge was bought by Chrysler in 1928 and in 1930 UK assembly was transferred to the Chrysler works at Kew. British content of Dodge commercial vehicles increased during the 1930s. From 1933 Dodge lorries (but not light vans) were British except for engines and transmissions; in 1935 a UK-designed and targeted 4-ton model was announced and in 1938 the range incorporated features from a new drawing and design section at Kew. The heavier, semi-forward-control chassis were particularly popular with sand and gravel hauliers, for example in their home region, the Thames Valley. Wartime production was devoted to the aircraft industry, in the London Aircraft Group, plus 5-ton chassis produced for civilian use and for the RAF. Post-war production resumed with the semi-forward-control models, which were replaced in 1949 with a restyled range, which continued until 1957. That year the model range became heavier, starting at three tons, with forward-control models sharing the Motor Panels LAD cab with Leyland and Albion. It also shared an earlier semi-forward-control cab, built by Briggs Motor Bodies, with Leyland.

Following the Chrysler-Rootes link-up of 1964, Rootes Motors Ltd acquired Dodge Brothers (Britain) Ltd in 1965. Production of Rootes and Dodge was concentrated at Dunstable. The Dodge range largely complemented Rootes' Commers and Karriers at the heavier end. Although there was some badge-engineering of lighter Commer models in 1968–70, Dodge maintained a distinct identity with its K series of forward-control, low-tilt-cab models. To this were added in 1975 artics and 8-wheel lorries produced by the Spanish Chrysler subsidiary, Barreiros. In 1976 the Commer marque gave way to Dodge-badging, then in 1978 Chrysler's European operations were sold to Peugeot, which in turn sold Dodge and Barreiros on to Renault Vehicules Industriels three years later. The Dunstable works was closed by Renault in 1993. **RAS**

Klapper (1973); Stevens-Stratten (1988 and 1978); S Young and N Hood, *Chrysler U K: a corporation in transition* (New York, 1975); '75 years in business', *CM* (22 March 1980), pp. 40–4; Millar (1997); Carverhill (2002)

Dogs were introduced by BRS's Carter Paterson (q.v.) unit in 1949 to counter pilferage, in the context of a shortage of van boys (q.v.). Examples of similar use of canine security, especially on parcels work, are to be found elsewhere in the industry. **RAS**

World's Carriers (15 October 1949), p. 44

Don-Bur (Bodies & Trailers) Ltd, of Longton, Stoke-on-Trent was formed in 1981 when Don Burton and John Archer bought out Welford Truck Bodies from Bristol Street Group International, vehicle dealers.

Don Burton had been managing director of Welford for nine years before the buy-out. He had served an apprenticeship as a coachbuilder and later joined Tom Byatt, a Bedford dealer in Stoke-on-Trent. The company subsequently formed a separate bodybuilding division and Don Burton became its director and general manager in 1960. Later the Byatt Group was taken over by the Bristol Street Group with him becoming manager of its bodybuilding companies, which were amalgamated to form Welford Truck Bodies.

When recession prompted the sale of Welford, Don-Bur took over most of the work-force, beginning with 70 staff and a £2.5 million annual turnover. Staffing totalled 600 by 2002, working from seven sites, with £36 million annual turnover. A substantial order from Tibbett & Britten (q.v.) helped get the new business under way and its range included bulk tipper and curtain-sided and panelled bodies for rigids and semi-trailers. Innovations included the Multilowda, an extra-low-height, level-floor, bulk-tipper and the Slide-a-Side body, a quick-opening, curtain-sided rigid.

More recent innovations include buckle-less curtains, air-operated curtains and air-operated rear doors. Double-deck trailers form an increasing part of production including temperature-controlled trailers with a second, moving deck. What the company calls air management systems encompass under-bumper air dams, cab air deflectors, cab side-collars and side-skirts on rigids. The company claimed in 2000 to build more double-deck trailers than any other bodybuilder, and to have a high percentage of the brewery market. **RAS/JMA**

MT Bodywork Supplement (14 September 1983) and information supplied by the company.

Doors (Figure 20) were a part of van bodies that for many years attracted little attention from operator or bodybuilder. Barn doors were most common, this being the usual term for hinged doors, with roller shutters (q.v.) often fitted at the rear, while sliding doors were sometimes specified on one or both sides. The Post Office (q.v.) required high standards for hinges and locks on its vehicles to withstand frequent use.

Bakeries often wanted rear doors hinged horizontally so that an upper door provided shelter for the driver while unloading in inclement weather. Use of trays or containers for carrying loaves and cakes also dictated particular features. For example, in the late 1960s the Rank Hovis McDougall group specified a nearside sliding door towards the front to give access to 21 trays while a conventional rear door gave access to 145 trays. At the same period Lyons (q.v.) bread vans had a central rear door hinged to the right and an extra slender door on its left and hinged to the left: this gave a wider doorway for depot loading of wheeled containers while the main door alone was sufficient for deliveries.

From the mid-1960s the general move away from platform vehicles caused a rethink. Tighter requirements and enforcement on individual axle weights also posed a problem on multi-drop work, since taking weight off the rear of a vehicle or semi-trailer first upset weight distribution. This led to a need for side access. Loading or unloading by fork truck is also quicker and easier with side access.

Curtainsided (q.v.) bodies were not always the answer, since they might not provide sufficient load retention, or could be damaged by continual rough handling. Sliding doors were the obvious answer, perhaps top-hung to avoid damage to tracks at floor level. Conventional pairs of sliding doors with one sliding behind the other intrude on the loadspace, and this was a particular problem when carrying (or wanting to) Continental pallets side-by-side within the legal limit for overall width, though the law changed early in the 21st century. One solution was with top-hung sliding doors which are released by over-centre mechanisms and then pulled out from the body side in order to slide.

Sliding doors of whatever design also add weight and Tate & Lyle (q.v.) pioneered the use of lightweight doors made of a honeycomb section. Then there is Boalloy's (q.v.) Linkliner which uses two sliding doors on each side, with between them a lockable hinged slim panel which has to be opened before a sliding door operates.

There have been developments with curtainsiders. Boalloy went on to develop insulated curtains, calling the completed bodies Insuliners, with Chipliners – to carry woodchips – another variant. Concerns about security with conventional curtains have led to various forms of strengthening being added. One example is the Body Armour fabric used by Southfields, which is bonded to the back of otherwise conventional curtains. Another approach altogether for operators who wish to retain the full side access to a vehicle but want better security is to use full length metal doors that are hinged horizontally at mid height and open outwards and upwards. These are often called gull-wing doors and are popular with breweries, but cannot be used where height is restricted as when fully opened they project well above trailer or body height. For speedier opening and closing without any problems with height Cartwrights developed the SafeSide. It is claimed to be ten times faster to open than a conventional curtain-sider and is power-operated and split into four horizontally-hinged sections rather than two so that intrusion above the roof of the body was minimised. Another variation of the conventional curtain-sider, by Marshalls of Cambridge, is the Combi-Roll which has the curtain rolling upwards (instead of sideways). A central furling bar provides some stiffening for the assembly.　　**JMA**

Dorman Diesels Ltd, see PERKINS ENGINE CO.

A **double-bottom** is a colloquial term for an articulated unit drawing a second trailer of similar size and capacity, common in Australia and the USA. Successful trials in British motorway trunk service were carried out by ERF and Volvo under special dispensation in the 1970s, but no sanction was granted for regular use of the practice.　　**GM**

Double-deck bodies offer greater capacity for any load that is high in bulk but low in weight and were widely used by the 1990s. Lorries with double-deck bodies were offered from at least the very early 1920s but were mostly one-offs. Some were used at an earlier date for cycle transport, including a modified railway container for Raleigh Cycles. Stork Margarine was another early user for palletised loads based on a low-loading well-type semi-trailer. They were also employed for small livestock, such as sheep, and for motor cycle transport. For example, Woodgate's Transport of Sheldon, which delivered new motor cycles for Triumph Engineering from 1955, bought a Bedford S with pantechnicon body by Wilsdon & Co. Ltd of Solihull, in *c*. 1961. Wilson Double Deck Trailers (q.v.) of Ireland claims to have introduced double-deck articulated trailers in the early 1980s. It was certainly the first company to exploit the concept on any scale. Initial City Link was one of the largest users in the 1990s and had 80, each carrying 43 roll cages. Dockspeed of Kent, part of the Norfolk Line Group, used Schmitz double-deck refrigerated lorries in the late 1990s and owned 35. With some double-deck designs the second deck can be lowered to rest immediately above the bottom deck, either for loading or unloading or to enable higher loads to be carried. Other designs enabled a second deck to be simply removed if required. They were increasingly used for deliveries to supermarkets, especially of temperature-controlled loads. The potential savings are a greater volume carried, fuel savings, lower ferry costs, less expenditure on tractive units, lower maintenance costs and fewer drivers.   **RAS**

CM (17 December 1988), pp. 58–9; R A Storey, 'Moving the product', *Warwickshire History*, 7, 1 (1987), pp. 19–21; *Coopers Vehicle Journal* (January 1922), plate 4144

Douglas timber tractors and shunters (the Tugmaster) are the two types of vehicle most relevant to road haulage made by the multi-product Douglas Equipment Ltd. F L Douglas had been a vehicle salesman with Armstrong-Saurer and Unipower before setting up on his own after the Second World War to convert ex-WD AEC Matadors into logging trucks. As supplies dried up, Douglas became more of an assembler, using components from AEC. The Douglas range built up with off-road and 4- and 6-wheel drive conversions for oil companies' overseas work and civil engineers such as William Press.

The shortening and modification of a Leyland Comet for Silver City Airways in 1954 led to the Tugmaster range and from the mid-1960s, when Douglas died, output concentrated on different versions of the Tugmaster, for airport and dock work in connection with the growth of ro-ro (q.v.) operations. These 'dockspotters' were fitted with an elevating fifth-wheel (q.v.) to enable them to handle semi-trailers with different coupling heights. In 1996 Trinity Holdings, which already owned Reliance-Mercury, acquired Douglas Equipment Ltd as well as Schopf Maschinenbau GmbH and in 1998 Reliance-Mercury production moved to Douglas's Cheltenham works. Douglas Equipment Ltd became independent again in 1999 and continued with Tugmaster and Davies Magnet apparatus production.   **RAS**

'If no one else makes it Douglas can', *Vintage Lorry Annual*, 1 (1979); *CM* (20 May 1999), p. 14; Nick Baldwin, 'A to Z of Classic Commercials' *CVC*, 6, 1 (July 2001), pp. 38–9

Downtime is non-productive time spent by a vehicle and driver, waiting to load or unload in ports, depots and supermarket delivery areas. It is not a new problem, having been especially associated in the past with the Liverpool and London docks, with their cramped layout for road vehicle access and difficult labour practices. The mechanical horse (q.v.) was promoted as a means of reducing vehicle downtime by servicing several trailers with one tractive unit. Downtime caused by manual handling has been reduced by the spread of mechanical handling (q.v.) techniques. In the late 1990s downtime, or excessive waiting time was often a problem when delivering to the regional distribution centres of some major supermarket groups.   **RAS**

M Brignall, 'Time is money', *CM* (15 June 2000), pp. 36–7

Drawbar outfits (Figure 104). From the start of mechanical road transport, towing an independent trailer was a relatively inexpensive way of increasing the carrying capacity of a vehicle. The trailer was usually attached by a solid bar, often supplemented by chains. Legislation soon demanded the carrying of a second man, an attendant (known as a statutory attendant) whose task was to operate the separate trailer brake lever in front of the passenger seat in the cab of the drawing vehicle. The primitive nature of this rod and lever arrangement was emphasised by the special footrest sometimes fitted, against which the attendant could brace himself to gain maximum leverage.

As a result of American influence in the Second World War, technical improvements enabled the brakes of both vehicles to be linked, with the trailer brakes being applied automatically at the same time as those of the drawing unit, but the legal requirement for an attendant persisted until 1970. The attendant could also help with loading or unloading and could fulfil a valuable security function.

A wide variety of operators used trailers, often on a regular basis for trunk runs. BRS (q.v.) was a big user in its early days, while a slightly earlier example was Salisbury Meat Haulage with its regular runs to London's Smithfield Market. Drawbars, also known as danglers, provided a relatively inexpensive way of increasing capacity at busy times, since a trailer was relatively cheap to buy and cost little when idle. To aid manoeuvring in yards and other tight spaces many operators also fitted coupling gear (and bumpers) to the front of drawing units.

Higher wages gradually changed the economics of drawbars, and the need for a two-man crew, plus the lower maximum permitted speed, led to a steady decline. Even after the second man requirement was removed there remained speed and weight limitations for many more years, and it was only with the current 44 tonne maximum that drawbars have been treated equally. They have steadily become regarded with more favour by operators moving relatively light but bulky goods. The flexibility of the modern drawbar

outfit has also gained it new users. Examples are the delivery of new furniture to individual homes, with the rigid vehicle alone used to those with difficult access, the trailer (fitted with security devices) being left in a lay-by or lorry park, and bulk milk collection from farms by road tankers, with the trailer detached while the drawing unit makes a separate round.

Development of demountable (q.v.) body systems from the 1970s gave some impetus to the use of drawbars, and from the 1980s a number of technical improvements added to their appeal. By the 1990s drawbar trailers might have a single, double or triple axle mounted centrally (called centre-axle drawbars), or conventional single, twin or triple axles (called steered or turntable drawbars), while complex coupling and control systems allow trailers to follow precisely the tracks of the drawing units.

Another disadvantage of the drawbar outfit was the problem of loading or unloading at a loading bay or bank, which could involve much trailer shunting. Walk-through designs became available where the front of the trailer body also had an opening door or doors, and a hinged bridging section, so that loaders or fork-lift trucks could reach the body of the drawing unit through the trailer.

For operators wanting the absolute maximum loadspace within the legal limit special designs of coupling gear provide the absolute minimum distance between the rigid and trailer, while meeting the legal limit when both parts are drawn up in a straight line. This space gives insufficient clearance when deviating from the straight but when turning the coupling gear automatically extends to prevent any collision between the two parts.   **JMA**

Driver agencies became established as a part of the haulage industry from the late 1960s when new hours rules and a driver shortage created a need for this service. An early entrant providing national coverage was Manpower, the recruitment agency. The demand for this service grew with the largest operators, including supermarket regional distribution centres, using drivers to cover holiday and seasonal peak requirements. Some agencies operated as franchises. There were problems over who was responsible for the drivers and their hours and tachograph (q.v.) records. The leading agencies shifted to have the drivers on contracts offering salaries, bonuses, sick pay, training, and uniforms. Not all users of agencies were happy with the services. There were problems with driver inexperience of the make of vehicle provided, or in handling the load. Drivers reported being given old, or poorly maintained vehicles, limited or unhelpful instructions, and being expected to break rules. Legal judgements in the 1980s and 2002 clarified the responsibilities of the agency and the hirer of the driver. Problems continued with agencies providing 'moonlighting' or unqualified drivers but reputable agencies ensured their operations met all legal requirements. **GM**

Drivers' Action Movement see PROTEST MOVEMENTS

Drivers' clubs were introduced by a number of manufacturers to foster interest in and enthusiasm for their products. Members usually paid a modest subscription and received a regular newsletter or magazine and a badge to display on their vehicle; sometimes clothing or accessories were offered at low prices and even life insurance. Among the most successful were those of Bedford, founded in 1934, and Perkins. The latter promoted its diesel engines which were offered as an option in a number of makes at a time when petrol engines were still widely used. The Headlight Drivers Association published a monthly magazine for lorry drivers and enquired into accommodation for them, as well as providing legal advice and insurance facilities.

Drivers' clubs provided a source of feedback for the manufacturer on how the lorry performed in operation and how it was perceived by drivers. They faded away from the 1970s.

An early example of a club was one begun in 1925 by Harris and Hasell Ltd, concessionaires for Reo, which provided free insurance cover of £100 for every member of its Reo Drivers' League if he was killed in an accident while driving a Reo. Hints and tips by members were also circulated to the membership at intervals. In 1939 Morris-Commercial launched a free employment bureau run in conjunction with and for members of its Drivers' Association: 'competent drivers and driver-mechanics' and operators of Morris-Commercials were all expected to benefit. **JMA**

John Reed, *Bedford* (Shepperton: Ian Allan, 1983); Hollowell (1968), p. 53

Drivers' hours and pay. The driver's working day has always been long. This is exacerbated by much of the weekly wage being made up of overtime, even in 2001. It is still common to see wage agreements guaranteeing a fixed amount of overtime, which is really the normal working week. In addition there are payments such as 'dark money' for working at night, probably the first recognition in the late 1930s of 'unsocial hours'. There was 'dirty money' for handling certain types of loads, such as carbon black, fishmeal, wet hides, when all such were handballed. Before universal car ownership 'penalty payments' were paid for starting at unusual hours, to cover the cost of taxis when public transport was not running. Bonuses were paid for getting lucrative return loads from clearing houses (q.v.).

The first attempt to control the hours worked by drivers was contained in the Road Traffic Act 1930, which ruled that drivers were not to drive for more than 5½ hours continuously and not for more than 11 hours in any 24-hour period. The Road & Rail Traffic Act 1933 followed with a provision that time spent with the vehicle or load was to count as driving time. This effectively meant that drivers should spend their daily rest period away from the vehicle (See DRIVERS' WORKING CONDITIONS). This resulted in drivers being paid subsistence money, which became specified in Road Haulage Wages Board/ Council orders. This became another vital part of drivers' remuneration. When the writer started driving in 1955 this was 10s per day soon rising to 12s 6d. per day. At this time bed, breakfast and evening meal was 6s 6d. Many lived entirely on what was usually called 'night out money' which paid for snacks, mid-day meal, evening meal, bed and breakfast, even the price of the 'pictures.' There was also the practice of the 'dodgy night-out'. This involved reaching the end of the legal working hours reasonably near to the driver's home, the vehicle was parked, generally at a café, the driver got a lift home from another driver, spent the night in his own bed, than got a lift back to the parked vehicle next morning.

Details of working hours can be found under log sheets (q.v.), which were the means of recording hours worked. The restriction to eleven hours per day was an improvement on the then current situation, but was only observed by large, often trade-unionised, firms. As these only formed about ten per cent of haulage, the myriad of small firms maintained their competitive edge by drivers working whatever hours were needed to do the job. With the demands placed on the expanding road haulage in the 1950s, coupled with slow vehicles and poor roads, working hours in excess of the legal limits was routine. The writer has had personal experience of working 108 hours a week on a regular basis at that time. There were large firms where it was well known that the fiddled log sheet was the norm. Again drawing on personal experience, the writer's work records were examined only three times in forty-two years: never in the era of written records; only after the universal fitting of tachographs (q.v.) in 1982. Research carried out by one of the Dutch universities in the early 1980s showed that throughout the western world the average working day in road haulage was twelve hours.

The biggest advance in drivers' hours and pay occurred in 1948/9 with nationalisation. Although with the move towards increased C licence (q.v.) operation and other moves by hauliers to avoid being nationalised (q.v.) plus genuine exemptions, the number of drivers benefiting from these advances did not form a large part of the workforce. Drivers' hours rules were enforced as strongly by the trade union as they were by the management. Throughout, BRS drivers were always the subject of ridicule by private enterprise drivers as they (the BRS men) were not able to work excessive hours and indulge in other practices to increase their wages except for the dodgy night out. Although even under that regime there was still guaranteed overtime. When the speed limit for Heavy Motor Cars (vehicles over 3 tons unladen) was increased from 20 mph to 30 mph there was an agreement for the working day to be decreased from eleven to ten hours. At that time the National Agreement for Operating and Other Wages Grade Staff (the Green Book) contained the words – an eleven hour complex has developed, this must be overcome. To make use of the extra speed, jobs were rescheduled to do eleven hours work in ten hours. Existing employees were paid a lump sum to compensate for loss of future earnings, until a satisfactory agreement could be reached. This resulted in a payment of 15 per cent bonus on top of wages. As an example, this is the payment for an eight-wheeler driver on night trunk (q.v.) in April 1961:

40 hours at basic hourly rate of 3s 4d	£6 13s. 4d
10 hours at time and a half (5s)	£2 10s. 0d
50 hours' dark money (20% of basic, i.e. 8d per hr)	£1 13s. 4d
	10 16s. 8d
Plus 15% 30 mph bonus	£1 12s. 6d
	£12 9s. 2d

The Green Book followed the Road Haulage Wages Board (q.v.) and Road Haulage Wages Council (q.v.) orders, in that there was no differential wage rate for female drivers of any class of vehicle. It did, however, specify 80 per cent of the male rate for female bank (q.v.) staff and porters (mostly in the parcels industry), ostensibly because they could not lift or carry the same weight as men.

The tachograph (q.v.) was the next attempt at controlling driver's hours. While it can show when a vehicle is moving, how fast and how far, other recordings depend on input from the driver. Thus like all methods of controlling driver's hours, discovery of contraventions depended largely on roadside checks. One year produces 150 million discs, so that although it is the employer's responsibility to check them weekly, unless a firm is targeted, a vehicle involved in an accident, or the driver checked at the roadside, enforcement is still tenuous.

The introduction of pan-European rules on driver's hours in 1986 did not improve things. Although the actual time at the wheel was reduced to eight hours, the on-duty time or spread-over was increased to fourteen hours. There is a statutory provision for a twenty-four hour break each week. However, these rules contain so many exemptions and provisions for deferment that most drivers find them impossible to follow. Firms have employed experts to work out driving rotas, exploiting every opportunity to have drivers work the maximum hours legally permissible. This law also outlawed many systems of payment by trip money, mileage or tonnage. It also removed the provision that the driver must spend his daily rest away from the vehicle, thus legalising the sleeper cab (q.v.) in Great Britain.

In April 2002 a survey by the BBC reported on Radio 4 revealed that 78 per cent of the drivers interviewed ignored the rules in some way or another. Some drivers had spent up to thirty-four hours continuously on duty. With the low rates being paid to the numerous owner drivers this is not surprising. Drivers are still not well paid. They work in one of the few industries where a minor error of judgement can produce a prison sentence.

Gibson (2001), ch. 14

Drivers' working conditions. The elite of drivers drove stagecoaches on the Royal Mail, yet they sat on an outside seat exposed to all weathers, the same situation as that of the lowly carrier. When mechanisation came, in the form of the steam engine, it did not seem necessary to make any changes. Not only was the driver exposed to the weather, now he had to contend with oil and steam from the exposed motion and heat from the firebox.

Things did not at first change with the arrival of motors. Weather protection on most lorries was a storm sheet tied round the neck until after the First World War. In the 1920s the enclosed cab (q.v.) quickly developed and then remained largely unchanged for the next thirty-five years, little attention being paid to comfort. Even on premium vehicles only a thin metal cover separated the driver from the noise of the engine and its heat in the summer, while conversely this was the only form of heating in the winter. When the diesel engine came along, it ran cooler, which was a benefit in summer but not in winter. Not until the late 1960s were cab heaters a universal fitment. It took the arrival of Swedish truck makers to give a boost to standards of driver comfort.

From the days when the drover and the carter slept in the hayloft, often behind an inn, the provision of food and accommodation for drivers has often been poor. The transport café (q.v.) was for long synonymous with meals of fats and carbohydrates necessary for heavy manual work which was part of the driver's job. Before power-assisted steering became universal, manoeuvring a heavily laden vehicle was a wrist- and shoulder-aching job. Delivering loads such as sugar or cement in one hundredweight bags was hard work too. In the 1970s palletisation (q.v.) and the fork-lift truck (q.v.) became universal. Today many drivers delivering to supermarkets neither load nor unload their vehicles and are sometimes called 'chauffeurs' in a derogatory manner.

The 1933 Road & Rail Traffic Act made it mandatory for the driver to spend his daily rest period away from his vehicle. This gave rise to the driver's digs. Sometimes the commercial hotel, which catered for commercial travellers and theatricals, opened its doors to drivers or a widow living near a lorry park took in a couple of drivers. Some establishments catered exclusively for drivers on a major lorry route. These were often akin to barracks. They had long rooms with a row of beds down each side, washrooms with a row of sinks and WC cubicles, and a large communal dining room. The best of these were those run by the Salvation Army whose standards of cleanliness were in stark contrast to some other establishments.

One retired driver recalls how, before he made his first long distance journey, his father, also a driver, said 'Don't get any big ideas, most people think of you as only one bit better than a tramp. That bit because you ride and he walks.' This perception can still sometimes be found even in the present century when there is a major shortage of drivers.

Why do drivers accept this situation? It revolves around the independent and self-sufficient type of personality which the job has attracted. It is difficult to do any other type of work after having been a driver for a time. This is why many drivers become owner-drivers hoping to stay in the business and make more money. Exploitation of this trait by customers and large haulage companies is making this enterprise probably less attractive than being an employed driver. Until very recently it was a job with minimal supervision, now the tachograph and more importantly the global positioning system has made it possible for the employer to know where his vehicles are to within a few metres. The major shortage of drivers shows that such restricted freedom is not proving attractive to modern youth.

Hollowell (1968)

Du Cros, W & G, Ltd, see W & G DU CROS LTD

Dunbar, Charles Stuart (1900–93), was a transport manager, organiser, writer and consultant. Transport management and journalism were the two themes of his long working life and each produced results on which his lasting reputation rests. These were respectively his foundation, and service as first chairman, of the National Conference of Express Carriers (q.v.), and two of his published works, *Goods Vehicle Operation Principles and Practice for Students and Executives* (1949, 1953) and *The Rise of Road Transport 1919–1939* (1981).

Beginning as an editorial assistant, Dunbar spent most of the 1920s as circulation and transport manager of various provincial evening papers. After three and a half years with the Birmingham & Midland Motor Omnibus Co., he started Red Arrow Deliveries (q.v.), based in Birmingham but aiming 'to provide a nationwide service by road for parcels and smalls'.

When Dunbar set up the National Conference of Parcels Carriers in 1937 (renamed the National Conference of Express Carriers in 1938), he brought to it a wide range of practical transport and business experience,

organisational skills, and a network of road haulage contacts from Red Arrow operations. He saw the need for the organisation of parcels carriers in the context of the government's intention that there should be a rates (q.v.) structure for road goods transport. It was vital to ensure that the special organisational features of parcels traffic were taken into account when a rates structure was fixed. An additional complication was the railway companies' 'Square Deal' campaign (q.v.) of 1938. In this connection, it is significant that, as well as members of the Commercial Motor Users' Association (q.v.), Associated Road Operators (q.v.), and other bodies, the National Conference also included some railway-controlled firms. Indeed, James Paterson of Carter Paterson (q.v.) became its president. It was important for the protection of express carriers' interests that their Conference was firmly in place before the Second World War further complicated the organisation of transport. After the war, the NCEC became one of the Functional Groups of the re-formed Road Haulage Association (q.v.).

By mid-1941 Dunbar had become manager of the smalls department of Hauliers Ltd (q.v.), moving to the Ministry of War Transport and other official posts, including the Inter-Allied European Central Inland Transport Organisation to 1947. He then embarked on the career of freelance writer and consultant, interrupted by an official post with the Commonwealth Development Corporation from 1950 to 1952. He was the first editor of *Buses Illustrated* and editor of *Passenger Transport,* 1961–3. *Goods vehicle operation*, a very practical manual when current, is now valuable as an inside view of the industry of its time. *The Rise of Road Transport* is one of the few authoritative, detailed works on the consolidation years of the industry.   **RAS**

Dunbar's papers, in particular as chairman of the National Conference, are in the Modern Records Centre, University of Warwick Library, MSS. 347.

Duple Motor Bodies Ltd. Although primarily associated with coach bodies, Duple of The Hyde, Hendon in its earlier years had a considerable involvement in goods body building. Indeed, the name Duple derives from its origins in producing the Bifort duplex body system, whereby a specially designed van top could be fitted over a car body. Between the wars lorry and van bodies provided a supplementary turnover when the bus and coach trade was depressed. As well as such work as semi-forward-control lorry conversions and the building of lorry bodies on former bus chassis, work for the Post Office was sufficient for a special department to be set up, in particular producing light vans on Morris Minor chassis for postal collection and telephone line work. **RAS**

Alan Townsin, *Duple: 70 Years of coachbuilding* (Glossop, 1998)

The **Duramin Engineering Co.** Ltd was founded in 1920 in Dartford, Kent, by E L Oglethorpe as Dartford Engineering to exploit duralumin, a new lightweight aluminium alloy he had encountered in the First World War. Duralumin had been developed and manufactured exclusively by James Booth & Co. Ltd of Birmingham. The first containers Oglethorpe produced were for J Lyons & Co. (q.v.) to carry tea. They were successful and the firm turned to the construction of various types of bodywork for commercial vehicles including horse boxes. He was soon joined by P A Bristow, an accountant, and these two families controlled the firm until the 1960s. In 1923 the firm outgrew its site and moved to north-west London and then in 1927 was taken over by Curtis Auto Co. and it moved to Abbey Road on the Park Royal estate. In 1929 it changed its name to Curtis Duramin until the mid-1930s when it dropped the 'Curtis'. It was a leader until the Second World War in offering alloy bodywork. It also made underframes and Red Line truck bodies. Its customers included Express Dairies.

During the Second World War the company made aircraft components and reverted to commercial vehicle bodywork afterwards. In 1950 a subsidiary to make radar cabins was established in Lydney in Gloucestershire and in 1958 the bodywork business was so good that it was moved from Park Royal to a larger site at

Ruislip. The United Transport Co. Ltd had put up some money to finance the move to Lydney in 1950 and in 1965 it took a controlling interest, the Oglethorpe and Bristow families ceasing to be involved in the business. At the same time vehicle bodywork production was consolidated on the Lydney site.

From 1968 the firm moved into a new business which was expanding rapidly, the manufacture of lightweight insulated containers for the international transport of perishable products. The boxes used glass fibre skins and polyurethene cores and by the late 1970s were being produced at the rate of about 80 per week. Some were also refrigerated. Thus Duramin were twice pioneers: in the use of light alloys for lorry bodies, minimising the unladen weight, and in producing insulated containers for international transport. **JA**

CM (10 February 1939); p. 5; *CM* (3 July 1953); *Railway Gazette* (3 July 1931), pp. 21–2

Dyson, R A, & Co. Ltd (Figure 149) of Liverpool, was founded in 1850 as wheelwrights, wagon builders and smiths, and for many years was among the UK's best-known trailer makers. The company expanded with the growth of Liverpool's shipping and commerce and continued to supply the Liverpool pattern of team wagon until the late 1920s. This was a design peculiar to Liverpool dock work, larger and wider than average and carrying 10 to 12 tons with two horses. As mechanical transport became important so Dyson began to cater for this market, concentrating on special-purpose trailers for both British operators and the Liverpool-based trading companies which had strong links with the British Empire, for example the United Africa Co.

Dyson was quite a small firm and lacked the capacity to cope with all orders received in the busy period after the end of the First World War, so made an arrangement with Cranes (Dereham) Ltd (q.v.) for them to manufacture to Dyson's designs, mainly drawbar trailers. Any trailers thus built were sold as Dysons. Cranes designed and built the well-known 100-ton trailer (q.v.) for Norman E Box (q.v.) but because it had been ordered through Dyson it was displayed on their stand at the 1929 Commercial Motor Show, a significant factor in Cranes' decision to end the relationship in 1931.

Dyson continued to build a wide variety of one-off designs as well as standard drawbar and semi-trailers: many were recognisable by the shape of the polished aluminium hub caps, with Dyson name embossed. The aftermath of the Second World War and the gradual decline of Liverpool's shipping and Empire-based trading together with the mid-1960s move to widespread use of articulated outfits hit Dyson.

It missed out on opportunities to offer a standardised range of semi-trailers conforming to the revised dimensions introduced in 1964, and allowed new entrants to trailer building to gain significant market share.

Dyson also lost the services of several local engineering sub-contractors for metal fabrication when these closed or moved away. Its own premises were unsuitable or incompatible with plans for a development area covering the mainly derelict docks and their immediate vicinity and this and financial constraints saw Dyson acquired by King Trailers in 1980. **GM**

E

The **Eagle Engineering Co. Ltd**, Warwick, was particularly associated with municipal vehicles, especially for refuse collection, but its product range in the twentieth century was at times more varied. Eagle was established as a limited company in 1911, when it took over the Eagle Works, Saltisford, Warwick, of William Glover & Sons, agricultural implement makers and vehicle builders. Between the wars, in addition to municipal and public utility vehicles, Eagle produced large numbers of drawbar and articulated trailers. Bodies were also built on rigids, including some for local operators. An attempt to move into third-axle conversion was stymied by a challenged patent and Eagle passed this work to Ferraris of Cricklewood, together with most of its tipper work. Close co-operation with Thornycroft is evidenced in the Eagle order-book for 1936, as are numerous orders from Scammell, and individual orders from haulage contractors and own-account operators, such as Hovis, and Dunchurch and Wiltshire Creameries.

After the war, Eagle advertised as a manufacturer of trailers, semi-trailers and commercial bodywork. An advertising record book of 1947–51 features a variety of products, from pole trailers for timber carriage to pantechnicon semi-trailers, with similar diversity for a single customer: 6-ton, 2-wheel tipping trailers for tractor use on site work and a 60-ton low-loading trailer, both for McAlpine, the contractors. Local operators, such as Red House Motor Services, Huckvale & Hemmings Transport of Warwick, the Motor Packing Co. and Saville (Tractors) Ltd of Stratford-on-Avon, feature in post-war orders. Those for national concerns included twenty 8-ton semi-trailers and one hundred 10-ton platform trailers for the Road Haulage Executive in 1950–1, 21 biscuit van semi-trailers for Peek Frean & Co. in 1954–6 and six for McVitie & Price Ltd in 1954.

In 1966 Eagle was taken over for a short period by Hanger Motors, then by Combat Engineering, but was finally acquired by the Hestair Group, a conglomerate which went on to buy Dennis Brothers of Guildford in 1972. Two decades of close collaboration followed between Hestair Eagle and Hestair Dennis; both passed to Trinity Holdings in 1989. A change of name and corporate identity to Dennis Group plc occurred in 1997. The following year a hostile bid by Mayflower Corporation plc took Dennis away from the Henlys Group, with which a merger had been agreed. Mayflower's main interest was in the bus business and in 1999 both the Douglas (q.v.) and Eagle parts of the former Dennis Group were acquired by NatWest Equity Partners. A management buy-out financed by Bridgepoint Capital took place in 2000. In 1985 Dennis Eagle moved to the Heathcote Industrial Estate on the outskirts of Warwick. Eagle's production at the end of the twentieth century was not limited to refuse-collection vehicles: in addition to a 1998 order for air-portable, 26-tonne refuelling tankers won from the Royal Air Force, Dennis Eagle low-access chassis were offered for airport vehicles, milk-collection tankers, utilities' special-purpose vehicles and urban delivery. **RAS**

Warwickshire County Record Office, CR 1372; N Baldwin, 'Eagle municipals', *VCVM*, 1, 3 (1985); pp. 22–4; *VCV*, (March 1999), pp. 14–15; B C Woods, *Municipal Refuse Collection Vehicles* (Appleby-in-Westmorland: Trans-Pennine Publishing, 1999); information from Dennis Eagle Ltd

Eastern Roadways (ER) was formed by J W Cook & Co. Ltd, Thameside wharfingers, in 1929. Its operations were confined to serving East Anglia. The main depot and workshops were at Bishop's Stortford, with other depots in London, Kings Lynn and Norwich. The ER trunk fleet initially comprised ex-army AEC Y-type articulated conversions, replaced by Scammell articulated units. These were later converted to Gardner LW engines and pneumatic tyres. Some remained in operation to be nationalised. As ER's fleet increased and other operators were acquired these were joined by Albion and ERF, while lighter vehicles for collection and delivery work were Ford, Dodge and Bedford. Major traffic was malt for London brewers, notably Watney, and imports of dairy products and parcels and smalls. ER acquired H C & L B A Day Ltd in 1935, the name being changed to Day's Transport Ltd, with depots at Ipswich and Colchester. Also operating from Day's Ipswich depot was another subsidiary, Orwell Transport Ltd. T C Grange Ltd, of Wells-next-the-Sea, Norfolk, also joined ER in 1935, operating a mixed fleet of 27 vehicles. Sheringham Haulage, with ten vehicles, acquired in the 1940s, was also based at Grange's depot. Suffolk Road Transport of Bury St Edmunds, was acquired in the early 1940s, operating 14 vehicles. Other subsidiaries were Mallon & Grange Ltd of Swaffham, Norfolk, operating a mostly Albion 15-vehicle fleet, with livestock and meat containers; R T Lawrence Ltd and F W Riches Ltd, both at Roudham, East Harling, Norwich, with eight vehicles with drawbar trailers and Robinson's Transport of Beccles with 22 vehicles. ER was nationalised, operating 200 vehicles. Some directors opened a clearing house at Tower Hill and at denationalisation re-entered the industry, tendering for special A licences to form East Anglian Carriers. **GM**

MT (17 January 1948), p. 20

Easyloader, see LOW HEIGHT VEHICLES

Ebro UK in 1983 began importing part of the Spanish-built Ebro range made by Motor Iberica. It offered 6 and 7½ ton chassis/cabs and 6 and 7½ ton vans, all powered by 3.8 litre Perkins engines also made, under licence, by Motor Iberica. The arrangement ended after Japanese maker Nissan acquired Motor Iberica. The large vans achieved a measure of popularity since no complete factory-built vans of this size were available from UK makers. Motor Iberica had been formed in 1956 to build bonneted British-designed Ford trucks under licence in Spain. **JMA**

Eccles Motor Transport Ltd of Gosta Green, Birmingham is an unusual example of a road haulage business which became the basis of a caravan manufacturer. Founded by H A Eccles as the Eccles Transport Co., it operated the short-lived French Mass front-wheel-drive lorry, produced only from 1912 to 1914. An advertisement by Eccles at the end of the First World War for further capital attracted Bill Riley senior and junior, who shortly before the war had begun to produce motor caravan designs. The Rileys became directors of Eccles, which changed its trading name in March 1919. Two new lorries were bought and Eccles continued in the administrative side of the business, but Riley junior turned to trailer caravan building and by 1921 Eccles had become solely a caravan manufacturer. It went on to dominate the UK caravan market from the 1930s to 1960. **RAS**

Andrew Jenkinson, *Caravans: the story of British trailer caravans & their manufacturers 1919–1959* (Dorchester: Veloce, 1998), ch. 2.

The **economic contribution** of goods road transport. Almost all economic activity is dependent to a greater or lesser extent on the transport of goods; but it is not easy to quantify the scale of its contribution to the UK economy, because the answer is concealed within the official statistics. One can start to build up a picture by first comparing goods road transport with the rest of the transport industry.

As shown in Table 3, public and private passenger road transport uses many more vehicles and generates the majority of road traffic. In relative terms, goods traffic has declined since the 1950s, partly as a result of increasing lorry size, which allows more goods to be carried with fewer vehicles, but chiefly because of the rapid growth in car ownership. Neither vehicle numbers nor vehicle-miles are good indicators, for goods road transport was equal in importance to passenger road transport in the period 1965–75 and suffered only a modest relative decline in the following decade (see Table 3), again because of the faster growth in the use of private cars. In absolute terms, goods transport has, of course, continued to grow (see GROWTH OF ROAD FREIGHT TRANSPORT).

Table 3: Passenger and Goods Vehicles and Road Traffic

	Percentage of all motor vehicles			Percentage of road traffic (vehicle-miles)		
	Passenger vehicles	All goods vehicles	Goods vehicles except light vans	Passenger vehicles	All goods vehicles	Goods vehicles except light vans
1939	84	16		73	27	
1949	77	23	11	59	41	27
1959	84	16	6	73	27	14
1969	89	11	4	81	19	10
1979	90	10	3	83	17	9
1989	90	10	2	84	16	7
1999	91	9	2	83	17	7

In the UK National Accounts the transport sector of the economy embraces only public carriers of goods, not own-account operation, which is treated as part of the particular industrial or service sector that it serves. The relative economic significance of these two modes of working is discussed in the article on STRUCTURE OF THE HAULAGE INDUSTRY, but summarised here in Table 4.

Table 4: Goods Traffic by Road and Rail

	Percentage of goods lifted by road and rail (tons)			Percentage of goods moved by road and rail (ton-miles)		
	Road: public carriers	Road: own-account	Rail	Road: public carriers	Road: own-account	Rail
1954	77	23		49	51	
1958	34	47	19	30	28	42
1969	42	47	11	47	31	22
1979	44	46	10	50	34	16
1989	52	40	7	61	27	11
1999	56	38	6	63	26	11

Tables 4 and 5 also illustrate rail transport's declining share and the effect on road transport's economic position. Water and pipeline transport are disregarded here, as neither has significantly affected this position.

Table 6 shows the percentage of the UK gross domestic product attributed in the national accounts to passenger and goods transport as a whole. As previously mentioned, this table ignores the value of own-account goods transport. Taking this and the previous tables into account, it is clear that the contribution of goods road transport to the UK gross domestic product remained fairly steady through the 1960s at 5½ per cent (a figure estimated from a survey of road freight transport costs undertaken by the Ministry of Transport in 1965), but from the early 1970s

began falling steadily to perhaps half this percentage by the 1990s. Some writers quote higher figures (7-10 per cent of GDP), but these are based on invalid calculations using gross expenditure on goods road transport, rather than the 'value added' by the industry after deducting the cost of goods and services bought in from other sectors. One important factor responsible for the relative decline has been the steady reduction in the real rates charged for road haulage, which has been a stimulus to many of the other sectors of the national economy. The dominant reason is the much larger share of the economy now filled by the financial, real estate, education and health sectors, which have been growing much faster than the production, construction and transport industries.

Table 5: Percentage of Users' Expenditure on Road and Rail Transport

	Passenger road transport	Goods road transport	Rail transport
1954	47	33	20
1959	47	37	15
1969	48	46	7
1979	52	43	5
1989	57	40	4

Table 6: GDP attributed to Transport Sector in National Accounts (%)

1938	7.4
1954	6.6
1959	6.2
1969	6.2
1979	5.3
1989	4.5
1999	4.5

In the 1990s the UK national accounts re-defined the transport sector to include the now closely-linked activity of storage or warehousing. At the end of the century the contribution of the freight component of this sector to the UK economy was comparable with the largest of the manufacturing sectors, food, drink and tobacco, and with the other large production sectors: oil and natural gas extraction, and electricity, gas and water supply. **GAB**

Highways Statistics, 1964–1973 and *Transport Statistics Great Britain*, 1974– ; *National Income & Expenditure*, 1956–1983 and *United Kingdom*

National Accounts, 1984– ; S L Edwards and B T Bayliss, *Operating Costs in Road Freight Transport* (c.1971); A H Watson, *Road goods transport* (*Reviews of United Kingdom statistical sources, 7*) (1978) p. 12

Edbro Holdings (Figure 105) producers of tipping gear and bodies, originated with Edwards Brothers of Bolton, incorporated in 1919, who developed the first successful hydraulic tipping hoist for commercial vehicles in Britain using oil rather than water. Steam vehicles were able to use their own water supply and pump this to raise the body, a means denied to petrol-engined vehicles. Other pioneering achievements included a swash plate hydraulic pump and a combined pump and power take-off unit which was simpler to make.

A major amalgamation created Edbro (Holdings) Ltd in 1952, under Eric Tonge as managing director, who had joined Edbro as works manager in 1943. Companies absorbed into Edbro included Bromilow & Edwards Ltd, Edbro Ltd, Edwards Brothers (Tippers) Ltd, Moveable Floor (Vehicles) Ltd, Pilot Works Ltd and Wood Hoists Ltd. By the mid-1970s, when Edbro, wanting extra capacity, made an unsuccessful bid for Anthony Carrimore Ltd, two thirds of group profits came from export sales, a substantial part from Europe.

In the 1970s Edbro embarked on a programme of expansion and diversification, acquiring a 75 per cent holding in Hydro Hoist Ltd, Eire, and all the share capital of one its distributors, Edbro (Scotland) Ltd. It also moved into waste compaction, setting up Solid Waste Engineering Ltd. In 1981 the company experienced the worst year in its history and first-ever loss, as well as the death of its president, Lord Coleraine, chairman from 1942 to 1971. There followed concentration of production on its extended main site in Bolton and on its core activities: the design, manufacture and sale of tipping gears, associated hydraulic products and truck bodies. In 1985 there were added the manufacture of hydraulic cylinders for major earth-moving machinery and fork-lift truck manufacturers and sizeable MoD contracts for army truck bodies.   **RAS**

Modern Records Centre, University of Warwick Library, MSS.226X/IND/273: Edbro annual reports, 1975–85

Eddie Stobart Ltd, see STOBART, EDDIE, LTD

Eight-wheeler, see RIGID EIGHT

Elddis Transport. Thomas Cook started in the haulage business in the late-nineteenth century with horses and carts, as the local carrier bringing goods from Newcastle to Consett, mainly for the local co-operative society. After the First World War, the business expanded into trunk haulage and into bus services. The buses were eventually sold to concentrate on the haulage side of the business and in 1942, when Thomas Cook died, his son, Siddle Cook, bought the shares of his brothers and sisters by borrowing money from a friend and formed Siddle C Cook Ltd.

Experience gained during the Second World War, when its vehicles were commandeered by the government for the carriage of war materials, allowed the company to expand more into the heavy haulage side of the industry. The company was nationalised in the 1940s but retained a small number of vehicles which were classified as 'special types' and therefore exempt from nationalisation.

After de-nationalisation the business grew by acquisition, concentrating on heavy haulage operations and operating vehicles with carrying capacities of up to 100 tons. Two companies acquired were Diamond Transport of Manchester and J & I Gordon of Bedlington, each with two vehicles.

In the early 1960s, the Cook family was approached by the holding company, Tayforth Ltd (q.v.), with a view to acquisition. Tayforth was strong in Scotland but wanted national coverage. At this time, the then Labour Government was insisting that the movement of all abnormal loads where practicable should be via coastal shipping (q.v.). Tayforth wanted to quote an all-in price for such movements from factory to site. Siddle C Cook Ltd was the only company of any substance which had not been acquired by one of the conglomerates; Pickfords was government-owned, Wynns &

Sunter had been acquired by United Transport, and McKelvies by Transport Development Group. The business was taken over by Tayforth on 1 July 1964 and was then operating 35 vehicles and 70 trailers. Siddle Cook retired and the company was run by his son, Geoffrey Cook. Under the Tayforth umbrella, the business grew to over 100 vehicles and 250 trailers and in 1968 Tayforth became part of the National Freight Corporation (q.v.).

After this takeover, Geoffrey Cook left and bought a small business of six vehicles and 11 trailers, Norwood Garages of Corbridge, and moved into rented premises at Greenside, joined by Bob Whinney and Austin Lawrie, both previous employees of Siddle C Cook Ltd. By reversing 'Siddle' the company was re-named Elddis Transport (Consett) Ltd and recommenced trading in 1971. Norwood had carried for Van den Bergh & Jurgens Ltd of Purfleet, the margarine manufacturers, and British Steel at Jarrow. The Van den Bergh's contract allowed Elddis to develop into the food industries and with the help of previous contacts to obtain work from companies such as Ever Ready, Procter & Gamble, British Steel at Consett and others. The margarine contract also meant work from other Unilever companies such as Batchelors, Brooke Bond, Lever Bros and Van den Berghs at Bromborough and Greenock.

In the early 1980s, the company was hit by several closures: British Steel at Consett and Ransome, Hoffman & Pollard Bearings, but won much new business in the area from companies such as Derwent Valley Foods, because Elddis was one of the few hauliers in the North East then which operated vans and curtain-sided trailers and offered warehousing facilities. Thus it could accommodate new industries.

Elddis continued to grow and in 2000 operated 130 vehicles and 230 trailers, supplemented by 250,000 sq. ft of warehousing. It had become one of the leading hauliers in the UK specialising in the timed delivery of goods to supermarkets.   **NC**

The **Electric Vehicle Association of Great Britain** was founded as the Electric Vehicle Committee in 1913 under the auspices of the Incorporated Municipal Electricity Association. It was reconstituted and renamed in 1938. Its members comprised manufacturers of vehicles, batteries and accessories and the electricity supply industry was also represented. The objectives of the EVC/EVA included promotion of the use of battery electric vehicles, the provision of facilities for electric vehicle users and the maintenance of a record of work done by such vehicles. During the Second World War the issue of standardisation was taken up by the EVA on the suggestion of the Ministry of Supply, but the worsening supply situation hindered production of a standard design. The changed nature of the vehicle manufacturing sector and the privatisation of the supply industry led to the closure of the EVA at the end of 2001.   **RAS**

Motor Industry of Great Britain (1933); Hills (1943*); Goods Vehicle Yearbook* (1964)

Electric vehicles (Figures 28 and 188) Electric cars enjoyed a brief period of popularity in Britain between 1900 and about 1910 because they did not require hand-starting, were quieter, cleaner, easier to drive and more comfortable than petrol-engined cars. It was soon realised that the limited range of operation of a battery-powered vehicle, which was maximised by driving slowly, was more suited to urban movement of goods.

Electric goods vehicles began to appear from about 1908 and may be divided into two groups. First on the scene were the heavy vehicles, fitted with various types of body and with capacities up to 5, and ultimately 10 to 12 tons. Small numbers were bought for trial on town delivery work by users such as railway companies and breweries. They were simple to maintain and many remained in service for 20 to 30 years, but their initial cost was high and few were built after the 1920s, with one notable exception. They were particularly suited to the heavy start-stop workload of refuse collection and found favour where there was a municipal tramway system with an electricity generating station.

The second group comprised panel vans of about 1-ton capacity whose introduction to Britain was led by US manufacturers, supplying direct, like the Walker Vehicle Co. of Chicago, or from factories established in England for assembling the vehicles of Edison (General Electric) and GV (General Vehicle Co.), from 1916 to 1935. The biggest users were London's department stores such as Harrods (q.v.), which bought its first electric vans in 1913, Selfridges, and Barkers of Kensington; they were selected for their quiet reliability, rather than economy. British manufacturers of the period included Electromobile Ltd of Otley (1914–33), Ransomes, Sims & Jefferies Ltd (q.v.) (c.1916–39), Richard Garrett & Co. (q.v.) (1917–37), Electricars Ltd of Birmingham (1920–35) which purchased Edison Accumulators Ltd's UK manufacturing rights, Clayton Wagons Ltd of Lincoln (1921–9) and Victor Electrics Ltd of Ormskirk (1927–61)

These electric goods vehicles made no significant impact, except on the two specific groups of users mentioned. By 1930 the number in use had risen to only 1752, at a time when there were still 7750 steam and 335,000 petrol-driven goods vehicles; by 1933 the number was falling. It was at this point that the battery-electric goods vehicle found its most successful niche — as a milk-, bread-, or laundry-delivery roundsman's vehicle. The credit for popularising this development is usually given to A E Morrison & Sons of Leicester which combined with GV in 1933 to produce a small lightweight van for a 10-cwt payload. In fact, Murphy Cars & Trucks Ltd of Maidenhead had been producing its Auto-Electric 3-wheel 'errand boy on wheels' parcel carrier since 1924 and 4-wheel models for 10–15 cwt payloads since 1928.

Many other manufacturers quickly entered the market, including Bradshaw, Cleco Electric Industries Ltd of Leicester (1936–57), Electruk (manufactured by T H Lewis 1937–61), Graisley (Diamond Motors Ltd of Wolverhampton 1937–9), Metrovick (Metropolitan-Vickers Electrical Co., Manchester,

1934–42), Midland Vehicles Ltd of Leamington Spa (1935–58), Sunbeam Commercial Vehicles Ltd of Wolverhampton (1937–40), Tumilty, Victor Electrics Ltd and Wilson (Partridge, Wilson & Co. 1934–1954). They offered a profusion of lightweight designs using car and motorcycle components: three-wheelers, with one wheel at either the front or rear, and 4-wheelers of 5-cwt to 2-ton capacity, and pedestrian-controlled three-wheelers of about 3½-cwt capacity. By 1938 registered electric goods vehicles had risen to 4340.

Replacement of the horse-drawn, cycle and hand-propelled milk delivery vehicles continued rapidly after the war. There was also a considerable expansion in the use of electric tractors and fork-lift trucks for internal work at factories, stations and airports, many of which were registered for occasional use on public roads. This accounts for the peak figure of over 50,000 registered electric goods vehicles in the 1970s; it had fallen to 10,800 by 1999.

As some pre-war manufacturers dropped out, others started up: Lancaster Electrical Co. of New Barnet (1941–52), Tomlinson (Electric Vehicles) Ltd (1940–61), Manuelectric (Sidney Hole's Electric Vehicles, later the Stanley Engineering Co.) (1948–c.1969), Helecs (Hindle Smart & Co. of Ardwick, Manchester, 1950–7), Electrojan (Trojan Ltd of Croydon) (1951–3). Two of the three post-war makers who enjoyed a lasting success were newcomers. The exception was A E Morrision & Sons which had merged with Electricars in 1935 to form Associated Electric Vehicle Manufacturers Ltd and in 1941 changed its badge from Morrison-Electricar to Morrison-Electric. An association with Crompton-Parkinson from 1941 went a stage further in 1948 when the company became Austin Crompton Parkinson Electric Vehicles Ltd, after Austin took a 50 per cent interest. In 1968 it became Crompton Leyland Electricars Ltd and then in 1972 Crompton Electricars Ltd. One experiment was the building of a battery-electric version of the Austin (or Morris) Minivan.

Wales & Edwards Ltd, later W & E Vehicles Ltd, was established in 1945 at Shrewsbury and built large numbers of 3-wheel milk floats, initially with a maximum speed of 8 to 10 mph. Larger motors and batteries allowed an increase of both speed and range and ultimately the company offered 3-wheelers for loads up to 1¼ tons and 4-wheelers for up to 2½ tons.

Northern Coach Builders (NCB), established at Gateshead in 1945, became the third of the major post-war manufacturers, from 1956 under the name of Smith's Electric Vehicles Ltd. An innovation was the Cabac milk float designed with driver safety in mind. The cab, which had no side doors, was entered from the rear via a gangway running across the vehicle, with the loadspace behind.

The potential environmental advantages inspired continuing attempts to develop a competitively-priced van with a speed and range suitable for a day's delivery work. These often had government backing and electric vehicles have been exempt from vehicle excise duty since 1980. The Post Office (q.v.) has provided facilities for in-service trials of electric vans since at least 1929. In the late 1970s Lucas built a number of battery-powered Bedford CFs, while Chloride joined forces with National Carriers Ltd (q.v.) to develop a larger van with a capacity of 3.65 tonnes, the Silent Karrier, later renamed the Electroflow, which was based on the Karrier (later Dodge) KC Walk-Thru. In the late 1990s Citroen's Berlingo van, designed from the outset for petrol, diesel or electric propulsion, seemed to be getting close to making the long-sought breakthrough. The electric version was priced competitively by excluding the battery; this was leased on a monthly rental, the cost of which — like petrol or derv — was allowable against tax and for the first time the total operating costs were competitive.

RFdeB/JMA/GAB

W Worby Beaumont, *Industrial Electric Vehicles and Trucks* (1920); Hills (1943); de Boer (1990); Georgano (1996)

Electricars Ltd of Birmingham (1920–39) acquired the manufacturing rights of Edison of London's range of electric vehicles in 1920. This coincided with a large order for refuse vehicles from Birmingham's salvage department, and the establishment of the first factory in Landor Street when an Electricars employee, Charles Pedley, moved to the salvage department at nearby Montague Street in 1924 where he remained for the duration of Electricars' existence.

In 1926 a range of 1-, 2½-, 4- and 5-ton designs was offered and by the end of the decade the firm had expanded into nearby Lawley Street. Not only dustcarts were built, but also electric lorries. Large users included Midland Counties Dairy with several depots scattered through the Black Country as well as Birmingham itself. Davenports Brewery used 2-ton lorries as did the Birmingham Co-operative Society in 1933, some lasting until 1969. Ten Acres & Stirchley Co-operative Society, covering south west Birmingham, began dairy horse replacement with two Electricars in the 1930s. Thereafter they standardised on Morrison chassis only. Birmingham Co-operative Society and its descendants almost exclusively used Morrisons.

In 1935 Electricars merged with A E Morrison & Sons of Leicester and two other companies to form Associated Electric Vehicle Manufacturers, a much bigger and more powerful player. Lighter models were discontinued in favour of Morrison designs.

By 1939 the works had moved again, to a larger site in the Birmingham suburb of Hall Green, and Electricars collaborated with Scammell of Watford to build electric mechanical horses (q.v.) which were mainly used in refuse disposal, the City of Westminster being a large user. Their trailers were built by Eagle (q.v.) of Warwick. The brand name of Electricars was last used in this year. From 1941 chassis produced at Hall Green bore the Morrison-Electricar marque.

The last heavy vehicles made were DV4 dustcarts for Birmingham. After 1944 other commercial vehicles were built at Leicester by Morrison. The Electricar name was revived in 1983 by M and M Electric Vehicles, which acquired the remnants of the original business, by then called Crompton Electricars. Harbilt and FMW were added in 1989 and all subsequent marketing was done under the Electricar name. **RFdeB**

Ellis, Jesse, & Co. Ltd, Maidstone, Kent were steam wagon builders between 1897 and 1907. Jesse Ellis was an inventive agricultural and haulage contractor, financially backed by Aveling & Porter (q.v.), owning over forty of their engines, and in partnership with one of the Fremlin brewing family. Most of the 45 wagons built by Ellis were overtype. They incorporated such safety features as pump and injector water feed and double safety valves. Some Ellis wagons were exported and others went to Fremlins Brewery, before a decline in contracting work brought the firm into receivership in 1907, although Ellis continued in business, but not as a wagon builder.

RAS/RWK

Whitehead (1992); *VCVM*, 41 (September/October 1992), p. 112.

Enthusiasts' and fan clubs are a late-twentieth century phenomenon now recognised by hauliers for their public relations value. The pioneer and largest is the Eddie Stobart Fan Club, with a membership in the tens of thousands. Other popular operator's clubs include those of James Irlam, Norbert Dentressangle, Pulleyn Transport and Stan Robinson. All provide fleet details, newsletters or magazines, memorabilia and web sites. Eddie Stobart, the leader in merchandising, advertises over 40 liveried models and toys, others offer limited editions. **GM**

Environmental issues. The government issued in 1999 a long-term strategy for freight in the UK, that aimed to promote a competitive and efficient distribution sector to support future economic growth, while minimising the effects on society and the environment. Heavy-goods traffic had increased by 14 per cent during the 1990s, 85 per cent of that load being carried by vehicles of over 25 tonnes gross weight. The strategy sought to stem the extent to which lorry movements increased with economic growth, by improving efficiency, making the most of rail, shipping and inland waterways, and improving the interchange links between the different types of transport.

The Road Board emphasised, in its first report of 1910–11, the need to reduce costs and alleviate 'the intolerable and injurious nuisance arising from mud and dust'. An estate agent had described to the Royal Commission on Motor Cars, in 1906, how such clouds of dust made the herbage along lengths of the London to Bath Road absolutely useless for feeding cattle and haymaking. It was impossible to sell or let some houses. The Royal Commission regarded the possibility of 'dustless' cars as a chimera. The solution was dustless roads. The Road Board investigated allegations that the residues of tar from newly-surfaced roads were polluting nearby watercourses, destroying valuable fisheries.

While it was known that asphaltic bitumen, derived from imported natural bitumen, had no polluting effect, the priority was to develop a relatively safe formulation of the obtained as a by-product from town gasworks. From trials supported by the British Road Tar Association and undertaken by the Alresford Station, it was confirmed in 1933 that there was no significant risk to neighbouring watercourses from a new dressing, Brotox.

Buchanan's commissioned report for the Minister of Transport, *Traffic in towns,* provided graphic illustrations of the intrusiveness of heavy goods vehicles in towns.

A further critique was offered by the Civic Trust in 1970, following Ministry of Transport proposals to increase the permitted maximum weight and size of lorries. Some 750 local amenity societies argued that the heaviest commercial traffic be confined to designated routes and prevented from entering residential streets, town centres, conservation areas and minor rural roads. Industry emphasised that the key to road haulage was its availability – there were few streets and lanes that had no demand for road goods – but the unloved lorry was increasingly perceived, in public perception, as 'a monstrous juggernaut' (q.v.). For some, it was symptomatic of the general deterioration of the environment in densely-populated Britain. A larger group resented having to share the road with large and slow-moving lorries. Ironically their greater speed in the 1980s and

1990s caused them to appear even more intimidating.

In such a context the newly-appointed Royal Commission on Environmental Pollution warned, in 1971, that it would be 'dangerously complacent' to ignore the revised forecasts of a doubling of motor vehicles by 1995, in terms of possible deterioration in air quality. By the time of the Royal Commission's eighteenth report, 25 years later, there was 'a deep and widespread concern' as to 'the unrelenting growth of transport'. The Department of Transport's most recent forecast for a doubling of road traffic between 1988 and 2025 was possibly 'the greatest environmental threat facing the United Kingdom'. Over and above the damage to the environment, there was a growing realisation that neither the existing, nor a larger, road programme could prevent congestion worsening. Solutions had to be found either through radical improvements in technology or changes in human behaviour and, most probably, through a combination of all available approaches.

Freight transport, as measured in tonne-kilometres, grew broadly in line with the economy. That growth arose not so much from the total weight of goods carried, as from the distance over which they were moved. Since 1983, it had been almost entirely due to road transport. Increasingly worried by the prospect of tighter environmental controls, the Freight Transport Association (q.v.) and Road Haulage Association (q.v.) commissioned in 1975 *Living with the lorry. A study of goods vehicles in the environment.* The report by an economist, Clifford Sharp, emphasised how environmental benefits, like any other 'good', had to be considered in relation to the costs of production. The possibility of a 'trade off' had to be explored. An 'optimum' technology would take account of such factors as fuel consumption, vehicle maintenance and wages, and of the social or external costs, such as those of noise, air pollution, accidents and road wear. A Committee appointed by the Minister for Science in 1963, identified road traffic as the principal cause of noise in London and other cities. The effects of exhaust emissions on personal wellbeing were less serious, and

more easily remedied. There was no technological problem in keeping smoke emission down to an acceptable level. Solutions had, however, to be sought over a much larger canvas, in that roads carried more than lorry traffic, and there were alternative modes of goods transport. While there were instances where further road-building and improvement should be limited because of damage to the environment, Sharp contended it was false reasoning to regard every deferment, or rejection, of such works as a triumph for the environment. A by-pass might bring immediate and much needed relief to many towns and villages.

Although the volume and nature of freight transport might be largely unavoidable in a consumer society, the Royal Commission of 1994 pressed for the transfer of as much as possible to rail and water, which were not only preferable on environmental grounds, but had capacity for additional freight traffic.

A measure of the concern felt by the Royal Commission was its decision to review developments in 1996, two years after its previous report. Within the freight sector, it noted how certain 6-axle vehicles had been allowed since 1994 to operate at up to 44 tonnes, when carrying containers, or 'swapbodies', in combined road-rail operations. That consent was extended in 1997 to lorries engaged in piggyback (q.v.) road/rail operation. Whilst welcoming that more integrated approach to transport policy, the Commission warned that 'the trend towards heavier goods vehicles is inconsistent with the objective of reducing the dominance of lorries in order to improve the quality of life'. The solution must ultimately be one of reducing traffic intensity. The Commission's report cited how, whilst there had been little change in the volume of food transport over 15 years, it was carried some 50 per cent further around the UK, largely as a consequence of the centralised distribution system of supermarkets and just-in-time deliveries. Food transport constituted over a quarter of the distance travelled by heavy-goods vehicles, more than for any other major commodity group. It was in this context that a Queen's Award for Environmental Achievement was given, in 2000, for the adoption of a re-usable transport packaging system, which represented a saving of over 50 per cent in space and vehicle journeys in the supply of Britain's largest chain of supermarkets.

By the early 1980s concerns were growing about potential harmful effects from vehicle exhausts. With petrol engines the main concern was over the addition of lead to the fuel and its use was phased out in the late 1990s. With diesel engines there was a reduction in the sulphur content of derv. Diesel had been regarded as 'cleaner' but concerns had arisen over the particulates found in the exhaust gases: these are minute particles formed during combustion. Also emitted are hydrocarbons, which consist of mainly unburnt fuel, and carbon monoxide, which is a colourless gas which is toxic. By the late 1980s fitment of special filters could remove 80 per cent of particulates, over 60 per cent of hydrocarbons and half the carbon monoxide.

Lower noise and emission levels became a major concern of the EC. Beginning with Euro 1 and progressing through Euro 2, emission requirements reached yet more stringent standards with Euro 3, which was current by the beginning of the 21st century. Euro 2 in 1996 had also more than halved maximum permitted noise levels. Each step involved engine and vehicle manufacturers in huge research projects and resultant costs, added to the complexity of engine and vehicle design, and in some cases worsened fuel consumption.

Environmental concerns of a different kind have also been reflected in bodywork specifications and the early 1990s saw varied approaches. York produced a box-van semi-trailer with a softwood floor instead of the usual hardwood, to reduce the requirement for felling hardwood trees. A whole host of special features was incorporated on a few vehicles for the Post Office, all liveried in green to emphasise their credentials. The largest was a Leyland-DAF FTG 95 three-axle artic with three-axle Cartwright semi-trailer. Features included a low-noise engine, air suspension, electronic tyre pressure monitors, catalytic exhaust system, aerodynamic skirts, automatic weighing of each axle and energy-absorbing rear bumper.

On new refrigerated vehicles the refrigerant has been changed, while Safeway commissioned a refrigerated semi-trailer with roof-mounted solar panels to recharge the batteries powering the fridge unit. Safeway has also been a pioneer in the use of gas-powered vehicles (see ALTERNATIVE FUELS). **JS**

B Bryant, *Twyford Down: roads, campaigning and environmental law* (Spon, 1996); Colin D Buchanan, *Mixed Blessing: the motor in Britain* (Leonard Hill, 1958); Civic Trust, *Heavy Lorries* (Civic Trust, 1970); J C Haller, 'Roads and road transport,' *Journal of the Institute of Transport*, 2, (1921), pp. 156–64; B de Hamel, *Roads and the Environment* (HMSO, 1976); Minister of Transport, *Traffic in Towns* (HMSO, 1963); Road Board, *First report* (HMSO, 1911), pp. 6–7; Royal Commission on Environmental Pollution, *First Report* (HMSO, 1971, Cmnd 4585); *Eighteenth Report: Transport and the Environment* (HMSO, 1994, Cm 2674); *Twentieth Report: Transport and the Environment – developments since 1994* (Stationery Office 1997, CM 3752); Royal Commission on Motor Cars (1906); C Sharp (1973); John Sheail, *Rural Conservation in Inter-war Britain* (Oxford, University Press, 1981), pp. 212–23; John Sheail, 'Road surfacing and the threat to inland fisheries', *JTH*, 12 (1991), pp. 135–47; J A Thomas, 'Can ecologists recreate habitats and restore ancient species?' in T C Smout (ed.), *Nature, Landscape and People since the Second World War* (East Linton: Tuckwell, 2002), pp. 150–60; C Williams-Ellis, *Roads in the Landscape* (HMSO, 1967)

ERF Ltd (Figures 17, 21, 22, 44, and 182) lorry manufacturer, was founded as E R Foden Ltd in 1933, E R being Edwin Richard (1870–1950), the fourth child of Edwin Foden (1841–1911), the founder of the Foden family concern. In his youth Edwin Richard made significant contributions to the development of the Foden range of overtype steam wagons, but as he approached retirement in 1932 he was convinced of the need for the firm to change over to diesel models and impatient at its reluctance to do so. After retirement Edwin, together with his son Dennis and a handful of others, developed a 'light oiler', a robust, Gardner-engined lorry, notable at the time for its use of bought-in, rather than in-house-manufactured, components. A third chassis was exhibited at the 1933 Commercial Vehicle Show. It was largely designed by Ernest Sherratt, another ex-Foden engineer. Edwin had concluded that 'the maximum load carrying capacity wagon to sell in any quantity must have an unladen weight of under four tons' and he began production in that taxation class. It had a Gardner 4LW engine, David Brown 4-speed gearbox and Kirkstall axles. Brakes were of the then new vacuum hydraulic type. Production started in a workshop rented from Jennings of Sandbach (q.v.), a company acquired by ERF in the early 1970s.

ERF introduced an 8-wheel lorry at the end of 1934, and a 6-wheel and a tractive unit in 1935. Orders were received from major operators such as Reliance Tankers and Beresford, Caddy & Pemberton of Tunstall, as well as from small hauliers. ERF output rose from 96 vehicles per annum in 1934 to around 400 by the Second World War. Wartime production at this level was permitted for military and essential civilian users, but it dropped to below 250 per annum towards the end of the war, as the result of materials shortages. Post-war production resumed with pre-war types, but in 1948 a new model with a more rounded front was introduced. This incorporated a stronger chassis and the Eaton 2-speed axle of 1946 and could be supplied with a curved dash-plate, which facilitated choice in bodybuilding. More radical changes came in 1956 with the KV (Kleer View) model, with a cab designed by Gerald Broadbent. Although the Gardner 6LX engine of 1958 worked well in the KV, customers were given engine options from 1958 and the ERF/Cummins combination dates from this time. A semi-forward control rigid version was introduced, popularly known as the 'Sabrina', and ERF annual production reached 500 in 1959/60. Significant post-war customers of ERF included Rugby Portland Cement, the Co-operative Wholesale Society and Wincanton Transport (q.v.) (from the mid-1970s).

Following the death of Edwin in 1950, Dennis became chairman and ERF went public in 1954. Dennis died in 1960 and was succeeded as managing director by his half-brother, Peter Foden, then aged only 30, who remained in that post until 1996. In 1970 Peter Foden tried to acquire Atkinson, but was foiled by a higher bid from Seddon. ERF's own independence was under threat from its debt burden in the recession of the early 1980s, but the support of Barclays Bank ensured ERF's independence into the second half of the 1990s. In 1996 the board decided that to survive the company had to be stronger financially and agreed to merge with Canadian manufacturer, Western Star, a company similar to ERF. Western Star was controlled by Terry Peabody who held 42 per cent of its shares. Less than four years later he sold ERF to the German manufacturer, MAN for over £110 million, a profit of £70 million. At the same time he sold Western Star to Freightliner in the USA which was a subsidiary of Daimler-Chrysler. Plans for a new assembly plant at Wrexham were abandoned in 1981 and a subsequent agreement with Hino (q.v.) to produce a range of smaller vehicles using some Japanese components was similarly shelved. ERF moved to a new assembly plant at Middlewich and began assembling Isuzu trucks which had previously been assembled at the Leyland factory. The lighter EP range continued to be imported from BMC in Turkey and ERF production of Commander-derived tractive units for Western Star's Antipodean market continued. Within two years MAN reported serious financial problems at ERF and manufacture of ERF trucks at Middlewich ceased in 2002.   **RAS**

Kennett (1978); *The ERF Story (Commercial Motor* for ERF, 1989); *Portrait of a Pioneer* ([ERF Ltd], undated); *CM* (17 February 2000), p. 15; J Semple, 'ERF-shaker', *Truck* (March 1997), pp. 50–2; 'ERF works', *Truck* (October 2000), pp. 44–9; *Truck* (April 2002), pp. 9, 15, 18–23; *MT* (4 April 2002) letter from Peter Foden

Ewer, George, & Co. Ltd is best known as the operator of Grey-Green Coaches from Stamford Hill, north London, but Charles George Ewer began in 1885 by hiring out handcarts to local tradesmen in Spitalfields. The family business acquired its first motor vehicles in 1919 in the form of Dennis lorries, convertible to passenger-carrying at weekends. From 1922 Fords were chosen for lorries, supplemented by two Leyland and three Dennis lorries in 1925. Ford remained the preferred choice for the van-hire fleets, typified by 18

Thames Traders with pantechnicon bodies operated in the early 1960s. Typical clients were the small clothing and furniture manufacturers of east London. Morris-Commercials and Bedfords were also operated, including a Bedford SB8, rebuilt from an accident-damaged coach. On a different scale five Scammell Routeman 8-wheel tankers were acquired in 1960/1 to operate on long-term contract to Shell for the delivery of heating oil from wharves to large institutions. In 1980 Ewer's successful car dealerships prompted a bid from T Cowie Ltd, the northern car dealers. In the same year Grey-Green van hire and haulage terminated. **RAS**

K Bateman and O Woodliffe, *The Grey-Green Story* (Harrow Weald: Capital Transport Publishing, 1986)

Exceptional loads, see ABNORMAL LOADS

Exel Logistics was the brand name adopted by NFC plc in 1989 for its new Logistics Division, comprising the SPD Group Ltd (q.v.), which was renamed Exel Logistics Ltd, and the Contract Services division of National Carriers Ltd (q.v.). It grew fast, partly through acquisition of subsidiaries in Europe, North America and the Far East, and profits rose steadily from £29m on a turnover of £339m in 1989 to £65m on a turnover of £718m in 1993, despite the recession. It was described as the jewel in the NFC crown.

In 1999 Exel set up two joint ventures. One, called Joint Retail Logistics (q.v.), was in partnership with the Tibbett & Britten Group (q.v.) to deliver Marks & Spencer merchandise through the UK. The other was in alliance with Rover Ltd, the car manufacturer then of Cowley, Oxford, to collect components from suppliers and ensure their timely and correctly-sequenced delivery to the assembly line via an 'integrated logistics centre' using Jungheinrich tractors towing containers on bogies.

Exel plc was the name chosen in 2000 for the company which emerged from the merger between Ocean Group plc and NFC plc. Ocean had strengths in moving freight between countries while NFC excelled in moving it within countries, so the merger was promoted as one of complementary businesses to create a truly global group. Prior to the merger Ocean had used the brand name MSAS (MacGregor Swire Air Services) for collection and delivery of its air freight business. **RAS/JA**

Metro (22 February 2000), p. 36; *Evening Standard* (21 February 2000); *Rover Oxford* (Oxford: the company, 1999); *CM* (20 May 1999), pp. 8–10

Express carriers, see PARCELS SERVICES

Express Motor & Body Works Ltd, of Clerkenwell, then Great Cambridge Road, Enfield, was the engineering and bodybuilding subsidiary of Carter Paterson & Co. (q.v.) and became the maintenance centre for the combined Pickfords and Carter Paterson fleet. It developed in the course of the 1920s. Express also acted as commercial body builders for a wider clientele, exhibiting at the Commercial Motor Show (q.v.) and advertising in the trade press. During the Second World War Express produced Halifax bomber parts. It lost its separate existence as a result of nationalisation, when it was sold to J B Osler & Partners, Osler having been until 1938 CP's chief engineer. Only the haulage part of the business was taken into public ownership, the maintenance and engineering side was outside the act. **RAS**

Allan (1946): unnumbered plate.

F

Falkland Services was established in 1952, when A T Marriott of Sheffield, a successful motor trader, sold an Armstrong-Siddeley car to Robert Jenkins of Rotherham. The two men realised they had a further business link. Marriott was considering diversifying into haulage, while Jenkins, a director of the eponymous engineering concern, had goods to transport throughout the country. So Marriott operated one lorry, probably an Albion, from premises adjacent to his home in Bridport Road, in the industrial east end of Sheffield.

Marriott was an 'A' licence (q.v.) operator and the firm expanded until five or six vehicles were on the road. The business of Robert Jenkins was highly valued, but Marriott carried for others as well, including Direct Motor Services of Petre Street, Sheffield, which is probably better remembered as Sheffield Haulage and Storage Ltd. In 1961 Marriott acquired another small haulage business in Sheffield known as Falkland Services, because the proprietor lived on Falkland Road in the Ecclesall area of Sheffield. Marriott liked the name and adopted it for the combined business. The Bridport Road premises were large enough to absorb the expansion.

In the 1960s a further haulage business was acquired and incorporated into Falkland Services. Involving around four lorries, it was based in Derbyshire and worked for Staveley Chemicals. In 1966 Mike Marriott, the son of the founder, joined Falkland and ran it for the remainder of its lifetime. It expanded slowly at first and then during the 1970s grew to more than 20 lorries. The fleet was mainly 4- and 6-wheel rigids, but some articulated lorries entered service in later years. The livery was maroon for many years, but changed later to blue and white, for what were mainly AEC and Leyland vehicles.

Much redevelopment took place in the east end of Sheffield and in 1972 the Bridport Road premises were subject to compulsory purchase.

Falkland Services occupied the Chelmsford Street site until 1986 when it was compulsorily purchased. Premises in Ecclesfield, to the north of Sheffield, had been vacated by the Shell and BP group and this became Falkland's last home. A large customer base was built up, but Robert Jenkins Ltd remained a loyal customer. Distribution of traffic for the steel stockholding firm of James Fairley Ltd was also undertaken. Falkland delivered all over Great Britain but its two specialist areas were Aberdeen, and Devon and Cornwall. It was also a specialist in 'multi drop' operations, with loads made up from a variety of smalls. It rarely sought return loads, finding it more cost effective to return empty to Sheffield. The lean trading of the early 1990s saw the fleet reduced to twelve lorries and it was deemed wise to wind up the business. Falkland Services ceased trading after 42 years. In addition to the road haulage activities the company also dealt in commercial vehicles, initially offering parts and service for Seddon Atkinson. It became an agent and distributor for this marque in the 1980s and also acquired the Nottingham dealership. These activities ceased on the winding-up. **MB**

Farmers for Action, see PROTEST MOVEMENTS

Febry, R & W, & Sons Ltd of Chipping Sodbury, Glos., became a significant west country fleet in the post-war period. The firm was founded in 1931 by Richard Febry, who had been a coal-lorry driver, and it operated 18 vehicles by 1939. Despite wartime requisitions, the fleet had grown to 22 by 1948, when it was nationalised, together with the ten vehicles of Richard Febry's brother William. For a few years the brothers turned to coaches. On partial denationalisation, the brothers returned together to road haulage, acquiring valuable A licences and a mixed fleet of vehicles from the BRS South Glos. Group. The fleet grew to 130 by 1961/2, with a tendency to standardise on Leylands. Much work was for Amalgamated Roadstone, later ARC, quarries and contracts were signed with cement producers for bulk transport. Febry invested in bulk units, both tippers and powder tanks, which operated in Aberthaw, Ketton and Tunnel Cement liveries. For a less usual contract with Ready-Mixed Concrete, Bristol, Febry provided mixer-drum vehicles; at the peak of these operations 23 Leyland 6- and 4-wheel lorries were engaged in the work. A wide variety of chassis was operated, but ERF became favoured. In the 1960s the firm had its own maintenance and bodybuilding unit. As well as contracts with the cement and concrete industries, Febry had one with the Severn Valley Brick Co. This exposure to a single sector of the economy brought problems with the decline in the construction industry in the 1980s. In their attempt to diversify into container traffic, Febrys opened a branch at Avonmouth, which eventually became their sole base. Vehicle ownership largely gave way to leasing and the business was eventually sold to the Renwick group.   **RAS**

CM (21 September 1962); A Cypher, 'Febrys remembered', *CVRTC News,* 8/2000 (November 2000)

Federal Express was formed in 1971 by Frederick W Smith and based at Memphis, Tennessee, beginning its service in 1973. It provided the first overnight air-express delivery service for packages and heavy freight to 25 cities in the US using 14 planes it owned, rather than commercial airlines. Operating as Fed-Ex it became a public company in 1978. As part of expansion into Europe, a Brussels depot was opened in 1985, the same year that Lex-Wilkinson (previously their British agent) was acquired. Despite further investment, trading conditions and the differences between handling air freight and parcels meant heavy losses and Lex-Wilkinson was closed, its hub being acquired by Lynx. Fed-Ex's main British base is at Feltham. Agents are used for British collections and deliveries.   **GM**

IDCH, 18 (1997), pp. 176-9; M Austin, 'The Wilkinson Transport finale,' *CVRTC News,* 9/10 (December 2001); A J Wright, *abc Cargo Airlines* (Shepperton: Ian Allan, 2001)

Felixstowe Docks, opened in 1886 by the Felixstowe Dock & Railway Co. (FDRC), had sunk into dereliction when acquired in 1951 for £50,000 by the East Anglian grain exporter, H Gordon Parker, who had become increasingly frustrated by the effects of the National Dock

Labour Scheme on his traffic through King's Lynn. Parker, with his colleague, Ian Trelawny, gradually turned the docks around, dredging, consolidating the surrounding site and developing new trade, notably the import of chemical solvents for the plastics industry. A subsidiary, Felixstowe Tank Developments, was formed in 1961 to handle this side of the business but the controlling interest was sold in 1975 to Tankfreight Ltd, the major road tanker operator. Other traffic of significance included cattle export and Carlsberg lager imports, both in Danish vessels, the latter giving rise to some bulk-tank road operation. From the later 1950s general freight-handling was stimulated by the introduction of pallets (q.v.) and fork-lift (q.v.) truck operation, the number of fork-lift trucks growing from eight in 1962 to more than fifty in 1975. By then container traffic had been handled for more than a decade at Felixstowe and other equipment included dock spotters, straddle carriers and straddle cranes. In 1980 independently-moving gantry cranes replaced straddle carrier operation. To permit expansion 60 acres of land was bought from the Ministry of Defence in 1971, ensuring that the 'container revolution' at Felixstowe proceeded unhindered. Rail facilities were developed for some of the new container traffic, but most was road-hauled. In 1975 the British Transport Docks Board put in a bid for the FDRC, which lacked the capital necessary for further investment in an inflationary period, but in 1976 European Ferries Ltd, which had for some years operated out of Felixstowe as Transport Ferry Services (TFS) and Townsend Thoresen, made a successful counter-bid. (TFS had already made a significant contribution to road haulage operations through Felixstowe by the introduction of roll-on, roll-off facilities in collaboration with FDRC.) Subsequently the Port of Felixstowe passed to Hutchison Whampoa. The port's success resulted from its freedom from the constraints and restrictive practices of the Dock Labour Scheme and consequent ability to mechanise handling. The Port also focussed on the growing international container business where its speed of handling and low costs attracted scheduled shipping services from other ports. Much of the growth was handled by road transport, with owner-drivers (q.v.) and small operators providing traction (q.v.). **RAS**

R Malster, *Felixstowe 1886–1986: 100 years as a working port* (Port of Felixstowe, 1986); *Felixstowe: a pictorial history* (Chichester: Phillimore, 1992)

Fiat, see IVECO

Fifth-wheel (Figure 106) was a term said to have originated in the American West, when fore-carriages of wagons and stages were so-called. It was a device to allow large wooden wagons to steer using their front wheels. On modern lorries the coupling device comprises a large, flat steel plate, its rear part ramped and divided by a large vee, to guide the trailer-attaching pin to its apex at the centre, where it is securely locked. With the growth in use of articulated vehicles (q.v.) it became the standard method of attachment between drawing-unit and semi-trailer. A major specialist manufacturer, the Davies Magnet Works Ltd, developed in Hertfordshire after the Second World War, first at Ware, then at Thundridge. It claimed to be the largest maker. By 2000 Davies' units were made by Douglas (q.v.). In the early 1960s York Trailer (q.v.) also established itself as a substantial manufacturer of fifth wheel couplings. Other makers included Crane Fruehauf (q.v.), Scammell, Taskers of Andover, Hands Trailers of Letchworth, Herts, British Trailer of Trafford Park, and Carrimore Six Wheelers of Stanley, Co. Durham. **RAS**

Rolt (1969), pp. 206–7; R Storey, 'Some aspects of transport in Ware', *Hertfordshire Past and Present*, 10 (1970), p. 46

Fish traffic (Figure 107). Transport of fresh fish over long distances became possible with the growth of the railway. Until then, inland towns had to rely on dried or salt fish. Fresh, sea fish was rarely carried further than a 10–15 miles radius of the fishing harbour. Indeed the major fishing ports, such as Fleetwood, Grimsby and Milford Haven, were largely developed by the railways, who provided fast overnight services to major markets. Delivery from the termini to the markets was for many

years the sphere for the railways' horse-drawn cartage services. In Scotland the railway carriers, such as Wordie (q.v.), collected catches after they were sold and took them to the nearest station for onward carriage. Carting nets and other gear was also a regular traffic at the larger fishing ports. The growth in use of motor transport after 1920 saw the first introduction of trunk services to carry fish to large markets. Real success came after 1934 with the introduction of the faster, smaller vehicles on pneumatic tyres able to take advantage of the 2½-ton 30-mph limit. Perhaps the biggest obstacle was the railways' attempts to prevent road trunk vehicles entering the railway-owned docks to load at the fish auctions. For example the LNER would not allow fish merchants at its Lowestoft docks to use road transport for distances over 12 miles. The legal case eventually reached the House of Lords, which ruled against the railway.

Operators, such as Charles Alexander, serving the Aberdeen area, using mostly Leyland flats, established overnight trunk services serving Manchester, Birmingham, Bristol and Billingsgate, with changeover points for drivers, or, for Manchester traffic, shunters. Manchester was particularly important until the 1930s as much of the fish supplied by the CWS to retail co-operatives went through there. Fred Cook, serving Hull, commenced his service by transferring the consignments outside the dock area and, having a shorter trunk to Billingsgate, could use heavier Armstrong-Saurer vans, despite the 20 mph restriction. The railway retained much fish traffic from Humber ports, Aberdeen, Fleetwood and Milford Haven, providing fast overnight services, although Marstons Road Service/Edward Box also had an overnight trunk service from Milford Haven to Billingsgate.

Billingsgate Market in Lower Thames Street was originally served by river, but by the early twentieth century cart delivery from London main line termini had become the principal mode of delivery. Numerous retail businesses were established in the vicinity and much street congestion was experienced even before road haulage with direct delivery superseded rail in the 1960s and 1970s. A lorry park created in 1940 was only a temporary palliative. Handling at Billingsgate was manual, with barrows, limited in size by City of London bye-laws, porters' trolleys and head-carriage on 'bobbin' hats. Upgrading Lower Thames Street resulted in the move of Billingsgate Market to North Quay, West India Dock in 1982.

The war saw much fish traffic restored to the railways. The return to peace saw growth of the road services, with Alexander, Cook and other operators introducing larger vehicles. Most Scottish vehicles, including Alexander's, carried a tow bar under the platform in case of a problem, so that progress could be made towards the market or nearest assistance. It was rare for a load to be transhipped. Alexander re-started at de-nationalisation in 1955 and quickly built the service, greatly assisted by a fortuitous rail strike. While the police might take an interest in their speed, to the end Alexander and other fish lorries were not stopped at a Ministry check. It was recognised that the nature of the traffic required high standards of maintenance, but also to get under the vehicle to check could mean a shower from the smelly, melting ice. Alexander was acquired by Transport Development Group in 1960, itself acquiring Rae Fish Transport serving the south west and Milford Haven Transport in early 1989 and integrating TDG's Link Fish Transport, Grimsby, into the Alexander network. Competition for the diminishing traffic to fewer fish markets caused TDG to close Alexander in 1991 despite their investment in refrigerated vehicles. Other Scottish fish specialists who successfully changed to handling chilled or frozen fish were Catto, Dyce, retiring in 1995, and Gibbs of Fraserburgh, which became primarily a meat transporter and closed in 2002. When BR ended their involvement with fish traffic in 1965, the Grimsby Wholesale Fish Merchants Association turned to BRS as their main transport operator. BRS introduced a fleet of Guy Big J articulated vans to some 30 depots and BMC FG or Terrier sided-lorries to the markets or other drops. This continued into the 1980s. The Fleetwood merchants chose to operate their own fleet. The growth of salmon

farming particularly in the Highlands and Islands, has brought a new traffic joining the catches of Scottish fish, crabs and lobsters, farmed fresh or frozen salmon out and their feed inwards. Currently much of the restricted British catches particularly from Scottish and West Country harbours, is exported, with most carried by transport operators, increasingly European-based, rather than own account fleets. An exception is the well-known fleet of W Stevenson & Sons Ltd, Newlyn, Penzance, who although using sub-contracted transport, also send their own refrigerated vehicles to the continent. The one-time famed AEC Mammoth Major refrigerated vans introduced by Sutton, from 1961 saw the transfer of the London fish traffic from BR to their new service. **GM**

Fisher Renwick Ltd was formed in 1874, becoming a large north-eastern shipowner, and was controlled by four generations of Renwicks. The opening of the Manchester Ship Canal led to George Renwick starting what became Fisher Renwick Manchester–London Steamers Ltd. The first sailing, on 3 December 1892, was from the temporary dock at Saltport, transferring to its wharf at Pomona Dock at the completion of the Canal in 1904. The London wharf was always at Shadwell Basin.

Major Gustav Renwick, a son of George Renwick, observed the French use of Knox tractors for tank transport, and became friendly with Colonel Alfred Scammell. Major Renwick received severe injuries in action on the western front in 1917. After recovery and demobilisation he returned in charge of the Manchester end of the steamer service.

He introduced the use of Ford T and war surplus Peerless lorries for local work. Contractors had previously carried out this work. He also purchased four of the first Scammell articulated lorries himself, operating as Fisher Renwick Transport from Pomona and Shadwell for local and direct services, using the steamers' facilities. This followed the demonstration of the first Scammell prototype, which pulled a 6-ton drawbar trailer, a type of operation stopped by the 1922 regulations.

His operation was successful, including the first non-stop London–Manchester overnight journey. A fifth Scammell was added with additional carriers (trailers), including cable floats. Fisher Renwick Transport became an integral part of the steamer operation in 1922. Fleet expansion followed with Scammell's updated heavier versions increasingly providing a complementary, faster direct service for more urgent traffic. They were first to introduce driver change-over in 1934, generally at Meriden, ending their drivers' nights out. The road 'Continuous Service' became a major reason for the steamer operation becoming un-competitive.

Major Renwick became a director of Scammell Lorries Ltd in late 1926, and was deputy chairman at the take-over by Leyland in 1955. The introduction of Scammell's Rigid Eight chassis which were to include the Luton bodied 'Showboats' led to the steamer service being sold to Coast Lines in 1938. This meant new depots. The first was opened at White City in 1940, Old Trafford was completed in 1940, that at Muswell Hill not until mid-1942.

Fisher Renwick maintained their Continuous Service throughout the Second World War, latterly as part of the Road Haulage Organ-isation, with most depots becoming RHO units. Major acquisitions provided Liverpool and Scottish direct services.

Fisher Renwick were a voluntary acquisition in 1949. This was not the end, for Renwicks entered into contract hire as Fisher Renwick Contract Services supplying fleets to famous businesses such as Brillo, Crosby Doors and Firestone. Again depots were required and existing garages were purchased at Hendon, and Didsbury in Manchester. Expansion and the requirements of the 1968 Transport Act led to new purpose-built workshops at Park Royal and Dukinfield.

Ironically, the existence of these purpose-built depots and the quality of Fisher Renwick Services, now operating 600 vehicles, caused Ryder (q.v.) to acquire various businesses except for the car distributors and dealerships. In 1972 Fisher Renwick ceased to be a transport firm. **GM**

Mustoe (1997)

Flagging out derived from the maritime practice of using flags of convenience for the operation of vessels. It came into general use in road haulage in 1998–9, as UK hauliers' dissatisfaction with government policy grew and registration of vehicles abroad was seen as a possible way of avoiding UK excise duty. A Transport Tribunal decision early in 2001 established the illegality of such a move in a case involving Irish-registered vehicles of Reeds Transport Co. Ltd of Ayrshire. The ruling held that an O licence obtained in Great Britain involved an obligation to comply in every respect with its laws. Those operators with depots and vehicles based abroad for undertaking haulage outside Great Britain, to which the term flagging out had been loosely applied, were not affected by this ruling. **RAS**

Truck (April 2001), p. 8; *CM* (15 July 1999), pp. 4, 11; *CM* (9 March 2000), pp. 23–6

Fleet numbering. This article illustrates methods whereby commercial vehicle operators identified the vehicles in their fleets, such identification being in the form of a fleet or stock number.

Fleet numbers are in basically two formats, numbers only or, much less common, letters and numbers. Pickfords (q.v.), a nationwide business, has always used a numerical system, commencing with 1 upwards but preceded by the letter M to indicate motor vehicle or PM to signify an item of mobile plant such as a crane. This, the first series, reached 9999 about 1957 when vehicles then in service and subsequent new or acquired stock were renumbered into a new series, commencing again at 1 but at the same time, the meat haulage fleet under the Hay's Wharf (q.v.) Cartage banner was numbered into a separate series prefixed with the letter X. A new series commenced in 1978 but this time starting at M2000 and has currently reached about 7000. The associated Carter Paterson fleet was also originally numbered from 1 upwards but to avoid confusion between the individual operators' vehicles employed on the Pickfords and Carter Paterson's parcels service, the CP fleet numbers had 10000 added, so that vehicle number 3000, for example, became 13000.

Brewery companies have identified their vehicles in different fleet number formats, one such operator being Whitbread. Initially, vehicles bore a number in a progressive numerical series but shortly after the Second World War, a letter and number format was introduced. This comprised a series commencing with 1 upwards for each chassis make, irrespective of body style, and prefixed by one or two letters. For example, A was used for Albion, Ae for AEC, At for Atkinson, D for Dennis, H for the Dennis Horla articulated outfit, S for Seddon and T for Thornycroft. In more recent times, fleet numbers have continued to be in a letter and number format but with the numbers being in a progressive numerical series, commencing with 1000 and currently reaching in excess of 8000 for all vehicles in the Whitbread Group.

Petroleum companies were another group of operators which identified their vehicles by fleet numbers. For example, the distribution fleet of Shell Mex & BP Group had fleet numbers comprising five figures, the first two digits indicating the vehicle type and the last three digits being progressive. For example 57019 was the nineteenth example of the three-axle Foden tractor unit, whereas the 49xxx series were applied to ERFs and the 75xxx series indicated Atkinsons. Previous to the current system, no fleet numbers were carried at all for a period but prior to that, the vehicles carried a letter and number scheme but with the letter or letters as a suffix, the letters again indicating the make and/or type of vehicle. During the Second World War, deliveries of petrol and diesel fuel were controlled by the government under the auspices of the Pool Petroleum Board (q.v.). All petroleum companies' vehicles were requisitioned, painted grey and allocated numbers prefixed by the letters PB or in the case of vehicles owned by the Anglo American Oil Company (Esso), the letters AA. In most cases the number portion coincided with the numbers carried by the original operator although new vehicles acquired during the war began a new numbering series of their own, such as International two-axle tankers which were 2201

onwards and Atkinson four-axle tankers commencing from 2601 onwards.

The TM Fairclough Group, which included subsidiary company Dawsons and the associated E R Ives Ltd, employed an interesting fleet numbering system where again, each chassis make was allocated a letter code. For example, FODE was an obvious choice for the Foden marque, whereas BED was visible on Bedfords and the non-logical letter E was allocated to Leylands. Vehicles owned by Dawsons were prefixed with a D, that is D.FODE 4 whereas Ives' lorries were prefixed G, that is G.FODE 2, the numbers not being repeated by a change of the single letter prefix. On the other hand, Fairclough's vehicles did not have the operator prefix.

Matthews & Co. Ltd, the meat hauliers, used a numerical system but this progressed in fives. For example, vehicle 980 was followed by vehicle 985 and then by 990 and so on. This is the only known example of such a system. J Reece Ltd (q.v.) also used a progressive numerical system but with a certain amount of 'gap filling', whilst the Davis Group (q.v.) of companies used a number system applied progressively irrespective of which company in the group the vehicle operated for.

These are only a few examples of the varied fleet numbering systems employed in the road haulage industry. Now, most operators which apply fleet numbers to their vehicles use numerical systems and the interesting variations which were once used are no longer in evidence. Some firms used names on their fleet, for example Fisher Renwick (q.v.) called their lorries after birds and Eddie Stobart used female names. **MD**

Paget-Tomlinson (1990), p.127

A **float** has a narrow body that sits between the wheels to produce a low-floored vehicle — even lower if the axle is cranked. It was originally introduced in the mid-nineteenth century as a 2- or 4-wheeled special vehicle for carrying difficult loads such as steel plates or crates of glass on edge. There were also floats specifically for livestock traffic (q.v.). In the twentieth century float bodies were fitted to both steam wagons, for example by Naylor & Co. of Hereford in 1906, and motor lorries.

The smaller 2-wheeled float used by farmers as a combined passenger and goods vehicle for attending markets and by dairymen and other tradesmen as a delivery vehicle seems to have come into use in the 1890s. Its low floor, usually entered from the rear via a step, made it a convenient vehicle for loading the larger milk churns in use at that date and for frequent alighting to make house-to-house deliveries.

GAB

Smith (1994); Russell (1995)

Flower traffic. Cut flowers have been transported by road for many years, certainly since before the Second World War. Often they comprised part of a general load of fruit and vegetables (q.v.) and, thus carried, overcame an official ban on their transport in the Second World War. Until the 1930s spring flowers from Cornwall and the Scilly Isles were brought to London's Covent Garden via the GWR; but then London & Southern Counties, known by its slogan as 'Spans the South' (q.v.) started running AEC Mandators, which were capable of carrying eight to ten tons, with loads of only two to two and a half tons. As a result they could make fast trips of between nine and ten hours, much quicker than the railway, and hence captured the traffic. Also in the 1930s flowers picked in Lincolnshire could be delivered to London's Covent Garden in five to six hours by road.

In the 1990s big increases in sales prompted mainly by the supermarkets saw the build of dedicated vehicles and trailers. Dutch flower growers in particular made daily deliveries with their own vehicles to the UK, often direct to individual retail outlets. Bodywork on these was often of the multi-compartment type with access by numerous side doors.

The need for longer shelf life before sale prompted the development of specialised trailers able not only to keep flowers cool in summer but also to maintain a reasonable temperature inside when it was freezing outside. Ventilation also needed to be controlled. There was also brief enthusiasm for trailer bodywork with provision for injection of an inert gas which could prolong the freshness of the flowers and which would also slow down the ripening process in certain fruits such as strawberries.

GM/JMA

OCBRH; Murphy (1968); Allan (1946), pp. 163–5

Fodens Ltd (Figures 1, 8, 17, 23, 25, 36, 45, 47, 49, 53, 59, 65, 90–1, 108, 143, 145, 158 and 174). Edwin Foden (1841–1911) produced his first steam traction engine in 1882 in Sandbach, Cheshire, which remained the home of the firm until the 1990s. The first steam lorry was made in 1900 and it was not until 1932 that production finally ceased. In 1902 the famous 5-ton lorry was first made, continuing in production until 1923. It was an overtype model with the cylinders and engine mounted on top of the boiler. The driver stood between chassis members and the steerer stood or sat outside, often using a fairing mounted on the nearside. In 1920 an improved 6-ton version appeared with many changes including a full-width open cab for two. During the 1920s taxation and other restrictions made steam lorries increasingly uncompetitive with petrol-engined vehicles. In 1930 Fodens moved into production of diesel lorries. The first model, of 6 tons, appeared in 1931. It was fitted with a Gardner engine, starting a long association with this supplier. A smaller, less remembered model in the early 1930s was a 3-ton 4-wheeler with Gardner 3LW engine, a 3-cylinder unit, and a 4-tonner with Austin 6-cylinder petrol engine.

Up to 1939 Foden produced a range of forward-control diesel-engined lorries from 4-ton 4-wheelers to 15-ton payload 8-wheelers, all having a distinctive radiator grille in an otherwise conventional design. It also manufactured diesel-powered timber tractors, and produced a 6-wheel timber carriage of 4 tons 8 cwt unladen weight with an oscillating rear bogie, for use with the timber tractor. During the Second World War 1750 vehicles were made for the War Department as well as 770 tanks and shells.

Civilian production re-started after the war with pre-war designs but soon the cab was redesigned with a modern curved front and the radiator blending into the outline. In 1946 the Steel Company of Wales ordered a large-capacity tipper lorry. This was the first of many large dump trucks that were subsequently made. At the time it was considered huge but has been dwarfed by more recent examples. Also in 1948 Foden introduced its revolutionary two-stroke diesel engine which was further developed and stayed in production until 1977: previously Foden had bought all its engines from outside suppliers. In 1956 power-assisted steering was introduced and in 1958 the first lorries with glass reinforced plastic-panelled cabs were offered. In 1960 the design was modified to allow the cab to be tilted forward, giving unobstructed access to the engine and other mechanical components. In 1968 some half-cab models mounted low on the chassis were made for fitting cranes and also for the movement of long structural girders.

In 1974 a new factory allowed production to increase to 6000 units annually. This brought financial pressures on the company that were only relieved by a large order for NATO. A world slump in demand brought economic problems. In 1977 new Fleetmaster and Haulmaster models with steel tilt-cabs were introduced. The Fleetmaster had either a Cummins or Rolls-Royce engine of 190 bhp, the Haulmaster 265 bhp Cummins, Gardner or Rolls-Royce engines. From 1979 both models were available, with a glass-fibre and aluminium cab.

1980 was a bad year with deep financial troubles again and this time a receiver was called in. The American Paccar company eventually took control of Foden in 1982. A new company, Sandbach Engineering Co., was set up though the Foden name still appeared on its vehicles. Just before the take-over the new S10 series was introduced and these have been updated since and the more recent 3000 and 4000 models were developed from them. Improvements were made in small steps, interior cab design and suspension was tackled, a wider engine choice introduced, and a major improvement in build quality resulted in a well-engineered product.

Chassis design advanced in the 1990s. Wheelbases could be specified in one inch increments by customers. The choice of drive-train was almost unlimited with fourteen options available, by Cummins, Perkins, Caterpillar and Gardner, matched to no fewer than twenty gearbox options. There was also a choice of axles and suspension could be by conventional springs, air or rubber. The Kenworth torsion bar suspension was available as was their multi-leaf rear spring design.

The policy of building to a customer's individual requirements with a wide range of components and equipment available is common in the USA but rare in the UK. Staff numbers fell to around 450, compared to some 3000 in the pre-Paccar days. The range now includes 6- and 8-wheel rigid chassis and 4×2, 6×2 and 6×4 tractor units with 6- or 9-speed gearboxes. An example of the custom-built vehicles of the recent past was the order for 71 KW C500 6×4 38 tonne tractor units for Shell which had steel reinforced cabs, Eaton drive axles, Cummins engines, Spicer gearboxes and Skidcheck anti-locking gear. They were not produced as a single run, but as and when called for by the customer. Following Paccar's purchase of DAF and Leyland in the late 1990s, vehicle production moved to the Leyland plant in Lancashire.

Paccar's acquisition of Foden led to other makes also being assembled from time to time. In 1986 and again in 1993 batches of Kenworths were built, the 1993 ones being 6×4 tractors for Israel. Between 1980 and 1983 Ford Transcontinentals were built, at a guaranteed rate of at least two a working day, after Ford closed its Amsterdam assembly plant. **GK**

Stevens-Stratten (1993); Paul Barden, 'Foden: A Family Affair', *Truck* (December 1986); Kennett (1978); Seth-Smith (1975); *Foden Society Newsletter*, 13, pp. 16–19

Ford (Figures 24 and 109) introduced its first commercial vehicles into Britain in 1912, offering the T car chassis for use with various bodies. Their reputation in the First World War caused them to become used by all types of operator. The first Ford TT one-ton chassis was assembled at the Trafford Park plant in 1918. Many firms began supplying conversion kits and modified chassis for heavier loads. In 1927 the Ford AA one-ton and 30-cwt chassis replaced the T. The BB, normal-control 2- and 3-ton chassis, retained the A 24 hp engine. The demand for Ford products led to the move to the new factory at Dagenham in 1931. The Fordson (used from 1933 to 1939) BBX forward-control chassis was the first to have longitudinal front springing, and was available from 1935 with a V8 engine. A normal-control Model 51 chassis was also produced. Besides a 10-cwt van, a 5-cwt van based on the Y model car became the basis for the unsuccessful Tug unit, intended for 3-ton trailers from 1935 to 1937. The A had been supplied with a six-wheel conversion by County Cars Ltd (q.v.). This was followed at County by the normal-control Surrey (6×2) and Sussex (6×4) conversions. The Fordson 7V forward-control chassis was introduced in 1937, 2- to 5-ton models and 6-ton six-wheel versions were listed. The E38 purpose-designed 10-cwt van was introduced in 1938, the E denoting English manufacture. The Sussex 6×4 version became the basis for RAF balloon-winch units. From 1939 to 1957 the commercial range was known as Fordson Thames. Beside the wide variety of military models built during the Second World War, many civil type 7V chassis were produced for the Auxiliary Fire Service, Ministry of Supply and essential users and also E38 vans.

A new forward-control range of chassis replaced the 7V range in 1949, the ET6 with the V8 petrol engine and the ET7 with a Perkins diesel engine. The County conversions continued to be listed. The Ford Cost Cutter diesel engine was first produced in 1953, becoming the 4D engine in 1954. The semi-forward-control Thames Trader series was introduced in 1962, with six models from 1½- to 7-ton payloads and a 13½-ton gross vehicle weight articulated unit. The Trader II versions increased the capacity to 7½ tons and the tractor unit to 17 tons gross vehicle weight. The County and special conversions by Vickers-AWD were also available. The Thames ET chassis continued as the Ford K model, now with the Cologne (Köln) built cab. The car-derived vans changed after the war,

with the Thames 100E 5-cwt Anglia-based and the 7-cwt Prefect-based vans. The E38 van was replaced by the forward-control 10- to 15-cwt Thames van in 1957 using the Consul drive line, a Perkins diesel option was available from 1962. Following the new 105E Anglia car in 1959, the Ford Thames 307E vans was introduced in 1961. The Ford Thames name was used from 1957 to 1965. From 1965 Ford was used with the model name. Production of Ford commercial vehicles transferred to Langley, Bucks, in 1960. This was to release space at Dagenham for growing car output and to provide more competitive production methods for a larger range of vans. The introduction of the first Transit van in 1965 was followed by the replacement of the Thames Trader range by the D chassis. The D forward-control range had tilt cabs and improved hydraulic braking, enabling Ford to compete in the 9-ton payload category for rigids. By 1972 low-loading rigid and articulated versions on 17-inch wheels were available and new heavy-duty drivelines enabled the heaviest models to be 24 ton gross vehicle weight 6×4 chassis. The K range ceased in 1972. The Transit van range, introduced in 1965, was built in a new factory at Southampton from 1971. The new Cargo range replaced the D series in 1981 eventually offering tractor units up to 38 tons gross vehicle weight. Ford introduced the H series Transcontinental model in 1975, to compete in the heavy duty 44 tons gross vehicle weight market. These used a modified Berliet (q.v.) cab, Cummins engines and Fuller gearboxes and were assembled at Ford's Amsterdam factory. After problems, the Transcontinental became highly regarded. In 1980 production was transferred to Paccar's (q.v.) Sandbach Engineering site and sub-contracted to Foden under a three-year contract with a commitment by Ford for a minimum production requirement. The site had better quality spares capacity. The decision had already been made to stop production, the last models were produced in 1982. Ford's Langley division and Iveco (q.v.) merged as Iveco Ford Trucks Ltd in 1986. The merger followed some poor years for sales of Ford trucks with the UK truck market declining. Ford claimed to have

1138 truck franchises in the UK in 1981, but two years after the Iveco merger the number had fallen to 577. Between 1991 and 1993 a new range was produced from 6-tonne to 44-tonne gross weight. The Langley assembly plant was closed in 1997, all Iveco Fords subsequently being imported from Italy. **GM**

Fordson. Commercial vehicles were always part of Ford's production programme, until the 1980s merger with Iveco (q.v.). From 1933 Ford began badging some of its commercials as Fordson: all carried that name from 1935. In 1939 medium and larger vehicles were given Thames badges but officially called Fordson Thames and after the Second World War this became the official maker's name. From 1957 to 1965 they became Ford Thames, but in 1965 a third change returned to the Ford name for all vehicles. The use of names other than Ford was said to be to distinguish between British-built models exported and models sourced from elsewhere. **JMA**
See also FORD

Fork-lift trucks are inseparable from modern distribution operation: loading and unloading vehicles and warehouse movements at the volume and speed required would be unrealisable without them. One forerunner of the fork-lift truck was the works truck (q.v.) with elevating platform. Hiscox stressed the value of the 'lever platform truck' as early as 1921. The main impetus to the introduction and manufacture of fork-lift trucks in the UK came from their employment here during the Second World War by the American services. The fork-lift truck, battery-electric, particularly for indoor use, or petrol- or diesel-engined, then increasingly became a feature of material handling and a variety of UK manufacturers appeared (such as Boss, Conveyancer, Coventry Climax, Matbro), and in some cases disappeared, sometimes losing their separate identity through merger, in the post-war period. Further developments towards the end of the century extended the concept of the fork-lift truck: the lorry-mounted fork-lift, the telescope truck and the heavy-duty fork-lift truck.

Two early forms of UK fork-lift truck were the Ransomes electric tiering truck and Wingrove & Rogers Ltd (BEV) high lift truck. The essential features of the fork-lift truck, the pallet-engaging prongs or forks which can be raised far higher than the limited lifting capacity of the elevating platform truck, were by 1943 fully recognisable.

In the early post-war period two directors of a newly-revived engineering company, Lansing Bagnall Ltd, made a fact-finding visit to the United States and in 1946 secured agreement with the Baker Raulang Co. of Cleveland as sole concessionaires for Baker electric fork-lift trucks. This provided a useful trading base whilst Lansing Bagnall developed its own pallet trucks. Demand for its new model P came to replace that for conventional platform trucks and variants with hydraulically-actuated lifting forks and telescopic tilting masts followed, before the Rapide series of substantial fork-lift trucks. In 1949 Lansing Bagnall moved from Isleworth to a new factory at Basingstoke and became a market leader. The company was restructured in 1966 with the formation of the Lansing Bagnall Group Ltd, of which a subsidiary was Fork Lift Rentals Ltd. In 1986 Lansing Henley, as it had become, was acquired by the German materials handling specialist Linde AG. In 2000 Linde, entered into a marketing deal with Komatsu Forklift of Japan. Internationalisation is a feature of the fork-lift industry. In 2000 the Finnish group Partek Cargotec, which owned Hiab lorry-mounted cranes (q.v.) and the Finnish heavy-truck manufacturer Sisu, added Moffett of Ireland to Princeton Piggyback in the USA and the Dutch firm Kooi. The Moffett-Mounty, devised by Robert Moffett as part of the range of his family's agricultural engineering business in County Monaghan, went into production in 1986, increasing from 15 units in the first year to hundreds as a successful sales campaign took off. The Moffett-Mounty and Kooi are lightweight models that are carried on the back of a rigid or trailer and demounted when needed by the driver for unloading all or part of the load without other help at the delivery point..

The telescope fork-lift truck is a development by JCB Industrial Products of JCB's wheel-digger/loader with telescopic arm for agricultural and construction industry use. The heavy-duty fork-lift truck, especially in the form of the container-handling fork-lift, evolved to meet the needs of international container transport at the port-shore and rail-road interfaces. Typical manufacturers of this type of equipment, which is essentially the conventional fork-lift truck on a large scale, include Boss (formerly Lancer Boss), Caterpillar, Hyster and Kalmar which owned Coventry Climax. In addition to manufacture, the hiring of fork-lift trucks became a major activity: by the end of 1999 Lex Harvey, after 25 years in business, had 12,000 trucks on hire or rental.

The side loader is a specific variation of the forklift mainly used in the sawn timber industry from the late 1960s. It is a platform truck about 15 ft by 8 ft with the cab set centrally to one side and an extending forklift mechanism set into the deck. It could be drawn up beside a vehicle or stack of timber, the forklift then extending from the side of the truck to pick up the timber. The fork is then retracted and the pack of timber placed on the deck of the truck. By the mid-1970s most major timber yards and builders merchants used them as did some steel stockists and tube works. **RAS**

W J Hiscox, *Factory Administration in Practice* (Pitman, 1921); H Pynegar (ed), *Mechanical Handling Yearbook and Manual* (Paul Elek, 1943); Anglo-American Council on Productivity, *Freight Handling: report of a specialist team which visited the United States of America in 1950* (AACP, 1951); British Transport Commission, *Freight Transport. Equipment used by British Railways and British Road Services* (undated: 1958?); British Transport Commission, *Mechanical Handling Equipment in British Transport* (undated); L T C Rolt, *Lansing Bagnall: the first twenty-one years at Basingstoke* (the firm, 1970); B Johnson, *Classic Plant Machinery* (Boxtree, 1998), esp. ch. 4; H J Sheryn, *An Illustrated History of Fork-lift Trucks* (Shepperton: Ian Allan, 2000); *Evening Standard* (21 December 1999)

Forward control (Figures 110 and 146). Most early vehicles were of normal control layout, with the engine ahead of the driver, though Karrier favoured forward-control for a period before the First World War. Forward control, now almost universal, puts the engine mainly beneath the driver to produce a more manoeuvrable and compact vehicle, or one with a longer loadspace, something that became important with the imposition of restrictive length limits. A half-way house is semi-forward control, where the engine projects partly forward of the cab under a short bonnet, with the back part of the engine intruding into the cab (q.v.).

By the early 1930s most production for the home market from the makers of heavier (and more expensive) trucks was of forward control layout, which at that time meant the driver was partly alongside the engine rather than above it. In the lower price, medium-weight field from manufacturers such as Bedford, Commer and Dodge, (as well as imported US makes such as Diamond T or Reo) only normal control layout was offered. The exception was Ford from 1937 with its 7V, also unusual in having a V8 engine. More surprisingly, Ford (or Thames as it then was) replaced the 7V in 1949 with a bonneted range. Not until the Thames Trader in 1957 did the maker return to forward control. Probably the most significant change came in 1950 from the largest volume truck builder, Bedford, with its forward-control S series, launched as the Big Bedford, with capacities up to 7 tons. Bedford had previously produced one forward-control model, the wartime four-wheel drive QL, built for the military in large numbers. **JMA**

The Foster Committee was set up in 1977. It met on 64 occasions and received written evidence from 196 individuals and organisations and oral from 50. This Independent Committee of Inquiry into Road Haulage Operators' Licensing was chaired by Professor Christopher Foster and reported in 1978 with 44 major and 47 minor recommendations, the report running to 162 pages. These were principally aimed at tightening up the O licensing system, which had been in place since 1968, by increasing enforcement activity against illegally operated and unsafe vehicles and giving greater powers to the licensing authorities (later called traffic commissioners (q.v.) to penalise errant licence holders. **DL**

Christopher D Foster, *Road Haulage Operators' Licensing: report of the independent committee of inquiry,* (HMSO, 1978)

Four-in-Line (Figure 111) was a name given to a particular layout of wheels and axle and also the name adopted by one semi-trailer builder which specialised in this configuration. The normal practice with a trailer was to have a single conventional axle with twin wheels and tyres at each side. The four in line spread the tyres and wheels equally along the axle, thus giving each tyre and wheel a more even share of the load carried. Tyre life could also be improved, it was claimed, partly because the layout eliminated the possibility of debris or a brick becoming trapped between twin tyres, as often happened with lorries on construction sites. The unladen weight was higher and changing a tyre on either of the inner wheels more difficult. When plating and testing legislation was introduced a single four-in-line axle was allowed to carry an extra ton. Several makers offered the layout for a time, but British Trailer Company made this feature a strong selling point and probably built more trailers to this configuration than other makers. **JMA**

Four Wheel Drive Motors Ltd came between the First World War Model B 4×4 truck of the Four Wheel Drive Auto Co. of Wisconsin and the AEC Matador 4×4 of 1938, which played a significant role in the Second World War and afterwards in civilian recovery and timber work. The American Model B was launched in 1912 and 3000 came to the UK for military use in the First World War. The British government's licence to produce the FWD as the British Quad was acquired by a company which was eventually based at Slough, building and rebuilding FWD vehicles. Close relations were developed with AEC and AEC components were utilised in FWD production. Four Wheel Drive Motors were incorporated in

1929 and in 1930 new products adopted the Hardy trade name for FWD road vehicles to avoid confusion with the US company. This name was chosen because an associated company, Hardy Rail Motors, during the 1920s converted FWDs to rail-going vehicles. Development work continued, including in-service trials of the R.6.8 commercial chassis, but in 1932 FWD's financial situation brought an end to independent production, AEC taking over the company, producing and marketing the 4×4s under the Hardy badge until the launch of the Matador. **RAS**

S W Stevens-Stratten, *AEC Trucks in Camera* (Shepperton: Ian Allan, 1984); B H Vanderveen; 'FWD', *OM*, 8, 3 (May/June 1974), pp. 220–9; FWD and Hardy minute books in Modern Records Centre, University of Warwick Library, MSS. 226/FW, MSS. 226/HA

Fowler, John, & Co. (Leeds) Ltd were principally known as makers of steam ploughing sets and heavy haulage engines from 1856. Fowler was noted for heavy haulage steam engines, examples of which served with such operators as Norman Box, the London Traction Haulage Co., MRS Ltd, Pickfords and E W Rudd. Some road engines were equipped with front-mounted cranes. Fowler went on to produce diesel engines from 1931 to 1935. Powered by their own engines, Fowler diesel lorries were over-engineered and correspondingly expensive, and had major problems in service, so production was short-lived, amounting to about 25 units. Operators included R V Morris Ltd, which ran a London to Norwich service, Commercial Roadways Ltd and Union Cartage, which acquired surplus tractor chassis that it fitted with Gardner engines. Fowler continued as producers of heavy-tracked tractors. **RWK/RAS**

CVRTC News, 1/98; Lane (1980); Nick Baldwin, 'Fowler oil-engined lorries' *OM*, 11, 5, pp. 366–76; Mc Taggart (1989)

Frameless tankers. Scammell introduced the frameless articulated road tanker in 1924 as an important weight-saving innovation. Road wheels and turntable coupling device, mudguards and other equipment were fixed to the tank itself, the front end of which was raised at about ten degrees. Shell-Mex was the first customer, but frameless tankers were subsequently used for a variety of liquids, including beer, milk and molasses. Scammell's largest supplier of frameless tankers was Thompson Bros of Bilston from the 1920s to the late 1950s.   **RAS**

Georgano (1997)

Francis, N, & Co. Ltd, parcels carriers. After the Second World War, London's commerce was close knit. There were lots of small shops: supermarkets did not exist and while the chains like Marks & Spencer and Woolworth existed, even their stores were small by comparison with today. Their delivery requirements were largely met by common carriers. One company dominated Greater London, Francis of Dalston.

The firm originated with a specialist piano business, which diversified into more general operations in the early 1920s. It head-hunted a manager from City & Suburban who brought a large client list and built on that. The operation was very slick. Shops ordered today from wholesalers who had a regular contracted call from Francis late afternoon whose vans brought the packages back to Dalston. Overnight sorting was undertaken and at 7 am drivers loaded their vans and started deliveries as soon as premises opened. At least 95 per cent next day delivery was normal. There was no perishable traffic and little house delivery as the distinction between wholesale and retail was virtually complete.

The area served was 'Greater London' within a 25-mile radius of the base. Francis were therefore not nationalised in 1948. BRS Parcels was no competition as it was heavily unionised and flabby. Francis worked from its base in Parkholme Road, Dalston. The vehicles were 2-ton diesel normal-control Fords. Bodywork was aluminium framed and panelled, with a Luton top and roller shutter (q.v.) at rear for access. Livery was plain dark green, later blue, lettered 'N. Francis Ltd – Parcels Carriers' in white.

There were about 65 routes, five of which were within the Square Mile. Thus mileages were low. The workshops were in Cremer Street, Shoreditch, the original base. Drivers stayed on regular routes. They were very hard working. 200-plus parcels and 50 or more deliveries were normal. Paperwork was all hand-written on large sheets. Valuable items, primarily the easily pilferable, such as nylons and chewing gum, were carried under a system of 'Specials' like Post Office registered traffic.

It was the best sort of family firm. Before the war drivers were paid a little more than the going rate and there was a small contributory pension. A day off for family funerals without loss of pay was in marked contrast to most employers. These conditions produced a loyalty and camaraderie. The founding family of Gozee, Shoreditch publicans, retired in the 1950s and a Glaswegian Scots accountant, William S McKay, led the compact administration. There was a traffic department, accounts and claims plus the engineers. When McKay retired in 1960 the company with 97 vehicles was sold to BRS. The market was changing: traffic congestion hampered operations. The altered patterns of manufacturing, of commerce, of distribution, and of shopping removed the world which Francis had served for nearly fifty years.   **TP**

Freight Rover was established in 1981 as the division of British Leyland responsible for the manufacture of the Sherpa van, which had been introduced in 1974. The name was retained after Leyland DAF Ltd was formed in 1987, changing to Leyland DAF Vans in 1989. From the Sherpa, which in 1989 became the 200 and 400 series, were developed the more sophisticated LDV (q.v.) Pilot and Convoy ranges of 1996.   **RAS**

The **Freight Transport Association** reflects two main influences in its history. First, the domination of goods transport by the railway companies and the resulting need for an effective voice for the rail freight customer. Secondly, the effects of the development of the internal combustion engine on haulage.

The date of birth which the Association officially recognises is 26 July 1889. It was on that day that the Lord Mayor of London called together companies and local authorities throughout the land to consider how best they might defend themselves against the power of the railways, and the Mansion House Association (q.v.) on Railway & Canal Traffic for the United Kingdom came into being. It remained in existence until 1969, the last five years under its new title the National Traders Traffic Association (q.v.).

On 3 November 1903 an exploratory meeting was held to consider the setting up of the Motor Van, Wagon & Omnibus Owners and Users Association. The Association was duly formed and four years later it changed its name to the Commercial Motor Users Association – the CMUA (q.v.). It remained in existence until 1944. It is interesting to speculate upon the shape and power of the commercial road lobby today if all parties had remained together in one organisation, but that was not to be.

During the years leading to the Second World War it became increasingly obvious that each of the three sections of the CMUA, the hauliers, the own account operators and the passenger transport operators were anxious to secure their own identity. In particular the own account traders (the C licence operators) wanted to ensure exemption from the restrictive measures which were being mooted for the haulage industry. In 1938 a conference of C licence holders had resolved that 'Traders shall have unfettered choice of the type of transport used to carry their goods and unfettered rights to carry their own goods in their own vehicles, anywhere'.

So at the end of the war the three sections went their separate ways as the Road Haulage Association (q.v.) Passenger Vehicle Operators Association and the Traders Road Transport Association. The TRTA settled down to the task of representing and protecting the freedom of choice of the own account operator of which, in 1949 there were 351,000. Meanwhile the MHA continued its role as the mouthpiece for the freight transport user, to be joined in that task by yet another body, the Traders Co-ordinating Committee on Transport (TCC). With many major companies being members of two, if not all three organisations, not surprisingly there was growing pressure to rationalise the situation and on 1 January 1969 the TRTA, NTTA and the TCC joined together to form the Freight Transport Association. Ten years later the British Shippers Council, representing the users of sea and air transport, became part of the FTA, creating one organisation covering the total freight transport interests of British trade and industry.

In 2000 the FTA had over 10,000 members, employed 360 staff and had an annual turnover in excess of £15 million. It had offices in England, Scotland, Wales, Northern Ireland and Brussels and an extensive and much admired portfolio of member services. It then represented both the transport operator and the transport user. From time to time it was suggested that the FTA and Road Haulage Association (q.v.) might merge, but the smaller hauliers, who dominated the RHA, saw the FTA as comprising its competitors – the large hauliers – and its customers, and were afraid of losing their separate identity. **GT**

Freightliners Ltd was created under the powers of the Transport Act 1968 as one of the subsidiaries of the new National Freight Corporation (q.v.) and on 1 January 1969 took over the network of Freightliner container services that had been built up by British Railways since 1965. BR was allowed to retain a 49 per cent interest. The concept of high-speed (75 mph) 'liner trains' dedicated to the transport of containers began with the London–Glasgow Condor service introduced in 1959 and the London–Manchester Speedfreight service of 1963. It was seen as a way of exploiting the economies of full-train operation for wagon- or lorry-size consignments, but the rail–road transfer costs at terminals proved to be a significant extra burden. The launch of Freightliner services also coincided with the increase in maximum gross vehicle weight from 24 to 32 tons and with the early years of the motorway construction programme. The minimum distance at which they could compete with throughout-road transport was thus higher than expected — 150–200 miles — and its share of the domestic freight market much lower than forecast in the 'Beeching' Report (*The Reshaping of British Railways,* 1963). The early years were also hampered by opposition from the National Union of Railwaymen to 'open terminals' (allowing road hauliers to collect and deliver the containers), which was not resolved until 1967. BRS's use of Freightliner services for containerised parcels was similarly delayed by the Transport & General Workers' Union.

Freightliner had been designed around the dimensions of the new international standard (ISO) containers. From 1968, as container ships began to replace cargo liners, its disappointing share of the domestic freight market was offset by the movement of maritime containers to and from container ports, particularly Southampton, Tilbury, Felixstowe and Liverpool. Freightliner was able to capture a large share of this market, because rail-road transfer costs were only incurred at one end of the journey. In 1969 its network had grown to 140 trains per day serving 33 terminals, with one of the largest fleets of articulated vehicles at that time for collection and delivery of containers and shorter–distance trunk hauls.

Freightliners Ltd was returned to BR ownership in 1978, initially retaining its autonomy. It was absorbed into Railfreight Distribution in 1988, but re-established as Freightliner (1995) Ltd in preparation for privatisation. It had suffered a decline during the uncertainties of impending privatisation, but recovered strongly following a management buy-out in May 1996, aided by the 44-tonne weight limit (q.v.) allowed for combined transport. A record number of containers being carried in 2000: over one million 20-ft equivalent units. In 1999 the company began to diversify into conventional trainload freight operation. The privatised company was at first called Freightliners Ltd, but was renamed Freightliner Ltd in 1997. Its road fleet in 2000 was down to 200 tractors and 400 trailers. **GAB**

M R Bonavia, *The Organisation of British Railways* (1971); T R Gourvish, *British Railways: a business history 1948–73* (1986) pp. 491–3, 544–7; Collins (1991); *OCBRH*; National Freight Corporation, *Reports and Accounts,* 1969–77; *Freightliner Yearbook,* 2000

Fruit and vegetable traffic (Figure 112) Growers, merchants and retailers were among the earliest users of mechanical road transport. Until 1914 this was usually as a replacement for horses, extending growers' access to merchants. Generally it was deliveries to the railway station or to a wholesale market or from the railway to market, or to the retailer. Imports followed a similar pattern, only local or short distance traffic going by road.

From 1919 there was rapid development in longer-distance haulage of produce. Strikes on the railways led to road offering an alternative, able to demonstrate the benefits for market deliveries. Not least were the freshness of the produce and greater flexibility in loading time, which was helpful with the vagaries of weather when picking, compared with the fixed departure times for rail. The growers also benefited by motor transport opening new markets. This particularly applied to fruit and vegetables with short seasons such as peas, spring cabbage, soft fruits and some top fruits e.g. cherries. The wholesalers in the large provincial markets in England and Wales extended their areas for deliveries to retailers, helping to raise the prices received for better quality, which was possible by less handling and shorter time delays. Glasgow market was a notable exception, deliveries to retailers not collecting their own supplies were by carriers, each wholesaler having regulars, and for the Greater Glasgow area, the Carriers Quarters dealt with individual localities. The higher legal speed limits of 1934 saw the introduction of nightly services from the major growing areas, Evesham, Kent, the Fens, Lancashire and Yorkshire, to major markets as far as Glasgow using smaller, faster vehicles with up to 5-ton payloads. The capacity of the vehicles could be limited by the type of produce carried. Heights and weights varied according to seasons and loads. Produce in crates could be stacked up to eight feet high in most cases and could be roped, often with corner boards. Some covered markets had entrances which restricted the height of the load. Many hauliers and merchants used slat-sided vehicles. These gave security for a varied load of crates, nets and punnets or chips, which were unsuitable for roping.

Methods of packing and packaging were quite different from today's non-returnable boxes or paper sacks. Weights too were different. Bushel or two-bushel crates were used for apples, peas were in 20 lb muslin nets or bags. Cabbages were packed in 40 lb crates or bags depending on the market and growing area. Beans were in 40 lb bags. Roots, carrots, parsnips, turnips and swedes were in 56 lb sacks. Main crop 'ware' potatoes were in 1 cwt sacks, the first new potatoes in 56 lb barrels, then 46 lbs sacks. Soft fruit was in punnets or chips. Generally these were not stacked above three high, and if wet were not covered to reduce the danger of heating up, causing mould. Fisher Renwick had a long-standing contract to deliver Kent strawberries in season for Marks & Spencer stores as far as Scotland, a light load for a rigid-eight van. Bouts/Holdsworth & Hanson group also handled considerable quantities of home-grown and imported produce for the northwest. Bouts had contracts for Lea Valley tomatoes. Most imports for provincial markets were handled directly from London docks or Covent Garden, some as return loads through agents, some by hauliers who specialised in this traffic, e.g. Bowker. Generally vegetables were not sheeted, even in rain, though in the winter if there was a possibility of frost during the journey, a sheet covered the front and top, but not the sides. Potatoes had a covering of straw on the bed, and between layers, and under the top sheet to reduce any frost damage. Flowers were also a specialist traffic. Before 1939, the railways retained much of this traffic partly due to the low weight per box, making it suitable traffic for special passenger traffic. The Second World War saw an increase in the use of road transport, particularly by wholesalers and grower merchants, caused by the need for supplies of homegrown produce for industrial areas and military camps and the difficulties encountered by the overstretched railways.

The railways continued carrying their Fens potato and roots traffic, because of the long established merchants' stores at Kings Cross and St Pancras. The growth of canteens and school meals needed arrangements for regular supplies. Licences to purchase vehicles for this category of user were granted, as were fuel allocations. From the beginning of the War wholesalers organised zoned or pooled deliveries, retaining their own vehicles or placing them into a central pool, appointing a controller or manager. Strict attention was also paid to the return of empty sacks and boxes. Reject egg crates and beer bottle crates were repaired and proved suitable substitutes for some produce. The Ministry of Food introduced price controls applying to the grower, wholesaler and retailer. One effect of this was that a one-cwt sack of potatoes was allowed to contain up to 6 lb of earth and stones (for picking in wet weather) and this became the norm. There was zoning of root crops, particularly potatoes, e.g. the Fens supplied potatoes to the Midlands and London. Generally controls were accepted and worked, but a ban on transporting flowers by both road and rail was evaded or ignored, resulting in official acceptance that flowers were essential for civilian morale and their transport was allowed. By 1946 the principal growing areas had hauliers providing nightly services as required to the main markets. At nationalisation some areas, notably Kent, the Fens and the Vale of Evesham, had all their hauliers working beyond the 25 miles radius acquired. This led to a considerable increase in C licences. At denationalisation units specialising in this traffic were almost without exception among the disposals. The introduction of containerisation and palletisation, with changes in the Construction & Use Regulations combined to change the pattern of the trade and vehicles used. Curtain-siders have become widely used. Much of the Port of London traffic now comes into Sheerness docks, requiring heavy investment in cool stores. This coincided with the development of supermarkets and the use of regional distribution depots. Grower-merchants also started their own packing stations and trunking directly to regional distribution centres, cutting out markets. This was encouraged by the EEC regulations requirement to fast-chill produce before distribution, requiring the use of temperature-controlled transport. The growth of supermarkets also reduced the number of general stores and greengrocers and saw fewer or smaller wholesale markets. The EEC, now a source of much of our fruit and vegetable supplies, requires refrigerated transport, with foreign hauliers carrying much of the traffic.

The forty years from 1960 to 2000 marked the greatest change in produce handling. In the early 1960s, the last of the companies which operated as a clearing house for returning empty packaging to growers ceased trading. Lightweight non-returnable boxes remained but cardboard became almost universal. Palletisation on a world-wide basis became the norm. A traditional box of apples from South Africa was handled manually 36 times before it reached the shop. Once palletised the total handlings were reduced to 12. Latterly, returnable containers, in washable plastics, have reappeared in response to environmental demands.

In 1960, the import market was dominated by marketing boards, whose merchandise went first across London markets to establish price levels. To match them, co-operatives of English growers came into being, Home Grown Fruits at Faversham being the largest. In 1965 the first container ship appeared and within five years most of the traditional ships and their companies had disappeared. European produce, traditionally carried by ship or rail increasingly travelled in through lorries which reduced transit time and handling and improved quality. The traditional ports, led by the Port of London, rarely touched produce. Fast palletised or containerised ships with turnrounds measured in hours not days discharged their UK segment in a morning in specialised facilities like Sheerness.

Through this period, the traditional markets diminished in volume and importance with the growth of direct delivery to the supermarket chains. When it opened in 1972 New Covent Garden was far too large for its volume. Other markets moved and rebuilt to operate more efficiently and to handle larger modern vehicles but all suffered a similar fate.

The traditional flat bed lorry with a high headboard disappeared. Louis Reece (q.v.) introduced the first-ever Boalloy curtainsided vehicle in 1968 and they became universal throughout the trade until demands for higher standards and European regulations led to full refrigeration even for citrus produce. International deliveries are often made direct into the reception facilities of the supermarket chains, where the cargo is mixed with other merchandise and delivered to store level.

GM/TP

Fuel supplies. In the earliest days petrol – then known as motor spirit – was sold in 2-gallon cans by chemists, ironmongers and blacksmiths. Vehicles expecting to cover any distance carried cans with them, usually on trays fitted beneath the chassis. Fisher Renwick (q.v.) trailers had a standard fitment of a fuel tank underneath, for use by the drawing vehicle. Even in the late 1940s trunk vehicles of J Lyons & Co (q.v.) still carried cans of fuel, plus water and lubricating oil, in case of problems on the road. Thomas Tilling (q.v.) claimed to be the first operator to have a bulk supply at a depot, when in 1905 it installed four petrol tanks with a total capacity of 1000 gallons at its Bull Yard, Peckham, premises.

The concept of the public petrol station was slow to be established and in the early 1920s in response to members' requests the Automobile Association (q.v.) opened its own filling station at Dunchurch on the A45 to provide a facility on an important trunk road where there had been none. Early petrol pumps were hand operated, quite heavy to work and only delivered a small quantity at a time. The gradual introduction of electric pumps (which were universal by the 1960s) made refuelling much quicker, and more profitable for the filling station owner.

Fuel and water supplies were a different problem with steamers. Typically they had a water tank with a capacity of 150 gallons sufficient for 20–25 miles running, and a bunker with a capacity of 4 cwt of coal or coke, sufficient for 50–60 miles. Water was not too difficult to obtain from hydrants in cities such as Liverpool, or (illegally) from fire pumps. When in 1917 Allen Knight & Co (Linthwaite) was contracted to move a 60-ton mill engine from Cornwall to Yeadon (near Leeds) it needed five motor wagons, all 5-ton Foden steamers. Each carried 15 tons of Welsh coal and 120 gallons of oil, as well as a quantity of spares. At the end of the first day of the outward journey, one Foden deposited its load of coal and oil, the process being repeated at the end of each day from another Foden, with the fifth steamer having sufficient coal to fuel all five – by then loaded – on the first leg of the return journey.

The number of petrol stations gradually rose with the growth in car usage, but the diesel engine initially caused problems: widespread availability of the fuel at filling stations did not come until the 1960s, and even then often consisted of just one pump at the back. Larger fuel tanks on vehicles was one answer. Pickfords' (q.v.) vehicles had tanks on both sides of the chassis, while Fisher & Ludlow vehicles had tanks carrying a sufficient supply for 500 miles. The economy of a diesel engine helped. The largest operators of diesel vehicles installed their own derv (diesel engined road vehicles) tanks at their depots while smaller operators often came to an arrangement with one local filling station. Clearing houses (q.v.) often made a point of supplying fuel at attractive prices, and some transport cafés also had pumps. Some operators had reciprocal arrangements: membership of the Transport Association (q.v.) in its pre- and post-nationalisation forms provided a facility still widely used.

The Suez crisis of 1956 caused a rethink by many. United Carriers, for example, doubled tank capacity at each depot, while some operators bought a secondhand fuel tanker to enable them to move supplies between depots.

The subsequent introduction of agency cards, initially by the major fuel companies, proved an attraction to many and cards which could be specific to one vehicle or one driver cut down on potential fiddles. Cards eliminated the need for operators to maintain their own tanks and they no longer needed to buy fuel in quantity in advance, assuming that the card prices were competitive. Other specialists also began to offer cards, and most provided add-on services such as analysis of fuel used per vehicle (with mpg figures) while many cards could be used in mainland Europe as well. Accounts are normally sent monthly.

The growing gulf between fuel prices in the UK and elsewhere in Europe in the 1990s led international operators to add extra tanks to their vehicles so that many can return to the UK with sufficient fuel for, say, 1,500 miles running. Vehicles makers offer optional extra or larger fuel tanks, but a specialised market has grown up for fabricators offering bespoke solutions for individual chassis.   **GM/JMA**
See also STEAM ROAD TRACTORS AND LORRIES and PETROLEUM TRANSPORT

Furniture removals, see REMOVALS

Furniture traffic (Figure 113) The high capacity van, both the pantechnicon (q.v.) generally called the box van, and the Luton van (q.v.) often called a furniture van, between them did more to improve the quality of life in Britain, than did the much-loved eight-wheeler (q.v.) and even more in making our way of life dependent on road transport. They started to make their presence felt in the early 1930s and immediately after the Second World War were the most numerous commercial vehicles on the road. While the eight-wheeler shifted the raw materials to the factories and the finished products to their end user or the docks for export, the van brought the home comforts to the High Street shops to improve the home.

Seth Smith's building of The Pantechnicon in 1830 and with it the advent of the pantechnicon van brought the idea of proper furniture removals and storage to the upper classes, those who had their furniture made by the cabinet-maker. At the other end of the social scale was simple furniture made by the local carpenter. Improvements in real incomes, materials and manufacturing techniques brought the price of furniture within the reach of a growing number, which led to factory-scale production. This in turn needed a steady supply of timber in quantity, which in the case of lower priced furniture was soft wood made to look expensive with thin veneers of more expensive wood. Thus furniture manufacturing grew in areas with easy access to imported timber in quantity. East London and Leeds were two of these, while High Wycombe expanded its already traditional industry of chair manufacture rooted in the bodgers of Burnham Beeches.

Cheap road transport just after the First World War opened up the British Isles as a market for mass-produced furniture. Furniture could be loaded into a van at the factory and delivered to the retailer without being re-handled. This had been done to a small extent with furniture being loaded into containers that were transhipped on to rail and then back on to a road vehicle. Later furniture was taken by motor to a railhead and transhipped into a specially built rail van. Both methods had a major drawback. Goods trains were made up by shunting trucks in sidings. Even with a huge amount of packing furniture did not withstand the massive deceleration experienced in shunting.

In the early 1930s vans became a common sight in High Streets. A small group of east London owner-drivers formed the Northern Motors Union, a co-operative, which specialised in connecting the manufacturers of east London with the markets of Glasgow and Edinburgh. Over the years furniture manufacture became more mechanised, producing even larger quantities, which demanded still more transport. Many larger manufacturers operated their own vans with ornate livery, which also advertised their products. At the same time specialist new furniture carriers came into being, some evolving from or in concert with embryo motor removals businesses.

In the first group came Harris Lebus, with a big fleet of vans and a vast loading bank where its own and hired transport was loaded by specialist van packers, together with Beautility, Austinsuite and Golden Key. There were Gomme and Ercol in High Wycombe and Silentnight, Sleepe'z'e and Myers in the bed and mattress industry.

In the second group, the carriers, there are too many names to mention all of them. There were many small fleets and many one-man bands. A & E Bristow, which specialised in East Anglia; Blue Bell Transport; Regal Transport; Hamilton's (Long Distance) Transport; Ralston's of Milngavie and G McIntosh, all Scots firms which specialised in that area. Wades, D & H, Alexandra, Coles of Twickenham (which went on to specialise in carrying for the film industry), G Ratcliffe Ltd (which started with a horse pantechnicon and also went into films); WT Noble Ltd; Griff Fender from Wales.

There were also large removal companies which carried new furniture as a back load or to utilise their vans when normal trade was slack. Firms such as Blatchfords and Tuckers from the West Country, Parkes of Portsmouth, Overs of Camberley, Wort & Son of Bournemouth and Poole.

During transport nationalisation there was a New Furniture Carriage Division, while Pickfords had a similar division piggy-backed on to its removal responsibility. In connection with NFCD one company worth a special mention is Deffries Transport. It was nationalised as Balls Pond Road depot. On denationalisation it was bought back by Charlie Dormer the old foreman, and operated as C E Dormer, Trnspt. As new furniture began to decline, he sold the van fleet and set up as a tanker haulier.

In the furniture field there were many small manufacturers of specialised products: kitchen cabinets, light-weight kitchen sets, cocktail cabinets, occasional tables, bookcases, folding beds (Zed Bed), folding settees (Put-u-Up). Much of the upholstered furniture, three-piece suites (known in the trade as soft suites) and easy chairs were also made by small firms. There were even two and three-man firms making ultra cheap bedroom and dining suites for the very lowest end of the market. Their output was too small to make up a full van-load so their goods were mixed into a load for the same area from a bigger firm.

The large number of high-capacity vans soon attracted the attention of the growing television industry of the 1950s because they were delivering to the High Streets and major retailers and their drivers were used to handling fragile goods. There was soon a demand either to add its products to the load or to hire complete vans to do multiple deliveries.

It became commonplace for van hauliers to load full loads from single customers, then to take them back to its depot where the van was emptied. The goods of numerous manufacturers were then mixed together and made up into van-loads for a single geographical area. This consolidation of traffic was no problem to the general goods haulier. It did however, create at least one interesting situation with an own account (q.v.) operator. Part of Lebus' fleet had been supplied by a haulier under a C Contract Licence. With the steadily growing demand for large capacity vans for all kinds of vulnerable traffic it was decided to put the whole Lebus fleet, owned and hired, on to a single A Licence (q.v.) which enabled anyone's traffic to be carried, particularly as a back load to cut down on empty running. It was to trade as Merchandise Transport and be operated by the haulier who had supplied the hired vans. This brought about one of the biggest Public Enquiries to be held by the Metropolitan Area Licensing Authority, something which is well known and documented as The Merchandise Case.

A 1600 cubic foot van could hold thirty six dining room suites (sideboard, table and four chairs) which took a full day to load. Developments with demountable bodies later allowed loading in advance, enabling vehicles and their drivers to be kept busy. White goods (cookers, fridges and freezers) were only ever very marginally involved in the van trade. One van carrier, Pitt and Scott, had a section which specialised in the carriage of Belling cookers. From the end of the Second World War it used a swap body system at Belling's works at Ponders End, now the site of Pickford's vast state-of-the-art removal warehouse.

Changing fashions in furniture, particularly the move to flat pack, did away with the biggest part of the high capacity van trade. The high capacity van of today is a 40-foot trailer delivering suites, beds and mattresses to a furniture retailer's central warehouse. The television trade has gone the same way.

Furniture Warehousemen & Removers' Association, see BRITISH ASSOCIATION OF REMOVERS

FWD, see FOUR WHEEL DRIVE MOTORS LTD

G

Gammons, Walter, pioneer freight manager, was born in Bedford in 1881, one of several sons of John Gammons, a Midland Railway employee. Completing his formal education at the age of 12, Gammons joined the staff of the Midland, at Cardington station, where his father was stationmaster. When 19 he accepted a new appointment with prospects to give wider scope to his initiative and, as it proved, skill in transport organisation. Gammons appreciated the benefits of own-account transport. When the Elstree photographic materials firm for which he was transport manager replaced part of its horse fleet by motor vehicles in 1905, Gammons deployed the motors on London delivery and return load runs, as well as local work. He had earlier persuaded the firm to establish its own transport, initially horse-drawn, to avoid the losses occasioned by indifferent railway cartage.

During the First World War he served as transport manager for a major aircraft manufacturer at Hendon, Holt Thomas, which hitherto lacked a central transport department and experienced the utmost difficulty with the Midland Railway in the supply of raw materials and delivery of products. Using his previous experience, Gammons overcame the embargo on deliveries to Hendon station because of congestion, effected substantial savings and utilised road transport where it proved more efficient.

Gammons had the foresight to leave before the Holt Thomas liquidation. In 1920 he joined the A.3 Transport Co. of Victoria Street, London, and acquired the firm the following January with the aid of a sleeping partner, renaming it W Gammons & Co., Shipping, Road & Rail Transporters. By insuring traffic at its own expense and contracting 'to pay promptly for any orders sub-let', Gammons made the exaggerated claim that he had been the first 'to visualise and regularise the clearing-house business'. The firm soon moved to Rood Lane, EC3, convenient for the foodstuffs and produce trade from the Thames docks and wharves and for the produce brokers involved. Gammons was joined by his daughter, Elsie, and son, Horace. Expansion meant a further move to Basinghall Street and the eventual opening of branches in Birmingham and Liverpool.

The addition in 1930 of a shipping department necessitated a move to larger premises in Chiswell Street, the department being registered independently as Cifco Ltd, 'the company, which specialises in CIF [cost-insurance-freight] quotations.' The business functioned by calculating the cost of delivering UK export orders to any major world port, Cifco at its own risk arranging collection and delivery to the customer, for a delivered price.

Throughout the 1920s Gammons engaged in strongly-felt and detailed discussion and controversy in the transport press on the principles of freight transport and charging, fiercely critical of the railways' attitude both to their own traffic and to their possible role in road transport. In 1921 he urged the railways to embrace containerisation, but when they did so in 1928 he accused them of window-dressing, to make it appear that the granting of road powers had enabled the railways to develop in this way. His independent stance was equally apparent in his criticism of the evidence submitted by the Long Distance Road Haulage Committee (q.v.) to the Royal Commission on Transport in 1930. **RAS**

Gammons (1931)

Gardner, L, & Sons Ltd (Figure 25) diesel engine manufacturers of Patricroft, originated in the machinist's business set up by Lawrence Gardner in Manchester in 1868. The firm began to make coal gas industrial engines in the 1880s and produced its first (marine) diesel engine in 1912. In the late 1920s Hugh Gardner, a grandson of the founder, was involved in the development of a new 6-cylinder diesel engine, which his father had initiated, with fuel injection into an open chamber in the crown of the piston. Its governed speed was not much less than that of petrol commercial vehicle engines of the period and a Leeds firm began making conversions for buses. Hugh and his brother, John, then designed the first Gardner diesel aimed specifically at the automotive market. Exhibited at the 1931 Manchester conference of the Municipal Transport & Tramways Association, it featured Gardner-designed, and made, fuel pump but with a CAV-Bosch cam-box, governor and injectors (the firm had had its own ferrous and non-ferrous foundries since 1912). Rated at just over 100 hp, it was produced, with derivatives, over 50 years. 4- and 5-cylinder versions were also built. It was the legendary economy of the Gardner engine and its ease of starting that made it so popular, aided by the level of craftsmanship and hand assembly: for example, matching individual pistons for each engine to much tighter tolerances than was practical for other engine builders who used less hand assembly, and semi-skilled rather than skilled labour for engine building. Gardner engine life was usually longer than that of rivals, and when improvements were made they were normally done so that inter-changeability was not affected.

After the Second World War, Gardner's main customers were the smaller vehicle builders including Atkinson, ERF, Foden, Guy and Seddon. Most of these also offered other engine options such as Perkins or, later, Cummins, and often charged a premium price for models fitted with Gardner engines, the price reflecting a certain amount of greed or opportunism rather than the true cost of the Gardner. Gardner also found it difficult, with its need for mainly skilled engineering staff, to meet sudden fluctuations in demand and there were periods when the company had to turn away orders. Meanwhile Cummins, after an uncertain start in the UK, developed a successful range of engines that were much lighter and rivalled the Gardner's fuel consumption.

Gardner was slow to develop more powerful engines to meet higher vehicle weights and high speed running on the new motorway network. A new generation of engines, the 6LX series followed the legendary 4LW, 5LW

and 6LW in the late 1950s: the figure in the engine nomenclature refers to the number of cylinders. Later derivatives were the 6LXB and 6LXC, the latter producing twice the output of the original 1931 6LW. An increase in cylinder bore size meant a much stiffer and fatter crankshaft could be fitted which ultimately meant that the engines could run at a faster speed than the 1700 rpm maximum, which had been a hallmark of Gardners for years. One aberration was an 8LX engine using mainly standard components: this made it much longer and caused installation difficulties with the rear of the engine projecting about 16 in (41 cm) beyond the back of the cab – a particular problem with artic tractors, which were the vehicles most needing extra power.

Rightly seeing a demand for yet more power, Gardner went on to produce an LG1200 engine in 1990, a 12.7 litre engine producing 275 bhp, though in overall size it was slightly smaller than the 6LX range. Emission controls were becoming widespread in the EC and elsewhere, and indeed the 6LXB had to cease production in 1993 as it did not meet the compulsory Euro 2 specification. Unfortunately, the easiest way to meet the ever-tightening emission requirements was to burn less fuel more efficiently by using turbocharging of much smaller engines, and Gardner had always been against turbocharging.

By the 1990s Gardner was concentrating on re-manufacturing engines. In earlier years the scrap value of a Gardner-engined truck had always been higher, because its engines could be rebuilt and reconditioned ad infinitum: many finished up in Chinese junks in Hong Kong. Hugh Gardner became company chairman in 1955, stepping down in 1975; two years later the business was sold to Hawker-Siddeley, which in turn sold it to Perkins Engines (q.v.) in 1985. Perkins later sold out to Caterpillar of America, but a management buy-out kept Gardner in Great Britain as L Gardner Group plc, producing engine components. Two main divisions are Gardner Aerospace and Gardner Automotive, and companies under their control include Gardner Parts Ltd. The Gardner Engine Forum was founded in 2000 to promote preservation and interest in the history of the Gardner engine. **RAS/JMA**

D Whitehead, *Gardners of Patricroft 1868–1968* (Newman Neame, 1968); obituary of (Joseph) Hugh Gardner, *Independent* (23 February 1989); K H Lindon, 'Only the best is good enough: the engine makers', *Precision* (Leamington Spa: Automotive Products, July 1965); Gavin Martin, 'Hugh Gardner and the transport diesel engine', *Buses* (May 1989); Geoff Burrows, 'Gardner Engines', *Classic Bus* (April–May 2001); Edge (2002)

Garford commercial vehicles were manufactured in Ohio, USA between 1909 and 1933, the range extending over time from one to ten tons (the latter an articulated unit). Garfords were extensively used in the First World War, and subsequently they and their components found their way on to the UK market. Toler Brothers, the London wholesale newsagents and contract hire specialists, are reputed to have assembled the Toler lorry for a short time after the war from Garford components; it is more likely that they applied their own badge to what was in essence a rebuilt Garford. The main UK rebuilder was E B Horne & Co. of Holloway and their work on reconditioning Garford chassis led to the Gilford marque. **RAS**

Marshall and Bishop (1979), pp. 110, 112; *Leyland Journal*, 31, 4 (July/August 1970), pp. 242–3

Garment carriage. Small quantities of clothes have been carried in gown vans (q.v.) for many years, but the hanging garment business is more recent.

Carrying hanging garments in quantity by road probably originated with multiple tailor Montague Burton, which in the 1950s used its own fleet to deliver unboxed or unwrapped suits, overcoats and raincoats. Almost all the three million suits annually produced went directly or through regional warehouses to 500 UK shops. Bodywork on vehicles and semi-trailers (Bedford-Carrimore) had a high standard of internal finish with smooth, easily cleaned surfaces and items carried on transverse, removable rails. A new Leyland articulated outfit built to the latest length limit in the 1960s could carry 4500 suits.

In the late 1930s Marks & Spencer and other large retailers had dresses and coats delivered to their stores hanging in railway containers. These were examples of road-rail-road traffic. The pioneer haulier which developed the concept more widely was Tibbett & Britten (q.v.), formed in 1958 to carry garments on hangers, and soon also to press them before delivery. Two subsequent changes in the retail clothing industry have contributed to the huge growth in the hanging garment handling business. One was the decision by Marks & Spencer, and later other groups, to devote virtually all shop space to selling, with stock held in warehouses (on which rates were lower) and then moved straight on to the sales floor. The other was the decline in the UK clothing industry with most items sourced from Eastern Europe, North Africa or even further afield. Handling garments in boxes takes up much more space and they ultimately have to be unboxed for display in the shops anyway. Distant sourcing also means that it is not practical to return goods to the manufacturer for minor faults such as missing buttons or incorrect labels to be rectified.

Some retailers developed large warehouses with mechanical conveyor systems designed to handle only clothes hung on rails, and which could be transferred to wheeled rails suitable for moving by lorry and then for display inside stores. A development of this is an automated system that virtually eliminates hand handling.

Most collecting, warehousing and ultimate delivery was by the end of the twentieth century handled by specialist transport contractors. They took summer delivery of winter clothes and stored until required. They offered computerised stock control, inspection, pressing, attachment of security tags and ticketing as well as actual delivery. Much of the work was on a low-cost basis per item: for example, in 2001 around 10p per item for changing a price tag. A spin-off was sometimes use of the same vehicle to carry cloth or buttons out to the manufacturer, returning in the same vehicle with finished goods. **JMA**

Garner Motors Ltd (Figure 26) was founded by Henry Garner, director of the Moseley Motor Works established in 1907 in Moseley, Birmingham. In 1909 he obtained exclusive Austin rights for the Midlands and bought out the Motor Works, which also made accessories including carburettors. During the First World War Garner imported the US Gramm-Bernstein trucks, which were marketed under the Garner name, with some success. Anglo-American Oil ordered 38 in 1917 and United Dairies had 80 by the end of the war. During the war Garner also imported Galloway tractors, but Fordsons' market domination brought this to an end and the Gramm-Bernstein connection continued under the Garner label. In 1920 the Garner Patent Busvan for country carriers was developed, with folding seats at the sides of the vehicle to adjust to passenger/goods requirements. In 1925 the English-manufactured Garner appeared, as a 2-ton lorry and small bus chassis, as well as specialised municipal vehicle chassis from 1923. The range included a 3-tonner, which could carry up to six tons as a tractive unit or as a 6-wheel rigid with a trailing axle. A new factory was opened at Tyseley in 1926 and forward control models were added to the range. A new private limited company, Garner Motors, was formed in 1927. Sentinel (q.v.) now began to acquire a financial interest in Garner and in 1933 Henry Garner's brother, James Parker Garner left the board and three new directors joined it from Alley & McLellan (Sentinel's parent) and Sentinel Waggon itself. J P Garner went on to found Midland Vehicles Ltd at Leamington Spa. In 1934 Garners' registered office and production moved to Shrewsbury. There followed a strange episode when Sentinel extended the range of commercial vehicles as Sentinel-Garner, but failed to market it forcefully, perhaps because it was seen as being in competition with Sentinel's steam wagons. Receivers were appointed to Garners in 1935 and Garner Motors Ltd were wound up in April 1937. However, a new company had been formed and production started, in Acton, in mid-1936 with a team of disaffected Dodge (Kew) staff. Lorries continued to be made into the early stages of the war, latterly including some 4×4 Straussler designs. A 1939 subsidiary, Garner Mobile Equipment, made trailers during the Second World War and post-war concentration was on bodywork and a lightweight tractor (1949–55). In 1956 Garner joined the bodybuilders Hawes at Sunbury, to become Hawson-Garner. Total production of Garner lorries has been guestimated at several thousand. **RAS**

Nick Baldwin, 'Garner' *OM*, 8, 5 (September/ October 1974), pp. 387–401; N Baldwin, 'Garner, a marque that vanished with hardly a trace', *VCVM*, 12 (January/February 1988), pp. 137–9, 142–3; *VCVM*, 4 (1985), p. 14; B Bell, *Fifty Years of Garden Machinery* (Ipswich: Farming Press, 1995)

Garrett, Richard, & Co. Ltd of Leiston, Suffolk, was a firm of agricultural engineers formed in 1783 and well-known later for its Suffolk Punch steam-driven tractor, portable steam engines and farm equipment. In 1904 it made its first undertype steam lorry. Examples of its Garrett Wagon six-wheeled steam lorry of the 1920s are preserved. In 1921 the company made a battery-electric vehicle and in 1928 began building trolleybuses. The only Garrett diesel-engined lorry was produced in 1930 with a Blackstone 6-cylinder engine fitted to a steam lorry chassis and cab. Steam and diesel lorries were generally used for heavy haulage of farm produce and aggregates. Alfred Manchester of Charlton in south-east London used Garretts in the 1920s and 1930s, operating a dozen in general haulage and sub-contracted to gas works for tar spraying. The firm was bought by Beyer-Peacock, railway locomotive engineers, in the 1930s and the manufacture of road vehicles phased out. **GK**

R A Whitehead, *Garretts of Leiston* (Percival Marshall, 1964); Stevens-Stratten (1993); Notes of a visit made by the Newcomen Society (1998)

Gas turbine engines made a brief, experimental appearance in UK road haulage in 1972, following the unveiling of the Leyland gas turbine at Earls Court in 1970. Leyland had tested a prototype as far back as 1954 and at the same time Rover had successfully developed a turbine-powered car, JET 1. After Rover joined Leyland in 1966 Leyland Gas Turbines Ltd was formed. At least five 6×4 tractor units were built, fitted with a cab styled by David Bache, and three went to oil companies, including Shell Mex-BP, in 1972 for operational evaluation. The engine was quiet and could be fitted with a Self-Changing Gears automatic gearbox and routine maintenance costs were predicted to be low. Although the Shell test vehicle could outperform a Scammell tanker, its fuel consumption was unacceptably high, especially in slow traffic, the gearbox gave problems and the heat exchanger, which raised the temperature of compressed air flowing into the combustion chamber, suffered from a chemical reaction between the fuel and the composition of its ceramics. In retrospect, the Leyland gas turbine would have been more suited to the higher operational weights which were subsequently permitted and to longer distance operations. In the short term the experiment came to nothing as a result of inadequate research-and-development funding and Leyland's internal politics, in the context of a world fuel crisis. Some of the trucks survive.   **RAS**

Bob Tuck, 'Whispering powerhouse', *Truck*, 25th anniversary supplement (October 1999) pp. 86–9

Gattie System. In 1919 a departmental committee of the Board of Trade assessed an elaborate transport system proposed by Alfred Warwick Gattie (1856–1926), inventor of 'co-ordinating springs' for vehicles, chairman of Gattie Springs Ltd, and a persistent self-promoter. Its essence was the establishment of distribution hubs based on specially erected rail terminals (central clearing houses) to handle all goods trains serving a particular town or district. Its justification was to minimise cross-town road traffic, especially in London. A building of several floors permitted access above rail level, with traffic stowed in containers, which was handled at the terminal by lifting machinery and continuous moving 'truckers' or electrically-driven carrying machines, with transverse transfer machinery. Traders' road vehicles would be replaced by motor lorries operated by the clearing house. Although it anticipated some elements of modern logistics, the Gattie System was too far

ahead of its time, too centralised (the proposed single London depot in Clerkenwell would have employed 3000 lorries) and costly to be a realistic proposition.   **RAS**

Peter R Jenkins, *The Other Railway Clearing House* (Pulborough: Dragonwheel, 1987); Reply of New Transport Co. Ltd to departmental committee's report (February 1920)

Geddes, Sir Eric Campbell (1875–1937), was born in Agra, India. His father was an engineer involved in the survey and construction of Indian railways. Eric's early business experience was gained there, in forest clearance and the laying and operation of many miles of estate railways. By 1901 he was traffic superintendent with the Rohilkund & Kumaon Railway.

In 1904 Geddes moved to England to a new job as claims agent with the North Eastern Railway. His career was meteoric, partly as a result of his friendship with the general manager, Sir George Gibb, partly because of his unbounded energy and flair for organising. By 1907 he was chief goods manager and in 1911 deputy general manager.

The First World War gave Geddes opportunity to display his energy and drive. He was one of Lloyd George's hustling businessmen brought in to boost flagging production of shells and other munitions in 1915. He was a great success and in 1916 he became director general of military railways in France and later director general of transport. He built miles of light railways to get munitions and food to the front. Geddes's role seems to have been crucial to the conduct of the war. Success in this position led to his appointment to reorganise shipbuilding. He was promoted to First Lord of the Admiralty and helped ease Jellicoe's departure.

After a 'good war' he looked set to revolutionise civilian transport as thoroughly as he had done military. He became a Minister without Portfolio on the understanding that he would become Minister for Ways and Means with the brief to put into effect the reconstruction of the run-down transport facilities of Britain. This was to include an 'integrated transport' approach, whereby

177

different modes of transport were co-ordinated and competition reduced, as each mode concentrated on the types of traffic for which it was best suited. In addition electricity production and distribution were to come under his remit because of its centrality in tram and train propulsion, both actual and proposed. Transport was seen by both Geddes and Lloyd George as central to the switch from war to civilian production, the construction of houses and the reconstruction of the economy. They favoured a continuation of war-time controls under the direction of the Ministry of Transport, which covered virtually all modes of transport including docks and harbours and merchant shipping. It was believed wasteful competition could be eliminated and ad hoc measures taken, as in the war, to get things moving. Little came of the grand schemes. Geddes was not a good parliamentarian and did not convince a House full of businessmen with vested interests in the transport industries that they should not be put back into private hands. Nor were the draconian methods of wartime seen as relevant to a peace economy striving for 'normalcy'. Also Lloyd George's power and political support were waning. The plan was so watered down as to be unrecognisable.

Geddes achieved three things. He was the first ever Minister of Transport, from 1919 to 1921. That role once inaugurated continued throughout the century. Secondly, Geddes played a large part in the railway merger and rationalisation scheme creating the Big Four companies which dominated the railway industry until nationalisation. Thirdly, he was crucial in introducing the system of grading roads as A, B or unclassified to denote their importance and the level of funding and hence quality of maintenance.

Once out of politics, Geddes continued to be involved in transport industries. He became chairman of the Dunlop Rubber Co. in 1922, famous for pioneering pneumatic tyres, which he turned around from making huge losses by diversifying. In 1924 Geddes became chairman of Imperial Airways and was instrumental in building up its long distance routes linking the empire to London.

Geddes died relatively young but packed an enormous amount into his life. He was involved at times with all modes of transport and pioneered the concept, if not the practice, of integrated transport which reappeared, at intervals, mostly ineffectually, throughout the century.

JA

DBB, 2 (1984), pp. 507–14; Keith Grieves, *Sir Eric Geddes, Business and Government in War and Peace* (Manchester University Press, 1989); Keith Grieves, 'Sir Eric Geddes, Lloyd George and the transport problem, 1918–21', *JTH*, 3rd series, 13, 1 (1992), pp. 23–42.

The **Geddes Committee,** was appointed in 1963 by the Minister of Transport, Ernest Marples, to examine the operation and effects of carriers' licensing 'in the light of present day conditions'. The committee was chaired by Sir Ross Campbell Geddes, nephew of Sir Eric Geddes (q.v.), and reported in 1965. The major recommendation was 'to abolish all restrictions on the capacity of the road haulage industry and on any work for which a lorry may be used'. Traders and manufacturers should be allowed to use their vehicles for any work they chose, including carriage for hire and reward. These, if accepted, meant that the licensing system, introduced in 1934 would be abolished. Anyone wishing to operate lorries could obtain a permit to operate. This was to be 'available on demand, but held subject to good behaviour as regards all aspects of safety'. Permits would be revoked or suspended if the holder failed in this. Geddes also recommended use of 'a readily visible form of permit plate' which could be 'summarily removed' if any lorry was found to be mechanically defective or overloaded. The Geddes Committee carried out checks on a sample of 15,000 lorries. It found a 'shocking state' with much overloading, limits on drivers' hours being ignored, and the system of record keeping quite inadequate. Barbara Castle, Minister of Transport when action was taken on the report, accepted that carriers' licencing should end for lorries under 3½ tons. For heavier vehicles, operators had to demonstrate professional competence, a form of 'quality licensing'. She also wanted a system of 'quantity licensing', limiting the number of lorries according to either need or the distance they could travel 'where under-used rail services were equally economical'. Both were included in the Transport Act, 1968, drafted under Mrs Castle but passed when Richard Marsh was the new Minister of Transport. The quality operator licensing was introduced in mid-1970 and carriers licensing abolished a little later. Quantity licensing was not introduced and the relevant legislation was repealed in 1981. **GM**

Bagwell (1988), pp. 322, 347 and 341; Aldcroft (1975), pp. 186, 195–8.

Gefco, see TRANSPORTS GEFCO

General Post Office, see POST OFFICE

General Roadways Limited. In 1925 H Daniels, a dentist, was persuaded to set up business in Cricklewood as a haulage contractor with his son, David, still in his late teens, taking control of the operation. The first vehicle was a Scammell artic, the largest lorry of its type at that time. Work was obtained initially from Cary Davis & Thomas, a clearing house, recommended by Col Scammell, based at Tower Hill in London. It was here that David Daniels first met Capt. Claud Barrington (q.v.) who had been injured on the Somme and was soon persuaded to move office with the latter to new premises in Shoreditch.

David Daniels and his manager, Larry Godfrey, expanded Daniels Road Haulage, registered as a private company in 1930, as commerce moved from rail to the faster and more flexible road transport provided by the long-distance hauliers. Standardising on Scammells, with much work coming from Tate & Lyle (q.v.), and Whitbread, General Roadways was formed in 1931 with 50 per cent held by Daniel, the remainder with CD&T. The directors were Barrington and Godfrey.

In 1933 the company moved to premises leased from the LMSR in Spring Place, Kentish Town, London NW5, where Louis Levy became leading driver/foreman. Prior to their move, Scammell at Watford had maintained the fleet, but now General Roadways had their own workshops at Kentish Town where their servicing was carried out. In 1936 Transport Services Ltd was formed at the instigation of Barrington with the backing of the city finance house, Charterhouse Investment Trust. Harley Drayton was chairman and major investor and General Roadways joined this firm. Daniels resigned in 1938, having become disillusioned by the prospects of the company within Transport Services. He reverted to his original professional aim of being an analytical chemist. By 1934 the firm was operating 10 vehicles and by 1938 18 Scammell artics on trunk services.

In 1941, General Roadways acquired C Durston of Stratford, E15 gaining 21 vehicles. During the war, it became Unit 5S3 of the Ministry of War Transport, and Barrington was a senior government adviser on road haulage matters. This in turn promoted him to the board of BRS on nationalisation in 1948, when General Roadways became BRS Kentish Town Branch, the main general haulage trunking depot for the Midlands, by which time the fleet comprised about fifty vehicles. **CRS**

Ingram and Mustoe (1999), pp. 19–20; David Daniels

The **General Strike** (Figure 114) of May 1926 was a time of national crisis which demonstrated 'the permanent importance of road transport to the whole community' (*Autocar*). Road haulage had a visible role, notably in the form of convoys with military escort to and from the London Docks. The scale of such operations was limited, so that they were largely symbolic, as an affirmation of the government's intention to protect the fabric of civil society. Even so, the establishment of the Hyde Park depot, serviced by road, the movement of, admittedly limited, quantities of food and fuel in convoys protected by the military, the safeguarding of petrol supplies, the inter-urban transport of mail (excluding parcels) by road, and the co-operative movement's use of road vehicles for essential food distribution, all these activities emphasised the significance of goods transport by road. The strike also had indirect effects. For example, Mrs Bessie Langdon of Taunton, consignor of eggs and poultry to London, hitherto by rail, acquired a motor lorry in 1927, to gain independence from strike-prone rail transport, thereby laying the foundations of Langdons' (q.v.) road haulage business.

A Supply and Transport Committee had been formed within the Cabinet in response to the 1919 rail strike and this mechanism was developed in subsequent crises. The country was divided into eleven divisions, with Road Commissioners in each, and Road Haulage Committees and Road Officers in each of the 82 sub-districts. The Automobile Association (q.v.) and the Royal Automobile Club (q.v.), both co-operated with government, organising volunteers and helping with convoy work (for which the AA was subsequently criticised by the trade union leader, W J Brown). The unofficial Organisation for the Maintenance of Supplies, set up by various establishment figures in 1925, was no part of the government's official planning, despite some incautious public support from Joynson-Hicks.

The General Strike exposed the weakness of trade unionism in the burgeoning road haulage industry. Many union members remained at work. In Glasgow and the Manchester area, the Scottish Horse and Motormen's Union and the United Road Transport Workers' Association respectively, gave only nominal support to the strike call. The number of defectors from the strike was large, but in Liverpool, Bristol and London support was strong. In London, some 1000 workers were victimised after the strike.

As far as possible, commercial practice, rather than direct government operation, was the preferred *modus operandi* for central government in road haulage provision during the emergency. Thus, even if lorries were requisitioned by Road Officers, the rate for the work undertaken by them was negotiated between customer and haulier, as far as possible in the normal way. **RAS**

M Morris, *The General Strike* (Harmondsworth: Penguin, 1976); K Laybourn, *The General Strike of 1926* (Manchester: Manchester U P, 1993); *The General Strike Day by Day* (Stroud: Alan Sutton, 1996); Glasgow (1926); Holder (2000); M Beam, 'H H Kemp & Son 1921-1972', *CVC* (April 1999), p. 34; Gibson (2001), pp. 169-76

General Trailers, see CRANE FRUEHAUF

Gibb, Thomas, (Fraserburgh) Ltd, haulage contractors, originated in 1895 with the horse-drawn transport of herring from Fraserburgh harbour. Motor vehicles were operated at least from the 1920s and James Gibb & Sons, registered in 1937, had a mainly Leyland fleet on nationalisation. Until denationalisation Thomas and James Gibb remained in transport by operating a small coach fleet, which was sold when they resumed haulage with two ex-BRS Albions. In 1959 the business was registered as Thomas Gibb (Fraserburgh) Ltd, with a largely Albion and Leyland fleet. Traffic included paper to London and countrywide timber, but fish predominated. For a time refrigerated containers were used for this traffic, but in the late 1960s the move was made to refrigerated trailers built locally by Gray & Adams with standardisation on Atkinson tractive units. These were followed by ERF, then DAF, and by the 1990s Scania units. By the time of the BSE crisis, c.1995, meat haulage accounted for 80 per cent of Gibb's business and 24 tractive units were operated, a figure which fell to 18, although their beef traffic was rebuilt. In 2002 fuel costs and the difficulty of obtaining satisfactory freight rates led to closure of the family firm. Gibb's assets included 16 vehicles, 24 trailers and a 3-acre site at Fraserburgh. **RAS**

B Gooding, 'Freezing all the way!', *VCV,* 143 (November 2001), pp. 16–19; *Truck* (May 2002), p.19

The **Gilford Motor Co. Ltd** evolved from E B Horne & Co. of London N7, which began as converters of Garford war-surplus vehicles. From 1925 it made its own Garford-inspired Gilford models and in 1927 moved to High Wycombe, where a range of new vehicles was produced, utilising engines of American design and some American components though British items were gradually substituted. Gilford was best known for its bus and coach production, but some lorries were made on public service vehicle chassis, such as the AS6 and DF6, and as late as the 1935 Commercial Motor Show

Gilford introduced a 4-ton lorry (unladen weight less than 2½ tons). Lorry customers included the Danish Bacon Co. (a 1931 AS6 survives in preservation), the Express Dairy Co. and Dominion Petrol. A distinctive feature of most Gilford vehicles was the vertical cylinders of the Gruss auxiliary air springs on the front axle. Gilford ceased business in 1935, having previously moved back into London at Brentside Works, NW10 and having built 2300 vehicles. The works were taken over by High Speed Gas (Great Britain) Ltd and a few producer gas HSG-Gilford vehicles were made before HSG were taken over by Sentinel. Horne Products of London N6, a company started by Horne after Gilford's closure, advertised itself as suppliers of 'reconditioned and MoT certified buses and coaches'. **RAS**

Stevens-Stratten (1988); *CM* (31 March 1931 and 8 November 1935)

Glass traffic (Figure 27). The earliest glass probably carried was on the back of an itinerant glazier, on its edge, on something like a rucksack frame called a 'frail'. 'Panes' of glass were about 18 inches square. As manufacturing processes improved the panes got bigger. Glass was then packed in crates to be carried on horse cart or rail. With the advent of motors, glass was carried inside a van still loaded a pane at a time by hand. The advent of suction grips helped in handling large panes, although this still takes much skill.

The glass leaned on a sloping frame, still called a frail, secured by poles slotted in the floor and tied at the top. Some vehicles had a canvas roof which could be rolled back to allow very large panes to be loaded by crane. Even bigger panes were carried on a frail secured to the off-side, which grew to 7.3 m (24 ft) long and 3 m (10 ft) high and was especially useful for panes of plate glass used in shop windows and more recently double-glazed units for floor-to-ceiling walls and patio doors. Flat glass traffic increased significantly in the interwar period as it was used in the burgeoning motor vehicle industry and for window glass in the housing boom. Similar circumstances occurred from the 1950s.

Mechanical handling came in the form of A frame pallets. The smaller sizes were still loaded in the traditional way but fork-lifted on to curtain-sided vehicles. There were specialised glass-carrying vehicles with a curtain-side on the nearside and a frail on the offside. The supply of stock from the glass works comes as panes 5 m long by 4 m high known as Jumbos. These are still loaded on an A frame which forms the floor of a special trailer with air suspension to lower the trailer to the ground.

Pilkington of St Helens used motor lorries to take cases of glass to Liverpool just before the First World War but it was in the early 1920s that they began to build up their own fleet starting with two Sentinel steam wagons. In the 1930s a Motor Transport Department was established and by 1936 it had 72 lorries. Some were based on bus chassis because their drop-frame design provided a lower loading height.

Glass was one of the earliest materials for recycling. Bottles and jars were collected, washed and re-used. Broken glass (cullet) was and is collected from glass works, bottling plants and in the twenty-first century re-cycling centres to be returned to the glass works.

T C Barker, *The Glassmakers: Pilkington, 1826–1976* (Weidenfeld & Nicolson, 1977)

Gosselin, C le M, managing director of the long-established Preston hauliers, H Viney & Co. Ltd (q.v.), at the time of nationalisation, was an important voice in the road haulage industry. He was an early user of costings and management records and gave papers to the Institution of Automobile Engineers, for example on 'The use and limitations of the steam wagon' (1922) and 'Goods carrying vehicles' (1930). Gosselin was particularly active in the 1930s as one of the road representatives on the Salter Committee (q.v.), president of the Institute of Transport (q.v.) and the Commercial Motor Users' Association (q.v.); and for many years he was prominent in the Road Haulage Association (q.v.). He also started Lancashire Petrol Deliveries, which went into Pickfords at nationalisation. In the early 1950s Gosselin founded a successful bulk gas and liquids business, Tyburn Road Tanker Services, at Wooburn Green, Bucks, which was later acquired by Calor Transport.

RAS/GM

A **gown van** (Figure 115) is a vehicle with a special body of added height to allow for the transport of hanging garments to reduce the risk of damage or creasing. The earliest was in use before the First World War. Usually coachbuilt for the clothing trade on a light van chassis, the body design enables the weight of the load to be taken by the roof rails. In the 1930s they were often on Bedford BYC car chassis, and were particularly popular with small Jewish clothing manufacturers in East London and Leeds who sold from their vans. So, many had a clerestory roof (q.v.) which allowed the salesman to stand upright in the centre gangway. The Ford E83W was often chosen in the 1950s as the basis of a gown van and examples of this vehicle/body combination were also operated by London Transport for uniform distribution. From the mid-1950s the Morris Minor van in chassis-cab form and with purpose-built bodywork, was used by the Burton Group, John Collier, and Kuperstein, among others. In the 1970s factory-built Bedford CF vans were popular and usually had part of the standard roof cut out with a raised section riveted in. The type continues in use for fashion wholesalers, usually based on box-bodied Ford Transits with security systems to deter theft.   **RAS**

See also GARMENT CARRIAGE

Ingram (1975), p.117, pl. 26

GPO, see POST OFFICE

Greenwood, Edward, established both Greenwoods Transport of Ramsey, Hunts and the St Ives Sand & Gravel Co. Ltd. Although Greenwoods Transport was set up in the 1920s, its fleet was initially horse-drawn. From the mid-1930s AECs featured in the fleet, which reached about 140 on nationalisation in 1948, when it formed the BRS Hunts & Isle of Ely Group. Many of the AECs were bought back by Greenwoods on denationalisation. The firm

maintained its own canteen and extensive repair facilities, even building its own cabs; it also had a wide spread of depots, including London, Birmingham, Ilkeston and Kent. Following the death of its founder in the 1960s, Greenwoods gradually dwindled, as other companies acquired parts of the business. The aggregate business had been founded before the Second World War, but grew particularly in the 1950s with the development of US air bases in East Anglia. As well as sand and gravel, it produced concrete items and ready-mixed concrete. Its early post-war fleet included several ex-military, normal-control, 6-wheel Fords and, later, 8-wheel AEC tippers. The business was acquired by Amey Roadstone in the late 1960s.

RAS

N Larkin, 'AEC memories', *CVC*, 6, 9 (May 2001), pp. 28–33

Growth of road freight transport. Graphs 7 and 8 show various indicators of the pattern of growth of the goods road transport industry through the twentieth century.

Until the 1920s the only available indicator is the estimated total number of goods motor vehicles in use, which shows accelerating growth up to 1914, a sharp decline during the First World War as vehicles were commandeered for military use, followed by rapid expansion as ex-military vehicles were sold for civilian use. During the inter-war period, 1920–38, this indicator shows continuing growth averaging 14 per cent per year until 1929, slowing to 4.6 per cent in the 1930s.

How many of these motor vehicles were a replacement for horse transport (q.v.), rather than for road traffic growth? Taking F M L Thompson's estimate of 832,000 carts, vans and waggons on the roads in 1911 and assuming that replacement was in the ratio of 3 to 1, about 85 per cent of goods motor vehicles were horse-vehicle replacements in 1922/3 and 50 per cent in 1938. The balance is accounted for by traffic captured from the railways, which began seriously in 1919, and new traffic arising from economic growth.

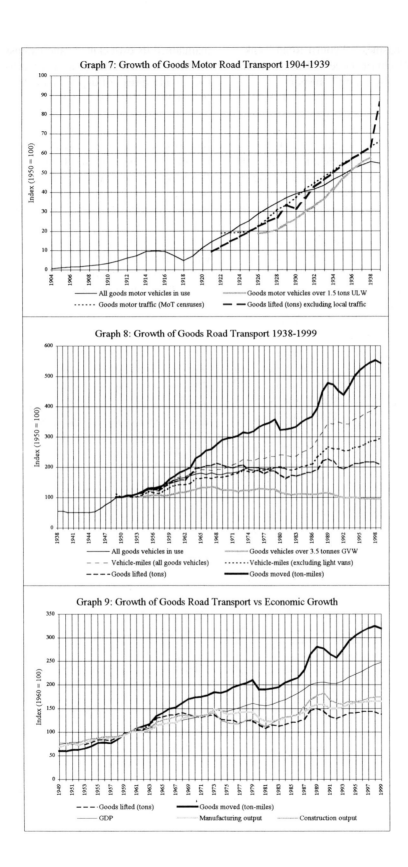

Graph 7: Growth of Goods Motor Road Transport 1904-1939

Index (1950 = 100)

— All goods motor vehicles in use
— Goods motor vehicles over 1.5 tons ULW
..... Goods motor traffic (MoT censuses)
— — Goods lifted (tons) excluding local traffic

Graph 8: Growth of Goods Road Transport 1938-1999

Index (1950 = 100)

— All goods vehicles in use
— Goods vehicles over 3.5 tonnes GVW
– – – Vehicle-miles (all goods vehicles)
..... Vehicle-miles (excluding light vans)
— — Goods lifted (tons)
— Goods moved (ton-miles)

Graph 9: Growth of Goods Road Transport vs Economic Growth

Index (1960 = 100)

– – – Goods lifted (tons)
— Goods moved (ton-miles)
— GDP
— Manufacturing output
..... Construction output

The number of goods vehicles is only a crude indicator, as it ignores the increasing productivity of motor lorries. Other indicators which now became available suggest faster growth in the 1930s. The proportion of lorries over 1½ tons unladen weight grew from 35 to 55 per cent between 1926 and 1938. The Ministry of Transport traffic censuses indicate an average growth rate in goods motor traffic (which is analogous to vehicle-miles) on class A and B roads of 7.3 per cent per year in the 1930s. Peter Scott estimated that the tonnage carried by road where it was in potential competition with the railways (i.e. excluding local traffic) increased by an average of 13 per cent per year.

During the Second World War, the numbers of goods vehicles might suggest that there was a significant reduction in goods road traffic, with priority given to use of the railways. However, by the end of the war the government's emergency control measures had become so effective that the fewer vehicles were probably carrying as much goods traffic as in 1938.

Post-war growth in the total number of goods vehicles was dominated by an enormous increase in the number of light vans. By 1981 over 70 per cent of goods vehicles were less than 1.525 tonnes unladen weight; from 1982 they were absorbed into a new 'Private & Light Goods' taxation class and ceased to be identifiable in the statistics. They are responsible for less than 6 per cent of freight tonnage and less than 5 per cent of ton-mileage, so their role was only small. The majority of light goods vehicles was used by service industries, building contractors, etc., rather than for the transport of goods.

The number of heavier goods vehicles (over 1.5 tons/1.525 tonnes unladen weight, later redefined as 3.5 tonnes gross laden weight) grew by 35 per cent between 1950 and 1967 but, following the successive increases in maximum lorry weights, has fallen back to its 1950 level. Average annual mileage per vehicle has continued to increase, however, reflecting improvements in vehicle technology and the road network. Since 1950 annual vehicle-miles have increased three-fold for heavier goods

vehicles and four-fold if light goods vehicles are included.

The tonnage of goods 'lifted' has more than doubled since 1950, while the ton-miles moved by road, which is arguably the most significant measure of goods transport activity, has increased no less than 5½ times. This means that in 1999 goods were being transported 2.6 times further, on average, than in 1950, which is partly the effect of winning longer-distance traffic from the railways — road transport's share of the road/rail total ton-miles increased from 44 to 89 percent over this period — and partly a result of the changes in patterns of production and distribution that advances in goods road transport have made possible.

The overall growth has been subject to some marked upward and downward variations, showing, as Graph 9 illustrates, that the fortunes of the road haulage industry follow the state of the national economy, particularly the manufacturing and construction sectors. **GAB**

F M L Thompson, 'Nineteenth century horse sense' *Economic History Review,* 2nd series, 29 (1976) pp 60–81; Peter Scott, 'The growth of road haulage 1921–58: an estimate', *JTH,* 19 (1998), pp. 138–55 *Highways Statistics,* 1964–1973 and *Transport Statistics Great Britain,* 1974– ; *National Income & Expenditure, 1956–1983* and *United Kingdom National Accounts,* 1984–

Guest Road Services Ltd, Bath and London, originated in 1926 with a Bath to Bristol parcels service operated by H H V Guest with a Ford 1-ton van. This grew to six vehicles, then in 1931 removal vans were bought and a depot acquired in Hackney, convenient for the east London furniture industry, and deliveries of new furniture from London to the west of England and south Wales commenced. Expansion also took place in and around Bath in the 1930s. Two carriers at Weston-super-Mare were acquired and Trader Motor Transport of Chard, where a depot was opened, providing parcels service over a large area. In 1933 Ward & Ling of Bath, operating a daily Bath to Bristol service and 30-mile radius newspaper delivery, was acquired. This was incorporated as Guest, Ward & Ling Ltd in 1937, expanding in the west of England and

London until the war, when it became a controlled company, priority being given to arms, aircraft parts and food transport. A number of vehicles were converted in wartime for meat haulage to Bath, Bristol and London. Normal business resumed after the war and two Bath removers were acquired, before the business was nationalised in August 1948 with 65 vehicles. On denationalisation, the Hackney depot and 11 vehicles were bought from BRS (q.v.) and Guest Carriers (Hackney) Ltd established. A depot in Edmonton was then acquired, at which loads of new furniture for delivery to Scotland were assembled, Guest Scottish Carriers Ltd being incorporated in 1955. A large depot in Bath and 35 vehicles, mainly platform and dropside lorries, were bought from BTC and daily trunking to London and regular services to all parts of the UK commenced. At the beginning of 1956 50 vehicles were operated by the three associated fleets, including 22 with Luton bodies, most being on Guy chassis. Following the decline of the Lea Valley and east London furniture industry in the 1970s, the Guest business came to an end. **RAS**

Dunbar Papers, Modern Records Centre, University of Warwick Library: MSS.347/D/10/6/2476; P Kirkham *et al.*, *Furnishing the World* (Journeyman Press, 1987)

Guy Motors Ltd (Figures 35 and 119) (1914–82), lorry, bus and trolleybus manufacturers, was established at Fallings Park, Wolverhampton by Sydney Slater Guy (1884–1971), who remained chairman and managing director until his retirement in 1957. His brother, Ewart, played a significant role as sales director. After an engineering apprenticeship at Belliss & Morcom, steam engineers, Sydney became repairs manager at Humber, 1905–08, then works manager at the Sunbeam Motor Car Co. Ltd 1908–13. Guy resigned from Sunbeam, following its refusal of a salary increase and share in profits, and set up his own works, with backers including Alfred Owen of Rubery Owen (q.v.).

The first Guy was a 30-cwt chassis for bus or lorry use. The new works was soon in war production, including depth charge firing

mechanisms, aero engines and Ministry of Munitions orders for 30-cwt vehicles for Russia. After the war V8 and 4-cylinder engined cars failed to give Guy a niche in an overcrowded market and development of the mainstream commercial range provided the way forward, although small diversions were undertaken, such as road-rail vehicles for South African Railways, battery-electric refuse collection lorries and producer gas vehicles and military half-tracks. The main product range expanded with 15-cwt (soon to become 1-ton), 2 - and 2½-ton vehicles and the B series of bus chassis from 1924. The 15- to 30-cwt vans found favour with prominent operators such as Whiteleys, John Barker and Allen & Hanbury.

In 1928 Guy bought its Wolverhampton rivals, the Star Engineering Co. Ltd (q.v.), reducing lorry production but continuing to offer cars, car-based ambulances and a specially developed newspaper van for the *Evening Standard*. In 1930 the civilian lorry range was extended to include the 6-wheel, 10-ton Goliath, but between the wars and during the Second World War the development and production of military vehicles increasingly became a major, even predominant, activity for Guy.

Its first military vehicle was produced with government subsidy in 1923, a rear caterpillar-tracked variant appeared in 1924 and a military six-wheel lorry with four rear-driven wheels on a rocking cross-shaft in 1926. An eight-wheel version followed in 1931 and in 1936 government requests for a light four-wheel vehicle led to the Ant and its four-wheel-drive derivation, the Quad Ant, in 1938. By this time all Guy civilian production had ceased and the company was exclusively on government contracts. By 1941 the need for civilian lorries to keep the war economy going at home was so great that, at government request, the angular cabbed and bonneted Vix-Ant was produced from Ant units.

Guy entered the post-war period strengthened by the reputation earned by wartime bus production, but its fortieth anniversary booklet indicates traditional attitudes: 'Mass production, in its usually accepted sense, is not attempted in Guy. Every vehicle is individually built for long life and low running costs'. Guy maintained a large service department for vehicles produced during the previous 25 years and there was a 'standing instruction that it is more important to supply a part required to keep a vehicle on the road than to produce a new one'. These attitudes suggest a longer-term view of customer satisfaction and loyalty than usual. In the early post-war years Guy consolidated its position in the bus and coach market and resumed production of its Otter, Vixen and Wolf commercials, introducing improvements such as the Motor Panels' all-steel cab for the Otter in 1953. In 1954 came the move to the heavier end of the market with the Big Otter (later Warrior) and a revival of the Goliath name (changed to Invincible to avoid a clash in export markets with the Borgward group's Goliath-Werke). This used an AEC chassis frame and a Gardner engine. Tractor versions of both the Invincible and the recabbed Otter were introduced and Guy received a significant order for nearly 400 short-wheelbase Otter tractive units from BRS.

In the mid-1950s, encouraged by its export successes and the importance of its South African market, Guy decided to open its own depots there, a costly decision which led eventually to the company's collapse in 1961. Meanwhile, the improved Invincible Mk 2 with Guy chassis and restyled cab, was introduced in 1958 and in 1960 the lighter Warrior 2 was launched. Despite its success with these models at the heavy end of the commercial range, the financial drain of South African trading, combined with the failure of the Wulfrunian double-deck bus with its related warranty costs, brought Guy into receivership in 1961. Rescue came in the person of Sir William Lyons, founder and head of Jaguar Cars, who wished to expand his company's scope, without the need to relocate to a development area. In accordance with this policy he had bought Daimler of Coventry in 1960 and in 1961 purchased Guy and simplified the commercial vehicle range. In 1962 the Invincible Mk 3 was

introduced and in 1964 the Big J (Big Jaguar) truck range was launched, developed by Cliff Elliott, whom Lyons had originally lured from Dodge Trucks to Daimler. Also in 1961 Jaguar bought Henry Meadows Ltd, gearbox and engine manufacturers of Wolverhampton. Founded in 1920 when they had attracted John Dorman and Dorman's designer, R S Crump, they had been suppliers to Guy. By now Lyons was in his mid-60s and wished to ensure his group's future as an autonomous part of a larger concern. With this end in view, in 1968 Jaguar joined the British Motor Corporation (itself a non-assimilated coming-together of Austin and the Nuffield Group) to form British Motor Holdings. The Big J was a success, but the acquisition of BMH by the Leyland Motor Corporation in 1968 was the beginning of the end for Guy, although closure, planned for the mid-1970s, was delayed by the Big J's popularity until 1982, with Fallings Park also assembling some Leyland models, such as the new Marathon. The eventual closure was received locally with incredulity and bitterness.

RAS

Anon, *40 Years of Achievement: 1914 to 1954* (Wolverhampton, 1955); Hannay and Broatch (1994); M Wells, 'The Goliath that became Invincible', *VCVM*, 32–3 (1991); B H Vanderveen, 'The Guy Ant', *OM* 8, 6 (November/December (1974), pp. 444–50; Baldwin (2001), pp. 17–20

GWK Ltd (Grice, Wood & Keiller) produced motor vehicles from 1911 to 1931 first at Datchet then at Maidenhead from 1914. They manufactured vans between 1914 and 1924, initially a rear-engined friction-drive light van, succeeded in 1918 by a front-engined van. Over 50 of this F type were ordered by the Post Office (q.v.) in its post-First World War move into mechanically-propelled vehicles for local work but reliability problems meant no larger order followed. **RAS**

Martin (2000), p. 26; Lord Montagu, *Lost Causes of Motoring* (Cassell, 1960), chap. 12

H

Half cab (Figure 183) The bus-type, driver-beside-the-engine half cab has from time to time appeared on lorries, for example, steel carriers, ready-mixed concrete vehicles, on/off road dump trucks, for hauliers who wished to prevent unauthorised passenger-carrying, and to give maximum visibility and reduce the risk of accidental damage. Foden built a number in the late 1960s but driver resistance led to few sales. Robinsons of Stockton used a few and although they saved weight and eased servicing drivers claimed they were cold in winter. **RAS**

Hallett Silbermann (Figure 116) was started by John Silbermann in 1946. He learnt his skills in operating low loaders working for CAEC Howard, then major civil engineering contractors and clearing house operators. After a year with Coupar of Acton, another clearing house (q.v.) dealing with low-loader traffic, Silbermann started his own clearing house business, Peterson Ltd, based in north London. This was partly because, having left Coupar, he was being asked by former customers for assistance. Around 1951 it acquired the business of Tom Hallett, operating a Canadian Dodge articulated low-loader. He also established Metroplant Ltd machinery removals and installation and West Bridgford Transport Co. Ltd (also a clearing house), in partnership with Annis & Co. (q.v.). During state ownership he operated an ERF low-loader on hire from Pickfords, which although allocated to Perivale depot with a fleet number of 52A60 did not have the lion and wheel symbol but carried Peterson's name and livery.

At denationalisation John Silbermann Ltd successfully bid for three Pickford low-loaders. It gradually expanded to 11 vehicles, despite opposition from Pickfords when applying for additional vehicle licences. In the mid-1950s HS acquired Annis's holdings in Metroplant and West Bridgford Transport. All vehicles adopted the Hallett Silbermann title. Acquisitions of small operators included A R F Foskett of Watford and Gliberry's Transport of

Hornchurch, primarily for their sites. Storage and distribution was started at a new depot at Feltham, to be acquired by Carryfast (q.v.) in 1971. Expansion in heavy haulage came with acquisition of Styring Transport Ltd of Rotherham and Reeves Transport of Acocks Green, Birmingham. The various trading companies became subsidiaries of Brent Group which was formed as a holding company. Cattermoles, London-based machinery movers, was acquired in 1974. The main London base for HS moved to Hatfield in the 1970s. HS employs a number of owner drivers mostly with lorry-mounted crane vehicles in HS livery. John Silbermann was chairman of the Road Haulage Association in 1978–80 and Master of the Worshipful Company of Carmen in 1999–2000. **GM**

Halley Industrial Motors Ltd, 1906–35, was a Scottish commercial vehicle manufacturer, founded by George H Halley as the Glasgow Motor Lorry Co. Ltd in 1901, changing its name when it turned from steam to petrol lorries. A wide range of vehicles was in production before the First World War, with fire engines a significant element, but wartime production concentrated on shells, with only 400 lorries going to the War Department. The effects of this move away from vehicle manufacture, in contrast to its rival, Albion Motor Co., combined with an initial post-war single model policy and the death of its founder in 1921, resulted in the decline of Halley into voluntary liquidation and its reconstruction as Halley Motors Ltd in 1926–7. The surprising feature of Halley's history is not that it ultimately failed, but that it took so long. Fire engine, municipal vehicle and passenger chassis manufacture helped prolong its life. Local loyalty was significant epitomised by a handsome confectionery sales van for the Scottish Co-operative Wholesale Society on a 6-wheel bus chassis in 1931, but some orders came from further afield, from customers such as Shell BP and Kent County Council. Halleys was acquired by the North British Locomotive Co., then went into liquidation in 1935. The Yoker site was bought by Albion for building completely-knocked-down chassis and for servicing; the spares went to R H Collier (q.v.). **RAS**

Klapper (1973); Stevens-Stratten, (1988); Glasgow Art Gallery & Museum, *Scottish Cars* (Glasgow, 1962); G Oliver, *Motor Trials and Tribulations* (Glasgow, 1993); Grieves (1998); Nick Baldwin, *OM*, 10, 5 and 6

Hallford lorry. About 3000 were built by J & E Hall Ltd, refrigeration and lift engineers of Dartford, between 1907 and 1926 as a diversification. Originally produced under licence from the Swiss firm of Adolph Saurer, Halls introduced their own engine from 1911 with the unusual feature of transverse radiator tubes. Hallfords were particularly popular with brewers. Other orders came from local government and hauliers and for export. Halls were associated with W A Stevens Ltd of Maidstone, from 1909 to 1911, in the production of petrol-electric vehicles, an association ended when Tilling acquired Stevens. First World War production was of 3-ton lorries which continued after the war still with chain-drive. After development of a battery-electric vehicle, it decided that the cost of a new range and production facilities would harm Hall's core business and the Hallford ceased, although a company provided spares back-up. **RAS**

H Miller, *Halls of Dartford 1785– 1985* (1985)

The **Hanbury Davies** distribution and container haulage group of Felixstowe (q.v.) was established by Glyn Davies in 1999, after his restrictive contract with Securicor (q.v.) had expired. His original business, Russell Davies Distribution, owned jointly with Ron Davies (no relation), was sold to Securicor in 1995. Russell Davies, although subcontracting much of its work, was a leading firm in container haulage, with joint ventures with Freightliner (q.v.); it developed major workshop facilities, servicing not only its own Iveco rental fleet on an agreed standard hours basis, but also maintaining the vehicles of other operators. By the time of its sale it was the largest privately-owned transport group in the UK. In 1995 Glyn Davies and Ian Wilson, who had been his deputy managing director and became chief executive of Hanbury Davies, joined Securicor and played a major part in developing Securicor Omega Logistics. After Glyn Davies left in 1997 he engaged in a number of diverse business ventures, moving back into transport by the purchase of Riverside Commercials in West Thurrock, a quality-used commercial vehicle dealer with a hire and contract fleet which had developed, as Hanbury Riverside, to 90 vehicles by 2000. Hanbury Davies began in mid-1999 with five vehicles, growing to 50, on distribution work, within seven months. There followed a move back into container haulage by the purchase of Goodway in 1999 and Loadwell in 2000, creating Hanbury Davies Containers with over 200 vehicles. Hanbury Davies concluded a four-year leasing contract with TIP (q.v.) for 45 Dennison sliding skeletal trailers at the end of 2000. **RAS**

J Semple, 'Business as usual', *Truck* (August 2000), pp. 56–61; *T ruck* (January 2001), p. 31

To **handball** is to load and unload by hand, without the benefit of mechanical handling equipment. Charlie Walker graphically describes the process of loading a Foden tipper with bricks in the 1950s: 'We never looked at the wagon, just the pile of bricks on the floor: bend throw, bend throw.' **RAS**

Walker (2000), p. 83

Handcarts formerly shared with cycle delivery (q.v.) the end position in the distribution chain. Their use persisted into the post-Second World War period, when battery-electric-powered, pedestrian-controlled vehicles replaced the traditional handcart or 'pram', especially for milk delivery. The milk pram was a three-wheeler, with a single small wheel in front and two large wheels behind, whereas the baker's barrow or handcart and similar delivery carts generally had two large wheels only. Some major coachbuilders, as well as smaller specialists, supplied what was, in its heyday, a very large market. In 1931 Lewis of Chalk Farm in north London, handcart suppliers to the Express Dairy Co. Ltd, was acquired by Express as its bodybuilding and maintenance department. Co-operative societies were large users of handcarts and the London Co-operative Society, which used milk prams into the post-war period, had its own bodyworks at Manor Park, east London. **RAS**

Backhouse (1982)

Hanson, Joseph, & Sons Ltd. The original business was started in 1830 when Mrs Mary Hanson, using packhorses, began serving the Colne Valley. Her son, Joseph, joined her, and developed the business. His son, James William, in his turn joined his father, but continued his own furniture removals business. Together they extended their service to include Manchester and Leeds. By 1900 they were also carrying Liverpool cotton. James died in 1911, the business continuing under the control of his sons, Joseph and Robert. At the outbreak of the First World War, all the Hanson horses and steam wagons were requisitioned, but they were later allowed to purchase six steam wagons and three motor lorries for essential transport. Hanson was awarded contracts to supply army horse remounts.

The furniture business now included a depository, destroyed by fire in 1919. The business was able to continue, but one customer sued for negligence and loss. Judgement went against Hanson, leading to further successful claims. The depository and its contents were not insured, forcing Robert Hanson into bankruptcy.

There was a relationship between Hanson and the Halifax-based Holdsworth (q.v.) business. Oliver Holdsworth gave financial and practical support and a new company, Joseph Hanson & Sons, was formed in 1920. Charles Holdsworth became chairman, Robert Hanson becoming manager, his brother Donald Hanson was secretary.

Hanson started a Huddersfield to London service in 1928, sharing Holdsworth & Hanson's London depot. A Huddersfield to Leicester service followed, then to Goole and Hull. In 1930 the Holdsworths and Donald Hanson transferred their Hanson shares to Robert Hanson, giving him control of Joseph Hanson. He was now able to develop Hanson,

acquiring a local carrier, Queen Carriage Ltd of Huddersfield, operating 28 vehicles. He also formed joint holding companies, with the Holdsworths acquiring Bouts Tillotson (q.v.) and Oswald Tillotson (q.v.). The later history is under Holdsworth & Hanson Ltd (q.v.). **GM**

Brummer and Cowe (1994); PRO: AN Files.

Harris, Brian, Transport, of Bovey Tracey, Devon, was closed by its owner in 2001, ending a business set up in Widecombe-in-the-Moor by his father and uncle in 1946, trading as Harris & Miners. The original V8-engined Ford lorries were joined by Albion, ERF and Guy vehicles. The business was nationalised in 1950, but restarted four years later. A long-distance link with Scotland, which persisted, began in 1948, with a contract from a local tile manufacturer to supply a customer near Glasgow. This developed into regular work to Aberdeen, Dundee and Edinburgh, with backloads of steel, paper and machinery, distributed by Harris throughout the south west peninsula. The smartly turned out fleet reached 23 by 1965 and stood at 31 vehicles on closure, it was all-British, the majority ERF: eight 6×4 and 16 4×2 tractive units, two 8×4 tippers and a 6×4 platform lorry. Brian Harris, who took over and renamed the business on the death of his father in 1978, attributed his closure decision to a number of factors, some of which were common to many small haulage firms. The chief problem was failure to reach agreement with the local authority on restricting operations in response to opposition from local residents, housing development having been permitted in proximity to the depot. Additional factors were the impact of fuel prices, rate-cutting, and the effects of the foot-and-mouth outbreak of 2001 on the delivery of agricultural machinery from one of Harris's main customers. Failure to modernise also played a part. **RAS**

C Sheer, 'Harris finally calls it a day', *Truck* (June 2001), pp. 19–20; D Lee, 'Brian Harris Transport', CVRTC *News*, 5/01 (June 2001); Corah (2002)

Harrods Ltd (Figure 28) of Knightsbridge, London's best-known department store, began a horse-drawn van delivery service in 1874, replacing handcart (q.v.) delivery. By 1903 six motor vehicles were in use and the first motor van produced by Dennis entered Harrods' service in 1904. About 1906, 21 Lacre 25-cwt vans and more than a dozen Albions were added. Harrods built their own bodies, a distinctive feature over a long period being an upright, rectangular cab-side window behind the driving position. Although horse-drawn transport continued to be significant for Harrods (111 horses were bought in 1909), the motor fleet grew to 200 by 1910, for free delivery in town (for which Walker, Edison and other electric vans were used) and to the suburbs, as far out as Maidenhead, Woking, Enfield and Bexley. The 1922 delivery fleet comprised 90 petrol and 70 electric vans. In 1937, 320 vehicles were operated. Smaller vehicles operated at different periods included a number of Warrick three-wheel parcelcars (replacing pedal-delivery) and a pair of Reliant three-wheelers, acquired for special town deliveries in 1938. In addition to delivery vans, Harrods ran a heavy removals fleet, including eight Foden steam wagons operating from the Barnes depository c.1915–22; a containerised service was offered, including to Europe.

Between 1936 and 1939 Harrods built 60 replacement electric vans, designed by J H L Bridge of Harrods Garage and utilising components from the Walker vans. These hybrids lasted until 1970. By this time over 150 vans were operated, more than half of which were on service, rather than delivery, work. Deliveries were also undertaken for other stores then within the group, such as John Barker and Dickins & Jones, and a separate removals fleet was still operated. Outside coachbuilders were supplying Harrods with vehicles by this time, for example Sparshatts with ten walk-through-bodied BMC JU vans in 1970 and two Luton-bodied Boxers in 1971. For central London customers Harrods had offered a daily delivery service even for items as inexpensive as a loaf of bread, but ultimately the cost of such frequent deliveries became too great and the delivery fleet had been reduced to about 40 vehicles by 1991. As a publicity device, a horse-drawn cart service was reintroduced for local deliveries and a number of Ford Transit-based Walker replicas fulfilled a similar function. The Barnes depository (a former soap factory, acquired in 1894) was closed in 1989 and replaced by a new warehouse at Osterley, with computerised racking systems. Harrods' fleet in 1998 was on contract hire and included 17 MAN and three Mercedes-Benz for heavy work, such as furniture delivery and daily produce collection from New Covent Garden. A dozen Ford Transit vans and the six Walker replicas dealt with deliveries. **RAS**

'Harrods' photo-feature, *Vintage Commercial*, 1, 4 (December 1962), pp. 123–5; J Aldridge, 'Delivery with a difference', *Commercial Vehicles* (December 1969); S Callery, *Harrods Knightsbridge: the story of society's favourite store* (Ebury Press, 1991); Georgano (1996), p. 22; R Coates, '150 Years of Harrods' Transport', *VCV*, 119–122 (November 1999–February 2000)

Hastie, James Barrie (189–1968) was born in Glasgow and joined the firm owned by his uncle, John Barrie, as a clerk. The firm offered contract carting services and Hastie used the opportunity to learn the road haulage business. After war service as a despatch rider, in 1919 he was installed as manager of Glasgow Hiring Co. Ltd, a firm acquired by his uncle. He introduced motor lorries and claimed to be the first firm to offer contract hire in a company's livery in Scotland. Among the contracts he secured was one with Royal Mail and another to provide vans for the Territorial Army.

Following nationalisation, Hastie became divisional manager for Scotland of BRS. After denationalisation he resumed his interest in Glasgow Hiring Co. Ltd, remaining even after it became a subsidiary of the Transport Development Group (q.v.). **JA**

Anthony Slaven and Sydney Checkland (eds) *Dictionary of Scottish Business Biography 1860–1960, 2: Processing, Distribution, Services* (Aberdeen University Press, 1990), pp. 289–90

Hauliers' & Farmers' Alliance, see PROTEST MOVEMENTS

Hauliers Ltd was established in 1939 by Reginald Hindley, who was treasurer of Associated Road Operators (q.v), and the financier Frederick Szarvasy (1875–1948) of the Dunlop Rubber Co. and numerous other businesses. The road haulage firm began with the amalgamation of Edward Box Ltd (q.v.), the heavy hauliers, and Beresford, Caddy & Pemberton Ltd of Tunstall, which carried groceries from Liverpool to the Potteries and china back to Liverpool and Manchester docks. During its first year, the Airlandwater Transport Co. Ltd of Bishop's Stortford, Butterwick Transport Ltd of Leeds, C F Denning (Transport) Ltd of Epping, Newcastle Transport & Trading Co. Ltd of Stockton-on-Tees, Walker Bros (Brighouse) Ltd and the Ware Transport Co. Ltd of Peterborough were taken over. The war weakened, and nationalisation ended, this firm. In 1948 they claimed to own about 600 vehicles. **RAS**

Dunbar (1981); Labour Research Department *Why Haulage must be nationalised* (1946); *DBB*, vol. 5: entry on Szarvasy; *MT* (31 January 1948), p.19

The **Hauliers' Mutual Federation** was founded in 1943–4 by E B Howes, at one time 'a fiery partisan of the small man' in road haulage. He had organised the Saunders Group at Harpenden to haul bulk commodities in tipper wagons. The HMF National Council in 1946 adopted a 16-point policy, strongly opposed to nationalisation and urged the 'release' of road goods transport to its pre-1940 position. It held that the peacetime planning of the details of traffic movement would be best prepared for each plant, not centrally, and claimed that small hauliers, linked by mutual arrangements with industrial traffic departments and/or clearing houses, formed efficient and flexible units. The HMF address in 1946 was the same as that of Federated Conveyers Ltd, a clearing house. Together with 'rebel local associations', the HMF made up the National Conference of Road Transport Associations (q.v.), in opposition to the Road Haulage Association (q.v.). Though widely discussed at the time, the HMF had no lasting influence and was essentially a one-man band, set up by Howe to facilitate the negotiation of increased compensation at nationalisation. This achieved, Howe lost interest and went to Kenya. **RAS**

J A Dunnage, *Transport Plan and Britain's Future* (Industrial Transport Publications, 1946); Labour Research Department, *Why Haulage must be Nationalised* (1946); Dunbar (1981), p. 67.

The **Hauliers' National Traffic Pool** was established in 1942 as part of the wartime emergency measures. Under these a hard core of commercial vehicles was chartered from private hauliers by the Ministry of War Transport. Because this fleet would not be big enough to handle all government-controlled traffic a number of pools were needed, comprising private hauliers, to whom traffic could be allocated. These became almost a form of clearing house for government traffic. Because the Ministry was slow to recruit vehicles, in 1942, whereas chartered vehicles carried about 77,000 tons, Hauliers' National Traffic Pool vehicles carried 500,000 tons. It gave rise to a huge bureaucracy and was not motivated to reduce the volume of road transport which was one of the government's aims, to economise on scarce petrol and rubber for tyres. It was largely superseded by the Road Haulage Organisation (q.v.). **JA**

Savage (1957)

Hays' origins go back to 1651 (see HAY'S WHARF). Hays' recent history starts with the closure of its last warehouse in the Pool of London and subsequent diversifications. In 1975 some 35 per cent was owned by St Martin's Holdings, which was acquired by the Kuwait Investment Office (KIO). The outstanding Hay's shares were acquired in 1980, enabling the Hay's properties to be merged with St Martin's for development. Hay's made a series of acquisitions in commercial, distribution, office support and later, personnel services. That of Farmhouse Securities in 1981, led to Ronnie E Frost becoming chairman and chief executive. He led the buyout of the KIO's involvement in Hay's in 1987, the KIO retaining a 25 per cent holding. Hay became a publicly-quoted company in 1989. Its transport interests within its commercial division included Hay's Mail and Express Services trading as Hays DX. This operated a country-wide document exchange service, for the legal, medical and financial sectors. There were subsidiary operations in France, Germany and Spain. Other sectors included archive management and storage and overnight delivery of spare parts for service engineers. The logistics division has dedicated distribution contracts for Waitrose, B&Q, Marks & Spencer, and Yates Wine Lodge. Its European contracts include Carrefour-Pormode in Italy, Staples in Germany, BMW parts in Bavaria and Iveco spares for Europe. Other services include overnight delivery of delicate high-value items and the Rentacrate crate hire service. It also provides controlled temperature storage and ambient warehousing. Home delivery services have become important, including a USA division.   **GM**

Hay's Wharf Cartage Co. (1947); Turnbull (1979); *FT* (9 September 2002), p.29

Hay's Wharf. Alexander Hay gave his name to a Wharf at Tooley Street in 1651, on leasing a brewery on the site and conducting business as a wharfinger. Despite fires and recessions the business prospered. In 1768 William Humphrey became associated with the business, eventually acquiring full ownership. The Hays preferred to change to lighterage. The Great Tooley Street fire in 1861, although costly, gave the opportunity to rebuild damaged warehouses and to pioneer cold stores. This needed capital and in 1862 Humphrey's grandson, John secured two new partners, Hugh Colin Smith and Arthur Magniac. The business, now known as The Proprietors of Hay's Wharf, became a limited company in 1907. The partners' purpose to extend Hay's Wharf to occupy the three-quarter mile stretch between London Bridge and Tower Bridge and to have the Provision Exchange move from the other side of the river to Tooley Street was achieved. Hay's now began their Carmen's and Cartage Division, at first trading as Cliffords Ltd to move thousands of tons of dairy produce

handled by Hay's Wharf together with imported meat and produce from the docks. The title changed to Hay's Wharf Cartage Co. Ltd in 1912. They then acquired Pickfords Ltd in 1920. The major attraction was its meat carriage although the other branches of the business, heavy haulage, provisions, removals and travel, were also developed. A new venture was into bulk liquid transport, by acquiring B T Norris of Tooting operating 14 vehicles. In 1923 Robert Hall Ltd, also a major meat carrier, was acquired, adding 20 Hallfords, six Ford T vans and four elderly CPT vans, a short-lived US-import, built by the Consolidated Pneumatic Tool Co. of Chicago. There were also 10 Foden 5-ton steam wagons, probably sub-contracted. Carter Paterson parcels' interests were excluded, but retained a close working partnership, and outside Greater London acted as agents for each other. In 1933 they created a joint subsidiary, Karriers Parcels Delivery service of Liverpool. Hay's Wharf invested heavily to develop the Pickfords businesses, including acquiring London Traction Haulage and Norman E Box Ltd (q.v.) in 1930, with six Fowler road locomotives and four Scammell low-loaders. At its acquisition in 1919 Pickfords had 1580 horses and 46 petrol and steam vehicles. In 1933 Hay's Wharf were operating 560 horses and 628 diesel, petrol and steam vehicles. In 1933 the railways jointly gained control of Hay's Wharf Cartage including Pickfords and also of Carter Paterson. Hay's Wharf Cartage Co. remained the holding company responsible for vehicles including licencing, and property. In 1944 Carter Paterson and Pickford's London parcels services were merged into Carter Paterson & Pickfords Joint Parcels Services with Carter Paterson having management responsibility. By 1946 the joint service took over responsibility for all the parcels business, including Sutton & Co. The railways transferred their holdings in Carter Paterson to Hay's Wharf Cartage Co. Ltd, still controlled and owned by them. The Hay's Wharf property and engineering divisions provided the administrative basis for the Road Haulage Executive acquisitions. Hays Wharf retained the Pickfords & Hay's Wharf

Shipping & Forwarding Co. Ltd, a subsidiary, started in 1922. **GM**

A Ellis, *Three Hundred Years on the River 1651–1951* (1952); Ingram (1993); Turnbull (1979)

Heanor Haulage Ltd started life in 1936 as Heanor Coal and Haulage, its main traffic being domestic coal deliveries from the local Derbyshire collieries. When the Second World War broke out the vehicles were acquired for use by the military, bringing the company to a halt during hostilities. In the 1950s the Searson brothers, Jack and Ken, purchased the company's three A licences and five B licences from nationalisation, thus re-launching the business, undertaking mainly bulk tipper work.

Some 6-wheel rigid lorries were acquired and these were employed on the haulage of pipes. One Scammell 6 wheeler was converted, by the company, into a tractor unit. This was coupled to a Dyson low-loading trailer and used to transport bulldozers.

During the years of carrier licensing the company expanded by acquisition. The business of Buckland Haulage was bought out, introducing four tractor units with A licences into the fleet. Graham and Brown Transport of Coventry and Thamesmouth Transport were also brought into the Heanor Haulage fold.

The company moved premises, within the Langley Mill district of Nottinghamshire, a number of times over the years to gain larger premises. The last move was in 1996. Throughout this time the company remained in the ownership and operation of the Searson family. Today the company specialises in the movement of abnormal loads in the UK, Ireland and Middle East. The specialist fleet can accommodate loads from 10 to 500 ton. **MB**

The **Heavy Transport Co. Ltd,** which became the basis of English China Clay's post-war transport operations, was founded at Charlestown, Cornwall, in 1919 as Neesham and Hodge for the transport of china clay, coal and cement. Its base moved to Truro after takeover by Simmonds Hodge in 1927. Shelabears of Walsall subsequently acquired

Heavy Transport, which was almost exclusively occupied with deliveries from Amalgamated Roadstone Corporation quarries during the Second World War. A post-war demolition removal contract was secured from Plymouth, but not renewed for 1947–8. At this time ECC were concerned that independent haulage contractors operating for them might be restricted by the provisions of the 1947 Transport Act. ECC therefore bought Heavy Transport with 23 vehicles in 1948, as fleets wholly-owned by a producing firm were not restricted. They had already acquired other transport concerns with double-figure fleets, such as Western Express Haulage Co. Ltd of St Austell with 16 vehicles in 1945. Heavy Transport became the ECC Transport Division in 1950, subsequently changing its name to Heavy Transport (ECC) Ltd, and continued to acquire other haulage businesses through the 1950s and 1960s, including Glover & Uglow Ltd of Callington with 75 vehicles in 1963. A much smaller fleet than Heavy Transport's was operated by ECC's Quarries Division. **RAS**

Hudson (1969), ch. 8

Hellmann Worldwide Logistics, a privately-owned international operator, was founded in 1871 in Osnabrück, north-west Germany, for the local movement of textiles. It entered the UK in 1988, buying the freight forwarder Mitchell Cotts, and developed three hubs, at Bradford, Rainham in Essex, and Fradley Park, near Lichfield. The latter £12 million complex was opened in 1999 as a base for trade to and from Europe. It has computer-controlled pallet- and parcel-sorting in the same building and Hellmanns developed an adjacent site as a hub for clients' warehousing. Fradley Park also served as Hellmann's UK head-quarters. In addition to the three hubs, there were also three other major depots in the UK and 55 parcels offices. UK turnover of £55 million was generated by air freight and ocean forwarding and European road services. Some 40 per cent of Hellmann's UK work is handled by owner-drivers (q.v.), but its UK direct operation is in contrast to most of Hellmann's overseas activity, including in the USA, which involves local haulier partnership. **RAS**

CM (7 October 1999), pp. 48–9

Henman, Philip S, see TRANSPORT DEVELOPMENT GROUP

Hilton Transport Services Ltd, as Roadships Ltd (they were renamed in 1974), was the subject of a Board of Trade Companies Act s.165(b) inquiry which cast unwonted light on some of the darker areas of road haulage. HTS was formed in July 1959 by Ralph Hilton (1923–81) and his wife Pearl, who assisted with the administration, a not uncommon division of labour in family haulage firms. Hilton, a London greengrocer's son, went into road haulage part-time in 1954. With the useful asset of a filling station, acquired in 1956, his fleet had reached 49 by 1959. During the 1960s HTS grew by the acquisition of smaller businesses for their A licences. Hilton worked hard with initiative and drive and what the inspectors' report described as 'a robust attitude towards business affairs'. Thus far, Hilton may be regarded as typical of the rough diamond which has often been evident in road haulage entrepreneurship. When HTS expanded from the late 1960s beyond his management capabilities, especially in the area of warehousing, its weaknesses and those of its founder came to the fore. Expansion included not only large and, in one case, unsuitable sites, but also larger haulage businesses than heretofore, such as the Joy Group, with 155 vehicles, which joined a fleet of over 400 operated at that time by HTS. The report of the inquiry criticised the flotation of HTS by the Industrial & Commercial Finance Corporation in November 1970. By that time the size of HTS had exceeded managerial competence and growing rumours should have been heeded. Yet HTS continued to grow: nine companies were taken over between May 1970 and January 1972, including the J & H Transport Group Ltd. The report considered that the HTS Management structure virtually collapsed from the autumn of 1971. Gallagher, the tobacco firm, dropped a takeover bid in March 1972

and an independent businessman was appointed as chief administrator, but to no effect and in March 1973 Cork Gully, the liquidation specialists, were called in. Hilton resigned in the following month, but until February 1974 he owned 35 per cent of the equity of HTS and forced the holding of an extraordinary general meeting in October 1973 and issued a 'Programme for Recovery' in January 1974, a few days before his arrest. He was acquitted of conspiracy but found guilty of falsifying accounts at his trial in June 1975. He went on to found Hilton Amalgamated Transport, which included WBS Transport of West Thurrock, Priestner Transport of Manchester, D W Woodward (Transport) Ltd of Hampshire, and Silvertown London Inland Clearance Ltd. Hilton died, relatively young, in 1981 and his son, Ralph John Hilton, took over control of Hilton Amalgamated, which called in the receiver in 1986, following the collapse of the WBS subsidiary, with 94 vehicles. **RAS**

B A Hytner and I A N Irvine, *Roadships Limited: report of an investigation under section 165(b) of the Companies Act* (1976); *DBB*, 3; R Hilton, 'Hilton Transport Services' in R Lynn (ed.), *The Entrepreneur: eight case studies* (1974); *MT* (26 October 1983 and 26 September 1985); *New DNB* entry (forthcoming)

Hinchcliffe, J & H, traces its history to at least 1850, from John and Mary Hinchcliffe, who moved from Yorkshire to near Bury. The business expanded under John's son, Joe, carrying for the local cotton mills. At the start of the First World War, all his horses were requisitioned. In 1919 the business re-started, now as a partnership with George Hopkinson, which was dissolved in 1924. The first lorries, four Pagefields, were placed in service in the early 1930s. These had the Pagefield system for transferring their loads. The slump in the textile industry led John's two sons, Herbert and John, now in the business, to extend their Glasgow–Bury service to London. Herbert moved to a north London base with additional new vehicles, including Reo Speed Wagons. Fisher Renwick (FR) acquired the business on 1 September 1939. The fleet now included AEC four- and six-wheeled lorries and it is believed that the immaculate fleet was requisitioned by the Army. There is no record of these being taken into the FR fleet. Hinchcliffe had been acting as sub-contractor to Fisher Renwick, particularly for Scottish traffic. The brothers remained to work for FR, being valued for their achievements in a wide variety of jobs. At the end of the war they elected to re-commence their own business, starting with two B licences, and second-hand Dennis Pax lorries delivering coal. Soon after they acquired Howarth Scholfield for its A-licenced vehicles. Working within the 25 miles radius, extended by their take-over of a Blackpool operator, they were able to avoid nationalisation (q.v.). The main traffic was cement and aggregates. They diversified into coach operation, but sold this off in 1975. The fleet mostly comprised Dennis lorries, converted to Gardner engines. Later, as the business expanded, Albion, Atkinson and ERF lorries and articulated outfits were purchased. They were one of the first to operate a Volvo, purchasing a LHD Volvo four-wheel lorry in 1966. It had been used by Ford UK for assessment. Between 1984 and 1986 13 Dennis with Gardner engines were added. Hinchcliffe took delivery of the last Seddon-Atkinson 411 artics with Gardner engines, also among the last to be built for lorries by Gardner. The fleet in 2000 was mainly ERF, with a few Mercedes. The traffic was largely for the paper industry, with some general haulage and storage and warehousing. Herbert's sons, Geoff and John were in charge, with Herbert still able to take an interest. In turn younger members of the family worked in the business. Among the facilities available at their Walmersley, Bury, base was an excellent traditional transport café (q.v.). The haulage business was closed down in September 2001 and the fleet and equipment sold by auction.

GM

The Hinchcliffe family; Mustoe (1997)

Hindley, E S, & Sons, of Bourton, Dorset, built a range of steam wagons, mainly 3 and 5 tonners, from 1904 to 1908 and is credited with putting Pickfords' (q.v.) steam fleet on a firm foundation. Competition from other, better remembered, steam builders made its success short-lived.

JMA

Hino, owned by Toyota, was the first Japanese heavy lorry maker to make inroads into the UK market, from 1980 onwards, although in small numbers, via an importer/assembler in the Irish Republic. Hino 6- and 8-wheel chassis were particularly favoured by earth-moving and demolition contractors.

RAS

Hiring Margin. Under a C licence the trader need not own its vehicles, but if it hired vehicles more or less permanently they could be authorised under this licence. The trader could, however, have a hiring margin in order that they could hire vehicles which might be required from time to time, up to the number specified. They needed to employ the driver for these vehicles. The licence disc (q.v.) belonging to the person lending the vehicles and who, for the time, was not using them, had to be removed and replaced by the borrower's 'hiring' disc.

Historic Commercial Vehicle Society. Response to a letter in *Veteran and Vintage Magazine* led to the formation of the Historic Commercial Vehicle Club under the chairmanship of Lord Montagu of Beaulieu in 1958. Citing current enthusiasm for car and steam traction engine rallies the letter had suggested something similar for commercial vehicles could be popular. The HCVC's first rally was at Leyland in 1958, with some 20 vehicles taking part, while the first of its annual Brighton runs was in 1962. In that year the vintage Taxi Club and the Vintage Passenger Vehicle Society joined forces with the club. Its aims are to encourage and promote interest in the preservation, ownership, history and running of historic commercial vehicles. A change of name in the early 1980s to the Historic Commercial Vehicle Society accompanied a change to charitable status.

The growing interest in preservation has more recently seen the emergence of societies and clubs with a narrower remit based on either a particular make, such as the AEC

Society, or an area such as the Lincolnshire Vintage Vehicle Society. **JMA**

The **Hixon disaster** of 1968 highlighted the meticulous care essential in the planning and execution of journeys involving abnormal loads. A double-ended low-loader operated by Robert Wynn & Sons was transporting under police escort a transformer from the English Electric works at Stafford to a depot at Hixon. Negotiating an automatic half-barrier level crossing, it appears that both the escort and the lorry crew were unaware of the short period of time allowed for clearance of the crossing once the barriers and related warning lights and bells had been activated by an approaching train. In this case a Manchester–Euston express travelling at 75 mph was unable to stop within the available distance and the ensuing collision resulted in eleven fatalities. The disaster was followed by a rare judicial enquiry and a heightening of awareness of the potential hazards and a tightening of procedures by all parties involved. Improved signage at level crossings and additional road signs where there was a risk of vehicles grounding were among the recommendations adopted.

This was a high-profile accident because there had been previous concern about the safety of introducing automatic, half-barrier crossings, the number of fatalities were high and the train came off as badly as the road vehicle, which was not the case with most level crossing accidents.

The report of the public inquiry into the accident was critical of virtually everyone concerned. The cause of the accident was judged to be the driver, Grover, failing to comply with the requirement to stop and phone the signalman before attempting to traverse the level crossing. The slow speed, 2 mph, aggravated this, as did Wynns' failure to ensure proper precautions had been laid down. The two police constables escorting the load were almost totally ignorant of how automatic crossings worked and the procedures required, and they assumed the driver knew what he was doing in attempting to cross the railway. The chief constable of Staffordshire and other senior police officers were condemned for failing to instruct their constables about the methods and precautions needed when using automatic crossings, especially the need to use the telephone. Most heavy haulage drivers assumed that when there was a police escort the latter assumed control. but in fact when problems arose they were only officially present in an advisory role. British Rail failed to disseminate information about automatic crossings to road hauliers, assuming the Ministry of Transport would do so, but the Ministry had failed to consider the need for special procedures for slow-moving vehicles. The Ministry and British Rail failed to collaborate or to appreciate the need for special measures. In this regard the Inspector of Railways, Col McCullogh was criticised. In the enquiry nobody came out well. **RAS/GM**

World of Trains, pt 8 (1991); Report of the Public Enquiry into the Accident at Hixon Level Crossing (HMSO, Cmnd 3206)

Holdsworth & Hanson Ltd (H&H). Starting in 1928 both Joseph Hanson Ltd (q.v.) and I W Holdsworth Ltd (q.v.) chose to operate most of their acquired companies as joint ventures with neither parent company having a controlling interest. These joint trading companies had the title H & H with the name of the operating base identifying each subsidiary, that is Chelmsford; Glasgow; Hull; Leeds; and London. The one exception was Hanson & Holdsworth (Birmingham) Ltd. J Hanson Ltd had acquired its Birmingham agent and reversed the sequence, Hanson preceding Holdsworth in this instance. There was one other joint trading company H & H (Estates) Ltd, this was formed to own and manage properties mainly used by the joint businesses. The other transport subsidiaries also owned jointly were Holdsworth and Burrill Ltd; Bradford–Leicester Transport Ltd; J Poulter & Sons Ltd and J S Hutchinson Ltd.

In broad terms the subsidiary companies carried out the trunking, while H & H did the terminal activities, such as collection and delivery, sorting and providing the depots. They preferred to use Morris and AEC vehicles. Some were open top wagons or trailers which were used in the wool textile trade to carry semi-finished and piece goods. The open top allowed overhead loading from the mills and a degree of flexibility in load height.   **GM**

MT (21 February 1948), p. 5

Holdsworth, Israel William, started his carrier's business in 1870, at first serving the woollen industry. His sons, Oliver and Charles, chose to operate separately their own business, retaining a working relationship with their father. On his death in 1905 they merged the businesses, trading as I W Holdsworth, their brother-in-law, Walter Dean, becoming a partner. Holdsworth also had contracts to supply the War Office with horses during the Great War. Losing horses and vehicles through requisition, they were subsequently able to purchase steam and motor vehicles.

After purchasing Walter Dean's shares from his widow in 1918, they formed O & C Holdsworth, trading as I W Holdsworth Ltd. They also acquired livery stables. Walter Dean's son, Norman, joined the business, starting Hebble Motors bus service. This expanded to operate some 90 buses in 1929, when it was acquired by the LMSR and LNER.

Holdsworth expanded its carriers and haulage businesses, with a Halifax to London service from 1928, trading as Holdsworth & Hanson (London) Ltd. Acquisitions soon followed including J W North and J W Benn. They both carried wool and textiles from Bradford to the Humber ports, as well as operating a removals business. They merged as J W North, followed by William Burrill of Littleborough. Holdsworth & Burrill Ltd (previously J W North Ltd), was formed to take over North. The business of William Burrill of Littleborough, was acquired in 1930, specialising in trans-Pennine textile traffic and continuing to operate as William Burrill until nationalisation.

J Poulter Ltd of Bradford, a smalls carrier serving the West Riding and Lancashire, was acquired in 1933, followed by Bradford–Leicester Parcels Express, providing a service to the Midlands; its title was changed to Bradford–Leicester Transport.

Both Hanson's and Holdsworth's directors were directors of the joint companies, setting the precedent of no single company controlling the trading subsidiaries.   **GM**

Brummer and Cowe (1994)

Holland Coachcraft. There was a fashion for streamlining both railway and road vehicles in the 1930s. At the road speeds then normal there was little or no benefit, but there was a considerable publicity value. Achieving the required curvaceous shapes on what would otherwise have been simple box bodies required considerable skills in panel beating: the metal had to be shaped to curve in more than one plane and the timber framing behind it also had to be shaped. The best-known was Holland Coachcraft of Glasgow, which supplied designs for other body builders. The first van, on a Commer Centaur chassis, was exhibited at the 1933 Commercial Motor Show. Unhappy with the way in which some bodybuilders were building its designs, the firm opened its own body building factory at Team Valley Industrial Estate, Gateshead, in 1938.   **JMA**

Home Delivery (Figure 118) is a well-known term, but its meaning has subtly changed in recent years. Deliveries of goods by traders (or contractors on their behalf) formed a part of the transport industry from its earliest days, whether by errand boy on a bicycle or by van, lorry or electric float. Before the day of the supermarket the local grocer usually delivered the week's order to his customers. Milk and bread were delivered house-to-house on a daily basis while at least in middle-class areas dirty washing was collected weekly and returned washed and ironed. Bread deliveries generally faded away in the 1960s, often after smaller local bakeries sold out to larger ones, while the development of the domestic washing machine killed laundry work. There were other regular deliveries, too: for example, wireless and electric shops would take away accumulators for recharging and deliver recharged ones to homes with wireless sets that had no electricity supply.

Universal availability of electricity, the growth of supermarkets and widespread car ownership meant that only milk deliveries survived to the end of the twentieth century, and even these were a shadow of their former selves. The once universal delivery of coal to virtually every householder dwindled after the development of gas and electric central heating systems, but oil-fired systems were also developed and users of these needed regular deliveries by tanker.

The 1990s saw the main supermarkets and some other food stores inaugurating home delivery services, often initially on an experimental basis, and not always successfully. These deliveries could be made in the evening or weekends, were charged for and made in high-specification vans with separate compartments for frozen and chilled food. In the 1980s the term home delivery had also been applied to a new specialist branch of the transport industry, where transport operators undertook not merely to deliver large electrical items by appointment with the householder but also to unpack and install them, and take the old unit away. Such operations usually took the goods straight from a warehouse (perhaps also operated on the store's behalf) rather than from the local shop or showroom where an identical item was on display. Despite the obvious attractions of the system and the high calibre of operators offering it, there have been difficulties in making it profitable. It proved hard to predict the time taken to install appliances and householders were not always at home when they had promised. Blocks of flats proved a particular problem if the lifts were not working. Retailers sometimes drove such hard bargains with operators that the work proved unprofitable.

Two types of home delivery that have remained relatively unchanged are of furniture (though development of tail lifts for vehicles has made this easier) and of mail order goods. Mail order was once seen as the favoured means of buying consumer goods by householders with lower incomes, but in recent years specialist mail order outlets have targeted other sectors of the market. Sales of goods through the world-wide web have not grown as quickly as expected, but it is now understood that success depends on reliable home delivery services. A number of parcels, mail order and other carriers carry out this work, which often involves evening and weekend working.

A distinction should be drawn between regular deliveries, perhaps daily, made of milk (and, in the past, bread too), and the kind of on-the-spot sales made by mobile shops (q.v) and also "rounds" where traders came round opportunistically selling soft drinks, fish or frozen produce or indeed anything else. Here there was no prior agreement to call or deliver and the trade depended on people happening to be at home when the vehicle or roundsman appeared and then wishing to purchase what was on offer.   **JMA**

The **Hope anti-jack-knife device** was developed in the mid-1960s and brought to the market in 1968, to counter the problem of articulated lorries jack-knifing when under sharp braking. It was developed by Fred Hope of Hope Transport (q.v.). It acted as a king-pin damping device, fitted to trailers to slow down trailer swinging. A multi-plate disc brake acted on the trailer king pin when the brakes were applied. The king pin was located by a tang in the vee of the fifth wheel of the tractor and was free to rotate in this mounting until the brakes operated. The device was manufactured by Self Energising Disc Brakes Ltd from the later 1960s and was for a time popular with safety-conscious operators, until the development of sensor braking systems. By 1980 it had sold 25,000 worldwide.   **RAS/JA**

Dickson-Simpson (1968); *CM* (12 January 1980), pp. 61–3

Hope Transport, general and long distance hauliers, was established by Fred Hope during the Second World War at Hounslow. The operating centre later moved to Bedfont. Using secondhand and ex-WD vehicles, on which he carried out extensive rebuilding, Hope built up a fleet which included seven Dodge T110s. The business grew with contracts from Taylor Woodrow, then Truscon and Tarmac. Hope expanded, like many concerns before 1968, by acquiring small hauliers to obtain their A and B

licences rather than their vehicles. Acquisitions included J Steele, livestock hauliers and royal warrant holders of Datchet, with a fleet of Bedfords, some with non-detachable Carrimore trailers, and Vulcans. Hope went on to acquire quantities of ex-BRS vehicles and a variety of semi-trailers, for in-house adaptation. In 1956 the first of six new AEC Mercury tractive units were added to the fleet and for a time Hope Transport expanded in long-distance haulage, for example, taking Channel Islands tomatoes to the north west and returning with clearing house loads. Hope decided to specialise in heavy haulage, acquiring two AEC Mandator and two Mammoth Major tractive units for the purpose. In the lighter sector of the firm's operations, the replacement of Fordson Thames ET6 tippers and flats by Thames Traders was regarded by Hope as less than successful. By the mid-1960s Hope's fleet had grown to 35 vehicles, but he required capital for the development of the anti-jack-knife device (q.v.) on which he had been working, with the result that Hope Transport was purchased by Speedfreights Ltd in 1966. In the 1970s Hope made trailer scrutineers and under-run devices.
RAS

F Hope, 'If in a hurry HAVE HOPE', *Classic Commercial* (1981), pp. 8–12, 16–17.

Horse boxes (Figures 119 and 124) were developed to meet the needs of those with valuable equine property to transport, whether racehorses, bloodstock, or hunters. Frequently they were constructed on coach chassis, to gain the advantages of extra length, lower chassis height and, especially, smoother ride. Vincents of Reading (q.v.) were pioneers of horse box design and construction and became leading suppliers. Lambourn (q.v.) and Oakley were later entrants to this specialist field. The necessary interior arrangements included stalls for the horses carried, a compartment for the groom or stablehand accompanying the horses and lockers for saddles, fodder, etc. Examples of passenger chassis-based horse boxes by Vincents included a Leyland Tiger 4-horse box for Lancashire Constabulary, 1939, a Daimler 3-horse box for the trainer, Fred Armstrong of Newmarket, 1947, and an AEC Regal III horse

box for George VI, 1949. British Railways and its predecessors operated horse boxes to connect stables, studs and racecourses with railheads, and in some cases undertake the entire journey by road. For this work a notable group of horse boxes with bodies by Thomas Harrington of Hove was commissioned. The first of these full-fronted, metal-panelled designs were mounted on Albion Valkyrie coach chassis for the LNER in 1938. Similar bodies were subsequently built on Maudslay Marathon coach chassis for the LNER and the Southern Railway, passing into British Railways' service. With a change of BR policy in 1963, these horse boxes were sold off; a batch of five previously based at Leyburn was acquired by a local haulier, George Wilkinson, Sons & Co. (Leyburn) Ltd to expand that aspect of his business. **RAS**

Stevens-Stratten and Aldridge (1987), ch. 3; *MT* (6 March 1964), p. 12; Vincent file, Words & Machines Collection; *Motor Body Building* (January 1929), p. 2

Horse-drawn transport (Figure 30) In the nineteenth century the spreading railway network almost eliminated medium- and long-distance road transport. Nevertheless, such was the demand for road feeder services generated by the railways, coupled with the general growth of trade, that according to F M L Thompson's estimate, the number of horse-drawn carts, vans and waggons increased by a factor of five between 1851 and 1911. The railways did not have things all their own way. For example, in connection with its recently-introduced parcel post service, the Post Office (q.v.) began to run road coaches in 1887 between London and Brighton and later on other roads. In 1900, however, the main task of the horse was to move goods around the towns, to and from railway goods depots, to and from the docks, between factory and warehouse, between wholesaler and retailer, between mill and station yard, between river or canal wharf and factory.

There were other non-urban services still in 1900 entrusted to horses. The country carrier working from a rail-served market town had long been a feature of rural horse transport, bringing provisions to the villages and consignments to individual houses. Then there were the tradesmen's vans, the butcher, the baker, the oil man, the fishmonger, operating a door-to-door service, along with what might be termed heavy rural transport, corn to the mill and flour and cattle feed from it, timber from the woods to the sawmill and from the sawmill to the station. Such traffic circulated within about a ten-mile radius of the nearest railway station, probably overlapping deliveries from the next station along the line, although some districts were more remote from railheads – North Devon, Lakeland, the Scottish Highlands – and here longer-distance transport prevailed such as fish-laden vans from Ullapool to Garve on the Kyle of Lochalsh line. Steam road vehicles also played a part in this rural traffic, especially in timber extraction and quarry and mine traffic.

Whereas rural road use was comparatively light, it was quite otherwise in the towns and particularly at the ports, where the ordinary business traffic of distribution to shops, of delivery of raw materials to mills, of finished goods to the station, was augmented by imports and exports to and from wharves and quays. The railways handled much of the traffic through their dockside goods stations, like the huge concentration of sixteen at Liverpool linked to the dock railway system, but there remained carts from quay to warehouse, from warehouse to railway, from railway back to quay. In those days of break bulk, with every item individual, there were sacks and barrels, carboys and crates, coils and baskets, drums and bales, an overwhelming medley of goods demanding carriage. In 1900 steam vehicles were in evidence on the docks, but horses did the bulk of the work and in the towns horse-transport in the railway service, either directly worked or in the hands of contractors (favoured in Scotland), offered as intensive a parcels service as the Post Office.

In urban work speed was not important as the density of vehicles, particularly round the docks, made swift operation impossible. Indeed traffic jams in the horse age were more tangled than today because of the unpredictable behaviour of horses. Accidents were frequent, with stumbles and falls, breakage of harness, poles and shafts, runaway carts and waggons, runaway horses, shafts goring horses, kicks and bites, all contributing at times to indescribable confusion. On the other hand horses were manoeuvrable and could back their carts and waggons into confined spaces with more success perhaps than a steam or motor lorry, useful accomplishments on a wharf, in a brewery yard, alongside a railway loading dock. Loads might pose problems of awkwardness rather than weight – bales of cotton, hogsheads of tobacco, piles of fish boxes – with instability a constant threat, especially with timber unless tightly secured. Heavy loads demanded teams of horses which led to manoeuvring difficulties, but most of the work was of a miscellaneous nature well within the competence of a single horse. Distance depended on stamina as did hours of work, but in towns activity was broken by long periods of waiting and the actual distances in start-stop delivery work were limited, so that a horse could handle refuse collection, milk rounds, beer deliveries, post and parcels, with ease. Great distances could be covered only by relays of horses, as in the days of the stage waggon and canal fly boats, but by 1900 few stage services were in operation.

Ten years on horse transport was in slow decline and sixty years on all but extinct. The reasons are clear: the development of the motor van and lorry, which could be designed for every need and built as required. When not working it was not, unlike the horse, consuming fuel, but was ready to go, night or day, at a swing of the starting handle. It was manoeuvrable too, indeed it had the advantages of the horse with more added. Against the motor's merits was its dislike of start-stop work, and its greater first cost. Its stabling needs were not dissimilar to a horse's and cost about the same, fitter's shop against farrier's, fuel tank against feed bin, petrol pump against water trough. A major triumph for the motor was the introduction in the early 1930s of the Karrier and Scammell mechanical horses (q.v.) which combined the manoeuvrability of the horse with the greater speed of the motor.

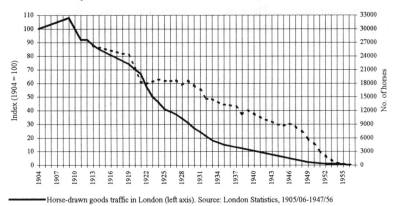

Graph 10: The Decline of Horse-Drawn Goods Traffic 1904-1957

———— Horse-drawn goods traffic in London (left axis). Source: London Statistics, 1905/06-1947/56

- - - - - Railway cartage horses (right axis). Sources: Railway Returns, 1913-1947; BTC Annual Reports, 1948-1957

The traffic censuses conducted by the Metropolitan Police indicate that the number of horse-drawn goods vehicles in London began to decline after 1909 (see Graph 10). By 1923 more than half of them had gone and the numbers of horse-drawn and motor goods vehicles passing the census points were about equal. At first sight it might seem surprising that the other half took another thirty years to disappear, but published costings demonstrate that for a long time the horse was more economical for short-distance collection and delivery rounds. For example, J S Holloway, a co-operative society transport manager writing in 1931, compared using a 3-ton capacity motor lorry and a 30-cwt-capacity horse dray on a coal- or grocery-delivery round; their respective costs, including driver, were 75s and 22s per day and their speeds were 10 and 2½ mph. While actually travelling, the cost per ton-mile of the horse dray was 2.35 times that of the motor lorry; but, if the loading/unloading time for the motor lorry were twice its travelling time – as could be the case on town rounds – the horse was more economical. The cartage work undertaken by the railways was nearly all in towns and cities, some of it in congested streets where a motor lorry could not maintain 10 mph. Thus, as the graph shows, the railways were slower than average in converting from horse to motor; indeed they were still constructing new horse-drawn vehicles until the Second World War.

This proved valuable during the war and the years of post-war austerity, when motor vehicles, petrol and tyres were in short supply. By then, however, the relative economics had changed and the end came quite quickly. Yet the value of the horse for start-stop work is still recognised, with the added attraction in this nostalgic age of publicity, of which breweries have taken advantage.

Operational problems occurred, since horses are self-willed animals. They cannot be completely under control, with the possibility of unpredictable behaviour. Accidents in horse-choked streets were as fearful as any modern pile up. Congestion was indeed the main problem, exacerbated by the slow speed. Rather than overtake, a horse followed in stately procession, but the procession could degenerate into a pushing, shoving melée where accidents were bound to happen. Weather conditions might hasten the deterioration. Rain, ice and snow caused slips and skids, even fatal falls where legs were broken, while on country roads the hazards were mud and floods. During the Second World War the blitz and fire were unlooked-for threats, stables were bombed and horses killed and injured. It proved necessary in Belfast, when fire destroyed stables, to let the horses escape and bolt with tails afire.

Whereas broken-down motors can be repaired and parts replaced, with sick and injured horses it is not so simple. Not only is treatment uncertain, there are the problems of infection and contagion against which drastic measures have to be taken. During equine epidemics it was usual to seal up water troughs, fumigate and disinfect, burn litter, whitewash floors and walls, and destroy infected horses. Glanders and farcy were the most lethal diseases, both causing ulceration of the air passages and other organs, and could spread so quickly as to threaten the entire horse transport system of a district. Slaughter was the only solution.

Vehicles followed two main patterns, two-wheeled or four-wheeled, the former limited to light work, except for the huge paired wheels of the timber carriage sometimes called a gill, the latter with a turning fore axle and usually rear wheels of larger diameter. Whereas the two-wheeled could be a flat float, a high-or-low-sided cart for bulk carriage, or a closed van body, favoured by butchers and bakers, the four-wheeler had infinite possibilities. There were high-sided floats with a deep well for sheets of glass or corrugated iron, standard platform lorries or lurries or rulleys for general cartage. There were extra strong team waggons for heavy loads, notably at the ports, open-sided and bow-fronted coal merchants' waggons called coal vans in the London area, low-sided trolleys for handling removals containers, covered pantechnicons, pole waggons for pipes, rails, shipyard plates whose rear axles could be moved to suit the length of load, tankers for oil and paraffin, drays for beer and wine. It was not practicable to go above two axles, but there were multi-wheeled bogies for teams handling heavy loads like boilers.

Traction depended on shafts and poles and traces. Two-wheeled carts were shafted and needed no more than a single horse, unless heavily laden or facing a hill, when a trace was attached. Four-wheeled waggons might have a single horse between shafts, a pair of horses between shafts, a pair divided by a pole, or work in tandem by means of shafts and traces, in other words a team. Harness or gears worked on the same general principles with variations, the pull coming from the collar pressed by the shoulders. With shaft harness

the breeching took the thrust when backing and enabled the horse to check the vehicle. With pole harness the horses could hold back the pole and might also employ breechings. For lighter vehicles the gears were also light, contrasting with the heavy saddles and back chains of waggon gears. Regional variations in detail were many, Scotland favouring the high-peaked collar and wide-spreading hames, Kent a low saddle and Liverpool a saddle with double girths. Bridles varied too, ones with blinkers were most usual although an open bridle was often used in Scotland.

Horses themselves were mixed, the main heavy breeds were the Shire, the Clydesdale, the Suffolk and the French Percheron introduced after the First World War. There was too the Irish Draught Horse, but breeds were heavily crossed, notably Shires and Clydesdales. For lighter vehicles came the Irish Cyp Horses and smaller vanners and Welsh Cobs, down to pony size, say 14.2 hands (a hand is 4 inches or 122 cm) as opposed to the 17.2 of the Shire and Clydesdale, while Cleveland Bays occupied an intermediate position at about 15 hands, good on express delivery of parcels. By 1900 an immense organisation had developed round the horse. Stables were universal in the towns, some several stories high with stalls for two hundred horses and ramps down to ground level. Within, the horses were tethered by loose halters so that they could lie down; loose boxes were for sick or injured horses. Harness was hung at the stall ends and there were water troughs on every floor as well as the yard. Near the stalls were the feed stores and there was a feed preparation plant, although this might be centralised somewhere and the feed, made up to the company's specification and sent out to each stable. Some stables also housed a goat, as goats gave early warning of fire and fire was a big risk in stables. A farrier's shop was a necessity, perhaps with several hearths in a big stable, and there was a saddler's, a wheel and cartwright's shop, and a veterinary surgery with the necessary equipment like stocks to hold horses during treatment. The collection and disposal of manure was a big task, the nightly amount running into some 15 cwt at a large establishment. Equally daunting was the provision of bedding; straw was not popular as it was bulky and harboured vermin, but peat moss was favoured.

Stable staff included stablemen, a provender man, farriers and a blacksmith, a cartwright and a saddler, under the yard foreman, but each carter had his own horse, staying with each other for years so that mutual trust and respect was built up. Horse transport could work in no other way. The carter was generally responsible for feeding, watering, grooming, harnessing and unharnessing, and cleaning the gear but at some large railway stables stablemen were employed for this work. In 1923 the LMSR made significant economies by introducing vacuum cleaners for grooming. The vehicles, kept often in the open, were under the care of the wheelwrights and cartwrights. Saddlers looked after the harness, which they altered to suit the individual horses, while a sailmaker might be employed to make and repair waggon cloths and horse cloths. Horse transport was a big undertaking and so it remained to 1945. **EWPT**

F M L Thompson, 'Nineteenth-century horse sense,' *Economic History Review*, XXIX, 1 (1976), pp. 60–81; Alan Everitt, 'Country carriers in the nineteenth century', *JTH,* 2nd series, 3, 3 (1976), pp. 179–202; Clark (1989); Smith (1994); Russell (1995); Paget-Tomlinson (1990)

Hoyer began in 1946 as a bulk liquid specialist with headquarters at Hamburg but it has operated in Britain since 1974. Besides road tankers it has had some thousands of ISO tank containers and swap bodies suitable for all categories of liquids, powders and gases. It was also a big customer of Railfreight. Among the British bulk liquid operators acquired in Hoyer's expansion were George Catchpole, Hipwood & Grundy, Bulk Liquid Storage, and an interest in Dennis Dixon of Middlesbrough. Subsidiaries include Thurroclean, providing a tank cleaning service for any operator's tanker or tank container. Hoyer continued to expand in Britain, opening a rail terminal at Workington, to handle Eastman Chemical using dedicated ISO

powder containers. It also won a contract to distribute Esso Petroleum. **GM**

Hurlock, William, Junior Ltd was established before the First World War by William and Charles Hurlock in south London, as component and secondhand car dealers. The business greatly expanded after the war through the purchase and thorough reconditioning of ex-service lorries, of which 180 had been processed as early as mid-1920. To a massive trade in spares were added Bean, Dennis and Willys-Overland-Crossley agencies, with a thriving ancillary business in trailing-axle conversion to six-wheelers. A growing commercial vehicle bodybuilding activity accompanied the continuing reconditioning of ex-service lorries, including post-war vehicles; the needs of civil engineering firms were especially catered for, as well as such prominent firms as Sainsburys. As time went by conversions became more radical, to compete with the standards of contemporary vehicles: four Thornycroft road tractors supplied to R Cornell Ltd of Smithfield for hauling meat trailers were to all intents and purposes new vehicles. In addition, secondhand buses were converted into pantechnicons and into vehicle-carriers for the business. To meet the space needs of their growing bodybuilding, the Hurlocks were attracted by the Thames Ditton plant of AC Cars, which had gone into receivership in 1929. They bought the works at auction in 1930 then changed plans, reviving the AC marque. Commercial vehicle work continued at their Effra Road, Brixton, site; from 1938 it was divided between the Thames Ditton works and a new site at Hounslow. The south of Thames agency for the Gardner diesel engine was acquired and Hurlocks carried out many conversions. An attempt was made to enter commercial vehicle manufacture by the acquisition of Arran Motors, which had gone into liquidation in 1937, but the compulsory purchase of Hurlocks' Effra Road premises put an end to this venture. The Hounslow premises were bombed; after the war there was a return to trading in ex-service vehicles at Kingston. The next generation of Hurlocks acquired Unipower in 1977 and a 70 per cent interest in the PEM bodybuilding business at Poole. **RAS**

Nick Baldwin and W D Hurlock, 'The Hurlock family', *OM*, 11, 4 (1971), pp. 314–27; J Mclellan, *Classic ACs Auto-Carrier to Cobra* (Thrupp: Sutton Publishing, 2000)

Hutchinson, Ernest Boyd (1884–1967) was a former railwayman turned bus pioneer, who created United Automobile Services in 1912 in East Anglia and the north east. In 1929 he sold out jointly to the LNER and Tilling & British Automobile Traction, following competition for UAS between these two interests. Hutchinson then turned to investment in road haulage, creating Ryburn United Transport, based at Leeds, from a number of small businesses, including a bodybuilder and trailer manufacturer. Ryburn, with about 100 vehicles, was acquired by Oswald Tillotson Ltd in 1934. Hutchinson also set up Transport Service Ltd, to provide trunk services between the industrial towns, with a fellow busman as manager. He had plans to incorporate air freight into these operations, but TSL collapsed during 1933, as the result of operating and record-keeping problems, which are analysed by Dunbar (p. 56). Following the sale of UAS, Hutchinson was encouraged by Junner, editor of *CM*, to make a tour of inspection of the haulage industry in the winter of 1929–30. His findings on the lack of organisation prompted Junner to call the lunch in April 1930 which led to the Long Distance Road Haulage Committee of Enquiry and then to the Long Distance Road Haulage Association (q.v.), of both of which Hutchinson was honorary secretary.

RAS

Dunbar (1981); John Hibbs, *The History of British Bus Services* (Newton Abbot: David & Charles, 2nd ed., 1989); Gibson (2001)

Igloo (Figure 31), see PALLETS AND STILLAGES

The **Independent Express Corporation plc** was set up in 1983 by former managers of the Independent Parcel Express Co., after it had been taken over by TNT (q.v.). The Transport Development Group (q.v.) made a large investment in an attempt to create a national overnight freight service, but it proved to be an expensive failure. It incurred substantial set-up costs before any freight was moved, notably for a site near Northampton, close to the M1, for a purpose-built hub and head office. In 1987 it was brought under a new TDG holding company, Express Development Services Ltd, then in 1988 it was absorbed by another TDG business, Tufnells Parcels Express Ltd, a 50 per cent share in which was sold in 1990 to the French parcels carrier, Ducros Services Rapide SA. **RAS**

TDG Annual reports

Indiana commercials were made in Marion, Indiana, USA from 1911 to 1933, but after control passed to White Motor Co., production moved to Cleveland, Ohio. 1936 sales amounted to 1706 units. There was some penetration of the UK market in the 1930s. Indiana Sales were based at Wolverhampton and Georgano reports an abortive plan to make Indianas there for the home market in 1937. In the same year A Comer Ltd at nearby Bilston was producing cabs and bodies for Indiana chassis, and Black & White Transport of Bilston (later Queen Street Motor Garage) operated eight Indianas with Boys (q.v.) conversions. **RAS**

VCVM, 41, p. 85; *VCV*, 126, pp. 40–1

Indivisible loads, see ABNORMAL OR INDIVISIBLE LOADS

Industrial relations. By the end of the nineteenth century, the road haulage industry had dramatically expanded to meet the demands of the ports, railways and cities for local deliveries and goods movement. Workers' pay, conditions and effort remained determined overwhelmingly by employers. Work was frequently casual. Collective bargaining, in the form of district agreements, was found only in the principal cities (often ports), where trade unionism had become established during the 'New Unionism' upsurge of the late 1880s and was then rebuilt in the period 1910–14. Even here, collective organisation was weak. The major exception was in Liverpool (see LIVERPOOL AND DISTRICT CARTERS' AND MOTORMEN'S UNION). Trade union organisation grew during the First World War, and a national joint industrial council was briefly established in 1919 but by 1921 it was moribund. In the subsequent bleak years trade union organisation retreated, hastened by victimisation in the aftermath of the General Strike (q.v.) of 1926. Continuous vehicle improvements allowed a new, long-distance road haulage industry to develop, characterised by an employer's prerogative untrammelled by trade unionism, statutory regulation or labour shortages.

The majority of road haulage unions had come together in 1922, as part of a wider amalgamation with dockers' unions, to form the Road Transport Commercial trade group of the Transport and General Workers' Union (q.v.). In the late 1920s, and throughout the 1930s, the TGWU, in the person of the RTC group's national secretary, Jack Corrin, and the union's general secretary, Ernest Bevin, fought to maintain and extend union organisation in the road haulage industry. Their basic problem was the workers', and hence the unions', lack of power. As a result road haulage companies were rarely compelled to negotiate. Many companies organised in the National Road Transport Employers' Federation wanted standard terms throughout the industry in order to regulate competition. Numerous aspects of road haulage (vehicle condition and operation, drivers' hours and pay) constituted a threat to public safety and governments took powers to intervene. The Road Traffic Act 1930 gave authority to supervise drivers' hours and vehicle design, operation (speed and loading weight) and maintenance; the Rail and Road Traffic Act 1933 introduced a licensing system (q.v.).

Attempts to establish a voluntary national collective agreement for the hire and reward sector soon collapsed in 1936. The National Road Transport Employers' Federation (represented by W Edwards) and the trade unions (represented by Bevin) made a joint approach to the National government for an inquiry into pay and conditions in the industry. At its subsequent hearings they proposed a joint policy of statutory regulation of the hire and reward sector, with a fair wages clause to extend comparable terms to the own-account sector. This became part of the inquiry's recommendations that formed the basis of the National government's Road Haulage Wages Act 1938. It marked another important step in the renewed commitment of the state to the extension of collective bargaining.

The RHWA 1938 established a central wages board, composed of representatives of employers' associations and trade unions and independent members nominated by the government, given the task of formulating recommendations for the wages and conditions of drivers employed by hire and reward companies. These were then submitted for consultation to area boards comprised of representatives of employers' associations and trade unions, before being embodied in a statutory instrument by the Ministry of Transport. To inhibit undercutting on the basis of cheap labour, a fair wages clause (with recourse to the Industrial Court for adjudication) was imposed upon own-account operators as a condition of their licences. The upshot was a significant and general improvement in drivers' pay and conditions.

During the Second World War, as with other sectors, there was a dramatic increase in trade union organisation and its acceptance by employers in the road haulage industry. In the war's aftermath the statutory system of pay and conditions was marginalised (the structure was reformed in 1948 when the area boards were abolished and the central board was renamed the Road Haulage Wages Council). A National Joint Industrial Council was created in 1947,

following a strike in that year to protest at the continuation of pre-war practices such as the accumulative week, whereby overtime was paid on a weekly basis only after the accumulation of 48 hours, with no daily maximum or minimum specified hours. The nationalisation by the Labour government of much of the privately-owned road haulage industry led to the formation of BRS, with its own structure of bargaining and consultation.

The return of a significant part of BRS to private ownership by the incoming Conservative government in 1951, and the subsequent expansion of the private sector during the years of economic growth in the 1950s and 1960s, led to revival of the importance of the RHWC. Road haulage companies co-ordinated their policy through the Road Haulage Association, and the RHWC employers' panel. The NJIC was all but moribund. The TGWU, organisationally sclerotic and obsessed by anti-communism, was incapable of initiating any effective campaign to strengthen union organisation in the industry, in spite of the energy of Frank Cousins (q.v.) who by now was RTC group national secretary. Companies obtained a wide discretion, within the minimum terms stipulated by the RHWC and drivers' statutory hours, to determine pay and effort through mileage, trip and return-load bonuses. In practice, of course, this was always restrained by the weakness of supervision over drivers 'on the road'.

The unions responded to the raising of the speed limit for heavy goods vehicles to 30 mph in 1956 by seeking a 15 per cent pay increase. This was only partially successful. Drivers at London's Smithfield meat market won the increase after a major strike in 1958 but no national campaign was attempted. In Birmingham Alan Law (q.v.), supported by TGWU regional officers, Jack Jones and Harry Urwin, led a sustained campaign to rebuild the TGWU 5/35 branch as an effective focus of workers' collective power throughout Birmingham and its hinterland. In 1967, following industrial action, the Birmingham differential (£1.50 above the RHWC rate) was established. Similar movements occurred in

Liverpool and central Scotland (the latter led by the Scottish Commercial Motormen's Union (q.v.) under its general secretary, Alex Kitson). The TGWU 6/541 Liverpool branch subsequently played a significant role in the defiance of the Conservative government's Industrial Relations Act 1971.

The response of many companies to the growth of trade union power was one of alarm and the RHA agreed in 1965 to meet the unions' long-standing demand for a national negotiating body — the National Negotiating Committee. Its life was brief. Union organisation was too uneven for sufficient companies to feel the need for a national agreement. Thus the way was left open for local and sectoral bargaining, which spread though the road haulage industry during the 1970s, encouraged by Jack Jones and Harry Urwin, now respectively general and deputy general secretary of the TGWU. A major unofficial strike by Scottish drivers in 1974 signified the new national dimension of road haulage trade unionism The unions had withdrawn from the RHWC in 1972 and it was finally abolished in 1978. At the insistence of the unions, 22 regional joint industrial councils were created for the hire and reward sector.

The RHA, in response to the growth of union organisation, was by now a much more coherent and disciplined body. Encouraged by the Labour government (1974–9), it resisted the TGWU RTC group's pay claim in 1978–9, for workers covered by JIC agreements in the hire and reward sector. Union activists became aware of the RHA's strategy and an unofficial conference in Liverpool galvanised the disparate mood of discontent into a powerful movement against the RHA and the Labour government, precipitating a major strike in January 1979 (one of the constituents of the so-called 'Winter of Discontent'). This was notable for the role of local, lay-member committees which directed picketing, embargoes and dispensations across the whole of the road transport and distribution sectors, as drivers, confronted by appalling weather, sought to prevent the substitution of strike-bound companies by the own-account sector and BRS and other hire and reward companies

that negotiated national agreements. The TGWU executive officers and committees fought hard, but often failed, to exert the union's authority over the course of the strike. The pay claim was won but at the cost of the Labour government's credibility, and it was replaced in May 1979 by a Conservative government led by Mrs Thatcher, committed to a reduction in the power of trade unions.

A number of factors combined to transform industrial relations in the road haulage industry after 1979: economic restructuring, innovation in work organisation and employment legislation. Large, dedicated distribution companies now dominate the sector. There has been significant erosion of the workers' collective power within the employment relationship, evidenced in the decline of trade union organisation. Regional collective bargaining has all but collapsed, to be replaced either by employers' unilateral pay determination or company collective agreements.   **PS**

Paul Smith, *Unionisation and Union Leadership: the road haulage industry* (Continuum, 2001)

Industrial tractors, see TRACTORS ON THE ROAD

The **Industrial Transport Association** was founded in 1927 as an organisation of transport managers (covering all transport modes) *inter alia* to improve the efficiency of industrial transport staff and 'to impress upon businessmen the vital national importance of a proper use of transport'. In 1931, when it published the memoirs of Walter Gammons (q.v.), the ITA had impressive patrons and vice-chairmen. The former included Sir Harold Bowden of Raleigh and E S Shrapnell-Smith (q.v.); among the latter were the transport managers of the Co-operative Wholesale Society and of Allen & Hanburys Ltd, the manufacturing chemists. As well as running a College of Advanced Transport, it published the monthly *Transport Management*. The courses were aimed at transport managers but were on freight topics only. The Association merged with the Freight Transport Association (q.v.) in the 1970s.   **RAS**

Inland waterways and road transport. Much traffic on inland waterways, especially that in general merchandise, has always relied upon road transport for collection and delivery. The development of improved road haulage services in the inter-war years, and the flexibility which these brought, contributed to the loss of canal traffics, as did the location of new customers whose facilities were designed for road transport. For instance, the inter-war Park Royal estate in West London was laid out primarily for road (and rail) transport, although some traffic developed upon the Grand Union Canal which ran through it. As road transport matured, few new waterside locations were laid out without road facilities; a late example was Westwood Power Station, on the Leeds & Liverpool Canal at Wigan, opened in 1951; this had only rail and water facilities. The impact of road competition upon railway rates and facilities also encouraged the decline of inland waterways traffic.

Some waterways carriers developed road services themselves in order to offer an integrated service. One of the earliest was the Rochdale Canal Company, which introduced motorised road vehicles in the Manchester area, before they were requisitioned for military use during the First World War. The Bridgewater Department introduced a lorry fleet for collection and delivery from Castlefield, Warrington and Runcorn in 1923, while the Aire & Calder Navigation developed road services in West Yorkshire from the 1920s, primarily to serve its depots at Wakefield and Leeds. In the 1920s Fellows Morton & Clayton acquired about 20 lorries to collect and deliver from its Midlands depots, and in the early 1930s, facing a financial crisis, contemplated transferring its traffics on north west canals to road. T & S Element of Salford Bridge, which survived to the 21st century, operated both road and canal transport in the Midlands canals between the 1930s and the 1970s. In the early 1940s the Grand Union Canal Company modernised its line to Derbyshire through the development of a series of road transhipment points. Extensive traffic developed around warehousing in the Birmingham area where the GUC Co. owned

three Bedford articulated lorries, and in 1945 the GUC Co. acquired the Brierley Hill haulage firm, Cartwright & Paddock; this was later transferred to the Road Haulage Executive. In the post-war period Philip Henman developed the TDG (q.v.) from his General Lighterage Co.

Modernisation before 1947 included the development of terminals which were based on road forwarding. These included those at Worcester and Stourport on the Severn, and two in Nottingham on the modernised Trent Navigation. This sometimes included transhipment from large vessels direct to road vehicles over former narrow boat routes, such as the Worcester & Birmingham Canal. New traffics also developed in petroleum products, including fuel for road vehicles, to new inland depots such as that at Colwick (Nottingham) and on the Manchester Ship Canal, which were road-served.

After 1947, when smaller waterways were nationalised and the major carrier Fellows Morton & Clayton was taken over, the BTC developed road haulage around a series of depots based on their warehouses and new ones built from the 1950s, including those at Knostrop (Leeds) and Enfield (1970). Although BRS vehicles were sometimes used, in the 1950s British Waterways developed a series of road transport sections to serve major depots for radii of up to 25 miles; the number of vehicles involved is indicated by the 57 drivers who received awards for safe driving in 1961, and in 1973 153 drivers. Many of these depots were eventually served by road transport only, such as those on the Leeds & Liverpool Canal, whilst others closed altogether. By 1988 almost all the eight which remained were devoted to road use, and were transferred, along with their remaining lorry fleets, to Leggett Freightways.

By 1970, when long-distance carrying by narrow boat ended, most traffics had either been lost to road (or rail) or had disappeared; very few long-term contracts to carry by canal were arranged after 1947, and remaining movements tended to be specialised. In the 1950s coal carriers like Barlows had increasingly turned to road transport, which after 1958 subsidised its canal traffics. In the 1970s British Waterways developed plans for new depots at Winsford and West London to interchange with road traffic from the M6 and M1 to serve the ports of Liverpool and London. Most of the inland waterways traffic that survived into the 21st century tends to be dominated by port-related traffics and much relies on loading to and from road transport.

JB

The **Institute of Logistics & Transport** was formed in 1999 by an amalgamation of the Chartered Institute of Transport and the Institute of Logistics.

It is no coincidence that the Institute of Transport, the first professional institute for those engaged in the non-engineering aspects of transport, was established in 1919, the same year as the Ministry of Transport, and that Sir Eric Geddes (q.v.), the first Minister of Transport, was its first president. Both institutions were the outcome of the intense public debate about how transport should be developed and organised after the First World War. The Institute was granted a Royal Charter in 1926 and changed its name to the Chartered Institute of Transport in 1971. Membership grew to 5000 in 1939, 10,000 in 1959 and 21,000 in 1984. Its presidents included a number of figures from the field of road freight transport, including Major General Russell (q.v.) and Dan Pettitt (q.v.) from the nationalised sector, E G Whitaker (SPD), R H Farmer (Atlas Express), Sir James Duncan (Transport Development Group) and Len Payne (Sainsburys). Its *Journal*, published until 1980, and the less-formal *Transport* which replaced it are both useful sources for historical research.

The origins of the Institute of Logistics can be traced back to the National Economic Development Council's desire to create 'centres of excellence'. The Centre for Physical Distribution Management was set up in 1971 within the British Institute of Management, under the chairmanship of Sir Reginald Wilson (q.v.). The term *physical distribution* had come into use from the late 1960s to reflect the trend for transport companies and transport managers to take on other functions in the goods distribution chain, such as warehousing, stock control, packaging and order processing. Out of the CPDM grew the Institute of Physical Distribution Management, formed in 1981 in response to the demand for a specialist professional body in this fast-growing field. It was initially administered by the BIM and in 1982, along with some other BIM departments, moved from London to Corby, which has remained the headquarters of its successors. In 1987 it became fully independent and widened its scope to encompass the entire range of logistics (q.v.) management, changing its name to the Institute of Logistics & Distribution Management. The ILDM was merged in 1993 with the Institute of Materials Management (formerly the Institute of Materials Handling) and renamed the Institute of Logistics. By then it had some 10,000 members. The Institute's journal, published since 1982, was originally titled *Focus*, but renamed *Logistics Focus* in 1993. It became *Logistics & Transport Focus* at the 1999 merger. The ILT also produces two academic journals: the *International Journal of Logistics: Research & Applications* (from 1998) and the *International Journal of Transport Management* (from 2002). **GAB**

Sue Wooley, *The First Seventy Years: a history of the Chartered Institute of Transport 1919–1989* (Glossop: Transport Publishing, 1992); Ray Horsley, 'The Institute: the first six years', *IPDM Yearbook 1986–7* (Kogan Page, 1986) pp. 7–10

Institute of Physical Distribution Management, see INSTITUTE OF LOGISTICS & TRANSPORT

The **Institute of Road Transport Engineers** was formed in 1944, initially as a limited company, mainly through the enthusiasm of Mackenzie Junner (q.v.). It originated in regular lunch meetings to discuss the design and suitability of goods vehicles for their operations, as suggested by Captain J B Walton, in charge of engineering at SPD (q.v.). The liveliness of the meetings convinced Junner that something more ambitious was needed, an idea he floated with articles in

Commercial Motor with the theme of 'let the operator advise the maker'.

Its creation filled a vacuum in that more than one professional body covered the operational and traffic sides of goods vehicle carrying, but there was nothing similar for the engineering side. The IRTE grew in numbers and stature, and by the 1980s had a membership worldwide of 16,500. As well as liaising with government departments and vehicle and component makers, it developed standards of education and skills and its corporate membership qualification gave a transport manager exemption from the need to take the Certificate of Professional Competence examination when that legislation-backed standard was introduced in 1978.

The IRTE introduced codes of practice on workshop standards, computerised vehicle maintenance reporting, tipper stability and braking on truck-and-trailer combinations and on many other aspects of transport engineering. From the 1970s its annual conference included a vehicle and component exhibition which by the 1990s when held at Telford had developed into the largest commercial vehicle show in the UK. In the late 1990s the show was merged into the Commercial Motor Show (q.v.) at the NEC in Birmingham organised by the Society of Motor Manufacturers and Traders. In September 2000 the IRTE merged with the Institute of Plant Engineers to form the Society of Operations Engineers, but continued as a professional sector within the new society.

A number of factors led to the IRTE management's controversial decision to merge with another organisation. The growing dominance of accountants in purchasing policies and decisions, the trend by breweries and others to give up running their own transport operations, inflation and pressures on operating costs all contributed to a decline in the number of transport engineers. Coupled with this was the continuing trend for vehicles to be contract hired or leased (rather than acquired outright) and for truck manufacturers to offer through their distributors complete acquisition, servicing and maintenance deals. This has meant that many transport operators of size no longer employed a fleet engineer.

Increasingly choice of vehicle specification to meet an operator's requirements, however complex, was left to the dealer's or bodybuilder's staff. **JMA**

G M Junner, *The Road Transport Engineer* (1957)

Institute of Transport, See INSTITUTE OF LOGISTICS & TRANSPORT

Institute of the Furniture Warehousing & Removing Industry, see BRITISH ASSOCIATION OF REMOVERS

The **Institute of Transport Administration** was formed as the Institute of Traffic Administration in 1944 to develop standards of knowledge, training, conduct and human relationships that were desirable in traffic administration, to encourage research and presentation of papers and to hold examinations. It also provided professional opinion on current and proposed transport policies. There are five grades of membership relating to skill and experience. Regular meetings are held at 24 local centres and a magazine, *Transport Management,* is published six times a year. **JMA**

The **Institution of Automobile Engineers** (until 1911 the Incorporated Institution of Automobile Engineers) was established in 1906 because the Institution of Mechanical Engineers, founded in 1847, did not adequately accommodate the aspirations of those involved in the new specialised branch of automobile engineering. Its field of interest was the use of both steam and internal combustion power in land, sea and air transport. The IAE was preceded by the Cycle Engineers' Institute, formed in Birmingham in 1898 and renamed the Automobile & Cycle Engineers' Institute in 1904. Its president for 1904–5 had been Herbert Austin. To avoid any division within the ranks of motor engineering, Col R E B Crompton (q.v.), first president of the IAE, and Rees Jeffreys (q.v.), secretary for the first four years and honorary treasurer for 22 years, persuaded the Institute to move to London and to be re-constituted as the IAE.

The inaugural meeting was held in 1906 at the Institution of Mechanical Engineers and the relationship between the two Institutions continued to be cordial. The IAE grew steadily and in 1938, when its membership reached 3000, it was granted a Royal Charter of Incorporation. Five years later, however, discussions about merging the two Institutions began, leading to the IAE becoming the Automobile Division of the Institution of Mechanical Engineers in 1947.

From 1909 the IAE was much involved in preparing standards for automobile components and materials and in research. In 1916 the government set up the Department of Scientific & Industrial Research to encourage the principal industries to establish research associations. Soon after, the IAE and Society of Motor Manufacturers & Traders (q.v.) created a Joint Technical Committee, which in 1919 became the Research Association of British Motor & Allied Manufacturers, based at Chiswick. In 1931 RABMAM and the Standards Department of the SMMT were taken over by the IAE's Research & Standardisation Committee, renamed the Automobile Research Committee in 1937. The research laboratories were moved to the Great West Road at Brentford in 1936. Its work was funded by some 400 affiliated companies, which received copies of its confidential reports. In 1946, in preparation for the IAE's loss of its independent existence, the ARC was taken over by the newly-created Motor Industry Research Association (q.v.), but the IMechE's Automobile Division is still represented on MIRA's Council.

The 41 volumes of the Institution's *Proceedings* are a record of the papers presented at its meetings and the discussions that followed. They often take the form of an historical introduction to their subject, followed by a survey of current practice. Since 1970 the Division has kept its members informed of developments through the magazine-style *Journal of Automobile Engineering,* replaced in 1975 by the *Automotive Engineer.* These publications form an important record of the development of motor engineering practice in the UK. **GM/GAB**

'Metamorphosis', the address by Frank G Woollard, last president of the IAE and first chairman of the IMechE Automobile Division, *Proc IAE,* 41 (1946–7), pp. 295–310; Shirley and Reid (1996); oral testimony of Captain G T Smith-Clarke

Intermediate bulk containers are small containers for liquids or solids, which can be transported within rail or road vehicles, ships or aircraft and may in some cases be pallet-mounted to facilitate handling. A variety of materials are used for modern IBCs, including stainless steel or aluminium for multi-trip containers, heavy duty plastics with the container being fitted into a metal frame for protection and handling, fibreboard, or wood.

RAS

Global Hazardous Cargoes (1998)

Inter-modal transport (Figure 120). The management of journeys involving more than one mode of transport was inevitably more troublesome than direct transits in the same ship, barge, railway wagon or lorry. Transhipment of goods from one transport mode to another at ports (see DOCK TRAFFIC) and at canal and railway depots generally carried significant cost and journey time penalties and the risk of loss through damage or pilferage. A number of different inter-modal techniques was developed to minimise these problems, some of them dating back to the nineteenth, or even the eighteenth, centuries. Their use mushroomed after the Second World War in response to the rapid rise in labour costs and the growth of international trade. Each is dealt with in a separate article: containerisation (q.v.), piggyback operation (q.v.) and road-rail vehicles (q.v.).

Like containers, pallets (q.v.) and stillages (q.v.) are a method of 'unitisation' of goods into larger, standard-sized units to minimise handling, and, like all the inter-modal systems, they also reduce or eliminate the cost of protective packaging for the goods. Pallets and stillages were developed primarily as a solution to the problems of loading, unloading and storage at warehouses and are not normally regarded as an inter-modal technique. Nevertheless, they have proved, in some circumstances, to be a cheaper and more convenient method of transferring goods between rail and road than containers, because they do not require high capital investment in large lifting equipment and heavy-duty roadways.

Inter-modal transport is also known as combined transport (q.v.).   **GAB**

International Harvester: between the wars this American company imported vans, trucks and road tractors into the UK through the International Harvester Co. of Great Britain Ltd, with head office in City Road, EC1, and exhibited at Commercial Motor Shows. There were importing depots in Liverpool and Leith. During the Second World War many International lorries came in under the lend-lease scheme, numbers being allocated to the Petroleum Board's fleet, some of which served with individual distribution companies after the Petroleum Board (q.v.) was dissolved in 1948. International Harvester had started to develop a site in Doncaster in 1938 and opened a second agricultural tractor manufacturing plant there in 1965. This was also used for the production (1965–9) of what was broadly a US truck model with detail modifications, as a two-axle rigid platform truck or tractive unit. Named the Loadstar it had lightness, speed and a relatively attractive cab to recommend it. It had normal-control, a configuration by then rare in the UK. As a result sales were disappointing but some operators, including Bradleys of Accrington, for example, built up a sizeable Loadstar fleet. Sales remained at about the first year's level of 500 so the production of Loadstars ceased. In 1974 IH acquired Seddon Atkinson (q.v.).**RAS**

Stevens-Stratten (1983), p. 65; Edge, *The Leyland Comet* (1998), p. 37; *CM* (10 November 1931); 13th International Commercial Motor Transport Exhibition, November 1937: *Catalogue*; information from Philip Scowcroft

The **International Road Transport Union** was founded at Geneva in 1948 to represent road transport generally. It has over 100 members in 50 countries; membership comprises road transport associations, associate membership includes commercial vehicle manufacturers. It acts for road transport at the highest levels, for example in relation to the United Nations, international professional bodies in related sectors, commercial vehicle manufacturers and academic institutions. It is at the service of road transport on a day-to-day basis, for example in the administration of the TIR (q.v.), customs system mutual assistance services, the issue of information, and intervention in emergency situations.   **RAS**

IRTU handout

The **International Transport Workers' Federation,** founded in London in 1896, is one of the few international labour movement bodies to be based in the UK. It moved to Hamburg in 1904 and was re-established in Amsterdam in 1919, returning to England in 1939 when the Second World War threatened. The logic of an international union as distinct from national ones was that so much transport was international and the trend was growing. Hence issues such as flags of convenience could not be tackled other than by supra-national bodies. The ITWF did not recruit individuals, but national unions, like the TGWU (q.v.), were federated to it. Between the wars the ITF organisation developed industrial sections, including for road transport workers. Hours and conditions of work for drivers have been a major concern since the 1920s and the ITF's 1999 day of action on the theme 'Fatigue kills' included a rally at Dover. The far-reaching effects of containerisation, telematics, the growth of cross-border road haulage and the increase in crime in international transport were major concerns of the ITF in the late-twentieth century and have underlined its significance for road haulage as a labour organisation with an international focus. In 1997 it set up a world council for employees of United Parcel Service (q.v.).   **RAS**

Solidarity: the first hundred years of the International Transport Workers' Federation (Pluto Press, 1996); B Reinalda (ed.), *The ITWF 1914–45: the Edo Fimmen era* (Amsterdam: IISG, 1997); N Baldwin, *The International Transport Workers' Federation Archive* (Coventry: University of Warwick Library, 1985)

Isuzu Motors Ltd was established in 1933 to produce standardised lorries for the Japanese army; its present title was adopted in 1949. In 1971 General Motors acquired a 35 per cent interest in Isuzu, which accounts for the marketing of some Australian-assembled vehicles under the Bedford badge. Isuzu entered the UK truck market in 1996 through Isuzu Truck (UK), largely owned by the Lex Service group. The first model was a 3/5-ton version and later it was joined by a 6.2-ton chassis. Isuzu trucks were assembled by Leyland (q.v.) for the UK market. Nikki King, managing director of Isuzu (UK) Ltd, introduced the unusual policy of selling direct, appointing agents for after-sales and service only. After Paccar's takeover of Leyland in 1998, assembly was moved to ERF at Middlewich and the range extended to 7.5 gross vehicle weight vehicles. By the end of 2000 there were some 50 agents, about a fifth being ERF dealers. The 6.2 and 7.5 tonne lorries are typical Japanese products and significantly different in design and engineering. Most noticeable is the use of small cabs and other lighter components, but combined with heavy-duty chassis engineering and larger under-stressed engines. Isuzu added a 12-ton vehicle to its range, which features a more modern cab and a chassis generally closer to European specifications. **RAS/GM**

Millar (1997)

Iveco (Figure 151) is the marque name of the Industrial Vehicles Corporation, a Fiat initiative of 1975, which brought together its Gruppo Veicoli Industriali and the OM (Officine Meccaniche) and French Unic marques, which had been acquired in 1933 and 1965 respectively. The German Klöckner Humboldt Deutz concern, producers of Magirus Deutz commercial vehicles, owned 20 per cent of Iveco from its foundation until 1980. Fiat had begun making lorries in 1903 and before the First World War Fiat vans sold well in London through Fiat Motors Ltd of Wembley. As Italy was on the allied side in this war the British government bought several hundred Fiat 1½-ton lorries some of which were rebodied for post-war use. Fiat light van and truck sales continued in the UK in the 1920s. After this Fiat did not re-enter the UK market until 1973, when the Fiat OM 55 and 75 integral 5½ and 7½ tonne vans were in the forefront of its market penetration. In 1986 Iveco attained greater significance when it entered into a joint venture with Ford (q.v.) for the operation of Ford's UK commercial vehicle production (excluding the Transit and smaller vans). Initially jointly owned at 48 per cent each, with a four per cent bank shareholding, Iveco became dominant in Iveco Ford Truck a decade later when it acquired the balancing bank shareholding. The Ford truck plant at Langley ceased production in 1997. Iveco in 1991 acquired ENASA, the Spanish state-owned parent of Pegaso, which also owned Seddon-Atkinson (q.v.). **RAS**

Sanguineti and Salazar (1994); Millar (1997); Ingram and Baldwin, (1977); 'A to Z of classic commercials', *CVC*, 7, 11 (July 2002), p. 45

J

Jeffreys, W Rees (1871–1954) formerly a civil servant at the Board of Trade, became secretary from 1901, and later chairman, of the Roads Improvement Association (q.v.). He was administrative (from 1904 technical) secretary of the Automobile Club of Great Britain & Ireland, secretary of the Motor Union 1903–10, and of the Motor Van & Wagon Users Association (later the CMUA). From 1910 to 1918 he was secretary of the Road Board. He was offered the chair of Lord Cowdray's Highways Construction Ltd, which introduced Mexican bitumen into the UK. Jeffreys declined, to avoid the monopolisation of his specialist knowledge by a commercial concern. After the Road Board was succeeded by the Ministry of Transport, Jeffreys became chairman of the British Organising Committee of the International Association of Road Congresses; in 1913 he was secretary of the third congress, held in London. In Plowden's words, he was 'a lifelong and fanatical roads lobbyist'. He is remembered by a scholarship and some of his papers are in the LSE library.

RAS

Plowden (1971); Jeffreys (1949)

Jempson, John, & Son (Figure 122) were transport contractors based in Rye since 1924. They were typical of the medium-sized family firm so common in road haulage. The firm began in 1924 when Arthur John Jempson purchased his first lorry, having gained experience of the business by working in his father's horse-drawn cartage business. The lorry, a Model T Ford, was financed by his father and used for short-distance haulage of the same type as the horse-drawn carts. It was rated at 1-ton but often carried up to 1½ tons. Within six months the loan from his father had been repaid. The firm grew, acquiring a Thornycroft J type and another Model T in 1926, and an ex-army Packard in 1927. The larger vehicles were recommended for up to 4 tons but were regularly overloaded. In the mid-1920s the firm started carrying fresh produce into London from local market gardens and fruit farms, with return loads such as flour, fertiliser often obtained at the docks, and cattle feed. Hops were a lucrative freight in the six-week autumn season, making one return trip per day to London.

In 1932 Arthur Jempson and Son was drawn up with father and son as equal partners, a Leyland Bull, 8-ton lorry was acquired and John Jempson spent more time in the office on management rather than driving. At the same time traffic in concrete kerbs and sewer pipes and bricks to feed the building boom was growing fast and Jempsons took over the transport fleet and work of Simpson & Co. which made concrete products. The business boomed in the late 1930s and profits were ploughed back in new lorries. Jempson's traffic was classified as essential in the Second World War and the drivers not called up and the lorries mostly not requisitioned. In 1940 the partnership was dissolved and John Jempson became the sole owner.

The post-war fleet was built up to 13 vehicles, mostly Leylands and Fords, when it was nationalised in 1949, at a good price for the Jempsons, and John remained as manager of the Rye Depot of BRS. In 1954 Jempson bought the depot back, as part of denationalisation, together with 24 vehicles, at a much lower price than he had received for it. The movement of building materials and agricultural products remained the mainstay of the business, the average journey became longer, and the lorry greater in capacity. Between 1955 and 1965 turnover rose from £60,000 to £91,000 with only a small increase in lorry fleet from 24 to 29. In 1961 the business became a private limited company but all the shares were retained by the family. In the mid-1960s John's son, Jonathan, joined the firm as a director and was soon running the firm. Rapid expansion occurred from 1965 to 1980, the fleet growing from 32 to 60, earnings rose from less than £100,000 to nearly two million, and annual profits rose tenfold. From the late 1980s Jempson were the main contractor for British Gypsum at Robertsbridge, carrying out European inter-working with bulk powder traffic to Germany and Belgium. As this work grew, Jempson set up a Midlands branch at Burton-on-the-Wolds, Loughborough to handle the gypsum traffic. They were members of the Palletway network. **JA**

Barker (1982)

Jennings, J H, & Son Ltd, (Figure 121) coachbuilders of Sandbach, Cheshire, claimed to have been founded in 1764. They began as wheelwrights in Little Warford, moving to Sandbach around 1900 when they acquired an existing coach-builder. They were especially known for the production of mobile shops, horse boxes and cattle floats. Between the wars they also built small motor coach bodies, motor caravans and, for a time, trailer caravans. There was close association with ERF from the beginning of that firm, which initially leased workshop premises from Jennings, who became virtually sole producers of ERF cabs until the early 1960s. Jennings' fortunes and their relationship with ERF deteriorated in the 1960s, when ERF sourced some of its LV glass-fibre cabs elsewhere. In the early 1970s ERF acquired Jennings. **RAS**

Kennett (1978); Walker (1997); Jennings' advertisements; Andrew Jenkinson, *Caravans: the story of British trailer caravans & their manufacturers 1919–1959* (Dorchester: Veloce, 1998)

Jensen Motors Ltd of West Bromwich, best known for their sports cars, also produced two types of lorry in the early post-war years, the JNSN 6-ton lightweight, especially suited to pantechnicon use, and the Jen-Tug mechanical horse. The JNSN lorry evolved in 1938/9 at the request of a customer, the Reynolds Tube Co., which required a maximum-length vehicle to carry their lightweight but lengthy goods. Commercial vehicle bodywork in light alloy was by then offered by several makers. The innovation introduced by Jensen was to design and build the chassis also in aluminium alloy. After a wide variety of war-work, which included fire tender and ambulance bodies, civilian production began in 1946 with the JNSN 6-ton, which used the experience gained with the Reynolds Tube lorries, and the Jen-

Tug 4-wheel mechanical horse which was based on a design rejected by British Latil, where Jensen's works manager, Colin Reikie, had previously been employed. The Jen-Tug was allied to a range of trailers with Jensen quick-release couplings. The Jen-Tug used a Ford or Austin engine, was under-powered, had rather flimsy couplings, and had a high tare weight compared to its load capacity. Customers included British Railways and the Corona soft drinks company and there were significant exports. An electric version, by Hindle, Smart & Co., appeared in 1949. Changes to the Construction and Use Regulations (q.v.) later lessened the advantages of lightweight construction and aluminium was more expensive than steel, so in face of cheaper competition, the JNSN lorry faded out in the mid-1950s and the Jen-Tug had ceased production by 1960, as also had a short-lived attempt to produce under licence the German Tempo. This was a small commercial load-carrier, produced by Jensen as a 25-cwt 'hydraulic elevator truck', that is with a variable load-platform height. **RAS**
See also LUTON BODY

N Baldwin, 'Jensen A lightweight heavyweight', *VCVM*, 43 (January/February 1993) pp. 186–9; K Anderson, *Jensen* (Sparkford: Haynes, 1989); Jensen records in the Modern Records Centre, University of Warwick Library, MSS.215

John Lewis Partnership. Soon after opening his first drapery shop in Oxford Street in 1864 John Lewis needed to deliver goods to his customers. His, and other department stores across the country, used not only their own horse-drawn delivery vehicles but also the country-wide carrier cart system. This entry will cover all the department stores and food shops within the John Lewis Partnership and includes references to the transport fleets of Bainbridge of Newcastle, Heelas of Reading and many London-based stores such as Peter Jones and John Barnes.

With stores operating not only a delivery service for goods but also a removals and storage facility there was a wide-ranging requirement for various types of vehicles. By 1887 Bainbridge had acquired the business of J

Pilgrim using horse-drawn removal vans whilst employing their own smaller two-wheeled carts for local deliveries, One of the first moves away from horse-drawn vehicles was also seen in Newcastle when Bainbridge purchased their first motorised van, a Panhard Levassor at the Paris Exhibition in 1901. Motor vans came into use around the beginning of the First World War with custom-built bodies, with steam wagons becoming popular for heavier removals work.

By the early 1920s Studebaker delivery vans were in use and in 1928 fleets of vehicles were common in department stores. For example, Heelas of Reading owned a large number of vehicles including a 25-cwt Fiat chassis with Vincent's (q.v.) cab and a van body (£366 5s); Albion chassis with Great Western body, Vandervell lighting, a 20-hp Model 20 van with custom tyres (£654); and Dennis chassis with Vincent's body, a 30-cwt van with straight-sided pneumatic tyres. These vehicles were maintained by the store's own garage and many remained in service until the Second World War.

Other stores had a more radical approach to transport. At Peter Jones in Sloane Square, London, the van fleet was sold in 1927 and replaced by a contract transport company. This decision was reversed in 1934 when the fleet was re-instated with a range of vehicles from Carrimore 1000-cu.ft capacity trailers for removals to 8-cwt Commer delivery vans. There were experiments with electrically-powered vans for John Lewis and Peter Jones in 1936.

In the 1930s other London stores such as John Barnes were using motor vehicles painted in the livery of the Selfridge Provincial Stores group which had acquired department stores across the country. Their London fleet included 3-ton Scammell tractor units with 3-ton Dyson trailers, Guy Otter chassis fitted with platform and double-driving cab with trailer, Morris Commercial 30-cwt vans, and a Commer 1-ton dropside truck with a body by Glover, Webb and Liversidge.

The John Lewis Partnership acquired fifteen department stores from SPS in 1940, and the transport operations of the two groups were amalgamated. By the mid-1950s the main garage was operating ten vans in London and twenty three in the provinces serviced by a central repair depot at Peckham and smaller garages on each site. The total mileage travelled in 1957 amounted to 175,320 miles, of which 42,709 was in the London area. A total fleet of 264 vehicles included 10 radio vans which provided service for those purchasing radios and televisions.

The company's food division, Waitrose, was employing 17 vehicles to deliver to their chain of grocery shops and supermarkets with the first tail-lift van being introduced in 1963 and the first refrigerated van in 1965. The 1960s saw a rekindling of interest in battery-electric vehicles with two in London for deliveries for John Lewis and Peter Jones.

BMC were the most popular vehicles used for customer deliveries but by the 1970s they were replaced by the Ford D0708 with a standard glass-reinforced plastic box body from Tidd of Biggleswade. These were later replaced by the new Ford Cargo 0709 and latterly by the 0811 and 0812 with many bodies being supplied by the Partnership's workshop at Bracknell. Later in the 1980s Fords were replaced by the Leyland Roadrunner and latterly the DAF 45, while smaller parcel deliveries have been carried out in either standard or customised Mercedes-Benz vans for the last 20 years.

Since the late-1960s the Partnership had relied on articulated vehicles for the movement of bulk stocks. Until reliability became an issue in the 1970s the Partnership sourced from Leyland, AEC and BMC. In 1975 the first DAF 2000 was purchased and since then DAF (95 and 85) and Volvo (HL and FM) have dominated. The design of trailers altered in the early 1980s and new semi-trailers built by Craven Tasker were introduced. This design became embryonic for the double-decker vehicle increasing the carrying capacity of existing trailers by 95 per cent. In 1998 a successful design devised by the John Lewis fleet engineers and Don-Bur (q.v.) of Stoke for a multi-decker trailer was trialed and won the Dry Freight Trailer award for 1999.

The Partnership (including Waitrose) in 2000 operated 1576 commercial vehicles ranging from small vans such as the Citroen Berlingo for service and workroom requirements to multi-deckers for bulk haulage.　　　**JF**

Joint Retail Logistics was established by Exel Logistics Ltd (q.v.) and the Tibbett & Britten Group (q.v.) in 1999 as a joint venture to transport Marks & Spencer general merchandise throughout the UK and the Irish Republic on a five-year contract. Based in Coventry, it took over the vehicles and 145 staff of BOC, Lex Transfleet and Christian Salvesen (q.v.) formerly engaged in M&S work and painted the 300 commercial vehicles and 700 trailers involved in JRL livery.　**RAS**

CM (20 May 1999), pp. 8 and 10

Joloda was a patented mechanical device introduced in the 1960s by George Bernard Johnstone for handling pallets or heavy items, mainly in box vans, occasionally curtainsiders. It has a capacity of 1½ tons per pallet. It is a means of taking items to or from the back of the vehicle for unloading by, or loading with, a fork-lift truck. A platform is moved relative to the chassis by a tommy bar in a pivoting block. It is raised so that the load is just clear of the floor. Thus it can be wheeled along the vehicle. This system can be mechanised. See PAPER HAULAGE. The system was in widespread use by the 1980s.　　**GM/JMA**

Jones, S, (Transport) Ltd, Aldridge, West Midlands was established in March 1999 after the original business had gone into receivership. Founded in 1913, three generations of the Jones family developed a group with three divisions: transport, container storage and engineering, and a truck franchise (ERF and Isuzu). The profitable transport operation was apparently brought down by problems in the other two divisions. The 1999 company, with David Vicary as chairman and James Weir as managing director, acquired the original Aldridge site, an Essex depot, 65 vehicles and a loyal customer base, which included contract tanker hire clients such as

Carless Transport. Jones also operated a spot-hire tanker fleet, an intermodal fleet on behalf of Combined Transport (CTL) and S Jones Bulk Services, bulk tipping. The fleet in early 2000 comprised seventy tractive units (mostly ERFs) and 82 trailers.　　　　**RAS**

CM (17 February 2000), pp. 40-2, (23 March 2000), p. 40

Jowett Cars Ltd. This Bradford-based firm produced light commercials for three decades, from 1924 to 1954. They were best-known for the 2-cylinder Bradford van, made from 1946 until the company's demise in 1954. Some 38,000 were manufactured as vans, utilities and light lorries, proving popular, despite handling limitations. The English and Scottish Co-operative Wholesale Societies, and London Meat Co. were among the larger customers. A replacement model, the CD had reached prototype stage when cash flow problems forced the parent company into liquidation in 1954. Spares back-up continued to be provided by a new company, Jowett Engineering Ltd. In earlier years Jowett's 7 hp flat-twin engine had powered the first production models of Karrier's innovative mechanical horses, the Cob and Colt, announced in 1930.　　**RAS**

P Clark and E Nankivell, *The Complete Jowett History* (Sparkford: Haynes 1991); P Landers 'The Jowett Bradford', *VCVM*, 15 (July/August 1988), pp. 6-9

Joynson-Hicks, William, (1865-1932) was born William Hicks, but after his marriage in 1895 he compounded his wife's maiden name, resulting in the nickname Jix when he entered politics. His father, Henry Hicks, was a director of McNamara & Co. (q.v.) (1887-c. 1910) and vice chairman, later chairman, of the London General Omnibus Company (1891-1912). His younger brother, (Lt. Col Sir) Maxwell Hicks, was receiver/manager, later chairman, of McNamara & Co. (1913-48).

Having qualified as a solicitor in 1888, he established his own practice and in 1892, through his father's influence, became the LGOC's solicitor. Thus began his expertise in road transport law. From 1896 he was legal advisor to the National Traction Engine Owners' & Users' Association (q.v.), becoming its president in the 1920s. He was joint author with Sir Montague Barlow of *The Law of Heavy and Light Mechanical Traction on Highways in the United Kingdom* (1906) and from 1908 to 1923 chairman of the Automobile Association.

His firm was soon the leading defender of commercial road transport interests in the courts, acting in some notable cases. For example, Joynson-Hicks & Co. acted for the Commercial Motor Users' Association (q.v.) in an important test case, which lasted from 1917 to 1922, on the powers of highway authorities to make claims for damage to roads by heavy vehicles that they regarded as constituting 'extraordinary traffic'. A major client was Norman E Box (q.v.). It is said that he never lost a summons that he defended for Box whose regard for him was such that he named his Fowler B6 road locomotive (16264) JIX. It has been suggested that his opinion on the possible direction of legislation influenced Box's decision to sell out to Pickfords in 1930.

Despite his busy legal practice, Joynson-Hicks was also active in politics. He was Conservative MP for North West Manchester (1908–1910), Brentford (1911–1918) and Twickenham (1918–1929). He served on the Treasury Committee on the Rating of Motor Cars (1911), the War Office Committee on Motor Transport (1916) and the Ministry of Transport's Advisory Committee on Road Transport (1922–3). In 1919–22 he was chairman of the Motor Legislation Committee, set up by the AA and Society of Motor Manufacturers & Traders (q.v.) to oppose the Lloyd George/Geddes (q.v.) plans for re-organising transport, and led a large group of pro-road parliamentarians in opposition to the 1921 Transport Bill.

He also took a great interest in aeronautics and was chairman of the Parliamentary Air Committee (1918–22) and a member of the Board of Civil Aviation (1922–3). He contributed to Lloyd George's downfall in 1922, by his exposure of the corrupt honours system. By then he was a senior figure on the right of the Conservative party and was quickly promoted through the ministerial ranks of the new government to become Home Secretary from 1924 to 1929. These years included the General Strike (q.v.) which brought into use his knowledge of commercial road transport, and the strains of office took a toll on his health.

He was created a baronet in 1919 and 1st Viscount Brentford in 1929. When he died *The Times* honoured him with an editorial as well as a 23 column-inch obituary; it summed him up as 'a thorough Englishman, with those strong beliefs which an Englishman's enemies call prejudices and his friends common sense …he was articulate in the expression of them'.

GM/GAB

Times, obituary, 9 June 1932; *Railway Gazette* (14 March 1919), pp. 499–500; Plowden (1971); H A Taylor, *Jix, Viscount Brentford* (Stanley Paul, 1933)

Juggernaut ('lord of the world') is one of the titles of the Hindu god Krishna, but the English mistakenly applied the word to the enormous car that was dragged in an annual procession, carrying an idol of the deity. It was said that in former times devotees threw themselves in front of it to be crushed under its wheels. From the early 1900s the word appeared occasionally in the daily press and in the parliamentary record as a colourful derogatory epithet to suggest the destructive power of the motor vehicle, particularly the lorry. From 1969, in the period of growing opposition to the government's road-building programme, it came into common usage to mean a heavy (then 30- or 32-ton) lorry, mainly by those opposed to the road haulage industry. **GAB**

OED; Seth-Smith (1975), pp. 38, 116

Junner, Gordon Mackenzie (1892–1980) as editor of *Commercial Motor* 1929–59 was an influential figure in the world of commercial transport and is credited with initiating the train of events which led to the foundation of the Long Distance Road Haulage Association in January 1931. Junner had commissioned E B Hutchinson (q.v.), founder of United Automobile Services, to travel the country in order to write on the haulage industry.

Hutchinson's findings, especially on the lack of organisation in the industry, prompted Junner to arrange a lunch meeting of prominent hauliers on 29 April 1930. This meeting set up a Long Distance Road Haulage Committee of Enquiry (q.v.) from which in turn derived the LDRHA. Another of Junner's foundations, in association with the technical editor of *Motor Transport*, P M A Thomas, was the Institute of Road Transport Engineers (q.v.). In 1957 he published a text book on road transport engineering. Junner had had a tough first-hand experience of transport before being appointed to the editorial chair. After a thorough grounding in vehicle engineering with AEC and coaching for his City & Guilds examinations in motor engineering from Leslie Hounsfield, the designer of the Trojan (q.v.), he was appointed a technical sub-editor on *Commercial Motor* in 1912. He was a military despatch rider throughout the First World War, on a half-pay retainer from the Temple Press, to which he returned in 1919. **RAS**

G M Junner, 'The annals of Mac', *CM* (19 March 1965), pp. 68–76; idem., *The Road Transport Engineer* (Temple Press, 1957); Dunbar (1981); A Smith, 'The hat fits', *CM* (2 March 2000), p. 22; J Durant, 'Editorial Matters'; *CM* (15 March 1980), pp. 42–3

Just in time (JIT) is a post-Second World War development in manufacturing, pioneered by the motor industry, in which the stockholding of parts or components is virtually eliminated so reducing inventory costs. Instead, contracted suppliers are given advanced and daily details of build programmes and have to deliver, say, already trimmed car doors in correct sequence for the production programme just a short time (perhaps an hour) before they are needed. The doors for successive cars on the production line will be of different colours or specification. For the car maker, the cost of stockholding is eliminated and production line layout simplified. The car door maker in turn has a more valuable contract, but with added onus and responsibility. If the factory is distant from the car plant a buffer store is probably necessary, while the whole system requires a high degree of reliability from the transport operation, and an absence of industrial disputes. The system was pioneered at the Toyota Motor Co. in Japan and called Kanban after the word for the cards attached to the containers of parts. It was also known as 'lean production'. It became fashionable in British manufacturing in the mid-1980s.

To serve one onerous JIT operation, TNT (q.v.) in the 1990s with bodybuilder Cartwrights of Altrincham developed a 13.6 m long semi-trailer with a king-pin and set of tandem axles at each end to allow access to both ends of the trailer. The trailer had roller shutters at each end and carried the wheeled bogies that carry parts within car plants. The bogies were coupled into short trains pulled by electric tugs. They normally have to be reloaded individually on the trailer by fork truck. This semi-trailer enabled them to be pulled on and off, always in the right direction and eliminated need for fork-truck reloading of them when empty. **JMA**

James P Womack et al, *The Machine that Changed the World* (Oxford: Maxwell Macmillan, 1990), pp. 11, 62 and 67: Malory Davies, 'Goods on delivery', *Global Transport* (Summer 1996), pp. 38–9

K

Karrier Motors (Figures 92, 96, 120–1, 123, 130, 159–60 and 186) originated in 1908 with Clayton & Co. (Huddersfield) Ltd, manufacturers of railway signal detonators, though the company name was not adopted until 1920. Although best remembered for the small and manoeuvrable Bantam series and, to a lesser extent, for the Cob mechanical horse, Karrier produced some 2000 3–4 ton lorries in the First World War under the War Office subvention scheme and military 6-wheelers between the wars and during the Second World War, when 4×4 lorries were also produced. Civilian inter-war models included the K6 12-ton tractor unit. A short wheelbase with a large load-carrying area and a powerful engine were Karrier features from the outset. In 1930 Karrier co-operated with the LMSR to produce a mechanical horse (q.v.), the Karrier Cob, in production mainly 1931–8, although some were produced after the war. It was derived from the Colt 3-wheel dustcart which had been commissioned by Huddersfield corporation. The Cob was in use by the four mainline railway companies, and the Colt continued to be offered as a load-carrying version. The Cob was initially powered by a Jowett engine, but this was replaced by a more powerful Coventry-Climax power unit. In 1932 the 2-ton Bantam was launched, to prove popular over a long period for municipal and delivery work, for example with McNamaras and Wordies. Although Karrier had a workforce of 1000 and a 10 acre site at the beginning of the 1930s, financial problems forced it into receivership in 1934, prior to its acquisition by Rootes Securities Ltd. In the following year Karrier production was phased in at Rootes' Commer (q.v.) works at Luton and these two commercial marques were thereafter closely related. The replacement for the Cob was a tractor version of the Bantam, which had been introduced in 1936. The tractor version was not in railway use until after the war, although Bantam parcels vans were. Karrier maintained close links with specialist bodybuilders, which helped to place their municipal vehicles with 600 local authorities by 1939, and to encourage the use of Karrier chassis as the basis of mobile shops. For example, in 1956 Karrier advertising made clear their co-operation with Smith's Delivery Vehicles Ltd of Gateshead, which resulted in bodywork 'specially designed for individual trades'. Karrier wartime production of more than 8000 vehicles had included gun tractors and CK6 6-wheelers. The Bantam was updated several times after the war and in 1953 the CK3 model was superseded by the Gamecock with a new-style cab. When the former Rootes commercial vehicle range was split in 1968, following the Chrysler takeover of Rootes in 1965, and Commer designated the lighter end of the range and Dodge (q.v.) the heavier, Karrier became a model, not a brand name for Dodge Karrier municipal and specialised vehicles.   **RAS**

Klapper (1973); Stevens-Stratten (1988) and (1978); Stevens-Stratten and Aldridge (1987); S Young and N Hood, *Chrysler UK: a corporation in transition* (New York, 1977); Aldridge (2000); '75 years in business', *CM* (22 March 1980), pp. 40–4; R J Anketell, 'Boosting trade by mobile shops', *MT* (9 March 1956); M Bates, 'Getting back to our Rootes?' pt 3, *Diecast Collector* (April 1999), pp. 16–21; Carverhill (2002); Karrier archives are held by the Museum of British Road Transport, Coventry.

Kennett, Pat, engineer and commercial vehicle journalist (1932–1998) began work with Leyland Motors in 1948, his seventeen year career with them including twelve years as a field engineer and then sales engineer in Latin America and other Spanish- and Portuguese- speaking areas and involvement with the major Cuban bus order. He subsequently became technical editor on *Motor Transport,* before becoming in effect joint founder of *Truck* magazine in 1974. He also wrote numerous titles in the authoritative 'World's Trucks' series in the 1970s.   **RAS**

A Frankel, 'Kennett's contribution', *Truck* (May 2001), p. 27

Kerr Stuart & Co. Ltd, locomotive builders of Stoke-on-Trent, was the first British firm to design and build a diesel-engined lorry, although it never went into series production. The Garrett prototype four-wheeled and six-wheeled lorries which preceded it were based on conversions of their steam wagons. Kerr Stuart had experience of McLaren engines in their diesel locomotives which were designed by K W Willans, who was previously with Sentinel, where he had been responsible for their entry into the rail market. The first production chassis, in 1929, used a British-built 60 hp McLaren-Benz four-cylinder diesel engine with a cone clutch. The larger engines were started by a J A P engine. The engine weighed some 23 cwt. The four-speed gearbox was mid-mounted with the final drive through 2½-inch chains. The unique rear axle suspension was mounted on two transverse springs, fitted to a central cross-member with their ends resting on axle pads located in the drums. It was claimed this gave flexibility without excessive movement. The prototype was exhibited at the Public Works Exhibition in London in 1929. The production chassis was able to use more stampings and was a lighter and stronger chassis. It also had Clayton Dewandre brakes. In the spring of 1930 Bonallack & Sons were appointed London agents. Unfortunately, despite the interest in a British lorry, available as an alternative to the Mercedes and Saurer diesel lorries, only a few Kerr Stuart lorries were produced. Its chairman, unknown to the board, had fraudulently used Kerr Stuart's assets as security to finance another business which failed, causing Kerr to be placed into receivership. The Hunslet Engine Co. Ltd acquired all its designs and patterns, but did not choose to start producing the lorry. **GM**

LTC Rolt, *Landscape with Machines* (Gloucester: Alan Sutton, 1971), ch. 8; Klapper (1973), p. 98

Kingston-upon-Thames Leyland works, see LEYLAND MOTORS

Knowles Transport Ltd of Wimblington, Cambridgeshire, was established by Gerald Knowles in 1932 at the age of 17, with a 2-ton Ford. Early traffic included sugar beet haulage to railheads. During the Second World War business increased with the transporting of caterpillar tracks for Manea-based contractor Derek Crouch engaged in runway building. After the war, prior to nationalisation, brick traffic from Whittlesey and Peterborough and market traffic in vegetables was taken on. Contract work with four new Bedford O vehicles was then undertaken for Whittlesey Central Brick Co., before Knowles obtained March, Ramsey and Whittlesey BRS depots on denationalisation, with a variety of vehicles, including Fodens, AEC, Maudslay and a Bedford QL breakdown truck. A licences were, however, transferred to the Bedford S type, which became the firm's preferred vehicle. Two examples, a tractive unit and a four-wheel lorry, have recently been restored and added to Knowles' fleet of some dozen preserved lorries, which includes Fodens and a Scammell. By 1980 the fleet, with the associated Wisbech Roadways, owned more than 60 bulk tippers and some 40 bulk trailers, operated by tractive units working part-time on general haulage; there were also 22 rigid 8-wheelers in the fleet at that time. Today the firm, run by the founder's sons, Gerald junior and Tony, operates 90 Volvos and Scanias from two Cambridgeshire depots with warehousing and food-packaging facilities. **RAS**

N Larkin, 'S Class', *CVC*, 6, 8 (April 2001), pp. 4–8; *MT* (6 December 1980)

L

The **Lacre Motor Car Co. Ltd** was founded in 1902 as the Long Acre Motor Car Co. Ltd, abbreviated to Lacre in 1904. Originally Albion's London agent, the first Lacre vehicles were cars and light vans. Lacre was to retain its London agency for Wolseley cars for some time. From 1909 a complete range up to 9 tons was available, with manufacture moved to a new factory at Letchworth.

Its 15-cwt chassis became a popular choice for carriers, railways and stores, for instance Shoolbreds of London bought a Lacre van in 1905 for deliveries and by 1911 had a fleet of 56. Harrods (q.v.) had twenty-one 1¼-ton vans in 1907. The co-operative movement were also customers. Lacre were best known for the O-type 2- or 2½-ton chassis. The output in 1914–1916 went to the Belgian army, but hundreds were later supplied to the American, British, Canadian and Indian armies.

Production after the war included a forward-control 2½-ton lorry, also produced as an early articulated unit, notable for its engine mounted on a sub-frame for ease of removal. A range of municipal vehicles helped the company survive until 1928. In 1923 Harry Shelvoke and J S Drewry, Lacre's chief engineer, left to set up the rival Shelvoke & Drewry. The company was reconstituted in 1928, as Lacre Lorries Ltd, operating from Kings Cross and later a new factory at Welwyn Garden City, building only road sweepers. It also owned Burford.

GM

Davies (2000); *Vintage Commercial*, 1, 4 (December 1962), p. 123; Stevens-Stratten, (1988); Marshall and Bishop (1979)

Laingfreight was the title of the road haulage division proposed in 1976 by the Laing construction group, which at that time operated nearly 3000 vehicles. Plans included a first depot at Andover, with 50 heavy lorries, with a second at Manchester, then others according to demand. The launch of this attempt at diversification came at a bad time, with substantial over-capacity in road haulage in a period of worsening recession. **RAS**

Guardian (18 August 1976)

Lambourn Engineering (Figure 124), horse-box manufacturers, evolved from Lambourn Racehorse Transport in the same Berkshire village, in the mid-1930s. It was founded by Lord Nugent, a gentleman engineer. A bold step in 1937 was production of a rear-engined horse-box, using a chassis designed by Nugent himself and built by Unipower. It provided a low frame height between the axles and used a standard Fordson V8 engine mounted at the back and coupled to the rear axle. Other components were also from Fordson. By the mid-1960s annual production included some 50 to 60 horse-box bodies, other special purpose bodies, and some 13,000 to 15,000 tractor cabs. The firm was built-up by the Nugent and Thatcher families and controlled by a Dublin holding company, O'Reilly Estates. The marque passed to Oakley coachbuilders, also horse-box specialists, of High Cross, Ware, Herts, in the mid-1990s. The firm had over-expanded and under-priced when the quality was considered. Lambourn Racehorse Transport was taken over by Merrick Francis, son of Dick. **RAS**

Guardian (20 October 1996)

Lancashire flats, or flat-bottoms, were originally large flat trays that fitted into a railway wagon or onto a horse dray and were brought into use in the 1890s by the Lancashire & Yorkshire, LNWR and Midland Railways for inter-modal (q.v.) movements of baled cotton yarn and cloth between mills and warehouses in the north-west that were not directly accessible by rail. They were transferred by an overhead crane with a spreader beam and four chains that hooked into the tray's lifting lugs. In the 1930s the LMSR replaced them with new open-topped containers (see CONTAINERISATION). About the same time they re-appeared in a different guise.

With limited exceptions, the Irish & English Goods Traffic Conference, which included all the railway and shipping companies operating regular services across the Irish Sea, did not carry loaded containers to Ireland, as most would have returned empty, occupying space needed for cattle, the main traffic for England. Lancashire flats therefore developed into a road/ship inter-modal system for Irish traffic, taking on the appearance of a flat lorry platform complete with headboard. When returning empty they could be stacked on top of each other, thus reducing the shipping charges as well as the space problem. They continued in use until superseded by the new ISO container shipping services in the late 1960s/early 1970s. Other versions of the flat tray were used as demountable bodies (q.v.) and load trays (q.v.).   **JMA/GAB**

Railway Clearing House, *Use of Mechanical Appliances and Labour Saving Devices in connection with Goods Train Traffic: report of sub-committee* (1918); LM&SR internal report, *Treatise on Container Transport* (1937)

The **Lancashire Heavy Motor Vehicle Trials**, popularly known as the Liverpool trials, were organised for commercial vehicles by the Liverpool Self-Propelled Traffic Association (q.v.). The first was held in May 1898, as a reaction to the 1896 Act freeing up motor traffic. The trials were important as they provided a showcase for manufacturers to display their products and promoted competition between marques to improve performance. Edward Shrapnell-Smith (q.v.) was appointed conductor of the first three trials, in 1898, 1899 and 1901. Test drives were mapped of 30 to 40 miles each day on four consecutive days, the routes picked to test hill climbing and manoeuvrability. The first prize was £100. Only four vehicles competed, a LIFU of two tons, a 4-ton Leyland, and two Thornycrofts, one of three tons and a 5-ton, 6-wheel articulated lorry. All were steam-propelled. The Leyland won first prize.

The second trials took place in summer 1899. Six vehicles took part, all steam- driven. Two Thornycrofts won gold medals. The third trials were held in 1901 and eleven vehicles took part, two were petrol-driven, eight were steam-propelled, and six gold medals were awarded. There was intense interest in the trials from War Office officials, the Local Government Board, the railways and politicians. The trials showed that the 3-ton tare limit imposed by the 1896 Act made it hard to construct an economic vehicle.   **JA**

T R Nicholson, *The Birth of the British Motor Car, 3: The last battle 1894–7* (Macmillan, 1982); Seth-Smith (1975); Kennett (1978)

The **Lancashire Steam Motor Co. Ltd** of Leyland, Lancashire, came into being in 1896 when James Sumner, a blacksmith, went into partnership with Henry Spurrier. Sumner had experience of steam mowing machines and moved into commercial vehicles in 1896 with a 1-ton steam van having a vertical oil-fired boiler and a compound engine with three speeds (2, 5 and 8 mph). By 1900 sales were being made of a 5-ton lorry with vertical boiler in front of the driver and underfloor engines with twin-chain final drive. They were popular and no attempt was made to alter the design, as the firm, called Leyland Motors Ltd (q.v.) from 1907, saw more future in petrol vehicles.
                                   RK

Turner (1971); Kennett (1983)

The **Land-Rover** is a 4-wheel drive vehicle launched by the Rover Co. of Solihull in utilitarian form in 1948. From the outset it functioned as a workhorse, for farmers and engineering contractors for example, rather than as a carrier *per se*. There are, however, some exceptions to this including its use by the Post Office (q.v.) for mail collection and delivery in areas of rough terrain and adverse climate and in a mixed role for passenger- and mail-carrying as Post Buses.   **RAS**

Post Office Vehicle Club (1995)

Langdons, the west country haulage and distribution company, had unusual beginnings. Mrs Bessie Langdon, who by the First World War had developed a significant business supplying eggs, poultry and rabbits from Somerset to London, became dissatisfied with the service provided by the GWR. As early as 1915 she replaced horse-and-trap collection with a Model T van and experienced the possibility of delivery by road during the General Strike. In 1927 she acquired a 3-ton Chevrolet for long-distance delivery. Return traffic began in 1933, but local collection by lorry with another driver between its London trips was the pattern of operations from the outset. By 1939 Langdons still had only a single lorry, but this now made intermediate-drop trips, as well as one direct run to London each week. Return trips carried animal feed and six vans were operated for local collection of produce. Vehicle requisitioning and zoning of food supplies cut back Langdons' business during the Second World War. It returned to lorry operation for its own business with two vehicles purchased in 1949 and 1950.

Following denationalisation, Langdons moved into road haulage proper with the assistance of a former local haulier, Sidney Pulsford, and established Tone Valley Transport Ltd at Wiveliscombe. This grew from two vehicles to 17 within two years, operating platform lorries as far afield as Cornwall to London. In 1960 Taunton Meat Haulage Ltd was established with Langdons' financial involvement and in the same year Langdons moved out of poultry and set up the West Somerset Warehousing Co. When Bill, one of Bessie's sons, died in 1967, his brother Philip took sole charge and remained in daily control after the business was sold to a mixed transport, timber and financial conglomerate, Price & Pierce, in 1974. In the following year, in response to troubled industrial relations, all Taunton Meat Haulage drivers were dismissed and replaced by owner-drivers. Price & Pierce were bought out by Tozer, Kemsley & Millbourn, venture capitalists and factors, in 1977. In the 1970s it operated Leylands and Volvos, and felt it was being persecuted by police charges over drivers exceeding hours, speeding and overloading. Until TKM lost its BMW franchise in 1980, this change of ownership was beneficial to Langdons and a new operating site was acquired at Walford Cross, between Taunton and Bridgwater. At the time of the move in 1981 Tone Vale operated 150 trailers, hired or owned, and 58 tractive units of owner-drivers.

A new managing director was appointed at Langdons in 1980 and Philip and other senior managers resigned in the ensuing years after various policy and personal differences. Equipment needed upgrading, but cash flow was precarious; initial approaches to TKM for a management buy-out were rejected, until it was seen as the only solution for both parties. It was operative from 1985. Costs were reduced by cutting warehousing, reducing 'running light' by seeking outward loads from closer to base, developing Truck Stop facilities at Walford Cross and upgrading the tractive unit fleet, gradually switching to company-owned vehicles with staff drivers. A major traffic breakthrough followed the acquisition of an old customer in Bridgwater, Quantock Jams, by Gerber Foods. Its need of chilled and sub-zero storage to buffer discrepancies between production and demand for different product lines led to Langdons' development of a new facility at Walford Cross and related penetration of regional distribution centres on a daily basis. This benefited local producers with small consignments. Langdons was unable to establish a network of hubs and considered a bid from a national haulier seeking a west country base, but arrangements with a long-standing storage customer, Tom Granby (Liverpool) Ltd, gave virtually nationwide coverage under the registered trade name Chillnet. By 2000 60 vehicles were dedicated to this operation and in the same year a hub in southern Ireland was established. A new 10-acre site was opened in Bridgwater in 1999 and a depot acquired at Blackburn for its major customer. As an important step in this development, Granby's transport operations were taken over in 1999, adding 50 vehicles to Langdons' fleet. By late 2000 this stood at 120 vehicles, of which 55 were rigids and 85 trailers. **RAS**

R W Holder, *Taunton Cider and Langdons: a West Somerset story of industrial development* (Chichester: Phillimore, 2000); A Salter, 'Trip wired', *Truck* (April 2001), pp. 52–5

Latil tractors were first imported in the 1920s. Their distinct feature was that they were all-wheel drive and all-wheel steer. In 1932

Figure 65 Accidents: Conventional timber-framed cabs offered little protection to drivers in an accident, as evidenced by this Foden diesel lorry of *c.* 1934. Note the AA badge on the radiator top. (Reproduced by kind permission of Colin Parrott)

Figure 66 AEC Mammoth Minor six-wheeler, here pulling a drawbar trailer and so, by law, required to carry a driver's mate, also pictured. The vehicle was photographed immediately after the Second World War, as shown by the Ministry of Transport number. It has a Duramin cab, is carrying flour and is outside the Princes Risborough premises of its operator H Hickman & Son. Note the early use of a tag axle. (Reproduced by kind permission of Nick Baldwin)

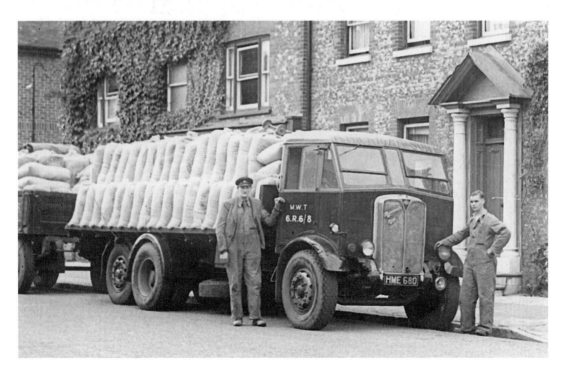

Figure 67 Aggregate traffic: this Volvo FM12 has underfloor tipping gear for added stability on uneven ground. It was photographed in 2001 delivering aggregate to the site of a new supermarket. It has a substantially constructed body with roller sheet to cover the load. (Kevin Lane Collection)

Figure 68 Agricultural traffic: this Dodge six-wheel T308 of 1964 with a Dunn-Spencer Bulkflo aluminium body and Edbro tipping gear was operated by Brummitt, a subsidiary of Spillers. The cab was a forward-control Motor Panels LAD. Engine-driven pneumatic and hydraulic equipment allowed the load to be blown into a silo as an alternative to tipping. (Reproduced by kind permission of the Museum of British Road Transport, Coventry)

Figure 69 Associated Daimler Co. was a joint venture between AEC and Daimler in the late 1920s. This ADC-badged model dates from the late 1920s and boasts pneumatic tyres on the front wheels, but solids on the rear. The three-tier load of empty barrels is well roped and centrally inclined. (Reproduced by kind permission of Nick Baldwin)

Figure 70 Atkinson manufactured this rigid-eight with Mark 1 glass-fibre panelled cab. It has just delivered a load of derv to London's Victoria Coach Station in 1963. The access ladder to the tank top is visible behind the cab. Regent Oil Co. was bought by Texaco in 1956. (Kevin Lane Collection)

Figure 71 Austin LD diesel-engined van of about 1965, which was well suited to deliveries as it had sliding doors, allowing the driver to exit safely. It sold well under a range of badges. (Reproduced by kind permission of Nick Baldwin)

Figure 72 Automatic coupling was an important advance for local collection and delivery work. This is a 1934 Scammell Mechanical Horse, showing the company's patented design of automatic coupling. (Reproduced by permission of Gordon Mustoe)

Figure 73 Bank: a busy loading bank at Fisher Renwick's Coppetts Road depot in Muswell Hill, London, in the 1940s. An amazing variety of goods is visible and the names of some of the cities served appear on the far wall. A pair of the famous Showboats are at the back. (Reproduced by kind permission of Guy Renwick)

Figure 74 Beck & Pollitzer: this Commer 7-ton FC pantechnicon body had a 45-inch Baico wheelbase extension, giving a total wheelbase of just over 17 feet. Notice the cyrillic script, as the vehicle was on its way to Moscow in 1961, carrying material for the international exhibition there. It was specially liveried for the occasion. Such long-distance work was rare at this time. (Reproduced by kind permission of the Museum of British Road Transport, Coventry)

Figure 75 Bedford: transatlantic styling was a feature of Bedford's S types introduced in the early 1950s. This tipper version of 1960 is diesel engined and four-wheel drive was added by United Service Garages of Portsmouth to cope with conditions such as those seen here. (Reproduced by kind permission of Vauxhall Motors Ltd)

Figure 76 Bishop & Sons are furniture removers and storers based in London. This Leyland chassis dates from the early 1920s, but carries a body modified from the days of horse-drawn vehicles. When lowered, the tailgate provided a ramp for access to the body. (Words & Machines Collection)

Figure 77 Bouts Bros ran a nightly trunk service between Lancashire and south Yorkshire and London. It later became Bouts-Tillotson, using this AEC Mammoth Major in the early 1930s, supplied by Oswald Tillotson. (Reproduced by kind permission of Nick Baldwin)

Figure 78 Brewery traffic: an ex-RAF AEC Marshall of about 1938 with flat-bed body, loaded with Threlfalls of Liverpool's crates of bottled beer and one crate of Gaymer's cider, ready for local delivery in the late 1950s. The badge on the radiator shows the vehicle has been re-engined by Perkins, who guaranteed a 'square deal all round'. (John Armstrong Collection)

Figure 79 Brick traffic: 1976 Volvo F86 8×4 30-ton platform body, with Selfstak integral crane for handling palletised bricks for the London Brick Co. (Reproduced by kind permission of Volvo Trucks UK)

Figure 80 Bristol was predominantly a bus manufacturer, but did produce rigid-eight chassis and articulated tractive units for British Road Services between 1952 and 1964, though production was not continuous. This eight-wheeler was based in Dunstable and has a sheet rack above the cab. (Kevin Lane Collection)

Figure 81 British Road Services had been divided into separate companies, though it was still part of National Freight Corporation when this photograph was taken in the early 1980s. The Mercedes-Benz artic has the New Generation cab and the awkward load looks rather clumsily sheeted. (John Armstrong Collection)

Figure 82 Bus chassis conversion into lorry. This former AEC Regal bus of Hebble Motor Services has been neatly converted to a crew-cabbed lorry and towing vehicle using part of the original Weymann bus body. (Kevin Lane Collection)

Figure 83 The **cab-over platform** is illustrated by this Volvo outfit with conventional flat drawbar trailer carrying old-style bales of straw or hay, photographed at Skipton in 1986. Use of the space over the cab gives valuable added capacity. (Kevin Lane Collection)

Figure 84 Car delivery: this Commer TS3 two-stroke tractor of the late 1950s is hauling a double-deck Carrimore car transporter with Rootes Group coupés for delivery. It is on contract from British Road Services. The picture was taken outside the Rootes Competition Department, Coventry. (Reproduced by kind permission of the Museum of British Road Transport, Coventry)

Figure 85 Car industry traffic: this busy shot shows Commer TS3 articulated lorries and a Merriworth trailer outside the Rootes parts distribution centre, formerly a Singer car factory, at Small Heath, Birmingham, in 1966. Note the use of stillages to hold parts and a fork-lift truck to load them. The vehicles were owned by Morton and employed on the Rootes contract. (Reproduced by kind permission of the Museum of British Road Transport, Coventry)

Figure 86 Carter Paterson was a long-lived firm of parcels carriers, here using Leyland X-types of the early 1920s with solid tyres, in a CMUA motor parade with both drivers and vehicles smartly turned out. These lorries have probably been refurbished in CP's own works, as shown by the name on the radiator. (Reproduced by kind permission of Nick Baldwin)

Figure 87 Cement traffic was carried in hundredweight bags, as shown by this shot of Blue Circle Cement being loaded onto petrol-engined AEC Monarch four-wheelers using sack trucks. Note the large number of men involved and the absence of nearside mirrors, though the vehicles do have trafficators. (Reproduced by kind permission of Nick Baldwin)

Figure 88 Chaplins was official carrier to the Southern Railway, having originated in the horse-drawn era. This Thornycroft JJ dates from the late 1920s and was based in Yeovil. (Reproduced by kind permission of Nick Baldwin)

Figure 89 Chemicals traffic: a 1933 Leyland Beaver operated by ICI to carry acids. Note the step access at the rear to the heavy-duty tank. (Reproduced by kind permission of ICI)

Figure 90 Chemicals traffic: a 1982 Foden S10 6×4 24-ton sleeper cab with a special box-van body for carrying hazardous chemicals. Note the HAZCHEM signs on the radiator and bumper: yellow for organic peroxide, red for flammable gas and black and white for corrosives. (Reproduced by permission of Fodens Ltd)

Figure 91 Chinese six: a 1935 Foden DG5 rigid six-wheel diesel lorry. The sheeting and roping are somewhat untidy: the hanging rope ends could whip out and hit cyclists. The bumper is an unusual addition. (Reproduced by kind permission of Colin Parrott)

Figure 92 Clerestory roof: this 1948-model forward-control Karrier Bantam of 2-ton capacity, exhibited at the Earls Court show, was built as a mobile shop and shows quite clearly the raised clerestory roof. The £430 price tag applied to the chassis. (Reproduced by kind permission of the Museum of British Road Transport, Coventry)

Figure 93 Coal traffic was a familiar sight in towns until the 1960s when it began to be displaced by natural gas as a result of clean-air legislation. This Commer N3 drop-side lorry of about 1936 was used for delivering coal in hundredweight sacks to domestic users by J Mason of Eversley, Hampshire. Notice the opening split windscreen, which was a legal requirement, and the taller coke sacks near the headboard. (Reproduced by kind permission of the Museum of British Road Transport, Coventry)

Figure 94 Commer 10-ton Rootes diesel tractor, with a TS3 three-cylinder, two-stroke engine, and a 2000-gallon tanker for petrol delivery, in the livery of Shell Mex and BP of the early 1950s. (Reproduced by kind permission of the Museum of British Road Transport, Coventry)

Figure 95 Commercial Motor Show: this overhead shot of the 1960 show reveals most of the Commer stand. The variety of customers and vehicles is emphasised by the many different liveries on display. (Reproduced by kind permission of the Museum of British Road Transport, Coventry)

Figure 96 The **Co-operative movement** was probably the largest operator of mobile shops. This Smiths-bodied Karrier Bantam of 1962 represented a popular combination and was used by the quaintly named Windy Nook and Felling Shore Co-operative Society, near Newcastle upon Tyne, as a mobile shop to serve their far-scattered members. (Reproduced by kind permission of the Museum of British Road Transport, Coventry)

Figure 97 Crow Carrying Co. Ltd were among the first firms to use tank wagons. This well-travelled AEC Y-type dates from before 1920. Note the solid tyres, substantial fire screen between cab and tank and short exhaust pipe and rear-mounted hand pump for petroleum. (Reproduced by kind permission of Nick Baldwin)

Figure 98 DAF: an early UK example, *c.* 1976, of this imported lorry. An eight-wheeler, it was operated by Goddards of Rugby. (Words & Machines Collection)

Figure 99 Daimler: this CK3 is being used for brewery traffic carrying barrels of beer and so has a 'boxing ring' body to help restrain the load yet allow easy loading and unloading. Note the open cab, solid tyres, low speed limit and artillery wheels. (Reproduced by kind permission of the Museum of British Road Transport, Coventry)

Figure 100 Demountable body: this Morris FG K80 4-ton lorry with the BMC FG Safety Cab of the late 1950s is picking up an Abelson demountable container. The cab was nicknamed 'a threepenny bit' and was no doubt chosen because the outfit was used on local collection and delivery work. (Reproduced by kind permission of Nick Baldwin)

Figure 101 Dennis vans owned by the Great Western Railway under contract to Cadbury Bros for local deliveries. They are London registered but are operating out of the Canterbury depot *c.* 1932. (Words & Machines Collection)

Figure 102 Dock work was carried out by this MAN, operated by Stockton Haulage, in 1986 at Teesport to carry steel. The semi-trailer has simple sideguards. (Kevin Lane Collection)

Figure 103 Dodge tipper loading peat at Fisons in Somerset in 1980. The timber additions to the top of the metal body were sometimes called 'greedy boards'. (Kevin Lane Collection)

Figure 104 Drawbar trailer: a 7-ton Commer lorry drawing a 3-ton drawbar trailer in 1957. It contains equipment for the Rootes stands at the Geneva Motor Show, carefully tarpaulined and tied down. (Reproduced by kind permission of the Museum of British Road Transport, Coventry)

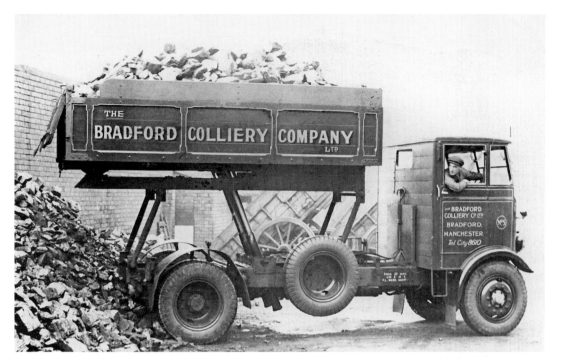

Figure 105 Edbro was formed in 1952 and one of the firms involved in this merger was Bromilow & Edwards, who made high-lift tipping gear like this one installed on a Leyland Badger in the 1930s. (Reproduced by permission of Gordon Mustoe)

Figure 106 Fifth wheel: this shot from above of a Dodge KP900 of 1966 shows clearly the fifth wheel for attachment of the trailer. This one was made by York and the groove and locking pin can be seen. The cab is in Turners livery and the badges on the front indicate Turners were members of the Transport Association. (Reproduced by kind permission of the Museum of British Road Transport, Coventry)

Figure 107 Fish traffic: Albion artic with platform semi-trailer, belonging to Chas Alexander, unloading fish for kipper processing in Aberdeen in the mid-1950s. (Reproduced by kind permission of Arthur Ingram)

Figure 108 Foden built this S-series rigid-eight in the late 1960s. It was operated by Foster Yeoman for stone traffic and has had a substantial height addition to the tipper body in the form of 'greedy boards'. (Kevin Lane Collection)

Figure 109 Ford Transit vans dominated the 3.5-ton market for many years. This example seen in 1999 has a less-common coach-built body with a stylish Luton head for transport of furniture, a light but bulky product. (Kevin Lane Collection)

Figure 110 Forward control: this Commer N3 of the mid-1930s was specially bodied for Robertson's Golden Shred to deliver their marmalade. The engine is in the cab, with the driver alongside it. As the vehicle's unladen weight was less than 2½ tons, it had a maximum legal speed of 30 mph. It has five separate compartments, which allowed the crew to 'pick and mix' retail deliveries. (Reproduced by kind permission of the Museum of British Road Transport, Coventry)

Figure 111 Four-in-line: this Scammell 15-ton frameless tanker shows the principle of four wheels in line on the rear axle of the trailer, an idea introduced by Scammell. This vehicle, of about 1928, was used for non-hazardous loads, and is equipped with a compressor. (Reproduced by permission of Gordon Mustoe)

Figure 112 Fruit delivery: this Commer 1½-ton lorry of the early 1950s was used by C E Wilkinson of Bedford to deliver Fyffes bananas in wooden crates to retailers. Note the extensive use of the vehicle for advertising. This cab is typical of Rootes design after the Second World War. (Reproduced by kind permission of the Museum of British Road Transport, Coventry)

Figure 113 Furniture removals: this handsome Luton body was owned by John Walton of Mere in Wiltshire in 1938 and was used for furniture removals. It is built on a Commer N3 forward-control chassis and has an illuminated headboard. (Reproduced by kind permission of the Museum of British Road Transport, Coventry)

Figure 114 General strike: this scene, featuring 17-gallon milk churns, probably in Hyde Park milk depot, shows how road transport took over the role of the railways, which were heavily unionised. The vehicles include a Ford T nearest the camera, and a removals van pressed into service. (Reproduced by kind permission of Nick Baldwin)

Figure 115 Gown van: this Austin, based on a Three-Way chassis cab but with coach-built bodywork of the late 1940s, was used to transport garments, as indicated by the signboard. (Reproduced by kind permission of Nick Baldwin)

Figure 116 Hallett & Silbermann were heavy-haulage specialists, as shown by this Scammell Constructor of the early 1960s pulling a large Grayston excavator on a 45-ton Crane trailer. (Reproduced by kind permission of Nick Baldwin)

Figure 117 Heavy haulage preceded motor transport, as is shown by this 40-ton boiler trolley owned by the Great Western Railway, built by the company in their Swindon works, and photographed here in about 1907. The double shafts indicate it was drawn by a team of horses. (Reproduced by permission of Gordon Mustoe)

Figure 118 Home delivery: this delightful period shot shows a Commer 20/25-cwt forward-control van of 1937 in Golden Crust livery, using the van side and cab top for advertising, outside a bread shop and tearoom. Notice the attractive period lettering and design. House-to-house bread deliveries were big business until the advent of the supermarket and rising delivery costs. (Reproduced by kind permission of the Museum of British Road Transport, Coventry)

Figure 119 Horsebox: a Vincent body on a Guy chassis of the early 1920s; this held two horses, both side loaded. Note the diagonal tongue-and-groove boarding for extra strength. The folding padded division being held open allowed easy access for the padded horse. (Words & Machines Collection)

Figure 120 Intermodal transport: this 1911 Karrier B50 2-ton flat-bed lorry is carrying a beautifully liveried lift van which can be craned off onto a railway flat truck, thus giving inter-modal transport. Note the chain drive of the Karrier. The vehicle is in the Northampton goods depot of the London & North Western Railway. (Reproduced by kind permission of the Museum of British Road Transport, Coventry)

Figure 121 Jennings bodywork: this convertible cattle truck of 1949 is based on a Karrier CK3 Gamecock chassis, with body by Jennings of Sandbach in the livery of T Hollamby & Son Ltd of Burwash, Sussex. It has an open top, covered by a tarpaulin, and the sides can be easily removed. The metal cab has a wood-grained finish. Jennings was later acquired by its neighbour ERF. (Reproduced by kind permission of the Museum of British Road Transport, Coventry)

Figure 122 John Jempson: an AEC Marshall Major of the mid-1970s, in the livery of long-established haulier John Jempson of Rye, carrying drums of hazardous chemicals as shown by the HAZCHEM sign on the radiator. (John Armstrong Collection)

Figure 123 Karrier: this fleet of Karrier CK3s was built for the Post Office telephone section in about 1937. Note the forward control position and tilt covers used to cover the load space. (Reproduced by kind permission of the Museum of British Road Transport, Coventry)

Figure 124 Lambourn Racing Transport chose Commer chassis for these horseboxes of 1972, used to carry the British Olympic team around Europe. The Commander Transporter on the left was able to carry nine horses and grooms. (Reproduced by kind permission of the Museum of British Road Transport, Coventry)

Figure 125 Leyland's T45 Constructor range came in several forms. This six-wheeler in Tarmac livery is delivering top dressing for road resurfacing in south London. The tipping body is insulated and a tarpaulin has covered and preserved the temperature of the load. (Kevin Lane Collection)

Figure 126 Livestock traffic: this Commer Superpoise of 1939 has been given a lift-off body for livestock carriage, with the Luton head above the cab to carry hay, feed or calves. (Reproduced by kind permission of the Museum of British Road Transport, Coventry)

Figure 127 London Brick: this AEC Mammoth Major rigid-eight of the late 1950s carries newly introduced mesh-panelled drop sides to retain hand-loaded stock bricks. In the 1970s, palletisation and strapping made this redundant. (Reproduced by kind permission of Nick Baldwin)

Figure 128 Lorry-mounted cranes were used to speed up loading and unloading at locations which had no mechanical handling equipment, such as building sites. This AEC Mammoth Major of 1975 in Ibstock livery has an on-board Hiab crane, though the unitised brick stacks can also be moved by fork-lift truck. The slung forks are in position at the rear of the body. (John Armstrong Collection)

Shelvoke & Drewry, the municipal vehicle and low-loader manufacturers, acquired from the French firm Automobiles Industriels Latil of Suresnes manufacturing rights of the Latil KTL road-going tractor (a cabbed tractive unit) for the UK and colonies. Between 1932 and 1937 some 150 tractors were produced. The range was marketed as the Traulier, presumably on the basis of it being a tractor for the haulier. It was used by the railway companies, timber hauliers, Guinness and Pickfords, and for dock work. From 1937 until the war the tractor was assembled by concessionaires in London; after the war until 1959 it was produced at Ascot by US Concessionaires Ltd and fitted with Meadows diesel engines. **RAS**

Law, Alan (1919–85) was appointed as a TGWU full-time official and secretary of the 5/35 branch in 1958. He brought to his post, as West Midlands region trade group officer for road haulage, experience as a post-war lorry driver and battery sergeant-major in the Second World War from which service he may have derived the deafness which became an increasing problem in his later years, as well as his determined — some said aggressive — character. Law's commitment was to the workers whose interests he successfully represented, rather than to any political party or doctrine. Exploiting the anomaly of a paid official also serving as a full-time branch secretary, Law used his bargaining skills and determination to create in 1966 the Birmingham differential in road haulage wages, which, by the end of the 1979 strike (which he had strongly opposed) had become the West Midlands differential. His tactics were to concentrate on firms where union success was likely, achieve this, and then use the result to put pressure on other employers. Significantly he had taken the BRS drivers, closely linked to the low Wages Council rates, out of the 5/35 branch. The employers he wished to drive out of business were the small, under-capitalised concerns, often operating badly-maintained vehicles and paying staff the lowest rates they could get away with. These were the 'cockroach capitalists' scorned by Jack Jones,

the TGWU General Secretary. The 1968 Act reduced, but did not eliminate them.

Law used the press, by which he was much maligned, to project a tough image, a process which may have had deleterious effects for the labour movement. He was well regarded by some employers because, once agreements were reached, he always ensured that employees kept to them. Although closely identified with the 5/35 branch, as a regional officer, Law's concerns were much wider, including, for example, oil and car transporter drivers, who were outside the branch, and he also had national responsibilities. His resignation as branch officer was forced on him by the TGWU regional executive in January 1978, following an irregularly-conducted ballot, but his retirement in the following year, on reaching 60, was a response to genuine health problems and not simply the result of the 5/35 leaders taking a line on the 1979 strike so much at variance with Law's. **RAS**

Corfield (1982); obituary in TGWU *Record* (December 1985); Thompson (1991), p. 49; Smith (2001), chap. 6.

Lawther & Harvey Ltd of Belfast, founded in 1857, were hauliers, shipping agents, customs and forwarding agents, warehousemen and managing agents in Northern Ireland for Anglo-Continental Container Services Ltd, which built up a road–sea–road container service to and from the province, via its Preston/Ardrossan–Larne shipping services. Following BRS's acquisition of ACCS in 1958 as part of its strategy to expand its Anglo-Irish business, it was logical for the Transport Holding Co. to take over L&H in 1967. The company initially prospered, particularly after it passed to the NFC in 1969, for example taking over Freightliners' collection and delivery work. However, this coincided with the beginning of Northern Ireland's civil disturbances. L&H's premises were burned down in the 1969 riots. Vehicles were often delayed at military checkpoints and sometimes hijacked. In 1975 its newly-rebuilt premises were partly destroyed by terrorists, together with one-third of its fleet of 80 vehicles. Every NFC annual report during these years had paid tribute to the L&H staff for their efforts in keeping the firm profitable, but the troubles were now affecting the province's economy and in 1978 the NFC decided to sell the site and merge L&H's general haulage, parcels, groupage and warehousing activities with those of Northern Ireland Carriers Ltd (see ULSTER TRANSPORT AUTHORITY). **RAS/GAB**

BRS, *Management Bulletin*, 74 (June 1966); National Freight Corporation, *Annual Reports & Accounts* (1969–78); Baldwin (1982)

The **LDV** series of vans dates back to the 1960 Austin/Morris/BMC J4 model. This was developed to comply with new Construction & Use legislation and became part of the British Leyland Austin/Morris van, being refined to form the Sherpa. It has since been part of British Leyland, Freight Rover, Leyland DAF Vans and finally, following a management buy-out in 1993, LDV.

Updated versions of the Leyland DAF 200 and 400 range were sold as the 2.2- and 2.8-ton Pilot and 3.5-ton Convoy, with Peugeot or Ford diesel engines as standard. A smaller, badged version of the Nissan 2.5-ton van made in Barcelona, was sold as the LDV Cub from 1998. A Royal Mail order for over 1000 LDV vans in late 1999 brought its LDV fleet to 9500. After Leyland DAF Vans' receivership, the joint design project formed with Renault was terminated. A joint venture with Daewoo arranged in 1998 was to develop two new ranges of vans, with production to be divided between LDV's Birmingham plant and Daewoo's Polish subsidiary, DMP Lublin works. Following Daewoo's financial problems in 2000 LDV bought Daewoo's share of the joint venture. **GM**

Legal lettering is the statutory display of the owner's identity and other information that has been required at different times on various types of road vehicle. The requirements relating to goods vehicles are set out in the Table 11.

The 1795 Act that introduced 'taxed carts' specified lettering at least one inch high, white on a black background or vice versa. This style became a common standard. The position specified for legal lettering varied: it was generally on the back for carts; on mechanically-powered vehicles it was usually on the side (initially the off-side, but from 1938 the near-side). **GAB**

Acts of Parliament; Statutory Rules & Orders (1904–49); Statutory Instruments (1950–)

LEP Transport & Depository Ltd was a leading importer and exporter of motor vehicles and components between the wars. The business was founded in 1910 by the London manager of the forwarding agents Langstaff, Erembert & Pollock (hence LEP), in partnership with Pollock who broke away from the original business. After the First World War, LEP used its expertise in handling, Customs procedures, insurance, packing and shipping for the two-way flow of motor vehicles, especially cars. It opened the first Customs-approved bonded warehouse for McKenna-dutiable material in 1919 and expanded to a new warehouse at Chiswick in 1923. A wide range of American cars was imported; the biggest UK exports were Morris and Morris Commercial. Packing for export was at first individual vehicle crating, but bulk orders were eventually handled by packing the parts for eight to ten cars in two or three packing cases, with vehicles in smaller consignments being partially dismantled. LEP built up a sizeable transport fleet at this time, including 50 ex-WD Lancias, Fiats, Chevrolets, Star, S&D and Foden and Sentinel steam lorries. By the 1930s the handling of cars gave way to car parts; the export of British lorry parts was also undertaken. There was still an export trade in Morris Commercial and imports of Diamond T, GMC and Studebaker trucks.

During the Second World War LEP handled some 360,000 military vehicles. After the war it continued as an international freight forwarder, with a fleet of 220 vehicles in 1964, but its business changed to concentrate on high technology products; it also moved into the property, security and services fields. In 1985 LEP absorbed the long-established Swift Transport Services, intending to use it as the

Table 11: Lettering and Symbols Required on Goods Vehicles

Period	Type of vehicle	Lettering or Symbols required	Purpose
1745–1869	Goods vehicles used in London	Owner's name (and address from 1832)	Prosecution of disorderly drivers
1795–1823	Carts that qualified for reduced taxation	Owner's name and address and the words A TAXED CART. Also on new carts from 1810 the price and the maker's name and address	To prevent evasion of annual luxury tax on carriages
1804–1854	Carts that qualified for exemption from taxation	Owner's name, address and (from 1833) occupation; until 1836 the words COMMON STAGE CART	
1854–1944	Horse-drawn goods vehicles that qualified for exemption from taxation	Owner's name and address	
1861–1930	Locomotives	Owner's name (and address from 1865); weight	Enforcement of Locomotives Acts
1896–1904	Light locomotives	Owner's name and address; unladen weight	Enforcement of use and construction regulations
1905–1931	Heavy motor cars	Unladen weight, axle weights and max. speed	
1910–1921	Petrol-engined goods vehicles	Owner's name and address	To prevent evasion of tax on motor spirit
1931–	Locomotives	Unladen weight	Enforcement of construction and use regulations
1931–1937	Motor tractors	Unladen weight; max. speed when drawing trailer	
1937–1957		Unladen weight; max. speed with the words WITHOUT TRAILER	
1957–		Unladen weight	
1931–1957	Heavy motor cars	Unladen weight; max. speed when not drawing trailer	
1957–1994		Unladen weight (from 1986 not required if shown on Ministry plate)	
1938–1968	Trailers fitted with overrun brakes	Unladen weight	
1934–1936	C-licence vehicles	Licence number (superseded by display of identity certificate on all goods vehicles)	Enforcement of licensing regulations
1925–1995	Vehicles used for selling meat; from 1939 ice cream; from 1956 all food	Owner's name and address	Enforcement of food hygiene legislation
1967–1995	Vehicles used for delivering food		
1937–1957	Motor vehicles and articulated trailers restricted to 20 mph	20 mph speed limit disc displayed on rear — white '20' on 8 in. black disc (or black on white from 1941)	Enforcement of speed limit
1937–1957	Motor vehicle trailers (other than artic. trailers)	White 'T' with inset red reflex lenses on rectangular black plate displayed on rear	
1957–1984		White triangle with inset red reflex lenses	
1962–	Vehicles with long loads projecting front or rear	Red and white striped triangles on end and sides of projection	Visibility to other road users
1971–1982	Goods vehicles over 3 tons UW and trailers over 1 ton UW	Reflective LONG VEHICLE plate(s) (yellow with red border) on rear of motor vehicles or trains exceeding 13m. length. Those up to 13m. have plates with red and yellow diagonal stripes.	Warning to drivers of overtaking vehicles
1982–	Goods vehicles over 7.5 tonnes gross and trailers over 3.5 tonnes gross	For vehicle built from 1995/6 the words LONG VEHICLE are omitted	

basis of development into Europe, but it came unstuck in the economic downturn of 1991–2 and sold Swift to a management buy out. **RAS**

K Desmond, 'LEP International Transports', *OM*, 9, 4 (undated), pp. 327–31; Watson (1997)

Leyland Motors Ltd (Figures 4, 32–4,76, 86, 89, 105, 125, 131, 151, 161, 176, 184 and 187). In 1907 the Lancashire Steam Motor Co. Ltd absorbed the steam wagon building business of Coulthard of Preston and changed its name to Leyland Motors Ltd. The works were expanded, bus building was taken on, and in 1912 the company built its first subsidy 3-ton truck, later to become famous as the RAF type. Before the First World War Leyland gained publicity by using its own products on mail contracts. Depots, including London, Liverpool and Southampton, were established which also serviced customers' vehicles.

The First World War brought huge expansion to the company. A new foundry plant was begun in 1913 at Farington and in 1914 the company took over an unused factory at Chorley, to which production and repair of steam wagons was transferred. At Leyland, the existing North Works was expanded by the erection of a new South Works. Nearly 6000 vehicles were produced for the armed forces, and for the first time Leyland saw the benefit of series production.

At the end of the War, the company took over the lease of a former Sopwith aircraft factory at Kingston-upon-Thames to recondition and rebuild nearly 3000 ex-RAF type lorries out of twice that number that were brought back. This was to prevent others from tarnishing Leyland's reputation by placing shoddy rebuilds on the road and was achieved at the expense of the Leyland works, which built relatively few new lorry chassis between 1920 and 1926. The rebuild work almost bankrupted the company. A huge injection of cash from the Spurrier family and the appointment of Aylmer Liardet as general manager at the behest of the banks saved the situation and Leyland became prosperous again by 1929. Liardet decided to remain with the company, ultimately as managing director. His

continuing guidance was an important factor in its success in the 1930s and later.

The works at Leyland re-focussed its efforts on building buses and bus bodies. A complementary goods range was introduced using similar components. G J Rackham, was appointed chief engineer in 1926 and he developed the low-loading concept a stage further with new models (Tiger and Titan) and a 6-cylinder engine (the T type). Rackham left two years later to join AEC, where he repeated his actions for Leyland's closest rival. Rackham's engine and designs were adapted at Leyland for a new range of lorries (Badger, Beaver, Bull, Bison).

Steam wagon production and repair ceased at Chorley in 1926, existing work passing to Atkinson-Walker. Chorley took on production of chassis frames and engines, special vehicles, overhaul of engines and vehicles on behalf of customers, and the manufacture of obsolete spares. The Kingston works phased out the reconditioning of War Office vehicles and from 1923 undertook the manufacture of Trojan cars and 5-cwt and later 7-cwt vans and some vehicle bodybuilding until switching, in 1930–1, to the production of a new light commercial vehicle (the 2-ton or Cub range), but the Cub models were too expensive to compete with the cheaper mass-produced vehicles then flooding the market.

The factories at Leyland continued during the 1930s with buses and a family of 4-cylinder and 6-cylinder goods vehicles using many common components with the passenger vehicles. The lorry range was expanded by the 3-axle Hippo and 4-axle Octopus, and a cross-country/military chassis named the Terrier. From 1933, both the engine ranges were available as diesel units, the 6-cylinder 8.6 litre engine being very well respected and continuing in production well into the post-war era, along with a new lighter 6-cylinder unit under development in the late 1930s which was adapted for use in military vehicles, enlarged to 7.4 litre capacity. A substantial export trade was built up between 1928 and 1940.

The Cub range, after a re-vamp in 1935 and the introduction of a diesel engine, was superseded for goods use by the Lynx in 1938.

This was followed by a military version for the Second World War, many of which were reconditioned at Kingston in 1945 before it was vacated in 1951. Fire engine manufacture at Chorley ceased in 1942, which continued to supply part-manufactured units to the Leyland sites and as a repair depot.

The war production of Leyland consisted of a large number of Retriever 6×4 petrol-engined lorries and Hippo heavy duty 6×4 diesel-engined lorries, before going over exclusively to armaments and tanks. Hippo Mk II military style lorries restarted road vehicle production in 1944, to be followed by the Interim Beaver civilian lorry in mid-1946. This was in fact a 2-axle truck built from existing stocks of parts intended for assembly into 3-axle Hippos.

The war over, the company embarked on one of its most prolific periods of production. The success was founded upon the new lightweight lorry, which replaced the range formerly made at Kingston and which took its name of Comet from one of the Leyland-built tanks. The power unit was a new 300 cu in capacity petrol or diesel engine. For the heavier vehicles there was a 600 cu in diesel engine, known as the 0.600, used to power buses and the heavier lorry range of four models, the 4×2 Beaver, the 6×4 Hippo, the 6×2 Steer and the 8×4 Octopus. Leyland's products were in great demand all over the world and in 1948 an Export Division under the guidance of Donald Stokes was established in London. 4×2 Super Beaver and 6×2 Super Hippo bonneted trucks were developed for export markets.

Over the next two decades manufacturing plants were established in Australia, South Africa and, by collaboration, in India (Ashok-Leyland). To increase the range on offer, Leyland acquired Albion Motors in 1951 and Scammell Lorries in 1955. The former added lighter and the latter heavier commercial vehicles to the range built by the parent company. AEC was subsumed by Leyland in 1962 along with its subsidiary companies. Several models were designed purely for assembly overseas. Bus production continued to be a core activity, but designs had by now diverged substantially from those of haulage vehicles.

For the commercial vehicle range, the 1960s was a decade of rationalisation. Many models were phased out and common components were supplied to many factories. The most obvious of these was the adoption of, first, the LAD cab by Leyland and Albion, and then the Ergomatic cab by Leyland (heavier range), Albion and AEC (1966–81). Before the integration of the goods range was complete there came the first of two entries into the field of cars which, unfortunately, presaged the demise of this great company. Standard-Triumph was absorbed in 1963, adding light vans and pick-up trucks to the commercial range and the burden of several car plants to the company's budget.

Bristol Commercial Vehicles and the ECW bus body plant at Lowestoft were absorbed in 1965, but in 1968 there occurred the most momentous take-over of all, when British Motor Holdings Ltd, combining Austin, Morris and Jaguar cars and BMC, Guy lorries and buses and Daimler buses were joined with Leyland Motors to form the British Leyland Motor Corporation. Just before the merger, the company had put together a team of engineers from various plants to develop a new fixed-head diesel engine, the 500, for use in lorries and buses. **ARP**

Kennett (1983); Turner (1971); Baldwin (1986); Peter Davies, 'Great Leyland lorries', *CVC* Supplement (September 2002)

Licensing Authority. When licensing of goods vehicle operators (q.v.), or carrier licensing, was introduced in 1934 under the terms of the Road & Rail Traffic Act 1933, the country had already been divided into Traffic Areas, each with Traffic Commissioners responsible for adjudicating on applications for public service vehicle (bus) licences under the Road Traffic Act 1930. The 1933 Act nominated the chairman of the Traffic Commissioners to be the Licensing Authority in each of the 11 Traffic Areas for adjudicating on applications for goods vehicle licences. The traffic area offices provided the administrative support for the LAs, the clerk having a similar function to that of the magistrates' clerk. Although LAs were individually independent, they operated within guidelines laid down by the Ministry of Transport. The senior LA advised on consistency.

The processing of all applications for grant or renewal of licences was notified to the public through weekly or fortnightly publication in each area of its *Applications & Decisions* (A&Ds). They were the means by which objectors were able to know that an application had been made. Objections had to be made within 21 days from the date of the A&D. The LA was required to hold a public hearing on all opposed applications. If an objector was unhappy with a LA decision, an appeal might be made to the Appeal Tribunal (q.v.) (from 1951 the Transport Tribunal).

The LAs were also involved in enforcement of the licensing and Construction & Use regulations. Routinely they brought cases, often in conjunction with the police, against offending operators in the magistrates' courts. Regular offenders could also be faced with a disciplinary hearing before the LA, at which their licences could be revoked or suspended.

During the Second World War, carrier licences were replaced by defence permits, issued by the LAs acting as regional Traffic Commissioners of the Civil Defence Regions under the Defence Regulations 1939. Applications for permits were not published, there were no public hearings and no right of appeal. After the war, it took until 1950 to replace all the defence permits with statutory licences.

The Transport Act 1947 renamed the LAs Licensing Authorities for Goods Vehicles. When carrier licensing was replaced by operator licensing under the Transport Act 1968, the LAs continued to be the granting authority. Their number was reduced to eight in 1991 and in 1995 they were re-titled Traffic Commissioners (Goods). **GM/GAB**

Annual Reports of the Licensing Authorities

Licensing of goods vehicle operators, also called carrier licensing, was introduced in 1934 under the Road & Rail Traffic Act 1933 to bring order to the road haulage industry and to protect the railways from unregulated competition. Licences were in three main categories: A, B and C. Public (hire-and-reward) carriers were granted A licences, while B licences were intended for limited operations for both the operator's own and other people's goods, while C licences covered private (own-account) carriers. There was also a Contract-A licence for use by a carrier when he had a vehicle or vehicles contracted solely for use by one hirer or customer.

What might now be called grandfather rights gave anyone applying for an A or B licence before 1 April 1934 a right to a licence for the same total tonnage as had been operated in the year beginning April 1932, providing this could be proved. Licences had to detail the unladen weight and registration number of each vehicle (and trailer weights, if applicable). The different classes of licence lasted for different periods, all of which were later extended, but renewal could be almost automatic, subject to satisfactory conduct.

Licence applications could be opposed by other transport providers (road or rail) on the basis that they were already providing sufficient facilities. Proof of need (plus a lack of suitable existing facilities) had to be provided by any applicant seeking to add additional vehicles or run heavier ones. Unfortunately, almost any bid for an increase gave rise to virtually automatic objection by the railways and not infrequently by other hauliers too. The railways normally claimed they had existing, under-utilised facilities, and other hauliers were not averse to claiming to be able to do the work without requiring additional vehicles. The needs of the customer, and in particular the speed or reliability of the service he needed, tended to be given scant attention. Railway objections in particular at the inevitable public enquiry were often fronted by a barrister, a luxury small operators could not afford, and many eminent barristers cut their teeth at traffic court hearings. Top-class barristers were sometimes engaged for important cases. Walter Monckton, (later Sir Walter and then Lord Monckton) who became legal advisor to King Edward VIII, did much traffic court work. Not only did the railways frequently appear as objectors at Licensing Authority hearings, they often subsequently appealed against any decisions in favour of road hauliers to the Transport Tribunal.

The effect of the A and B licences was to restrict the growth of public haulage, but there was no constraint on the issue of C or Contract-A licences. One result was that it gave a value to a public haulier's business, this value being intrinsically linked to the number and size of vehicles licensed. This, rather than the actual worth (taking into account the age or state of repair) of the vehicle, became the defining factor in the price when businesses were offered for sale.

Another result of the difficulty in obtaining an A licence for additional vehicles was that either traders themselves took out a C licence and ran their own vehicles, or the haulier provided vehicles exclusively for them with a Contract-A licence. As the UK moved out of recession in the mid-1930s the numbers of C licences rose rapidly. It was the enormous growth in C licences after the Second World War that defeated the main intentions of the 1947 Transport Act.

At denationalisation vehicles purchased from BRS came with a Special A licence, sometimes known as an S licence.

This 'quantity' licensing was swept away by the Transport Act 1968 and replaced by 'quality' licensing of operators, or O licensing, introduced in 1969–70. Suitability of operator and premises (see OPERATING CENTRE) and financial backing became the criteria.

GM/JMA

Annual Reports of the Licensing Authorities; Dunbar (1981), p. 137

Lifting axles are used on multi-axle vehicles or trailers to reduce tyre wear and fuel consumption when a vehicle is lightly laden or unladen. Then the axle is raised and makes no contact with the road surface. When in the down position they are useful in spreading the load on a part-loaded vehicle, when it is easy for an individual axle to become overweight. Their position may vary, for example lifting

pusher axles may be found in the centre of a three-axle tractive unit.

Their usage began gradually as it was not covered by existing legislation; for example, maximum permitted rear overhang was limited to 60 per cent of a vehicle's wheelbase so a lifting rearmost axle altered this calculation when lifted. The main impetus came from the high tyre wear experienced with tri-axle semi-trailers while changes since the early 1990s in vehicle taxation have favoured multi-axle layouts. A 23-tonne rigid 6×2, with a lifting axle, has a more favourable tax rate than an 18-tonne 2-axle vehicle, and a greater payload.

Lifting axles are offered by all trailer makers as every leading suspension manufacturer now has suitable equipment, but the first to achieve popularity was the York Trailer (q.v.) Hobo, launched in 1976 (hobo being the US name for a hitchhiker). **JMA**

Lift-van was the name given in the nineteenth and early-twentieth centuries to the covered container, which could be transhipped by crane from railway flat truck to horse-drawn trolley or steam or motor platform lorry. Built of metal or wood, they were especially used for furniture removal. See CONTAINERISATION.

RAS

Dunbar (1981), p. 137

The **Liverpool & District Carters' & Motormen's Union** was formed in 1889 as the Mersey Quay and Railway Carters' Union, organising mainly Orange workers employed in firms owned by Liverpool's protestant ascendancy. The usual chequered history followed, but the union was reconstructed in the years immediately prior to the Liverpool transport strike of 1911, where it played a vital supportive role that is frequently overlooked. Its protestant origins and constituency were both a resource and a threat to its unity and links with catholic dockers organised in the National Union of Dock Labourers. The threat was contained by banning discussion of all religious and political issues.

The LDCMU (which name the union adopted in 1918) was the most powerful of all road transport unions, hence it held aloof from the formation of the TGWU (q.v.) in 1922. The union enforced union-preference on Liverpool's waterfront and a range of working rules, which were upheld during the bleak interwar years against the depredations of employers and the fragmentation of workers' discipline. It gave strong support to the General Strike (q.v.) of May 1926.

Co-operation with the TGWU during the interwar years, in particular the campaign to unionise the growing long-distance haulage sector, laid the foundation for an amalgamation of the two unions from 1 January 1947. The LDCMU's tradition of disciplined if passive union organisation was transferred to the TGWU, where its direct successor, the TGWU 12/41 branch (later the 6/541 branch) played a major role from the mid-1960s in rebuilding trade unionism and district bargaining, defiance of the Conservative government's Industrial Relations Act 1971, and leading the 1979 hire and reward strike. **PS**

The **Liverpool Self-Propelled Traffic Association** was a branch of the Self-Propelled Traffic Association (q.v.). The Liverpool branch was founded in October 1896. Its president was the Earl of Derby and its honorary secretary was Edward Shrapnell-Smith (q.v.). It brought together many of the businessmen of the city who were concerned about Liverpool's position vis-à-vis Manchester, a long-standing rivalry. The opening of the Manchester Ship Canal in 1894 allowed ocean-going ships to go direct to Manchester, cutting out some of Liverpool's trade which had then been transhipped to Manchester, by rail. To try to compete, Liverpool merchants pressed the railway to reduce its charges but, having a virtual monopoly, it resisted. The merchants saw mechanical road transport as a possible alternative to rail goods traffic and a bargaining counter to persuade the railway to relent and reduce its freight rates. Because of this concern for goods transport, from 1898 the Association promoted and organised a series of trials for commercial vehicles known as the Lancashire heavy motor vehicle trials (q.v.). These were

instrumental in getting the pioneers to develop the lorry. **JA**

T R Nicholson, *The Birth of the British Motor Car, 3: The last battle 1894–7* (Macmillan, 1982); Plowden (1973), pp. 8, 10 and 14; T C Barker, 'Slow progress: forty years of motoring research', *JTH*, 3rd series, 14, 2 (1993), pp. 149–50

Livestock traffic (Figures 121, 126, 163 and 184) by road has a long history from the time of the drovers, at its high point in the eighteenth and first half of the nineteenth centuries, when cattle moved on the hoof, for example from the Welsh borders, through the English midland counties to the London market. Even geese, 'shod' for the journey, were driven from East Anglia in the autumn to London. One drawback of droving was that livestock lost weight as they walked, whereas transport by rail, and later road, was quicker and required less effort from the beasts and so they lost less weight. The development of the national railway network and of reliable long-distance road transport in the nineteenth and twentieth centuries respectively allowed the long-distance transport of carcasses. At the same time, local livestock markets and abattoirs provided for local needs, served by local livestock hauliers with small fleets, typically Bedfords, with such marques as Commer or Thornycroft for heavier-weight vehicles, or by farmers operating a single cattle truck. When transporting small animals, such as sheep and pigs, double-deck (q.v.) lorries were used to maximise revenues.

In the late twentieth century new patterns of animal traffic developed, which were highlighted by the outbreak of foot and mouth disease in 2001. This new traffic was occasioned by the closure of many smaller local abattoirs in the previous two decades and the national purchasing and slaughtering policies of some major food retailers. The reduction of abattoirs had come about from a combination of factors, including the reaction to e-coli and BSE infections and the over-zealous UK interpretation of EC regulations. The vehicles of livestock carriers and meat and dairy concerns have been the object of arson attacks by animal rights activists. **RAS/JMA**

K Bonser, *The Drovers* (Macmillan, 1970); *CM*: 'Transport for Agriculture' special issues

A **load tray** (also set or sett) was an early method of combining smaller items of traffic, such as cartons or sacks, into a larger unit for lifting by crane, thereby reducing the labour and time involved in loading and unloading lorries. It took the form of a tray with four lifting points, comparable in size to the pallet (q.v.), by which it was superseded after introduction of fork-lift trucks (q.v.). It dates from the horse-drawn era and was largely replaced by the pallet from the 1950s. **GAB**

Loading and unloading. This topic can be divided into two distinct aspects. One is the need to gain access to premises in order to collect or deliver consignments. The other is the physical handling of such items on or off the lorry. As far as access was concerned, although most of the vehicles were smaller than their modern day counterparts, many industrial sites predated the motor vehicle and were of a size and density totally unsuited to its application. Given that power-assisted steering was rare before the 1970s and self-steering trailer axles were not prevalent until the 1980s, the efforts required from the driver were greater.

The size of businesses varied greatly and the premises reflected this. Sometimes they could be so small that lorries were unable to enter, and loading or unloading took place in the street. Very often there was insufficient room for a lorry to turn round inside the premises and it was necessary to reverse in. At the time under discussion the mirrors in use were more perfunctory than now. Furthermore, when reversing from outside on a sunny day the loss of vision when entering a poorly-lit bay was quite alarming.

When delivering to large premises the complexities encountered could present problems. Firms had their own procedures and protocols, which were familiar to their own employees and regular visitors, but were an obstacle course for drivers delivering there for the first time. With some firms it was necessary to report to a central point on arrival and then be sent on to a specific part of the site. Others were content to have a load directed straight to the relevant location. When a driver arrived at a large industrial site the time taken up between arrival and finding the actual point of loading or unloading could be considerable. This problem was exacerbated when a lengthy wait at one point resulted in rejection because the delivery notes had not been presented at some other point beforehand. The procedures connected with the documentation could be as time-consuming, and sometimes more so, than the physical process of loading or unloading. This was the case particularly, but not exclusively, with docks traffic.

Some firms weighed lorries on arrival and departure. Modern premises installed weighbridges which were large enough to accommodate today's lorries, older premises tended to have inadequate facilities. Such shortcomings brought about the need to disconnect from the trailer in the case of articulated vehicles or drawbar combinations, and worse still, the time-consuming and inaccurate practice of double-weighing. This was adopted where the lorry, rigid or articulated, was too long to fit on the weighbridge, and was weighed in two movements. The lorry was driven onto the weighbridge, a chalk mark made on its side at the point immediately above the end of the weighbridge plate, and the vehicle weighed. The lorry was then driven forward until the chalk mark was directly over the front edge of the plate, and a second weighing took place. The sum of the two readings was taken to be the true gross weight of the vehicle. The inadequacies of this method are not difficult to understand, but even the dubious practice of double-weighing was better than the total inability to weigh, which was the case at many premises. These failings meant that drivers and operators were constantly vulnerable to prosecution for overloading, while being denied the facilities for prevention. Having to rely on information stated on consignment notes was all the more questionable in a business environment where carriage was charged according to weight.

Any goods which lorries carried needed to be lifted on and off. Consignments of freight varied from small, light items which a person could handle with ease, to large and heavy loads requiring special lifting equipment. Vehicle loads could be entirely of one product or could be a mixture of different types; the complete load might be for one destination, or might be consigned to a number of locations.

All the above factors had a bearing on the way in which lorry drivers carried out their work. The best time to think about unloading a consignment was when it was loaded. The intended recipient might not have the same lifting facilities as the sender, and the traffic had to be loaded with this in mind. Drivers who delivered to the same places on a regular basis were aware of the specific methods used, and loaded accordingly. When offloading facilities were an unknown quantity, the best thing was to load in such a manner that all eventualities were anticipated. To offer an example, steel bars are always loaded onto battens, never straight onto the platform, to allow chains or forks to have access. If these were loaded by magnet crane it would be easy to do away with battens when loading; but, if the bars could not be lifted off by a magnet the unloading was quite an ordeal. It was the driver who worked on the back of the lorry, and acted as slinger to the crane driver, so it was the driver who had the problem of ensuring accessibility.

The logical sequence of the deliveries also impacted on the loading of mixed traffic. It was perfectly acceptable to load items on top of a consignment of steel plate, providing they were delivered first. If the plate was to be delivered before the other goods it could not have them placed on top. The driver who loaded traffic which he also delivered planned his journey to his own preferred choice, subject to any customer priorities which prevailed. The driver who delivered consignments loaded by someone else was at the mercy of the latter's expertise, both in terms of making everything accessible at the right time and being able to follow a logical route. Where circumstances dictated this way of working, trunk operations with collection and delivery functions at either end being a good example, the best people to carry out the local collection work were those who had experience of long distance deliveries.

General haulage operations, with mixed traffic, presented some interesting challenges to drivers in terms of accommodating everything within the parameters of compatibility.

A factor to be considered was axle weights. It was easy to break the law, albeit unintentionally, by overloading an axle while keeping within the legal gross vehicle weight. This problem was also encountered by distribution operators because of the weight transfer effect of unloading progressively from the rear forwards, which increased the weight applied to the front axle. This phenomenon resulted in a revival of the twin-steer rigid lorry for that type of work.

The proliferation of curtain-sided lorries, rigid and articulated, in the 1990s reduced the need for traditional ropes and sheets. In the 1950s these were the rule, rather than the exception, requiring a level of skill in their proper use which was a source of professional pride to most drivers. To the casual observer a sheet, when not covering a load, is simply rolled up and secured onto the lorry, yet even this has its proper method. A sheet was folded so that when it was placed on top of the next load, near, but just short of the front, as it was unrolled the front of the sheet reached over the headboard, the sides fell over the load to left and right and the back portion of the sheet was unrolled as much, or as little as was needed. In this way loads, full or part, of all shapes and sizes could be protected. The sheet was then pulled tight and secured at the front and rear corners, followed by securing at the sides. It was important to get the sheet as tight as possible to prevent it billowing in transit, especially on long motorway journeys. If two sheets were used because one was not long enough the rear sheet was put on first so that the front sheet overlapped it. This prevented the headwind from getting under, and lifting, the rear sheet. For high loads on long journeys extra protection was obtained in the form of a fly sheet, an additional sheet on top of the standard sheet, covering the top of it from front to back, impervious to the worst weather.

When roping the starting point was dictated by which portion of the load was to be delivered first; the rope was finished off at the point where it would be undone first. Other little tricks of the trade were employed, such as avoiding tying off at a rope hook immediately behind a wheel, to prevent having to handle a sludgy mess after a journey along wet roads. Over time, mechanical handling has become normal with fork-lift trucks (q.v.) or on-board cranes to move loads. Tail-lifts (q.v.) are widely used on vehicles or trailers carrying easily divisible loads which can be wheeled or carried on or off. **MB**

C Clark and R Munting, *Suffolk Enterprise* (Norwich: Centre of East Anglian Studies [2000], p. 94; The day books of the Haverhill Rope Twine & Sack Co. for 1948 to 1972, with drawings of customised lorry covers and tarpaulins, are held by the Haverhill & District Local History Society.

Locomotive was the nineteenth century legal term for any mechanically-propelled road vehicle, but in the twentieth century it came to mean a heavy vehicle designed to haul up to three trailers. **GAB**

Log sheets were introduced by section 19 of the Road & Rail Traffic Act of 1933. To demonstrate that they were driving legally, drivers had to complete and preserve log sheets showing the times of driving periods and breaks. Employers were required to issue such sheets and ensure they were completed and preserved. These rules also applied to drivers' mates when these were legally required, as when a lorry was pulling a trailer. Log sheets were subject to random — if infrequent — roadside checks by the enforcement staff of the licensing authorities.

Gilbert Walker, writing in 1942, thought that the log sheet requirement 'has been reasonably well enforced', but others such as Murphy suggest there was much falsification and failure to record hours worked until afterwards and inaccurately, as the chance of being discovered or stopped en route was small. In addition, drivers who were observing the hours limits nevertheless found completing log sheets a chore, and often did not bother.

Also the limit on hours encouraged drivers to speed in order to pack as many miles as possible into the driving shift. Hollowell argued that in the early 1960s 'offences relating to records' were the most common grounds for prosecutions relating to goods vehicles and most of these referred to log sheets. The process of falsifying the log sheets was known as to 'flog' one's log sheets. Falsification of records was so widespread and persistent that various mechanical devices were introduced to record driver hours, such as the Servis (q.v.) recorder in the 1930s, the Rotherham Recorder and the Tachograph (q.v.) in 1968. Fitment and use of the tachograph later became a legal requirement, virtually replacing log sheets. **JA**

Hollowell (1968), pp. 33–34; Walker (1942), pp. 23 and 94; Murphy (1963), pp. 21–2; *The Roadway* (March 1957), pp. 3 and 31

Logistics is the time-related positioning of resources. The term is derived from military deployment. Expressed simply it describes getting the right item to the right place at the right time and in the right condition.

David Lowe defined it as 'the planning and organising of the supply and movement of materials or goods from their original source through the stages of production, assembly, packing, storage, handling and distribution to the final customer. Distribution is but one element of the whole logistics concept, and transport only a single element of physical distribution.

The fashion for incorporating 'logistics' in the title of transport companies, which came into favour in the later 1990s, is rather misleading, as the Chartered Institute of Logistics and Transport pointed out, because they are components of the process but cannot themselves plan and organise the total process. It also includes reverse logistics, which refers to the taking back of used packaging and the return and recycling of items that are unsold or faulty. See also JUST-IN-TIME **JMA**

David Lowe, *Dictionary of Transport and Logistics* (2002)

London & Southern Counties Transport, see
SPANS THE SOUTH

The **London Brick Company** (Figures 79, 127 and 128) (LBC) eventually emerged in the 1930s as the predominant producer of Fletton bricks after a complex evolution, which began with the sale of the Fletton Lodge Estate near Peterborough in 1877 'with good brick earth on the estate'. 'London' in the company title referred to the principal market anticipated, not to the Fletton brickmaking sites, which lay on the Oxford Clay belt from Peterborough/ Fletton southwards through Cambridgeshire to Bedfordshire and Buckinghamshire. Until the mid-1930s distribution of bricks was by rail, involving multiple handling from kiln to building site and likely damage in transit, for example by shunting. Although road distribution came to predominate, 446 million bricks were moved by rail from the Peterborough area in 1964 and ten years later 10 per cent of LBC production was rail-distributed: the Fletliner system (whole trains of bricks carried by Freightliner) was introduced in mid-1973.

It was not until 1936 that the LBC transport department began operation, initially without covered accommodation and with a fleet of sixteen cars, eight lorries and a bus. By 1939 the LBC fleet comprised 58 Leyland Cub and Lynx lorries, 238 AEC, 38 Morris-Commercial Equiload and Leader, 4 Bedford and 2 Thornycroft lorries. There were five fleet depots, at Peterborough, Bletchley, Arlesey, Stewartby and Calvert, the principal one being Peterborough/Fletton. Duramin (q.v.) alloy cabs and bodies were fitted to the Cubs and AECs to reduce weight, enabling the Cubs to travel at 30 miles per hour. The predominance of AEC persisted, two thirds of the fleet comprising this marque up to the 1960s.

The Second World War brought accelerated demand followed by a decline, with the stockpiling of millions of bricks. When the stockpiled bricks were sold to meet the high post-war rebuilding demand, they were heavier to transport, having absorbed water; 57 LBC vehicles were requisitioned for war service, including some which were used for food distribution in their normal operating area; some second-hand vehicles were acquired as replacements, of which a number were in turn requisitioned.

Despite the acute post-war vehicle shortage, LBC quickly managed to obtain 34 Equiloads and 35 AEC Monarchs and Matadors. The latter were of the post-war haulage type and operated with 28 Tasker drawbar trailers. There were also big purchases of AEC Mammoth Major 8-wheelers and in 1950 a large number of Albion FT37 Chieftain platform and tipper lorries. The tippers delivered bricks to the East Midlands and returned with coal. Common as opposed to facing bricks could be tipped, as a skilful driver caused less damage than from handballing (q.v.). LBC, operating on C licences, was able to obtain return loads of coal for use in its own kilns from nearby pits. Longer distance delivery journeys were generally in the hands of private hauliers.

From 1953 AEC Mercury 4-wheel platform lorries, initially still with Duramin cabs and bodies, later with glass fibre cabs by Road Transport Services (Hackney), entered the LBC fleet in some numbers. Their greater speed meant that even careful hand-stacking could not guarantee a stable load and hinged drop-sides from Duramin were fitted. When AEC proved unable to meet all the fleet's demands for new vehicles, Albion CH3 Chieftains were purchased. In 1966 the decision was taken to acquire 6-wheelers for the carriage of about 7,000 bricks per load, which led to the purchase of the AEC Marshal.

From 1971 onwards Volvo supplied its F86 6-wheelers; a variety of chassis types and configurations also entered the LBC fleet with the purchase of Marston Valley in 1968 and Redland's Fletton works in 1971. By the early 1970s the LBC's fleet size was nearly 500. By the late 1990s it had returned to approximately that of the late 1930s. LBC was itself purchased by the Hanson Trust in 1984; rationalisation and improvements in the product followed, and in 1995 all the Trust's brickworks, including the Butterley Brick Co. acquired in 1968, were amalgamated under the

Hanson Brick title. Fletton production continued at Peterborough and Stewartby.

As well as its brick delivery fleet, two other LBC vehicle operations should be noted: its works and landfill fleets. The works fleet included seventeen ex-WD 4×4 Chevrolets fitted with new tipper bodies, delivery vans and a large bus fleet after the war to carry the firm's immigrant workers. The last were replaced by contract vehicles from 1971. The post-war acquisition of ex-WD Matadors, later replaced by Scammells, gave LBC its own recovery capability.

Mechanical handling played a significant part in LBC transport operations and in the manufacturing process itself with the introduction of Shelvoke & Drewry Freight-lifter kiln-loaders, developed on the lines of the American Hyster. In the 1960s the brick industry was among the first to use pallets (q.v.) and fork-lift trucks (q.v.) to cut labour costs in handling and later it used shrink wrapping making it a pioneer in mechanical handling. A search for increased transport efficiency after 1968 led, via crane experiments, to the Selfstak gantry system, developed from a Canadian original and manufactured by Primrose Engineering Co. It consisted of a light-weight gantry travelling along body side-channels, with a power-driven hoist and grab. In the 1980s cranes were fitted to some new vehicles and in the 1990s all new lorries had hydraulic cranes.

In the 1970s a different type of vehicle operation was created by LBC's land reclamation activities. London Brick Land Development Ltd was set up in 1970 to make the best use of LBCs existing derelict land, for example by a joint Central Electricity Generating Board-British Rail operation to bring in pulverised fuel ash from power stations. The following year LBC acquired the waste disposal firm, Easidispose of Bletchley, and in 1977 it set up London Brick Landfill Ltd, catering for household and industrial dry waste. Under a 1977 agreement with the GLC, waste from Barnet, Brent and Camden was processed at Hendon for rail containerisation to Stewartby. AEC Militant 6-wheel tractors were originally used with Tasker trailers. These were replaced by Nord-Verk 6-wheel transporters, carrying waste containers from the railhead to the tipping face. The landfill operation was sold off by Hanson after its acquisition of London Brick.

In its heyday the fleet in its red and black livery served as a positive publicity agent, even if the headboard legend Phorpres Bricks (denoting bricks made by a four-pressing system) mystified the uninitiated. **RAS**

Aldridge (1998); R Hillier, *Clay that Burns: a history of the Fletton brick industry* (1981); *OCBRH*

London Lorries Ltd was a firm of coach-builders of Kentish Town, London, which achieved some reputation for its passenger bodywork in the 1920s, and was mainly a builder of coach bodies. A small group of surviving records shows that, at least in its final years, it was concerned with goods bodywork as well. A 'Rough Book' containing quotations for jobs between October 1930 and January 1933 includes pricing for 5-ton Luton bodies for Trutime, for the production and fitting of lifeguards to 13 steam lorries, one Leyland and 30 Ford lorries and 21 Ford trailer units for J H Beattie & Co., coal merchants, and for bodies for Morris Cowley Post Office vans. A book recording sales contacts, 1931–2, shows approaches by letter or circular to Luton Industrial Co-operative Society Ltd, Chance Caterers of Acton Vale, the West Middlesex and Curzon laundries of Acton and to W H Nevill Ltd, wholesale butchers of King's Cross, who had just renewed its fleet, the order going to Robsons. A call was made on Commer Cars of Luton, but they did their own commercial bodies, although there might have been scope for reciprocal recommendations for passenger bodies. London Lorries succumbed to the depression of the early 1930s and were acquired by Duple (q.v.) in 1932, whose production capacity at Hendon absorbed any outstanding orders. **RAS**

V&A Archive of Art & Design (AAD/1997/17); A. Townsin, *Duple. 70 Years of Coachbuilding* (Glossop, 1998)

The **London lorry ban** was enacted by the Greater London Council shortly before it was abolished in 1986. It was initially administered by the London Residuary Body, which was set up to handle 'left-over' functions of the GLC. From 1987 the ban was run by the London Boroughs Transport Committee, which formed a Lorry Control Unit. Responsibility later passed to Transport for London in the London local government changes that created a London Assembly.

The ban covered lorries over 16.5 tonnes on all roads within Greater London except trunk roads, banning them from 9 pm to 7 am Mondays to Fridays, after 1 pm on Saturdays and all day Sundays. Condition 5 of the ban also required vehicles with legitimate and essential business to minimise use of restricted roads, a definition that included parts of the A2, A4, A5, A13 and A 20. The ban on the A13 made it a virtual cul-de-sac, despite all these roads being part of London's official strategic road network. This A13 ban barred use of the road to reach the southern end of the A1, a four-mile journey and required a long deviation round the North Circular road (the A405). The aim of the ban was said to be to remove large and noisy lorries from roads with substantial housing along them.

To use any other road an operator needed to apply to the Lorry Control Unit, and fill in a 10-page application form. It required information on each vehicle an operator might wish to use, including its engine make and model code, design features and even the likely date of replacement of the vehicle. Non-compliance could result in fines of up to £1000: fines of £400 plus costs on operators and £200 plus cost on drivers had become common by the early 1990s. If granted permission an operator had to fit an exempt plate on each vehicle and also display a permit in the form of a disc in the cab window.

The proposals for the ban brought over 3600 individual formal objections but no public inquiry into the proposal was set up, and subsequent legal challenges were unsuccessful. Applications to use otherwise-banned roads could be for individual journeys, or for regular journeys for which a permit might be granted for one year. Criteria for rejection (not infrequent) or approval were never clearly defined and an expensive legal appeal by Parcelforce failed.

Not every London Borough was a member of the scheme and by 1993 membership had dropped to 20 (out of 33 London boroughs), partly on account of the cost: each borough paid £40,000 a year.

A condition that caused considerable controversy was the insistence on fitment of air brake silencers to vehicles. Operators and trade associations had misgivings over a successful attempt in one area to impose new design criteria on vehicles that were not considered nationally to be of benefit: if such actions were allowed to proliferate operators might end up having to face conflicting conditions in different areas served by the same vehicles.

Another grouse by operators came from the continuation for some time of the ban on four-wheel vehicles over 16.5 tonnes when the weight limit nationally had risen to 17 tonnes: the limit subsequently rose to 18 tonnes, a figure that was later accepted by the LBTC.

All roads affected by the ban have to be suitably signed. Quite separate from the London Lorry Ban is a restriction on vehicles exceeding 12.2 m in length from central London at all times unless carrying out collection or delivery at specific addresses within central London. **GM/JMA**

Trucking International (September 1998), p. 73

Long, Major-General Sidney Selden CB (1863–1940) was a pioneer of military logistics, his service career culminating as Director of Supplies and Transport at the War Office between 1914 and 1916. Long resigned as a result of political differences over vehicle procurement. He joined Lever Brothers in late 1916 and began a second, pioneering, career in civil transport, serving as a director of Lever Brothers and chairman of SPD Ltd (Speedy Prompt Delivery) (q.v.) until the end of 1931. Between the wars Long played an important role in national transport bodies, serving as president of the Commercial Motor Users' Association (q.v.) and chairman of the

Transport Committee of the Federation of British Industries.   **RAS**

Reader (1969); J Fortescue and R H Beadon, *The Royal Army Service Corps, a history of transport and supply in the British Army* (2 vols, 1930-1)

The **Long Distance Road Haulage Committee** was established in 1930 to provide evidence to the Royal Commission on Transport chaired by Sir Arthur Griffith-Boscawen (q.v.) which sat from 1928 to 1930. The LDRHC was chaired by Sir Maxwell Hicks who was a director of McNamara (1921) Ltd. (q.v.) The Committee represented a small number, some 25 or 30 of large firms who carried out long distance haulage and as such was quite unrepresentative of the industry as a whole. Despite this, Sir Maxwell's views carried much weight with the Royal Commission. Hicks gave evidence casting doubt on the value of small firms and owner-operators (q.v.), claiming they cut corners on safety and working conditions. He called for the Traffic Commissioners, who had been established to licence bus traffic, to cover goods haulage as well. He was in favour of the licensing of hauliers and clearing houses (q.v.). In 1931 the name was changed to the Long Distance Road Haulage Association to recruit and represent professional hauliers. About 150 companies joined, representing about 1500 vehicles, still a small minority of the total industry. E C Marston was elected chairman. He was from the Liverpool firm specialising in abnormal loads. In April 1932 the LDRHA decided to amalgamate with the Short Distance Road Hauliers Alliance (q.v.) to form the Road Haulage Association (q.v.).   **JA**

P E Hart, 'The restriction of road haulage', *Scottish Journal of Political Economy*, 6 (1959), pp. 119–128; Seth-Smith (1975), p. 115; Dunbar (1981), pp. 78–9; Gibson (2001), pp. 213–16

Lorry (also larry, lorrie, lory, lurrie, lurry, rolley, rolly, rulley, rully, trolley or trolly) were all words that came into use during the nineteenth century for a 4-wheeled horse-drawn goods vehicle, smaller than a dray (q.v.), but similar in that it usually had a flat body. It might have a headboard (q.v.), removable or drop-down sides and ends, or removable vertical stanchions and connecting chains. It might also be fitted with a tilt (q.v.) or more-permanent canvas cover. A lorry was commonly fitted with a pair of shafts for haulage by a single horse, but for heavier loads they could be replaced by a draught pole for a pair of horses, one on each side.

The terms lurrie and lurry seem to have been particularly associated with west Yorkshire, Lancashire and the North West; rolley, rolly, rulley, and rully with east Yorkshire and the North East; trolley and trolly with London. Railway company usage followed a similar regional pattern: 'lurry' on the Lancashire & Yorkshire and London & North Western Railways, 'rulley' on the North Eastern Railway, and 'trolley' on the GWR and LMSR.

At the turn of the century the word lorry was applied to steam vehicles and then petrol-driven vehicles with the equivalent style of body, although for several decades the term 'motor lorry' was used to distinguish it from a 'horse lorry'. Already the words lorry/lurry and wagon/waggon were being used interchangeably for all large mechanised goods vehicles. Lorry became predominant, at least with the general public, until overtaken by truck (q.v.) in the 1970s.   **GAB**

OED; Thompson (1980); Smith (1994); *Oxford Dictionary of English Etymology* (1966), p. 357; Smith (1988)

Lorry-bus, see CONVERTIBLE BODIES

The **Lorry Driver of the Year competition** originated in Coventry in 1951 when the Coventry Road Safety Officer, Mervyn Miles, presented safe driving awards at the Standard Motor Co. One recipient of this award was Jack Patience, a Transport and General Workers Union shop steward and a member of the Coventry Road Accident Prevention Council and the Coventry Courtesy Club. Patience and Miles, in conjunction with the chairman of the Accident Prevention Council, Bob Brain, agreed to hold a competition for lorry drivers and one was held in 1952 for lorry drivers from the Coventry area. In 1953 there were so many entries that the event had to be held over two days. In 1954 Portsmouth joined with Coventry and the official title 'Lorry driver of the year' was initiated as suggested by Raymond Baxter of the BBC. The event grew in numbers of entrants and geographical spread. In 1957 there was even an Anglo-French contest at Versailles. In 1965 Coventry road safety office passed the organisation over to *The Commercial Motor* and the finals moved to HM naval base at Bramcote in Warwickshire. In previous years it had been held at Fort Dunlop and Coventry airport. In 1974 a Lorry Driver of the Year Association was established.

The qualification for entrants was that they were professional drivers who had not had an accident which was their fault or a licence endorsement in the last twelve months. There were eight classes by type of vehicle, four rigid and four articulated. By the early 1970s there were forty centres throughout the kingdom. The contest comprised a written paper on the *Highway Code* and very awkward manoeuvring tests. The first woman champion occurred in 1973 in class A..

The aim of the competition has always been to promote road safety and encourage drivers to take a pride in their driving. It also acts as a showcase demonstrating the care and concern of the industry to be good citizens and so counteracts any bad publicity implicit in the term 'juggernauts' (q.v.).

The competition began to lose support in the 1980s, partly because the introduction of Heavy Goods Vehicle licensing required practical demonstrations of the driver's ability to manoeuvre similar to the exercises of the competition, partly because the accident rates of commercial vehicles were falling. **JA**

Seth-Smith (1975), pp. 151–4; *Official programme* (1974)

The **lorry-mounted crane** (Figures 33 and 128) can give increased flexibility to a vehicle's operations, freeing it from dependence on fixed or mobile cranes (q.v.). This came at a cost in terms of installation costs, extra weight, and a little less load space. It also speeded up loading and unloading and reduced the increasingly-expensive labour costs. One of the best known types from the 1960s onwards was the Hiab, for which George Cohen 600 Group were the UK agents. Hydrauliska Industri AB was founded in Sweden in 1944 by Eric Sundin and Einar Frisk to exploit the power available from a truck engine via hydraulics to lift loads. Two years later they had the HIAB 19 prototype, and in 1947 began series production of the HIAB 190. By 2000 over 400,000 of these had been sold. The main other maker is Atlas Terex. Earlier commercial models were launched by Lorry Loaders of Ealing in the early 1950s, and even earlier in 1933 an Albion 6-ton lorry was fitted with a self loading crane, but this was probably a one-off and had hydraulic-mechanical operation.

Lorry-mounted cranes had wide acceptance in the building industry. Builder's merchants regularly delivered intermediate bulk containers of sand or ballast, pallets of bricks or blocks and packs of timber to building sites without the use of site labour. In the same way articulated vehicles can deliver full loads of bricks or blocks to building sites entirely unaided whereas before the early 1970s this would have involved the driver throwing the bricks off seven at a time to be stacked by the site's labourers. With a crane it was often possible to deliver palletised bricks and blocks to the second lift of scaffolding. It was also used considerably by machinery removal and plant hire firms. **RAS**

The Engineer (20 November 1953), p. 674; Nick Baldwin, *Heavy Goods Vehicles 1919–39* (Andover: Almark, 1976), pp. 62–3

Lothian bus chassis were assembled by the Scottish Motor Traction Co. Ltd, Edinburgh, between 1913 and 1924, mainly for their own use. However, a few were supplied as 3-ton lorries to other firms, including William Anderson of Newton Mearns, coal merchant, haulage contractor and garage proprietor. After the war, SMT assembled some American Bethlehem and Reo trucks. **RAS**

Grieves (1997); M Worthington-Williams, *The Scottish Motor Industry* (Princes Risborough: Shire, 1989)

Low-height vehicles were typically associated with municipal operations, especially for refuse collection, but could also attract commercial operators such as dairies, breweries, food producers and others. In the 1920s the average commercial vehicle had large solid tyres and stood high off the ground, which made loading and unloading difficult, even though drivers were then expected to lift and carry weights that would now be illegal. This led to the development of the unique Freighter by a new company in 1922, Shelvoke & Drewry and soon to a host of imitators. Most came from established makers which merely fitted small wheels to existing designs. Particularly half-hearted efforts came from makers such as Dennis and Halley, whose so-called low-loading vehicles were of standard design with normal front wheels, but small rear wheels.

S&D's purpose-designed Freighter was copied by Easyloader, Electricar, Karrier, Low-Deck, Pagefield and W&G, plus Dearne and Allan Taylor, the last two basing their models on the ubiquitous Ford model T. More successful were Guy and Vulcan, but the Karrier Bantam and the S&D Freighter continued to be improved and remained in production for many years: construction of Freighters lasted from 1923 to 1947.

The similar, but short-lived, Easyloader like the Freighter, but unlike many of the others, had front wheels behind cab and engine, its small wheels giving a 2 ft platform-height and ground clearance of 7 in. It was made in north London between 1928 and 1933, and had a claimed road speed of 30 mph with fuel consumption of 15 mpg. Customers included I Beer & Sons Ltd, wholesale provision merchants, who operated eight by 1930.

Many years later there was renewed interest in vehicles with low-loading bodies, mainly for the brewery and soft drinks trades. By the 1980s tyre makers had developed low profile tyres suitable for fitment to most rigid vehicles, while a more expensive approach to the same requirements was the replacement of the standard chassis of a vehicle from behind the cab by a completely new structure. This often took the form of two longitudinal members running at low height as far as the back wheels, where they stepped up to clear the axle before lowering again. Such a modification was the more popular, with AWD, Ford and Mercedes-Benz chassis being among those modified, while bodybuilder Don-Bur (q.v.) had a production line carrying out the work for some time. The dimensions of a double-drop frame usually provided for three rows of pallets to be carried on the main drop section, one row over the axle, and a further row behind it. A different approach was offered by Leyland-DAF, with a vehicle with a single central spine behind the cab, sufficiently strong to support the whole body. The spur for these developments came from the brewery trade in particular, which wanted to reduce the number of crew members carried on its delivery vehicles. Making unloading easier was seen as the key to this. Another approach to the problem was the Bruce, a vehicle developed by Alan Bruce of Scottish & Newcastle Breweries, in which the engine and gearbox were turned round, giving front wheel drive so that no prop-shaft intruded in the load-carrying part of the body. Some users built up considerable fleets of low-height vehicles: for example, Whitbread bought its first drop-frame in 1982, and by 1990 had some 220, mainly Ford Cargos suitably modified. By that time it was paying a premium of about ten per cent over standard vehicle prices, and was about to replace its oldest drop-frame rigids with new.

Enthusiasm for such vehicles faded away in the 1990s, perhaps partly because of the cost but also because the whole delivery operation was contracted out. In addition, a lower deck-height was also obtainable by using an articulated outfit with low-profile tyres and a low-height fifth wheel, and such a combination also had a taxation advantage. A special display of brewery vehicles held in 1985 by Leyland-DAF showed a wide diversity of thought, with a twin-steer 3-axle rigid with smaller wheels being yet another approach.   **RAS/JMA**

Baldwin and Negus (1980); *OM*, 2, 6 (June 1980), pp. 34–7; *CM* (1 April 1930), advertising supplement, p. 103; Klapper (1973), p. 159

The **Luton body** (Figure 129) is so called because it was originally developed for the

Luton straw hat trade, which was characterised by an exceptionally high volume-to-weight ratio. In pre-motor days the Midland Railway developed a special high-volume lightweight van body to fit its standard flat dray for collection of the hats and delivery of the returned empty hat boxes. The Luton body for a rigid motor vehicle, developed in the 1920s, is taller than the normal van and features the Luton head extension, which increases the available load-space by extending the bodywork forward over the cab roof. In the later 1920s it began to appear in its more familiar guise as a removal pantechnicon (q.v.) and also for carrying other large-volume, low-weight products such as furniture and mattresses. In the 1930s and for some years after the war it was also widely used for parcels trunking work.

After the war a Luton head extension was often specified with custom-built bodywork on vans. The Jensen was probably the ultimate in lightweight Luton van building. As much as possible of it was aluminium. On larger rigids the advent of the tilt cab made provision of a Luton extension difficult, but this was solved by a hinged floor in the Luton section which could be lifted when the cab was tilted – provided the vehicle was empty.   **JMA/GAB**

Lynx Express (Figure 34) is a descendant of BRS Parcels Ltd and National Carriers Ltd (Parcels Division), which were merged in 1986 under the latter's name. During its first year, the merged company traded as National Carriers-Roadline, delivering only to commercial and industrial addresses. It was re-launched in 1987 under the brand name Lynx Express Delivery Network, with a new livery for its vehicles and depots. In 1992 it acquired the former Federal Express hub at Nuneaton, but the ensuing operational reorganisation did not go smoothly, causing a loss of £10.1 million in the following year. In 1995 the company was again profitable and was formally renamed Lynx Express Delivery Network Ltd in preparation for its sale. It was sold to its management in 1997 for £35 million.

In 1999 Lynx Express took over Red Star Parcels Ltd, the former British Rail fast registered parcels service, which had been the subject of a management buy-out in 1995 (see RAILWAY-OWNED ROAD TRANSPORT). However, the Red Star concept proved to be incompatible with the disaggregated, privatised railway and it was closed in 2001. The combined companies had a turnover of £170 million, ran about 2000 commercial vehicles, and had nearly 200 depots.   **RAS**

Freight (July 1997); Karen Miles, 'Unions want talks on Lynx changes', *CM* (7 January 1999); J Hobbs, 'Lynx with the past', *VCV*, 126 (June 2000), pp. 16–19

Lyons, J, & Co. Ltd (Figure 130), caterers and food manufacturers, were registered in 1894, having been set up as outside caterers as an offshoot of the tobacco business of the Gluckstein and Salmon families, who remained in control, with a family trust, into the late 1960s, when the introduction of outsiders to the board preceded a change of ownership and direction. A large site in Hammersmith, formerly a piano factory, was acquired in 1894 and the head office, Cadby Hall, and manufacturing departments were established there. In the same year Lyons' first tea shop opened, in Piccadilly, to be followed by the first of four Corner Houses, at Coventry Street, in 1909. By the inter-war period the company had nearly 200 tea shops, mostly in London, with some on the south coast and in major cities. To source these outlets and the retail trade generally, as well as major outside functions, Lyons built up a substantial transport fleet, as well as employing outside contractors, under strict control as to standards. In 1903 the delivery of tea, c.o.d., by Carter Paterson (q.v.) to retail outlets began; this became so successful that Lyons soon took over the distribution with its own fleet, initially with horse-drawn carts, boldly lettered 'Lyons Tea'. The lettering and livery of Lyons' fleet were distinctive throughout most of its existence: dark blue and light grey panels, with gold leaf, white-edged lettering. Local deliveries continued to use horse traction into the inter-war period, but by the mid-1920s the fleet was slightly balanced towards motors: over 800, including 300 1-ton vans and almost 100 4- and

6-ton petrol and steam wagons and trailers; there were 800 horse-drawn vehicles in the fleet at this time. A presentation booklet of 1926 indicates that Lyons were keen users of mechanical handling devices, Fordson (industrial) tractors and S&D Freighters. Much of this equipment was used at their second, much larger site at Greenford, Middlesex, about ten miles west of Cadby Hall, acquired in 1920. It offered road (with Western Avenue and Great West Road improvements in prospect), rail (GWR) and canal (Grand Junction) access (Lyons owned sixteen barges). Tea- and coffee-packing plant and grocery products factories were built there as Lyons became a mass-producer of certain food lines, in particular tea, coffee, ice cream, packaged cakes and bread. A standard unit wooden 'service tray', moved in the factory on a racked trolley, was developed to handle goods for local delivery, typically by a 2-horse van or 30-cwt. motor, although some early morning deliveries were made by 4-ton electric or petrol vehicles. These 'tray body' vehicles included side-loaders on Dennis single-deck bus chassis. Ice cream was at first carried by 1-ton Ford vans in 1-gallon cans buried up to their necks in crushed ice, then American 'Bath' (bulk) bodies were used, before Lyons developed vehicles with their own refrigeration unit, with dynamos powered from the engine. For bulk loads wooden containers ('skips') were gradually replaced after 1921 with aluminium containers by Duramin (q.v.) with significant benefits in container weight-to-contents ratio and life-span. In 1919 Walter H. Gaunt, a former distribution superintendent for the Board of Trade, was appointed as Lyons' distribution manager and his career reflects Lyons' significance as a major transport operator. He served during the General Strike (q.v.) as a member of London Division Haulage Committee, in charge of local food distribution. In 1932 he was appointed by the Standing Joint Committee of Mechanical Road Transport Associations (q.v.) to serve on the Salter Committee and in 1939 he was appointed transport adviser to the Ministry of Food. From 1942 to 1951 he held the position of transport director at Lyons. Over the years

Lyons operated a variety of marques; pre-1914 these included Buick, Ford, Renault and some battery-electric small vans. Lyons were large Albion users; at different periods their fleet also included Commer, Karrier, Guy, Leyland and Maudslay vehicles and such vehicles as Trojan vans, S&D low-height lorries for promotional mobile shops and insulated box traffic from the Cadby Hall ice cream factory to Addison Road (Kensington) station, as well as several types of Pagefield lorries in the 1930s, with flat or box bodies. Scammells featured in the fleet for many years, and in 1929 Lyons pioneered the use of the American Trailmobile automatic coupling system in the UK. By this time Lyons' use of the steam wagons was coming to an end; it began in 1915 with four Aveling & Porter wagons and three A & P steam tractors. After the First World War, however, the decision was taken to standardise on Sentinel steam vehicles, the fleet eventually taking in 29 standard Sentinels, three Super Sentinels and one DG6 in 1928, the last steam road vehicle bought by Lyons. In 1921 Lyons founded Normand Garage Ltd, as an in-house bodybuilder and maintenance works, one intention being to facilitate greater discounts on new vehicles than were then available to fleet operators. In 1923 it was decided to expand Normand's operations by becoming a commercial motor retailer, although it continued to rely heavily on Lyons' work, until it became wholly committed to the retail market in 1960, ceasing to manufacture new bodies in 1963. In 1925 Normand moved to a large factory at Park Royal. The wartime production of Normand Ltd (as it had become in 1941) included special vehicle bodies, tank transporters, a variety of equipment for the armed services and small trailers for emergency 'blitz feeding'. In 1974 Normand obtained a franchise for Mercedes-Benz lorries. After Normand ceased to be Lyons' bodybuilder, other firms received orders, such as Sparshatts (q.v.), which built refrigerated vehicles for Lyons and in 1970 received an order for 50 bakery delivery vans on BMC FG360 chassis.

In the post-war period the inadequacies of Lyons' management system and structure, with the persistence of strong family involvement, combined with new trends in food production and marketing and changes in consumer tastes to bring about the eventual demise of the company as it had operated in its inter-war heyday: in 1978 Lyons lost its independence to Allied Breweries. Many of the attempts made by Lyons to arrest this decline were themselves the occasion of further problems; even their famous LEO (Lyons Electronic Office) computer system, developed in-house and sold to other concerns, could be seen as a costly diversion from their core business. Between 1958 and 1962 Lyons' manufacturing departments became divisions and the Transport Department was disbanded, with transport responsibilities passing to the individual divisions.

External transport developments, notably the closure of railway stations and branch lines even before the Beeching report of 1963, forced new responses by Lyons. For the distribution of ice cream a road network based on a series of cold depots (36 by 1955) was established; further changes occurred after Lyons acquired the Neilson and Eldorado ice cream brands in 1962. Alpine Refrigerated Deliveries Ltd was set up to handle ice cream and frozen food products and Glacier Foods Ltd, a holding company set up to take over Lyons' ice cream division, was able to halve its van fleet as part of the rationalisation process. For bread a series of regional and provincial depots was established to compensate for the former reliance on rail; these were supplied mainly from Cadby Hall. Lyons kept its lead in the packaged cake market and decided in the early 1970s to modernise manufacturing capacity by setting up a new cake bakery. The site chosen, at Carlton near Barnsley, was distant from the main market in southern England, adding to transport costs.

With the passing of Lyons as a separate entity a major operator left the transport scene. At various times its road fleet included eleven bread handcarts, 1000 horses, more than thirty steam vehicles and 2750 motor vehicles (1957). Lyons' fleet was noteworthy not only for its size, but also its variety and the development of specialised vehicles to meet its particular needs, assisted by an in-house bodyworks. The integrated use of road, canal and rail transport, assisted by mechanical handling and controlled by the company's Transport Department provided an object lesson to other companies when Lyons was at the peak of its success.

RAS

London Metropolitan Archive: Acc/3572; *DBB*, 2 (1984) M Gluckstein; 3 (1985) Sir Joseph Lyons; 5 (1986) H Salmon; P Bird, *The First Food Empire: a history of J Lyons & Co.* (Chichester: Phillimore, 2000)

M

MacBrayne, David, Ltd (Figure 35). In 1879 David Hutcheson & Co., a company founded in 1851 to take over the shipping services of the Western Highlands and Islands of Scotland, adopted the name of David MacBrayne, the last of the original three partners still in the business. It became David MacBrayne Ltd in 1905. Its ships carried passengers, livestock, parcels and 'light goods', including groceries and the other needs of the Highland and Island communities and the output of their distilleries. From 1880 it held the contract for carrying mail, but in 1928 it precipitated a crisis by not tendering for its renewal; after government involvement, a new company was formed, David MacBrayne (1928) Ltd, owned jointly by the LMSR and Coast Lines Ltd. It again became simply David MacBrayne Ltd in 1934.

MacBrayne began operating bus and charabanc feeder services in 1906, some also carrying mail and parcels. These expanded, particularly after 1928, partly to replace uneconomic Highland steamer services, which also required the provision of lorries for carrying the luggage and goods. At this period MacBrayne found itself facing competition from new motor bus and carrier services, to which it responded by setting up competing road services or by buying out the competitors, becoming the dominant operator of bus and road haulage, as well as shipping, services in the region. Nevertheless, by 1940 the proportion of its freight revenues from road operations had risen only to 11 per cent. Its first lorries, purchased in 1928, were Albions, but other pre-war purchases included Bedford, Foden and Morris vehicles; AECs were added during the war.

In 1929 MacBrayne established Glasgow–Inverary–Ardrishaig passenger and goods road services to meet the competition from similar services that had been operated by Link Lines Ltd since 1927. In 1931 it transferred the goods service with its two lorries to Clyde Cargo Steamers Ltd, in which it had a financial stake and which was in a better position to compete with Link Lines. When in 1932 Link Lines offered itself for sale, MacBrayne took its buses and CCS its eight lorries. By 1939 CCS was wholly-owned by MacBrayne and had been renamed the Clyde & Campbeltown Shipping Co. Ltd; partly as a result of the delays to shipping caused by the Clyde defences during the early months of the war, much of its shipping traffic was diverted to the road service, and extended to Campbeltown.

In 1939 MacBrayne bought two Fort William firms: A & J Macpherson which operated two lorries alongside its tourist bus fleet; and the haulier R H Drummond, with four lorries, which operated a daily Glasgow–Fort William goods motor service from 1932. At the request of the Road Traffic Commissioner, this service was suspended from May 1943 to September 1946 to conserve petrol and tyres and its traffic diverted to steamer.

At nationalisation in 1949 the CCS road haulage business became part of BRS 66B Argyll Group. Its mixed fleet of 24 lorries comprised AEC, Bedford, Maudslay (reflecting Coast Lines' influence) and Thornycroft; some were convertible to cattle floats. One of the Maudslays was the last of the rare Mikado eight-wheelers to be built.

The LMSR's 50 per cent interest in MacBrayne was transferred to the British Transport Commission in 1948 and to the Transport Holding Company in 1963, but MacBrayne continued to retain its operational independence. Its road haulage services, which in 1951 employed 23 lorries, were beyond BRS's sphere of interest and continued to expand and make acquisitions. Motor vehicle ferries before the war had allowed lorries to start penetrating to places such as the Isle of Skye. In 1949 and 1950 two second-hand Scammell mechanical horses were acquired. These were replaced in 1962 by new Scarab models to shunt the articulated trailers as MacBrayne began to operate roll-on roll-off vessels on their shipping routes, allowing an increasing proportion of goods to be carried throughout by lorry. MacBrayne's road fleet now included containers and articulated units. In 1969 the nationalised interest was vested in the Scottish Transport Group, which also acquired the Coast Lines' share. MacBrayne's bus services were integrated into other STG companies in 1970–2, the shipping services were absorbed into Caledonian MacBrayne Ltd, the road freight operations became MacBrayne Haulage Ltd.

A 1983 Monopolies & Mergers Commission report found that Caledonian MacBrayne had abused its monopoly by giving undue preference to the haulage company. The government decided that MacBrayne Haulage should be sold by tender. Billy Walker, trading as Kildonan Transport Ltd of Turriff, acquired the company which become Kildonan MacBrayne. In 1994 the firm appeared before the Scottish Licensing Authority, which found that it 'operated on the edge of the law', referring to its cavalier attitude to servicing and maintenance, drivers' hours and the licensing laws. The Licensing Authority halved its authorisation to 45 vehicles and 90 trailers, thereby breaking its dominant position. It was re-formed as Kildonan International Forwarding and again appeared before the Licensing Authority in 1996; its licence was suspended for two weeks, causing it to be placed in liquidation. **GM/GAB**

PRO, files in RAIL 425 series; Monopolies & Mergers Commission, *Caledonian MacBrayne Ltd* (HMSO, 1983, Cmnd 8805)

McCurd commercial vehicles were introduced in 1912 by W A McCurd, a central London car retailer. The first model was a 3½-ton lorry with a worm-driven back axle, probably powered by an engine produced by Tylor Ltd, another London firm. Customers included H Tate & Son, the sugar producers, Yeomans of Canterbury, Mex Petroleum and the City 'motor contractor' Chas A Wells. During the war a new factory was opened in Cricklewood, but it was taken over as an experimental tank workshop. Wartime civilian deliveries included five lorries to Lever Bros. McCurds' post-war history is obscure, with changes of location in greater London. When a new 40-/50-cwt goods chassis was launched in 1925 the firm's advertising referred to its deliberate suspension of manufacture for the previous five years in view of the abundance of ex-service vehicles. In 1928 the firm came to an end, after going into receivership in 1927. **RAS**

N Baldwin, 'London's Forgotten Makers', *VCVM*, 16 (September/October 1988), pp. 46–7. M Worthington-Williams, 'Finds and Discoveries', *Automobile*, 15, 6 (August 1997) pp. 68–9

Mack, M & W, started as a family-run produce dealer in Covent Garden. It still exists as the Mack Organisation, one of the largest fruit and produce distributors in the UK. It moved into haulage initially of fruit and produce from the docks using horse-drawn vehicles, and collection and delivery. The first motor lorry was a Milnes-Daimler acquired in 1910. After 1920 there was considerable expansion of the transport business to include contract hire and bulk liquids. The fleet size and the introduction of licensing led to a separate business, Mack Hauliers, in 1934.

One large part of its business was the new bulk liquids division, as the company saw the need for bulk liquid tankers following the phasing out of the 2-gallon petrol can. This was based at a purpose-built depot at Barking pioneering a tank-cleaning facility with provision for disposal of the residues. By 1934 it was operating some 72 tankers on contracts or spot hire, mostly with petroleum products, bitumen, tar and beer. Vehicles used were Scammell 6- and 8-wheel articulated tankers, some converted from solid tyres, Leyland Hippo rigid 6-wheelers, some on a Cleveland petrol contract, and a few smaller tankers. The large tankers did about 150 miles per day.

Another aspect of the firm's business was general haulage including fruit and produce, beer, wine and spirits, paper and groceries. The firm used AEC, Bedford, Dodge, Guy, Mercedes-Benz and Scammells for this traffic and also mechanical horses (q.v.). The contract hire customers included Elders and Fyffes for banana deliveries. The firm was also cartage agents for shipping and forwarding companies.

In 1950 the firm was nationalised, becoming part of BTC (q.v.). It was still family-run and had depots in London, Salford and Southampton. About 200 vehicles were operated. Mack did not re-enter the industry at denationalisation. **GM**

Ingram and Mustoe (1999), p. 44; *World's Carriers* (16 September 1929)

McLaren, J & H, Ltd of Leeds, steam engineers, produced steam road locomotives (but not wagons) from 1880 to 1936 and gear-driven steam road tractors from 1909 to 1936. Its products were of a high quality and reliability. UK users included Road Engines & Kerr (Haulage) Ltd, Norman E Box Ltd (q.v.) and Allan Knight of Huddersfield, but much of its output was for colonial use. Between 1926 and 1940 it built oil engines to Benz, and then Ricardo, design. Most were used in agricultural tractors, but one powered a unique heavy haulage road tractor built for Pickfords in 1940 and bodied by Roe (q.v.). Of forward-control layout, it had small front wheels with pneumatic tyres and larger solid rubber tyred rear wheels. A 1918 McLaren of Pickfords had earlier been converted to diesel by Fowlers, producing a rather intractable machine. **RAS**

McTaggart (1985, 1986, 1989); G Lumb, *Charles H Roe* (Shepperton: Ian Allan, 1999)

McNamara & Co. Ltd (Figure 131) of Finsbury, London was perhaps the largest operator of goods vehicles for 'hire and reward' still outside railway ownership at the outbreak of the Second World War. Although there was continuity in the trading name, the firm went through three periods of ownership.

The original firm of Arthur McNamara & Co., founded in 1837, was a general carrier and a cartage agent for the Eastern Counties, later the Great Eastern, Railway. In 1852 it became a contractor to the Post Office (q.v.) for carting mails between London post offices and stations. It remained the Post Office's biggest transport contractor and this was its main source of income for nearly a century.

Following the death of Arthur McNamara junior, the company and its assets, which included 462 horses, 111 mail vans, 73 railway vans and 28 other vans, were sold in 1887 to a new company, McNamara & Co. Ltd. Its chairman was [Sir] John Pound, a London

businessman who was already chairman of the London General Omnibus Co. Henry Hicks, father of [Sir] William Joynson-Hicks (q.v.), was a director. Among the assets taken over by the new company was the contract for the first long-distance road service for the Post Office, carrying parcel post in pair-horse vans from London to Brighton and soon afterwards to Tonbridge, Windsor and Oxford.

In 1905 the company had 1300 horses, all stabled on the upper floors of its premises and approached by a ramp from street level, an arrangement which McNamaras claimed to be the first to adopt (see HORSE TRANSPORT). The vans were parked on the roof. They were built in its own workshops, which were subsequently adapted for building bodies for, and maintaining and overhauling, motor vehicles.

The company bought its first two motor vehicles for trial in 1904: 4½ hp German chassis on which it fitted horse mail van bodies, giving 7 cwt capacity. Following experience with motor operation of the existing parcel post services, beginning with the Brighton service in 1905, new longer-distance night services were introduced, using Dennis and Leyland vehicles: to Southampton and Portsmouth in 1908 and Bristol in 1911. In 1907 McNamaras won a contract to supply wholesale druggists and in 1910 it began wholesale delivery of newspapers. In these early years McNamaras also introduced night services for market produce and other goods between Worthing and Brighton and London.

To raise money for expansion and investment in motor vehicles, the company's £120,000 capital was supplemented by the issue of £50,000 of 5 per cent and then £50,000 of 8 per cent debentures. McNamara misjudged the costs of operating motor vehicles and in 1913 it went into receivership, with Maxwell Hicks, an accountant and brother of Joynson-Hicks, acting as receiver and manager. At this date it employed some 700 horses, 140 motor vans and 850 men. Because of the war it was not until 1921 that the company could be reconstructed under the name of McNamara & Co. (1921) Ltd, which reverted to the name McNamara & Co. Ltd in 1938. Hicks (by now

Sir Maxwell) became chairman of the new company and remained so until nationalisation.

During the First World War its long-distance services were discontinued because of the lighting restrictions, but in 1919 McNamaras pioneered regular long-distance services for parcels and smalls, establishing a network linking depots at London, Bristol, Birmingham, Leicester and Liverpool, at each of which it had its own collection and delivery vehicles. In 1937 the trunk services operated thrice weekly. The Birmingham operation was originally Allied Transports Ltd (founded in 1919 as the Liverpool Road Traction Co. Ltd and renamed in 1922), which became a subsidiary of McNamara in 1925.

In the 1930s the range of services operated by McNamara was exceptionally wide, including contracts and daily and short-period hire; the mail contracts; and the scheduled parcel services (but no longer railway cartage). In 1937, when its activities were probably at a peak it had 140 horse vehicles, 660 motor vehicles and 1200 employees, including 750 drivers. At nationalisation it still had 33 horses on Post Office work and 415 motor vehicles, mainly Bedford, Commer, Morris and Karrier vans, with Scammell and Mercedes articulated tractors for parcels trunking and general haulage. Its 98 trailers included 26 built in the McNamara workshops. **GAB**

Dunbar (1981), pp. 52–3; McNamara & Co (1937); *Post Office London Directories,* various dates; Post Office contracts, 1847 & 1853: Post Office Archives, POST 10/174–5; Board of Trade dissolved company files: PRO, BT 31 series; Report of working party to consider future of McNamara & Co., Feb. 1949, PRO, AN 13/669

McVeigh Transport Ltd was set up in Grimsby in 1934 by John James McVeigh, a foreman pile-driver. He began the business with two articulated lorries on timber transport, loading by day and delivering by night. The business had six lorries by the outbreak of war and worked mainly for the Ministry of Defence during the war, being allocated two Maudslays to augment its fleet. The founder of the firm was the eldest of six brothers and several joined him in its management.

When it was nationalised in 1949, J J McVeigh became BRS's group manager at Grimsby, Joseph group traffic superintendent and David district manager at Lincoln, so that BRS in Lincolnshire was said to be McVeigh-owned. In 1953 David joined the Ross Group, trawler owners and fish processors, as traffic manager, preparing the way for a joint offer in 1954 by McVeigh and the Ross Group, for the main part of the BRS Grimsby fleet to be operated as McVeigh Transport Ltd. Activities included warehousing, removals, refrigerated traffic, bulk tanker operation and general goods carriage. Regular overseas runs were developed, including the trailer service from Immingham to Gothenburg, backed by a Swedish bank. A joint Freightliner (q.v.) service with British Rail, in which McVeigh assisted with the design of equipment, was less successful: consignors preferred the security of transport by the same lorry throughout and the cultures of the two undertakings differed greatly. AEC and Leyland predominated in the fleet, with a few Scammells, until dissatisfaction with Leyland led to a change to Atkinson.

Following acquisition of the Ross Group by Imperial Tobacco, its haulage interests were sold and Associated Fisheries bought McVeigh in 1970, merging it with its Humber Warehousing Group subsidiary, which it had bought in 1965 with some 60 vehicles. Two members of the McVeigh family moved to the new firm, Humber McVeigh Transport Co., which brought together refrigerated and general haulage specialisms. Another McVeigh set up Anglo Danish Food Transport at Grimsby, for the distribution of Danish Bacon Board products. Humber McVeigh over-extended to more than 500 vehicles and 22 depots by 1975. A new managing director, J Holt ex-Transport Development Group (q.v.), reduced the fleet to some 50 vehicles with five depots. In the early 1980s Humber McVeigh was merged with Associated Cold Stores Ltd of London. **RAS**

'Brotherly business', *CVC*, 6, 8 (April 2001), pp. 16–19, *CVC*, 6, 9 (May 2001) pp. 12–15; *CM* (1 August 1981); 'Brothers in road transport', *The Road Way* (September 1957), pp. 16–19

Magirus-Deutz was a German bus and lorry manufacturer, formed in 1938 by the coming together of the Magirus and Klöckner-Humboldt-Deutz vehicle, machinery and engine-making concerns. In the mid-1960s the Blundell Group of Kent, vehicle distributors, hauliers and contractors, became M-D concessionaires, but collapsed within two years. M-D then entered into an agreement in 1967 with Seddon to form Seddon-Deutz Ltd, a joint marketing organisation, with the possibility of some local sourcing. The Deutz engine was an air-cooled diesel which Seddon hoped would make them popular for site work. This was soon overtaken by events. In 1971 M-D joined with Volvo, Saviem and DAF in European Truck Design, the 'Club of Four' (q.v.), then in 1975 M-D took a 20 per cent share in Iveco with Fiat owning the rest. In the late 1960s and early 1970s, finally through Magirus-Deutz (GB) Ltd, M-D made some penetration into the UK market, mainly with 6×4 and 8×4 normal-control and forward-control tippers, capable of on-site as well as road work. Wimpey, the contractors, bought more than 100 and in 1978 Toleman, the car transporters, ordered 150. Premises were opened at Winsford in 1972. Assembly took place there, until rendered unnecessary by a lowering of import duties in the mid-1970s. Magirus-Deutz (GB) Ltd and Fiat Trucks UK were merged into Iveco UK Ltd in 1980. **RAS**

Observer's Book of Commercial Vehicles (Frederick Warne, 1971); Nick Georgano, *World Truck Handbook* (1983); F Tisdale, 'Triumph over adversity,' *VRS* (2002)

MAN trucks (Figures 5, 19, 20, 56, 60 and 102) began to enter the British market in 1974, a process given impetus by setting up the MAN Volkswagen import centre at Swindon in 1980, in which Lonrho took an 80 per cent interest in 1984. As part of Lonrho's asset disposal programme, Swindon was sold back to MAN in January 1992, 1336 MAN registrations having been made in the UK in 1991. The 28-dealer network was not affected by the 1992 change. MAN lorries were high quality, with an innovative design and the 5-cylinder diesel

engine. They were much used for trunk services.

The Maschinenfabrik Augsburg Nurnberg began producing commercial vehicles in 1915, moving to a new plant at Munich in 1957. Co-operation with VW from 1976 resulted in a jointly-developed range of light trucks, between VW's heaviest and MAN's lightest models. In 1990 the Steyr Daimler Puch truck division was acquired and Steyr cabs were introduced on MAN's lighter models. In 2000 MAN bought ERF from Western Star.   **RAS**

Millar (1997); MAN advertisement (1986); Lonrho annual report (1985)

The **Manchester lorry** was produced between 1928 and 1932 by Willys Overland Crossley Ltd at Heaton Chapel. WOC was established by Crossley in 1919 to utilise the former National Aircraft Factory which it had established and run at Heaton Chapel during the war. The Overland car of American origin did not sell in sufficient quantities to be profitable. Car-derived vans and the American-designed Willys trucks were also produced. The light (25- and 35-cwt) Manchester lorry which succeeded the Overland range was a semi-independent design, which extended the life of the Heaton Chapel factory for five years, before the building was sold to Fairey Aviation. It was quite popular.   **RAS**

A Robson, 'B Line from Manchester', *VCV*, 100 (April 1998), pp. 42-6; A D George and B Champness, *Commercial Vehicle Day School Proceedings* (Manchester: North West Industrial Archaeology Council, 1998); Eyre (2002)

Mann's Patent Steam Cart & Wagon Co. Ltd, Leeds (1900–28) was the successor to the partnership of J Mann and S Charlesworth, which in 1897 began to produce a 'steam cart' to the patent design of P J Parmiter. This was essentially a small steam tractor with a large transport box over the rear wheels. This load carrier was pivoted and could be tipped, then detached. Although this basic design remained in production until after the First World War, the company also developed a range of undertype and overtype wagons. By 1924, when the advanced, superheated Express model was added to Manns' range, it was too late to reverse falling orders in an increasingly petrol-oriented transport world and in 1926 a receiver was called in. Customers included breweries, tar-sprayer manufacturers and the contractors, Beck & Pollitzer (q.v.), which acquired many of Manns' remaining spares, the rest going to Atkinson-Walker Wagons. **RAS**

'Mann's Patent Steam Cart & Wagon Co. Ltd', *VCVM*, 12 (January/February 1988), pp. 126–7

Mansel Davies & Son Ltd was founded in 1875 in Llanfyrnach, Pembrokeshire, as an agricultural merchant and local distributor of goods from the village's rail sidings. It continued operating on this small scale for the next 85 years, changing only from horse to motor traction. In 1956 D M K (Kaye) Davies, Mansel's grandson, purchased the business from his father and began its expansion from the then total of four vehicles.

In 1963 the Whitland—Cardigan rail branch closed, forcing the company to change direction. Surplus railway land was purchased as the basis of the company's premises and A licences attached to a total of nine businesses were purchased to enable longer-distance work to be carried out. Early areas of activity were milk in churns to the Milk Marketing Board creamery at Whitland (at the time a 'closed shop' to new entrants), and quarried aggregates. Much of this was agricultural lime, retaining the link with the farming community, but delivery of granite was also developed. Kaye Davies's son Stephen joined the business in 1979 and succeeded as managing director in 1994, during which period the company expanded and diversified further. In particular it entered a dealership for Volvo, beginning as a distributor in 1982 and becoming the main dealer for the whole Dyfed peninsula west of Llanelli from 1988. It had previously operated mainly Volvo trucks and switched almost entirely to them.

The principal impetus for growth, however, was the change and deregulation in the dairy industry which began in 1990. The MMB underwent a long-term programme of closing its smaller creameries, many of which were purchased by small specialist producers. Thus the creamery at Felinfach near Lampeter turned to products for which quantities of processed whey were required beyond those available locally, and Mansel Davies became involved in its inward delivery in liquid tankers. Dansco, a subsidiary of McCain, purchased the Newcastle Emlyn creamery for the production of mozzarella cheese; Mansel Davies undertook collection of milk from farms, delivery of finished mozzarella in refrigerated trailers to pizza manufacturers, and transport of whey from Newcastle Emlyn to Felinfach. The closure of the former MMB Whitland creamery in 1994 necessitated movement of the milk being produced in West Wales to manufacturing plants elsewhere in the UK. Delivery of milk and cream to mainland Europe was also developed, with fruit juice and vegetable oils as return loads.

The company also carried increasing quantities of grain and animal feed products between farms and mills. In 1998 a feed mill in Carmarthen was sold by Dalgety to a consortium of three owners. Mansel Davies had previously provided transport for Bibby, one of the three, and this led to five of its vehicles being based at the mill. The business's warehousing activities were limited compared with others, but the storage at Llanfyrnach housed sugar beet pellets used as animal feed, and it continued as an agricultural merchant. Seasonal delivery of local potatoes to the UK retail market also became important.

While 80 per cent of the business continued to be agriculture-related, other activities were developed. The company became one of seven approved contractors for British Steel/Corus Strip Products, specialising in coated steel from South Wales plants. A waste disposal business, Pembrokeshire Environmental, was operated but sold to Shanks McEwan in 1998. In its place Pembrokeshire Freight Ltd was set up as a subsidiary, jointly owned with a partner in Wexford and specialising in unaccompanied trailer movements by ferry between Pembroke and Eire; this generated about 160 loads per week, for which Mansel Davies provided traction involving perhaps 15 tractor units.

At the end of 2000 the group of companies employed 200 and owned 55 rigid vehicles and 85 articulated tractor units, with 200 trailers; these were based at 12 locations, all within the south-west Wales peninsula, but managed from the single office in Llanfyrnach. Its 1996 turnover was £14 million. D M K Davies became chairman of the group in 1994. **DMH**

'Men of Haulage', *CM* (27 June 1996) p. 45; 'Haulier to get MBE for services to community', *Western Mail* (30 December 2000); interview with D M K Davies and Stephen Davies.

The **Mansion House Association** was formed in 1892 by the merger of the Mansion House Committee and the Railway & Canal Traders Association. The Mansion House Committee had been established in 1889 by the Lord Mayor of London (hence the name), Sir James Whitehead. It resulted from widespread unease with railway freight rates and the desire to negotiate lower charges with the railways and act as a pressure group on government. In 1897 the Mansion House Association absorbed the Lancashire & Cheshire Conference on Railway & Canal Rates, which had similar aims. The Mansion House Association then became the main body representing railway users and pressing for lower rates and better services.

In the early twentieth century, the MHA tended to support road haulage, partly as an alternative to, and check upon, railway charges, partly because it was a new industry and very much the underdog compared to the old-established and near-monopolistic railways. Hence the MHA gave evidence to the 1928 parliamentary joint committee set up to consider the railways' request to operate road traffic largely in favour of hauliers and also to the Royal Commission on Transport appointed in the summer of 1928. In 1931 the MHA changed its name slightly, to the Mansion House Association on Transport. In 1938 it was involved in the debate over the railways' Square Deal Campaign (q.v.). Another change of name came in 1964, to the National Traders Traffic Association. Five years later it amalgamated with the Traders Road Transport Association and the Traders Co-ordinating Committee on Transport to form the Freight Transport Association (q.v.). **JA/JMA**

OCBRH, p.312; *Freight Transport* (August 1989); Geoffrey Alderman, *The Railway Interest* (Leicester University Press, 1973)

Manton lorry, see RUTLAND LORRY

Market garden produce lorries (Figures 133 and 168) supplying the capital typically had slat-sided bodywork, surmounted by raves (a framework of vertical rods, held in place by horizontal members). These bodies, originating in the horse-drawn era, gave extra load capacity and accessibility: the spacing of the uprights allowed for the insertion of the loader's foot, to enable the side to be climbed and the dimensions were related to the stacking of bushel boxes. The slatted sides facilitated washing out of the load space, which was essential when return loads comprised manure. One of the leading market garden lorry builders, J Gibbs of Bedfont, founded in 1844, was well placed to meet demand from the horticultural area west of London, which supplied the capital. The chassis used were usually the lighter sort, such as Austin (for which Gibbs was a dealer), Bedford, Commer and Ford. **RAS**
See also FRUIT AND VEGETABLE TRAFFIC

B Moorman, 'Commer GF 212', *CVC*, 5, 6 (February 2000), pp. 28–31; Gibbs' trade advertising

Marketing by hauliers to the general public via press or radio advertising would be a waste of money as the services offered are targeted at other businesses not the average consumer, except for express package carriers. Thus marketing in the form of advertising has not been a feature of road haulage, except, perhaps, in its campaign against nationalisation in the 1940s.

Marketing by hauliers was closely related to the livery and turn-out of their vehicles. Smart, well turned-out vehicles in a distinctive livery with clear lettering created favourable public awareness; the 'Well driven?' campaign of the late 1990s is an extension of this public relations activity. The name, address and telephone number of the haulier might be accompanied by a slogan such as 'Any ware to anywhere', or a more specific indication of regular services between major locations; a suggestion of dependability could be given by the date of the establishment of the business. The lining of panels, shading of lettering and inclusion of such devices as the buckler or the Staffordshire knot served as a link back to horse-drawn haulage. In the 1990s the appearance of the Stobart (q.v.) fleet, with the positive use of the display potential of curtain-sides, and the introduction of the Transport Development Group's (q.v.) juggler logo are indicative of the importance of vehicle presentation. Enthusiasts' and fan clubs (q.v.) are an aspect of public relations (and were sometimes a source of profit) but do not contribute directly to winning business. The choice of a vehicle such as the Scania T-cab or a north American tractive unit, with its rarity value in the UK, may also be seen as an aspect of marketing. Letterheads have been used as a kind of advertising medium, and advertising within the trade through a journal such as *World's Carriers* was a way of keeping a presence among fellow hauliers. At a local level, advertisements were sometimes placed in directories or town or district handbooks to supplement personal contact and word-of-mouth recommendations.   **RAS**

Marples, (Alfred) Ernest (1907–78), was Conservative Minister of Transport 1959–64. A chartered accountant, he entered the building industry in 1929 and established Marples, Ridgway & Partners, contractors. After war service in the Royal Artillery, he became a Conservative MP in 1945. During his time at Transport, his self-projection identified him with numerous issues coming to the fore, particularly those concerned with the regulation of motor traffic, even though they may have predated his term of office, to such an extent that there was eventually a good humoured 'Marples must go' campaign. He was an excellent self-publicist with a strong bias in favour of road transport. He is widely — but wrongly — credited as the prime mover behind

the first part of the M1 motorway, but it was his predecessor, Harold Watkinson, not a man who courted publicity, who gave the go-ahead.
                                            RAS
DNB

Marshalls of Cambridge began as a hire car business established by D G Marshall in 1909. It became distributor for the new range of Austin commercials and a depot commenced in 1939 came into use as the Airport Garage in 1945. In the early post-war period Marshalls began a long involvement with Services vehicles, setting up a servicing depot at Bourn airfield for government vehicles and stripping and refurbishing military vehicles, an activity which lasted into the late 1980s. Hugh Gordon, who had been general manager of Shorts' Sebro Stirling works at Cambridge, was appointed to establish a commercial vehicle bodybuilding division for Marshalls. St Clair Marshall of Spurlings was recruited as manager and D G McMillan of Express Motor & Body Works as chief designer. Gordon returned to aviation with BEA, but Marshalls became well established as a commercial bodybuilder, securing through personal contact such prestigious customers as Chivers of Histon and Whitbreads, the brewers. Marshall Motor Bodies Ltd was formed in 1948 and customers included the Post Office, brewers and livestock carriers. In the 1960s Marshalls' Body Division developed a container to ISO and Lloyds' standards, but the firm was careful not to get over-involved in this market. Marshalls continued to win military body-building contracts and was unusual, if not unique among bodybuilders in having a rust-proofing plant in which complete bodies could be dipped. Civilian customers for Marshalls' commercial bodies declined, with exceptions such as Whitbreads and John Lewis, as lower quality but cheaper bodies dominated the market. This trend was partly offset by Marshalls' appointment as distributors for the American Thermo King vehicle refrigeration equipment. Then in 1993 Marshalls became vehicle producers with the acquisition by its special vehicle division, Marshall SPV, of AWD. There was a limited home market, especially from some brewers, and civil and military demand in the developing world for AWD's rugged products. As this dried up, Marshalls SPV moved to a niche market with the Utility. This was aimed in particular at the refuse vehicle market and at specialised delivery activities, such as those of brewers. In 1999 ERF (q.v.) bought the Bedford spares business (to serve over 20,000 surviving Bedfords) and some designs from Marshalls, which henceforth concentrated on its bodybuilding activity. **RAS**

A Marshall, *The Marshall Story* (Sparkford: Patrick Stephens, 1994); Millar (1997); *Homme et Camion*, 13 (January 1999), pp. 78–9; *VCV*, 115 (July 1999), p. 6

Marston Road Services (Figures 134 and 166) was founded by Ernest Charles Marston, who started his transport business at Lightbody Street, Liverpool, in 1920. During the First World War he made friends with Lt Colonel Alfred Scammell. Starting with ex-WD Daimler and then Leyland lorries, he soon added Scammell articulated lorries, including low-loaders to move export locomotives from Manchester to Liverpool docks. He probably sold Scammells too as an agent in the early days. In 1926 he purchased the business of Edward Box (q.v.), which gave him the capability to move the largest export locomotives to Liverpool Docks. The business was reorganised as MRS Ltd in 1926 claiming to operate 74 vehicles, mostly Scammell, together with 20 AEC Mammoth Major six-wheelers for a contract with Tate & Lyle. This led to financial problems, mostly the unprofitable contract with Tate & Lyle, which also utilised sub-contractors. The fleet included four Fowler road locomotives, including the 'Duke of York' equipped as a crane engine, new in 1928 (now preserved). These had 'In Association with Edward Box Ltd' as part of the title. About this period he spoke out against clearing houses, saying that owner-drivers would be better served acting as sub-contractors to larger haulage concerns. An associated business, A C Marston Ltd, operated as a clearing house. Walter Gammons (q.v.) took exception to Marston's remarks and attacked Marston's claims that 10s. per ton for loads carried on his 15-ton Scammells was profitable, compared with £1 per ton for a 6-ton lorry. Marston further claimed that cost per day or week was a better basis for costing than cost per ton-mile. He stated that Gammons had never met him and never owned vehicles, whereas his own wages bill was £700 per week and the last year he had used 320,000 gallons of petrol. At a meeting in May 1928, Major Renwick told the Fisher Renwick directors he had withdrawn from acquiring an interest in MRS, after careful assessment, considering the business to be under-capitalised. In 1929 Marston, as MRS, asked Scammell to design and supply a low loader to carry locomotives from Manchester to Liverpool (see SCAMMELL 100-TON TRANSPORTER). His involvement with the business ended in 1930, after poor results caused his brothers to force him out. Marston was closely involved in the foundation of the Road Haulage Association (q.v.) becoming its first president in 1932.

A severe fire at the Liverpool depot in 1934 damaged many vehicles, including the AECs and destroyed many tons of goods including sugar, which led to the bankruptcy of MRS. The Scammell 100-ton Transporter and the Fowler Duke of York were among those rescued, with many of the Scammell articulated lorries also away working. Marston died from a brain tumour in April 1934. MRS were taken over by Colonel Hudson, with his son John Donaldson Hudson becoming manager and the trading name changed back to Edward Box Ltd. A new depot was built at Speke Hall Road. In 1935/6 Pickfords took action to stop this use of Box, considering only they had the right to trade under the Box title. They were defeated and Pickfords ceased using the title Norman E Box. Heavy haulage operations continued to be the major business, now with offices or depots at London, Birmingham, Glasgow, Manchester, Sheffield and Bradford. Shortly after it became a founder subsidiary of the publicly-quoted Hauliers Ltd (q.v.). MRS continued with specialist operations, including a Bradford–London textile trunk service, and a trunk fish service from Milford Haven to Billingsgate, using Bedford and Morris-

Commercial vehicles, within the 30 mph limit. They also accepted some general freight traffic. The mixed fleet comprised mainly Scammells at nationalisation. **GM**

Road Locomotive Society Journal and Portfolios; Lane (1980); Mustoe (1997)

The **Maudslay Motor Co. Ltd** (Figure 135) of Coventry was established in 1902, as an engine and car manufacturer. Commercial vehicles were offered from 1903. New 30-cwt and 3-ton lorry designs appeared in 1912 and the latter, with a 40-hp engine, was produced to War Office Subsidy (q.v.) specifications and built by both Maudslay and Rover in the First World War. These early Maudslays were unusual in having overhead camshaft engines.

Passenger chassis were increasingly important between the wars, though a wide range of lorries was offered. In the 1930s the firm's output dwindled and a major outside shareholder, O D Smith, a Birmingham builder, was brought in to pull the company round. This he did, with the aid of designs by Siegfried Sperling, a refugee Austrian from Gräf und Stift, the Austrian commercial vehicle manufacturer. Sperling was briefly interned in the Isle of Man, but rejoined Maudslay, and retired in 1953.

The range included the Six-Four, which carried six tons but weighed under four. It later came with a Gardner engine and in 1938 became the 7½-ton Mogul. The war delayed the introduction of this new range of heavier commercial vehicles, which appeared in 1939, with the exception of the Mogul and Militant, which were produced for civil and military use respectively. The 1,000th Mogul came off the assembly line in February 1948.

Among commercial vehicle customers the GPO Stores (later Supplies) Department is worthy of note. Local patriotism in the West Midlands may have helped Maudslays' order book; firms such as GEC (Stoke Works); Hurst & Payne Ltd; ICI Metals Ltd; and Tan-Sad Ltd were customers, as were John Morton (q.v.) and Red House Motor Services.

During the Second World War Maudslay bought a 400-acre estate at Great Alne near Alcester. It subsequently became its sole factory. In 1948 Maudslay and Crossley joined AEC in Associated Commercial Vehicles, which marked the beginning of the end of Maudslay as a distinct marque. The AEC diesel engine had become a predominant Maudslay power unit. After 1955 Maudslay vehicle production was restricted to bonneted specials and AEC dump trucks, which were not suitable for Southall's production lines. The Castle Maudslay workforce actually increased, with axle production, special version AEC engines and outside work, but in 1972 Leyland, which had taken over AEC in 1962, sold Maudslay to the American axle producer, Rockwell International. **RAS**

N Baldwin, 'Phoenix of the forties', *VCVM*, 1, 4, pp. 22–5; 'Maudslay. A family affair' *VCVM*. 32, 4 (1991); Stevens-Stratten (1988), pp. 88–92; C Wright, *Post Office Stores and Telephone Vehicles* (Nynehead: Roundoak, 1991), pp. 37–40; Modern Records Centre, University of Warwick Library, MSS.226X/MA/1–10

Maybury, Sir Henry, (1864–1943) civil engineer. His work had a two-fold significance for the development of motor transport in the UK. The first phase comprised his professional service with public bodies, civil and military, local and national, at a crucial period for the physical development and administrative control of roads and motor transport. After his retirement from public office, active involvement in business followed, especially in the road materials industry.

An 'indefatigable' character of 'remarkable vitality', Maybury was Kent County Engineer and Surveyor from 1903, gaining his reputation from the Sidcup trials of road surfacing. He became chief engineer of the Road Board in 1913. From 1914 he was responsible for road works undertaken for the War Department and in 1917 he went to France, with the rank of brigadier-general, as director of roads. He was appointed director general of roads in the new Ministry of Transport in 1919, a post he held until retirement in 1928, after which he continued as consulting engineer and adviser until 1932. He is credited with negotiating road schemes for the relief of unemployment in the post-war period, during which time he held three presidencies: of the Institute of Quarrying (1919), the Institute of Transport (1921–2) and the Institution of Civil Engineers (1933–4).

After retirement he took up a number of directorships and was instrumental in effecting some rationalisation in the road materials industry, bringing eight quarrying companies, including John Arnold Ltd of Chipping Sodbury, into one, the British Quarrying Co. Ltd.   **RAS**

DNB; Plowden (1973); P Johnson, *Consolidated Gold Fields: a centenary portrait* (Weidenfeld & Nicolson, 1987), ch. 6; Earle (1971)

Meadows, Henry, Ltd, see GUY MOTORS LTD

Meat transport (Figures 37 and 136). The development of refrigerated ships in the early part of the twentieth century brought increased business to road transport in two ways: the carriage of frozen carcases from docks to Smithfield (London) or Liverpool markets or to cold stores (usually nearby) and from cold stores to inland wholesale markets or very large buyers. After sale at markets there was transport to shops. The deliveries to most retailers were carried out regularly by specialist carriers, some of whom were also longer distance carriers.

Previously most meat was either fresh and slaughtered and sold locally, or salted and brought from further afield. Animals were also imported on the hoof, mainly from Ireland, and slaughtered in the UK, often after a final journey by special trains, while until the 1920s drovers still delivered some animals direct to market in rural areas. Some markets, such as Smithfield, were rail-connected. Imports of livestock for slaughter on occasions came from as far afield as America.

Loading and unloading of frozen meat at docks was mainly by manual labour, usually highly unionised. Carcases such as sides of beef were hung in the vehicle but frozen sheep were stacked on the floor, the former giving rise to employment of a specialised 'puller-back' who was responsible for filling the whole of the vehicle interior and of unloading it without damage. Meat porters – those at Smithfield were called bummarees – were another feature of major markets and had sole rights to load and unload vehicles: this led to two public inquiries, which basically concluded that a closed shop was operating and the men were highly paid, but quick and efficient.

Most frozen meat was imported through London or Liverpool docks, whether from Australia, New Zealand or (usually south) America. Vehicles or trailers used for dock work had substantially built boxvan bodies or liftable containers on platform bodies, always insulated. Two of the London hauliers, E W Rudd (q.v.) (with its meat department at Poplar) and T M Fairclough of Stepney, built their own bodies, using 6 in of cork insulation. In the London docks containers and bodies were loaded through end doors, while those of Liverpool carriers had side doors. Most London carriers first used horse-drawn vans, then drawbar trailers hauled by a tractor (later tractors were usually short-wheelbase lorries with a ballast box over the rear axle and, finally articulated trailers. In London operators were allowed to use one tractor to pull two empty trailers from market to docks. Horses continued to be used for a considerable time to move empty trailers alongside ships. Once a ship docked considerable resources were used to unload it quickly.

Much of the meat trade was in the hands of the Vestey chain (as Dewhurst and British & Argentine Meat Co. shops) while the co-operative societies also had a big role. The general pattern continued unchanged until the 1960s, after which the burgeoning supermarket groups began buying direct, with most wholesale markets declining or even closing.

Bodywork of vehicles carrying meat had to be strongly built and where carcases were hung from ceiling rails a considerable strain was put on the roof structure. Containers with lifting hooks or rings were widely used and carried on platform-bodied rigids or drawbar trailers, some of which (for example, those of United Carriers) were floor-less.

Until meat rationing finally ended in 1954 meat transport was handled by the Meat Transport Organisation Ltd (q.v.), usually known as MTOL, but considerable changes came to those hauliers carrying for the MTOL after nationalisation of much of the haulage industry. Pickfords (q.v.), like Hay's Wharf Cartage (q.v.), already had a large meat-carrying set-up. As the BTC compulsorily acquired hauliers, the vehicles and operations of those with substantial meat work were passed to what was originally the Meat Cartage Department of Pickfords. Well-known names absorbed included E W Rudd, T M Fairclough, R J Weeks of Hackney Marsh and E Wells & Son of Rotherhithe. The fleet was smartly liveried in cream and dark blue, ultimately becoming BRS (Meat Haulage) Ltd. Operations were modernised with insulated containers. Drawbar trailers continued to be widely used for dock work.

Man-handling was reduced by special trailers with racks that could be raised and lowered mechanically and which could carry 24 sides of beef. A much earlier example of mechanisation had appeared at the 1931 Commercial Motor Show (q.v.) when Duramin Engineering (q.v.) exhibited a bonneted diesel-engined Mercedes-Benz six-wheeler for Hay's Wharf Cartage's Scottish meat traffic. It had an all-metal insulated body with a moving endless overhead chain system from which meat was hung. Similar bodywork was fitted to an early oil-engined (but forward-control) AEC Mammoth.

By the early 1950s the pattern of meat haulage was changing, with greater home production and fewer imports. When rationing ended MTOL closed, but United Carriers was formed in replacement as a clearing house, with much of the BRS (Meat Haulage) fleet chartered to it. The BRS work produced a poor return. Denationalisation plans following a change of government saw BRS (Meat Haulage) offered for sale in late 1954 and again in 1956, but to no avail. A few years later, as it was making losses, United Carriers closed. In 1966 Union Cartage, part of the Vestey empire, bought a major shareholding, leaving the Transport Holding Company (q.v.) with a 35 per cent interest: that too was acquired by Union Cartage a few years later. Even by 1966 the fleet numbered only 150 vehicles, a huge drop from 500 in the early post-war years.

Higher standards of insulation came in the 1950s and in the 1960s refrigeration equipment designed specifically for use on commercial vehicles became available. The total number of vehicles engaged in meat transport fell as market conditions changed. Imports of frozen meat continued to fall. Supermarkets buying direct led to the run-down of many wholesale markets and the number of high street butchers reduced as meat consumption per head dropped and more people shopped at supermarkets.

While beef, lamb, pork and bacon consumption fell, sales of chicken and then turkey (usually sold frozen) rose dramatically. Some hauliers, including United Carriers, diversified into frozen food and ice cream transport.

As standards improved, new problems emerged, such as carcases of beef on hanging rails leaning against the body sides, thus disrupting the flow of air. To overcome this special types of aluminium (and later plastics) panels were produced for interior lining.

From the 1980s sales of chilled meat, particularly poultry, grew steadily, needing higher quality refrigeration equipment on a vehicle to keep a constant temperature. New European Community regulations imposed many improvements and standards at supermarkets and other suppliers improved.

The activities of animal rights protesters and their arson attacks on some operators' premises led to many operators adopting a low profile with their vehicles painted plain white. At the other end of the spectrum, some Scottish beef was exported in 44-tonne outfits with operator's name and cargo displayed in large letters to disassociate them from English foot-and-mouth concern.

Hanging rails and a connecting frame that lowers a carcase to shoulder height became standard equipment on vehicles delivering to local butchers, while most meat taken by supermarkets is pre-packaged and can be delivered with other food products. **GM/JMA**

The **Meat Transport Organisation Ltd** evolved from the 'pool' which was set up by the largest meat carriers based on London's Smithfield Market. They were aware of the problems that decentralisation of London's wholesale markets and diversion of imports from London, Liverpool and Southampton to other ports would cause their customers in the event of war. They held three meetings in 1938 and 1939, finally creating their pool scheme to serve London and the Home Counties. Named the Wholesale Meat and Provisions Transport Association (WMTA), the 'Provisions' was later omitted. The major problem was in obtaining the support of the smaller operators with their particular concerns about payment for their services. The three principals behind the creation of the WMTA, P J R Tapp, F H Minter and G W Quick-Smith (q.v.), produced the system of paying for the payload capacity of vehicles in the pool. The pool became the operating unit, each of the members kept their identity and management responsibilities for drivers, maintenance, etc. Payment was determined by dividing meat transport revenues received in a chosen year by the payload capacity of the operator, to give an income base. This could be adjusted as needed to meet changes in costs to give operators a profit in the war pool years to equal the profit of the selected year. The WMTA asked the Board of Trade to recognise it and agree to use it in the event of war. This happened in 1939 when the BoT Food Defence Plans department asked the pool to start work at once, but without any terms for payment. They began removing meat and butter and other provisions from the port's cold stores and warehouses. Smithfield Market was removed in its entirety to the allocated depots. With no agreement for payment the major founder operators gave guarantees to the bank to enable small operators to have payment of their invoices to date. The Ministry of Food (MoF) took over responsibility for the working of the pool, with rationing introduced from 1940, also making payments for transport. The WMTA extended the pool to cover the whole country, in 10 days. At the same time the MoF opened area meat and livestock offices, to be responsible for transport instructions. In 1941 the pool was transferred to the MoT, and now included livestock transport. P J R Tapp and Claud Barrington were appointed Chief Road Transport Officers, at the MoT. Shortly after,

in 1941, the Road Haulage Organisation (RHO) (q.v.) was created, the meat pool becoming the meat section under Minter. This continued until the RHO finished in August 1946. The pool agreed to carry on to December 1946. By then the agreement leading to the MTOL was concluded with the intention that it should continue to December 1948, or with six months notice from either side, so long as rationing continued. In the event it was 30 July 1954 before meat rationing finally ended. The MTOL was then closed. An attempt to continue as a clearing house followed when United Carriers Ltd (no relation to the entry of that name) was formed. This eventually failed under the conditions of a free market, although in 1958 United Carriers had claimed to have 800 vehicles at its disposal with BRS (Meat Haulage) Ltd among its chief suppliers. Vehicle owners in effect hired to United Carriers on charter, United making no profit.

GM

Mechanical handling is the essential prerequisite of modern road haulage and logistics systems. Lansing Bagnall, a pioneer of material handling equipment in the UK, employed the slogan 'Mechanised muscle — to lift the load and lower the cost', which encapsulates a process involving a series of technical developments throughout the twentieth century. Their cumulative effect has been to reduce drastically, if not eliminate, the manual handling of goods in transit, referred to as 'handballing' (q.v.). In a very elementary form the application of mechanical handling can be seen in the sack truck. Although operated by human power, the sack truck, with its use of the lever principle around the axle of its two wheels (which, together with the load platform, took the load off the handler's back or arms), embodied the basic features of mechanical handling, albeit at its simplest.

The handling of stillages by works trucks (q.v.) was accelerated by the needs of industry in the First World War and was one of the lines of development leading to the use of the fork-lift truck (q.v.) and pallet (q.v.) in and after the Second World War, stimulated by the example of American practice. Throughout the century the mobile crane (q.v.) developed in manoeuvrability and lifting capacity and during the post-war period the fork-lift truck grew enormously in lifting capacity. It gave an impetus to the use of the curtain-side body (q.v.). Both crane unit and fork-lift truck can now be made available as lorry-mounted equipment, thus further enhancing their usefulness. **RAS**

The **mechanical horse** (Figure 137) was originally a three-wheeled tractor with a 2- to 6-ton capacity, designed to replace the horse on railway collection and delivery rounds in towns. The Karrier Cob appeared in 1930 as a joint development venture with the LMSR. The rival Scammell Mechanical Horse appeared in 1933 after Scammell had purchased a project developed by D Napier & Son Ltd (q.v.) for the LNER. Apart from their manoeuvrability in confined spaces the other notable feature of mechanical horses was the automatic coupling (q.v.), which allowed the driver to couple up to, and uncouple from, semi-trailers rapidly, without assistance and, as fully developed, without leaving the cab. A handful of prototype Karrier Cobs were supplied to the railway companies for trial use with existing horse drays (with the shaft removed), but this idea of using horse drays without at least substantial rebuilding was quickly abandoned.

In 1935–7 Ford tried unsuccessfully to enter the market with the 3-wheeled Ford Tug. Because the Cob, with its narrow back axle, had a tendency to be unstable, Karrier introduced the 4-wheel Bantam mechanical horse in 1936, which largely superseded the Cob. After the war Jensen Motors Ltd brought out the 4-wheeled Jen Tug and several manufacturers of electric vehicles (q.v.) produced 4-wheeled 'electric horses'. Scammell continued to dominate, however; in 1948 its Mechanical Horse evolved into the Scarab and in 1964 into the Townsman, the latter with a fibre-glass cab. At some major goods depots the railways made use of battery-electric mules to position empty trailers.

The railways and railway cartage contractors were the biggest single users of mechanical horses – British Railways' fleet reached a peak of 10,000 in the mid-1950s – but there were as many employed by BRS and a variety of other in-town users, such as brewers, millers and waste paper merchants. There were also substantial exports in the 1950s and 1960s. The 1966 Construction & Use Regulations, with their implications for vehicles with non-braked single-steering wheels, and the changing nature of railway freight operations, led Scammell to cease production. **RAS/GAB**

Twells and Bourne (1983); Stevens-Stratten and Aldridge (1987); Georgano (1997); Aldridge (2000); Earnshaw and Aldridge (1997); idem, *Great Western Railway Road Vehicles* (2000); Carverhill (2002)

Mercedes-Benz (Figures 9, 13, 38, 61 and 81), the German manufacturer, was formed in 1926 by the merger of the Daimler and Benz concerns. In the following year it imported the first diesel-engined lorry to be seen in the UK, where it won the Dewar prize for engine efficiency in 1928. A marketing organisation, British Mercedes-Benz Ltd, was set up in London and built up a small clientele in the 1930s, although high cost (plus import duty) and residual anti-German feeling kept UK sales down. Customers included McNamara, H & G Dutfield and Gamman & Dicker, the Sussex parcels carrier. Mercedes' re-entry to the UK after the Second World War was gradual, after exhibiting at the 1960 Commercial Motor Show. Both the dated normal-control LK322 and 327 models, as tippers, and the forward-control LP322 and 327 found a variety of customers. Some, such as R Hanson & Son Ltd and Placketts Transport Ltd took several, but sales figures were small, at about 25 per annum in the early 1960s. The models surpassed UK vehicles in several respects, such as a superior cab and exhaust brake, but relative costs (including a 32 per cent import duty) and lingering prejudice against German products restricted sales. To support the UK sales figures, rights for the Unimog 4×4 cross-country vehicle were acquired in 1961. The UK M-B lorry franchise passed to Normand in 1964, as the permitted gross weight for articulated vehicles was raised to 32 tons. Normand took advantage of the opportunity by acquiring a cancelled-order batch of right-hand-drive LK 327 tractor units. M-B growth in the UK was assisted by its New Generation range in 1974, relaunched as the SK in 1988 and replaced by the Actros introduced in the UK in 1997. Its van sales were boosted by the Sprinter, which sold 11,000 in the UK in 1996 and the Vito, imported from Spain via Portbury. To assist UK sales a 100-acre site at Wentworth Park, near Doncaster was opened in the mid-1980s as a preparation centre. **RAS**

Millar (1997); N Baldwin, *Lorries & Vans* (Marshall, Harris & Baldwin Ltd, 1979); F Tinsdale, 'How Mercedes arrived', *VCV* (1998–9); ibid., 'Mercedes pioneers', *VRS,* 17, 65 and 66 (2000–1), pp. 10–13, 70–1; Dunbar (1981); Ingram (1975); *Truck Star Actros* supplement (March 1997)

Mickey Mouse, see NICKNAMES

Midland Motors of Oadby, Leicestershire, serves to illustrate some of the connections between operation, dealing and preservation (q.v.). This well-known scrapyard and source of vehicles for preservation closed in 1999, having been relatively inactive since the early 1990s. The site had its origins in a War Agricultural Executive repair depot and the business originated, *c.* 1947, as J B Coleman, general hauliers, mainly operating Scammell Rigid Eights. Coleman also refurbished war surplus lorries in that vehicle-hungry period. When he ceased trading about 1960 the yard was taken over by the commercial vehicle breakers Rush Green Motors of Hitchin, Herts. Oadby provided a convenient staging-post between the auction centres at Measham, Leeds, Irthlingborough and Garrett Lane, London, for vehicles to be prepared for resale. Business was at its height in the second half of the 1970s, when up to 18 Scammell trailers a month were processed. **RAS**

'Oadby. The final countdown', *CVC*, 4, 7 (March 1999), pp. 6–9

Midland Vehicles Ltd of Leamington Spa was founded in 1935 by James Parker Garner after he had left Garner Motors (q.v.) because it was losing its independence to Alley & McLellan. He decided to break into the battery-electric

door-to-door vehicle market and started the firm in Upper Grove Street, Leamington Spa. The vehicle range went from 10-cwt to 1¼ ton. During the Second World War it appears one or two chassis were built. Hinckley, Nuneaton and Rugby Co-operative societies were moderate users, but by far the largest customer was the Midland Counties Dairy where over 100 floats were employed. Other users for milk delivery included the Nottingham and Royal Arsenal Co-operatives and private dairies such as Piper of Dymchurch, Kent, Evesham Dairies, and J Cleaver of Leamington. Bread delivery versions were used by Portsea Island Co-operative Society, Bradford's Bread and Hawleys Bakery of Birmingham. Ipswich Co-operative ran Midland mobile greengrocery vans.

Cash flow problems began to occur in the 1950s, when their invoicing system was notoriously slow. As a result the site was sold to a nearby engineering firm owned by G Gulliman which wished to expand and so let the electric vehicle side decline. The driving force of Midland, Major Pickin, died in 1958 and this sealed its fate. The firm's models were too small and outdated by the late 1950s. The roundsman disliked having to do a double-run (going back to the depot to load extra crates) as rounds became longer in an attempt to reduce costs, something not necessary with modern larger vehicles. **RFdeB**

R F de Boer, 'Midland Electric Vehicles', *Wheelspin*, 21 (July/August 1978), pp. 19–21; R A Storey, 'Midland Vehicles Ltd', Society of Automotive Historians, UK Chapter, *Newsletter,* 17 (January 1988), pp. 3–4

Milk transport (Figures 11, 39, 138 and 140). The long distance transport of milk goes back to 1865 when the government ordered destruction of all London cattle because of an outbreak of rinderpest. George Barham, an enterprising pioneer in the marketing of milk and dairy products, had set up the Express Dairy Company in Bloomsbury two years earlier and foreseen that the development of London would gradually engulf the grazing land. So he made connections with farmers further afield to supply him with milk conveyed in churns on Great Northern Railway trains coming into Kings Cross station.

By the mid-1920s over a thousand million gallons of milk were produced annually by the dairy herds of England and Wales. This enormous quantity had to be conveyed distances of up to 150 miles to the consumer, not at infrequent intervals, but in daily deliveries, seven days a week and fifty-two weeks a year. Apart from the use of milk in its natural form, about five million gallons were used for the production of cream and butter, while large quantities were made into cheese, condensed, dried and otherwise subjected to manufacturing processes. Speed, hygiene and economy in handling being factors of prime importance in the transport of milk, the railway network played an important part. Conveyance from farm to distant creamery involved the use of churns of various sizes which were susceptible to damage, content contamination and extremes of weather.

The coming of reliable mechanical road transport made the operation somewhat easier in that farmers could speedily transport their produce, still in 10-gallon churns with their own brass identity plate, to the local station for onward transmission instead of relying on the horse and cart method used hitherto.

In the United States, development of bulk liquid tankers had already taken place and in 1923 the Liverpool firm S Reece & Sons (q.v.) Ltd, purchased two glass-lined steel tanks each with a capacity of 1250 gallons. These, mounted on Leyland chassis, conveyed milk in bulk the 35 miles from their farm depot at Malpas in Cheshire to their bottling plant in Liverpool. Previously this trip had been made by rail in churns. The new method offered significant economies in labour and equipment and also made possible doorstep delivery of a much fresher product.

Following this pioneering success, others took up the idea on a much greater scale. The London area relied on supplies from outside and in 1926 Viner and Long of Frome in Somerset took delivery of two 6-wheel articulated tankers from Scammell Lorries Ltd, to provide a daily service over the 110 miles to London. These had a capacity of 2620 gallons

and were equipped with the then latest method of electric lighting. The tanks were built by the Aluminium Plant & Vessel Co. of London. They were insulated by six inches of granulated cork, to keep the milk at a relatively constant temperature in transit. After discharge the tanks were washed out with hot water prior to the return journey. A contemporary report stated that 'There is no comparison between the railway rates and the costs of the daily road runs to and from London whilst the tankers are much more hygienic'.

In the early 1930s road-rail co-ordination was in vogue and several road trailer manufacturers produced tank trailers which could be conveyed by rail in dedicated special trains over longer distances. In 1931 R A Dyson & Co. (q.v.) produced a solid-tyred trailer on which was mounted a 2000 gallon tank built by Butlers (London) Ltd, to the order of the Co-operative Wholesale Society for conveyance by rail between their creamery at Bruton in Somerset and their bottling plant at Clapham Junction, London. The SR produced special flat wagons incorporating various features to secure the road trailer during the railway transit. The use of the road/railer did not find universal approval as tank capacity was restricted by the railway loading gauge.

The Milk Marketing Board was formed in 1933 to co-ordinate the collection, marketing and distribution of milk on a national basis. Many new specialist milk haulage contractors were established including such well-known names as Bridgnorth Milk Transport, Bulwark Transport and the Wincanton (q.v.) Transport & Engineering Company. Larger dairy groups such as Express Dairy Co., United Dairies and the CWS Dairies provided tankers to link their own creameries and distant bottling plants. In the 1950s the MMB established its own dedicated fleet of vehicles based at regional centres in milk producing areas and included 'reload' sites where milk was transferred from churns to road tankers for trunk movements.

The development of larger and more reliable road tankers led to a decline in rail traffic and the last milk train ran in the late 1960s. Road tankers increased in size from the 8-wheel rigid to the maximum capacity articulated outfit which increased flexibility and productivity, as did the expanding motorway network.

Transporting milk churns from the farm survived until the late 1970s when the labour-intensive and less hygienic methods were replaced by refrigerated bulk tanks at farms from which the insulated road tankers could collect directly for conveyance to processing plants. Drivers have to take, and check, samples from each farm tank before loading. Tankers with drawbar trailers have enjoyed some popularity, the trailer can be parked en route while the rigid unit makes some collections. Rear-steer axles on some rigids and artics are other recent innovations.

In 1984 milk quotas were introduced. Many farmers found it uneconomic to continue and gave up the business. Traditional milk haulage companies who for years had collected from farms in their area were also seriously affected and whilst many turned to other work, others came out of transport altogether, for example, Bridgnorth Milk Transport. Abolition of the MMB in 1994 led to a further upheaval, which resulted in many long-established milk hauliers losing contracts or deciding to give up. The MMB's successor, Milk Marque, operated on a different basis.   **SW**

Alan Jenkins, *Drinka Pinta: the story of milk and the industry that serves it* (Heinemann, 1970); Bryan Morgan, *Express Journey 1864-1964* (Newman Neame, 1964); Edith H Whetham, 'The London milk trade, 1900–1930', in Derek J Oddy and Derek Miller (eds), *The Making of the Modern British Diet* (Croom Helm, 1976), pp. 65–76

Milnes-Daimler began with lorries made by Milnes and fitted with German Daimler engines, but soon changed to German-produced chassis, bodied in England. Production began in 1901, in which year Milnes lorries took part in the Lancashire Heavy Vehicle Trials (q.v.) winning a gold medal, and the War Office Trials (q.v.) at Aldershot. A Milnes lorry became the first petrol-engined vehicle to carry the Royal Mail. The original participants were G F Milnes & Co. Ltd of Hadley, Shropshire, tramcar builders, and a Daimler licensee. Milnes' works manager and the founder of Milnes-Daimler was H G Burford (q.v.) and

the specifications of Milnes-Daimler's original lorries were drawn up by F R Simms (q.v.). By 1907 the firm had built 300 commercial vehicles. The successful performance of Milnes Daimler vehicles on mail runs from London to the coast from 1907 gave the marque valuable publicity. The GWR operated a 1904 lorry and a later parcels van and converted some M-D buses to lorry use. (The GWR's subsequent orders for Burford vehicles may be traced back to this Milnes-Daimler connection). Despite the predominance of bus orders, 2- and 4-ton goods models continued to feature in the M-D range. Later Mercedes cars were also sold, but the First World War and the German connection effectively killed it. Milnes-Daimler-Mercedes, as the company became, was wound up in 1916 under the Trading with the Enemy (Amendment) Act.   **RAS**

Lord Montagu and D Burgess-Wise, *Daimler Century* (Sparkford, 1995), p.76; John M Aldridge, *British Buses before 1945* (Shepperton: Ian Allan, 1995; Miller (1982); P Darke, G and J H Pick, 'Milnes-Damiler', *Old Motor and Vintage Commercial*, 3, 3 (September 1964), pp. 86–94); Aldridge and Earnshaw (2000)

Mitsubishi Motors have supplied pick-ups and light vans to the UK since 1979, but the Canter lorry (1964 in origin) has only been available in the UK since the Japanese company's 1998 agreement with Volvo Trucks to distribute and support the Portuguese-built range here. The 7.5-tonne truck usefully supplemented Volvo's heavier series and 3.5- and 6.3-tonne models were also available. The latter had a factory-built crew-cab and was therefore popular for light recovery (q.v.) work; customers for the main model ranged from local tradesmen to large distribution concerns. 1200 Canters were sold in the UK in 2000. UK distribution of Mitsubishi trucks passed to Mercedes-Benz UK in 2001, following Volvo's sale of its stake in Mitsubishi to Daimler Chrysler. This ended plans for the joint development of a successor to the Volvo FL.   **RAS**

CM (31 August 2000), pp. 27–31; *Truck* (June 2001), p.12, (August 2001), p.18; Bob Tuck, 'Canter balance', *Truck* (November 2001), pp. 68–73

Mobile cranes are self-propelled lifting machines which found a significant role in inter-modal traffic after the Big Four railway companies introduced standard rail/road containers (q.v.) in 1928 for a variety of traffics. They transferred the containers between the two forms of transport. Mobile cranes could be battery-electric, petrol, diesel, petrol-electric or diesel-electric powered. There was a small number of manufacturers particularly associated with their production, including Ransomes & Rapier of Ipswich, Pagefield (q.v.), Coles Cranes Ltd and Jones of Letchworth (manufactured by K & L Ironfounders). The success of Coles' EMA range and the resulting service orders revived the firm. In 1939 it was taken over by Steel & Co. of Sunderland, which was anxious to diversify away from shipbuilding-connected engineering, but the Coles trade name was retained. 20 years later two other crane manufacturers, Neal of Grantham and F Taylor & Sons (Manchester) Ltd joined the Steel Group, the latter bringing hydraulic crane experience. A subsequent merger brought Steel within the Acrow Group in 1972 and later into Grove International. Mobile cranes were used for lifting heavy or awkward loads such as main frame computers in the 1970s, air conditioning units, and printing presses. Some firms specialised in such awkward deliveries, such as Vanguard of Greenford. **RAS**

M Wilson and K Spink, *Coles 100 Years: the growth story of Europe's leading crane manufacturer 1879–1979* (Harefield: Coles Cranes, 1978); H J Sheryn, *An Illustrated History of Cranes* (Shepperton: Ian Allan, 1997)

Mobile shops (Figures 96 and 139) and display vehicles have operated since the early days of the motor vehicle. Mobile shops brought a selection of goods to potential customers, rather than delivering ordered items as the van did. The first examples were conventional vans or small lorries on which various goods for sale might be hung or otherwise displayed. A recognised type was the hawker's van, with side apertures covered by roll-up canvas curtains. A Jowett example of 1937 exists in preservation. Purpose-built vehicles gradually evolved. The true mobile shop had displays and counters, an entry step or steps and often an internal aisle for customers. The need to make entry and exit as easy as possible led to widespread use of bus and coach chassis from the early 1930s, since these had a lower frame height than goods vehicles. In more recent times the lower cost of a goods vehicle chassis has made these the usual choice.

In the 1920s and 1930s mobile shops sold meat or general provisions, fruit and vegetables or household goods. They brought to villages items that otherwise might only be obtained from towns some distance away. After the Second World War there was an increase in their numbers, partly fuelled by the post-war housing boom which meant that on many new estates the houses were built long before the shops and amenities were added. Except in a few areas, the use of mobile shops has subsequently declined, though the dwindling number of fishmongers' shops has spurred use of small vans selling fresh fish. Mobile fish and chip shops are also found plying their trade in country areas. More stringent hygiene regulations mean that hygienic surfaces and washing facilities have to be provided for the driver and staff.

Retail co-operative societies have been notable operators of mobile shops, with bodies built by the movement's own bodyworks. During the Second World War retailers such as J Sainsbury (q.v.) brought a number of mobile shops into service and J Lyons (q.v.) introduced 'Emergency Teashop' trailers to replace blitzed facilities. In the post-war period the Karrier Bantam, bodied by Smith's Delivery Vehicles (later Smith-Appleyard Ltd) was a popular choice for a mobile shop. Its low frame for ease of entry and economic 4-cylinder engine for stop-start work were combined with a body providing nearside sliding door access to the sales area. Electric vehicles were also used as the basis of mobile shops in suburban areas, for example by the Express Dairy. In the 1950s former buses and coaches were converted into mobile shops, including fish-and-chip vans. Vehicles providing mobile service points, such as mobile libraries, mobile banks and even mobile building society offices (for example one operated by the Stroud Building Society), share some of the basic bodywork requirements of the larger type of mobile shop, such as the clerestory roof (q.v.), with a single coachbuilder offering a range of such vehicles, for example, Road Transport Services (Hackney) Ltd.

Designs of mobile shops have varied from the strictly practical to the stylish, with some striking displays of the bodybuilder's art. Large window displays were often a feature. An example of the latter was a bonneted Albion 'super demonstration van or travelling showroom' exhibited at the 1934 Scottish Motor Show for a Glasgow confectioner and baker. Its streamlined body had numerous curves and chrome-plated sweeps, windows of different shapes and sizes and extra batteries and converter equipment to power its neon advertising signs. Rather different, though built in the same year, was a mobile shop on a Leyland Cub public service vehicle chassis for an Ilkley firm of grocers and provision merchants. Its 20-ft long body contained showcases, meat rails and a bacon slicer, clock, mirrors and a marbled metal counter running the width of the vehicle at the rear. Interior cabinet work was in mahogany with chromium-plated metal fittings.

Mobile demonstration vehicles were operated by some well-known food suppliers to enable their wares or new products to be sampled. When use of gas or electric cookers was not widespread, their makers often operated mobile showrooms that visited new estates, or towns or villages where a gas or electric supply was being provided for the first time.   **JMA/RAS**

Karrier Motors Ltd Sales Division, *Motor Transport* offprint (9 March 1956); *JS 100: the story of Sainsbury's* (the firm, 1969); P Bird, *The First Food Empire* (Chichester: Phillimore, 2000), p. 121; P Galvani and A F Arnell, *Going Self-service?* (Sidgwick & Jackson, 1952), ch. 19; J Woodhams, *The Bedford OB and OWB* (Twickenham: DPR, 1986), p. 80; G I J Orton, *An Illustrated History of Mobile Library Services in the United Kingdom* (Library Association, Branch & Mobile Libraries Group, 1980); A Kermatschuk and M Osborne, 'Jowetts in the blood', *Classic Van and Pick-up*, 2, 4 (February 2002), pp. 22–5

Model vehicles for many decades provided children with an introduction to the world of road transport and they continue to exercise a fascination which for some extends into adult life and to the development of collections such as the Tiatsa model museum of the late Tibor Reich, now in the Museum of British Road Transport, Coventry.

The earliest models, generally at least ten inches in length, were of wood or brightly coloured tinplate, with printed detail and a clockwork mechanism. Germany was a leading manufacturer of tinplate vehicles, but in the 1930s in the UK the Triang 'Minic' series produced by Lines Bros introduced a new sophistication into tinplate motors: smaller models, with separate keys, bearing more than a passing resemblance to actual vehicles.

The future lay with diecast models, of which the pioneers in the UK were Dinky Toys. Introduced in 1934 by Meccano Ltd of Liverpool as 'Modelled Miniatures', they were intended as lineside accessories for their Hornby Railways and were in competition with the imported Tootsietoys from the USA. The first MM set included non-specific dropside and box-bodied lorries and in 1934 a set of six commercial vehicles (petrol tanker, market gardener's lorry, etc) was introduced, to stay in production until 1950. These were generic designs not based on actual models. Most of these models were relatively costly so only children of well-to-do parents could afford them, though a few cost as little as sixpence. A mechanical horse, delivery and postal vans and a striking Holland Coachcraft (q.v.) van followed before the Second World War, during which Dinky production ceased, although a 'Pool'-liveried tanker did make an appearance. New commercial vehicle models were produced after the war, including lorries to a larger scale ('Supertoys'); both these and new, smaller-scale commercials were more accurate representations of actual vehicles.

Dinky at first had some rather crude rivals, such as Moko, Morestone and Timpo, but by the 1960s the threat to its position came from the Lesney 'Matchbox' and 'Models of Yesteryear' series, to a smaller scale, but with a remarkable degree of detail and accuracy, and from Corgi and, for a time, Spot-on models: the last being a subsidiary of Lines Bros. In recent decades the UK model vehicle industry has undergone changes of ownership and sourcing, especially from Asia, but there are still UK series catering for the collector at whom most of the model ranges of the late twentieth century were aimed. The use of models to promote a particular product or operator is long-established, a specific livery often adding verisimilitude, although the marketing of anachronistically liveried vehicles by operators' fan clubs strikes a somewhat false note. **RAS/JMA**

Cecil Gibson, *Commercial Vehicles* (Nelson, 1970); idem., *A History of British Dinky Toys* (Eton Wick: Mikansue, 1973); Marcel R Van Cleemput, *The Great Book of Corgi 1956–1983* (New Cavendish Books, 1989); David Pressland, *Pressland's Great Book of Tin Toys* (Golden Age Editions, 1995); Sue Richardson, *Minic: Lines Bros tinplate vehicles* (Windsor: Mikansue, 1981); Mike and Sue Richardson, *The Great Book of Dinky Toys* (New Cavendish Books, 2000)

Morris Commercial Cars Ltd (Figures 100, 139 and 141) 1924–54. Morris Motors built light delivery vans from 1914 to 1917 and again after the war based on their Cowley and then Oxford car chassis. Morris wanted to produce a heavier one-ton chassis to compete for the growing market being met by imports, notably Chevrolet and Ford. The liquidation in 1923 of E G Wrigley & Co. Ltd, of Soho, Birmingham, an original supplier of components to Morris, enabled William Morris to buy the assets and start Morris Commercial Cars Ltd. The chief draughtsman, Percy G Rose, designed the first chassis to be built, the one-ton capacity, T model. The first chassis left the works in May 1924. The earlier models used many Morris car components including the Hotchkiss engine.

In 1926 Morris-Commercial became the title cast in the radiator header. The range was extended with the Z 25- or 30-cwt model, available from 1926 to 1931 and the TX 30-cwt heavy duty chassis. These were designed for export, but were equally popular in this country. It was uprated to 35/40-cwt, and then to a 45/50-cwt version.

An R type 30-cwt range was introduced in 1929, being superseded by an improved model in 1931. Variations of the R model included the 'ton economy' chassis and the RD version. This had twin rear axles and was designed to carry bulky loads and was available from 1930 to 1932. To meet the demand for a heavier capacity vehicle the P Leader 3-ton chassis was available from 1931 to 1934 in both long- and short-wheelbase models, and normal and forward-control versions.

There were too many chassis models in the range, not all of which were competitive. The move to the ex-Wolseley works at Adderley Park in 1933 allowed the production of a new range of chassis, the C type. This competed with the comparable Bedford and Fordson chassis. The first models available were 30-cwt and 60-cwt vehicles with the option of normal or forward control. The 5-ton Leader introduced in 1936 was only available with normal control.

In the early 1930s heavy trucks were built, primarily on the bus chassis designed by Charles K Edwards, previously at AEC and later with Guy. A unique feature was that engine, gear box and front axle could be withdrawn from the front of the chassis as a single unit. Users of Morris-Commercials included the Holdsworth & Hanson Group, the Post Office, McNamara, J Lyons & Co., the co-operative societies and the railways. They were in widespread use by the haulage industry. The army also bought considerable numbers of medium off-road 6×4 chassis.

The LC 25-cwt and the CV Equiload 30 and 40-cwt and 3/4 ton and 4/5 ton chassis were produced for the 1937 Commercial Motor Show. An addition to the range in 1939 was the PV (parcels van), a forward-control 15/20-cwt capacity van intended to compete with electric or horse-drawn vans. The production of a limited number of commercial vehicle chassis was allowed during the war for operators granted Ministry of War Transport approval. Production of the PV and the Equiload range recommenced in 1945, although only the 4-cylinder engines were available. In 1948 a full forward-control chassis, the FV, came into production, retaining the four-cylinder petrol engine. The cab was notable for the rear-hinged 'suicide' doors. The FVO version with a new six-cylinder diesel engine, using Saurer patents was also available. Unfortunately the diesel engine was less successful. The merger of Austin and Morris Motors Ltd to become British Motor Corporation in February 1952 had a gradual effect. The FV was produced with a six-cylinder petrol engine. The new 30-cwt LC series Equiload truck and the LD, the replacement for the PV, used Austin 16 2.2 litre engines. A replacement for the FV, part of a new common range, with a pressed steel Willenhall Motor Radiator cab, also used by Austin, was introduced in 1954. A BMC six-cylinder diesel engine was available from 1955. The use of the Morris-Commercial name ended in 1956 when the name Morris was adopted. Soon after commercial vehicles were badged as BMC. Possibly the last evidence of Morris was the innovative, ergonomic, angle-vision 'threepenny bit' cab for the FG range introduced in 1960. **GM**

See also STEWART & ARDEN and CABS

Harvey (2000); Harry Edwards, *Morris Commercials – the first years* (1989); *OM* (July and August 1974); Nick Baldwin, 'Morris-Commercial', *VCV*, 3, 9 (1987), pp. 8–10

Morris Motors Ltd (Figure 40) of Cowley began building cars in 1914, with production including some vans based on car chassis. From 1924 vehicles of 1 ton and over were produced by Morris-Commercial in a separate factory, but the car plant continued to manufacture smaller commercials, some of which sold in considerable numbers. The first major success was the Minor van, built from 1930, with the Post Office (q.v.) taking large quantities from 1934 to 1940. The Royal Mail version differed considerably from the standard van. From 1936 10 cwt (½-ton) vans were of semi-forward control layout, with the engine angled to the left to permit a shorter length while still offering generous loadspace compared to rival makes. Synchromesh gearboxes and hydraulic brakes were features.

A further step in van design came in 1948 with the forward-control J series of 10-cwt capacity, a design that was later improved with the JB and J4 series. Some common panels lasted into the Sherpa range, which however was of forward-control layout.

The new Minor van introduced in 1953 was based on the Issigonis-designed car, and initially used an 803 cc engine. With larger engines, initially 948 cc and then 1098 cc, and other improvements it remained in production until 1971. Unlike the car, the van retained a separate chassis. Van production totalled over 337,000, with the Post Office (q.v.) taking 50,000 for mail and telephone work. **JMA**

Morton, John, & Co. Ltd of Coventry was founded in 1866 as a remover and horse-charabanc operator. By the early twentieth century 120 horses were used by the firm. With motorisation, passenger work was dropped in favour of haulage, especially for the Coventry motor industry. Between the wars Dennis and Maudslay lorries were particularly favoured by Mortons, with Eagle of Warwick (q.v.) trailers. AEC, Bedford, Commer and Morris Commercial vehicles were also included in the fleet, which reached 100 by 1935. A Morris car- and van-body delivery contract was of particular significance for Morton, double-deck vehicles being employed; some bus and coach chassis were used as lorries by Morton. Although the firm developed into a specialist vehicle transporter, inter-war traffic also included coal from the Coventry Canal and grain, sugar and general merchandise. Mortons had so much London traffic that it established a London hostel for its drivers in 1933.

Most of the firm was nationalised as part of the Transport Arrangement Realisations in 1948 along with the Klondyke Garage in London but not the own-account work, carried on under C licences, such as coal traffic, furniture delivery, and contract work including delivery of Ferguson tractors. It went on to develop car transport for Rootes. This work was acquired during the 'backdoor nationalisation' phase in 1966, although it retained its identity as Morton's (BRS) Ltd; the car-carrying business was absorbed into Cartransport in 1972. **RAS**

'One hundred and twenty not out', *VCVM*, 2, 7, pp. 116–17

Moth, J Coventon was the managing director of Commercial Car Hirers Ltd, a subsidiary of Commercial Cars Ltd, the makers of what became known as Commer commercial vehicles. Formed in 1909, the subsidiary offered vehicles for contract hire, with or without a driver, to transport goods or run bus services. This was an early move — perhaps the first — by a vehicle maker into contract hire. Not until well after the Second World War did many other vehicle manufacturers offer their own contract hire schemes. The Hirer's business operated well away from the maker's works, initially near Oxford Circus in London and then at a former horse tram shed in Holloway. The business went into liquidation in 1923, not long before Commercial Cars itself failed.

In the mid-1920s Moth set up another contract hire business, Coventons Transport Ltd, using Scammell artics. These carried fleet numbers consisting of a white letter C followed by a number. An identical style of fleet number was used by Herbert Crow beginning with AEC lorries, which has led to suggestions that there was some connection between the two businesses. **JMA/GM**

Motor cycle combinations (Figure 140). Between the wars the motor cycle with purpose-built sidecar (such as a trade-box body) had a role in commercial delivery, one promoted by the British Cycle & Motor Cycle Manufacturers' & Traders' Union, the trade association for the two related industries. During the mid-1920s it organised demonstration tours by commercial motor cycle combinations and in 1927 published an illustrated booklet, *Carry by Sidecar*. Arguments put forward in its favour included that 'the horse eats its head off when standing idle' and the assertion that the motor van was often used for 'absurdly light loads'. Sidecars could be used as milk floats, bill-posters'

trucks, motor cycle-carriers, ice cream vans, or service vehicles and a Pratts Golden Pump Maintenance combination was shown in this role. The Union's advocacy also extended to three-wheel commercial vehicles, such as the Warrick, built at Reading 1900–31. Less likely commercial uses of sidecars included livestock-carriers for small animals and the delivery of coffins to a local workhouse for paupers' funerals. The employment of purpose-built sidecars in a service role continued into the 1960s by the road rescue organisations, the AA and the RAC. An attempt to produce a motor cycle-based workhorse, the By-Van, and a three-wheel load-carrier, the Tri-Van, by Light Delivery Vehicles Ltd of Wolverhampton in the late 1940s is described by Boulton and Parsons. **RAS**

Modern Records Centre, University of Warwick Library, CMCA archive, MSS.204; J Axon, *Sidecars* (Princes Risborough: Shire, 1997); J Boulton and H Parsons, *Powered Vehicles made in the Black Country* (Black Country Society, 2nd ed., 1990), pp. 99–100

Motor Haulage Service of Leamington Spa, Warwickshire, was an example of a haulage business which diversified from its haulage origins, as opposed to businesses such as coal merchants which diversified into road haulage. It was established in the early 1920s by William Henry Yardley after an earlier transport business in which he had been a partner, the Spa Transport Co., had come to an end. Yardley had been a lance corporal in the Royal Engineers in the First World War, but he began MHS with two new Ford TT one-ton lorries, fitted with balanced tipping bodies. A close relationship with local builders developed, for the transport of men and materials to sites within a ten-mile radius. Foreseeing that the builders would in due course acquire their own motor transport, future business was secured by the leasing by MHS of its own source of sand at nearby Lillington. This side of the business, which traded as Midland Sand Supply, continued into the Second World War and led MHS into contracting through its acquisition of a Blaw-Knox excavator.

As well as tippers, MHS operated Bedford platform lorries, primarily for brick haulage from local brickworks, but also for the longer-distance delivery of other local products, such as the carriage of produce from Stratford market to local retailers. Some deliveries of Flavel gas cookers were undertaken, but a contract for the carriage of brake parts from Automotive Products of Leamington to Morris factories at Ward End and Cowley came to an end when Morris's 'Buy British' policy extended to the exclusion of 'foreign' origin vehicles making deliveries and MHS were operating Bedfords, a subsidiary of the American General Motors. Although predominantly Ford and Bedford, the fleet also included individual examples of Leyland and Maudslay and a secondhand Pierce-Arrow. Steam vehicle operation, a secondhand Foden from Flowers' Brewery, lasted only one year. Some MHS lorries were fitted with moving floors (q.v.) to facilitate the handling of cement in bags from Rugby.

Between the wars MHS ran on 60-mile radius B licences; after the war, A licences were successfully applied for. MHS acquired a base in central Leamington, formerly Leamington Mews and Royal Repository and latterly a brewery store, and covered accommodation for 24 vehicles (the size of the fleet on nationalisation) was provided. In the Second World War MHS became a 'controlled undertaking' for South Warwickshire, with Yardley as Unit Controller. After nationalisation he served for eleven years as BRS superintendent at the local Milverton depot After MHS was nationalised, its garage was used by Flavel & Co's transport department. **RAS**

R Storey, 'A pioneer Leamington haulier', *Warwickshire History*, III, 1 (Summer 1975), pp. 37–40

The **Motor Industry Research Association,** commonly known as MIRA, was set up in 1946 as successor to the Automobile Research Committee of the Institution of Automobile Engineers (q.v.), which in turn had grown out of the Research Association of British Motor and Allied Manufacturers, with origins just after the First World War. All were based in laboratories on London's Great West Road.

Its move in 1952 to a former airfield at Nuneaton enabled it to build up a comprehensive range of test facilities for cars, trucks and buses, including a number of road circuits. One of these included a half-mile section which randomly replicated a stretch of rough Belgian pavé (or cobbles) copied from a road near Brussels. It proved invaluable for commercial vehicle makers as the pavé revealed any weaknesses quickly: one mile on the pavé was said to be the equivalent of 1000 normal miles.

Gradually other facilities were added. They included a ride and handling circuit, washboard or corrugated tracks to simulate unpaved roads, watersplashes and wading troughs and a dust tunnel. There were short artificial hills of varying gradients, a wind tunnel able to accept full-sized trucks and a 24 ft diameter screen on which visibility from cabs could be accurately measured. Other equipment was concerned with crash testing and vehicle noise measurement and in emission measuring and monitoring. **JMA**

Shirley and Reid (1996)

The **Motor Legislation Committee** was established in 1919 by ten organisations of which the most important were the Automobile Association (q.v.) and the Society of Motor Manufacturers and Traders (q.v.) to put pressure on government to aid motorists. Initially it wanted wartime restrictions removed, motor fuel made more available, and roads and bridges restored and strengthened. Later it opposed the 20 mph speed limit and other restrictions on motoring. Its chairman was William Joynson-Hicks (q.v.) and vice chairman was Rees Jeffreys (q.v.). Corporate members included the RAC and CMUA. It lobbied against the formation of the Ministry of Transport because it feared that the railway interest would retard the interests of motorists. Throughout the 1920s and 1930s the MLC lobbied government to reduce taxation on motorists and to oppose regulation of motor vehicles and their drivers. It seemed concerned to put the financial burden of road maintenance and improvement entirely on commercial users, so it was seen as representing the extremist end of the private motoring sector. In 1943 it was dissolved, and its work taken over by committees of the SMMT. It had always been dominated by the AA and its stance was seen as too extreme in the new atmosphere of partnership in the war effort.   **JA**

Plowden (1973); Sean O'Connell, *The Car in British Society: class, gender and motoring 1896–1939* (Manchester University Press, 1998), pp. 137–9; Hamer (1987), pp. 29–32

Motor Panels (Coventry) Ltd, now part of the Mayflower group, was founded in 1924 to produce wings, panels, bonnets and other bodywork components for the motor industry. It was acquired by Rubery Owen (q.v.) in 1943 and played an important role in commercial vehicle production after the war by its output of all-metal cabs, not only for smaller manufacturers such as Guy, Seddon and Thornycroft, but also for Leyland. 135,000 examples were produced of the shared LAD cab design of 1958, utilised by Leyland, Dodge and Albion. Motor Panels subsequently produced cabs for Leyland's T45 range. It made the steel cabs for many heavy vehicles in the 1960s and 1970s including Foden and Scammell. It also manufactured panel units for such van makers as the Standard Motor Co. and Morris Commercial and more recently modified Ford Transit vans to provide a higher capacity by raising the roofline.   **RAS**

N Baldwin, 'New cabs for old', *VCVM*, 51 (January 1994), pp. 215–17; 'Cabs off the peg', *Vintage Lorry Annual*, 1 (1979) and 3 (1981)

The **Motor Union** was created by the Automobile Club of Great Britain and Ireland (later to become the Royal Automobile Club) in 1903. It was formed to represent the growing number of motor owners while retaining the exclusivity of the Automobile Club. It became independent of the RAC in 1907 and then the Automobile Association took it over in 1910. It grew rapidly, having more than 11,000 members by 1906, over three times as many as

its parent body, the RAC. It was founded to act as a political pressure group, and it tried to reserve this role to itself, leaving the AA to organise road patrols and the RAC to deal with sporting events. Things did not work out so neatly and rivalry continued until the merger in 1910. Its role was to pressure government into freeing up road traffic and oppose any pending legislation it deemed anti-motorist. In 1908 it accepted the principle of the introduction of motor taxation, providing that the proceeds were used to improve the road system. It also encouraged innovative thinking in motor transport, for instance, offering a prize in 1906 for an essay on the use of alcohol as a motor fuel at a time of concern over petrol supplies. Its first and only secretary was W Rees Jeffreys (q.v.).   **JA**

Plowden (1973); Seth-Smith (1975); Hamer (1987)

The **Motor Van, Wagon & Omnibus Owners & Users Association** was an offshoot in 1903 of the Motor Union (q.v.). In 1907 it took the shorter name of the Commercial Motor Users Association (q.v.). The Association gave evidence to the 1903 Committee arguing for a maximum tare weight for commercial vehicles of six tons. Anything less was uneconomic, as had been shown in the Lancashire Heavy Motor Vehicle Trials (q.v.), because the load carried was too small. In 1905 the Association was willing to accept taxation on motor vehicles providing that the money so raised was spent on improving the roads. Its secretary was W Rees Jeffreys (q.v.) and its chairman was R E B Crompton (q.v.). In 1906 it was involved in discussions with the War Office over the shape and scale of the subsidy scheme (q.v.) that the WO might introduce as a method of obtaining mechanical goods transport in an emergency.   **JA**

E S Shrapnell-Smith, 'Five decades of commercial road transport with inferences about its future', *The Journal of the Institute of Transport* (1946), pp. 214–29; Gibson (2001)

Movers Institute, see BRITISH ASSOCIATION OF REMOVERS

Moving floor (Figure 141). In the First World War some Army Roads Department lorries were fitted with the Wilkins patent movable floor. The hand-operated, continuous belt was a popular method of loading and unloading lorries in the 1930s, before the introduction of the hydraulic ram and mechanical handling equipment. Modern developments of the basic design are still built.

C H Johnson & Sons Ltd of Manchester produced a moving floor system (patent no. 293,997 of 1928) of a flexible rubber composition, under geared control, and hand powered from either end of the vehicle. Longitudinal operation was normal, but an either-side discharge was available. Claimed advantages were the capacity to load as well as discharge; the elimination of chassis strains caused by a tipping body; the ability to discharge a bulk load on uneven terrain or in restricted height areas where a tipper would be at a disadvantage; and the combination of flat and tipper body features in a single vehicle. Customers included the GWR, Hovis, the Cement Marketing Co. Ltd and W E Chivers & Son Ltd of Devizes. The Principality Wagon Co. Ltd of Cardiff produced a similar system in the 1930s (perhaps as successors to Johnsons). Its customers included the GWR and the North of Scotland Coaling Co. Ltd of Aberdeen. In 1933 Shelvoke & Drewry acquired the patent of the Principality moving floor refuse collector for its sole use. Principality was taken over by Bromilow & Edwards of Bolton (see EDBRO).

Other moving floor makers included Transport Engineering Ltd of London SE1, which produced both rubber moving floors and some of rust-proofed steel slats of a patent hollow section, enclosed between two longitudinal steel channels, hand-operated and driven by roller chains. Customers included the LMSR. The Eagle Engineering Co. Ltd of Warwick (q.v.) displayed an Eagle 6-ton patent moving floor general purpose trailer at the 1937 Commercial Motor Show.

The moving floor was also used for carrying products such as powdered material that are of low weight and therefore liable to stick if tipped in a conventional tipper. Today such products are carried in a tanker and unloaded by pumping or air pressure.

A form of moving floor — the roller-bed floor — was used on vehicles collecting the igloo-type goods containers carried on aircraft. Today's main use is on semi-trailers carrying bulk waste to tips where unstable ground makes use of tippers hazardous. It is also claimed to be superior to ejector bodies, since its mechanism can be mounted below floor level and does not occupy loadspace. Typical moving floors are made of high-grade aluminium slats with seals between each one and powered by a pump driving a hydraulic system. The US-built Keith Walking Floor is widely used and sometimes called a running floor because of its relatively high speed.

Other examples of moving floor usage include Castle Cement, which uses curtain-sided trailers to deliver cement to London and returns with scrap tyres for burning in its Leicestershire kiln, and Edgar Shepherd of Darlington which has a trailer for carrying woodchips: it can discharge a load in eight to ten minutes. A 1934 Foden with drawbar trailer, both fitted with a moving floor, have been preserved by F B Atkins & Sons of Derby.   **RAS/JMA**

R&RTHC *Newsletter*, 6 (August 1994), p. 6; *CM* (26 March 1919), p. 257; (8 November 1935); p. 102; Commercial Motor Transport Exhibition 1937 *Catalogue: Railway-owned Commercial Vehicles* (1987); *VCV* Supplement (April 1999), p. III

Muck-away (Figure 142) is a term which has come into general use in the haulage industry since the Second World War to describe operations, often by specialist contractors, involving the removal of demolition spoil. The activity itself has a longer history; for example, Hales Waste Control, the Ready Mixed Concrete (q.v.) subsidiary, was established in the late nineteenth century to supply clinker and remove and dispose of construction rubble. Hales Clinkers was bought by St Albans Sand & Gravel and passed with that business to RMC when it was sold by the Berk group, in 1970.   **RAS**

Michael Cassell, *The Readymixers: the story of RMC 1931 to 1986* (Pencorp, 1986)

N

Napier, D, & Son Ltd, of Lambeth then Acton, were precision engineers, who became best known as producers of quality cars and of London taxi-cabs, 1908–11. A few commercial vehicles were produced from 1901, but a Business Vehicle Department was not opened until 1912. In the following year W&G Express Carriers (q.v.) rebodied some of their Napier cabs for van service and W&G's fleet of 100 Napier vans was used in advertising for Napier Business Vehicles. Output of business vehicles reached 91 in 1912, 121 in 1913 and 363 in 1914, though the last figure includes some army lorries. Many body types were tried, including tipping wagons, mail vans and lorries. Napier followed with heavier chassis, including a 2½-ton lorry for the Army. This became a 2-tonner and the sole commercial chassis offered by Napier after the war. From 1920 Napier concentrated on aero engines, although a prototype three-wheeled mechanical horse (q.v.) was developed in conjunction with the LNER in 1931, before a change of plan led to the sale of this design to Scammell.   **RAS**

C H Wilson and W J Reader, *Men & Machines: D Napier & Son 1808–1958* (Weidenfeld & Nicolson, 1958), pp. 94–102

The **National Alliance of Commercial Road Transport Associations & Federations** was formed in the First World War in response to the pressure from the National Transport Workers' Federation (q.v.) for national awards for carters and a national joint industrial council. The Alliance, which agreed to the Liverpool employers remaining outside, as their rate was already above the national claim, was one of three employers' bodies represented on the short-lived NJIC of 1919.   **RAS**

Coates and Topham (1994), pp. 651, 696

National Association of Furniture Warehousemen & Removers, see BRITISH ASSOCIATION OF REMOVERS

National Carriers Ltd was created under the Transport Act 1968 to take over the unprofitable Sundries division of British Railways and in 1969 was transferred to the new National Freight Corporation (q.v.). Its assets were 215 depots (many of which were already closed, a dowry that was to bring great financial benefit to the NFC in later years) and 6600 motor vehicles. In 1968 it had carried 1.9 million tons of less-than-wagonload goods or 'smalls'. NCL also took over the rest of BR's cartage fleet (2900 vehicles with drivers) used primarily for the Rail Express Parcels Service, but also for full-load goods traffic (principally steel), and henceforth provided BR's cartage requirements under a contract hire agreement. In total NCL inherited 24,700 former BR staff. (See RAILWAY-OWNED ROAD TRANSPORT)

The government immediately put pressure on the NFC to merge NCL, which was making heavy losses, with BRS Parcels, then making only poor profits. The NFC resisted. The two were complementary rather than competing, serving different markets: the packages carried by BRS were generally less than 1 cwt, whereas NCL's were generally in the range 1 cwt–3 tons; NCL delivered to commercial and industrial premises, whereas BRS, like REPS and the Post Office, also had a share of the home delivery market. The NFC would also have faced strong opposition to a merger from the two unions involved, the National Union of Railwaymen for NCL and the Transport & General Workers (q.v.) for BRS.

In 1971 it was decided to phase out most of the inherited fleet of articulated vehicles engaged in local collection and delivery work in favour of integral vans of 600 or 700 cu ft capacity. Studies had shown that the pattern of traffic handling did not benefit from the use of artics, which cost more to buy and run. 324 vans on BLMC FG, Commer KN40 and Bedford J3 chassis were bodied by Freight-Bonallack over a six-month period, 129 of them carrying REPS livery. All weighed just under 3 tons unladen, so their drivers did not need a heavy goods vehicle driving licence.

In its first year NCL had made a trading loss of £15.1m on a turnover of £47.4m, but the 1968 Act provided for government grants to cover a 5-year transition to profitability. By abolishing quantity licensing, however, the Act had also opened up the market to free competition. Although NCL made considerable progress in reducing costs, both its own traffic and that of its biggest customer, REPS, was declining. It began to diversify into much more profitable fields. Fashionflow Ltd, a specialised distribution service for packaged clothing launched in 1974, was followed by Chinaflow for the pottery and glass industries in 1976 and Newsflow for the newspaper industry in 1986. A total distribution service for contract customers was launched in 1976. In 1977 NCL at last produced its first trading profit. By this time it had reduced its depots to 85, its fleet of motor vehicles to 6,100 and its staff to 13,500. As a reward for this progress, the Transport Act 1978 wrote off £34 million of NCL's capital debt, reimbursed its payments in respect of the pension and concessionary travel rights of its ex-BR staff, and provided for £15 million of investment grants.

In 1983 the old and new services were separated into a Parcels Division and a Contract Services Division respectively and the first steps made towards a merger of the former with Roadline UK, the renamed BRS Parcels. In Scotland the two had already been brought together in 1981 under the name of Scottish Parcel Services Ltd and full integration was well-advanced. The union problem still remained, however. The local TGWU officials did not want a merger but preferred that NCL should be closed, so taking all the job losses. However, in 1986 the NFC decided to close Roadline's home delivery service and absorb the rest into NCL's Parcels Division. This then traded briefly as National Carriers-Roadline and then from 1987 as Lynx Express Delivery Network (q.v.). Scottish Parcels Service was brought under its management in 1988. The division was formally renamed Lynx Express Delivery Network Ltd in 1995 and sold to its management in 1997.

In 1988 NCL's Contract Services Division became part of the NFC's new Logistics Division and began trading under the Exel Logistics (q.v.) name. In 1995 the NCL name was formally extinguished when it was amalgamated with Exel Logistics Ltd and British Road Services to form NFC (UK) Ltd, still trading as Exel Logistics. **JA/JMA/GAB**

NFC, *Annual Reports & Accounts*, 1969-99; Freight Integration Council (1970); National Board for Prices & Incomes (1971); Thompson (1991)

The **National Freight Corporation** was formed in 1969 under the provisions of the Transport Act 1968 to bring together the remnants of the nationalised road transport industry that had been nationalised in 1948 and partly denationalised in 1953-6. Its main components were British Road Services (q.v.), BRS Parcels (q.v.), Pickfords (q.v.) and Tayforth Ltd (q.v.), taken over from the Transport Holding Company (q.v.), and National Carriers Ltd (q.v.) and Freightliners Ltd (q.v.) from BR. It inherited 66,000 staff and 29,000 motor vehicles. The first chairman was Sir Reginald Wilson (q.v.), followed by D. E. A. [Sir Daniel] Pettit (q.v.).

Facing serious competition from private road haulage firms, the NFC set about rationalising its services and assets and reducing the labour force. By 1975 the staff had been reduced by a third and the vehicles by a quarter. In 1971-2, in anticipation of the UK's accession to the EC in 1973, it embarked on expansion into Europe under the name of Pickfords International Ltd, through purchase of haulage firms in Belgium, West Germany, Netherlands and France. A trading loss of £14 million in 1969 was transformed into a trading profit in 1972, but the oil crisis of 1973/4 hit NFC hard and in 1975 it reported a trading loss of over £7 million. The corporate management was strengthened in 1976 by appointing Peter Thompson (q.v.), previously managing director of BRS, executive vice-chairman operations and then chief executive. He set about bringing financial probity, withdrawing from the loss-making European ventures, further reducing the work force (down to 30,600 in 1980), retiring older, bureaucratic managers and promoting younger, entrepreneurial ones, persuading the government to write down the capital debt, so reducing interest charges, and decentralising much of the decision-making.

In 1979 the Thatcher government came into power with the aim of reducing the role played by the government in economic affairs. It wished to reduce government subsidies to loss-making industries and hand some back to the private sector. The NFC was a prime candidate for such a process, but partly because of the economic downturn of the early 1980s, problems over pension provision (or the lack of it), and Thompson's advocacy of an alternative course, this did not take place. The management team led a buy-out, but not as then fashionable a management buy-out, but rather an employee buy-out, whereby all the workers could buy shares and indeed were encouraged to do so. The advantage to the government was that it started the privatisation programme, got it moving quickly and with much good publicity compared to the likely effects if the firm had been sold to, and rationalised by, a rival. Inevitably the employees could not raise all the money, and a consortium of banks put up about 20 per cent of the equity. Employees, their families and pensioners put up the vast majority of the equity finance, about £7 million in all. The total price was about £53 million. The NFC became the employee-owned National Freight Consortium plc in 1982, with Peter Thompson as chairman (Sir Robert Lawrence had been chairman since 1979 during the long privatisation process).

The new company was committed to expanding profits and employment, particularly through expansion overseas, but needed to reduce costs. Its considerable portfolio of surplus property, following rationalisation of its overlapping networks of depots, was sold. Roadline UK Ltd (the renamed BRS Parcels) and the parcels division of National Carriers were merged and given the name Lynx Express Delivery (q.v.). The overseas expansion was led by Pickfords Removals Ltd, which acquired an Australian removals business in 1981, followed by others in Europe, North America and the Far East. In 1988 it bought the largest removals firm in the USA, Allied Van Lines, and began to adopt Allied Pickfords as its world-wide brand name.

At home the recession of the early 1980s and the prevailing management theory that firms should concentrate on core business encouraged manufacturers and retail groups to hire-in their transport and distribution requirements. The NFC, which was already operating a wide range of specialised services such as contract distribution, truck rental, cold storage, tank storage and distribution, and waste management, was well placed to become market leader. The acquisition in 1985 of the SPD Group (q.v.) was followed by the creation of NFC's highly successful Exel Logistics Division (q.v.), which also began to make acquisitions in the USA, western Europe and the Far East. The NFC's profit increased steadily from £23 million in 1983 to £117 million in 1993, a return on capital of around 20 per cent, while employment grew by about 10,000. In 1989 the company abbreviated its name to NFC plc and was granted stock exchange listing, so allowing some of the employees to cash in their much-enhanced shares and allowing the firm to draw on a wider pool of capital. In 1991 Sir Peter Thompson was succeeded as chief executive by James Watson, his deputy. Watson took a more profit-orientated view and had to be more aware of City sentiment. Thus in 1991 about five per cent of the staff were made redundant at the same time as further acquisitions were made abroad to give NFC a more international scope. In 1991–2 Pickfords Travel was seen as peripheral to the core business and sold. In order to reduce gearing, in 1993 a rights issue was launched to raise £263 million. In 1994 a new chairman, Sir Christopher Bland of London Weekend TV, was appointed. By 1998 the employees owned only 7 per cent of the shares and the unique ownership pattern no longer existed. In further rationalisations, the NFC sold Lynx Express to a management buy-out in 1997 and in 1999 it sold its Allied Pickfords Moving Services division to concentrate on logistics in the retail, consumer, automotive and electronics sectors. NFC lost its identity in 2000 when it merged with Ocean Group plc to form Exel plc.   **JA/GAB**

NFC, *Annual Reports & Accounts*, 1969–99; Turnbull (1979), p. 178; Pryke (1981), ch. 7; Thompson (1991); *IDCH*, 6 (1992), pp. 412–14; McLachlan (1983); *Private Eye* (25 December 1998); *Evening Standard* (21 February 2000)

The **National Road Transport Clearing House Ltd** was registered in 1921, with the head office in Holborn and a countrywide network of offices. It was launched with a full front-page advertisement in the *Daily Mail* in May 1922, setting out a table of standard rates, but it proved to be over-ambitious and short-lived. According to Gammons (admittedly not a neutral commentator), some of those involved lacked the necessary transport experience or training. Publication of its rates, even though these only applied to class 3 traffic in 1-ton lots, enabled independent hauliers to profit by under-cutting. The company was dissolved by court order in July 1923 at which time Sir Maxwell Hicks was in control and its 20 Scammells were sold. Earlier J F Shaw had been managing director. Two of its directors, A M Davis and Claude Barrington (q.v.), subsequently appeared as directors of a clearing house under the title Carey, Davis & Thomas Ltd. **RAS**

Gammons (1931); Dunbar (1981).

The **National Road Transport Employers' Federation** was founded in 1920 by fifteen local associations of cart and lorry owners. One of the largest of these was the London Association which included Carter Paterson and Pickfords. The Federation's secretary was R P Bailey, who was also secretary of the London & Home Counties Haulage Contractors' Association. It came to include the National Alliance of Commercial Road Transport Associations & Federations and the National Union of Horse & Motor Vehicle Owners' Associations.

In 1929 P R Turner, vice-president of the Federation, giving evidence to the Royal Commission on Transport, claimed the Federation represented about 3000 firms owning 80,000 horse-drawn vehicles and 50,000 motor vehicles. By 1938 G W Quick-Smith (q.v.) was assistant secretary and was

instrumental in finding a rapprochement between the railways and road transport interests over the rates for carrying small parcels. **RAS**

Birch and Harper (1995); Dunbar (1981)

The **National Road Transport Federation** was established in 1945 to deal with matters of common interest to the Road Haulage Association (q.v.), the Traders' Road Transport Association (q.v.) and the Passenger Vehicle Operators' Association. For a period the Federation provided common secretarial services and joint premises for the three bodies. In time its constituents wished to act completely independently and voluntary winding-up was approved in 1963, although the RHA chairman at the time, Derek Good, regretted the loss of a body which could speak for the entire industry. **RAS**

Birch and Harper (1995), pp. 41, 72, 215–16

National Safety First Association, see ROYAL SOCIETY FOR THE PREVENTION OF ACCIDENTS

The **National Traction Engine Owners' & Users' Association** was established in 1893 on the initiative of the Kent County Engine Owners' Association, one of the members of which was Jesse Ellis & Co. Ltd (q.v.). Supported by a number of engine manufacturers, the Association had as its legal adviser William Joynson-Hicks (q.v.), who marshalled its evidence to the Select Committee in 1896 with beneficial effects for the operators of traction engines on roads in the ensuing Locomotives Act 1898. He also won a notable victory for engine owners in the case of Monmouth County Council *v.* Scott, a quarry owner prevented from using a traction engine on public roads. **RAS**

R A Whitehead, *The Age of the Traction Engine* (Shepperton: Ian Allan, 1970), ch. 4; McTaggart (1987), p. 18; The Association's records are in the Rural History Centre, University of Reading

The **National Traders Traffic Association** was the new name adopted in 1964 for the Mansion House Association (q.v.), the change being motivated by the wish that it should be self-explanatory whereas the previous title was far from that. The Association took the side of the user of goods transport and kept an eye on the railways and road haulage firms. It ceased to have a separate existence in 1969 when it amalgamated with the Traders Road Transport Association and the Traders Co-ordinating Committee on Transport to form the Freight Transport Association (q.v.). **JA**

The **National Transport Workers Federation** was founded in 1910. It brought together unions of seamen, dockers and carters; railwaymen and road passenger workers held aloof, considering the NTWF to have little substance, although licensed vehicle workers and tramwaymen joined later, in 1916 and 1918. Its immediate aims were to prevent overlapping of membership in the transport sector, to achieve a general recognition of the cards of each member society, and to promote better organisation. A national seamen's and dockers' strike occurred soon after its foundation. The NTWF district committee in Liverpool, led by Tom Mann, played an important role in that city's disputes of 1911. Nationally the NTWF's reaction was more cautious and in the shipping and docks disputes of 1912 it suffered setbacks, as its call for a national strike failed and some of its constituent unions lost members. However, the NTWF had a threefold significance for road transport industrial relations. Firstly, as recognised by the young Ernest Bevin from his experience at Bristol, common union membership by carters and dockers strengthened the position of both. Secondly, the action of the NTWF during the First World War in organising sectional conferences of carters and making a national wage claim helped pave the way for the post-war National Joint Industrial Council for the road haulage industry. In the event this proved to be short-lived, but it prefigured the Road Haulage Wages Board (q.v.) introduced in 1938. Thirdly, the NTWF helped prepare for the amalgamations which resulted in the Transport & General Workers' Union in 1922, hastening its own demise in 1927. **RAS/PS**

Hugh Clegg, *A History of British Trade Unions since 1889*, 2: *1911–1933* (Oxford: Clarendon Press, 1985); Arthur Marsh and V Ryan, *Historical Directory of Trade Unions*, 3 (Gower, 1987); Coates and Topham (1991)

The **National Union of Vehicle Workers** was the direct successor to the London Carmen's Trade Union, formed in 1888 as part of the 'New Unionism' upsurge in London's East End. Membership in 1889 stood at 6,067, but then quickly fell to 2,068 by 1892. The union held on and the organisation was rebuilt: by 1910 it had 5,690 members in 102 branches. The change of name adopted in 1912 reflected the goal of creating a national industrial union for workers in road transport. In 1920 it amalgamated with the Association of Dairymen's Assistants, a London-based organisation of milk roundsmen.

In 1921 the NUVW held detailed negotiations with its main rival, the United Vehicle Workers' Union (q.v.), which was mainly a road passenger union, to form a new organisation for all road transport workers. These talks were aborted, however, when the NUVW decided to join the amalgamation with the dockers' unions to create the TGWU (q.v.). The core of the NUVW remained in London's East End and was a key component of the TGWU Area 1 Road Transport Commercial trade group, which gave solid support to the 1926 General Strike (q.v.). **PS**

Nationalisation (Figure 143) of inland transport as a means of achieving an integrated or co-ordinated national transport system (rather than just railway nationalisation which was a much older idea) began to emerge as a loosely-defined political aim as early as 1917. Although the Labour Party adopted a general socialist policy of nationalisation in 1918, its immediate aim was confined to railways, coal and electric power. The principle of nationalising all transport was adopted by the Labour Party Conference in 1932, but it was the practical experience of government control of transport during the Second World War that provided the foundation for the proposals in the Labour Party's 1945 election manifesto. The form of nationalisation that was proposed was an independent body under public control, modelled on the London Passenger Transport Board, which had been operating with manifest success since 1933. The subsequent Transport Bill was vigorously opposed by the Road Haulage Association (q.v.) and British Road Federation (q.v.), but passed into law as the Transport Act 1947.

With effect from 1 January 1948 the Act created the British Transport Commission and, beneath it, a number of Executives, including the Road Transport Executive — renamed the Road Haulage Executive on 20 June 1949 to allow the formation of a separate Road Passenger Executive. The BTC was required to take over firms involved predominantly in 'ordinary long distance carriage for hire or reward' and from February 1950, the BTC was given sole rights to operate such services. Long distance was defined as a journey of 40 miles or upwards or one extending more than 25 miles from the vehicle's operating centre (q.v.). The term 'ordinary' indicated that some types of cargo requiring specialised vehicles were excluded from this legislation: liquids in tankers; goods for which there was a statutory requirement for specially-designed vehicles (i.e. explosives and inflammable goods); furniture removals; meat; livestock; felled timber on specially-constructed vehicles; and abnormal indivisible loads. Nevertheless the BTC became involved in several of these 'excluded' traffics through its inheritance of Pickfords Ltd (q.v.).

The BTC took over four classes of road haulage firm. Firstly the 45 railway-owned companies (see RAILWAY-OWNED ROAD TRANSPORT) vested in the BTC from 1948; secondly, the principal haulage companies ('primary undertakings') acquired by agreement as quickly as possible so that their assets and management could form the skeleton of the transitional organisation; thirdly other significant companies ('secondary under-takings') acquired by agreement or, after 1 October 1948, by compulsory purchase; finally the remainder: small firms acquired by compulsory purchase. Initially firms retained their own company structure and name, but with the insertion of '(BTC)' and were kept as independent units with their own trading accounts, but the secondary and remainder undertakings were put under the direction of a primary undertaking.

By August 1949 the RHE was ready to merge all the individual general haulage and parcels companies and the branches of the national undertakings that it had inherited and acquired into a national organisation called British Road Services (q.v.). Thus within twenty months more than one thousand and ultimately nearly four thousand companies, none of which were of more than modest size, were shaped into a single giant enterprise while maintaining continuity of the service to customers — a significant achievement. What had been the most competitive of all industries after agriculture was now a monolithic structure, although not truly a monopoly because customers continued to have the option of using their own C-licence vehicles (see LICENSING OF GOODS VEHICLE OPERATORS). Indeed one effect of nationalisation was a rapid rise in the applications for C-licences (see STRUCTURE OF THE INDUSTRY).

The process of acquisition and compensation was subject to the independent control of the Transport Arbitration Tribunal (q.v.). The compensation prescribed in the Act to be paid to the owners of compulsorily-acquired undertakings was calculated in three parts: the replacement cost of the vehicles, less depreciation; the market value of other property; and, in consideration of cessation of the vendor's business (goodwill), a sum between twice and five times its average net annual profit over the previous three years depending on the likelihood of this level of profit being maintained. Terms 'corresponding as closely as possible' were offered for companies that were acquired by agreement, but erred on the generous side. Another incentive to voluntary acquisition was payment in cash. Compensation for compulsory acquisitions was generally given in British Transport stock, although payments of up to £2000 could be in cash.

From the appointed day, operators of A- and B-licence vehicles could not use them further than 25 miles from their operating centre unless issued with a permit by the BTC, but long-distance carriage of the 'excepted' traffics was exempt. It was originally intended that C-licence vehicles would be similarly controlled, but this provision was withdrawn by the government in response to strong opposition from trade and industry, not least from the influential Co-operative societies (q.v.). Hauliers licensed to operate long-distance services in November 1946, but not nationalised, were entitled to 'original' permits, which the BTC could revoke or modify after one year; if such a haulier were refused an original permit, or if the permit were revoked or modified in a way that substantially interfered with his business, he could require the BTC to acquire the business. 12,035 original permits were issued in 1950, but they were reduced to 6806 after one year. In addition there were 2500–3000 ordinary permits and 25–100 job permits current at any one time.

By the end of 1951 the RHE had acquired 3766 undertakings, employed 80,212 staff and owned 41,265 motor vehicles. It also acquired its own body-builder, Star Bodies (BRS) Ltd. There were still several thousand small firms waiting to be served with acquisition notices when the process of nationalisation came to an end by the election in 1951 of a Conservative government committed to allow private hauliers to re-enter the business (see DENATIONALISATION). **GAB**

G W Quick Smith, *The Transport Act, 1947, as it affects the road transport industry* (1948 edn); British Transport Commission, *Annual Reports and Accounts* (1948–1951); P S Bagwell, *The Railwaymen: the history of the National Union of Railwaymen*, [vol. 1] (1963) pp. 370–2, 619–21; Bonavia (1987); Coates and Topham (1991)

Nevile, Sir Sydney Oswald (1873–1969), brewer, made significant contributions to the development of brewery transport (q.v.). While head brewer at Brandon's Putney Brewery he introduced in 1900 a road tank wagon to deliver beer in bulk from brewery to bottling store. Its success encouraged him to patent the system and set up the Bulk Beer Delivery Co.

for bulk deliveries to public houses. He joined Whitbreads as a director in 1919, initiated motorisation of their fleet and road tankers for bulk delivery. With experience of electric vehicles while at Brandon's Brewery he influenced Whitbreads' acquisition of 15 GV electric wagons for London local delivery, arguing that conversion to electric vehicles was easier for horse-men than learning to drive a petrol lorry with gears. **RAS**

Ingram (1992); *DBB*; Sydney Nevile, *Seventy Rolling Years* (Faber, 1958)

Neville Industries Ltd was built up by George Neville III in the post-war period to exploit various commercial-vehicle innovations. He was already undertaking forward-control conversion on various bonneted chassis to meet the demand for greater load-carrying length, when he developed what was one of the first tilt-cabs, filing a patent in 1944 (see CABS). Vehicles such as Bedford and Thornycroft were ordered as bare chassis. Neville then moved driving seat, steering column, dash and pedals forward about two feet and added an all-new, curved cab shell. The effect was to increase the body length by about 3 ft 6 in, but access to the engine for maintenance proved a problem, leading to the 'swinging' or tilt-cab, at first moved manually, then handle-wound with a double rack-and-pinion. Neville was also a Bedford dealer. In the 1950s Neville Industries was appointed agents and converters for the Henry Meadows diesel engine. In 1964 the company moved into former BR premises at Mansfield; this became the Coalite Group's Neville-Charrold, as George Neville sold Neville Industries in 1968 to pay death duties. From the mid-1960s Neville concentrated on tipper construction. Lighter, simpler extrusions were used for van bodies. The Dumptrailer was introduced, based on the American configuration of a chassis-less, single-axle trailer, pivoting on the axle to tip. In 1986 George Neville handed over the managing directorship of George Neville Truck Equipment Ltd to his son, Michael, and set up George Neville Transport Safety Systems Ltd, concentrating on such devices as swing-out trailer landing legs and the Easysheet for the sheeting and unsheeting of a load single-handed from ground level. **RAS**

Truck (June 1986), pp. 66–7, 91

Newspaper traffic (Figures 41 and 144). Newspaper companies were among the first to use motor van delivery for short distances. Most long-distance newspaper traffic was in the hands of wholesalers like W H Smith or John Menzies, who used railways, with horse, then motor servicing of their wholesale depots. In August 1906 Pickfords carried the *Daily Mail* and *Daily Mirror* to south coast seaside towns using a 2-ton James & Brown van. The *Newcastle Chronicle* employed six Clement-Talbot vans each carrying 15 cwt of newspapers from 1903 and by 1912 the *London Chronicle* used 30 one-ton vans for delivery. Newspaper-delivery vans, sometimes on car chassis and in distinctive liveries, have been a feature of London and other large cities for speedy delivery to sales points through dense traffic, especially of evening papers. Their manoeuvrability, speed and flexibility made them ideal for this. Examples include Alvis-based vans for the *Midland Daily Telegraph,* a specially developed Star van for the *Evening Standard* in 1928, at least ten Dodge 15-cwt vans for the London evening paper the *Star* in 1938, Humber Super Snipes in 1947 with angular, purpose-built bodywork operated by United for the *Evening Standard* and Austin FX taxi-based vans for the *Evening News*.

Larger vehicles were needed for delivery to mainline stations for rail distribution to the provinces, such as McNamara's 1-ton Commers for *The Times* in 1937 with replaceable name-panels for daytime change of use, the 1955 fleet of Guy Wolf vans for the *Daily Mirror* group with special Boalloy bodies and the 1958 Dennis Heron 2-ton lorry for the *Sunday Pictorial*. Special vans were also commissioned for longer-distance road delivery, such as the *Belfast Telegraph* Austin Sheerline custom-built van of 1951, which travelled over 50,000 miles per annum on its Londonderry distribution run. In 1934 W H Smith set up WHS Transport Ltd, operating

vehicles on A and B licences to take advantage of regular daily slack periods for a variety of traffics. The change of the licensing system led Smiths to enter parcels traffic in the early 1970s. Townsends Carriers Ltd of Higham Ferrers, acquired in 1972 in connection with the project, was sold to Lex Wilkinson (q.v.) in 1974. Bedford TJ, CA, CF, and TL, Ford Transit and Cargo, and Leyland 45 models featured prominently with WHS from the 1960s to the 1990s. Whilst WHS operated more than 500 vehicles itself, 300 were on contract hire from Toler Hire, a major Bedford user, and a further 300 were provided by contractors. Toler Hire also provided a fleet for London evening paper deliveries. The move away from Fleet Street to Docklands in the 1980s and the Wapping dispute of 1986, which saw TNT (q.v.) create Newsfast to move *The Times* from the new production site by road rather than rail, marked the end of long-distance rail services for newspaper traffic, with their travelling packers. Firms like Newsfast and Exel took over this role. In the 1990s the Daily Mirror Group split its road distribution between Eddie Stobart (q.v.) for the south of the country and TNT, (not Newsfast) for the north. **RAS**

CM (1906 and 1912); C Chesterton, 'First with the News', *Heritage Commercials,* 153 (September 2002), pp. 53–5

NFC, see NATIONAL FREIGHT CORPORATION

Nicknames (Figure 145) which have been applied to particular vehicle and body types or specific models include: 'boxing ring', a brewers' dray body, with load-restraining chains mounted on metal stanchions around the edge of the platform; 'Chinese six' (q.v.), the six-wheeled chassis configuration with the twin steering axles at the front of the vehicle, which seemed to lorry drivers to be back to front; 'greedy boards' are additional removable boards placed above existing high sides to enable a larger quantity of a relatively light but high volume load such as coke to be carried; 'drag' or 'dangler', a drawbar trailer; 'Flying Pig', a Dennis 40/45-cwt chassis of 1935 with its engine ahead of the front axle; 'Mickey

Mouse', a Foden S21 fibre glass cab design which had prominent black wings like Mickey's ears and headlamps for eyes; 'Noddy van', the specially-designed BRS parcels van, named after Enid Blyton's famous children's character; 'reefer', a refrigerated lorry or trailer; 'Sabrina', the semi-forward-control ERF of 1957–63 after the well-endowed show business personality of that time (this had a three-man cab, useful for brewery deliveries, but never sold well, only 126 being built; it was unusual in being semi-bonnetted but the bonnet did not open, access to the engine being in the cab); 'Showboat', the van-bodied Scammell Luton van, which resembled a Mississippi paddle steamer; 'Sputnik', an alternative name for the Mickey Mouse Foden which had a futuristic appearance. **RAS**

N Larkin, 'Sabrina style', *CVC*, 7, 6 (2002), pp. 4–9

Nissan, the Japanese vehicle manufacturer, is best known in the UK for its cars and light commercials. The Nissan Motor Co Ltd was established in 1934. Its car connections with the UK date back to 1953, when licensed production in Japan of the Austin A40 and A50 began. A factory in the UK for car production was opened at Sunderland in 1985. Commercial vehicle penetration of the UK market has been restricted to light commercials, produced in Barcelona, and was particularly associated with the tradesman's workhorse, the Cabstar light lorry. Renault acquired a 36 per cent stake in Nissan in 1999. **RAS**

transporte mundial: Catalogo 2000; Truck (February 2001), pp. 38–9; Modern Records Centre, University of Warwick Library (MSS.226: passim)

Noddy van, see NICKNAMES

Nomenclature. A number of lorry manufacturers have favoured names for their vehicle types, sometimes in series. Perhaps the best known and most memorable was the inter-war Leyland zoo: the 4-wheel Badger, Beaver, Bison, Buffalo and Bull, the 6-wheel Hippo and Rhino and the appropriately-named 8-wheel Octopus. The lightweight Cub could appear as a lorry as well as a bus, with the Lynx as a variant. There were also the Terrier of 1928 and a later development, the Retriever. An ingenious animal name was the Steer, a twin-steer 6-wheel lorry. After the war, the Comet normal control four-wheeler marked a breakaway from the traditional system.

Broadly contemporaneous with Leyland's zoo was AEC's group of M names, denoting authority and power: Majestic, Mammoth, Mammoth Major, Mandator, Matador and Monarch, or speed: Mercury (and also Ranger). A less prominent range, Walker Brothers' Pagefield series, also bore names with a common initial: Paladin, Paragon, Pathfinder, Pegasix and Plantagenet. A poignant name was that of Guy Motors' final lorry design, the Big J of 1964. This denoted the Big Jaguar, a reflection of Sir William Lyons' attempt to graft a commercial vehicle range to the Jaguar-Daimler marques. As well as being memorable brand names, the word-association conjured up favourable attributes such as power, size, or speed or made inanimate objects seem more friendly.

The naming of individual vehicles by their owners is a feature of some fleets, such as that of Eddie Stobart (q.v.), each carrying a woman's first name. Other operators' sequences included geographical names, birds — Fisher Renwick (q.v.) — or, in the case of small fleets, the names of the owner's wife and family. Such naming is held to contribute to fleet identity and driver loyalty. **RAS**

Norbert Dentressangle (Figure 42) started in transport in 1974, joining his father's business in St Vallier, near Lyons. Two years later he decided to expand by offering a service from the Rhone Valley to Britain and in 1978 started his own company, based in London, originally named ND European Transport Ltd, but soon known as Norbert Dentressangle.

Within Britain there were several businesses, the ND Packed Goods operation, the chemical and powder tanker division and acquired companies. The first acquisition, in 1991, was Aston Clinton Haulage of Aylesbury with 40 vehicles, followed by Professional Tanker

Services with 30 tankers. Sheddick Transport of Newport, operating 110 articulated vehicles, was taken over in 1995 and AJG International Transport in 1997. TDG's French subsidiary Translittoral was taken over in 1993. It was then making heavy losses and ND received £12.5 million to cover the costs of redundancies and closure liabilities. Translittoral became a profitable division.

In 1994 Norbert Dentressangle Groupe became a French publicly-quoted company, the family remaining the largest shareholders.

In 2000 the Group's British logistics operation employed some 450 staff and 300 articulated units operating from 8 facilities. Together with the specialist bulk transport movements some 6000 cross channel trips were made in 1999. The company was probably the largest single user of Eurotunnel's service. **GM**

Normand Ltd, see LYONS, J,& CO. LTD

North, Oliver Danson, was Scammell Lorries' first chief designer. A Cambridge graduate, his early employment included Daimler and Straker-Squire. He joined Scammell Lorries in 1922 and was responsible for the development of the original Scammell Six-wheel lorry, followed by the rigid 6×4 Pioneer chassis. This became the basis for the tank transporters and recovery tractors used in the Second World War and after. He designed the 100-ton transporters, at that time the largest lorries in the world, and the rigid four and rigid six chassis. By 1933 he had developed the Napier design into the Scammell Mechanical Horse (q.v.). 1933 also saw the LA articulated and LS rigid-six vehicles, with Gardner 6LW diesel engines, using his six-speed gearbox and rear axle. The gearbox had a gate change, which meant that drivers had to work through each gear in sequence. Despite this it continued in use well into the 1960s. Scammell offered a drivers' course which covered this and other Scammell idiosyncrasies. The rigid-eight, with a front steering bogie, followed in 1937. Only the Auto-Van, with front-wheel-drive and a three-cylinder radial engine was a failure. North retired in 1952. **GM**

The **Northern Ireland Road Transport Board,** 1935–48, was an unusual example of transport nationalisation, introduced to deal with the problems of transport in Northern Ireland, in particular the losses suffered by the railway companies. Sir Felix Pole, former general manager of the GWR, was asked to investigate and produce a report, published in 1934. He recommended all public road services, passenger and goods, should be placed under one authority. The Road & Railway Transport Act 1935 established the Board. Belfast Corporation Transport Department, cartage firms operating within Belfast and Londonderry, furniture removers and cross-border operators were excluded. The lorry fleets of the railway companies were taken over first, then those of smaller operators, bought out with 'great generosity'. With no goods vehicle licensing system, some started up again in competition. Some traders acquired their own vehicles in anticipation of higher freight charges by the Board, which operated in a hostile atmosphere and was subject to an Inquiry in 1938 (Cmd.198 NI). The Act provided for a Joint Committee with the railways and a system of pooled receipts, but it never operated. The Boards's lorry fleet rose from 250 in 1935 to 1169 in 1938, then following rationalisation to 661 in 1940. It rose again to meet the demands of wartime and post-war reconstruction to 981 by its merger into the Ulster Transport Authority (q.v.). Fleet rationalisation 1936–9 involved the acquisition of 179 Leyland lorries, mostly diesel-engined, and from 1940 to 1948 of over 200 Bedford OW, some 200 Commer Q and numbers of Scammell mechanical horses, as well as 28 International/Fruehauf articulated units supplied under Lend-Lease. The Board established its own bodyworks. Many of its freight depots were on railway premises. Lorries were run on contract for some customers, including 17 tankers for Lobitos, a contract formerly held by the Irish Road Transport Co. Ltd of Portadown. **RAS**

Dunbar (1981); Wright (1986); Boyle (1999)

O

O licence, see LICENSING

One stop shopping was offered by some manufacturers to provide certain popular, standard types of bodywork, without the necessity for the customer to purchase a chassis/cab unit and then arrange with a bodybuilder for its completion. As an example, the Ford Motor Co. in 2000 offered off-the-shelf box-van, dropside, tipper and curtain-sider bodies on the new version of the Transit van, under its One-Stop programme. An earlier variant of this service was offered by large dealers, such as Arlington Motors, which had their own bodyworks. From the 1970s manufacturers of light commercial vehicles began making provision for quick deliveries of vans, and sometimes light trucks, to fairly standard specifications by providing what was called bank stock. Bodybuilders were allocated unsold chassis on which they could build bodies, the completed vehicles then being held to await orders from customers. A more recent variation of this for larger vehicles initiated by Leyland DAF and Boalloy (q.v.) was for the bodybuilder to establish a small assembly operation in premises near or next to those of the chassis builder. **RAS/JMA**

The all-new Ford Transit (Brentwood: Ford Motor Co., September 2000, ref. FA/1374/2), pp. 36–7.

The **operating centre** is an important element in the operator's licensing system. The idea was introduced in the 1947 Act as the point from where the twenty-five mile radius was measured. This was reinforced by the Transport Act 1968, subsequent regulations, and the Goods Vehicle (Licensing of Operators) Act 1995. Operating centres must be of sufficient size to accommodate all the vehicles used under the operator's licence for that location and satisfy environmental criteria. Proposals for a new operating centre have to be advertised in a local paper. Objections may be made to the grant of an application by a number of statutory objectors. This includes residents 'in the vicinity' but they can only object on environmental grounds, such as noise, not on grounds of road safety. Copies of any letter of objection to the local authority had to be sent to the haulier, which acted as a deterrent to action. The local authority and police are other statutory objectors who may oppose an application. Traffic Commissioners have considerable powers in respect to the road safety and environmental implications of a proposed operating centre. For these reasons the operating centre has been described as 'the cornerstone of the operator's licence'.

RAS/JMA

Transport Manager's and Operator's Handbook (1998); 'Legal Bulletin', *CM* (7 October 1999), pp. 29–32.

Operating costs and their calculation were among the content of the earliest transport magazines. They became important reading with the expansion of haulage and helped many new entrants into the industry after 1920. *Commercial Motor* had a weekly feature, 'Solving the Problems of the Carrier', possibly the most famous, and influential, contributed by Harry Scott Hall, under the nom de plume STR, until the 1950s. It was continued by S Buckley who moved the emphasis to management. STR had considerable influence and was widely quoted and accepted. He also gave answers to questions posed by operators covering a wide range of traffics, from livestock to bricks. The answers now have an historical interest as a guide to how a particular traffic might be handled at that date. *Motor Transport* chose to publish periodically tables of costs relevant to the vehicles of the period. Steam disappeared as heavy multi-axle diesels took over. The main costs then, as to-day, were standing charges and running costs. Standing charges covered wages, vehicle insurance, health insurance, vehicle licence, establishment, depreciation, and profit allowance. Running costs covered fuel, lubricating oil, tyres, maintenance and profit allowance. As the size and type of vehicles changed over time, so were the cost tables modified. This is shown by allowing for the cost of extras, such as refrigeration units, tail-lifts, cranes and curtainsiders. Although the publication of regular articles on costings has been superseded by the introduction of the Certificate of Professional Competence and its module for business and financial management, both *CM* and *MT* publish cost tables. The former is sponsored by a manufacturer, and *MT* has a supplement, with features advocating efficient operations or cost savings. Other road transport periodicals include references to costs within the contents.   **GM**

Operation 'Carter Paterson' was the codename given to one part of the Berlin airlift of 1948–9, when the Soviets cut road, rail and water links from the three western zones of Germany to Berlin deep inside the eastern zone. The Allies chose to fly in all the requirements from coal to flour to keep the inhabitants of the city supplied. In fourteen months over 270,000 flights were made. The code name was chosen because Carter Paterson (q.v.) was a well-known firm of carriers moving a wide range of goods. As the aim of the airlift was to supply all the necessities of life to the Berliners, 'Carter Paterson' seemed a peculiarly apposite code name. However it misfired, as the Russians claimed CP were a firm of removers and hence perhaps the name indicated the British were preparing to move out of Berlin. As a result in early July the operation was re-named 'Plainfare'. Unfortunate code names seemed to have been a common problem at the time, as operation 'Carter Paterson' replaced operation 'Knicker' in late June. The latter was a plan to supply the British garrison alone — no civilian supply was envisaged — by air and was drawn up in May 1948.   **JA**

Robert Jackson, *The Berlin Airlift* (Wellingborough, 1988), pp. 44–5; Arthur Peercy, *Berlin Airlift* (Shrewsbury, 1997), pp. 33–4, 138; Ann and John Tusa, *The Berlin Airlift*, (Staplehurst, 1998), pp. 115 and 150

Operator licensing, see LICENSING

Oswald Tillotson Ltd, see TILLOTSON, OSWALD, LTD

Outsourcing is the use of outside contractors or service providers for the provision of all or part of operations or services previously undertaken directly by the business concerned. An early example was the use of contract hire for postal services before the First World War, and the railways in the 1920s running vehicles in livery for customers such as Cadburys. The logic of such a move was to draw on the high level of expertise offered by the provider which cut costs and improved efficiency. In the 1980s when there was a move against diversification and towards concentrating on core business, outsourcing became a popular strategy. This included the supply and garaging of the vehicle, with or without a driver. The use of the local agent for servicing of vehicles was also a type of outsourcing. Some operators transferred their workshops to the distributor, who also serviced outside vehicles. The danger with this is being too tied to one manufacturer. In the late 1990s there was a choice of options, often the haulier or ancillary user leased vehicles for a fixed period with servicing and buyback arrangements at the end of the lease. The customer had a choice of options extending to full management responsibility for the supply chain which might include a retail distribution depot with the contractor having responsibility for receiving all stock, order picking for individual stores and delivery as required. This type of contract could include responsibility for the design and construction of the retail distribution centre and its equipment, staffing, etc. There was considerable capital investment involved, including the latest software. The transfer of investment allowed the client to concentrate on its particular business.   **GM**

Overnight express services. The first guaranteed national next-day delivery service was claimed to be National Carriers' (NCL) (q.v.) Diamond Service of 1969, though at first it depended on the railway for trunk routes. Its success meant it was extended to cover all major destinations. The road parcels carriers continued to provide their nominal next day, 24-hour service for local traffic, otherwise 48-hour or 72-hour service was normal. The

British Rail service using passenger expresses provided a competitive, if not guaranteed, service, until it was discontinued in 1981. A courier service for special consignments became available in 1984. The pioneer of this was Securicor (q.v.), which developed a service to meet the needs of banks, stores and other users of their money transport service to collect and deliver computer tapes. The first central hub for parcels was opened at Nuneaton in 1981 by Wilkinson (q.v.), a major parcels carrier. It used computerised sorting and documentation. There was rapid expansion led by the Australian-owned TNT (q.v.) entering the UK parcels industry, and then introducing their premium 'overtime' service. Skilful marketing made a guaranteed 24-hour service a requirement for many users. Other carriers then began to offer a similar service. Atlas Express started their Gold Band service. United Carriers were late in providing a nationwide, 24-hour service, but the acquisition of Atlas in 1984 allowed them to continue Gold Band as their dedicated service together with a short-lived multifreight service based on the use of small containers intended to reduce handling of consignments.

A new category of courier parcels service came into being, based on a franchised service. The franchisor provided the central sorting hub, the trunk service and usually arranged contracts and invoicing of customers for the service provided. The franchisee received payment by a mixture of commission and scale rates. Franchisees work to instructions on the type, dimensions and weight of consignments accepted. Because of the limitations of time at the hub, now known as 'sortation stations', the awkward or industrial type traffic is excluded, brown paper-wrapped or cartoned consignments meeting the required dimensions are the acceptable norm for their systems. The remaining traditional express carriers, notably Blue Band (q.v.), Crowfoot (q.v.) and to a lesser extent United Carriers' Ripponden Motors division, accepted much more diverse, awkward traffic of the kind which was acceptable for carriers up to the 1980s. From the late 1990s there has been considerable change in services and ownership influenced by economic conditions and more freedom for the Post Office. **GM**

B Carroll, *Hurry Back: an illustrated centenary history of Mayne Nickless* (Melbourne: Mayne Nickless, 1986)

Own-account operator, see ANCILLARY USER and LICENSING

The **owner-driver** has been a part of the haulage industry since before the motor age, when the country carrier (q.v.) plied his trade between outlying areas and the nearest market town. His urban or industrial counterpart was able to make a living at the service of the manufacturers, to supplement their own workforce of employed carters. Many small scale road transport operations were started up during the years between the cessation of hostilities and the inception of the licensing system. This was the case for both goods and passenger transport operators, indeed it was common practice then to operate a vehicle during the week with a lorry body fitted, and exchange it for a passenger body at weekends. By the late 1930s specialisation and legislation resulted in the virtual disappearance of the multi-purpose carrier, operating both goods and passenger vehicles. In the early years of motorised road transport the mixed traffic enterprise was commonplace.

The perceived freedom of self-employment appealed to the lorry driver as much as to any other type of worker. The reality was very often that the owner-driver was at the command of the manufacturer as much as an ordinary employee, and possibly not as well off financially. The owner-driver, as well as helping to cater for peaks in demand while being an escapable cost during the troughs, was of strategic benefit to a large manufacturer. The owner-driver as an individual wielded little or no power in relation to the manufacturers or the larger hauliers, however, as a collective entity, they are a key feature of the industry.

To appreciate this, it is necessary to examine the position of the owner-driver in the social hierarchy of the road transport industry and its customers. In this context the owner-driver can be seen as something of a pariah. The relationship between owner-drivers and employed drivers has always been an uneasy one. Employed drivers are well aware that owner-drivers have an incentive to maximise their workload and achieve it by whatever means prove necessary. Employed drivers see the owner-driver as a restriction on their own bargaining power, because the personal agenda of the latter may ensure they will disregard working agreements and defy picket lines in order to make their living.

To the haulage contractors owner-drivers were a mixed blessing. Their existence was very useful to a contractor experiencing peaks in demand. The lower overheads of the owner-driver meant that he might be willing to take subcontract work with the main contractor retaining a percentage of the rate charged to the consignor. The availability of owner-drivers strengthened the contractors' bargaining power with their own employed drivers. They could be the contractors' means of fulfilling delivery commitments, thus limiting the power of industrial action by their own employees. On the other hand, owner-drivers also posed a threat to the contractors because, having obtained traffic on a subcontract basis, they gained knowledge of the consignor's identity and the rate being charged. In this way they were in a strong position to compete with the original contractor for the traffic.

To the manufacturers, owner-drivers were a resource to be exploited which lacked power. The owner-driver was called upon to move traffic in the event of industrial action by employed drivers, either those working for the manufacturers or those working for the haulage contractors. The knowledge that they could be brought in also influenced the haulage contractors to be less demanding when rates were being negotiated.

The owner-driver lived in a constantly invidious position. He had usually been an employed driver, but was perceived by his peers to have deserted them and, worse still, sought to better himself, financially and socially, to the detriment of the working conditions they had sought to secure. He was exploited by the haulage contractors, who used him when it suited, but restricted his growth through fear of being usurped. The owner-driver was, at best, a peripheral player, unloved by employed drivers because he was perceived as a threat, but shunned by established operators as being just a lorry driver; no more, no less.

Under the system of carrier licensing (q.v.) there was limited scope for the owner-driver. Most were restricted to B licence activities, but, providing there was a continuity of direct traffic, were able to make a reasonable living. Those who depended largely on subcontract work were very vulnerable. The 1968 Transport Act, in opening up the market to all hire and reward operators, offered an opportunity for the owner driver to compete for any traffic. He was free to obtain work anywhere, and also to seek a return load, or a load for elsewhere, after completing the outward journey. Under the old system, licensing conditions placed severe constraints on the ability to do this, or limited the operating distance to the point where it was not worthwhile to seek a return load. Despite the influence of the large fleet operators, and the presence of multi-depot networks the owner driver has always played an important role in the road haulage industry, and seems set to continue in that vein. This was reinforced in the 1980s and 1990s when many large fleets, such as those in the cement (q.v.) and aggregate industries, shifted from direct employment to contracting out to self-employed drivers as a means of reducing labour costs and providing greater incentives. The largest class of owner-drivers in 1999 were those providing what is called traction (q.v.). They own a tractive unit and haul semi-trailers belonging to others. Use of owner-drivers is particularly strong in container haulage. Owner-drivers' efforts to protect their interests resulted in the formation of the British Association of Owner Drivers (q.v.). **MB**

P

P & O: Peninsular & Orient began in 1837 as a shipping line. The first joint venture container service, Overseas Containers Ltd (OCL), was introduced in 1969, P & O being one of the first British shipping companies to participate. Its major advance into road transport was in 1971, when P & O acquired Coast Lines, whose road haulage subsidiaries included Thomas Allen Ltd, Robert Armstrong Transport Ltd, Coastal Roadways Ltd, John Forman Ltd, James Hemphill Ltd, A S Jones Ltd and Henry Smither & Son Ltd, increasing its fleet to 6000 vehicles, of which 1500 were bulk liquid or powder tankers. The road-based subsidiaries became P & O European Transport, P & O Roadways, P & O Roadtanks, Ferrymasters, Northern Ireland Trailers and Pandoro. A re-organisation in 1990 saw the transport subsidiaries become P & O Distribution, P & O European Distribution Services (POETS), P & O Ferrymasters and P & O Roadtanks. There were further changes, the cruise operation Princess Cruises, de-merged in 1999. P & O then comprised Ports & Ferries and Logistics. The Logistics division gave an integrated supply service serving the UK and much of Europe. There was a major subsidiary operating barge services along the Rhine. P & O Cold Logistics provided temperature-controlled storage and transport in Australia, South America and the USA. P & O Trans European is generally concerned with distribution contracts, receiving orders, sorting and packing and delivery. It also operates Unit Load (Groupage) services, this includes container services. The main traffics are automobile parts, consumer goods, chemicals and bulk liquids. There are about 200 warehouses, with 2000 tractor units, 2400 trailers and 55 swap bodies for intermodal services. The Unit Loads services operate 320 tractor units, with several hundred traction sub-contractors. **GM**

Paccar, the American parent company of Foden since 1980, was established in 1905. As the Pacific Car & Foundry Co., it first made motor vehicles in the Second World War. Some examples of its output of over 1200 heavy tractive units found their way into civilian use in Europe and the UK after the war, including a 1944 vehicle modified by Wynns (q.v.) for heavy haulage in 1950. Pacific bought the American truck manufacturer Kenworth in 1944, and Peterbilt in 1958, running them as autonomous units. Paccar's involvement in the UK was increased when it bought DAF and its Leyland DAF subsidiary in 1996 and Leyland Trucks in 1998. Production of the former Leyland DAF 55 was transferred to a plant near Quebec. A few Kenworth trucks have been operated in the UK by owner-drivers and small fleets, such as John Golding of Kingswood, Gloucestershire, who operated five Kenworth units, as well as Mack, Peterbilt and White on heavy haulage, until type-approval problems resulted in their phasing out. **RAS**

B Tuck, 'Class pays', *Truck* (October 2000), pp. 72–5; Millar (1997); Martin (2000), p. 80; 'Americana, John Golding style', *CVRTC News*, 1/2001 (February 2001)

The **Packard Motor Car Co.** of Detroit, USA began making cars in 1900 and produced commercial vehicles from 1905 to 1923, developing a 3-ton capacity truck in 1908. English agents for Packard cars and trucks and sole concessionaires 1915–20 were Gaston Williams & Wigmore Ltd of Kingsway, London. Known English users of Packard trucks included the Western Ways Transport Co. Ltd of Sherborne, Dorset, and Beck & Pollitzer (q.v.) in their capacity as passenger agents, handling baggage. During the First World War thousands of Packard trucks were in military use, including by the British army. After the war the company specialised in cars, but Packard trucks, including war surplus vehicles, survived into the 1930s. **RAS**

F C Lane and B H Vanderveen, 'Packard', *OM&VC*, 4, 6 (January/February 1966), pp. 174–81.

Pagefield was a product of Walker Brothers (Wigan) Ltd whose Pagefield Iron Works made mining and general machinery. They entered commercial vehicle production in 1907 and were active in this field (latterly as Walker) until 1955. Over 500 type N 3-ton lorries were produced under the subvention scheme (q.v.) for military use in the First World War. After the war, an approach from Southport Corporation resulted in the Pagefield System of refuse collection (Patent no. 189,880 of 1921), ultimately used by numerous local authorities in the 1920s and 1930s. It was an early demountable (q.v.) system. Special horse-drawn, low-loading refuse containers on twenty inch wheels when full could be drawn onto two parallel tilting tracks on a Pagefield lorry which had previously off-loaded an empty container. The lorry then made the longer journey to a refuse dump. Some lorries for general commercial use were produced in the 1930s, customers including J Lyons & Co. Ltd (q.v.), who bought twenty. Diversification into mobile crane production occurred from 1929, initially for the LMS for handling 5-ton containers. Subsequent models were of 6- to 8-ton capacity. Their employment gave greater flexibility of container-handling than did the rail-mounted cranes on parallel tracks. Walmsleys of Bury, paper machinery engineers, took over Walkers in 1947/8 and motor work ceased by the mid-1950s, although a 5-ton general purpose chassis was developed in 1948 with an eye to the export market and a Swedish order for 40 chassis was met. Walkers & County Cars Ltd linked Walker Bros and County Commercial Cars (q.v.) in refuse vehicle development between 1948 and 1966. An earlier, unsuccessful liaison had been with Atkinson & Co. of Preston. It ended in 1930. Pagefield Paragon chassis were supplied to Northern Coachbuilders for conversion to battery-electric municipal vehicles. **RAS**

Meadows (1997); N Baldwin, 'Pagefield', *OM*, 9, 1

Palladium Autocars Ltd (1912–25) were one of a number of short-lived vehicle manufacturers in greater London, like McCurd, Napier and du Cros (q.v.). Palladium was established by Dr J R McMahon to assemble cars from French components. Vans were also made with colonial sales handled by Tozer & Kemsley. With the onset of war, a lorry to Subsidy standards was developed, eventually to be offered with Dorman engines. New works at Putney Bridge were opened and lorries, probably several hundred, produced for essential civilian use and colonial export: a late 1917 advertisement claimed 97 vehicles to E G Brown of Birmingham, 30 to the Bombay Cycle & Motor Agency and 20 to the Whitehead Aircraft Co. of Richmond for the carriage of fuselages. There were other, smaller orders, including by well-known manufacturers, and Pratts Petroleum distribution produced sizeable orders. Munitions work took over by 1918, but a new 4-ton chassis, the YEE, appeared in 1919, to take advantage of an active market for about another year, after which commercial vehicle production tailed off. After the firm's demise in 1925, spares went in bulk to two north London car dealers in succession, keeping existing Palladiums on the road for some years. **RAS**

N Baldwin and J M Bland, 'The Other London Palladium', *Vintage Lorry Album* (1980), pp. 84–7; N Baldwin, 'Forgotten London Makers', *VCVM*, 16 (September–October 1988), p. 49

Pallet distribution networks operate on the basis of one or more hubs serviced by companies which are members of the network. These companies can then offer, via the hub operation, deliveries of goods carried on one or more pallets to locations not covered by their own vehicles, enabling smaller companies to provide a national service otherwise beyond their individual resources. There are three principal networks in the UK: Palletways UK, Palletline and Pall-Ex. The first was Palletline, a co-operative formed in 1992 by 19 privately-owned regional hauliers to offer a nationwide distribution service. All members hold shares in Palletline plc, which runs the major hub in Birmingham. There are also two regional hubs run by member companies. On its first night of operation Palletline carried 51 pallets, but within ten years the nightly figure was almost 7000 pallets handled by 45 members.

Pall-Ex was founded in 1996 by Hilary Sharples to provide just-in-time palletised distribution and had 64 members by 1999. Its central hub was just off the M1 at Nottingham. In 2000 Pall-Ex took over Focus Parcels, a franchise operation, and in the same year sold it on to Blue Band Motors (q.v.). **RAS/JMA**

CM (18 May 2000), pp 28–9; *Midlands Business* (July 1999), p. 7; *CM* (21 February 2002), pp. 36–8

Pallets and stillages (Figure 43) allow goods to be combined into larger, standard-sized units suitable for mechanical handling. Originally developed to facilitate movement and storage in factories and warehouses, they were then used as a means of 'unitising' goods for transport, thus reducing the cost and risk of damage associated with loose-loading of individual items by hand. They could also reduce the protective packaging required. In this role they superseded the load tray (q.v.).

The two terms have at times been used imprecisely, but the British Standard *Glossary of Terms Used in Mechanical Handling* (BS 3810-1: 1964) makes the following distinction. The original stillage was a rectangular timber platform formed of planks nailed to a pair of transverse bearers underneath, which could be raised and moved by a form of works truck (q.v.), known variously as a lever platform truck, transveyor, jack truck or stillage truck, with an elevating platform that fitted between the stillage's bearers. The system was in use by 1920. The pallet was a 1930s or 1940s development of the stillage, with a third, central bearer to increase its safe working load. It is manoeuvred with a pallet truck, which has two forks that slot under the pallet on either side of the central bearer.

Pallets may be single- or double-sided (with platforms above and below the bearers) and may be two-way, four-way (permitting entry of the forks on all four sides) or even eight-way (also permitting diagonal entry) As the use of pallets spread, it became important to standardise their sizes, but this proved to be difficult because of the variety of sizes already established, in the UK or Europe, before the first British Standard of 1955, none of them compatible with ISO container dimensions. In 1988 three standard sizes were settled on: 1200×800 mm (48×32 in), 1200×1000 mm (48×40 in) and 1140×1140 mm (a new size designed to fit within an ISO 8 ft-wide container), but in the meantime eight other standard sizes had been adopted and subsequently dropped.

The use of pallets has been extended by the development of banding (steel banding from the 1950s and later plastic), which secures the load to the pallet during transit and allows loaded pallets to be stacked by fork-lift (q.v.). This has been partly superseded by shrink-wrapping, which also provides extra protection against the weather. Bricks are banded together into 'self-palletised' blocks, with gaps left in one of the lower rows of bricks for the forks of the truck to engage, eliminating the need for a separate wooden pallet. The loading of pallets on lorries was much eased from the early 1970s by the Joloda (q.v.) retractable roller conveyor.

There is also a great variety of box, or cage, pallets and stillages which were introduced in the late 1970s: for example, steel heavy duty stackable cage stillages for engineering components; and tall light-alloy stillages with collapsible mesh sides for retail use. Variants with wheels may be called roll-cages. Confusingly, the roll-cages introduced by the Post Office c.1998 for transporting trays of sorted letters are called York containers.

Very large pallets are used for air freight, commonly 88×108, 88×125 or 96×125 in., and may be fitted with a retaining net. The solid-walled igloo pallets, shaped to the aircraft contour, were developed in the late 1970s; Roy Bowles Transport and York Trailer developed trailers to accommodate them.

Plastic pallets came into use in the 1990s. Although not pallets or stillages, stacking plastic crates are a form of unitisation. They are a convenient size for lifting by one person and moving by sack truck. As well as being lighter and more robust than the traditional wooden crate, they greatly reduced the cost of returning empty crates, being designed to fit inside one another. An early use was to replace wooden fish crates in the 1970s and from the early 1980s they were hired out for office removals. By the 1990s they were widely used for shop delivery.

By far the largest pallet and crate hire company at the end of the century was the Anglo-Australian company Chep (Common wealth Handling Equipment Pool), founded 50 years earlier in Australia and introduced to the UK in 1974. In 1980 it had 50 million wooden pallets. By 2000 this had grown to 150 million and 30 million crates. It claimed to be ten times the size of its nearest competitor. **RAS**

British Standard Specifications; Gordon Jackson, *The History and Archaeology of Ports* (Tadworth: World's Work, 1983) pp 152–3; *Daily Telegraph* (4 August 2001); *CM* (17 September 1976), p. 137 and (1 March 1980), pp. 33–5

Pannell, A, Ltd, general and specialist haulage contractors, of Golders Green, Vauxhall, Surbiton and Borehamwood, Herts, is an example of a haulage concern which grew by diversifying out of another occupation involving transport. Albert Pannell, a Kent farmer, set up a greengrocery business in Vauxhall in the late nineteenth century and used a horse and cart to transport his surplus produce to the London markets and to bring back stock for his business. To utilise the cart fully, he undertook removals and local delivery, then gained contracts for sand and ballast and spoil removal in connection with road and tramway works. Pannell built up a large horse and cart fleet, retaining some horse transport until 1948. Its first motor vehicle was not employed until the early 1920s, although by 1933 Pannell had 41 lorries. The business expanded between the wars under the founder's sons and refuse (q.v.) contracts were taken on, and industrial waste such as power station fly ash and clinker, and some long distance haulage. Pannells' first multi-axle tippers, four Bedford-Unipower conversions, were acquired in 1935. Pannell had a 14-vehicle contract using Bedfords and Seddons to do collection and delivery work for Fisher Renwick of Muswell Hill in the mid-1940s. After the war, Leyland Hippos were succeeded by AEC

Mammoth Majors and Fodens. The latter included tankers in 1958 for a Shell-Mex & BP fuel oil contract. From the 1960s diversification occurred, including into gully cleansing, warehousing and commercial body-building, although recession reduced the group fleet to fifteen vehicles by 1983. It had ceased business by 1990. **RAS**

'From greengrocery to refuse', *Classic Commercials* (1983), pp. 24–8

Pantechnicon, meaning *every process of workmanship,* was the name coined for a business opened in 1831 by Seth Smith in Motcomb Street, Belgravia, London, that combined a saleroom for carriages, arcades of shops, a bazaar and storage for carriages, furniture, wines and other property of Belgravia residents when they shut up their houses and left for the country. By 1860 storage had become the predominant side of the business, which now emphasised that it was 'The Pantechnicon', because the word was being adopted by other depositories. Some of them had started to offer themselves as packers and carriers for household removals (q.v.), although The Pantechnicon itself does not seem to have done so until about 1872.

Thus the word *pantechnicon* came to be associated with the furniture storage and then the removal trades. By 1892 *pantechnicon van,* later shortened to *pantechnicon,* was being applied to furniture vans. Within the trade the term has sometimes been confined to certain types of furniture van, but with conflicting definitions of what constitutes a pantechnicon.

Although The Pantechnicon company moved to Turnham Green in about 1966, parts of its original premises were listed and have survived. In the late 1980s the company was acquired by a group formed in 1986 by the merger of Midland Van Lines, Briggs of Lincolnshire and Fox the Mover of South Wales, which adopted its prestigious name. Sadly The Pantechnicon Group changed its name to Fox Group (Moving & Storage) Ltd in 2000, reportedly because it was difficult for customers to remember or pronounce the historic name. **GAB**

OED; Christopher Hussey, 'Future of the Pantechnicon', *Country Life*, 139 (1966), pp. 714–16; *Removals & Storage*, 306 (January 2000), p. 6; *Post Office London Directories*, various years

Paper traffic (Figure 147). Paper, in a continuous strip wound onto a reel, has been available since 1805. There are two main consumers for paper delivered daily, the newspaper and the packaging industries. The first rotary newspaper press came to Britain in 1857, while Linotype, making high speed production possible was available from 1896, the year the *Daily Mail* was founded. In the early days railways played a major part in the distribution of the product, and were used to bring the paper from the mills to a railhead, for final delivery to the printer by horse and cart and later by steam wagon. There were also deliveries to stationery manufacturers, book and general printers, even bulk tissue to toilet roll and paper handkerchief makers. All were handled in a similar manner.

The packaging industry uses two different type of paper, one called liner board or kraft liner, in 2½ to 3 ton reels, which is the raw material for corrugated cardboard for carton making. This can take place in a single factory, from the raw material (wood pulp and waste paper) through making the linerboard, turning that into corrugated board, to the finished carton, made and printed to the end users' specification. Famous names doing this are Thames Board Mills and Reeds. The mills were generally rail-connected so that the reels of linerboard could be transported by rail to manufacturers. The other paper, white or grey board, comes in cut sheets about 48 in × 40 in (1220 × 1000 mm) for sheet-fed machines generally making cartons.

Between the wars, much of the movement of paper, both British-made and imported, was by road. For instance Bowater used Foden steam wagons, carrying about twelve rolls including those on the drawbar trailer, up to 1932. These were often hired, but in that year they decided to start owning their lorries. By 1933 they had 26 petrol-driven lorries and four steam wagons. They soon switched to oil-fuelled vehicles and by 1949 were using AEC Mammoth 8-wheelers, capable of carrying eighteen rolls. The massive decline of the British paper-making industry after the Second World War meant that most paper was then imported from Scandinavia, so transport was from docks and wharves. Handling paper needs much care as it is very liable to damage by moisture, requiring skill in sheeting and roping. It is also susceptible to foreign objects becoming embedded in the reel. If the reel is dropped, the tube can be crushed, making the reel useless to the printer.

Reels of paper were transported in two ways: 'on the roll' or 'on end'. Until the mid-1950s the former was the most common. Originally reels were handled by standard docker's techniques with a rope strop or special clamp and a crane, initially steam-powered and rail-mounted, later, fully mobile diesel-electric. Until the end of the 1980s one London press still required its reels to be loaded with a rope strop round each for unloading by a gantry crane at the press. The paper mills' and dock cranes were eventually superseded by the pole truck, a fork-lift truck (q.v.) with two 6 foot 6 inch (2 m) long round poles in place of the normal flat blades. These came into general use along with the clamp truck, which is a fork-lift truck with hydraulically-operated jaws, which can pick up and rotate reels. Specialised machines could tilt the reel from the 'on end' to 'on the roll' position, or vice versa.

The type of press used dictated the width of paper (and thus of the reel). For many years newsprint was the benchmark, with 'mains' at 7 feet, halves at 3ft 6in, and quarters at 1ft 9in, thus reels could be loaded one, two or four across the lorry. Today reels come in all widths. Paper mills with lorries dedicated to supplying the newspaper trade had bodies built so that a 'main' just fitted between the raves. When a lorry was loaded 'on the roll', each reel had to be positioned tight against its predecessor and scotched into place with wooden wedges. This was done with a paddle or reel-bar, originally shaped from wood, in later years an aluminium tube flattened at one end. The final row was secured with a long triangular timber, a 'back scotch', which had a length of rope permanently fixed to each end so that it could be tied in position with 'dollies' [see SHEETING AND ROPING]. A second tier of reels was loaded in the valleys ('cuttings' or docks) formed between the reels of the bottom tier. For certain operations a third tier was added; 7 + 6 +5 making 18 reels in all, a full load of newsprint for an 8-wheeler.

Unloading was generally done by reversing the lorry up to a loading bank (q.v.) knocking out the scotches and rolling the reels off. 'Dropping' or 'barring down' the second tier required skill and effort on the part of the driver. Dropping the third tier required even more skill as the second and third tiers had to be dropped simultaneously. All these operations were done with the aid of the reel-bar.

Widespread use of the clamp truck and the advent of the curtain-side trailer (q.v.), slowly from the late 1960s, but especially in the 1980s, revolutionised paper transport. There was no longer need for skilled drivers able to load and unload reels on the roll and to sheet and rope. Reels can be stored and delivered on end obviating much damage due to dropping and rolling. Even the 3-ton reels of linerboard can be handled this way. In the newspaper industry this was taken one step further with the system trailer with 'Joloda' (q.v.) track containing a pneumatically-operated lifting strip along the floor. The rear doors are opened and the corner posts swung out. Then the trailer is reversed up to a suitably equipped bank, and locked in position with a modified fifth wheel (q.v.) fitted under its tail. The driver connects an airline to the pneumatic system; four mechanical skates run out from the bank along the channels under the entire load; the pneumatic system inflates and lifts the 'skates' so that the reels clear the floor, then the whole load is drawn off in a single operation. Once in the plant the reels are handled by a computer-controlled clamp crane. At delivery points without a system bank the driver can bring the reels to the back of the trailer one at a time with a manual Joloda skate, which means that the curtains do not have to be opened for side unloading, reducing the amount of space needed to unload.

Pallets of cut board for the carton industry are delivered from docks, and palleted bundles of completed cartons are often taken from the carton makers by the same vehicle. There is a return trade. Bales of waste paper and returned scrap cartons are recycled at one of the few remaining paper mills. In the mid-1990s Aylesford Newsprint was set up on Reed's site in Kent to produce newsprint from British waste paper and pulpwood.

W J Reader, *Bowater: a history* (Cambridge University Press, 1981), pp. 94–5

Parades were a regular feature of the commercial vehicle scene until the Second World War. They succeeded parades of horse-drawn vehicles, though a few of these lasted into the 1960s. Whereas the latter had encouraged attention to the health and welfare of horses and also the cleanliness of their carts, the main focus of the commercial vehicle parades was the condition and cleanliness of the vehicles, and occasionally the appearance of their drivers: uniforms were rarely provided in the 1930s even, and might consist of just a cap, or a cap and an apron. Most parades were held on a Sunday and usually organised by the Commercial Motor Users' Association (q.v.), though some local authorities organised them for their own fleets. **JMA**

Parcelforce, see POST OFFICE

Parcels by bus, see BUS CARRIAGE OF GOODS AND PARCELS

Parcels by tram, see TRAMWAYS

Parcels services aimed to provide a virtually nationwide 24-hour parcels and smalls service. This became possible after the First World War with the combination of suitable vehicles and available trained drivers and fitters. At first progress was limited to regional services, London–Manchester being about the longest possible owing to speed limits and the limitations of vehicle design. Fisher Renwick (q.v.) was famed for its 24-hour continuous service, although at first it regarded itself more as a smalls service. Development of suitable chassis and the introduction of the 20 mph limit in 1930 allowed growth in these services.

Charles Dunbar (q.v.) started his Red Arrow (q.v.) service in 1933, serving Birmingham, London, Bristol and Leicester. By inter-working arrangements with other independent carriers he created a network of services to all the major conurbations with a next day service. Other large carriers whose depots served much of the country had also built up their own exchange arrangements, but the Red Arrow network was arguably the most comprehensive and even during the war was able to continue, albeit with longer timings.

To overcome various problems, such as claims for damage or loss and missing items, Dunbar set up the National Conference of Parcels Carriers in 1938, soon to become the National Conference of Express Carriers (q.v.). This produced a national set of conditions of carriage (q.v.). A number of carriers joined, notably Carter Paterson and Pickfords, with Sutton & Co. and the independent Atlas Express, McNamara and Youngs serving Scotland and the north down to the midlands, and the Holdsworth & Hanson group. The service was needed because the Post Office (q.v.) never set out to offer next-day national delivery and restricted parcel weight and size.

On nationalisation in 1948 all the long-distance express carriers and the railway-associated parcels companies acquired by BTC were absorbed into BRS. Although next-day deliveries were generally provided by depots for their area, it was normal for a 48- to 72-hour service to be provided and accepted by customers. De-nationalisation in 1955 created BRS Parcels as a separate trading division, and the emergence of new independent parcels carriers, e.g. United Carriers, and Wilkinson, which expanded to give nationwide services but arguably did not bring a return to the pre-war next-day standard.

There were next-day services for regional traffic provided by long-established local carriers, e.g. Bridges (q.v.), Ripponden, Crowfoot (q.v.) and Blue Band (q.v.). Changes led to Blue Band becoming virtually a nationwide service, while Crowfoot covered the midlands and north west. The development in 1981 by Wilkinson of its central hub using computer-based conveyor sorting and documentation made them the first independent to give a next-day guaranteed service. This was closely followed by the Australian-owned TNT (q.v.) which opened a new central hub at Atherstone for its 'Overnight' service. These hubs have generally excluded awkward or fragile traffic referred to as 'Uglies'.

Changes occurred in customers, traffic and distribution with the development of super-markets and retail parks and the decline of ironmongers, off-licences and furniture stores from the mid-1970s. The entry of new names, e.g. TNT and Target, the growth of some established local carriers and the expansion of the 'Courier' overnight service have led to intense competition and the receivership or closure of some firms, such as Elan which ceased operations in 1991, and Placketts which operated over 600 vehicles until its demise in 1994, and Blue Band which folded in 2002. Overnight or, more correctly, 24-hour services were widely available in the late 1990s but several specialist companies also offered cheaper two-, or even three-day services. The new pallet (q.v.) inter-working networks are the latest chapter in the provision of an express service able to deal with awkward or difficult traffic within the limitation of a pallet's dimensions. **GM**

Allan (1946): unnumbered plate

Parcels to Ireland, based in Rugby, Warwickshire, is an example of a relatively recent (founded 1988) and small (10 vehicles), business which established itself in its self-defined sector of road haulage. This was the collection of parcels, or more accurately freight, from the area between Telford, Peterborough, Sheffield and the M25, and delivery to Northern Ireland and Eire. Hauliers which delivered freight from outside this collecting area for onward shipping provided some 10 per cent of revenue. A depot is no longer maintained in Ireland; Parcels to Ireland has two partners for driver-accompanied delivery to Belfast or Dublin and two other partner firms for final delivery. The Parcels to Ireland fleet comprises Mercedes-Benz Sprinter vans, a Mercedes-Benz Actros tractor unit and Scania curtainside rigids. **RAS**

O Dixon, 'Success made simple', *Truck* (February 2001), pp. 58–61

Park Royal Coachworks (later Park Royal Vehicles) is best known as a builder of bus bodies, but at times it bodied considerable quantities of vans and trucks. In the mid-1930s nearly 250 bodies were built for the telephones section of the Post Office, including 129 line-inspection vans on Morris Minor chassis, and there were also cabs for AEC lorries. Wartime building totalled 16,000 cabs and bodies, including quantities of the latter on Ford four-wheel-drive chassis for the army and AEC Matador military tractors. After coming into Associated Commercial Vehicles in 1949, it again began building cabs for AEC lorries, work which continued on-and-off until 1972. Some later cabs were of glass fibre. Other work included bodies for military vehicles and 138 box van bodies on Thames 3-ton chassis for Kraft Foods in 1956–7. **JMA**

Alan Townsin, *Park Royal Coachworks* (2 vols, Glossop: Transport Publishing, 1979–80)

Parrott, W T. In the late nineteenth century William Parrott (1880–1933) started as a general trader in his home town, Leighton Buzzard. He moved to Luton *c.* 1900 and worked as transport manager at a garage owned by B E Barrett. By 1907 William invested in a horse-drawn cart designed to carry petroleum products, paraffin for lighting and heating around the villages, and petrol to the up-and-coming Vauxhall Motors.

His transport company was soon formed, comprising horse and cart, in the early 1920s Sentinel steamers and, later, the new Foden diesel lorries. While working at Barretts William conceived the Luton (q.v.) body for the transport of hats from Luton's many hat factories.

He was joined in business in 1925 by his two sons; Rex (1905–66) who had finished his apprenticeship at Barretts, and Frank (1908–55). Long hours were worked and after a day delivering, often the evening was spent at Leighton Buzzard quarries hand-loading silver sand to be brought back to Luton to be bagged and sold locally to pet shops for the bottom of bird cages.

The Parrott family were staunch Methodists (William was a local preacher) and it was this that brought Foden wagons into the Parrott family business via the Luton Redcross Band, the famous Mortimer brothers and Rex Parrott's in-laws where one of the brothers lodged while principal cornet player in the band. Mr Rex, as he was universally known, soon became excited about the new diesel lorries from Sandbach and he became a close friend of the Foden family.

William Parrott died comparatively young in 1933 leaving the business to be run by his sons, Rex concentrating on the engineering and Frank on management and book-keeping. As Luton grew, so did the haulage business and contracts were won for the movement of all Laporte Chemical products from the new Luton site, with Alcock Chemicals, the Cement Marketing Company at Houghton Regis and much other general haulage. The fleet grew to about 20 wagons.

Drivers were expected to use their own initiative to obtain return loads wherever possible, which resulted in two pay days; bonus day for obtaining return loads was Thursday and normal pay day was Friday. An early diversification by the brothers was into the Beech Hill Safety Coach Co. with a well-known Luton Methodist family Snoxell. In 1934 a subsidiary of W T Parrott was formed, West Park Engineering Ltd, primarily to repair and maintain the growing fleet of Fodens and the first ERF eight-wheeler, which had been bought by Fred Gilbert of Leighton Buzzard on the recommendation of his cousin Mr Rex.

On the declaration of war, Frank was called up. Rex carried on the engineering side and drivers were promoted to take over Frank's role. The engineering side prospered and was a major supplier of fully-tested reconditioned Gardner (q.v.) engines to the government and armed forces. Being main agents for Foden and

ERF provided much work for the employees bolstered by directed labour. During the war the fleet remained static. Immediately after the war, orders were placed for new vehicles, but these were not delivered until after nationalisation and so became part of W T Parrott BTC, of which Rex was appointed senior engineer, Luton and Leighton Buzzard Area BTC. Frank retired, but was retained by BTC as a consultant.

On denationalisation W T Parrott disappeared from the roads. Both Rex's and Frank's health had deteriorated. West Park Garage carried on as vehicle repairers and Rex's sons Colin and Norman owned the properties bought by their family some eighty years before. **CRP**

Paterson, James (1884–1964) was a member of the Paterson family of Carter Paterson & Co. (q.v.) and played an active part in the direction of this and related firms within the Hays Wharf group. A graduate of Merton College Oxford and barrister of the Inner Temple, he served with distinction in the First World War, being awarded the MC. He wrote *The History and Development of Road Transport*. A somewhat jejune book by modern standards, it nonetheless carries the authority of a transport professional. When the railway-owned road haulage companies joined the National Conference of Express Carriers (NCEC) in 1938, Paterson became active in its affairs, serving as its President. Surviving correspondence with Charles Dunbar, the NCEC founder, witnesses both to their friendship and to Paterson's professionalism. In July 1942 Paterson, in a letter to Quick-Smith (q.v.), copied to Dunbar, makes a telling analysis of the legitimate cost differentials of various prominent smalls carriers. Paterson was a director, and later managing director, of the family firm for many years. He resigned in 1943 at what he considered the extreme rationalisation following the merger of Carter Paterson and Pickfords. After nationalisation of Carter Paterson, he remained chairman of Express Motor & Body Works Ltd (q.v.), Tersons Ltd and a number of other former Carter Paterson subsidiaries. **RAS**

Paterson (1927); *Directory of Directors* (1949); Merton College register; Turnbull (1979)

Peck Express (PX) dates from 1896 when A Peck purchased a country carrier's business, based at Wollaston, serving Wellingborough daily and Northampton twice weekly. He moved to Rushden in 1913, having acquired another carrier serving Kettering and purchased his first motor, a Lacre van. During the First World War he regularly operated to London, particularly to collect imported hides. In 1918 he started a daily service to Leicester and in 1919, because of the rail strike, a daily London service. A son, William J A Peck became managing director. From 1919 to about 1927, two of the fleet were convertible to char-a-bancs for excursions. Its title was now Peck's Road Transport and Motor Service Ltd. A new depot was built at Rushden, followed in 1928 by Leicester. A depot at Poplar, London, opened in 1930. With continued growth, in 1934 the name was changed to PX Ltd. Bert Scroxton & Son Ltd, Rushden, was also acquired in 1934. It operated a parcels service to South Wales and a removals service. The fleet was now based on Leyland, Bedford, Fordson and Morris-Commercial vehicles, mostly vans. Further acquisitions included Nutt, Harpole and Essam, three small general carriers. The latter served Bristol, but PX ceased operating this, preferring to interwork this traffic via Red Arrow (q.v.). In 1938 Central Transport, Wellingborough was acquired to serve Liverpool and Manchester. This was followed by an interworking with Youngs of Glasgow, for PX Scottish traffic, exchanging with their Midlands traffic. This led to the creation of Central Carriers of Birmingham. In 1945, C Watling of Norwich, previously used for interworking, was acquired for an East Anglian service. PX was a voluntary acquisition at nationalisation to form part of Northampton Parcels. W J A Peck resigned to develop Vehicle Hire & Supply Co. Ltd, operating the Calor Gas contract, which arose from PX's success in delivering the Calor Gas cylinders during the big-freeze in the winter of 1945–6. His brothers remained as managers, Frank becoming group leader. **GM**

Peerless truck production in the USA had a short run, from 1911 to 1918, at Cleveland, Ohio. Peerless trucks were among the thousands of surplus military vehicles which finished up at the contentious Slough (q.v.) depot and so entered the UK post-war lorry market. Some 4- and 5-ton lorries were reconditioned and sold, first by the Slough Trading Co., then by Slough Lorries & Components Ltd. In 1925 the Peerless Trading Co. Ltd, also based at Slough, took over the reconditioning business, utilising the remaining spares and an increasing percentage of new components to refurbish 3000 Peerless lorries. The new company introduced the 8-ton Tradersix, which retained solid rear tyres and chain-drive, as did the Tradersix 90, which had its engine mounted forward of the front axle. Other models, including forward-control, were introduced, but assembly ceased at the end of 1933. Some vehicles were sold as Peerless Traders or just as Traders. Gravel haulage firms in the Slough area were keen Peerless customers; one of the last Peerless lorries to be built was for I Beer & Sons Ltd, the London bacon wholesalers. Fisher Renwick (q.v.) used ex-army Peerless lorries from the early 1920s for collection and delivery. In 1933 some Peerless directors broke away and acquired the agency for Studebaker lorries. **RAS**

Klapper (1973); Cassell (1991); *MT*, 50 years Ago series; Roy Larkin, 'The dump', *Roads & Road Transport History Conference Newsletter*, 22 (2000), pp. 18–19

Pengco, see CRANE FRUEHAUF TRAILERS LTD

Penman patent containers were produced by A C Penman Ltd of Dumfries. Founded as coachbuilders in 1887, the firm built car bodies from 1902 to 1929 and commercial vehicle bodies in the First World War and again from 1929. A Penman advertisement in 1958, showed a demountable livestock body. The same source claimed that the container could be removed or refitted 'in a few moments without assistance'. The Penman system was in trial use by British Railways in the late 1950s for the transfer of standard rail containers from railway trucks to road vehicles without the use of a crane. Pull-out metal rollers at each corner of the container engaged with and moved on parallel raised rails with a slight incline at each end. A shunting engine or wagon tractor pushed the container in the rail-road exchange process. It was an experimental system and did not gain widespread use. By the late 1960s Penman was building modern, conventional demounting systems of various sizes. One large user was kitchen cabinet maker Hygena, which had 57 demountable Luton bodies in use on 42 Dennis Pax four-wheelers, while a demount system in which landing legs dropped down automatically was developed for Transits and Bedford CFs in 1970. **RAS/JMA**

Freight Transport Equipment used by British Railways and British Road Services (1958); Penman's advertisement, *CM* (27 June 1958), p. 24; N Walker, *A to Z of British Coachbuilders, 1919–1960* (Bideford: Bay View Books, 1997)

Perkins Commercial Services, specialist builders of tippers on small chassis, of London E10, had their origins as a cycle shop, J Perkins & Son, of Leyton High Road in 1886. The family opened a garage in 1936, which became an agent for Anthony tipping gears and built tipper bodies. On the retirement of Sydney Perkins in 1961 the business was sold to Harry Terry. In 1967 he and his son Ian had the idea of the specialised production of tipping bodies for small chassis such as the Ford Transit, with the tipping mechanism powered by a CAV electric motor operating a hydraulic pump made by Gowring Engineering, a firm started by Ian Terry. The first production model appeared the following year. Co-operation with manufacturers resulted in PCS tippers on Volkswagen LT and Toyota Hi-Ace chassis. Tipmaster Ltd separated to produce bodies for larger chassis. They became popular with small builders and some councils. **RAS**

MT: Perkins Tippers Special (9 March 1979)

Perkins Engines Co., diesel engine manufacturer, was established in Peterborough in 1932 by Frank Perkins and a number of close associates, including Charles Chapman, who had previously been with Beardmore (q.v.) and Petters. Perkins came from an agricultural engineering background, working with Barford & Perkins of Peterborough and then elsewhere in the Agricultural & General Engineers group, where he was involved in diesel engine development. AGE went into liquidation in 1932 and constituent companies were sold off individually. At this juncture Frank Perkins set up his own diesel engine business. Commer was an early customer, for the Wolf diesel, and one-off, replacement engine orders were also met. Earlier, less successful, engines before the Wolf were the Vixen and Fox. A larger, six-cylinder engine, the P6, was produced from 1936 into the 1950s and within five years of its foundation Perkins had developed diesel engines for vehicles from half- to six-ton capacity. In 1938 an engine replacement scheme, the Perkins Perpetuity Plan, was introduced. After the war, major orders from agricultural tractor manufacturers justified a new factory in eastern Peterborough. In the post-war situation Perkins found a ready market for bought-in engines with numerous marques, from Austin to Vulcan, and including the Bedford O series. The R engine of the early 1950s damaged Perkins' reputation and Leyland took advantage of this by supplying their engines as original equipment and as replacements. In 1958, with the threat of opposition from vehicle manufacturers making their own diesel engines, Perkins accepted takeover by a prominent customer, Massey-Ferguson. By 1966 Perkins had four plants in Peterborough, employing 7600, and a central parts operation in a former wartime aero engine plant at Urmston. About half a million diesel engines were made annually. There were overseas manufacturing subsidiaries, such as Moteurs Perkins SA at St Denis, established in 1954. The trademark was 'square deal all round' and promotional methods included sausage suppers at transport cafés, hosted by Frank Perkins for owner-drivers to persuade them to change their engine to Perkins. These were sometimes held in conjunction with dealers and arose because most engines needed rebuilding after 40,000 or 50,000 miles. In the mid-1960s Perkins published a house journal, *Perkins Echo*, and other titles, as well as issuing promotional and instructional films. In the late 1970s Perkins acquired Gardner (q.v.) of Patricroft. Dorman Diesels Ltd of Stafford was acquired by the Perkins Group in 1994, to become Perkins Engines (Stafford) Ltd. The Dorman business had been founded in 1870 to produce machine tools for the shoe industry. By 1903 it designed and manufactured petrol and paraffin car engines and it introduced a diesel engine in 1929, finding a receptive commercial market in the 1930s. At the time of acquisition it produced engines for power generation and marine uses. Perkins' parent, Massey-Harris-Ferguson, wishing to distance itself from its image as a farm equipment manufacturer, changed its name to Varity Corporation in 1986. Varity Perkins (as Perkins was renamed in 1996) was sold to the American earth-moving machinery producers and engine builders, Caterpillar Inc. in 1997, despite the benefits from sourcing Lucas' fuel injection system, predicted when Varity and Lucas merged in 1996. Soon after the sale the Perkins name disappeared from truck engines.

RAS/JMA

J C Thompson, 'Francis Arthur Perkins', *DBB*, 4 (1985); *all about Perkins* (the firm, 1966); Nick Baldwin, *Proprietary Engines for Vehicles* (2001)

Peterson Ltd, see HALLETT SILBERMANN

The **Petroleum Board** and the Lubricating Oil Board were wartime agencies, formed and operated by the industry with government approval, to organise and run the production and distribution of non-branded 'Pool' petrol and oil during the Second World War. The Pool system was retained until 1952-3. The establishment of the Boards on the outbreak of war followed talks between the big four distributors and the government in 1938; the Boards were answerable to the official Oil Control Board. All the industry's resources were pooled for the duration and Pool tankers operated in grey livery with white lettering. To meet wartime demands, new vehicles were added to the Pool tanker fleet, including Bedford OY, Maudslay and Atkinson tankers, as well as some International vehicles supplied under Lend-Lease. **RAS**

British Oil Distribution in Wartime (reprint from *Petroleum Times,* 1945); Edge (1998), pp. 102–7

Petroleum transport (Figures 44, 94 and 150) Frederick Simms (q.v.) is credited with coining the word 'petrol'. Working near Putney Bridge Station on the application of the Daimler internal combustion engine to river launch and car use, Simms approached distilling company Carless, Capel & Leonard, which had been established in Hackney Wick in 1860. No suitable fuel was available for the engine. Under Simms's direction the firm produced a 'double-distilled deodorised spirit' and took up his suggestion made in 1893 that it should be called petrol. 'Petrol' is first recorded in a letter written in 1876 by German engineer, Eugen Langen, but Simms was probably responsible for its introduction into English. William Leonard (1857–1923) persuaded the railways to distribute petrol, thus promoting car usage in Britain. In pre-tanker days, petrol was carried in two-gallon cans for delivery to blacksmiths, chemists and ironmongers who served as the earliest filling stations. Originally by horse cart from railheads, but quite quickly by motor lorries with a special slat-sided body, this was a most expensive method. By 1935 the 2400 gallon tanker had replaced 1200 of these cans. The tank was filled once and emptied once, these two operations comparing with 2400 in the case of the cans.

The first road tanker produced by Scammell was built in 1920 for Shell-Mex. This was a six-wheeled articulated vehicle with a stepped rectangular-section tank mounted rigidly by wooden bearers on a drop frame. It had a capacity of 2000 gallons of fuel oil and was fitted with a single cylinder Kelvin engine driving a Fueherd pump for loading and unloading the contents. To warm the load, the exhaust gases from the engine were taken through the tank.

Following this, the company produced a tank wagon without the wagon section, and in 1926 filed the first patent for a frameless tanker (q.v.), and from this grew the well-known articulated frameless tanker. The design secured a low centre of gravity and considerable saving in weight and permitted a greater payload to be carried for the same gross weight. This new frameless construction meant that the tank shell had not only to be leak proof but was also required to stand up to considerable vibration and road shocks, especially when on solid tyres. These two hazards were virtually eliminated by the adoption of the single, large, low-pressure pneumatic tyre. By 1926 Crow Carrying Company (q.v.) had a solid-tyred AEC four-wheeler converted to an artic with a stepped-frame trailer carrying two tanks.

Petroleum spirit involves more peculiarities in the chassis and tank design than does any other liquid. By the 1930s petrol tankers were made in capacities as much as 2500 gallons for use in this country and up to 4000 gallons or more for operation abroad. In the case of road tankers for use in the UK, for quantities in excess of 1500 gallons, the sanction of the Home Office had to be obtained, both as to the construction of the tank and its materials, and the design of the chassis, with particular reference to the axle weights.

The Petroleum (Regulation) Acts of 1928 and 1936 specified details of design to ensure safety, such as compartmentalisation, baffles, and manholes and also that these petrol tanks were divided into compartments and none must contain more than 600 gallons. Moreover the baffle plates had to be fitted in each compartment to minimise surging of the liquid. A manhole or mann-way is fitted to each section and the cover embodies the filling apparatus. The filling pipe has to be designed to afford a liquid seal and any opening in it is usually covered by Davy gauze, to stop external ignition sources lighting the vapour. Because of the volatility of the load, tankers in accidents, could cause horrendous damage, as in 1976 when a Texaco tanker carrying 6000 gallons hauled by a Guy Big J tractor skidded on greasy roads, wet after a long dry spell, in Westoning, Bedfordshire, causing an explosion which consumed several houses.

Up to the increase in gross vehicle weight in 1964 the Scammell artic with its frameless 3500 gallon tank was the standard workhorse for petrol companies and specialist tank hauliers. Such names as Pickfords, Stevenson,

Hardy Ltd, Thomas Allen Ltd, Crow Carrying Company, and Smith & Robinson Ltd dated back to solid tyres. Various mergers and take-overs saw them in Tankfreight or P&O Road Tanks.

The increase in gross vehicle weight in 1964 to 32 tons, and subsequent weight increases, brought steady gains in tank capacity. In 1964 a maximum capacity tanker carried 18,000 litres (4000 gallons), by 2002 this had increased to around 43,000 litres, a huge advance. The increased size initially caused problems with stability, so research took place on producing a trailer with a low centre of gravity. One outcome was the use of alloys with benefits in payload at the expense of more costly materials. By the 1970s alloy tanks for non-pressure operation were fast becoming the norm for low-flash and fuel oil products. Alternative materials were tried, such as glass-reinforced plastics for fuel oil grades, but production costs were high and today all large tankers on petroleum distribution are of aluminium while smaller vehicles on local delivery are of steel. Petroleum tankers were among the first to use electric lighting as the nature of the loads made oil lamps something of a hazard.

By 2000 long-standing UK regulations had been adapted to meet European ADR (q.v.) regulations on the carriage of dangerous goods. Earlier, rules on wiring, fire extinguishers and containment of a cab fire had been introduced. The search for stability led in the late 1980s to the Lowmax trailer with lower suspension, smaller-diameter twin tyres so that the trailer height was no greater than the cab, so improving stability and handing. Tightening safety regulations and environmental considerations have led to tanks being loaded from the bottom, instead of through an open manhole with a drop pipe. This method of loading contains the petrol vapour, allowing it to be recovered and reprocessed.

The other major change since the mid-1980s was the move by the refiners to use smaller fleets with very tightly scheduled deliveries to their own outlets. At the same time they employed contract hauliers to provide vehicles and distribution and the large supermarket operators started to operate filling stations with supplies being delivered by vehicles in the supermarket's livery. The development of pipelines to deliver fuel in quantity both added work to and took work from road haulage. The first UK pipelines were built in the Second World War to provide direct supply to some RAF airfields. A pipeline was constructed to serve London's Heathrow airport, while growing demand for fuel resulted in many rail-served small terminals being closed in favour of a single large terminal to which supplies were piped direct from a refinery. Kingsbury in the West Midlands is the best example of a new terminal well-sited to serve a large and mainly industrial area. **SW/BV**

Edge (1998); Edward Living, *Pioneers of Petrol: a centenary history of Carless, Capel and Leonard 1859–1959* (Witherby 1959), plates xvi–xviii; *CM* (17 September 1976), p. 2, (30 April 1976), p. 26

Pettit, Sir Daniel E A (1915–2000) was educated at Quarry Bank High School in Liverpool and read history and modern languages at Fitzwilliam College, Cambridge, as well as winning a blue for soccer four years in a row and representing Britain in the 1936 Olympics. He was a master at Highgate School from 1937 and after war service in Africa, India and Burma in the Royal Artillery, ending with the rank of major, rejoined the school until 1948 when he joined Unilever at Port Sunlight on the personnel and training side.

In 1954 he joined the Unilever transport arm, SPD (q.v.) as personnel manager, being promoted to the board in 1958 and a year later changing to commercial director. In 1961 he was made chairman. During his time at SPD it was shifting from moving most goods from factory to warehouse and thence to retailer, to direct delivery, cutting out the storage depot. This saved both lorry movements and warehouse space. At the same time SPD increased substantially the proportion of non-Unilever business, so that by 1962 about a third of customers were not part of the group. Then SPD owned over 750 vehicles of which 320 were refrigerated, reflecting the growth of Birds Eye and other frozen food business.

In 1971 Pettit joined the National Freight Corporation (q.v.) as chairman and chief executive, having been a part-time member of the board since 1968. He had great personal charm and charisma, according to Thompson (q.v.), and had a vision of European-wide road haulage in the recently-joined European Economic Community. This led to a couple of unfortunate acquisitions of European hauliers which were losing money and never turned around. Combined with the oil crisis of 1973/4, this precipitated huge losses and led the government to decide on managerial changes leading to Pettit's retirement in 1978. He was knighted in 1974, after he had chaired a committee looking into why there was resentment against lorries, given their economic benefits. This had been appointed by John Peyton, then Minister of Transport, and the group was representative of road haulage interests. Not surprisingly their report was up-beat, suggesting additional road building and judicious traffic management should solve the problem. During his career he served on a number of transport-related councils and bodies, such as the Freight Integration Council, National Ports Council, the council of the British Road Federation (q.v.) and the Worshipful Company of Carmen (q.v.); he was founding president of the Lorry Driver of the Year (q.v.) Association, and president of the Chartered Institute of Transport in 1971–2. **JA**

Reader (1969); Thompson (1991); *Who's Who 1997*; *Report of the Lorries and the Environment Committee* (HMSO, 1973); Sue Woolley, *The First Seventy Years: a history of the Chartered Institute of Transport 1919–1989* (1992), pp. 149–50

Pickfords (Figures 148, 156 and 165) commenced business before 1756 as a common carrier between Manchester and London using horse-drawn wagons. This makes it the UK's oldest road haulage business. Under the leadership of James, it ran a twice-weekly service, taking eight or nine days on each leg which required a total of six wagons and fifty horses. By 1777 the service was thrice weekly and by 1788 daily (except for Sunday). In the 1780s and 1790s the firm began diversifying its routes and also started using the Grand Junction Canal to move goods to London, and by the 1810s this was the dominant mode for goods traffic to London, requiring the firm to invest in canal barges. In 1814 Pickfords introduced high-speed vans on the London to Manchester route which did the journey in thirty-six hours, a tribute to road improvements. New partners were introduced in 1817 following a liquidity crisis, among them Joseph Baxendale, and in 1846 the last Pickford in the firm, Thomas, died so severing the firm from the family.

In 1837 a rail link between London and Lancashire was opened and this marked radical changes in Pickford's business. It terminated its fast van service and by 1847 its road service had virtually ceased and all long-distance goods were moved by rail. The canal traffic was similarly run down, ceasing around 1850 after a decade's decline. The spread of the rail network meant that by 1850 Pickfords could offer a comprehensive carrying service by rail to all the major towns of England and Scotland. From then until about 1900 Pickfords were essentially railway carriers by horse and cart.

Pickford first used motorised road vehicles in 1903 when they purchased two Wallis and Steevens traction engines which drew trailers carrying 5 to 8 tons. They then experimented with steam wagons, buying five from S Hindley and Sons of Dorset in 1905. They also tried petrol-driven lorries, in 1907 buying six 5-ton Commers and in 1910 eight Thornycroft 2-ton petrol-driven vans were employed. In 1912 the meat department began using mechanical transport, and lift vans were employed for household removals for easy transfer of the containers to railway wagons. Also in 1912 the firm bought more petrol motors for suburban delivery but steam remained superior for heavy haulage and in 1919 Pickfords had fifteen petrol wagons but thirty steamers, mostly Fodens. From 1899 Pickfords actively contemplated merging with its great rival, Carter Paterson & Co., for competition was ruining their profitability. In 1907 Pickfords, Carter Paterson and Beans Express co-operated on fixing rates but this collapsed by 1911 as outside firms undercut their fixed rates. As a result in 1912 a full amalgamation took place between Pickfords, CP, Beans and London Parcels Delivery Co. The balance of power lay with CP, which absorbed Pickfords, ending its independence.

In the early 1920s Pickfords began buying Swiss-made, petrol-driven 5-ton Saurer lorries with 5-ton trailers, eventually owning over 100. These replaced the Foden steam wagons. The first pneumatic tyres were used in 1924 for household removals and in 1932 Pickfords commissioned AEC to build a temperature-controlled lorry to carry 110 sides of beef from Aberdeen to London. Steam continued to be used for many years for some heavy haulage work. For example, in 1941 three Fowler road locomotives were used to move a 117-ton hammer block from Sheffield on a 64-ed wheel Crane trailer with solid tyres.

In 1919 Hay's Wharf Cartage Co. made a successful bid for the non-parcels work of Pickfords, namely heavy haulage, household removals, and dock work, especially meat traffic. The Pickfords motor fleet then comprised 46 vehicles, but by 1933 this had risen to 628. In this year Pickfords, with CP and Hay's Wharf, became the joint property of the four mainline railway companies after negotiations lasting four years, and L H Baxendale (q.v.) resigned, ending that family's connection with the firm.

It was both inevitable and ironic that Pickfords should be nationalised. Inevitable because it was already owned by the four main line railways, themselves nationalised from 1 January 1948, but ironic because many of Pickfords' operations were outside the scope of compulsory acquisition: heavy haulage was excluded, as was short-distance haulage such as carrying meat from the docks to cold stores. Pickfords was acquired as a subsidiary of Hay's Wharf Cartage and the new British Transport Commission (q.v.) gained large heavy haulage and meat transport fleets and also one involved in household removals, bulk tankers and contract hire. It also retained much of its parcels interests in the provinces. In 1950 Pickfords became the Special Traffics (Pickfords) Division of BRS (q.v.). As operators were steadily acquired by the BTC so the fleets, or parts of fleets, of many came to be passed to Pickfords' operations, often with their depots.

Numerous vehicles of varying age and size were added. Among bulk liquid hauliers passed to Pickfords were Goldsmith (from Bow, East London), Imperia and Lancashire Petrol Deliveries. Heavy haulage included several previously controlled by E Box & Co of Liverpool, E W Rudd of Stratford (also in meat haulage), Premier Transport of Birmingham, John Young of Glasgow and Scottish company Road Engines & Kerr. Removal vans came from a number of companies including the Newcastle upon Tyne fleet of Currie, which had been railway-owned, and from Parks of Portsmouth. Several specialised meat hauliers were acquired.

Pickfords Household Removals had run Bedfords, but experience with Guy Vixen 4-ton chassis taken over from smaller operators led to them becoming standard: their forward-control layout gave a usefully large load capacity. However, new Bedford OL models continued to be bought for other operations, including the meat haulage section, which also acquired new Austin K2s, as well as some AEC Matadors. A number of small operators compulsorily acquired had specialised in collecting new furniture from factories and this led to considerable expansion of Pickfords New Furniture Carriage Service.

What could be termed the second stage of denationalisation, under the Transport (Disposal of Road Haulage Property) Act 1956, set up five new nationalised companies with some 15,000 vehicles, of which 1350 were allocated to BRS (Pickfords) Ltd, 1000 to BRS (Contracts) Ltd, and 500 to BRS (Meat Haulage) Ltd. The contract hire fleet continued to expand, though as vehicles were in customers' colours it was not particularly obvious. The tanker business did particularly well, and what had been mainly a liquid-carrying business became much wider, with powders, pellets and granules, and gas carried on rigid and articulated vehicles in bulk tanks of mild steel, aluminium or stainless steel according to intended load. Scammells were still the mainstay in tank and heavy haulage.

The 1960s saw removals traffic developing to include runs to Europe.

Following the winding up of the BTC in 1963 control of the publicly-owned road transport companies passed to the new Transport Holding Company (q.v.), BRS (Pickfords) becoming plain Pickfords Ltd. In 1965 the THC acquired 75 per cent of the Tayforth Group (q.v.), its bulk tanker work passing to Pickfords. The 540-strong tanker fleet of Harold Wood & Sons was acquired and attached to Pickfords, giving it a tanker fleet of 965 vehicles, but the declining BRS (Meat Haulage) business was merged with Union Cartage Co Ltd.

The THC was wound up in 1969, in favour of the new National Freight Corporation (q.v.). Pickfords became several separate companies, according to their work, in 1971. They became Pickfords Removals Ltd, Pickfords Tank Haulage Ltd, Pickfords Heavy Haulage Ltd, and Pickfords Management Services Ltd, but Pickfords (Contracts) Ltd was transferred to BRS. A further new company was Pickfords International, formed by amalgamating Containerway Europe Ltd, Pickfords Shipping & Forwarding Co Ltd, and Rod-Air Cargo Express (International) Ltd. Tank haulage work was merged in 1972 as Tankfreight Ltd, comprising Pickfords Tank Haulage, Harold Wood, and Caledonian Bulk Liquids, another company taken over.

Recession in the early 1980s hit the heavy haulage business, which was renamed Pickfords Industrial Ltd, a title more accurately reflecting its work. The 1980 Transport Act effectively denationalised NFC, which soon mounted a successful employee buy-out, Pickfords Espana was set up in the mid-1980s, and Hoults Ltd of Newcastle upon Tyne was acquired but continued to run separately. It soon gained two more acquisitions, Pitt & Scott Ltd, and Hilton Removals (established at Burgess Hill in 1882). Another acquired was John Julian of Cornwall, dating from 1836.

A later restructuring of NFC left the Pickfords name only on removals vehicles, and in 1988 agreement was reached with Allied Van Lines of America for Pickfords to acquire it. The name Allied Pickfords was adopted, and gained the US fleet's orange livery for that part of the fleet working on corporate and international moving. In 1999 Pickfords was merged with North American Van Lines through a holding company for the merged business. NFC plc, Pickfords former parent, had a 20 per cent shareholding.   **JA/JMA**

Turnbull (1979); *IDCH*, 6 (1992), pp. 412–4; Hay's Wharf Cartage Co., pp. 35–41; Ingram (1993)

Pickin, G, & Sons, haulage contractors of Rotherham, were founded in 1850 and had built up a fleet of 115 horse-drawn vehicles by 1914. They later introduced steam, then petrol-engined lorries. By 1937 their fleet included nine Scammells: three mechanical horses, four Rigid Sixes and the first two production models of the Rigid Eight. Pickins were nationalised in 1949 and on denationalisation in 1954 part of their former fleet was acquired by S Harrison & Son, Sheffield steel hauliers.   **RAS**

Georgano (1997), p 65

The **pick-up truck**, essentially a post-war phenomenon, possibly influenced by the wartime Austin utility or 'Tilly', is a small van with open, low-sided bodywork behind the cab, perhaps with a tilt or flat cover. Originally car-derived, for example the Austin A40, Morris Minor and Mini, in the 1990s 4-wheel-drive versions, sometimes with a double-cab, became popular, introduced from North America and Asia. Like the Land-Rover, the pick-up was a work-horse, popular with farmers, garages and as part of a works transport fleet, with the benefit of a low loading-height. Factory-built bodies were normally metal-panelled, sometimes plywood-lined.   **RAS**

Classic Van and Pick-up, passim; M Schofield (ed), *The Complete Book of Pick Ups and Vans* (Los Angeles: Petersen, 1972)

Pierce-Arrow Motor Car Co. was founded in Buffalo, New York. It manufactured commercial vehicles between 1910 and 1932 and is worthy of note on two counts. At the outset senior engineering staff in its truck division were from the UK: David Fergusson, whose brother was an engineer at Leyland, John Younger, formerly with Dennis, and H Kerr Thomas, ex-Hallford. Secondly, some of the firm's greatly increased wartime production of lorries went to the British army and thus found its way on to the UK used vehicle market in the early 1920s, for example via Lawson Piggott Motors of Ealing. New Pierce-Arrow lorries were advertised in the UK during the war. The business merged with Studebaker in 1928.   **RAS**

'P-A memories', *Automobile,* 13, 10 (December 1995), p. 62

Piggyback transport of road vehicles on railway wagons is intrinsically a relatively inefficient form of inter-modal transport (q.v.). The unit being transported is more expensive than a container and its extra weight, together with the space occupied by its running gear, increase the transport cost and reduce useful capacity. If the road vehicle's own wheels are used for loading and unloading, there will probably be some compensating saving in transfer costs, but not if it is lifted on and off the wagon in the same way as a container. Nevertheless, the principle has found application from time to time.

From 1830 private carriages, complete with their occupants, were transported on flat railway wagons attached to the rear of passenger trains. The first piggyback transport of road vehicles carrying what might be classed as goods was in about 1838 when, for a few years, mail coaches were conveyed for part of their journey on passenger trains, until Post Office carriages on the expanding railway network entirely supplanted the mail coach. From about 1850, long-distance removals (q.v.) were normally undertaken by furniture vans carried on railway flat trucks, until they were gradually superseded in the twentieth century by containers. From 1892 the LSWR used a fleet of road vans to transport American frozen meat from Southampton Docks on special trains to its Nine Elms (London) goods depot, whence they were taken by horse to Smithfield Market. These were also replaced by containers in the 1930s, but around this time piggyback transport of milk, beer and other

bulk liquids began, using specially-designed 4- and 6-wheel road tanker trailers. These disappeared in the 1960s.

Interest in piggyback transport was revived in the UK in the late 1980s as a result of developments in the USA and Europe, where two different types of operation could be found. In the first, only the road trailer was carried on rail. Reversing trailers onto a long train of railway wagons is scarcely practicable, so in most cases this is a lift-on/lift-off operation. However, the first of the new generation of British piggyback carriers was designed to allow each trailer to be backed directly onto its wagon at any position in the train. This was the Tiphook Piggyback swing-deck wagon, whose very low central deck between the bogies could be slewed outwards to permit loading. Its advantage was that railhead terminals could be established quickly, without the need for special facilities. The major drawback was that the semi-trailers were non-standard and of restricted height to fit within the British railway loading gauge. A private company, Charterail Ltd, in which British Railways had a 22 per cent interest, was established in 1990 to exploit piggyback and road-rail vehicle (q.v.) technology. As the new Tiphook Piggyback wagons were delivered during 1991–2, Charterail began running trains from Melton Mowbray to London, Manchester and Glasgow for Pedigree Petfoods, between London, Warrington and Glasgow for various users, and from Harlow, Essex to Bellshill, Lanarkshire for Safeway. The road trailers' restricted height meant their maximum payload was only 22 tons. The rates necessary to attract the business were uneconomic and the company soon went into liquidation.

In 1994 the Piggyback Consortium, a pressure group representing a wide range of freight transport interests, published a plan for enlarging the loading gauge of one of the south-north railway routes to allow piggyback transport of 4-metre-high semi-trailers between the Channel Tunnel and the Midlands, North West, Glasgow and an Irish Sea port. The estimated cost was relatively modest and it might have become a government- or European Community-funded project, had it not fallen victim to the upheaval of railway privatisation. The Consortium's studies did result in the production of some simpler, lift-on/lift-off piggyback wagons for operation within Britain and, together with the earlier Tiphook wagons, they have been operating services since 1998, chiefly for chemical tank trailers which fit more readily into the railway loading gauge.

The other type of piggyback operation is the 'rolling highway', the drive-on/drive-off transport of complete lorries on flat trains. This requires an even larger loading gauge. The only UK example is the Eurotunnel freight shuttle service through the Channel Tunnel (q.v.), opened in 1994.   **GAB**

G A Boyes, 'The furniture van or pantechnicon' and 'The pantechnicon: further notes' (Railway & Canal Historical Society, Road Transport Group, *occasional papers*, 95 (1997) and 122 (1998); 'Trucks for conveyance of road trailer milk tankers, Southern Railway', *Railway Gazette*, (9 October 1931), pp. 464–5; Twells and Bourne (1983), ch. 14; 'Pedigree Petfoods—bi-modal pioneer', *Modern Railways*, 49 (1992) pp. 20–3; *Working to put Trucks on Trains* (Piggyback Consortium brochure, 1995)

Platers, see CAR DELIVERY

Platform body. The simplest, commonest and oldest body design on a van or lorry is a flat platform. It is also the most versatile, since most loads can be carried on it. Until speeds and weights rose, and the skeletal trailer (q.v.) was introduced, platform bodywork was often used to carry old-style containers, which were secured to the bodywork with just a chain or rope fastening.

The earliest development of a platform body saw the addition of hinged dropsides (which were easily removable), typically to retain materials such as sand or gravel. A platform body normally had a headboard at the front, to prevent the load moving forward on heavy braking and spilling, or damaging the cab.

Use of platform and dropside bodies has gradually declined since the 1960s, in favour of enclosed bodywork, mainly curtainsiders (q.v.). Sheeting and roping (q.v.) a load needed some skill and time. The latter became more important with the tightening of drivers' hours (q.v.) requirements and rising labour costs. The nature of goods being carried and their packaging was also evolving. Bottles were no longer carried in wooden boxes and stout cardboard boxes gave way to shrink-wrapped goods, often on pallets (q.v.), and the weight and casing of large household appliances (brown goods) changed, so methods of handling had to alter too.

The platform body — a design dating back to horse-drawn days — lives on. For example, pallets of bricks and concrete blocks as well as other building materials are still carried on basic platform bodies, usually with simple dropsides and often with a vehicle-mounted crane fitted for unloading.   **JMA**

Plating and testing. Public concern about the condition of some motor vehicles, particularly their brakes, led the Ministry of War Transport Committee on Road Safety in 1944 to recommend the establishment of public vehicle testing stations, following the example of some US states. The annual 'MoT Test' was eventually introduced in 1959, initially for cars and light goods vehicles up to 30 cwt unladen weight more than ten years old, but by 1966 the age qualification had been progressively reduced to three. Testing of heavy goods vehicles soon followed, but would have been ineffective without parallel measures to prevent brake efficiency being impaired by vehicle overloading.

The Construction & Use Regulations 1966 required motor goods vehicles registered from 1968 to be fitted with a plate (sometimes called a manufacturer's plate) showing, *inter alia*, the design maximum axle weights, gross weight and, if appropriate, train weight (that is including any trailers). Trailers exceeding one ton unladen weight manufactured after this date were likewise required to carry a similar plate.

'Ministry' plating and testing for goods vehicles exceeding 1½ tons and trailers over one ton unladen were introduced on 1 August 1968 by the Goods Vehicle (Plating and Testing) Regulations 1968. Vehicles must be submitted for testing within one year of registration (or within one year of the first sale of the chassis in the case of trailers and semi-trailers) and annually thereafter. On successful completion of the test, a goods vehicle test certificate is issued, valid until the next test is due; without it a motor vehicle cannot be re-licensed. In the case of trailers, which are not subject to licensing, a test date disc is also issued and must be displayed on the nearside.

Initially Ministry plating coincided with the first heavy goods vehicle test, the 'plated particulars' being determined by examination of the vehicle. Following the introduction, under EEC legislation, of a system for awarding 'type approval' to goods vehicle manufacturers, since 1983 plating has taken place at first registration. The particulars are entered on a plating certificate, for retention by the operator, and on a Ministry plate, which is displayed in the vehicle cab or, for a trailer, on the nearside. The term 'plate' is here slightly misleading. Unlike the manufacturer's plate, which is made of metal, the Ministry plate is more modestly of paper enclosed in plastic laminate. The design was later enhanced in line with an EEC directive to include the EEC maximum permitted weights and also length and width dimensions. **GAB**

Statutory Instruments. *Goods Vehicle Tester's Manual* (1984); later editions titled *Heavy Goods Vehicle Inspection Manual*

Pool petrol, see PETROLEUM BOARD

The **popular culture of goods road transport,** as expressed in British literature, art, music, drama and popular entertainment, has always been overshadowed by that of passenger road transport. Although it was a less-popular subject than stage coach travel, artists such as John Constable and writers such as Charles Dickens and Thomas Hardy, were able to portray horse-drawn goods transport with understanding and a degree of affection. In the following century, however, the motor lorry generally failed to inspire similar feelings and was eclipsed in the creative arts by the tram, charabanc, bus, car and bicycle.

The lorry has been ignored by artists, except by those such as Peter J Davies and Alain Spillett who started in the 1990s to produce paintings specifically for lorry enthusiasts. There is no twentieth-century counterpart to Constable's famous painting of *The Hay-Wain* (1821). Some distinguished commercial artists have from time to time been commissioned to work on road haulage themes, for example, Frank Newbould painted a cover for Cadbury's house magazine in 1925 and the cover of the 1977 TDG (q.v.) annual report was by Anthony Colbert.

Twentieth-century writers have often preferred to look back with nostalgia to the horse-transport era; Israel Zangwill's *Jinny the Carrier* (1919) and S L Bensusan's *Marshland* novels and short stories (1932–55) both featured Essex country carriers, for example. In Bernard Ash's *Silence for His Worship* (1953), which may be semi-autobiographical, the self-made hero builds up a substantial haulage business in London, but gives it away; the successful transition to motor-traction by the new owner is dealt with perfunctorily. R E Delderfield's epic trilogy of novels about a nation-wide carrier — *God is an Englishman, Theirs was the Kingdom* and *Give us this Day* (1970–3) — ends with the entry into service of the company's first motor vehicle.

The Brothers, a long-running popular BBC TV Sunday-evening serial of the 1970s, epitomises the failure of the haulage industry to make an impact on the popular imagination; although nominally about a family-owned haulage company, the saga concentrated exclusively on the family relationships, largely ignoring the haulage activity. It is ironic that one of the most-enduring popular images of twentieth-century goods road transport is David Jason's role as the cycle delivery boy for Arkwright's corner grocery shop in the BBC TV comedy series *Open All Hours* (1976–85).

In fiction and screen drama, lorries and vans have been chiefly associated with crime — carrying stolen or smuggled goods, being high-jacked or carrying illegal immigrants — most frequently in television police drama series. The film *Hell Drivers* (1957) also portrays the road haulage industry in a poor light: the lorry drivers, working for a corner-cutting firm, have to drive their Dodge tippers dangerously fast to earn a bonus; violence, macho behaviour and cut-throat competition are suggested as a normal part of the industry. In the same year *The Long Haul*, starring Victor Mature and Diana Dors, featured road haulage as involved with law-breaking. A murdered lorry driver is the subject of Alan Hunter's detective novel *Gently Where the Roads Go* (1962), but in *They Drive by Night* (1938) and *The Hi-jackers* (1963) the lorry drivers take part in solving the crime. Alfred Hitchcock's *Frenzy* (1972) used Covent Garden Market as one of its principal locations, with road haulage playing a part in the plot.

If the road haulage industry has generally not been effective in promoting its public image, this cannot be said of the period when it was controlled by the British Transport Commission. The documentary films produced by British Transport Films to promote British Road Services are of the highest standard. They include *Dodging the Column* (1952), *They Take the High Road* (1960), and *Ferryload* (1960).

A similar pattern can be seen in the field of music. Charles Woodhouse's orchestral *Wait for the Waggon*, Sir Edward Elgar's *The Waggon Passes* from the *Nursery Suite* (1931) and the part of Hobson, the carter, in Benjamin Britten's opera *Peter Grimes* (1945) are examples of retrospection by twentieth-century composers. The music-hall song made famous by Marie Lloyd in 1919, *Don't Dilly Dally*, with its chorus *My old man said "Follow the van"*, is about furniture removal by horse-drawn pantechnicon. The only British music celebrating the motor-lorry era is the specially-commissioned incidental music for some of the films that have been mentioned, such as Kenneth V Jones's score for *They Take the High Road* and Edward Williams's for *Ferryload*. Vehicle building was one of the industries associated with brass bands, the Foden's Motor Works (formed 1902), Morris Motors (1924) and Leyland Motors Concert Bands being among the most celebrated.

In the USA, the long-distance road train (the 'big rig') acquired an image of glamour and awe. A 1970s television advertisement for the Rowntree Yorkie chocolate bar humorously suggested the extension of this image to the British articulated lorry. In spite of the 'juggernaut' epithet popularised by the anti-road lobby at this period, the well-known 'Trucking Song' sketch in the satirical comedy programme *Not the Nine O' Clock News* (BBC2 TV, 1979–82), with its driver fearlessly squashing hedgehogs, confirmed that it was never a serious possibility. Road freight is hugely important in modern life, but popular culture scarcely reflects this. **PLS/GAB**

Philip L Scowcroft, 'References to road transport in English literature' and 'Roads and road transport in music' (Railway & Canal Historical Society, Road Transport Group, *occasional papers* 5 and 9, 1992); Ian Yearsley, 'Road transport as portrayed in literature', *Roads & Road Transport History Conference Newsletter,* no. 19 (October 1999); 'Hell Drivers', *The Road Way* (August 1957), p.15.

The **Post Office** (Figures 123 and 151) became by far the largest UK operator of commercial vehicles, until the separation in 1981 of Post Office Telephones, a move that more than halved the fleet. The modern Royal Mail fleet is huge by any standards, at around 29,000 vehicles, including small numbers of cars and battery-electric trucks.

The GPO was an early user of motor vehicles. In 1897 a steam motor van ran between London, Croydon and Redhill and in 1898 it tried a motor vehicle operated by Stirling's Motor Garage Co. of Inverary for the 26.5 mile run to Ardrishaig, but winter problems forced a return to horse haulage. In 1910 an Arrol car was tried for about a year, but not until 1914 did a motor vehicle become the permanent choice. The GPO's early motor ventures were cautious, with almost all the vehicles run by contractors. Largest of these was McNamara (q.v.), which with Dutfield was still providing some vehicles in the late 1940s. Nationalisation of road haulage prompted a decision to run all its own fleet.

Horse transport survived a surprisingly long time, partly because much decision-making lay with 450 local postmasters. For example, well into the 1920s the Cardiff postmaster decided to retain horse-drawn vehicles because introducing motors would have necessitated rebuilding its premises. Mechanisation of deliveries was slow, walking or cycling being the predominant forms well into the twentieth century. It was not until 1914 that 20 motorcycle combinations of three different makes were bought to replace postmen on horseback. Otherwise the early use of motor vehicles was in the stores department (which from 1905 started owning the motor vehicles it used), for medium-distance carriage of mailbags, or for local runs between sorting office, post offices and railway stations.

The first significant conversion came in June 1905 when a Thomas Tilling (q.v.) Milnes-Daimler replaced horses on the London–Brighton parcels service, and by 1909 there were some 60 motor mail van services. By 1911–12 the number had risen to 120, including a London–Birmingham run, while the 1921 total reached 1200. Many motor mail services needed just one vehicle, but some required several and one needed a fleet of 70. At least some of the motor runs had been introduced to counter dissatisfaction with the railways over punctuality or high rates: back in 1898 a Daimler had been used between Reading and Newbury because of unpunctual running of a GWR goods train between the two towns. Earlier, a nightly horse-drawn service between London and Brighton had begun in 1887 to break the expensive rail monopoly.

Contracts with providers of transport were stringent, and in the earliest days involved three signatories: the GPO, the contractor and an insurance company to indemnify against loss or damage. Motor vans had to be thoroughly watertight, provided and lighted with suitable lamps and fittings both inside and outside and with a fire extinguisher. Spare vehicles and lamps had to be available, and there was a five shilling penalty if a van was over 10 minutes late arriving more than once in a week: more than 30 minutes late saw the penalty doubled. A guard (provided by the GPO) had to travel with every van, and its driver had to be provided with a GPO-style uniform, with GPO badges, at the contractor's expense. Motor vans had to run at a minimum speed of 10 mph (against 8 mph for horse-drawn ones) and motor drivers had to be not under 25 years old or over 50, whereas horse drivers, while still

needed to be 'steady and sober and competent' could be aged between 18 and 60. Another feature of the contracts was precise measurement of each journey length, a very complicated matter with, for example, central London contracts involving a vehicle making numerous short trips to and from sorting office to railway station, and local post offices. Every journey (and its timings) was scrupulously recorded and measured, with distances calculated to the nearest yard, and paid for accordingly.

By 1907 the GPO's own fleet numbered just three vehicles, and ownership did not get under way until after the First World War. Contractors included well-known names and even Leyland Motors at one stage provided a fleet. Some contractors had a very long relationship. Manchester-based George Richard & Sons began horse-drawn postal work in 1843: mail had previously been conveyed by stage coach, and by 1924 Richard had just replaced its last 70 horses on mail contracts.

A Motor Transport Scheme was set up in 1919, and bought over 650 mechanically-propelled vehicles from the Disposals Board (q.v.). Of these 500 were motorcycle combinations. A big step came in 1920 when 50 new GWK vans were bought. However, they were a bad choice and all had gone by 1925. Nearly 300 Fords bought at about the same time proved more reliable but buy-British pressure saw two Morris and a few Trojan vans acquired. This began a long association with Morris and Morris-Commercial that still survives with the LDV van successor. The Ford fleet totalled 625, including many reconditioned after war service, before the Morris association got into full swing. Cost studies at the time showed Fords were costing only £5 a year more to run than a motorcycle combination on a daily average mileage of 50, and were cheaper for 70 miles a day: higher maintenance and depreciation charges for the motorcycles were the culprits. Not until 1984 were Fords again bought in quantity.

In some respects GPO thinking was remarkably ahead. Each motor vehicle had a 'life history' book which not only recorded every item of expenditure on it, but also charged against it the cost of hiring a substitute in the event of a breakdown, while there was sometimes a charge for the theoretical cost of a parking space. A 1920s internal report felt that 'so large a user of vans as the GPO should have no difficulty in the long run in securing production of a type of van suited to its requirements'. This probably explains the long relationship with Morris, which from 1934 was producing a rather different version of its Minor van just for the GPO. Morris and successors including LDV were willing to build and complete vans on the production line, whereas even in the 1960s most other makers' production systems were insufficiently flexible and could not or would not complete internal fitments and livery on the line.

By 1933 the mechanised fleet totalled nearly 8000, with 2700 Morris and 320 Ford vans, plus 1200 motorcycle combinations for postal use. The telephone side included 500 Morris vans, 500 Albion lorries and over 2100 motorcycle combinations. Solo motorcycles jumped in number from the mid-1930s when they became widely used for delivery of telegrams. Combinations declined, because their limited capacity saw Morris 5-cwt vans come into favour. From 1934 the Minors were actually a van version of the Morris 8 car, with a different wheelbase, different wheels and other details unlike those of standard Minor vans. Pre-war Minors usually had GPO-designed bodies built by a number of contractors, including Bonallack, Duple and Park Royal. A striking feature of those for telephone linesmen was an additional angled windscreen above the normal one, so that telephone wires and telegraph poles could be inspected while driving along. Even when the Minivan was introduced in the 1960s, GPO versions were for a time specified with a smaller engine.

Motor vehicles were not generally used for local mail delivery and collection from post boxes in rural areas until well into the 1930s. This followed a decision that reorganisation 'had not to adversely affect any personnel with any appreciable length of service'. Thus introduction of vans on this work followed staff retirements.

Another practice established quite early, and which was to endure, was for specification of body sizes in terms of cubic foot capacity, which in turn was based on the theoretical capacity of a mailbag. Standard sizes became 35 (originally 30), 70, 105, 160, 250 and 340 cu ft, the smallest being the Minor van. In the 1950s sizes changed to 50, 100 and 150 cu ft, plus 240 and 360 cu ft, the last two having coachbuilt bodies. Concurrent with the growth of the motor fleet in the 1930s came establishment of a network of road transport workshops for vehicle repair and maintenance, together with a number of central repair depots for heavier work. Not until the 1980s did this system begin to change, as intervals between routine servicing were extended and vehicle durability improved. The last of the central repair depots closed in the mid-1990s. In the 1980s the Post Office Corporation began using its enormous purchasing power to buy more vans annually at keen prices but kept them for much shorter periods.

The 1930s saw a few specialised vehicles added to the fleet, including a streamlined van (with very low load capacity) on a Morris-Commercial chassis finished in the blue of the Air Mail service, and two mobile post offices for use at open-air events, with Morris-Commercial tractive units pulling Brockhouse semi-trailers. They were notable for the registration numbers GPO 1 and GPO 2. This series should have been allocated to Somerset, but was transferred to London County Council which used it entirely for GPO vehicles, almost all of which were registered to London. From about that time the organisation was allocated almost complete series of registration letters, as annual purchases climbed to two or three thousand.

Difficulties in the Second World War saw acquisitions of further motorcycles and motorcycle combinations. From 1941 Morris vans (and some Fords) were standard factory products bought complete, rather than with coachbuilt bodies, though they were subsequently fitted out and modified for GPO use by bodybuilders. Since then all deliveries of smaller vans have been standard products, albeit with Crown locks, security grills and other features.

Motorcycles continued to be used for telegram delivery, with the first BSA Bantams bought in 1948. This became the standard telegram bike, a last batch of 400 Bantams being acquired in 1970–1. Mopeds then became the only two-wheelers bought.

The early 1960s saw more use of road vehicles for parcels work, with a pioneering East Anglian Road Service based in Canning Town in east London and Liverpool Street station no longer used. Morris FF tractive units undertook much of this work, drawing Brockhouse drop-frame boxvan trailers with a 1300 cu ft capacity. Vehicles generally became more varied, for example with Land-Rovers being introduced on a number of rounds serving rugged rural terrain. In the late 1950s the Morris LD van became the standard large van in various sizes, and continued to be bought into the early 1970s. All told some 2170 Morris LDO vans were bought between 1957 and 1971. It was replaced by the Leyland EA, and after that van ceased to be built in the UK, with its production line moved to India, the guaranteed spares supply was also sourced from India. An indication of the importance of the Post Office to Leyland came when delays in production of the larger version of the new EA van led to production of LDOs being recommenced, just to meet Post Office requirements. While diesel power ultimately became the norm for this (and larger) sizes of vehicle, it was not until 1985 that the smallest vans were specified with such engines. A year before that, deliveries of new small mailvans had included Austin Metros and Maestros and Ford Escorts and Fiestas. Earlier, the Morris Minivan had not proved very successful, with its limited ground clearance and low loading height, and various alternatives had been tried, including (in 1970) 50 Reliant Supervan III three-wheelers (made of a special fire-resistant resin): these were all sold after less than four years' use. Minivans were also used for telegram delivery work, but telegram delivery ceased in 1982. Other small vans included Bedford HAs, bought between 1975 and 1979.

The GPO became the Post Office Corporation in 1969, at which time its fleet (including staff cars) totalled 61,368. This change made it responsible for vehicle licensing and taxation, matters from which it had previously been exempt as a government department. Then the British Tele-communications Act in 1981 split the business into two separate nationalised organisations, the Post Office and British Telecommunications. The latter was subsequently privatised. Within the Post Office a further change in 1986 moved parcels work. For a short period in 2001–2 the parent company was renamed Consignia, but was soon replaced by Royal Mail plc, and the operating divisions Post Office Ltd and Parcelforce Worldwide retained their titles. At one time the postal and telephone fleets were of similar size, but the huge growth in phone use meant that at the time of the split a fleet of 53,970 vehicles passed to BT. After the formation of the POC vehicles were registered and taxed by the local postmaster or local telephone manager.

By 1982 the fleet included 12,000 50 cu ft vans and 6600 150 cu ft vans, mainly for delivery work, with 2100 240, 2450 360 and 1050 600 cu ft vans all for inter-office and rail station work. There were also 740 tractive units with 1600 semi-trailers, plus various other types in small numbers, including a number of post buses, which combined mail delivery and collection work with fare-paying facilities for the travelling public in rural areas. The first postbus service began in 1969 and the concept was gradually extended, initially mainly with Commer PB minibuses suitably adapted. As the network grew a number of Land-Rovers were also used, with the most rural services often provided by cars suitably adapted. The 1980s saw the return of mopeds, usually for rural post rounds of about 15 to 20 miles, where they replaced pedal cycles. From 1983 personnel carriers began to be used in quantity as new sorting facilities were often opened on industrial sites away from town centres. From 1987 increasing numbers of similar vehicles of 150 cu ft capacity were used also to take postmen out to their rounds: some of the vans could also carry bikes, which returned to favour on some urban delivery rounds. The vans were known as Postmen Accelerators and were also used as conventional mailvans.

The parcels side increasingly followed its own vehicle purchase policy, and on its formation it ordered 4,000 new vehicles. It set up its own sorting offices, and quickly moved away from use of rail. What became the Parcelforce fleet included many large Mercedes-Benz and Iveco Ford panel vans, and it also developed a 530 cu ft collection and delivery van based on what was then the Leyland-DAF van chassis but with lightweight coachbuilt body incorporating an electrically-operated nearside door to make entry and egress easier.

The letter side of the POC moved away from complex rail links to road for journeys of up to 80 miles in the late 1980s, and then in the mid-1990s developed its Railnet operation which used a smaller number of faster mail-only trains linking a number of purpose-built terminals which are fed by road vehicles. The largest road-rail interchange is at Willesden, London, and one quarter of all mail is said to use Railnet at some stage. **JMA**

Daunton (1985); Wright (1987); Post Office Green Papers on cycles 11 (1935), air mail operations 23 and 45 (1936 and 1939) and motor transport 28 (1936)

The **Post Office parcel post** service commenced in 1883. This followed the Universal Postal Union's agreement to start an international parcels service. The railways were unsuccessful in objecting to the new service and ultimately agreed to a contract to run for 21 years to carry this traffic. Post offices had to be equipped to receive the new business, and then to deliver the parcels. Heavy duty skips were at first used for the railway services. To reduce its costs, the Post Office introduced sacks and horse-drawn parcel coaches, using contractors. The first was the London–Brighton run. By 1890 there were eight services, all running nightly and having armed guards.

The first motor run, in 1905 was again on the London–Brighton service. By 1914 there were some 38 services serving the major conurbations. These ended at the outbreak of the First World War.

After the war only 5 per cent of the post went by road and under a new agreement with the now amalgamated railways they were to receive 44 per cent of the postage charge, with the Post Office not to convey more than 10 per cent of the parcels traffic by road. The railways also competed for Post Office traffic, including special rates for major customers.

Between the wars the Post Office service continued without much change or profit. Indeed it was 1967 before small-wheeled containers were introduced together with the first mechanised sorting hubs. There were to be 31 dedicated parcels depots.

In 1984 the weight limit for parcels was raised to 25 kilos, keeping the flat rate of £3.95. The RHA (q.v.) complained to the Transport Secretary about alleged unfair advantages the Post Office had over the independent carrier, notably the 10-hour day, and exemption from fitting tachographs.

The Post Office introduced separate management for letters, parcels and counters. In 1989 Royal Mail Parcels became Parcelforce, with a new livery, with a diamond logo, and retaining the royal crown. It has its own independent management, and invested in new purpose-built depots. A major change was the agreement with unions to negotiate separate pay and conditions for parcels and letters staff. Parcelforce provided a range of services for the British Isles, Europe and virtually the rest of the world. **GM**

The **Potter Group** of Ripon, Ely, Droitwich and Selby was founded by Derek Potter at Ripon with one vehicle in 1965. It had grown by the end of the century to some 40 lorries with a new rail-linked depot at Knowsley opened in 2000. Its distinctive character derived from its multiple road, rail and storage activity, rather than a simple road haulage operation — few other hauliers owned and operated their own shunting engines. Potter's concept was that of a mixed structure in transport provision, assisted in practice by the rail connections in existence at Ely (opened 1981) and Selby (1983), both former sugar beet factory sites, although rail freight take-up was slow and this aspect of the group's operations was in effect subsidised by its storage activities. **RAS**

MT (4 May 2000), pp. 14–15; *Rail*, 421 (31 October 2001), pp. 44–8

Powder traffic (Figure 45) operation was not unknown before the Second World War: for example, the Standard Pulverised Fuel Co. Ltd operated Dennis and Commer/Hands/ Butterfield units with twin hoppers in the late 1930s for the transport of 'Pulverite', which was discharged by air pressure. However, it was the need for the cement-producing companies to meet the demands of post-war reconstruction which led to the wholesale introduction of bulk powder transport in the UK. Initially box-like, covered tipping bodies were utilised, but the demands of motorway construction led to the use of tankers, which blew powdered cement into silos, which in turn fed automatic concrete- making plants. By the second half of the 1950s companies such as Blue Circle and Rugby were using blower pots [hoppers] or tanks on Leyland Comet and Thames chassis, the blowing equipment being located in the passenger seat area of the cab. It additionally gave the vehicle the ability to self-load from bulk rail trucks, using the lorry's blower unit to pipe compressed air to the rail truck, feeding the cement powder into the lorry's tank by another pipe. From the 1950s onwards increasing quantities of cement and other powder or small grain commodities, such as flour, sugar, salt, sand and lime, were transported in bulk tankers. Carmichaels of Worcester and Interconsult of Slough were amongst the prominent makers of pressure discharge tankers at that period. **GMcB/RAS**

Wright, (1986) and (1989), p. 18; B Tuck, *Classic Hauliers 2* (1991), ch. 8

The **preservation** and enthusiast movement, comprising individuals, clubs and societies, museums and publications, has done much to encourage the growth and spread of interest in the history of all aspects of road transport, including road haulage, by ensuring the survival of artefacts, records, photographic collections and information and the display and running of vehicles. The doyen of commercial vehicle preservation bodies is the Road Locomotive Society, founded in 1937. What is now the Historic Commercial Vehicle Society (q.v.), is the national society catering for all owners and enthusiasts of commercial vehicles manufactured twenty or more years ago; it organises the London to Brighton run and publishes an illustrated magazine, *Historic Commercial News*. Commercial Transport in Preservation is a recent breakaway from the HCVS in the west country. The Commercial Vehicle & Road Transport Club, founded in 1965, publishes a newsletter and organises the Classic Commercial Motor Show, which held its twenty-first anniversary in 2000. The Transport Trust, which was also founded in 1965, aims to facilitate the preservation of items of all modes of transport of historic or technical interest, including books, papers, ephemera and photographs. The Trust attempts to co-ordinate the whole transport preservation movement, seeing itself in an advisory and enabling role. It maintains a library and archive at Ironbridge and publishes *Transport Digest*.

There are also numerous one-marque bodies, which play an important role in raising awareness of the marque, locating specimens for preservation, assisting with spares and bringing specialist knowledge together; most publish a newsletter or journal for members. The AEC Society was founded in 1983; the newest is the Leyland Society, founded in 1998. Most clubs are members of the Federation of British Historic Vehicle Clubs. In 1997 this produced, in collaboration with the School of Information Studies at the University of Central England, an important report on the historic vehicle movement in Britain, *Preserving the Past for the Future*. The UCE, together with the University of Brighton and the Universita Ca'Foscari di Venetia, supports the Historic Vehicle Research Institute based at Brighton, which was established in November 2000. The Roads & Road Transport History

Conference (q.v.), founded in 1992 and renamed an Association in 2002, provides a unique meeting ground for amateur and professional road transport historians. There are numerous museums with some relevant holdings; the following may be singled out: the British Commercial Vehicle Museum at Leyland, and the Science Museum vehicle collection at Wroughton Airfield, near Swindon, Wiltshire, though the latter is only open to the public on a few days a year. The Milestones Museum, Basingstoke, which opened in November 2000, houses Tasker (q.v.) and Thornycroft (q.v.) vehicles; there is an important collection of electric vans at the Wythall Museum of the Birmingham & Midland Motor Omnibus Trust. The National Motor Museum, Beaulieu and the Museum of British Road Transport, Coventry each have some commercial vehicle exhibits, but have a strong emphasis on cars and the British Motor Industry Heritage Trust collection at Gaydon, Warwickshire is almost exclusively car-related. There is a National Association of Road Transport Museums to provide a forum. Interest in preservation is stimulated by several magazines which are widely available. *Vintage Commercial* (first published in 1962 and merged with *Old Motor*) was a pioneer; other titles are listed in the bibliography. The Post Office Vehicle Club was founded in 1962 to bring together the activities of a number of observers of the GPO fleet. Its range has extended and includes a monthly journal, *Post Horn*. Scrapyards, many of which are currently closing and being cleared as a result of EU regulations, have been an important location for the survival at least of chassis and engines. Bodywork tends to suffer from decades of exposure to the elements, so that many restored commercial vehicles have completely rebuilt or new bodies; fortunately the dedication and skill of preservationists usually ensures that authentic replicas are made. Many lightweight lorries, particularly Bedfords, have been kept alive beyond their normal life-span as horseboxes. Numerous commercial vehicle chassis also survive in active use by showmen, often drastically altered to serve as generator-trucks, tractor units, or transporters for fairground rides. **RAS**

N Baldwin, 'The making of an enthusiast – preservation becomes paramount', *VCVM*, 3, 9 (July/August 1987), pp. 22–5; W A Briggs, 'The Road Locomotive Society', *Yesteryear Transport*, 12 (1982), pp. 27–8; R Coates, 'Wiltshire's Aladdin's caves', *VCV*, 123 (March 2000), pp. 20–5; Jenkinson (1977); *Daily Telegraph* (25 November 2000), Motoring, 15; Post Office Vehicle Club, *Tenth Anniversary supplement* (1972); Malcolm Slater, *Travelling Fair* (Driffield: Japonica, 2002)

Preston, Richard, & Son Ltd (Prestons of Potto) traces its origins to 1936, when Richard Preston senior formed a partnership with a farmer, William Thomas, to carry out agricultural contracting. Following Thomas' death within a few months, Preston continued the business single-handed. Originally it specialised in corn threshing, but diversified during the war into timber cutting and in the late 1940s into grass and grain drying, for which a suitable building was constructed at Potto Station, near the village of Potto (at that time in the North Riding). A further diversification was into cable laying for the GPO, at the time undertaking a major expansion of the telephone service.

Power for the business's various activities was generated by steam engines. In 1957, at the time of the Suez crisis, shortages of diesel fuel were being experienced. A brick manufacturer, Crossleys of Hurworth near Darlington, was having difficulty delivering bricks for a major contract involving construction of the chapel at Ampleforth College when one of its directors, passing through Potto station, noticed a former fairground engine at work and asked Preston if it could carry bricks. For the next three months the steam engine, 'Lightning II', carried bricks from Hurworth to Ampleforth on a two-day cycle. The significance of this event was both to move the Preston business into mainstream road haulage and to explain the business's continuing involvement in steam engine restoration and events.

In the late 1950s the focus of activity was agricultural and brick traffic, and this continued into the early 1960s when the first loads for ICI, at the time Europe's fastest growing chemical manufacturer, were obtained. In 1965 Anne, Richard Preston (junior's) wife, whom he had married in 1960, joined the company, bringing with her a transport and administration background. The rail line passing through Potto had by this time closed and the opportunity was taken to purchase most of the surplus railway land in the area for future expansion. It was desired to take advantage of proximity to the steel industry of Teesside, but entry for a newcomer was difficult. The problem was resolved by purchase of two businesses holding steel contracts, C W Tinkler and Freeman, Volkers and Stuart (FVS), both of Stockton; the Tinkler name was dispensed with and its premises kept for the short term until the Pickfords Stockton depot became available. The FVS name and identity was retained for steel and other bulk commodities, operating from the Stockton depot but co-ordinated where appropriate with the parent Prestons business, which became Richard Preston & Son Ltd in 1969.

The long-distance trunk movement which developed from the early 1970s created a need for a southern depot, which was created at Eaton Socon, Bedfordshire; the strength of this location was that it lay on the A1 trunk road, could be used as a base for work generated by growth in light industry in that area, and was also at an economic distance for a round trip from Potto within drivers' hours regulations. Customers attracted by the Eaton Socon base included British Sugar, Pedigree Petfoods and London Brick (q.v.) (part of the Hanson group); later part of the Potto premises were developed as the northern distribution point for London Brick.

In 1993 Prestons developed an intermediate depot at Knottingley, South Yorkshire, near the A1/M62 intersection, particularly to serve the nearby Coca-Cola-Schweppes plant for which the UK trunking contract was secured. Other smaller operating centres (q.v.) have since been established. In 1991 the business comprised 170 tractors, 400 trailers and 250 employees; this increased by the end of 1999 to 195 tractors but 580 trailers, reflecting greater

use of sub-contractors. The turnover for 1999 was £18 million, some of it generated by diversification from mainstream haulage into warehousing, supply chain management and employment agency work. The proprietors still see its focus as a family-owned and controlled general haulage business, willing and capable of undertaking most types of traffic. As the steel and chemical industries declined, other sectors were developed in their place, in particular food products to the distribution centres of supermarket groups, but Prestons continued its activity in other sectors including bulk powder tankers. Reflecting the desire of British Steel (later Corus) to deal with a smaller number of distribution contractors, Prestons formed a consortium with R Durham and Son of Billingham, TSD, to carry the reducing quantities of steel traffic (q.v.).

The company's strengths were in three features, two of which were its location and its management. Its headquarters and principal operating base remain at Potto, which lies close to the A19 trunk road connecting Tyneside, Teesside and the A1. It is close to the industry of Teesside but within the county of North Yorkshire, where business costs are lower; at the same time it is close to, but outside, the North York Moors National Park. Employee relationships in rural areas are traditionally better, and this interacted with the quality of management to develop a strong feeling of loyalty and identity with the local community. The continuity of family control is also a factor. By the end of 1999 Richard (jnr) had become chairman with Anne Preston and their son David, who had returned to the company after a period gaining wider experience with Transport Development Group (q.v.), as joint managing directors. Anne Preston in particular was heavily involved in RHA affairs, becoming the first female member of its National Council, chairman of the Long-Distance Committee and chairman of the North-East District. She was awarded the MBE for services to transport in 1987 and continued to serve on the RHA Executive Board, of which she was also the first female member.

The third element was a matter of being in the right place at the right time. In common with other businesses, Prestons benefited from a number of factors encouraging the trunk haulage industry from the late 1960s. These were improvements to the national pattern of trunk roads; increases in maximum permitted tonnage; and the replacement of A, B and C by O licensing from 1969. Originally the company favoured Atkinson trucks with Gardner engines, but by the 1980s it was turning to European manufacturers, in particular Volvo. Since then it has operated most major brands including ERF, DAF, Mercedes-Benz and MAN. Until the 1990s tractor units were retained for about ten years but then moves were taken to standardise on Scanias and keep them no more than three years. Prestons became a member of the Transport Association (q.v.) in 1999.   **DMH**

R Tuck *Classic Hauliers 2* (1991); 'The Iron Lady', *CM* (2 March 2000), pp. 43–4; interview with Richard and Anne Preston

The **Proctor** was a short-lived (1947–52) lightweight, forward-control vehicle, designed in 1939, with a post-war prototype built at Edmonton, but production took place at a new factory near Norwich. With a Perkins diesel engine, its specification was similar to Seddon and Vulcan. BRS was a significant customer, notably for its Coventry and Hereford depots. After component supply problems contributed to the end of the marque, its Hereford distributors, Praill's Motors Ltd, built up a few from spares.   **RAS**

Baldwin (1982)

Producer gas (Figure 152) was used to a limited extent in the Second World War to power buses, though even London Transport achieved fewer than 200 conversions, including only five of its large service lorry and van fleet. The logic behind these conversions was that coal-based fuels were local and plentiful, whereas oil-based fuels were scarce in wartime and needed to be imported through dangerous seas. Whether fitted directly on the vehicle, thereby taking up load space, or carried on a trailer (Brockhouse had the main contract to supply them), producer gas units, burning solid fuel such as anthracite, adversely affected the converted vehicle's usefulness in terms of range, speed, pay-load and servicing requirements. Some commercial vehicles were converted to on-board producer gas units, but they were in a small minority. Carter Paterson operated some 2- to 4-ton Albion box-vans with producer gas trailers. Pickfords built up a fleet of several hundred but only operated about 50 per cent of them. Savage estimates perhaps 725 converted goods vehicles were on the road by June 1944. A Directorate of Producer Gas Vehicles was established at the Ministry of War Transport in 1942 and transferred to the Ministry of Fuel & Power in 1944. Further experiments on diesel engines were carried out in the 1950s.   **RAS/AGN**

A G Newman, *London's Wartime Gas Buses* (Capital Transport, 1997); Sedgwick, (1980), p. 63; Savage (1957), pp. 435–7; J Aldridge and A Thomas, *Licensed to Carry* (1976), p. 85; PRO, MT55

Protest movements by road hauliers against government policy were a feature of the closing years of the twentieth century. Opposition centred on two issues, the level of taxation on fuel and the rate of vehicle excise duty. Fuel taxation had a dual aspect, created by the 'escalator', introduced by the Conservative government in 1993, which initially imposed an annual rise of 3 per cent additional to the rise related to the retail price index. The escalator, which subsequently rose to 5 per cent in November 1993 and 6 per cent in 1997, was abolished by the Labour government in the 2000 Budget. The industry had long been accustomed to strike action by drivers seeking to improve their rates and conditions, but direct action by operators, for example by a slow-running convoy, was a new phenomenon. This entered the politics of road haulage in the UK with the formation in 1998 of the direct action group Trans-Action by a number of Kent hauliers. The influence of French *manifestations* may be detected, such as the 1996 blockade, so costly to UK hauliers caught up in its effects. The immediate occasion for the establishment of Trans-Action was the diesel duty rise in the March 1998 budget, combined with the imminent ending of cabotage restrictions in the UK, which would enable foreign hauliers to pick up and deliver loads in the UK between dropping their incoming load and returning abroad. A slow drive in central London in April 1998 was followed in June by the creation of long tailbacks on the M6 in the West Midlands and the disruption of traffic in central London by about fifty lorries. Another organisation advocating blockades at this time was the Drivers' Action Movement. A 'rolling blockade' of central London, concentrating on Westminster and organised by Trans-Action, on 22 March 1999 continued the protest. It was followed by the government's establishment of a road haulage industry forum for discussions with the industry. Its first meeting was held on 8 April 1999, a few days before convoys demonstrated at a number of locations throughout the country. A go-slow on the M25 in May was less well supported and resulted in summonses against some participants. Direct action was for a time followed by more conventional campaigning, especially by the Freight Transport Association (q.v.), which conducted a press campaign in autumn 1999. Representing large operators rather than the smaller haulier, it had kept itself more remote from the demonstrations than the Road Haulage Association (q.v.). The March 2000 Budget, reduced vehicle excise duty on some categories of trucks and froze it on others, ended the escalator and announced the introduction of 44-tonnes on six-axle vehicles in January 2001. These measures were insufficient to meet the demands of the industry, although the FTA was less critical than the RHA. Farmers joined the smaller hauliers in a new protest movement and Farmers for Action was the chief instigator of the fuel supply blockades of early September 2000. The blockades seemed to take the general public, the media and, more surprisingly, the government unawares, despite the pattern of protest evident for more than two years, which also included British Hauliers

Unite, the Hauliers' and Farmers' Alliance and the People's Fuel Lobby. The immediate occasion for the September protests had been a wave of demonstrations in France against the low level of fuel tax cuts. This demonstration against cuts emphasised the high level of fuel tax in the UK, against which arguments about higher continental levels of corporate tax and other charges including road tolls had little persuasiveness. The co-ordination and spread of the action owed much to the mobile phone. After the September 2000 blockades ended, no effective protests followed a sixty day stand-off in the UK. Further palliative measures were introduced by the government in November, notably a freeze on fuel duty until April 2002, cuts in vehicle excise duty with a proposed simplification of the rate bands, a 'Brit Disc' for foreign lorries working in the UK and the establishment of an investment fund for the industry. For the agricultural lobby a freeze on the duty on red diesel and the abolition of vehicle excise duty on tractors and agricultural vehicles were offered. By the end of 2000 it was possible to discern only an uneasy peace: fuel taxation, resented as an indirect and therefore regressive tax, remained at a high level and concerns about the level of penalties for the unwitting conveyance of illegal immigrants continued to be expressed by hauliers and drivers. Comments by the media, politicians and sections of the general public in the autumn of 2000 had shown in many cases a lack of sympathy with and understanding of an industry perceived as polluting, overcrowded and bullying in its tactics. Yet the blockade's effects proved beyond doubt that the road haulage industry was essential to the functioning of society and the virtual collapse of the railway system after the Hatfield crash of October 2000 silenced those who had advocated a wholesale transfer of traffic from road to rail.   **RAS**

CM (12 October 2000); R Storey, 'The nation protests', R&RTHC, *Newsletter,* 23 (November 2000), pp. 3–4; A Rawnsley, *Servants of the People* (Harmondsworth: Penguin, 2001), ch. 20

Q

Quality assurance arose from the problems found in inspecting munitions during the First World War. At the Armistice some 1500 inspectors were employed in the directorate responsible. From these came the formation of the Technical Inspection Association in 1922, later the Institute of Engineering Inspection. The depression of 1929–32 caused a decline in membership, but from 1935 concerns for re-armament saw the IEI grow and form new branches. The three services each had their own Inspectorate. The Second World War saw the addition of the Aircraft Inspectorate Department. Inspection had shown its value and the IEI remained influential after the war. By 1954 the British Productivity Council was happy for the IEI to promote quality as a partner to inspection. The first National Quality and Reliability year took place in 1966 and there began a close association with the Institute of Production Engineers. As part of the IEI's policy of improving its status, a new examination structure was introduced and the IEI journal become monthly.

In 1972 the IEI became the Institute of Quality Assurance. Quality assurance and management in distribution and haulage was sought by many customers in the 1980s. Quality management was part of Margaret Thatcher's and President of the Board of Trade, Michael Heseltine's efforts to improve the efficiency and competitiveness of industry. It gained an official status as BS 5750 pt 2/ISO 9002.1987. Until the 2000 revision, ISO 9002 was the appropriate standard for the haulage industry, BS 5750 pt 1/ ISO 9001 had a clause for design, which was rarely applicable to haulage, while BS 9002 did not cover design. (When the Ford truck plant at Langley became part of Iveco, it was registered for BS 9002, because design work was transferred to Italy.) To be assessed, accredited and registered as holding BS 9002, with entry in the DTI Register, required a working quality system audited by an independent third party, who had been registered and recognised as

competent. The standard was revised every five years, the latest version being BS.ISO 9002.2000. It used a plan-do-check-act methodology and increased emphasis on meeting customer requirements.

The most recent changes to the standard paid attention to environmental requirements and to improving customer service. BS 5750 remained current until 2003 and provided the principles on which to base the quality manual, which covered quality management of the business. Other procedures covered processes, either as a section or in a separate manual. These covered the ways of working and operations involved in the business. The quality manual should have been prepared by the owners and/or managers but the procedures needed to be produced with input from employees who carried out the process covered.

Not all operators regarded quality assurance as being needed or useful for their business. Some, in hazardous traffic or involved with the automobile industry, have been required to have at least ISO 9002 registration. Many made the point that registration did not bring a higher rate. Others found that customers, even those themselves registered, used unregistered suppliers, because of their lower rates. A typical quality system had procedures for the traffic office, dealing with orders, use of sub-contractors, job sheets, and processing to invoicing. Customer complaints and dealing with them was a major concern, especially the corrective action taken. Drivers had to have a handbook, covering use of the tachograph, vehicle checks, loading and load security. Its contents depended on the type of traffic and activity. Many of the procedures were already carried out, without being fully written up, as part of the requirements of the Vehicle Inspectorate or the operators licensing provisions. These included drivers' daily defect reports and vehicle inspection and maintenance records. The disposal of worn or scrap parts, tyres and used lubricants became part of quality control. Calibration covered compressors, use of gas welding equipment and tyre depth gauges, as well as requirements for tachographs and speed limiters. Training had to be recorded, as did methods of assessing driving technique. There was a requirement for auditing, covering each clause and procedure at least once a year. The internal auditor had to have been trained, and preferably also accredited. The audit should be carried out by an independent person.   **GM**

Queen Mary trailers (Figure 153) were 45 ft long, and 60 ft including the tractor, thus exceeding normal limits. Intended for moving aircraft fuselages, they were built by Taskers of Andover (q.v.) from the late 1930s as a result of War Office contracts in the rearmament drive. The prototype design was made in Meccano at home in 1938 by Tasker's chief designer, H O Doughty. The original model had lattice-girder side-members and could carry fighter fuselages. Later a 5-ton version was developed for bomber fuselages and over 3500 vehicles were produced in the war. The tractor (q.v.) units for these vehicles were usually Bedford, Commer, or Crossley. After the war the Queen Mary was the basis of other types of vehicle including the Easiload for pantechnicon use and in the late 1950s one firm built their own car transporter on a Queen Mary chassis.   **JA**

Rolt (1969); Stevens-Stratten (1988); *Heritage Commercials,* 147 (March 2002), letter from Russell Doughty

Quick-Smith, George William (1905–86) was educated at the University of London where he took a LLB and then went on to become a barrister of the Inner Temple, completing both by part-time study while working at various jobs in shipping. He was a member of the British employers' delegation to the International Labour Office from 1935 to 1948, representing the National Road Transport Employers' Federation (q.v.) of which he was assistant secretary. He was also secretary to the Road Haulage Association (q.v.) until 1948. He played a crucial role in persuading the railways and road hauliers to agree rates for small parcel carriage in the late 1930s.

After the war and the nationalisation of much of British transport, in 1949 Quick-Smith was appointed secretary and legal adviser of the Road Transport Executive later the Road Haulage Executive. Quick-Smith played a part in pushing through the various acquisitions and then organising this huge undertaking into a workable hierarchy with proper reporting lines, procedures and rules. Following the re-election of a Conservative government in autumn 1951, denationalisation was proposed. Accordingly in 1953 the Road Haulage Executive was abolished and replaced by the Road Haulage Board with Quick-Smith as a member until 1959. Quick-Smith had been important in carrying through the nationalisation process, but even more instrumental in the disposal into private hands of about 20,000 lorries and several hundred depots. For his efforts he was awarded a CBE in 1959. 'Q.S', as he was always known, was seen by some as the consummate bureaucrat or a Vicar of Bray figure, moving from advising private enterprise up to 1948, then switching to aiding the process of nationalisation, only in the early 1950s to shift into disposing of vehicles back into private hands with equal conviction. Quick-Smith wrote and published many articles on road haulage, especially explaining the legal aspects and how changes in the law affected road transport, including the definitive guide to the Transort Act 1947.

From 1959 to 1962 he was an advisor on special projects for the British Transport Commission and from 1962 to 1967 secretary and for 196970 chief executive of the Transport Holding Company, which replaced the British Transport Commission once rail, London Transport, docks and waterways had been hived off into separate boards. He was briefly deputy chairman of the National Freight Corporation in 19701. From 1973 to 1977 he was a member of the Transport Tribunal. Quick-Smith was a committed Christian, being a churchwarden of All Saints, Margaret Street, London, for many years and involved with the Society for the Propagation of Christian Knowledge, latterly as its vice president.   **JA**

Bonavia (1987); Ingram and Mustoe, (1999); *WWW,* 8

R

Racing pigeons (Figure 46). Carriage of these birds and their subsequent timed release for races was steady business for British Railways and its predecessors for years. Special rates were offered to pigeon fanciers, who sent their birds by passenger train in special wicker baskets to a distant station. There the staff released them at an agreed time, the baskets (now empty) being returned to their owners in more leisurely fashion. The Beeching era and staff cuts on the remaining rail network ended this traffic with a number of hauliers acquiring specially bodied vehicles or trailers to handle this work for their local pigeon federation. The multi-compartment bodywork was designed to give the birds protection when in transit but also incorporated a quick-release mechanism so that all the birds were freed at the same time. Some pigeon racing federations made use of specialised road haulage equipment in the 1930s: 40 years later road gained a virtual monopoly.

JMA

Railway-owned road transport. Most of the early railway companies subcontracted collection and delivery of merchandise and parcels to road carriers. Some, like Chaplin & Co. (q.v.), Pickfords (q.v.) and Wordie & Co. (q.v.), were already old-established firms and were brought in to establish goods or parcels services for the railway company and to act as their goods or parcels agents, undertaking the handling work, accountancy and revenue collection, as well as the cartage, at a network of depots. Most, such as McNamara & Co. (q.v.), were cartage agents in only one town. By 1900 most railways had taken over the operation of at least some of their cartage services by buying out their subcontractors or taking over their assets; this process continued until the 1930s. However, some continued to operate under the former owner's name, as in the case of the Great Central Railway, which in 1887 purchased its Manchester cartage agent,

Thompson, McKay & Co. Ltd, with 700 horses.

The first mechanically-powered vehicle used on railway cartage work seems to have been a covered steam wagon built by the Liquid Fuel Engineering Co. of Cowes, Isle of Wight, which began carting goods and parcels in Swindon for the Midland & South Western Junction Railway in 1897. This was followed by trials of a Daimler parcels van by the LNWR in 1898–9; it may have been the same vehicle that went to work on the Belfast & Northern Counties Railway in 1899. Despite these early examples, the railway companies were at first slow to adopt motor vehicles for goods and parcels work. The GWR with 91 vehicles in 1914 and the LNWR with 50 were exceptional. There were only three other companies with more than 15. Lorries at the heavy end of the range fulfilled a need where there were large quantities of heavy traffics to be carted, particularly in hilly districts. For example, the Great Northern Railway in 1919 found it worthwhile to replace all 30 horses at its Hunslet goods depot in Leeds, where the principal traffic was bales of wool and cloth, with eight 3½-ton-capacity GEV electric lorries. But at this stage the motor vehicle was generally regarded as an uneconomic replacement for the single-horse van or dray on short-distance deliveries. The LNWR in particular was early to recognise the motor vehicle's potential for extending road delivery services beyond the range of the horse and in 1914 was the first to appoint a road motor superintendent to lead its development.

In 1919 the Ministry of Munitions loaned 1200 war-surplus motor lorries to the railways to relieve the congestion caused by resource shortages. Some were used for short- and medium-distance road trunking between depots, initially as an emergency measure, but then as a more efficient permanent arrangement. However, most companies had no statutory powers to carrying traffic throughout by road, a position they wished to regularise. In 1921 the government appointed a Departmental Committee on Road Conveyance by Railways to consider the question, but it failed to agree: the chairman, J H Balfour-

Browne KC, and the two members representing the railways recommended that such powers be granted, while those representing the road transport interests, the Federation of British Industries and the Association of British Chambers of Commerce were opposed. These powers were not therefore included in the Railways Act 1921 which established the Big Four railway companies.

From the mid-1920s the railways, led by the LMSR and GWR, responded to growing competition with a range of innovative services, all seeking to match road transport's door-to-door capability. The North Eastern Railway from 1904 and the GWR from c.1912 had used motor vehicles to extend collection and delivery services into rural areas. Such services were considerably expanded from the mid-1920s and in the 1930s were jointly marketed by the Big Four companies under the brand name Country Lorry Services (q.v.). The larger radius that could be served by motor vehicles was also used to introduce zonal schemes, whereby deliveries and collections were made directly by road from a main depot, eliminating the extra time of routing them via the nearest small station. In 1924 the GWR began offering to manufacturers of food and household products what it at first called 'bulking contracts': their packages for individual retailers in the same town or district were made up at the factory into a bulk package, which was carried by rail at an advantageous rate to a railhead, where it was broken down and the individual packages delivered by motor vehicle. The service was soon taken up by the other railways and expanded to include storage at the railhead, making-up of individual orders, stock control and delivery vehicles in the customer's own livery (or with the customer's name on a removable side-panel); the only employee that the manufacturer needed in the district was a salesman. This became known as railhead distribution or the Railhead Service and was the forerunner of contract distribution and logistics (q.v.) services. This creative period also saw the introduction of container services in 1926 (see CONTAINERISATION) and piggyback transport (q.v.) of road tank trailers

in the 1930s. One of the most significant technical innovations was the mechanical horse (q.v.), the viable alternative to the horse on short delivery rounds. Following its introduction in 1930, the average number of motor cartage vehicles purchased each year by the railways increased from 340 to 750. In about 1932 the cartage work performed by motor vehicles began to exceed that of horses. By 1938 the railway-owned cartage fleet exceeded two per cent of all registered goods motor vehicles.

Table 12 : Railway-owned cartage fleet

	Horses for road vehicles	Goods & parcels vehicles		
		Horse-drawn vehicles	Motor vehicles	Trailers
1913	26,270	32,657	191	
1919	24,259	33,329	654	
1929	18,575	32,281	4,011	
1939	12,106	24,615	10,728	
1947	8,555	26,340	11,828	13,965
1957	90	457	15,839	30,004
1968	–	–	9,611	23,136

Meanwhile the railway companies again lobbied for general road transport powers. This time the argument that road hauliers and carriers were under threat from the railways lacked conviction; Parliament was sympathetic to the railway companies' case for equal treatment and duly enacted each of their four identical Railway (Road Powers) Acts 1928. This allowed the LMSR to share in the rescue of David MacBrayne Ltd (q.v.), in which it took a 50 per cent interest. Apart from regularising their own relatively small-scale direct road services, the railway companies' aims seem to have been, firstly, to share in the profits of road transport through investment in existing companies and, secondly, to form allegiances with the larger road transport operators which, generally, also favoured some form of regulation of road transport. It was the LNER that took the first step in 1930 by acquiring a 50 per cent interest in Currie & Co. (Newcastle) Ltd, which had long been the North Eastern Railway's cartage agent in the North East. In 1938 it purchased the Bathgate haulier, James W Petrie Ltd with 21 vehicles.

In 1932 the LMSR bought the Manchester-based haulier, Joseph Nall & Co., and a 51 per cent interest in Wordie & Co., its Scottish cartage contractor. Then in 1933 the four railways jointly completed by far their largest purchases: Carter Paterson (q.v.) for £1,343,000 and the Hay's Wharf Cartage Co. (q.v.), with its subsidiary, Pickfords, for £840,000. Several other firms were later acquired through Wordies, CP and Pickfords, notably Chaplin & Co. and Sutton & Co. By 1939 the railways had invested a total of £4½ million in these acquisitions.

After nationalisation, the railways' road interests, other than their cartage services, passed to BRS. When the Transport Act 1962 dissolved the association between British Railways and BRS by abolishing the BTC, it debarred BR from again engaging in direct road services. The cartage fleet had been declining steadily from a peak in 1956-7, primarily through loss of goods, rather than parcels, traffic, but it still numbered 9,600 vehicles when it was transferred under the Transport Act 1968 to National Carriers Ltd (q.v.). BR's sundries (less-than-wagonload goods) business became the nucleus of NCL, but NCL's biggest single source of income was from contract hire of vehicles and drivers to BR, chiefly for the Rail Express Parcels Service but also for delivering steel and other full-load goods traffic. The principal customers of REPS, however, were the mail order companies that sold through weekly savings clubs. Easing of consumer credit regulations made this form of shopping redundant and in 1981 REPS was closed down. Meanwhile in 1963 BR launched Red Star, a premium parcel service offering same-day and overnight long-distance transits between pairs of stations that were linked by a direct passenger train service. In the early 1970s the service was expanded by arranging for parcels to be transferred between connecting trains. Road transfers between London termini were operated by the newly-established London courier, City Link, whose expansion into a national firm was associated with the introduction of collection and delivery services for Red Star parcels in the early 1980s. Red Star began to incur losses in the early 1990s and was sold to its management in 1995 for £1 as part of BR privatisation; it was subsequently re-sold to Lynx Express (q.v.). BR had resumed operating its own vehicles in 1978, when Freightliners Ltd (q.v.) was transferred back into its ownership. As well as road collection and delivery, the Transport Act 1978 gave it freedom to carry a limited number of containers throughout by road. Under the derogation given in 1994 for combined transport it became the first operator of 44-tonne lorries in the UK.   **GAB**

See also ROAD-RAIL VEHICLES

Railway Returns, 1913-1938; BTC and BRB, *Annual Reports & Accounts*, 1947-1968; Hoole (1969); Kelley (1973; 1982); Twells & Bourne (1983); Geary (1987); Stevens-Stratten & Aldridge (1987); Paget-Tomlinson (1990); Adrian Vaughan, *The Great Western at Work 1921-1939* (Sparkford: Patrick Stephens, 1993); Russell (1995); Earnshaw & Aldridge (1997 & 2001); Aldridge & Earnshaw (2000)

Ransomes, Sims & Jefferies Ltd, of Ipswich, Suffolk, produced what was probably the first British traction engine in 1842, but the firm concentrated on portable farm engines. Later diversification included the manufacture of aircraft and hangars in the First World War, grass-cutting machinery and electric vehicles. Some road locomotives were produced and as late as 1920 Ransome brought out an overtype steam wagon, of which only 34 were made. In the same year they made a more successful incursion into battery-electric commercial vehicles, under the Orwell marque, having produced industrial trucks during the First World War. Electric lorries were also produced, seven going to the GWR. The last road-going electric vehicles delivered were a batch of trolleybuses in 1946, although industrial truck production continued in the post-war period.

RWK/RAS

D R Grace and D C Phillips, *Ransomes of Ipswich* (Reading: Institute of Agricultural History, 1975); Aldridge and Earnshaw (2000); Brian Bell, *Ransomes, Sims & Jeffries, agricultural engineers* (Ipswich: Old Pond Publishing, 2001)

Ready-Mixed Concrete Group (Figure 154). The production of concrete is a major user of cement and in 2000 a significant vertical integration occurred when the RMC Group plc acquired the Rugby Group plc, cement manufacturers. In 1930 the British Steel Piling Co. operated a Paris Transit Mixer on a Sentinel DG 6 chassis. It was claimed to be the first such portable plant in the UK. RMC's first plant was established by a Danish engineer at Bedfont, Middlesex in 1930. This was in the heart of an aggregate-rich area and close to the greater London market for the product. Its first vehicle was a 6-wheel Chevrolet; by 1935 its fleet of 15 transit-mixers included six of this marque and some Studebakers. Rival producers rose and fell, including Balfour Beatty's Express Supply Concrete with 12 imported transit- or truck-mixers, a fleet rising to 30 before it was killed off by the Blitz. Only four plants, including RMC's, survived the war. It redeveloped at Bedfont in 1950 and was operating 12 Commer and 14 Dodge truck-mixers in 1952, when it was acquired by the leading Australian ready-mix company, a control from overseas which lasted until 1963. RMC subsequently made a number of significant acquisitions of aggregate suppliers, in some cases with haulage and contracting interests and sizeable transport fleets. These included St Albans Sand & Gravel in 1967/1970, bringing in Hales Containers; Hall & Ham River in 1968, 700 of their vehicles being replaced by 500 new ones; Pointer Group Holdings of Norfolk and Suffolk in 1970, with a transport fleet of over 500 units, later sold to Mitchell Cotts. Anglian Building Products, acquired 1965/6, also brought in Readicrete, with 17 depots. By the mid-1980s RMC operated some 370 plants in the UK and hundreds of others overseas.

The vehicle used in the ready-mixed concrete industry is typically a 6-wheel lorry-mounted mixer, which rotates slowly whilst the liquid concrete is being delivered from the mixing plant, to prevent it hardening in transit. Stothert & Pitt of Bath were major manufacturers of the mixing drum equipment; others have included Aveling Barford, D Wickham of Ware (Ritemixer) and Winget. Foden were attracted into the ready-mixed market by one of their customers, Gibson's Ready-mix Concrete of Gosforth, for which Fodens developed a hydraulic drive power take-off; some models used the heavy-duty, half-cab chassis. Fodens went on to sell modified 4-, 6- and 8-wheel chassis not only to contractors but also to the mixer producers. Special requirements for the base vehicle include power-take-off to operate the mixer-drum and possibly anti-roll bars and helper springs, to counteract the high centre of gravity of the drum. Lorry-mounted concrete pumps, such as those manufactured by Schwing, may be needed on site for higher level delivery. RMC has in addition an aggregates division, operating tippers, Leyland DAFs, formerly mainly Fodens, and a specialist fleet of nearly 400 vehicles operated by Hales Waste Control, serving the retail trade, commerce and industry.

RAS/GMcB

Michael Cassell, *The Readymixers: the story of RMC 1931 to 1986* (Pencorp Books, 1986); Nancollis (1995), p. 83; McBirnie (2002)

Recovery service vehicles (Figures 47 and 155) grew larger and their equipment and operations became more complex in the period since the end of the Second World War, to cope with the larger commercial vehicles, often carrying hazardous loads. The development of motorways and dual-carriageway roads increased the likelihood of multi-vehicle accidents (q.v.), often occurring at high speeds, which present recovery problems far beyond the scope of the early breakdown lorry. In the inter-war period this might have been no more than a heavy, quality car chassis with its body cut down and converted to a pick-up and equipped with a recovery crane. The Ford Motor Co. in the early 1930s provided to selected dealers more than 500 'service cars', a purpose-built breakdown lorry on a Ford AA chassis, with a Weaver crane, of which at least one survives in preservation. The civilian availability of ex-WD recovery vehicles after 1945 radically changed recovery operations. The AEC Matador and Diamond-T were prominent among this generation of recovery vehicles; a few individual recovery concerns subsequently acquired examples of other North American marques, such as Kenworth, but Scammell, together with

ERF and Foden, formed the mainstay of UK recovery fleets. A post-war curiosity, which apparently went on to serve with BRS, was a crated armoured vehicle which Robson's of Carlisle (q.v.) built up into a recovery vehicle. The basic breakdown crane, such as that manufactured for many years by Harvey Frost, which became part of the Brockhouse (q.v.) group, was joined by the twin-boom apparatus, pioneered by the American Holmes concern and introduced into the UK in the 1960s by W Jackson of the Chaseside Motor Co., Hertford, who set up Dial-Holmes (England) Ltd, with sole European marketing rights. This has a main frame with winches operating via two booms, which can act independently of each other. Airbags are now a regular feature in recovery work, to increase the speed of recovering vehicles which have tipped over and to reduce the risk of further damage to such bodies as frameless tankers. The interests of recovery operators are represented by the Association of Vehicle Recovery Operators, a group of the Retail Motor Industry Federation. Over 500 vehicle recovery operators belong to the Road Rescue Recovery Association founded in 1986.

RAS

Thomas (1987); 'Recovery time', *Leyland Journal*, 31, 4 (July/August 1970), p. 226; Tuck (1990), p. 18; Programme of Truckfest 2001, p. 34; Graham Edge, 'A nightshift to remember', *CVRTC News* (April 2002)

Red & White group were involved in both passenger and goods road transport. In the 1920s the Watts family of Lydney and the Bowns of Brynmawr built up a considerable bus and coach network in the Welsh borders. To bring the independently operating businesses together, Red & White Services Ltd was founded in 1930, succeeded by Red & White United Transport Ltd in 1937. A new head office and workshops were established at the former Bulwark military camp, Chepstow. After the Road & Rail Traffic Act of 1933 R&W moved into haulage, acquiring Freeguard Brothers of Newport, who ran regular services to Birmingham and London. In 1937 Freeguard and three other firms were merged to form All British Carriers. When R&W bought the London coach operator, Blue Belle, part of its coach station became the London depot of All British Carriers. R&W also developed the bulk liquid specialist carriers, Bulwark Transport, in response to a request to take over some tankers and a milk contract to London. In the late 1930s J H Watts took a financial interest in the amalgamated Pye and London & Counties business and in 1938 Mechanisation Ltd of Cheltenham became part of the R&W group, with 60 vehicles, some on GPO contracts. R&W's road haulage interests were nationalised in 1948. Bulwark escaped nationalisation by the specialised nature of its activity and became part of Red & White United Transport. Much of Red & White's activity now concentrated on road transport in east Africa and bus operation in Guernsey, but from 1959 United Transport re-acquired substantial holdings in UK road haulage. Having chosen ex-military Albions on technical grounds when building up their initial fleet, R&W were noted users of Albion vehicles for both passengers and goods. Watts Factors of Chepstow, owned by R&W, held thriving Albion and Gardner agencies. **RAS**

C Taylor, 'United Transport', *VCVM*, 3, 9 (July/August 1987), pp. 269; Dunbar (1981), p. 71; Ingram and Mustoe, (1999), p. 39; W Dowding, *30 Years of Progress in Passenger Road Transport: a history of the Red & White Group of omnibus companies 19191949* (Chepstow: Red & White United Transport Ltd, 1950)

Red Arrow Deliveries was the creation of Charles Dunbar (q.v.) who joined the Birmingham & Midland Motor Omnibus Co. Ltd (Midland Red) in 1930 to re-organise their expanding parcels service. A half share of Midland Red was bought by the GWR (20 per cent) and the LMSR (30 per cent) which led to Midland Red's parcel services being merged into Pickfords' Birmingham operation. Dunbar decided this was the opportunity to create a new road express parcels service serving the whole country based on interworking with other carriers. He entered into an agreement with Hurst & Payne Ltd, who among their operations had hired vehicles to Midland Red Parcels. Hurst had spare capacity for suitably licensed vehicles and a new warehouse at Yardley,

Birmingham, able to provide a 300 foot-long loading bank. RA began operating on 28 December 1933, with five vans for local collection and delivery work. At first Carter Paterson did the London deliveries and Hurst did the London collections until RA could open its London depot at Malt Street. Soon after Speed Lines of Chiswick was acquired as the second London depot. RA concentrated on serving the Midlands, London, and the Bristol region, with traffic to most of the rest of Great Britain served by interworking with key regional carriers.

Unfortunately Dunbar had no financial interest in RA, which affected his influence when Hurst sold its interest to Scribbans Bakery in 1935, Scribbans being one of its biggest customers. Because of the problems Dunbar found in setting up his inter-working arrangements, particularly documentation, he arranged a meeting at Birmingham in 1937 of the carriers who were interworking with RA. From this came the formation of the National Conference of Parcels Carriers, to deal with specific items of concern to members, including rates. Most regions had formal or informal arrangements for rates and services covered by members (which would be illegal today). A meeting in 1938 approved the rules and actions taken, changing the name to National Conference of Express Carriers. RA now had the routines for interworking in place and was able to increase the service offered to the extent that the service it provided was hardly bettered by current standards. Dunbar left RA in 1941 to start Central Carriers, based on the old established businesses of Picton & Co, Hauliers Ltd (B C & P) parcels traffic, PX and Youngs Express. He was not able to repeat his success, resigning in 1943. RA, operating 47 vehicles was nationalised in 1949, together with Hurst, with 63 vehicles and 10 drawbar trailers, which had continued their provision and servicing of the vehicles. **GM**

Dunbar papers, Modern Records Centre, University of Warwick Library

Reece, Louis, Ltd. At the end of the Second World War, one of the big four importers of fruit and produce was Louis Reece Ltd.

Founded in 1919 by a Jewish émigré, Louis Olins, by the early 1950s it had a commanding position in Australian apples and pears and substantial operations in most other trades. It owned a fleet of traditional flat bed trucks, principally Leyland Comets, to move its goods from dock to market. Reflecting the changing patterns of the produce world, by 1960 most of the fleet had been moved to a depot in Horsmonden, Kent.

This depot was developed with chill storage and packing facilities as well as the transport fleet, partly to serve a co-operative of English growers called Checkers. In pursuit of higher standards, and to give the growers greater economic strength in dealing with the increasing power of the supermarkets, Louis Reece provided packing, marketing, movement and accounting facilities. This was combined with an ever-increasing variety of imported operations, which enabled the company to provide a continuity of supply both to traditional markets and to the supermarkets.

As disposable incomes rose, so did the demand for new tastes. There was a constantly evolving range of exotics, partly dependent on airfreight. In particular the Israelis developed their marketing and distribution systems to match. Combined ship and lorry operations through Marseille gave a four-day transit to Horsmonden, where order picking to market and supermarket was carried out.

Louis Reece transport was integral to its working. The old flat beds were replaced by articulation from 1964 onwards. In 1967 the first curtainsided Tautliner (q.v.) ever built joined the fleet. It gave superior load protection and a speedier operation. A Volvo F86, one of the first in the country, followed the same year. At a similar purchase price, that vehicle produced a reliability and economy of operation which the traditional Leyland had lost. Over the years vehicle size and performance increased, eventually to 38 tonne three-axle tractors with 13 metre trailers on air suspension and with full refrigeration. These vehicles gave flexibility and rapid operation. They could load on farms or in docks and deliver, be it to market or supermarket depot. Spare trailers were placed at farms to be loaded as needed. Palletised working

Figure 129 Luton body: AEC Y-type of about 1919 running on rear solid tyres, but with a pneumatic conversion on the front. The vehicle was owned by W T Parrott & Co., who claimed to have developed the Luton body. (Reproduced by kind permission of Colin Parrott)

Figure 130 J Lyons & Co.: this small-wheeled Karrier Bantam tractor of 1946 has a Normand body, Scammell automatic coupling, and drop-frame semi-trailer turned out in distinctive Lyons livery. (Reproduced by kind permission of the Museum of British Road Transport, Coventry)

Figure 131 McNamara was an old-established haulage firm which did much work for the Post Office. This Leyland Beaver of 1933 is hauling a drawbar trailer. The low body height suggests a dense, high-value load. (Reproduced by kind permission of Nick Baldwin)

Figure 132 Mack lorries were rare on the British scene, but have been favoured by some individualistic hauliers. This bonneted version, photographed in Rotherham, was also unusual in 1982. (Kevin Lane Collection)

Figure 133 Market garden produce: a solid-tyred Federal lorry at Covent Garden, *c.* 1918, owned by Harold Bessent of Grove Park Farm, Chiswick, and stacked high with fruit and vegetable baskets. The method of loading looks hazardous. (Reproduced by kind permission of the Slide Centre)

Figure 134 Marston Road Services were involved in carrying abnormal loads, as shown by this Scammell SI5 four-cylinder petrol-engined outfit of the early 1930s with four-in-line trailer. The over-size load comprises the frame and cylinders of a steam locomotive. (Reproduced by kind permission of Nick Baldwin)

Figure 135 Maudslay Meritor forward-control rigid-eight with a 3000-gallon tank body of the late 1940s for carrying kerosene from the docks to distribution centres, modified to conform to petrol-carrying regulations. It has a fire screen between the cab and tank and a front-mounted exhaust. Kerosene (paraffin) was much used for domestic heating at that time. (Reproduced by kind permission of Nick Baldwin)

Figure 136 Meat transport in the early years after the Second World War is typified by this wartime-built Bedford OW, with flat platform and lift-off ventilated container, operated by a Smithfield contractor. (Kevin Lane Collection)

Figure 137 Mechanical horses were much used by British Railways for local deliveries. This pair of 3-ton Scammell Scarabs of 1954 shows the variety of goods carried in a busy goods terminal. (Reproduced by kind permission of Nick Baldwin)

Figure 138 Milk traffic: this Commer N3 lorry of the late 1930s has sides which drop to allow easy loading, and also restrain the load when upright. It is in the livery of the Bristol Pure Milk Co. and carries the later 10-gallon milk churns. (Reproduced by kind permission of the Museum of British Road Transport, Coventry)

Figure 139 Mobile shop: this Morris-Commercial 1-ton van of about 1930 has been bodied as a mobile shop for the Leicester Institution for the Blind. The bodywork was by W K Goddard of Blaby, whose works can be seen in the background. Some of the goods are displayed on the insides of hinged doors. (Reproduced by kind permission of Nick Baldwin)

Figure 140 Motorcycle combination: this 986-cc, 10-hp BSA of the mid-1920s could be used for delivering milk or parcels. It carried three churns, each of 17 gallons, and each full churn weighing about $2\frac{1}{2}$ cwt. Milk was then delivered to householders and sold by the jug measure. (Reproduced by kind permission of Nick Baldwin)

Figure 141 Moving floor: this Morris-Commercial Leader lorry has a Principality moving rubber floor installed to speed up loading and unloading. Once the hinged tailboard was dropped, the handles at the rear were turned to operate the moving floor. (Reproduced by permission of Gordon Mustoe)

Figure 142 Muck away: an AEC of *c.* 1936, with long-wheelbase non-tipping drop-sided body, is seen on a weighbridge with spoil to take away. This was not an ideal vehicle for the trade, as it needed hand unloading. It seems to have had a hard life. (John Armstrong Collection)

Figure 143 Nationalisation: a Foden DG6/8 eight-wheel lorry with six-cylinder Gardner engine in *c.* 1948. It was acquired voluntarily at nationalisation and displays its former owner's name but with the addition of 'BTC' as part of the livery. Note the trade plates and the 'hungry lion' logo of BTC on the cab door. (Reproduced by kind permission of Colin Parrott)

Figure 144 Newspaper vans were among the first uses for motorised vehicles. This is an Austin FX4 taxi chassis with special body, of about 1960, built for the *London Evening News*. The taxi chassis had an excellent lock, but was expensive to build and run and the length was a disadvantage at the base. (Reproduced by kind permission of Nick Baldwin)

Figure 145 Nicknames: this Foden design with the S21 cab of the mid 1960s was nicknamed Mickey Mouse because the headlamps and curved front wings reminded drivers of Disney's hero. Cyril White was a prominent Peterborough haulier specialising in brick and produce traffic. Castellated chassis side members were a hallmark of York Trailers. (Reproduced by kind permission of Nick Baldwin)

Figure 146 Normal control: this Commer N2 biscuit van of about 1938 shows the 'normal control' or 'bonneted' position. The large roof rack was used for returned empty tins, which were the normal method of distributing biscuits to retailers before individual packages were introduced. Folding steps by the door provide access to the roof rack. (Reproduced by kind permission of the Museum of British Road Transport, Coventry)

Figure 147 Paper traffic: this AEC Mammoth of the early 1930s is delivering rolls of newsprint in the Fleet Street area from Bowaters. Samuel Rogers was a well-known firm of hauliers and wharfingers. In the early 1930s Bowaters began to build up their own delivery fleet. (Reproduced by kind permission of Nick Baldwin)

Figure 148 Pickfords were heavy-haulage specialists, as shown by this picture of a large boiler being drawn by a Scammell. The slow speed at which the load is moving is shown by the assistant inspecting the corner. The expandable trailer was designed for this sort of traffic. (John Armstrong Collection)

Figure 149 Pole wagons were used for long loads, such as steel girders or tree trunks, and were adjustable for length. This Dyson export model dates from the early 1960s. (Reproduced by kind permission of Nick Baldwin)

Figure 150 Pool petrol was a wartime standardised product, here carried in an AEC Monarch of about 1940. Note the white edges to the wings to show up in the blackout and the shrouded headlamp. The vehicle was originally in the Shell Mex fleet, carrying bitumen, and has just come from the workshops. (Reproduced by kind permission of Nick Baldwin)

Figure 151 The **Post Office** used rail transport extensively until the late 1990s. Road–rail interchange scenes like this were common at mainline stations. The vehicles are typical 7.5-tonnes, a Leyland-DAF Roadrunner on the left and an Iveco-Ford Cargo on the right. (John M Aldridge Collection)

Figure 152 Producer gas: this Commer Q4 bonneted lorry of 1943 was modified to run on producer gas, that is, anthracite was the fuel. In the Second World War, oil supplies were vulnerable to enemy attack whereas home-produced coal was much less so. Wartime tyre shortages meant the spare-wheel carrier behind the back axle is empty. Note the white edge on both wings to show up in the blackout. (Reproduced by kind permission of the Museum of British Road Transport, Coventry)

Figure 153 The **Queen Mary trailer** was developed by Taskers of Andover in the Second World War to carry aircraft fuselages and wings. This shot from 1953 shows a postwar 5-ton model drawn by an Austin Loadstar. (Reproduced by kind permission of Nick Baldwin)

Figure 154 Ready-mixed concrete deliveries: three Dodge 300 lorries of the mid-1950s, with Motor Panels LAD cabs. (Reproduced by kind permission of the Museum of British Road Transport, Coventry)

Figure 155 Recovery vehicle services were provided by this late 1960s AEC operated by BRS Rescue. It is seen in its Southampton depot in 1988. BRS Rescue successfully exploited a niche market and by the early 1980s had become the UK's largest heavy-vehicle repair and recovery operation. (Kevin Lane Collection)

Figure 156 Removals traffic often used pantechnicon vans such as these being operated by Pickfords. They had a large cubic capacity, including a Luton head over the cab to maximise available space. These examples are a Volvo F6 and a Bedford of the early 1980s. The F6 has side loading access for Pickfords' container service. (John Armstrong Collection)

Figure 157 Ridge pole body: this Commer N1 20/25-cwt forward-control van of 1937 was used by Strawsons of Portsmouth for household delivery of soft drinks. It has a reinforced cab roof with rack for returned empty bottles. (Reproduced by kind permission of the Museum of British Road Transport, Coventry)

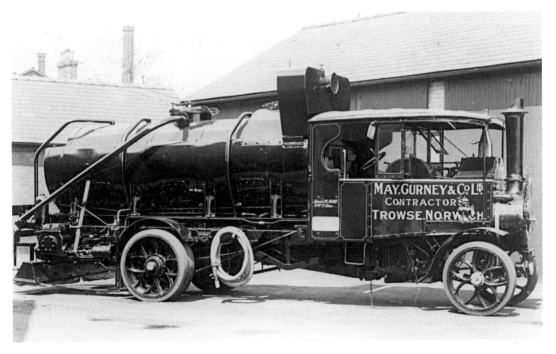

Figure 158 Road pavement: this Foden was converted into a tar sprayer for road surfacing in 1933. It was operated by May & Gurney of Norwich into the 1950s. The tar tank had a separate furnace to bring the tar up to working temperature. (Reproduced by permission of Gordon Mustoe)

Figure 159 Road-rail vehicle: a Karrier in road mode but as yet unbodied, as supplied to the London North Eastern Railway for permanent way and signalling maintenance in Scotland. (Reproduced by permission of Gordon Mustoe)

Figure 160 Roller shutter door: this Karrier Gamecock CK3 baker's van of 1950 had a capacity of 555 cubic feet and a wide roller-shutter side door to give easy access. It is in Bilsland of Glasgow's livery. Note the unusual set-back front axle. (Reproduced by kind permission of the Museum of British Road Transport, Coventry)

Figure 161 Roof rack: Leyland RAF model with box van body for W & R Jacob & Co. Ltd of Liverpool, *c.* 1920. Note the solid tyres and disc wheels. The roof rack was a normal feature for biscuit firms, which used them to carry the returned empty tins.

Figure 162 Roping and sheeting: these two Dodge KP900 tractors and York trailers were employed by Ind Coope to deliver aluminium kegs of beer in the mid-1960s. They are part sheeted and neatly roped. Notice the cab-top headboards. The semi-trailers have the four-in-line wheel configuration. (Reproduced by kind permission of the Museum of British Road Transport, Coventry)

Figure 163 Rowe Hillmaster of the late 1950s showing the typical muddy, sloping conditions encountered on farms. Note the Road Haulage Association logo on the front of the cab and the locally built, livestock-carrying, double-deck body. (Words & Machines Collection)

Figure 164 Sawn timber is being loaded onto this AEC bonneted Matador articulated outfit in Surrey Commercial Docks in 1935. Note the dangerous position of the loader. Thomas Hewstone was a well-known London-based firm of timber hauliers. (Reproduced by kind permission of Nick Baldwin)

Figure 165 Scammell was renowned for its heavy tractors, such as this Cummins-powered 240-ton Contractor of 1967, used by Pickfords for abnormal loads. Note the walking attendants clearing the path. (John Armstrong Collection)

Figure 166 Scammell 100-ton transporter being operated by Marston Road Services in the mid-1930s to carry an AEC railcar to Park Royal Vehicles for a body to be fitted. (Reproduced by permission of Gordon Mustoe)

Figure 167 Security vehicles, like this Commer Highline of the mid-1970s, were highly specialised. Note the air conditioning, reinforced windscreen, ventilation and armoured body. (Reproduced by kind permission of Nick Baldwin)

Figure 168 Selden: a Selden lorry of about 1918 seen at Covent Garden, loaded high with wicker hampers, operated by E James. Note the Ford Model T van behind, operated by the same firm. (Reproduced by kind permission of the Slide Centre)

Figure 169 Sentinel High Speed Gas lorry of about 1938, running on producer gas. Gilford had pioneered this form of propulsion in 1935 and was taken over by High Speed Gas, which was subsequently acquired by Sentinel. (Reproduced by permission of Gordon Mustoe)

Figure 170 Sheeting and roping: this AEC Marshall of the mid-1950s is neatly sheeted and roped so trailing rope ends do not hit the cyclist being overtaken. The front nearside seems to have had a recent bump. Coward Bros were a long-established firm of Grays in Essex who did much London dock work. (John Armstrong Collection)

Figure 171 Sleeper cab: 1974 Bedford TM sleeper cab with plaid weave on an uninviting bunk. (Reproduced by permission of Bedford Motors)

Figure 172 SPD ran this Sadgrove Special, which was a cheap pantechnicon body designed for the Container Recovery Service run by SPD in the Second World War. This model was photographed in the early 1960s, after a hard life, with St Pancras Borough Council. (Words & Machines Collection)

Figure 173 Steel traffic: this Commer Superpoise 5-ton platform lorry of the late 1940s had a 14-foot wheelbase and was used for steel deliveries by S W Farmer of Lewisham. Note the heavy-duty bolster behind the cab to protect the cab and support any long load. (Reproduced by kind permission of the Museum of British Road Transport, Coventry)

Figure 174 Steel traffic: 1970 Foden 28-ton rigid-eight with flat-bed body, in the livery of Johnston & Nephew of Ambergate, carrying steel wire in coils. It has a strengthened headboard. (J H Edser Collection)

Figure 175 Stobart was one of the best-known hauliers in Britain in the 1990s, thanks to its fan club and the ubiquity and smart turnout of its vehicles. This Volvo FL10 is making deliveries in the late 1980s. Note the female name assigned to each lorry, the cab-top deflector to reduce fuel consumption and the side guards. (John Armstrong Collection)

Figure 176 Sugar traffic: Leyland model OQ2 8-ton overtype, with tank body, for Fairrie & Co. of Liverpool, sugar refiners, *c.* 1920. Note the solid tyres and artillery-style wheels, and the granite-sett road surfacing.

Figure 177 Suttons of St Helens displayed their services on this Atkinson Silver Knight outfit with a Gardner 150 engine. The load is carefully sheeted and roped. (John Armstrong Collection)

Figure 178 Tartan Arrow: using a Dodge KP900 tractor and York trailer, this London-based haulier ran an overnight freight and smalls service between Scotland and London. Notice the use of the body to advertise the service and the illuminated cab headboard. In the 1970s the company organised a dedicated rail service for the trunk haul. (Reproduced by kind permission of the Museum of British Road Transport, Coventry)

Figure 179 Temperature-controlled transport was in its infancy when this prototype of the early 1960s Homalloy-built cab and body with its early wraparound windscreen was built. It used a Prestcold-Lucas refrigeration unit. (Reproduced by kind permission of Nick Baldwin)

Figure 181 Tilt cab: a Dodge K800 of the late 1960s with tilt cab showing 45 degrees of tilt to give easy access to the engine. This lorry body has a Luton head with hinged sections to clear the cab when tilted. (Reproduced by kind permission of the Museum of British Road Transport, Coventry)

Figure 180 Three-wheeled vans like this Raleigh were used for local deliveries by small traders. This picture of Tooley Street in 1936 captures a wide variety of goods traffic, including the Metropolitan Transport Supply Co. lorry with lift-off container. It was taken by the London County Council to illustrate traffic congestion. (Reproduced by kind permission of Nick Baldwin)

Figure 182 Timber haulage: timber for paper making is being carried on this drawbar outfit, consisting of an ERF EC10 6×4 and close-coupled trailer, in 1999. The timber is side loaded, which is now regarded as the safest method of carriage. (Kevin Lane Collection)

Figure 183 Tipper: half-cabs were attractive to tipper operators because they reduced the all-important unladen weight – and insurance costs were lower too. Ham River bought a number of these AEC Mercurys in the late 1950s. (John M Aldridge Collection)

Figure 184 Triple-deck cattle float, showing the arrangements for loading small livestock, especially sheep, up wooden ramps. The arrangement for the top deck, with no roof and slatted sides, would be illegal if operated today. The body is mounted on a Leyland forward-control Comet chassis. (Reproduced by permission of Gordon Mustoe)

Figure 185 TIR traffic: this late-1960s AEC Mammoth Minor was an early entrant to international routes. Notice the TIR badge on the top of the tanker. It has the Ergomatic tilt cab common to AEC, Albion and Leyland. Thomas Allen became part of P&O in 1971, when P&O acquired Coast Lines, among whose road interests was Thomas Allen. (John Armstrong Collection)

Figure 186 Van boy: this 1948 picture of a Karrier Gamecock CK3 forward-control 3- to 4-ton low-height lorry shows the van boy hard at work delivering mineral waters and Smiths potato crisps. The latter were kept in lockers below the main load bed. (Reproduced by kind permission of the Museum of British Road Transport, Coventry)

Figure 187 Viney, H, & Co. Ltd of Preston: Leyland model Q2 6-ton carrying a load of bales of sheepskins, *c.* 1920. Note the CMUA logo high on the garage wall, the driver and his mate, the solid tyres and artillery wheels, and the stone road surface.

Figure 188 Walk-Thru van: Commer introduced this model in 1961, its low step height, uncluttered cab floor and sliding doors allowing easy and cross-cab access. This is the uncommon battery-electric Electraflow version produced in conjunction with Chloride, and originally called the Silent Karrier. This one is badged Dodge. (John M Aldridge Collection)

Figure 189 Wartime: a completed Second World War Austin with drop-side body stands outside the works of Bromilow & Edwards in Bolton. The front bumper, edges to the wings and running board are painted white, the headlamps are masked and the glass of the sidelight has a white spot in its centre, all to meet blackout regulations. A further legal requirement was for vehicles to be immobilised in some way when left unattended. (John Aldridge Collection)

Figure 190 Wynns were famous for their ability to handle abnormal and heavy loads, as demonstrated by this shot of a transformer needing double-headed traction. Note the fleet number as well as the name 'Dreadnought' on the tractor. The tractor is a rebuilt version of a US-manufactured Pacific. (John Armstrong Collection)

reduced handling and raised quality. It became the norm to pack in the early afternoon and deliver to the supermarket depot in the evening whence they distributed to their stores all over the country by 0800 next day.

The company was not unique in this but it did establish a reputation for quality and reliability. It was a very early example of fully integrated logistics. Increasingly the race was going to the bigger organisations. The capital requirements for vehicles and equipment soared and in 1985 the company merged with the Glass Glover wholesale fruiterer organisation.   **TAP**

Rees Jeffreys see JEFFREYS, W REES

Refrigerated transport (Figure 48) see TEMPERATURE-CONTROLLED TRANSPORT

Refuse collection lies outside the scope of this work, although some methods of operation, such as the low-height vehicle (q.v.) and the mechanical horse (q.v.), were common. Some chassis- and body-builders, such as Pagefield (q.v.) and Eagle Engineering (q.v.), were noted for products relevant to refuse collection as well as to road haulage. There is, however, one aspect which crosses over into road haulage.: the longer distance, bulk movement of refuse to landfill sites at some distance from city collection areas. One example is the contract work of A Pannell Ltd (q.v.), of Golders Green, which in the 1950s had 16 AEC Mammoth Major 8-wheel tippers, succeeded by Fodens. These were top-loaded by grabs at Embankment Wharf by the Thames on a bulk refuse contract for Lambeth Borough Council; similar work was subsequently undertaken for St Pancras. Another north London contractor, Drinkwater Services Ltd, used the Walkers & County Cars Ltd maximum payload system, involving the compression of refuse at a central processing plant, a resultant slug of material being rammed into a huge cylindrical body for road transfer. In the provinces, Sheffield City Council operated one or more 8-wheel Fodens on bulk refuse haulage.

In addition, the local collection of refuse was sometimes undertaken on contract by haulage contractors; for example, Pannells operated SD

Freighters for various outer north London boroughs by the early 1930s and Hawkins Brothers, proprietors of Scarlet Pimpernel Coaches, won a 5-year contract from Minehead UDC in 1936 to collect refuse with two Karrier Colt Chelsea-bodied 3-wheelers.

Growing environmental concerns since the 1970s have led to the controlled development of landfill sites on a large scale, with major commercial and road haulage involvement. By the nature of their activity, extractive industries such as aggregates, brick- and cement-making have become involved with landfill operations, in order to make profitable use of their holes in the ground assets. One example of this is Hales Waste Control, a division of Ready-Mixed Concrete (q.v.).   **RAS**

B C Woods, *Municipal Refuse Collection Vehicles* (Appleby-in-Westmorland: Trans-Pennine Publishing, 1999), pp. 4, 27, 33; 'From greengrocery to refuse', *Classic Commercials* (1983), pp. 248; S Gibbard, *County: a pictorial review* (Ipswich: Farming Press, 1997); M Hawkins and R Grimley, *A Century of Coaching on Exmoor* (Dulverton: Exmoor Books, 1998), pp. 1278; H J Sheryn, *An Illustrated History of Dustcarts* (Shepperton: Ian Allan, 2000), especially pp. 1238

The **registration and licensing of vehicles** for the purposes of regulation and taxation (q.v.) go back to 1637 when licences were introduced for London's hackney carriages, partly to reduce street congestion and partly to raise revenue. From 1662 'figures or markes of distinction' (the first licence plates) were issued to identify licensed hackney carriages.

The first registration of goods vehicles was also in London. An Act of 1745 required every cart, car or dray to be registered with the Commissioners for Licensing Hackney Carriages and to display its registration number and owner's name in some conspicuous place – the first example of legal lettering (q.v.). The purpose here was not taxation, but to assist in identifying and prosecuting disorderly drivers. Registration (but not the legal lettering requirement) was discontinued in 1832.

Licensing of stage coaches was required from 1779 to assist the collection of a mileage tax. Other carriages were not licensed until 1870, even though they had long been taxed; carriers' waggons that conveyed occasional fare-paying passengers were included, but vehicles used solely for the 'conveyance of goods or burden in the course of trade or husbandry' were exempt (provided they carried the required legal lettering). There has only ever been one scheme for general licensing of animal-powered goods vehicles; introduced in 1783 to hinder smuggling, it lasted only a few months.

The Highways and Locomotives (Amendment) Act 1878 authorised annual licensing and taxation of mechanically-propelled vehicles by English and Welsh counties to compensate them for the excessive damage caused by steam road locomotives to the road surface. A vehicle using the roads of more than one county required a licence from each of them. From 1 January 1899, under the provisions of the Locomotives Act 1898, it became a requirement for locomotives (but not the new light locomotives, which were exempt from these acts) to display a licence plate showing the date and number of the licence and the name of the issuing council. A new plate was issued each time the licence was renewed.

From 1 January 1897, under the provisions of the Locomotives on Highway Acts of 1896, light locomotives, later called motor cars were licensed and taxed as carriages; but if they were used solely for carrying goods they were exempt. From 1 January 1904, the Motor Car Act 1903 required all motor cars, including those designed to carry goods, to be registered by the county, county borough and large Scottish burgh councils. To enable speeding and dangerous drivers to be identified, each vehicle had to display plates on front and rear (and, where applicable, on the rear of the trailer), showing its registration number preceded by a code of letters indicating the registering authority. Registration and licensing of motor cars continued as two separately-administered requirements for the next 17 years, but from 1 January 1921 the Roads Act 1920 introduced a single system, under the administration of the county, county borough and burgh councils, that combined registration and licensing and embraced all mechanically-propelled road vehicles. For the first time the motor lorry became licensed and taxed.

This arrangement continued until it became possible to bring all the vehicle registration and licensing records together into a single computerised system for the whole of Great Britain. In preparation for this the Vehicle & Driving Licences Act 1969 authorised transfer of responsibility to the Ministry of Transport, implemented on 1 April 1971. The actual transfer of duties and records to the Driver & Vehicle Licensing Centre (DVLC) at Swansea and its Local Vehicle Licensing Offices around the country took place in 1974 to 1978. On 2 April 1990 the DVLC became an executive agency of the Department of Transport and was renamed the Driver & Vehicle Licensing Agency. **GAB**

Philip Riden, *How to Trace the History of Your Car: a guide to motor vehicle registration records in the British Isles* (2nd edn, 1998); S Dowell, *A History of Taxation* (1884)

The **Reliant Engineering Co. (Tamworth) Ltd** was arguably the most important UK producer of three-wheel vans (q.v.). It was established in 1934 by Tom Williams (d. 1964), who had been made redundant when the Raleigh Cycle Co. decided not to proceed to long-run production of their three-wheel car. The Hodge Group bought a majority interest in Reliant in 1962, selling it to the Nash family in 1977. The company faltered in the difficult trading conditions of the 1980s and 1990s, undergoing several changes of ownership and going into receivership twice. After a promising new start under Jonathan Heynes in 1996, control was taken by his chief backer, who moved production then ceased manufacture in 2000. In 2001 a Suffolk firm reached agreement to produce Robin cars under licence, on rolling chassis made at Cannock. After 1998, to assist its dealers, Reliant imported the Italian Piaggio Ape (Bee) three-wheel van, which had considerable popularity on the continent for urban delivery and small-scale farming work. Reliant's first van was 7-cwt capacity, but the range extended to 12-cwt by the Second World War, when about 1000 vans had been made. Their motor cycle derivation clearly showed in the front wheel fork-system and upright stance. After wartime munitions work, van production resumed in 1946, resulting in another 2000 units before the Regal car appeared in 1953. The Regent van of 1950–6 was followed by the Regal, Robin and Rialto models. Nearly 2000 Ant TW9s, with an Ogle-designed cab, were produced between 1967 and 1987; a more upright and robust vehicle with a wide range of possible applications, it failed to make much UK market penetration, although it sold well in Greece where it was assembled. In 1969 Reliant took over the rival three-wheel vehicle manufacturer Bond Cars Ltd and stopped production of Bond's 875 Ranger van. Reliant vans were especially well suited to urban delivery and as general runabouts: the LMSR bought some for express parcels work, BOAC used a number at Heathrow Airport, the RSPCA had a fleet of 40 presented by Pedigree Pet Foods in 1975. **RAS**

D Pither, *Reliant Regal & Robin* (Thrupp: Sutton, 2001); N Wotherspoon, *'Lawrie' Bond: the man & the marque* (Minster Lovell: Bookmarque, 1993)

Removals. (Figures 76 and 156) Specialist firms of furniture removers began to emerge in the late 1850s and 1860s (see BISHOP'S MOVE GROUP). The earliest mention in the *Post Office London Directory* was in 1866, when seven such firms are listed. Specially-designed furniture removal vans appeared in the 1850s, having a cranked rear axle to permit a deep well in the floor of the rear half of the van; this allowed easily-damaged furniture to be carried, rather than lifted, in and out and increased headroom for tall pieces such as wardrobes. At this stage it still had low sides and the traditional tilt (q.v.) cover. For longer journeys the vans were loaded onto flat railway wagons — an early example of piggyback transport (q.v.) — but when goods train speeds began to exceed 20 mph, something more substantial and weatherproof was needed.

The classic horse-drawn wooden-bodied furniture van that later became known as the pantechnicon (q.v.), was developed in the 1860s; some examples survived in use until the Second World War. The bodies were usually covered with diagonal tongue-and-groove board, single-skinned for local work, but double-skinned for despatch by rail, in case the outer skin got damaged. Large rear wheels were inset into recesses in the otherwise flat body sides, but the front wheels were small enough to allow the steering carriage to turn a full 90 degrees either way. There were double rear doors above a large tailboard, which served as a loading ramp. On short road journeys, the tailboard might be supported by chains in the horizontal position to form an extension of the loading platform and top or rounding, boards, about 1 ft deep, fixed around the roof to contain smaller items loaded on top. The driver's seat on the front end of the roof was collapsible on vans designed for rail transport. A later variant, designed to fit within the railway loading gauge and introduced from about 1898, had four equal wheels, a flat floor and curved roof and was known as a tunnel van.

1888 has been quoted as the date of introduction of the lift-van or sling-van, which was in effect a removable body of a furniture van. For long-distance removals only the lift-van was transhipped for the rail or sea portion of the journey. From the early 1930s the railway companies became more directly involved in furniture removals, building a large fleet of containers, classified type BK, specially fitted out for this traffic. Some of their cartage contractors, such as Chaplins (q.v.) and Pickfords (q.v.), had long catered for furniture removals and, particularly after their purchase by the railway companies, were entrusted with developing this business. (See also CONTAINERISATION.)

Many large removal firms employed steam vehicles for their biggest jobs: at first traction engines hauling up to three horse vans; later flat lorries that could carry a lift van and haul van. Flat-bodied motor lorries with lift vans appeared just before the First World War, followed after the war by high-capacity vans and in the 1920s by Luton (q.v.) vans. At the top end of the range were coach-built Luton bodies, with comfortable large cabs for the removals crew, by firms such as Sparshatts. The light nature of the traffic allowed furniture vans to be designed with relatively small wheels and low floors, for ease of loading; bus chassis were often used. The total mileage undertaken is not high and the modern tendency is to buy good quality re-conditioned secondhand chassis and fit new bodies or refurbished exsting bodies.

The methods of packing and loading house contents have changed relatively little. The 'wrappers' carried in the van to protect the polished furniture were originally hessian sacking, supplied by firms that specialised in unpicking sacks and washing the squares of sacking used to wrap imported Polish bacon. These 'bacon cloths' were considered the best, being softer and closer woven. Two world wars provided a vast supply of cheap blankets. In more recent times padded fitted covers for standard shapes of furniture have become the norm. Glass and china were packed into second-hand tea chests with large amounts of newspaper. In recent years removers have gone over to cardboard boxes with foam, bubble-wrap and expanding corrugated sleeves. Another innovation is the wardrobe carton, in which clothes are hung on their own hangers. In past times a dustsheet was laid on the bed, the clothes removed from the wardrobe and wrapped into a bundle, which was stuffed into a suitable space.

It is usual for the driver to pack the van, after an initial survey of the house to see what is involved, while the porters carry the goods out. It is also usual for the driver to take instruction as to what goes where at the delivery end. For long-distance moves, the driver undertook the trunk haul alone and picked up a local crew from the firm's own depot, or that of an associated firm, for the delivery. At the top end of the market the removal contractor arranged carpet fitters, even soft furnishers to hang curtains. On this type of job the contractor sent a surveyor to note the client's wishes for the layout of furniture in rooms and also note positions of books in bookcases, clothes in closets and similar details. Most recent removal vehicles have a number of hinged doors on the nearside to accommodate standard-sized boxes that are now widely used in the industry.

At the other end of the social scale, many household removals have always been undertaken with do-it-yourself methods, using a handcart or a local tradesman's pony cart or the late twentieth century equivalent: the hire-van,

self-drive or with a driver. The customers might do their own preparatory packing of china and glass for a small removal firm.

Two major post-war developments must be mentioned. The first was the use of vans, rather than containers, for removals to Britain's off-shore islands and to the Continent following the introduction of roll-on/roll-off ferry services; containers are now confined to inter-continental removals. The second was the emergence of an important new market: office removals. **GAB**
See also BRITISH ASSOCIATION OF REMOVERS.

Robert Coates, 'Bishops Move', *VCVM*, 76 (April 1996), pp. 6–9, 77 (May 1996), pp. 12–17; M W Wahlen, 'History of the industry and advertising', *Trade Practice: a series of lectures...* (National Association of Furniture Warehousemen & Removers, *c.*1935); *Post Office London Directories*, various years

Renault Véhicules Industriels (Figure 42), the French commercial vehicle manufacturer, ultimately derives from Louis Renault's establishment as a car producer in 1898, followed in 1900 by commercial vehicle production. Renault penetrated the UK market after the First World War, with a full range of lorries, though light vehicles predominated. RVI evolved from Renault's acquisition of Latil and Somua in 1955, merged to form Saviem; in 1975 Berliet was acquired and in 1979 Renault took a 20 per cent share in the US truck manufacturer Mack, which subsequently became complete ownership. The Renault name replaced Saviem and Berliet in 1980 and in the following year Dodge truck production in the UK and Spain was bought from Peugeot, which had acquired Dodge with Chrysler's European operations in 1978. The former Commer plant at Dunstable continued in operation until 1993, the Dodge name being phased out during the 1980s. When it closed production of the Dodge/Renault 50 van ceased and the Midliner truck moved to France. The former Barreiros plant in Spain produced the Renault Major R series until 1996. The top of the range Renault AE Magnum was launched in 1990. The large high cab, despite difficult access, was eye-catching and offered an exceptionally good environment for the long-distance trunk driver. Despite its introduction in

1991, Renault's share of the UK truck market was only 4 per cent in 1994. The Midlum 7.5-tonne introduced in 2000 gained significant fleet orders, including Securicor Omega Express, and Renault's UK market share rose by over 30 per cent. In April 2000 Volvo acquired RVI in a cross-share deal, following the European Union's thwarting of Volvo's acquisition of Scania; in 1999 Volvo and Renault together shared 28 per cent of the UK market for lorries over 16 tonnes. **RAS**

Observer's Book of Commercial Vehicles (Frederick Warne, 1971); Millar (1997); *Homme et Camion*, 13 (January 1999), p. 25; *MT* (27 April 2000); *Truck* (February 2001), pp. 8–9, 14–15, 62–7; *Charge Utile*, 111 (March 2002), p. 27; Carverhill (2002)

Reo was one of the American truck makers which made some inroads into the UK market between the wars. Founded by R E Olds in 1904, the business was eventually acquired by the White Motor Co. in 1957, being consolidated with Diamond T in 1967. In 1915 Reo introduced the 1-ton Speed Wagon and, with extensive modifications over time, this range persisted into the late 1930s. In 1925 they offered the Reo Major chassis to carry loads of 36-cwt for £450, whereas the Speed Wagon was £320 for a 25-cwt load. They promoted the vehicles by a play on their name as 'Reliable economical operation'. Under the slogan 'Reorganise your transport with Reo' Reo Motors (Britain) Ltd of Hammersmith undertook a major campaign in 1935 to launch the more rounded streamlined version of the Speed Wagon. A ten-page feature in *Commercial Motor* listed main dealers, with illustrations of vehicles supplied, and described technical features, such as four-wheel internal hydraulic brakes and the Gold Crown engine introduced in 1929. Vehicles illustrated included platform, tipper, articulated and box-van types, three of the latter in the liveries of parcels carriers. Reos were offered in Britain until the early 1950s and many trucks remained in use long after. **RAS**

CM (15 February 1935), Adverts, pp. 12–21

Replica vans, see VANS

Return loads. The availability of a further load to be transported in the opposite direction after a vehicle had delivered its outward load made a big difference to the profitability of the work. Clearing houses (q.v.) played a large part at times in providing return loads, though there has been criticism of the rates they offered. It is much easier to find return loads when vehicles are engaged in regular runs, while the essence of tramping (q.v.) was the willingness to accept loads almost irrespective of destination.

Environmentalists and others have long criticised the number of vehicles running empty, but there are many instances where return loading is impractical. Tankers carrying milk or petroleum products and skip lorries are obvious examples, and even a tipper carrying coal or aggregate on its outward run is unlikely to be able to obtain a return load. On short runs, too -- and the average distance travelled by a lorry with a load in 2000 was only about 60 miles -- the time needed to secure a return load can make it unprofitable. As standards of product quality rose, so risk of contamination of a load rose as well, and this also mitigated against finding return loads as did restrictions on drivers' hours.

There is often a natural imbalance in traffic availability. Much of Scotland, for example, receives far more inward traffic, so rates for outward traffic may be low (and to the detriment of Scottish hauliers) because rates are driven down by the number of vehicles returning to England and seeking loads.

Where traffic carried is consistent, there is a greater likelihood of regular return loads. More extreme examples of adaptability of design and equipment have included flat platform vehicles carrying empty plastic or rubber roll-up tanks which are unrolled and filled on the return journey. Specially-designed curtain-sided trailers which carry sawdust on outward runs and the completed product, hardboard sheets, on the return are another example.

While carrying return loads whenever possible has long been regarded as important in reducing the number of goods vehicles on the roads, and worthwhile for their operators in producing a better financial return, the official attitude in the early days of goods vehicle licensing was strongly against the idea. For example, in 1935 the Appeal Tribunal totally agreed with the Metropolitan Licensing Authority that 'carriage of goods on return journeys was not generally desirable and constituted unfair competition with other hauliers.'   **JMA**

Richards, Jack, & Son Ltd, hauliers of Fakenham, Norfolk, were founded as J W Richards at Haddenham in 1956 by Jack Richards, the son of a Leicestershire miner, who had settled in East Anglia after marrying there whilst in the RAF. After six years driving for an aggregates firm, he set up on his own with a single vehicle. Experience showed the need to develop full loads by regular overnight trunking, initially to Nottingham and then to Derby, Leicester and London markets, a policy which proved successful. Some secondhand vehicles were acquired as part of the process of gaining A licences; new vehicles included Albion 6-wheel dropsides, Bedford S and TK, Seddons and Dodge four-in-line articulateds. The firm's close association with ERF began with the purchase of a secondhand example in 1965 and an invitation to visit the works; standardisation on the marque followed from 1973. Fakenham was opened in 1971, initially as an additional depot, with five new Scammell articulated units, Haddenham remaining in operation until the late 1970s. The nature of Richards' traffic changed, from market delivery to contract haulage. The firm was a founding member of Palletways, handling collections and deliveries of palleted goods within the Norfolk postcode area. A depot was opened in Warrington in 1996 and Stobart's former Wisbech depot taken over as a base for 20 vehicles; the Fakenham site of 6.5 acres provides 60,000 sq ft of warehousing. Fleet size at the beginning of 2001 was 124, with 32 more ERFs on order.   **RAS**

B Tuck, 'Jack comes up trumps', *Truck* (April 1999), pp. 60–3; *Truck* (June 2001)

Richardson, Don and Roy, now best known for their property development in Birmingham and the Black Country, began their business careers in transport around 1946. Originally selling ex-army vehicles and spares, they expanded by selling used, re-furbished commercial vehicles and also developed an export division including buses. Their success saw the expansion of their large Oldbury base, with workshop and warehousing and storage facilities.

De-nationalisation in 1954 saw them making successful tenders for BRS units with their special A-licensed vehicles. One such tender was for the entire High Wycombe fleet of 50 vehicles which was taken en-masse to Oldbury. These vehicles were sold on to new or re-entrants to the industry.

They also acquired the Rugeley depot and fleet in 1955 to operate as Richardson's Transport (Rugeley) Ltd. Richardsons had acquired a reputation for fair dealing and good back-up service. From this they were able to take advantage of periods of low demand for new vehicles, acquiring Bedford's available production of standard TK chassis over a period, offering immediate delivery of these, including tipping and skip-loading vehicles. Their success saw them repeating this with AEC chassis. Despite becoming recognised as appointed dealers for Bedford and AEC, changes in the market saw their withdrawal from the business of vehicle sales in the early 1980s and of haulage in 2000, to concentrate on their property business, refurbishing now redundant factories and developing the Merry Hill Centre. In recognition of their role in the re-generation of the Black Country the brothers were awarded Honorary Fellowships by Wolverhampton University Business School in 2002.

They were involved in the efforts to avoid Foden going into receivership in 1979, including the purchase for re-sale of the stock of unsold chassis. Richardson's Transport (Rugeley) Ltd was closed, because of the closure of major customers and the unprofitable rates offered for their other traffic. The 90 vehicle fleet including specialised trailers was sold by auction in May 2000.   **GM/JMA**

The **ridge pole body** (Figure 157) was a version of the tilt body, in which the load-covering sheet was draped over a horizontal ridge pole fixed longitudinally over the load-carrying platform, to which the cover was attached by lacing. It was also known as a pole wagon and was used, for example, by the GWR and Sutton of Manchester. **RAS**

Twells and Bourne (1983), pl. 256

The **rigid eight,** or 4-axle non-articulated lorry (also known as the eight-wheeler), was legally recognised by the Heavy Motor Car (Amendment) (No. 2) Order 1930, which came into force on 1 October 1930. It was allowed a gross weight of 22 tons, compared with 19 tons for a 3-axle vehicle, which gave a net payload advantage of 2½-tons within the same maximum length of 30 ft. It also had an advantage by the mid-1930s of being able to run at 20 mph while a vehicle and trailer or an artic was limited to 16 mph. The term was coined by Scammell to distinguish its non-articulated from its articulated models.

The first rigid eights were Sentinel steam wagons, the DG8 in 1930 and the S8 in 1934, but the heyday of the steamer was past and only a handful were built. The first production diesel rigid eight was the AEC Mammoth Major early in 1934, although there were some earlier conversions of 6-wheeled lorries. Within 2–3 years most of the UK heavy lorry manufacturers were offering rigid eights. From then until the early 1960s they dominated the long-distance haulage scene and in the late 1950s – to some the halcyon days of the British lorry – were being produced by eleven UK manufacturers.

From 1942 rigid eights were allowed to haul a drawbar trailer, initially as a wartime economy measure, provided power braking was fitted. Considerable use was made of this arrangement for trunking services, notably by Sutton & Son (St Helens) Ltd (q.v.) and BRS, until it became uneconomic as a result of the increasing cost of employing the trailer attendant and changes to the speed limits (q.v.) and gross weight limits (q.v.) that favoured articulated vehicles.

Originally there was little to choose between the rigid eight and the 8-wheel articulated lorry in terms of carrying capacity: both were allowed the same maximum gross weight; the articulated lorry was allowed an extra 3 ft of overall length, but this did no more than compensate for the

unusable gap between the back of the cab and the front of the trailer. In 1964, however, the maximum gross weight was increased to 32 tons for the articulated lorry, but only 28 tons for the rigid. Subsequent changes reduced the weight advantage of the 8-wheel articulated lorry, but increased its length advantage. From that time articulated vehicles began to dominate British long-distance haulage and some makers deleted rigid 8-wheelers from their ranges. Nevertheless they were still considered superior for some purposes. When fitted with a tipper body, its robustness and stability on uneven ground made it particularly suitable for the movement of dense bulk products such as coal, spoil and stone. The increase in permissible weight to 30 tons in 1973 brought a revival. European makers exporting to the UK, such as DAF, Magirus-Deutz, MAN and Volvo even added eight-wheelers to their UK ranges and some proceeded to sell them to their home markets for the first time. **GAB/JMA**

Billings (1982); Wright (1983); Davies (1985) and (1995)

RMC, see READY-MIXED CONCRETE

The **Road Carrying Co.** was one of the pioneers in carrying goods by motor lorry. It was set up in Liverpool in the spring of 1902 by Lord Derby, Sir Arthur Stanley MP, and Edward Shrapnell-Smith (q.v.) with a capital of £20,000. The aim of the company was to test the viability of using steam engines to carry goods on a commercial basis.

The three sets of trials held by the Liverpool Self-Propelled Traffic Association (q.v.) had shown that it was technically possible to operate motor lorries, but no trial had been made of the economics of regular lorry use. The company stuck to the legal limit of 3-ton tare weight even though this kept down the size of the load that could be carried. The 14 vehicles were used mostly for short-distance traffic to and from the docks. They did not prove successful. They were effectively limited to loads of about four tons on the lorry and an extra two or three in a trailer. This was too little to be commercial. In addition the state of the roads hindered vehicles and breakdowns and mechanical failures were common. Within a year the experiment ceased.

JA

E S Shrapnell-Smith 'Five decades of commercial road transport', *Journal of the Institute of Transport* (1946), pp.217–29

Road Haulage Association. Two distinct, although related, organisations have represented the interests of road haulage contractors as both a trade and employers' organisation under the title of the Road Haulage Association. The first had a life of only three years, from 1932 to 1935. Its origin was the Long Distance Road Haulage Committee of Enquiry (q.v.), established following a lunch in April 1930 at Pagani's Restaurant convened by G Mackenzie Junner (q.v.), editor of the *Commercial Motor,* in order to give evidence to the Royal Commission on Transport. In the following January the committee gave rise to the Long Distance Road Haulage Association. In the same year Frank Fowler, a south west London tipper operator and chairman of Murrell's Wharf which was a major operator with a large up-to-date fleet, founded a Short Distance Hauliers' Alliance (q.v.). These two organisations then amalgamated as the Road Haulage Association in 1932 with E C Marston (q.v.) as president and Roger W Sewill, previously managing director of London & Southern Counties Transport Co. Ltd, as secretary. Membership, organised in 1934 into 14 areas, grew to over 7000 by 1935, rising to nearly 9000 by the winding up of the RHA in August of that year. The character of the RHA, and its title, changed with its amalgamation with the Motor Hirers' & Coach Services' Association to form the Associated Road Operators (ARO), registered on 12 July 1935. The Motor Hirers' organisation had been set up in the 1920s by the coming together of 22 local associations of horse vehicle owners, with both goods and passenger operations, in the process of conversion to motors. By this amalgamation the RHA lost both its unambiguous title and its distinctive character. Amalgamation negotiations in 1936 with the Commercial Motor Users' Association (q.v.), the ancillary users' body, came to nothing and in the following year a specific

parcels carriers' organisation was founded on the initiative of Charles Dunbar (q.v.). To add to the complexity of the politics of road transport at this period, the recently founded British Road Federation (q.v.) also concerned itself with operators' interests, as well as the issue of road provision. Thus, as the 1930s ended, the representation of British road transport interests was still in a state of confusion, with a multiplicity of organisations, some overlapping, some conflicting. Under the dual pressures of war and the emerging threat of nationalisation, as well as the inevitable increase of government intervention in wartime, the road transport industry, through existing machinery, worked out a more rational system of post-war representation of its interests. In February 1939 the Standing Joint Committee of Hauliers' National Organisations (SJC) arranged a link with the National Emergency Co-ordination Committee and at another restaurant meeting, Kettner's on 10 May 1939, the idea of three autonomous bodies, for hauliers, ancillary users and public service vehicle operators, was put forward by J H Watts. In October 1942 the SJC set up a Road Transport Organisation Joint Conference with a planning sub-committee, from the deliberations of which emerged the RHA in its second creation, the Traders' Road Transport Association (q.v.) and the Passenger Vehicle Operators' Association, linked in the National Road Transport Federation (q.v.).

On 25 October 1944 an extraordinary general meeting of the ARO unanimously accepted the articles of association of the proposed RHA, which was incorporated as a company limited by guarantee on 14 December 1944. The organisation included a large national council, executive and finance committees, a range of standing committees, nine functional groups and committees, ranging from express parcels to heavy haulage, and a number of panels related to the Ministry of War Transport Road Haulage Scheme (q.v.). The RHA established 16 geographical areas. The most obvious deployment of the new RHA's collective power went into its anti-nationalisation campaign, from mid-1945 onwards, utilising public and special meetings, including a conference of national trade associations, parades and films, such as

When the Wheels Slow Down. With the loss of the political battle (although nationalisation was not as sweeping as many had feared), the RHA, whilst adhering to the principles of free enterprise, made clear its readiness to co-operate with the BTC, which was somewhat in contrast to its original refusal to negotiate with the government. A liaison conference held its inaugural meeting on 11 May 1949. At the same time, the RHA helped its members apply for 'original permits', which entitled holders to operate for the time being more than 25 miles from base after the appointed day. Advice on a wide range of topics has always been a principal benefit of RHA membership. Similar help was extended to members after the Transport Act 1953 introduced partial denationalisation: Transport Unit Finance Ltd (q.v.) was established and RHA members' purchasing interests and related information were processed and advice given to the Road Haulage Disposal Board (q.v.). Nonetheless, the RHA suffered a set-back when the Transport (Road Haulage Property) Disposal Act left BRS with a much larger fleet than the 1953 Act had provided for. The expansion of private enterprise which followed partial denationalisation benefited the RHA in terms of membership potential and in 1964 the Council approved the admission of BRS companies to a special category of membership, which would not allow them to gain control of RHA affairs.

From the 1950s through the 1970s a number of issues became of increasing significance to the RHA. It looked to a wider world, rejoining the IRTU (q.v.) in 1957 and setting up an International Road Transport Committee in the same year. At home the docks (q.v.) gave rise to serious concern from two aspects, one more or less replacing the other. Initially the problem was identified as delays at the docks. In 1955 a conference on the subject highlighted hauliers' frustrations at operating in an environment restricted not only physically by a layout not designed for motor traffic, but also restricted by problems which seemed to derive from management and labour attitudes. The solution to dock delays, by replacing handling across PLA quays with containerisation (q.v.), was in turn to present the RHA with another major problem, caused by the dockers' rearguard action to try to claim groupage work outside the docks as the dockers' prerogative, a claim which led to severe industrial action. By the early 1970s this second docks problem had become acute. In 1972 the RHA applied to the National Industrial Relations Court for an interim order restraining Liverpool dockers from blacking vehicles, the RHA claiming that 'groupage' had always been a road transport operation. Picketing and blacking worsened, leading to the dramatic resignation of the RHA's chairman, J P Wells, in 1975, when he put his 130 year-old family firm into voluntary liquidation, following unofficial blacking. At the end of the decade the hire and reward sector of the industry was involved in a fierce wage claim dispute with both the Labour government and the RHA during the so-called 'Winter of Discontent' of 1979. Paul Smith considers that the RHA failed 'disastrously' in its opposition to the union's wage demands (although raising the cost of winning the increase), but was partially successful in maintaining the national character of the eventual agreement, even though bargaining was regional in form. In his view, the RHA showed a considerable degree of unity and determination and emerged 'intact, if bruised'. In 1981 the incoming Director-General, F J Plaskett, faced a substantially declining membership (from 14,117 at the end of 1980 to 11,726 at the end of 1982) with a consequent loss of resources. The successful response was to replace areas by larger districts, sell off surplus property, move out of central London and modernise administrative methods.

Shortly before his retirement, Plaskett was presented in December 1987 with a merger proposal by the Freight Transport Association (q.v.), which was rejected by the RHA. In the following April the FTA amended its memorandum and articles of association to enable it to encompass membership from the hire and reward sector. It was made known that this change was in response to the growth of distribution systems and the ensuing complexity of the road haulage industry and the RHA and FTA accordingly moved towards closer liaison. A testing time for this relationship came from one of the principal challenges which faced the road haulage industry as the twentieth century ended. This was literally an escalating problem, the Fuel Duty Escalator (q.v.), introduced by the Conservative government in March 1993, ostensibly for environmental reasons. Opposed by the industry from the outset, the Escalator's rise to 6 per cent in 1997, a further rise of 1p per litre on diesel in 1998 and the rise of the Escalator to 11 per cent brought about a virtually unprecedented protest movement (q.v.) conducting a direct action campaign under various banners in 1998 and 2000. The debate served to highlight growing differences within the industry between smaller hauliers and the major undertakings deriving from road haulage which now regarded themselves as logistics companies. The RHA was criticised by Trans-Action for less than wholehearted support of the mass lobby of March 1999, whereas the FTA distanced itself from direct action and launched a major media campaign in September 1999 in an attempt to put pressure on government. Although some haulage firms had joint membership of both the RHA and FTA, some smaller hauliers, under pressure both from the Escalator and from larger rivals, saw a conflict of interests between the typical membership of each organisation. A joint steering group of the RHA and FTA was set up in December 1998 to 'manage and direct the co-operative action to be taken in 1999 for the benefit of members', but the tensions evidenced by responses to the Escalator increased and the sudden departure of the RHA's director Steven Norris in September 1999 made progress towards unification seem problematic. From 1997 to 1999 Steven Norris, former Conservative MP and under-secretary of state for the Department of Transport 1992-6, was director general of the RHA. He raised its profile, against the background of the protest movements (q.v.), partly by opening an office in Westminster. However, the RHA recorded pre-tax losses in 1998 and after what some described as an internal 'power struggle', Norris left on 'mutually agreeable terms'. The grass roots direct action on fuel prices in autumn 2000 further exacerbated differences between large and small operators and their views on representation. **RAS**

Records in the Modern Records Centre, University of Warwick Library comprise RHA secretary's department files, 1950–1960s, and industrial relations officer's files, mainly 1960s–1970s (MSS.234). Topics covered include delays at the docks, RHA/BRB/BRS tripartite machinery, 1963-7, containerisation, West Midlands disputes. Harper and Birch (1995); W P Clegg, *Docks and Ports*, 2: *London* (Ian Allan, 1987); F Lindop, 'The dockers and the 1971 Industrial Relations Act, pt 1: shop stewards and containerisation', *Historical Studies in Industrial Relations*, 5 (1998), pp. 33–72; P Smith, 'The "Winter of Discontent": the hire and reward road haulage dispute, 1979', *HSIR*, 7 (1999), pp. 27–54; P Newman, 'One for the road', *CM* (8 April 1999), pp. 42–3; A Hill and F Worsford, 'Haulage in crisis: Stuck on the escalator', *Truck* (July 1999), pp. 42–5; *CM* (26 August 1999), p. 2

The **Road Haulage Disposal Board** was set up by the Transport Act of 1953 and was in existence for some three years, until August 1956. Its chairman was Sir Malcolm Trustram Eve. It was part of the process of denationalising long distance road haulage. The Board's title was something of a misnomer, since its role was that of a court of referees, rather than the active vendor of BRS units, as selling was left to the initiative of the British Transport Commission. In the Board's first progress report to the Minister it emphasised that it had not been given by Parliament the duty of disposing of BTC road haulage assets. In a subsequent report the Board praised the advice which it had received from the Road Haulage Association (q.v.). **RAS**

Birch and Harper (1995); Ingram and Mustoe (1999); Bonavia (1987), pp. 158–64

Road Haulage Executive, see NATIONALIS-ATION

The **Road Haulage Organisation** was a body set up by the Ministry of War Transport in 1943 to coordinate the movement of goods by road. It comprised mostly long distance hauliers which were taken over and controlled by the RHO. At its peak it controlled about 34,000 vehicles in twelve areas. Its achievement was to economise in the use of tyres, fuel, and vehicles by maximising back loading and minimising journeys loaded only one-way. In this sense road haulage was better organised than before the war. The existence of the RHO also allowed the government to mobilise lorries in a national emergency, such as sending 500 vehicles into South Wales in autumn 1943 because the railways could not cope with the volume of freight traffic. The RHO was dissolved in August 1946 and the vehicles returned to their private owners. The economies achieved in road haulage under the RHO encouraged the belief that national control under one body (that is nationalisation) should result in similar savings in operating costs.   **JA**

Savage (1957)

The **Road Haulage Wages Board** was set up in 1938 under the Road Haulage Wages Act of that year. It established a scheme for the statutory determination of the wages of drivers and their mates. It arose out of the failure of previous attempts to fix the wages of road haulage drivers. In 1919 a Joint Industrial Council had been established to recommend wage rates in road haulage and Ernest Bevin had led the workers' side. But the wages could not be enforced and a severe industrial depression meant the JIC was dead by the end of 1920. Another attempt was made in 1934 to set up a framework for wage determination. A National Joint Conciliation Board was set up with fifteen members to each side, the workers led again by Ernest Bevin, but it was not satisfactory and in 1937 the Baillie Committee (the Committee on Regulation of Wages and Condition of Service in the Road Motor Transport Industry (Goods), Cmd. 5440) was set up to investigate the matter. It recommended a national board which would cover drivers of A- and B- licensed vehicles but not those driving railway-owned lorries. The railways saw this as a means of removing sub-standard wage rates which created unfair competition for them.

The result was the RHWB which comprised the national Road Haulage Central Wages Board and a number of Area Wages Boards. The Central Board had three independent members, about twenty members representing the employers and the workers, and representatives from each of the Area Boards. They made recommendations to the Minister of Labour who could issue an order enforcing the rates. The act was cautious about C-licensed drivers but gave them the right to appeal to the minister about 'unfair wages', which was referred to an Industrial Court which could fix a rate applicable for three years. The bill was backed by the Associated Road Operators (q.v.), which represented the larger hauliers operating A and B licences, as it thought it would bring a reduction in competition from under-cutting small firms and owner drivers.

The system was reformed in 1948 when the area boards were abolished and the Central Board was renamed the Road Haulage Wages Council. From then until the 1970s wage rates were set by the Minister of Transport based on the recommendations of the Wages Council, with rates depending on the weight of the lorry driven and the region in which it was based. The unions withdrew from the Council in 1972 and it was finally terminated in 1978.   **JA**
See also INDUSTRIAL RELATIONS

The Road Way (May, 1938), pp. 19–22; Gibson (2001), pp. 262–7

The **road pavement** (Figures 125 and 158). Developments in the design and construction of the road pavement in the twentieth century have progressed largely in response to the development of the road vehicle itself. The 'pavement' is the technical term for the part of the highway upon which the road traffic runs and the modern road pavement performs three distinct functions. Structurally, its function is as a means of spreading the loads applied to the road surface by the wheels of traffic so that at the bottom of the pavement, where it is in contact with the natural soil (the subgrade), the applied stresses and strains have been reduced to a level which the subgrade can withstand without significant deformation or failure. Secondly, the surface of the pavement should provide a protection against the entry of surface water into the pavement and subsequently into the subgrade soil, since keeping the pavement and the subgrade dry is important in maintaining structural strength and stability. Thirdly, for modern traffic the pavement surface should provide a skid-resistant, low noise surface for the safe passage of vehicles on the highway.

Towards the end of the nineteenth century, most town centre roads were paved, usually either with stone setts or wood blocks (to reduce noise levels from horse-drawn traffic) although some use was made of natural rock or mastic asphalt from the mid-nineteenth century. In other areas roads were normally of the water-bound macadam type, a legacy of the pioneering work in the nineteenth century by Thomas Telford and John McAdam. These pavements were generally made up of layers of broken stone, progressively smaller in size towards the surface with a surface layer of fine broken stone or gravel. Water was used as an aid to compaction of the materials and also as a binding agent in the road surface. Such road pavements were adequate for slow, horse-drawn vehicles with iron tyres.

During the latter part of the nineteenth century, due to the widespread use of coal gas for lighting and power, increasing quantities of coal tar became available which could be crudely distilled to increase its viscosity. Tar began to be used in road pavement construction either to grout existing water-bound macadam roads or for pre-coating stone. The need to stabilise the water-bound road surface was given additional impetus by the coming of the mechanically-propelled vehicle, initially with metal or solid rubber tyres and later with pneumatic tyres, and travelling at much higher speeds. Such vehicles caused major damage to the water-bound macadam pavement. The vehicle tyres plucked loose stones from the road surface, leading to the rapid development of pot-holes and the loose fine surface material was quickly blown away in the form of dust clouds. Refined tar was used to surface dress the water-bound surface, a layer of tar being sprayed on the road and covered with stone chippings or gravel. After the First World War a new industry developed from the early beginnings of the late nineteenth century to produce coated macadams, crushed stone or gravel which was pre-mixed with a quantity of tar or bitumen (a by-product of the burgeoning petroleum refining industry) to give a material which produced a stable, water-resistant road surface when laid

and compacted. From these early developments sprang the modern array of road building materials. By suitably adjusting the size and grading of the stone in combination with an appropriate quantity of bituminous 'binder' the industry has made available a variety of materials, varying from the traditional open textured tar and bitumen macadams to high density, high strength asphalts which must be laid hot and which gain much of their strength and stability from the rapid increase in the viscosity of the bituminous binder as the material cools.

Although there had been some use of concrete as one of the layers of a flexible pavement, the construction of wholly concrete rigid road pavements did not develop significantly in the UK until about 1920 when some experimental pavements were constructed. These early trials led to the wide-spread use of concrete pavements. One of the weaknesses in the use of concrete for pavements has been the need to provide joints in the pavement structure to allow for shrinkage and temperature-induced expansion and contraction of the material but very recent developments have begun to eliminate this problem.

Alongside the development of improved pavement materials has proceeded the development of structural design methods for road pavements. The design process involves the selection of the type and thickness of the materials in the layers of the pavement to enable it to distribute the traffic loading. Since it is estimated that the damage inflicted on the road structure by a single vehicle wheel increases by the fourth power of the wheel load, increasing vehicle weights have made it necessary to increase the number of axles and wheels in order to restrict the applied load from each wheel.

Until quite recently, pavement design methods have been based on the results of road trials of differing materials laid in differing thicknesses, the performance of the experimental sections being monitored over a long period and design recommendations modified accordingly. A measurement of the strength of the subgrade soil (for example the California Bearing Ratio Test) is frequently a starting point for such empirical design methods. Since the 1970s design methods based on an analysis of stresses and strains in the pavement structure and the subgrade soil coupled with a more detailed knowledge of the properties of the pavement materials have been developed. It is necessary to consider not only the load applied to the pavement by each individual wheel but also the cumulative number of load applications expected within the design life of the pavement. This required an estimate of the volume and weight of vehicles over a period of 20 to 40 years. In some design methods only the numbers of commercial vehicles are considered (for example those with an unladen weight exceeding 1500 kg), the loads imposed by cars and light vans being considered of little significance.

Mechanisation of road pavement construction led to the development of specialised vehicles, such as large capacity dump trucks for earth moving operations, insulated lorries for carrying high temperature pavement construction materials, paving machines for laying the pavement materials and steel and pneumatic-tyred rollers for compaction. Large scale road construction requires a considerable fleet of tipper lorries for muck shifting and aggregate transport.   **RC**

D Croney, *The Design and Performance of Road Pavements* (HMSO, 1977); Earle (1974); M G Lay, *Ways of the World* (Rutgers University Press, 1992); C A O'Flaherty, *Highways* (Edward Arnold, 1967), Reader (1980); Road Research Laboratory, *Bituminous Materials in Road Construction* (HMSO, 1962); T Salkield, *Road Making and Road Using* (Pitman, 1936); R A B Smith and T R Grigson, *Design and Construction of Concrete Roads* (Concrete Publications, 1946); Graham West, *The Technical Development of Roads in Britain* (Aldershot: Ashgate, 2000)

Road-rail vehicles (Figure 159). A vehicle able to run on both railway tracks and roads would, in theory, offer the benefits of inter-modal transport (q.v.) without the costs and delays associated with lifting containers. Bi-modal vehicles for transporting maintenance personnel and materials on remote railway lines were tried in the 1930s and since the 1980s there has been increasing use of bi-modal shunting tractors in sidings and bi-modal personnel carriers and maintenance plant to facilitate quick access to work sites. The few attempts to produce such a vehicle for commercial service in this country have never got beyond the development stage.

The first was the LMSR's Ro-Railer bus that ran experimentally in public service in 1931, but the first bi-modal freight vehicle did not appear until 1960. The Roadrailer was a joint initiative of British Railways and BRS (q.v.) developed for them by the Pressed Steel Company from a design operating on the Chesapeake & Ohio Railroad in the USA. Roadrailers were semi-trailers with alternative rear axles, one for road and the other for rail, the changeover being effected by a pneumatic mechanism. On the road the vehicles were hauled by standard tractor units. In rail mode they were coupled together with the front of each vehicle supported by the rear of the vehicle in front; the leading vehicle was coupled to a special adaptor truck behind the locomotive. (It was intended that the Roadrailers would run as separate trains, not in conventional freight trains.) Following trials with van- and flat-bodied prototypes, fifty vans were built for a London–Newcastle–Edinburgh service running at a speed of 80 mph. Its announced inauguration in September 1963 was delayed first by the need for technical modifications (completed by April 1964) and then by the 'open terminal' dispute with the National Union of Railwaymen which ran on until 1967 (see FREIGHTLINERS LTD). By then the Roadrailer's 24 ft body and 11-ton payload (16 tons gross) had fallen well behind the latest length limits (see CONSTRUCTION & USE REGULATIONS) and weight limits (q.v.) for articulated lorries. The opportunity to win customers over to the concept had been lost and it would have been necessary to start again. The project was quietly abandoned and the stored vehicles sold for scrap.

There was renewed interest in bi-modal semi-trailers after 1985, again as a result of successful developments in the USA, and prototypes of the Trailer Train appeared in 1986 and the RoadRailer in 1992. These were much larger than the 1960 design: 13.6 m long with three road axles. On rail they ran on two 2-axle bogies which also supported the adjoining vehicles. The air-suspension was used to lower the Trailer Train vehicle onto the rail bogies before retracting the road wheels. The RoadRailer had air bellows incorporated in its road running gear which raised the vehicle while being coupled to the bogies; the bellows were then exhausted, lifting the road wheels clear of the ground. The rail bogies were left behind when the vehicles ran in the road mode, thus not contributing to the gross road weight. Even though the vehicles had to be strengthened to withstand the longitudinal loads when marshalled within a conventional goods train, their payload of 23–4 tonnes was only slightly less than the standard 38-tonne articulated trailer. There was, however, some loss of volumetric capacity because the top of the body had to be shaped to fit within the railway loading gauge and the initial cost for such a specialised vehicle was much higher. Although the sets of prototype vehicles have been used from time to time for carrying commercial traffics, the idea never took off and has again been overtaken by increased lorry weights. **GAB**

1960 Roadrailer:- PRO, AN 120/305; *Modern Railways*, 13 (1960), pp. 685–6. Trailer Train:- David Ratcliffe, *Modern Private Owner Wagons on British Rail* (Wellingborough: Patrick Stephens, 1989), pp. 110–12

Road Services (Caledonian) Ltd was the name given to the BRS (Caledonian) Group assets including 83 vehicles in south west Scotland by Walter Alexander when they were acquired on denationalisation in the early 1950s. Expansion to some 450 vehicles took place, with a string of depots reaching London. The livery changed from green to light blue in the early 1960s and Caledonian joined other Alexander transport interests in the Tayforth Group, which was bought back into state ownership in 1970 by the Transport Holding Company (q.v.). A sister company serving the east side of Scotland was Road Services (Forth) Ltd. It too was based on former BRS units but operations remained more regional. It too went into the Tayforth Group in the 1960s. **RAS**

Truck (September 2000), p.88

Road tests of commercial vehicles have been undertaken by professional transport journals since well before the Second World War. *Commercial Motor* began publishing road tests in 1929 and by October 1938 had completed more than 280 of them. Before then it had carried technical descriptions of the specification of new commercial vehicles but not of how they behaved on the road. In the early days these were often rather amateur and gentlemanly affairs and in some cases testing was carried out by the factory or works driver with the so-called tester following in a car. Often a common route was favoured by a particular journal for most of its tests. Emphasis was usually on hill-climbing ability, with radiator water temperature being taken before and after a particular climb, which was also timed. Actual criticism of a vehicle, or any part of its design, was rare.

After the Second World War a more scientific and critical approach developed. Until the 1960s timed acceleration and measured braking tests were usually carried out on public roads, but a greater emphasis on safety and the increasing weight of traffic led to the use of test tracks or other special facilities for these. Today well-qualified staff with an engineering or operating background are used by the magazines and undertake all the driving. Modern test routes are carefully designed to include different road conditions and, depending on the type of vehicle being tested, usually include a mix of motorway, dual carriageway, A road and urban running. Particular attention is paid to fuel consumption, special meters being used, and vehicles are invariably loaded to their full payload. Manufacturers take great care before submitting a vehicle to road test, running it in over a considerable distance before releasing it to critical outside eyes. Road tests were sometimes used to highlight general deficiencies in design. For example, from the 1950s *Motor Transport* put all vehicles it tested through a visibility test at MIRA (q.v.) which showed poor visibility or 'blind spots' in many cabs. Ultimately cab and vehicle designers produced new models which eliminated these failings, and *Motor Transport* dropped this procedure from its road tests.

Manufacturers saw road tests as publicity which might at least make their product better known and hopefully help sell more of it. They ordered reprints of particularly favourable road tests to distribute to potential buyers. They also did not offer for road test a model or range which they felt did not show up particularly well against its rivals. It is difficult to estimate how influential road tests were but serious criticism, though not common, can certainly dampen sales. Certain aspects such as fuel consumption were widely studied and regarded as more credible and comparable than figures put out by the makers themselves.   **JMA**

The **Road Transport Board** was an inter-departmental body set up in February 1918 in the context of the petrol shortage which had not been averted by the establishment of the Petrol Control Committee in 1916 or by the limited introduction of town gas as a fuel for road vehicles and the extension of the use of battery-electric vehicles for delivery work. 13 Divisional RTBs and 84 Area Committees were set up, registration of goods vehicles by the end of July 1918 was required and the RTB took over the work of the numerous local transport sub-committees of the Food Control Committees. The end of the First World War in November 1918 meant that the RTB hardly had the opportunity to show its potential, although its Return Loads Bureau and encouragement of delivery co-ordination schemes showed practical results in the few months of its wartime existence. Its chairman, Sir Evan Jones (1859–1949, civil engineer), gave interesting evidence to the Select Committee on Transport in October 1918, although he made it clear that he foresaw only a limited role for motor transport of goods after the war, as a feeder to the rail and waterway systems and for independent local traffic, rather than as a trunk service provider to areas already served by rail or canal. Although the RTB was only intended as a wartime provision, it was again in action, located within the Ministry of Food, in the national railway strike of late September and early October 1919. Several thousand lorries were placed under instruction under a Road Transport (Registration) Order activated when the strike began. They carried milk and essential foodstuffs and, in the case of London, hay for its still large horse population.   **RAS**

Gibson (2001), pp. 108–16, 138–40, 147, 201; *WWW*, 4

Road Transport Executive, see NATIONALIS-ATION

Roadline Ltd, see BRS (PARCELS)

The **Roads Campaign Council** was set up in 1955, largely on the initiative of Wilfrid Andrews of the Royal Automobile Club and the SMMT to press for much more government spending on roads. It was backed by the RAC and AA (q.v.), the SMMT (q.v.) and the BRF (q.v.), as well as by motor agents, bus operators and motor cyclists. It resembled the Roads Improvement Association (q.v.) in trying to be a non-party organization which informed and influenced parliamentarians. It was a tireless advocate of motorways and by-passes, publishing pamphlets and reports such as *Road Matters, Highway Times* and *Missing Links* which drew attention to traffic congestion and the benefits of new motor roads. In 1963 it lost the support of a few backers, like the Automobile Association and SMMT, which joined instead the British Road Federation because of the tone and content of some of the RCC's broadsheets. The split was patched up in 1970 and the RCC reconstituted. It then became largely a parliamentary arm of the BRF, organising the All Party Road Study Group. In 1965 it pressed for £7 billion to be spent on roads over the next fifteen years.

It was largely successful in its campaigns in encouraging the government to build motorways. These were a great advance for road hauliers (the Road Haulage Association (q.v.) was a member from 1955) in speeding up freight transport and cutting costs.   **JA**

Hamer (1987), pp. 18–19; Piers Brendon, *The Motoring Century* (1997), pp. 264–6

The **Roads Improvement Association** was formed in 1886 by cyclists to put pressure on government to improve the roads. The two cycling organisations, the Cyclists Touring Club and the National Cyclists Union, financed and promoted it. Its aim was to improve the quality of road repair, administration and maintenance. It lobbied road surveyors, highway authorities and county councillors. It published pamphlets and circulated them to both professional road repairers and the public. By 1890 the RIA had inspected and reported upon more than thirty roads but by 1893 was virtually moribund and in financial difficulty. It was revived in the late 1890s when the motorists took up its cause. William Worby Beaumont, one of the editors of *Engineer* and a great advocate of motoring, became vice chairman of the RIA and in 1901 the Hon. Arthur Stanley MP, the Hon. John Scott Montagu MP, and Earl Russell joined the RIA council. They were all keen motorists and served on the committee of the Automobile Club. The RIA carried out experiments and trials with different sorts of road surface, and in 1907 offered prizes for suitable tar preparations and tar-spreading machines. It took on a major role as a parliamentary lobby in favour of road expenditure, and in 1908 organised the first international road congress in Paris.

One of the driving forces behind the RIA was William Rees Jeffreys (q.v.) who was a long term advocate of better roads and the cause of automobilism and the RIA's secretary from 1897 to 1910 and later its chairman. Partially because of RIA lobbying, in 1903 a departmental committee of the Local Government Board was established to look into the road problem. It recommended a national classification of roads into three categories, national, county and district, with administration by the Local Government Board and grants available for their maintenance and improvement. Nothing came of it immediately, but by 1905 RIA and other pressure groups had been so effective that a Royal Commission was appointed which advocated the establishment of a road fund to deal with the issues of motoring danger, dust and road cost. An outcome of this was the establishment of the Road Board (q.v.)

and the Road Fund in Lloyd George's 1909 budget.

By 1918 William Joynson-Hicks (q.v.) a persistent promoter of the motor car, was vice president. Until then the RIA had been open to individual private motorists, but in 1919 it went on a membership drive and allowed commercial users to join.

In 1927, when Churchill made his famous raid on the Road Fund, transferring £12 million from it to general purposes, the RIA tried to raise opposition to the move but with no success. It continued to advocate the cause of better roads. In 1929 the Transport & General Workers Union became a corporate member with Ernest Bevin as their representative. In 1932 when the British Road Federation was founded it usurped the RIA's role and the RIA declined in political importance. Rees Jeffreys, who became chairman in 1918 after he left the Road Board, had a combative and autocratic approach which fomented disputes and dislikes and contributed to some organisations resigning. **JA**

Plowden (1973); T R Nicholson, *The Birth of the British Motor Car*, 3: *The last battle 1894–97* (Macmillan, 1982); Earle (1974), pp. 10–11; Seth-Smith (1975); Hamer (1987), pp. 23–36

Roadships Ltd, see HILTON TRANSPORT SERVICES LTD

Robey & Co. Ltd of Lincoln built tractors from 1865 and later made a type much used by showmen. They also made steam lorries with the front axle as far back as possible to provide a smaller turning circle. They were overtypes, many with tipping bodies. They also made steam rollers and steam road tractors, at least one of which was operated by the lighterage firm, Clarkes of Erith in 1924. A light prototype 3-ton lorry with pneumatic tyres, developed in the late 1920s, seems not to have gone into production. Between 1870 and 1891 Robey also built some fifty Thomson 'road steamers' to special order. **RWK**

Robson's Distribution Services of Carlisle was established by Stanley Robson at Hethersgill in 1925, with a home-converted pick-up based on a Ford Model T car. For a few years hard work on local authority roadstone contracts built the fleet to four, but a reduction in public expenditure ended this work and only the original vehicle was retained. Robson then moved into Carlisle and with a brother built a Reo-based lorry, which was used for hauling plaster, with cattle feed as a return load; intensive family involvement contributed to the build-up of the business. Robson's (Hauliers) Ltd was founded in 1936, with a helpful accountant, N T O'Reilly, as co-director, and it was decided to introduce new and heavier vehicles to the fleet. Foden were contacted with this end in view and by 1940 the fleet had seven vehicles, four of them Fodens. These were assigned to the Ministry of War Transport and a secondhand eight-wheeled Foden was acquired. During and after the war, expansion occurred by purchasing vehicles for the sake of their A licences, as well as for the vehicles themselves, a useful acquisition for continuity in the event of nationalisation being the seven-strong churn-carrier fleet of F Laidlaw's milk collection business. Robson increased its productivity by sending a cattle float to the dairy to collect empty churns, getting return loads of cattle feed on the empty churn-carriers. The ex-Laidlaw operation became Border Hauliers (Gilsland) Ltd, the main business became Robson's Hauliers (Carlisle) and two other businesses were founded, each with two vehicles, to reduce corporate tax liability. In February 1947 the Robson fleet doubled in size by the purchase of Thistle Transport, with a wider range of operations. Then in mid-1949 the non-milk transport element of Robson's group, amounting to 52 vehicles, was nationalised. The founder contracted, but survived, tuberculosis, acquired a farming estate and continued with milk haulage and C licence work, using a single vehicle on several contracts, until denationalisation (q.v.) offered new opportunities. Robson secured the services of the BRS Carlisle traffic superintendent, George Flenley, who had formerly been with Hauliers Ltd (q.v.) as manager of Robson's Border Transport Ltd, founded February 1953 with five ex-BRS Jensens and a Bedford.

A variety of secondhand vehicles entered the Robson fleets, including six Scammell Rigid Eights (q.v.) originally with Young's Express; new vehicles were initially Ford Thames and Traders, but as the business grew through the 1950s and early 1960s, exceeding 100 vehicles in 1958, the acquisition of new Fodens reflected the founder's preference. To cater for this growth a new HQ with warehousing and ample parking space had been opened in 1956 on a Carlisle trading estate. The single depot concept was supplemented by a chain of agents and return loads were additionally facilitated by the contacts Flenley brought from his previous posts. Trunking and day shunting into London and some points in the south and east were facilitated by the employment of a number of drivers, eventually 15, at Biggleswade, Bedfordshire. Trunk drivers from Carlisle and Biggleswade normally interchanged at Knutsford, Cheshire and Micklefield, West Yorkshire, with Biggleswade shunters serving London and parts of the south and east. These complicated arrangements depended on the intensive use of the telephone and the dedication of Robson's staff.

The 1970s were a time of great change for Robson's, culminating in new ownership and including the introduction of foreign chassis. Milk traffic, which had been a steady activity for decades, was changing from churn to tanker collection: Robson's decided against investment in tankers, continuing churn collection with existing platform lorries whilst demand lasted. Robson himself passed normal retirement age and had been shaken by the national drivers' strike of 1976–7, when the company had been refused the union dispensation offered to firms undertaking to pay the agreed rate when it had been decided on. Both the National Freight Consortium (q.v.) and the Transport Development Group (q.v.) had expressed interest in Robson's 180 vehicle fleet, but he preferred to negotiate with the group distribution manager of United Glass, Herbert Nettleship. His objectives were to reduce the excessive number of UG warehouses and bring down costs by operating their own vehicles. To deal with the problem of obtaining return loads and avoid empty running, Nettleship decided on the acquisition of an established haulier. Despite the recession, the sale of Robson's to United Glass took place on 3 November 1980. Under new ownership, the fleet operated as United Distribution Services until December 1984, when it was renamed as Robson's Distribution Services (a trading division of UG) to reflect its origins. However, subsequent developments outside road haulage resulted in further changes of ownership: UG had been jointly owned by the Distillers Co. and Owens of Illinois since 1966. When Distillers were taken over by Guinness in 1986 agreement was reached between the various parties to sell UG in its constituent parts and Robson's Distribution Ltd was bought by the Bunzl Group in January 1988, becoming part of United Carriers (q.v.), but remaining only a short time within the Bunzl group, as a result of its reassessment of its businesses. **RAS**

Tuck (1990)

Roe, Charles H, Ltd, coachbuilders of Leeds, established in 1917, are generally associated with the production of bus and coach bodies. However, in the firm's early years a variety of commercial vehicle bodies was manufactured, including pantechnicons, vans and mobile shops. In addition, Roe produced heavy duty trailers suitable for use in conjunction with Leeds-manufactured steam road engines, such as Mann and McLaren. For these manufacturers Roe also produced cabs and bodywork, including for the McLaren heavy haulage road tractor supplied to Pickfords in 1940. Wartime production for the services and civil authorities included 12 articulated kitchen vans for the Ministry of Works Flying Squad, 48 articulated sleeper trailers and 68 printing press bodies for the services on Foden 6-wheel chassis. Roe was taken over by Park Royal Vehicles in 1947 and thereafter concentrated almost exclusively on passenger bodies. **RAS**

G Lumb, *Charles H Roe* (Shepperton: Ian Allan, 1999)

Roll cages are a late-1980s addition to the range of equipment designed to reduce manual handling and are widely used by supermarkets. They consist of a skeleton base with a folding mesh floor panel running on small wheels, two fixed, two as castors. On to this fit four mesh panels about 2 ft wide and 6 ft tall when transported empty. They enable orders to be picked from bulk stock in a warehouse, the roll cage can then be wheeled to the loading bank, into the trailer, from the trailer to the store bank or onto a tail lift, then right to the display on the shop floor. With the roll cage came the special dry freight trailer to carry it, although they can equally be loaded into a refrigerated trailer. These have a completely smooth inside ideal for food stuff transport. There is a 'rubbing strip' along the bottom to protect the panels while at waist height is a end-to-end strip with holes to accept spring loaded cross poles or special ratchet straps. Thus a full width row of three cages can be secured safely at any point allowing for progressive unloading.

Roller shutters (Figure 160) provide a useful space-saving alternative to hinged doors for vehicle loading and unloading, especially in confined spaces such as narrow streets. The Post Office was a major user. One of the best-known types was the Brady patented shutter, produced by G Brady & Co. Ltd of Ancoats, Manchester, makers of shutters since the 1880s. They claimed in their advertising to have originated the use of shutters in vehicle bodywork in the 1920s. Remarkably they offered an airborne repair service in 1949 provided by their own aircraft and pilots, to serve any part of the country. In use, regular maintenance was essential for the easy operation of the shutter. Until the 1960s shutters consisted of narrow slats of timber or aluminium on which paintwork was easily damaged by heavy use. New systems with wider slats then became available and were soon widely used. Lettering in particular was easier to apply and did not damage. Later insulated slats also became available for refrigerated bodywork. **RAS**

Brady advertising 1949

Roof-racks (Figures 146 and 161) were a feature of box vans used, especially up to the Second World War, for the delivery of such goods as biscuits and potato crisps. Taking the form of one or two thin metal rails supported by uprights and sometimes with metal mesh infilling, they provided extra space for the return of empty tin containers. Early contract mail vans and Harrods delivery vans were also equipped with roof racks, the latter in some cases bearing boards showing the areas covered.   **RAS**

Grieves (1999)

Rotinoff Motors Ltd (Figure 50) was founded at Colnbrook in 1952 by the Russian-born engineer George Alexander Rotinoff, to produce a heavy haulage tractive unit which he had designed. He had originally used Diamond T vehicles on post-war heavy haulage contracts. Competition from the Thornycroft Mighty Antar and Rotinoff's premature death in 1959 meant that total production of Atlantics and Super Atlantics was 35, of which only one went to a UK haulier. This was used by Sunter Brothers of Northallerton for a demanding contract moving 238-ton boilers on the last stage of their journey to Bradwell power station. In 1962 Atkinson acquired the design rights for the Rotinoff.   **RAS**

B Tuck, 'King George', *Truck* (February 2000), pp. 62–4; F Tinsdale, 'The Rotinoff story', *VRS,* 17, 68 (2001), pp. 153–6

The **Rowe Hillmaster** (Figure 163) was a bus and truck chassis built in Doublebois, Cornwall, between 1953 and 1962 by a Cornish coach operator. It offered two and three-axle chassis and an artic, with a choice of four different makes of engine. Most of its relatively small production was bought by Cornish operators. The maker exhibited opposite the Earls Court, London, Commercial Motor Show: it was not a member of the SMMT (q.v.) so could not have a stand inside, but instead rented a piece of ground opposite the exhibition hall, on which it showed part of its range.   **JMA**

The **Royal Automobile Club** was founded in 1897 as the Automobile Club by F R Simms (q.v.) and played an important part in the early development of commercial vehicles. It was associated with the Commercial Motor Users' Association (q.v.), having founded its predecessor, the Motor Van, Wagon and Omnibus Users Association (q.v.), in 1904. The

RAC organised Industrial Vehicle Trials in 1907, taking one month and visiting major towns. A wide variety of petrol and steam vehicles took part, with varying degrees of success. The results proved the supremacy of the internal combustion engine over steam power, though steam vehicles won class awards, the Burrell for example gaining a gold medal.

Later RAC activities concentrated mainly on cars and motor cycles, plus small vans, but its own van fleet grew considerably from the late 1950s when patrols gave up their motor cycle combination in favour of four-wheeled vehicles, initially mainly BMC Mini Vans. From 2000 the RAC fleet was provided and managed by Lex Vehicle Leasing. By 2000 the RAC was offering a Commercial Vehicle Assistance scheme for vehicles over 3.5 tonnes or 5.5 metres in length, and also a mechanical breakdown insurance scheme on commercial vehicles between one and 44 tonnes for up to four years from purchase.   **JMA**

P Brendon, *The Motoring Century* (1997)

Royal Mail plc, see POST OFFICE

The **Royal Society for the Prevention of Accidents** evolved in 1924 out of the National Safety First Association which in turn grew out of the London Safety First Association which was formed in 1916. Its aim was to reduce the high number of deaths and injuries caused by accidents of all kinds, including motor accidents. The NSFA made awards to safe drivers and some firms encouraged their drivers to enter, for example newspaper deliverymen working for the *Star* and *Daily News* from 1923. It has been seen as an example of independent experts coming together to solve a technical problem but O'Connell has argued that it was a puppet of the motoring interests. It was funded initially by Gordon Stewart of Stewart and Arden (q.v.), Morris agents in London, and had many prominent motoring men as its officers. It eschewed legislation, preferring educational campaigns which often stressed the responsibility of pedestrians and cyclists in road accidents. It opposed the introduction of a driving test in 1934. O'Connell considers it maintained a laissez-faire approach to motorists and represented the class interests of those who could afford motor cars. It took little interest in commercial vehicles.

It played a large part in reducing accidents at work, but rather less in road safety. Indeed in the late 1940s and early 1950s the Pedestrians' Association complained of its 'motorist bias' while the cyclists resigned from it.   **JA**

Sean O'Connell, *The Car in British Society: class, gender and motoring, 1896-1939* (Manchester University Press, 1998), pp. 123-36; Plowden (1973), pp. 342-4; *CM* (7 May 1928), pp. 426-7; *Railway Gazette* (14 March 1919), pp. 499-500

Rubery Owen. The heavy components industry's contribution to the development of the transport of goods by road has been highly significant and within that industry the role of Rubery Owen & Co. Ltd of Darlaston, Staffordshire has been outstanding. Alfred Ernest Owen, who joined John Tunner Rubery in 1893 as partner, was a pioneer in grasping the significance of the first automobile and the dawning of a great new industry. By 1898, Rubery Owen was already supplying a superior car chassis frame to the Daimler company, instead of their own design, which was cracking up. The concept of the chassis frame soon became relevant to the early commercial vehicles. In those early days frames were unduly heavy and cumbrous affairs, consisting of rolled steel channel and tubular members, though some makers successfully used steel-flitched timber frames well into the 1920s. The inventive mind of A E Owen conceived the pressed steel channel with tubular members and soon almost the whole motor industry became dependent on Darlaston's Motor Frame Department.

A 1500-ton 'upstroking' press was bought in the 1920s as the length and weight of chassis frames increased and by 1938 a side-loading mechanical 2000 ton British Clearing press had been installed. Smaller presses made cross-members, both hot- and cold-pressed, which enabled the chassis to be welded or riveted together. Some manufacturers assembled their own chassis, whilst others were despatched already assembled.

After the Second World War the length of side-members increased still further with the growing carrying capacity of trucks, so chassis had to be made in thicker and higher tensile steel. To enable this to be achieved, a 3000 ton British Clearing press was installed and in the 1960s a side- and end-loading 4000 ton, 42 feet long Weingarten press was installed. This was the ultimate development of cold-pressed side-members and was soon working three shifts to cope with the heavy demand for trucks, both for the home and export markets in the late 1960s.

The other interesting development in Motor Frame department in the 1930s was the Scott patent rear axle-casing for light commercial vehicles. In this process a piece of seamless tube with a slit in the middle was expanded through a hot press, so that the housing enclosing the gearing was entirely weldless. Immediately after the Second World War a new department called No. 11 perfected in principle the welded heavy axle-case. This consisted of a pressing made in two halves then welded together, with hubs flash-welded then friction-welded together, both concepts pioneered by Rubery Owen research engineers. A G B (later Sir Alfred) Owen, who had taken over from his father when the latter died in 1930, had the foresight to negotiate a deal with the Eaton Corporation of the USA to make and market the Eaton two-speed axle. This enabled trucks to run with existing gear-boxes much more economically on long distance trips and at much higher speeds.

From the 1970s road transport became dominated by the tractor and semi-trailer combination. Rubery Owen developed the frames for the early versions of these long trailers and perfected the so-called semi-trailer non-drive (dead) axle. This was done in Dept 11 by flash-welding and then friction-welding hub ends into seamless or welded tube. These were then assembled at the Warrington factory alongside the Eaton axles. Demand became so great that a separate factory was built at Llay, Wrexham, and a joint company formed, Rubery Owen Rockwell (ROR) which dominated trailer axle products in the UK until the end of the 1990s. A whole concept of 'running gear' was developed, comprising axles, brakes, suspensions, spring brakes, which were developed as an homogenous package for both tandem and triaxle configurations. Well over 50 per cent of production was exported.

A human element runs through Rubery Owen's achievements. Because the tradition of the Black Country in the nineteenth century was one of steel making and manipulating metal, the area was the natural place to develop this aspect of the commercial vehicle industry. Even with these native skills, design engineering capacities and productivity improvements were essential if the industry were to remain competitive. After the First World War A E Owen determined to attract the best employees. He was a founder-member of the Industrial Welfare Society and built a works canteen with adjacent sports facilities, including a bowling green. Such was the relationship between management and workforce, that in the slump of the early 1930s when A G B Owen, who had left his studies at Cambridge to take over the running of the company, had to go down to the shop floor and negotiate a 25 per cent reduction in wages, the workforce responded magnificently.

After the Second World War a very good apprenticeship scheme became the backbone of the development of the various departments. Some of the apprentices became department managers and many went into the toolroom, drawing offices and production control departments to develop more efficient ways of managing production.

The purchasing departments of the commercial vehicle manufacturers were very good at playing off suppliers against each other, so salesmen needed to be fully trained engineers. It was no good just sending a salesman to sell a chassis frame – he had to understand the quantities involved, what variants there would be to a particular model, whether new chassis frames could use any of the tooling already in existence, which might save costs, and whether some of the difficult cross-members had to be hot- rather than cold pressed. Each component had a proper cost price attuned to volume, which was essential to the profitability of a department. The other important facility needed was a research and development department, which could test the various capabilities of newer steels in order to lighten vehicles. Newer steels could crack if there was

too much variance in the carbon content. When a power-press of up to 4,000 tons hits a long piece of steel and then bends it into a side-member, the stresses are great. A manufacturer needed confidence that his component supplier had this technical knowledge and the ability to deliver on time to meet the schedule imposed by a new model. This customer confidence was particularly important for ROR as it developed its overseas business. It was deemed best to have companies in the larger European states which were effectively run by the nationals of the state concerned. Unlike the Americans, ROR sold a package of running gear to its customers and therefore had to be absolutely sure that what it was selling was suitable for that particular application. Thus in Australia or Sweden, for example, axles had to stand considerable 'overload' in the Outback or the northern forests.

From an organisation with 14 companies and associate companies in 1950, ROH grew to 66 UK and 18 overseas companies in 1969. This was its peak in terms of employment and manufacturing output. The decline of the UK vehicle industry in the 1970s and the recession of the early 1980s and particularly the demise of British Leyland, where 70 per cent of Rubery Owen Darlaston's supplies went, led to the closure of its main manufacturing plant at Darlaston. Rubery Owen Holdings Ltd continued to operate from Darlaston. Its Motor Panels subsidiary at Coventry went from strength to strength in the 1980s and 1990s and eventually became part of the Mayflower Group. Rubery Owen Rockwell (ROR) became a major supplier of trailer axles, supplying over 70 per cent of the UK trailer market and exporting over 50 per cent of its production, mainly to Europe. Rockwell International (later Meritor) bought ROR in the mid-1990s and still operates from its Wrexham factory.

The firm's own transport arrangements were based on a works fleet for deliveries mainly in the West Midlands, whilst it used haulage contractors for its long distance work. The works fleet consisted of around 50 vans and medium-sized trucks, mainly supplied from BMC, who were its largest customer. The familiar orange livery and RO logo could be seen on many roads, particularly in the Black Country and the wider West Midlands.   **ADO**

Based on personal knowledge. Rubery Owen records are deposited in the Modern Records Centre of the University of Warwick Library: MSS.338: *Sources Booklet No. 9* (1997)

Rudd, E W, Ltd, haulier of east London, was active in meat transport from the 1890s and in heavy haulage, by virtue of its base close to the shipping-related engineering industry of east London. It was taken over by Thomas Tilling Ltd in the mid-1930s. Rudd was a committed steam wagon and traction engine operator, with Coulthards, a Foden and Garretts. In the 1904 dock strike Rudd is reported to have used a steam wagon to head a picket-breaking convoy.

Rudd became agent during the First World War for the American Knox-Martin tractor, an articulated 6-wheel lorry, which influenced Alfred Scammell's designs, for Rudd was a founding director of Scammell Lorries. At the end of 1922 Rudd was recorded as operating thirty Knoxes, as well as six Scammells, twelve Foden and six Garrett steamers, and smaller Commer and Dennis vehicles. Between the wars Scammells provided the mainstay of Rudd's heavy haulage fleet, yet traction engines were still used by Rudd on heavy haulage in the 1930s, being hired-in from other firms where necessary. McTaggart describes a spectacular accident at Cobham in 1936, involving two Fowlers and a Burrell moving a transformer; an uncoordinated move resulted in the ditching of the two Fowlers, one of which was Rudd's. In addition to heavy haulage and meat transport, Rudd operated vehicles on contract in customers' liveries. Rudd's wartime traffic included concrete barges for the invasion of Europe and their wharf handled Sherman tanks and many other incoming heavy loads. The firm was nationalised in 1948.   **RAS**

McTaggart (1989); Georgano (1997), pp. 8–9, 13; Anon, *The War that Went on Wheels* (Tilling, 1945; Bradford: Autobus review, 1978)

Russell, Major-General George N 'Charles' (1899–1971) after schooling at Rugby was commissioned in the Royal Engineers in 1918 and attended the Royal Military Academy at Woolwich. He served in India, Iraq and Canada. In the Second World War he specialised in transport, being Director of Movements, Middle East; Deputy Quarter-master General, Movement & Transportation, India; and Transport Adviser to the Special Commissioner in South East Asia. In 1948 he was appointed chairman of the Road Transport Executive, at a salary of £5000 p.a., soon to become the Road Haulage Executive. This involved him in creating a single organisation from ovr 3000 separate businesses incorporating over 40,000 vehicles and 80,000 staff. He served as chairman until 1959, having to reverse his activities after 1953. He was a member of the Eastern Area Board of the British Transport Commission from 1957 to 1962 acting as chairman in 1961–2. He had little time for the 'integrated transport' approach, seeing the long-distance hauls as the most remunerative and so established a network competing with the railways rather than complementing them. He was instrumental in 'adjusting' uneconomic rates, which rose sharply from 1948 to 1951, but despite this BRS's return on capital employed was poor, around 2½ per cent.

In 1960 Russell chaired a committee to consider traffic strategy on both rail and road, including co-ordination between modes, pricing policy and traffic analysis. After the British Transport Commission was split up in 1962 he served on the British Railways Board for a couple of years.

Russell was energetic, agile, extrovert and outspoken, sometimes irascible and short tempered. He was keen to go on field trips and spent much time on inspections. His nickname in the army because of his vigour was 'Cyclone Charlie'. He married twice and had five children.   **JA**

Bonavia (1987), pp. 53–4, 70, 80, 161–2, 177–8; *WWW*, 7; T R Gourvish, *British Railways: a business history* (Cambridge, 1986); David J Jeremy and Geoffrey Tweedale, *Dictionary of Twentieth-Century British Business Leaders* (Bowker Saur, 1994)

The **Rutland lorry,** also marketed as the Manton (after its creator) and the MTN, was devised by Frank Manton, who set up a commercial vehicle repair business in Croydon in 1946, after he had left the Royal Navy the previous year. He saw the market for a simple, rugged chassis, especially for exports and established strong links with Spain through agents in Madrid. Approximately sixty chassis were built in the first five years of operation, most being exported. In 1952 Motor Traction Ltd was founded with new works at New Addington, Surrey, and Frank Manton as managing director. Much of the capital came from his father's business, Manton Motors Ltd, Commer dealers, also in Croydon. To avoid commercial confusion Manton vehicles were badged as MTN or Rutland (where the family originated). About 75 per cent of production still went to the Iberian peninsula, including the twin-steer Stuka for Spanish fish traffic. The basic product was a 13 ft 6 in wheelbase 4-wheel lorry for 12 tons gross vehicle weight, but there was a great variety, to meet customers' needs. UK customers included the CWS, which ordered six 6-ton lorries for North Wales, and G L Baker (Transport) Ltd of London E15. Crane-carrier and passenger chassis were also built. Production ceased in 1956, as the scale of output was too small to make them competitive and there were no real distinctive features.   **RAS**

'The Rutland story', *Move*, 10 and 11

Ryder Truck Rental began operating in the USA in 1939, and showed its determination to succeed in Britain when it bought Fisher Renwick's contract businesses in 1973, Ryder having some contracts, but limited maintenance facilities. Fisher Renwick had opened new depots at Dukinfield, Manchester, and Park Royal, London, with the latest facilities. Their contracts included Crosby Doors, Kraft Foods, Procter & Gamble and Johnson Wax. In 1974 Ryder claimed to be the largest contract hire fleet in the world with 43,000 vehicles. Some remain Ryder's customers today. The business extended into offering distribution contracts, typical of these was its 1993 contract with Nissan providing just-in-time deliveries, using the 'linehaul' system developed for North American contracts. Ryder's German truck rental division, already supplying Mercedes-Benz tank transporters to the British Army of the Rhine, served with the British peace-keeping troops in Bosnia. A contract with Milk Marque proved to be unprofitable, despite acquiring a successful long-established haulier, because of the complexity of the hours regulations for milk collection, and the variations in milk production. Others had a similar problem with their contracts. The appointment of former vice-admiral of the United States Navy Ed Straw in 1998 to be in charge of its Integrated Transport division indicated that Ryder sought contracts giving a 'global supply chain management' for multinational businesses. It was therefore a surprise when they announced their truck rental, contract hire and domestic logistics operations were for sale. No acceptable offers for the businesses were apparently received. Ryder then announced it was to retain its British interests and would expand when suitable opportunities occurred. Ryder have some 14,000 vehicles in service, many in customers' livery, with a discreet Ryder logo.   **GM**

CM (13 September 1974), advertisement

343

S

Sabrina, see NICKNAMES

Sainsbury, J, was established in Drury Lane in 1869 as grocers and provision merchants. From the start it needed transport for home deliveries, and by the 1880s was using horse vans for such work. By 1890 it had five single-horse vans and three two-horse vans. It also employed delivery lads on bicycles or tricycles with baskets on the front until the First World War. In 1915 it bought its first motor delivery van, a Ford Model T and by 1928 had 37 Ford and 80 Morris delivery vans. Home deliveries (q.v.) were an important aspect of gaining middle class customers and up to four were made each day. The delivery lads could graduate from their bicycles to a motor van. The Second World War saw home delivery much curtailed and Sainsbury's move into self-service from 1950, initially at its Croydon store, removed the need for home delivery. The widespread use of cars compounded this.

The other area in which Sainsbury needed transport was the heavier and longer distance side of restocking branches from depots. As Sainsbury's branch network grew and it opened branches outside London the horse-drawn van became increasingly inadequate and in 1907 it bought two Foden steam wagons to deliver to south coast branches. These had drawbacks, needing a crew of two men who were too dirty to help unload the foodstuffs. This did not aid Sainsbury's image of hygiene and cleanliness. So in 1911 it tried 1½- to 2-ton Milnes-Daimler lorries. They were petrol-engined, so cleaner to operate and seven were purchased. Considerable ingenuity was displayed in getting goods to stores. Just before the Second World War the Norwich branch had an arrangement with Caleys, the local chocolate maker. As Caley's lorries had considerable loads down to London but no back cargo, they hauled Sainsbury's goods back to Norwich. Both parties benefited.

In 1919 Sainsbury bought six Leyland lorries from the RAF to carry goods to more distant branches. They were more efficient than horse vans, in part because they put in longer — sixty six hour — working weeks. The 1933 Act governing lorry speeds and drivers' hours led Sainsbury to have built a lightweight body on a Bedford chassis weighing under 50 cwt which could run at 30mph.

After the Second World War, as a result of the increase in branch numbers, Sainsbury initiated a number of out-of-London warehouses and moved into frozen and chilled storage and distribution. Most was done by its own fleet, but overnight fresh fruit and vegetable distribution to reach the stores by 7.30 am was delegated to W J Sims Ltd. In the late 1950s, before the changes, over 300 lorries were loaded overnight at Blackfriars depot for deliveries to branches. To cope with perishables, in 1962 they started purchasing 12-ton Bedford TK refrigerated lorries. The lorry fleet was maintained in-house until the 1980s when Sainsbury began using outside contractors to warehouse and distribute. Its own fleet fell from 425 vehicles in 1981 to 386 in 1990, but rose again later when small vans were acquired for home deliveries. **JA**

Bridget Williams, *The Best Butter in the World: a history of Sainsbury's* (Ebury Press, 1994)

The **Salter Report** was published in August 1932. It was the result of the committee chaired by Sir Arthur Salter, which had been established in spring 1932 by the Minister of Transport, P J Pybus, in Ramsay MacDonald's government. Its remit was to examine the regulations needed for goods traffic by road and by rail, and to look at highway costs and how various groups should contribute to these. The background to the committee was pressure from railway trade unions and chambers of commerce which felt that the railways were suffering from competitive disadvantage and road vehicles were not bearing the cost of maintaining the highways. The composition of the committee was half railway representatives, and half road freight representatives. Inevitably, the road members represented the larger firms, such as J Lyons (q.v.) own account operators, and H Viney (q.v.) of Preston. Although no official record of the deliberations was kept, the report was unanimous.

It recommended that taxation on goods vehicles be revised. The existing system placed no more burden on a 10-ton lorry than on a 5-ton, as this had been the largest normally used when the system was devised. It also advised a full system of licensing for goods vehicles and considered heavy goods traffic should not be further directed from rail to the road. The recommendations on tax were particularly harsh for heavy steam wagons. The annual tax recommended by Salter for a 5-ton steam wagon would rise two and a half times and for a 10-ton three and half times. Although the actual rates introduced in the 1933 budget were not as high, heavy steam wagons faced a doubling of licence duty for 5-tonners and a threefold increase for 10 tonners. Despite these steep rises, heavy steam wagons paid the same or less tax than equivalent-sized petrol or diesel-engined lorries. Yet both Kennett and Seth-Smith attribute the death of the steam wagon to the Salter report and the ensuing rise in duty. They also suggest that the oil companies may have influenced the committee to be anti-steam, in order to boost the consumption of petrol and diesel. The fact that there were no oil company representatives on the Salter Committee is ignored. The Salter Committee did not discriminate against steam wagons but removed most of their special privileges and brought their taxation level more into line with those of diesel- and petrol-engined lorries.

The Salter Committee also endorsed the suggestions of the Royal Commission on Transport of 1930 that a comprehensive system of goods vehicle licensing was needed. The road representatives on the Committee deplored the cut-throat competition and particularly the small scale operators who cut corners. Its recommendations were largely implemented in the 1933 Road and Rail Traffic Act.   **JA**

Bagwell (1988), pp. 253–7; Kennett (1978), pp. 122–4; Seth-Smith (1975), pp. 110–1; Barker and Savage (1974), pp. 202–3

Satchwells' Road Transport of Balsall Common near Coventry began as a country carrier with a horse and cart in the 1920s,

offering collection and delivery within a twenty-mile radius. Four generations of the family developed the business for more than half a century, with a long loyalty to the Bedford marque, the fleet growing to twelve box-bodied vehicles of 3-ton to 8-ton capacity by the 1960s, including A, O, S and TK types. By this time the daily delivery radius had extended to almost 100 miles: six vehicles serviced the Birmingham area; four others operated to Northampton, Rugby/Banbury/ Oxford, and Corby/ Peterborough. In addition one long-serving driver operated to Wellingborough/ Kettering/ Rushden, on most days, with a return load from the Weetabix breakfast-cereal mill at Isham. One vehicle was normally kept in reserve for emergencies and the fleet was serviced by a single fitter. New vehicles were supplied by C/E Motors; the Bedford S was acquired secondhand, formerly operating with Heinz. Fleet livery was dark blue with white lettering. Both Collins' Parcel Services and United Carriers put in unsuccessful bids for Satchwells, which was acquired in the mid-1970s by locally-based Capels Transport, which itself went out of existence at the end of the century.   **GMcB**

Personal experience as a delivery driver for Satchwells in the1960s

Saurer, see ARMSTRONG-SAURER

Sawn timber transport (Figure 164). Movement of sawn timber by road has been subject to considerable change. Until the early 1960s it involved a great deal of manhandling. Even when it was lifted on to the lorry by a crane in a 'set', the set had been hand stacked by sawmill workers or dockers. Once the set was on the lorry the driver would then 'turn it down' to make a solid level load. Until the late 1960s the measure of timber carried was the Baltic Standard of 165 cu. ft. Moisture content and species make a big difference to the weight of a standard. A full load on the eight-wheeler was 5½ standard of soft wood but as little as 4 standard of hardwood.

From 1904 to 1969 large amounts of timber came from the Baltic and Canada into the Surrey Commercial Docks in London. The move down river had already begun in 1966, Macmillan, Bloedel and Meyer Ltd, Canada's largest forest products company, opened a dedicated berth in Tilbury to handle timber, plywood, prepared timber and linerboard. The timber was packed for mechanical handling at every stage, two packs went side by side on a trailer and each pack consisted of pieces all one size i.e 50×25 mm, 150×25 mm (still in 2002 called in the trade 2×1 and 6×1, the imperial measure) cut to a specific length with both ends square (length packs) again marked on the pack in metres and converted to Imperial by the trade, thus it was possible to work out a full load on a trailer in advance. The Scandinavian countries followed suit although some mills still produced packs of a standard width and height but made of various lengths so that only one end was solid and square, called 'truck packs' or 'randoms.'

Length packs produced a dense load, requiring no more than 6 ft high on the trailer to load the vehicles to full gross vehicle weight. However, a load of truck packs requires 10 packs which involves a much greater fully loaded height which requires a lot of skill on the part of the driver in the placing of the 'bolsters' when loading and the handling of the vehicle on the road, particularly on sharp bends and in observing overhead obstructions and bridges. Despite lorry length rising from 24 ft to 40 ft such a load only amounts to 6½ standards.

The rigid eight was popular for timber, even after the big move to articulation, probably because of its stability with high loads. AEC Mammoth Major and Leyland Octopus were fitted with a bolster so that extra load could be carried projecting over the cab. Artics only came into widespread use with the growth of 'pack' timber. Some docks would not load more than two packs high so artics could be used. With the widespread use of Tautliners timber was often loaded into them. This is useful with kiln-dried timber as it does not need sheeting.

Much sawn timber was carried by merchants' own transport. As a low priced commodity it was equally a low rate traffic often done as a back load and never overly popular with drivers or hauliers. In addition to imported timber, there was some home-produced but this was only of marginal importance, despite the efforts of the Forestry Commission, established in 1919, which supplied large amounts of pulpwood.

Scammell, G, & Nephew Ltd began as handcart then horse-drawn vehicle builders in Spitalfields around the middle of the nineteenth century, later taking on steam and motor vehicle repair and becoming an agent for Commer and a leading London Foden agent by the First World War. George Scammell, the founder, was joined by his nephew, Richard, and his great nephews Alfred and James. During the war they prepared a large number of requisitioned Foden steam wagons for the Army Service Corps, as well as producing gun carriages; Alfred, who rose to the rank of lieutenant colonel and was awarded the DSO, returned with valuable experience of military transport. In the immediate post-war period the firm now run by Alfred and James, converted ex-WD vehicles. In 1919–20 Percy G Hugh, the chief designer, conceived an articulated lorry for which 50 orders were taken at the 1920 Commercial Motor Show. By the mid-1920s their Fashion Street premises could handle 60 to 70 vehicles at a time. After Scammell Lorries Ltd became a separate concern in 1922 and moved to Watford for the production of its 'six-wheel carrier-lorry', Scammell & Nephew continued with refurbishing and bodybuilding, acquiring the Steel Barrel Co. of Uxbridge, which produced many of Scammell's frameless tankers (q.v.). Bodybuilding continued after the Second World War until Scammell & Nephew were taken over by York Trailer (q.v.) in 1965. **RAS**

Georgano (1997); J E Fardell, 'A history of Scammell Motors', *Journal of the Watford & District Industrial History Society*, 12 (1982), pp. 8–22

Scammell Lorries Ltd (Figures 29, 72, 111, 116, 134, 137, 148 and 165–6) was formed to take over from G Scammell & Nephew Ltd of Spitalfields the design of, and their works at Watford manufacturing, the Scammell six-wheel lorry from 30 April 1922. Lt Colonel Alfred Scammell, who had been managing director of G Scammell & Nephew, was managing director of the new business. Percy G Hugh, formerly technical director, held the patents for the new six-wheel lorry, which was designed by Oliver North (q.v.). Also a director was E W Rudd (q.v.). The Scammell was inspired by the American Knox, which Lt Col A Scammell had witnessed in use by the French as a tank transporter. A major feature of both was the turntable, mounted on springs bearing directly onto the chain-driven rear axle of the tractor. Scammell were able to improve on this design, and also the carrier. Scammell preferred carrier rather than trailer braking, operated by a handbrake through a rod and bell crank arrangement. E W Rudd was operating some 30 Knox tractors at this time, being their agent, and advised on the Scammell's design. Rudd had a large fleet of Scammell lorries, notably for meat traffic and for heavy haulage. The Scammell engine, at first 47.5 hp, had the same dimensions as the Knox. It was later developed to 70 hp. The first lorries carried 7½ tons, meeting the legal requirements for a lorry that no axle should carry more than six tons. By 1924, a change in regulations allowed the introduction of the S10 10-ton and the S12 12-ton models, finishing with the S15 15-ton range, with the carriers having the 'four-in-line' axles. The engine now developed 85 hp. The introduction of the frameless tanker (q.v.) carrier in 1924 allowed less stress, with reduced weight and, for a time, was a major proportion of their sales. The Autovan, for 2½ ton loads, designed in 1925, with a three-cylinder radial engine and front-wheel drive was a failure. It over-heated and had carburation problems. The first rigid chassis, the Pioneer 6×4, designed for overseas cross-country duties, was also developed into a tank transporter and tractor versions. It had O D North's patent beam bogie rear axle. Many of these were built for overseas, one-off special uses. Rudd were the first to operate one as a heavy haulage tractor. The first rigid lorries were introduced in 1929, basically longer-wheel-based versions of the tractor unit. Although having a shaft drive, chain drive remained an option. The majority were supplied on pneumatic tyres. This was overshadowed by the production of the 100-ton lorry, which was built to E C Marston's requirements for his company, MRS, particularly to transport locomotives to docks. A second unit, based in

Cornwall, pulled a Garrett ore-crusher and was acquired by Pickfords in 1934. Both remained in service until 1953, when legislation prevented their further use. The first Rigid 6 chassis was introduced in 1933. This retained chain drive, but was on giant pneumatic tyres. It was superseded in 1934 by the lightweight LA articulated units and Rigid 6 chassis. These had Gardner 6LW engines, North's new 6-speed, constant-mesh gearbox with a shaft drive to the new epicyclic rear axle. The Rigid 6 had rubber suspension, with giant single tyres all round. The 45-ton articulated heavy haulage unit continued, with chain drive and on solids. The forward-control Rigid Eight 8x2 was introduced in 1937 with optional rear rubber or steel suspension. Pioneers built from 1939 for military use had Gardner 6LW diesel engines. After the Second World War a number were supplied as 80-ton heavy-haulage tractors. The Pioneer was replaced by the Explorer. This had front-wheel-drive and retained a constant mesh gear, modified for front-wheel-drive, retaining the bogie rear axle. The Meadows 6DC650 diesel engine, converted to petrol by Scammell for military orders, replaced the Gardner unit. Rolls-Royce or Meadows engines were also specified. Among the drawbar tractors produced were 18 Showtracs, specially built for fair showmen from 1945 and having a dynamo and winch. Others had earlier been supplied for this purpose. Scammell also produced their mechanical horse (q.v.) from 1933, having acquired the design from Napier (q.v.) in 1932. The prototype was modified by North and was used by the railway companies and many ancillary and transport operators. It had a separate sales department, using dealers. It saved Scammell from failure in the difficult trading conditions of the 1930s, outselling all its other products by about five to one. Some 14,000 mechanical horses were sold, before being replaced by the Scarab in 1948, which became the Townsman in 1964. More demanding braking regulations came into force in 1968 which would have meant fitting front wheel brakes, so Scammell discontinued the model. It was used by many municipalities with a variety of functions. Diesel and battery versions became available, as did a rigid version, named the Trivan. A four-wheeled version, the Scarab Four, first seen in 1962 became available in 1964, and was withdrawn the same year. It was based on a Standard Atlas chassis, was under-powered and an ill-considered adaptation. In addition demand was declining. The Bedford-Scammell combination became available in 1939. Intended for 8-ton payloads for trunk duties, it remained in production for the services and essential users during the Second World War. After the war almost all makers offered tractors with Scammell couplings. For a period it was the preferred articulation system for British Road Services (q.v.) and BRS Parcels. Bonneted LA15 and 20 and the 45/60-ton units were built in limited numbers for essential users during the war. Scammell was acquired by Leyland in 1955, becoming the Special Vehicles Division. The Rigid Eight was replaced by the Routeman in 1958. The major difference was the Leyland chassis and engine and a fibreglass cab. This was superseded in 1962 by the Routeman II with the Michelotti cab and Kirkstall rear axles. The Routeman III had an Albion double-drive rear axle, becoming the basis for the Leyland-badged Constructor in 1980. The LA articulated units were replaced by the updated Highwayman in 1955 with an optional Leyland engine which continued to 1970. A forward-control version, the Handyman, was later introduced, incorporating Leyland components. Unfortunately it proved to be less reliable than its predecessors. It was replaced by the Handyman II with Michelotti cab in 1965. The Trunker II 32-ton gross vehicle weight tractor from 1966, with a twin-steering axle in front of the rear axle was used particularly for bulk liquids. The Crusader, originally designed as a 6×4 tractor unit for 40 tons, modified as a 4×2 32-tons gross vehicle weight, became BRS's trunk tractor unit in the 1970s. Scammell is remembered for its post-war export lorries and heavy haulage tractors. These were the Mountaineer, for maximum 45-ton gross vehicle weight, available in 4×2 and 4×4 long-wheelbase versions. The 6×6 Constructors and Super Constructors were the first to have the SCG gearbox and the 6×4 junior Constructor and the 6×4 Contractor from 1966 in 125 or 240

ton gtw versions were made with either a Fuller or SCG box with a two-speed splitter box. Pickfords experienced problems in service with early versions of the SCG transmission. Scammell's trailer division was acquired by York (q.v.) in 1977. Scammell assembled the S24 and S26 heavy-haulage units and the Commander tank transporters until the works was closed in 1988, following DAF's acquisition of Leyland in 1987. Scammell's business, but not the marque name or the factory, was purchased by Unipower (q.v.). **GM**

Georgano (1997); Billings (1982); Kennett, *World Trucks 8*

The **Scammell 100-ton Transporter** was probably the largest load-carrying vehicle constructed in the UK to that date. It was built in 1929, following a request to Scammell by Ernest Marston for a vehicle built as one unit, reputedly able to carry 250 tons. What he received was a Transporter, designed by O D North, able to carry 100 tons without assistance which was delivered to MRS as KD 9168 in 1929. It had a rivetted box-plate frame, using Scammell's four-cylinder petrol engine now 80 hp, a four-speed gearbox, with reduction gears to give a high range when empty and a low range when carrying a load, providing a total of eight speeds and using four duplex chains driving the four-in-line wheels, on two oscillating axles. The carrier had a swan neck, connecting two girder beams to the rear bogie. This could be either eight-wheeled for 100-ton loads, with the rear set of wheels equipped to steer, or a four-wheel version, using the rear set of wheels only and also able to steer, limited to 65 ton capacity. It was to carry a wide variety of loads in service, the heaviest probably a 165 ton ingot mould. The only major modification made was the lengthening of the front of the chassis frame for the installation of a Gardner 6 LW diesel engine in 1932 by the Pelican Engineering Co. Ltd. The fuel consumption improved from two miles per gallon of petrol at worst to 4 miles per gallon of diesel. It was reported Scammell undertook that no other abnormal low-loading trailer would be supplied to a competitor for two years. The second Transporter tractor unit was delivered to H E Whey Ltd, of Dartford, Kent. It spent its first four years with a 65-ton ore treatment mill, built by Richard Garrett of Leiston and operated by the Metallic Ore Production Co. Ltd of St Austell, Cornwall. In 1934 it was acquired by Pickford's, and registered as BLH 21. This was then similarly fitted with a Gardner 6LW engine. Its 100-ton trailer was built to the Scammell design by Crane Ltd of Dereham. Both were to remain in service until approximately 1953, when new regulations restricting axle loading and use of solid tyres forced their withdrawal. Both are preserved. **GM**

Georgano (1997); Ingram (1993); Crane (1991)

Scania trucks (Figures 46 and 64) trace their origin to the founding of the Swedish railway rolling stock manufacturer, Vabis, in 1891. The Scania company was founded in 1900 and bought the English Humber Company's Swedish subsidiary, beginning to build cars and lorries in the following year. It merged with Vabis in 1911. Restructuring followed the post-First World War recession, car production ended in 1924 and in 1940 the decision was made to concentrate on heavy lorry and bus manufacture. From 1950, Scania developed its export potential, establishing overseas manufacturing plants in Argentina and Brazil, and in the Netherlands to get a foothold within the EEC. The UK offered a market within the European Free Trade Association, as yet little penetrated by other European heavy vehicle manufacturers. It was also a market which needed larger vehicles if it were to participate in the growing long-distance haulage in Europe, utilising ro-ro ferries and the TIR customs convention (q.v.) and sharing in the growth of containerisation (q.v.). Thus Scania Vabis Great Britain Ltd was set up in 1964. The start of truck sales in the UK was related to the ending of tariffs between EFTA members in 1967. 150 of the LB76 type sold in the first year of Scania's UK operation, rising to 1500 per annum by 1979/80. In 1968 the Swedish Wallenburg empire merged Scania-Vabis with another of its enterprises, Saab. The new company was named Saab-Scania and brought cars back into the fold. The recession of

the 1980s obliged Scania to buy a number of its UK distributors and major fleet operators took up 75 per cent of Scania's UK sales. In 1999, following the sale of its car side to Ford, Volvo began to buy into Scania, but its take-over was vetoed by the European Union in 2000 on monopoly grounds and Volkswagen acquired a large minority stake in Scania in 2000. **RAS**

Building a Legend, Truck special Scania centenary supplement (1991); E Gibbins, *Scania* (Motor Racing Publications, 1980, 'Trucks Today' series)

The **Scottish Commercial Motormen's Union** (SCMU) had originally been formed in 1898 as the Scottish Carters' Association, which became the Scottish Horse and Motormen's Union in 1908, when it had 3,300 members, and the SCMU in 1964. Unlike a number of other Scottish road haulage unions, it refused to join the TGWU (q.v.) in 1922 and retained its separate identity. During the General Strike (q.v.) of 1926, it avoided calling out its members by the ruse of the liberal issue of emergency transport permits. By the late 1930s its organisation was extremely debilitated, but the creation of a separate Scottish Area Wages Board under the Road Haulage Wages Act 1938 preserved its role, although the union remained weak and beset by internal problems. In 1969 Alex Kitson became general secretary and initiated a process of institutional reform and a successful campaign to establish effective union organisation in road haulage. In 1972 the SCMU joined the TGWU's RTC group. In 1974 a major unofficial strike by Scottish drivers signified the now national dimension of road haulage trade unionism. **PS**

Tuckett (1967)

Scottish Co-operative Wholesale Society, see CO-OPERATIVE MOVEMENT

Scottorn Ltd of Victor Works, New Malden, Surrey, were noted for rebuilding ex-military vehicles such as AEC Matadors and Diamond T 6x6 trucks in the late 1940s, also for bodybuilding and single-axle trailer production. In 1956 a Scottorn subsidiary, Victor (Swedish Vehicles) Ltd, was formed to test the UK market for Volvo (q.v.) commercial vehicles and buses, however activity was limited and Victor's contract was terminated in 1958. Scottorn Trailers Ltd later joined the Boughton Group (q.v.). **RAS**

M Wells, 'Volvo in the UK', pt 1, *VCVM*

Securicor plc was founded in 1935 as Night Watch Services to provide cycle patrols of residential property in London. In abeyance during the war, it was revived in 1945 to provide security for commercial premises, its first contract being a Vauxhall Motors spares depot. In 1960 Keith Erskine, a solicitor, became managing director after he had persuaded his brother to acquire Securicor (the name was registered in 1953) as a subsidiary of Kensington Palace Hotel Ltd. Erskine, in many ways an idiosyncratic leader, took Securicor into cash-in-transit, initially with six Morris J series vans. Until 1968 Securicor faced the problem of obtaining 'A' licences, giving rise to a network of regional offices; despite the licensing problem and the competition from the Armoured Car Co., Security Express and the Swedish Securitas, Securicor operated 200 armoured vans by the mid-1960s. In 1965 it opened the first purpose-built security centre in Europe at West Drayton and began Data Transit Service with a few Ford cars (succeeded by a fleet of Ford vans) in response to the developing demands of computer activity. From this grew overnight parcels delivery (to become Securicor Omega Express), as well as other transport operations and Securicor's delivery services were boosted by the major postal strike in 1971. To ensure the supply of Ford vehicles, gain higher discounts on purchases, and develop in-house servicing and bodybuilding, Chiswick Garages Ltd, R J Bown Ltd and Bedwas Bodyworks Ltd were acquired. The latter introduced a sliding-door parcel van on the Transit chassis in 1986. These businesses were sold off in Securicor's restructuring in the 1990s. Keith Erskine's premature death in a road accident in 1974 was followed by reorganisation under his successor as group chairman, Peter Smith. In 1977 parcels operations were restructured by Peter Towle, who had been appointed special services director in 1976, to provide a clearly defined range of services in the UK and Europe, involving larger terminals, more staff and more, and larger vehicles. In 1979 a new '2/50' service was inaugurated with articulated vehicles, offering two-day delivery for parcels up to 50 kg. In practice this duplicated the existing parcels distribution work and was reunited with it. The Pony Express motor cycle courier business was bought in 1981 from Air Call. Developed by Securicor as a country-wide franchise, it became Omega Same Day in 1997. Cash processing and distribution by Securicor Cash Services grew to 1500 vehicles and 57 processing centres in the UK by 1997. The Datatrak vehicle location and monitoring system, developed to protect its cash-in-transit vehicles, eventually attracted 14,000 outside customers. A service of compact secure vehicles, Business-Link (originally Cash Guard), was introduced to serve smaller businesses. Significant developments occurred in the 1990s on the parcels side to strengthen Securicor as a logistics operator. Securicor Omega Express was founded in 1990; the UK domestic customer base of Federal Express was acquired in 1992 and Scottish Express International in 1993, with international air and sea freight and new customers, such as IBM. In 1995 Russell Davies Distribution of Ipswich, Britain's largest privately-owned transport group, was bought for £50 million, becoming Security Omega Logistics; Russell Davies Container Transport undertook major development at Felixstowe (q.v.) and elsewhere. A £30 million distribution centre was opened at Hatfield, Hertfordshire in 1997, by which date the Omega Express fleet amounted to 4,000 vehicles, as part of a group total of nearly 10,000. In the same year John Miller Transport was bought by Securicor. Deutsche Post acquired 50 per cent of Securicor Omega Express in 1998 as part of its global expansion programme. **RAS**

S Underwood, *Securicor: the people business* (Oxford: CPL Books, 1997); J Semple, 'Business as usual', *Truck* (August 2000), pp. 56–61

Security Express Ltd, cash and bullion movement specialist, was founded in 1960 by a partnership between De La Rue, the security printers, and the American security carrier, Wells Fargo, the latter giving up its holding after a few years. The firm, headed by the former police and security chief, Sir Percy Sillitoe, employed ex-policemen as drivers. By 1968 it had a fleet of 300 vans and by 1983 with its subsidiaries it operated from 60 depots, offering a 24-hour courier service as well as cash movement. Security Express was the target of a number of spectacular robberies, notably of £450,000 in 1971, the largest since the Great Train Robbery of 1963, £750,000 in 1978 and £7 million in 1983, when its London cash-in-transit depot was raided. Mayne Nickless, the Australian transport group, which had moved into security transport in the UK in 1972 with the acquisition of Armaguard of Nottingham, raised the possibility of buying Security Express in order to expand. Nothing came of this initial approach, but 'a friendly association' developed between Mayne Nickless and De La Rue, and Security Express was assisted by a Mayne Nickless executive when it experienced operating difficulties when it moved into fast-parcels. Security Express Courier Services was formed in the mid-1970s as a subsidiary to carry small high-value items for next day delivery. It soon became Courier Express, then about 1980 De La Rue Parceline and acquired J Brevitt of Willenhall in the early 1980s. The original ambition of Mayne Nickless was realised in July 1985, when it acquired Security Express with its two associated companies. It was taken over by La Poste, the French post office, in 2000. **RAS**

Times (5, 6 and 7 April 1983), p. 2; B Carroll, *Hurry back: an illustrated centenary history of Mayne Nickless* (Melbourne: the firm, 1986)

Security vehicles (Figure 167). The Bank of England and major banks have used special vehicles to transport large sums of money or bullion for many years. In the 1920s transport contractor McNamara (q.v.) was building special bodies for vehicles it operated, while Thomas Tilling (q.v.), another contractor, commissioned two new vehicles for Barclays Bank in 1934. Based on three-axle Dennis Ace chassis with Dennis-built metal bodies, they were designed to carry £1 million in 10s (50p)

and £1 notes (a huge sum of money in those days). They had an enclosed driver's cab with a large windowed compartment behind for bank staff. The final section was enclosed behind a double-folding wire mesh door, fastened by a cross-bar with padlock. Rear double doors were fastened and locked from inside. Vehicles and crew were and are mainly provided by specialist contractors. Bullet-proof panels and glazing as well as other security protection for crew and load are key features of these vehicles.

The increasing crime rate and widespread provision of automated cash machines has spurred development by contractors of small security vehicles to collect and deliver cash to or from banks, automatic teller machines, shops and businesses. Typically these vehicles are based on 3.5 tonnes gross vans and chassis. A few bodybuilders specialise in producing them. Their heavy weight, armour, bullet-proof glass and other provisions such as radio, tracking devices and time locks require careful chassis specification to keep within their gross vehicle weight. Until quite recently petrol engines were used as the lighter engine weight made up for the additional load imposed on the front axle by the very heavy bullet-proof windscreen. Today the use of Kevlar and other costly materials developed for aviation and space reduced armour weight yet offer superior resistance to bullets.

Security is tightly controlled in building the vehicles, and at the end of their working lives dismantling is undertaken by specialists under secure conditions, to prevent widespread knowledge of the security equipment. Most of these vehicles are operated by a few specialists in cash-handling, such as Securicor (q.v.), and Post Office Counters. **JMA**

Seddon Atkinson began with the partnership of Foster and Seddon in 1919 as charabanc operators, based on Salford, which expanded into vehicle dealerships. In 1929 Foster & Seddon Ltd was established. In the same year, to offset a costly insurance claim, the firm branched out into lorry reconditioning and in 1932 they further consolidated their position in the commercial vehicle field by taking on a Reo dealership. Robert Seddon was encouraged to develop long-nurtured plans for an oil-engined lorry capable of carrying six tons, but weighing in under 2½ tons to qualify for the 30 mph limit. The vehicle was said to be the first designed around the new Perkins P6 diesel engine and the six-ton lorry was in production by the end of 1938. Pilot Works of Bolton built the cab and axles were imported American Timken units. Output rose to 7 to 8 weekly until the war, by which time some 200 Seddons were in use. Wartime production was largely restricted to military trailers, but some three civilian lorries a week were also made. In 1947 an improved version of the original chassis, the Mark 5, appeared and Seddon's success led to purchase of a former aircraft carburettor factory at Shaw near Oldham and of a Ministry of Supply factory in the vicinity, which housed Seddon's bodyworks as Pennine Coachcraft. Seddon did well in the post-war European export market and also received fleet orders from firms such as Spillers Ltd and BRS (via an initial order from Fisher-Renwick). As well as heavier vehicles, such as a 24-ton tractive unit, a 25-cwt model featured in the range developed during the 1950s. Seddon Motors Ltd was founded as a public company in 1951. Foster & Seddon Ltd had by then been bought out by the Seddon brothers and Harry Redmond and traded as an independent distributor. In 1957 Halls (Finchley) Ltd, a Standard-Triumph as well as Seddon distributor, was purchased by Seddon.

Range rationalisation began in 1962. A decision was taken to drop the eight-wheel lorry, a standardised cab panelled in glass-fibre was introduced, and a new model designation system was initiated whereby, for example, '18-6DD-400' indicated an 18-ton 6-wheel lorry with double drive bogies and a Leyland 0.400 engine. When the new 13: four model (a 16-ton gross two-axle truck) came in 1964 it was built to a standard specification with fewer options. It enabled Seddon to switch to flow-line production and reduce prices dramatically. Bus manufacture became for a time an important part of Seddon's activity, with Pennine Coachcraft also building bus bodies on other chassis. The Seddon Pennine IV bus chassis was used as the basis for pantechnicons built by Boalloy (q.v.). Another aspect of Seddon's production was the

municipal vehicle, its growth accommodated by the cutback of coachbuilding. By the late 1960s a workforce of 1000 plus produced 2200 chassis per annum. Seddon-Deutz Ltd was set up in 1967 as an associated company with Klöckner-Humboldt-Deutz, manufacturers of Magirus-Deutz (q.v.) commercials. Mutual handling of products by some distributors, provided there was no clash of types, was envisaged with limited local sourcing. The context changed, however, and the Middleton works was bought by Magirus.

The founding Seddon brothers, Robert and Herbert, died in 1968 and 1971 respectively, but chairman Harry Redmond, whose connection with Seddon began as auditor in 1926, remained and in 1970 Seddon entered the contest for the control of Atkinson. There was no love lost between Atkinson and Seddon at any level and senior Atkinson personnel resigned at, or soon after, the take-over, with the exception of Stan Husband, who became manufacturing manager of Seddon Atkinson. Engineering integration proceeded more smoothly than personnel reconciliation. Seddon's hub-reduction axle was adapted for both marques and a new cab design could also be jointly applied and savings were made in bulk purchase of such units as engines and gearboxes. The numerous Atkinson subsidiaries were closed down, or more frequently sold off, over several years. Seddon Atkinson itself then became the object of an outside take-over, by International Harvester. They had tried to manufacture trucks in the UK in the 1960s, with limited success, and had been involved in talks with Seddon in 1971 and, informally, at an earlier date. The acquisition was made public on 1 July 1974. Under IH, Seddon Atkinson developed as a major heavy truck producer, even though there was strong shop floor suspicion of, and opposition to, the North American management culture introduced.

In 1975 a new joint model series, the 400, with a safety-engineered Motor Panels cab, was introduced, followed a year later by the lighter 200 series; the range was completed in 1978 with the 300 six-wheel lorry. By this time annual production was 5,000 chassis and the Redmond family connection came to an end when Geoffrey, one of Harry's sons, resigned as managing director. The 2–400 series were replaced by the 201, 301, and 401 in 1981/2, with a new style of grille, which included the popular circled A Atkinson logo. Then in 1984 IH ownership ended when restructuring of the parent company led to the sale of Seddon Atkinson to the Spanish ENASA concern. The next model series 2-11, 3-11, and 4-11 appeared in 1986/7; a special version of the 2-11 with Alexander crew cab was produced as the Britannia for the municipal market, bodied by Jack Allen of Birmingham. The new top-weight Strato with Cabtec (ENASA/DAF) cab was introduced in 1988, with a light-weight version of the cab for other models in 1990/1. In early 1991 Iveco (q.v.) acquired ENASA and Seddon Atkinson with it and Iveco Euro and Eurostar cabs were introduced. From 1997, in addition to the conventional Pacer refuse collection vehicle, the company built some 60 of the radical low-entry, centre-steer Leader which was introduced for municipal and urban delivery work. Seddon Atkinson later built its own version of a low-entry municipal vehicle cab for the UK and European use by Iveco. Seddon manufacture was transferred from Oldham to Madrid in 2002. **RAS**

Kennett (1978); Millar (1997); D L Collinson, *Managing the Shopfloor* (Berlin, 1992); R Coates, 'All of a Seddon', *VCV*, nos. 109–11 (January–March 1999), pp. 30-3, 16–20; Baldwin (1990); Atkinson Shareholders' Committee files, Modern Records Centre, University of Warwick Library, MSS.290; *CM* (28 March 2002), p. 7

Selden truck (Figure 168) manufacture began in 1913, two years after Henry Ford had successfully contested George B Selden's attempted hold over the US automotive industry by his 1905 patent. After the outbreak of war, representation of the Selden truck was established in the UK. The New York firm of Gaston Williams & Wigmore (GWW), which already had a showroom and depots for other US firms in the London area, received a contract to handle all Selden sales outside the USA from 1915. From 1916 Selden was involved in the development and manufacture of the 3- to 5-ton Liberty truck for the US Army.

After the war, GWW appointed a number of UK agents for Selden trucks, including Rootes of Maidstone, and well-known customers included Crosse & Blackwell, the food manufacturers. However, competition from ex-WD vehicles (including Seldens reconditioned by Robbins of Putney) cut back new Selden sales and the firm, which was taken over in 1929 by the Hahn Truck Co., ceased production in 1932. **RAS**

Old Motor & Vintage Commercial Magazine, November 1964; letters in *VCVM*, 59 (September 1994), p. 125 and 61 (November 1994), pp. 204–5

The **Self-Propelled Traffic Association** was formed at a public meeting held at the Cannon Street Hotel in London in December 1895 attended by between 300 and 400 people. Its objectives were to act as a lobbying group on parliament in favour of powered road traffic, to popularise all kinds of self-propelled vehicles, and to encourage their technical improvement. Its first president was Sir David Salomons, an electrical and mechanical engineer, mayor of Tunbridge Wells, and motoring pioneer and publicist. The council members included representatives from a range of related organisations such as the Society of Cyclists, the National Agricultural Union, the Cyclists Touring Club, a couple of MPs, and several industrialists. The secretary was Andrew Barr, who was also secretary to the Institute of British Carriage Manufacturers.

In February 1896 a delegation from the Association called upon Henry Chaplin, president of the Local Government Board, to urge removal of the restrictions placed upon motor traffic. The Association, through Salomons, played a large part in the drafting of the 1896 Locomotives on Highways Act which freed up 'light locomotives' of less than three tons unladen weight and increased the maximum speed limit to 12 mph for vehicles of less than 1½ tons. Vehicles of between 1½ and 2 tons were restricted to 8 mph and over 2 tons to 5 mph. Thus this act made life much easier for motor cars but changed almost nothing for commercial vehicles.

The SPTA came to be seen as no longer vigorous enough in its promotion of the motor car and rather out of the main stream. In 1898 it merged with the Automobile Club, which had been founded in July 1897 by Frederick Simms (q.v.) and Charles Harrington Moore, and hence lost its separate existence.   **JA**

See also the LIVERPOOL SELF-PROPELLED TRAFFIC ASSOCIATION.

T R Nicholson, *The Birth of the British Motor Car. Vol. 3. The Last Battle 1894–97* (Macmillan, 1982), passim; Plowden (1973), pp. 8, 10 and 14

Self-tracking axles, or positively steered axles, first became popular on the Continent, particularly in Italy, where they were widely used both on trailer and rigid multi-axles. In the UK they have generally been confined to specialist applications where optimum manoeuvrability is essential, or — more commonly — on heavy haulage trailers. Scania also made a self-tracking lifting mid-axle a popular option with its 6×2 tractors from the mid-1990s.   **JMA**

SELNEC Parcels. Many tramway and bus undertakings carried parcels, but a few created something much wider in scope: Manchester Corporation and Midland Red were notable examples. The Manchester operation became Selnec Parcels when the South East Lancashire North East Cheshire Passenger Transport Executive was formed in 1969 and compulsorily acquired the bus operations of several municipalities in its area including those of Manchester Corporation.

The Manchester Carriage & Tramways Company had offered a parcels delivery service well before the start of the twentieth century. When Manchester Corporation took over the network in 1897 and electrified it, the service was discontinued, but after pleas from traders restarted the operation in 1905, an event that immediately led to local general carrier Suttons issuing a writ, alleging the Corporation was exceeding its powers by acting as a general carrier. Judgment was given in favour of the Corporation, which nevertheless decided to scale down the operation and sold by auction its 90 'useful horses', 60 sets of harness, 39 vans and nine 'lurries' and also closed some of the larger depots.

Despite this the operation thrived. Parcels could be handed to 'guards' (conductors) on trams or into one of the 37 offices, depots or receiving points. Parcels were sorted at one of two distribution points, then moved by single-deck electric baggage cars to an appropriate depot, for final delivery by uniformed boys with hand-carts or by horse-drawn cart. For a time a cash-on-delivery service was offered, with payment for goods supplied by 'leading Manchester stores' being made on delivery. Prices for many years began at 4d for up to 14 lb in weight and same-day delivery was guaranteed for parcels handed in by 3.45 pm, though for delivery to the City of Salford and outer areas the time limit was 12.45 pm.

The parcels department bought its first motor van, a Ford T, in 1916 and in the early 1930s some 60 Ford vans replaced all the parcels tramcars. By this time size and weight limits were much more generous than those of the Post Office and even chairs or small trees would be carried. After the Second World War the fleet became more varied with mainly Bedfords and Commers, totalling 191 in 1950.

The headquarters and 40 of the vans of Selnec Parcels (as it had become) moved to the closed Parrs Wood bus garage in 1971, and was reformed as the Selnec Parcels Express Company with a fleet of 108. But it lost its biggest customer, Great Universal Stores, and profit or surplus of £19,182 in 1972 fell to £2,381 the following year. A 15-month accounting period to 31 March 1975 saw a loss of over £95,000 caused by inflation, recession and two of the slackest spells in a year included in the period. Diversification into van rental with a fleet of 46 hire vans still left annual losses of over £70,000, though a small surplus was earned in 1978–9. A new company was set up in 1981, Parcels Express, jointly owned by the PTE and United Carriers (q.v.). Less than a year later United Carriers bought the PTE's shareholding (by now it had become the Greater Manchester PTE) of 76 per cent for £75,000, and the Parrs Wood depot. United Carriers was able to transform the finances of Parcels Express by discontinuing a free laundry collection and delivery service and delivery of school meals, both undertaken for Manchester City Council at no charge. **JMA**

Ian Yearsley and Philip Groves, *The Manchester Tramways* (Glossop: Transport Publishing, 1988) pp. 179–80; Michael Eyre and Chris Heaps, *The Manchester Bus* (Glossop: TPC, 1989); Stewart J Brown, *Greater Manchester Buses* (Harrow Weald, Middx: Capital Transport Publishing, 1995)

Sentinel diesel lorries (Figure 169) were produced by the steam wagon manufacturer of Shrewsbury for a decade after the Second World War. In 1937 Sentinel had acquired H S G Gilford Ltd (q.v.), after owning Garner, and experimented with producer gas lorries. Sentinel's horizontal gas-powered engine was succeeded by the development of horizontal petrol engines. Following the war, Sentinel marketed its DV44 7/8-ton horizontal diesel-engined lorry in 1947, after a year's evaluation. Its underfloor engine made it unusual among truck designs but had considerable affinity with Sentinel's bus chassis of similar layout. Putting the engine below chassis frame height gave a flat surface for the body and lack of engine intrusion in the cab allowed seating for three. Production ceased in November 1956 after 1000 lorries had been built. The Sentinel Waggon Works was bought by Rolls-Royce for engine production and the manufacturing rights of Sentinel Road Vehicles Division passed to Transport Vehicles (Warrington) Ltd. As well as the DV44 (4-cylinder, 4-wheel), the Sentinel diesel range included the DV46 (4-cylinder, 6-wheel) and DV66 (6-cylinder, 6-wheel). Sentinel operators included breweries (which appreciated the three-man cab), BRS, British Railways, the British Oxygen Co. and the R E Mason Group. **RAS**

Matlock (1987); N Baldwin, 'The Sentinel diesels', *VCVM*, 14 (May/June 1988), pp. 218–19 and 222–3

Sentinel steam vehicles (Figures 51 and 52). Alley & McLellan, of Sentinel Works, Polmadie, Glasgow, entered the steam lorry field in 1905 with a simple undertype having no gears, but a three-way variable cut-off. The wheels were unusual, having wooden segments between core and rim. The front wheels were dished to enable the king pins to be at the steering centre. The Sentinel took up a large part

of the undertype market, but the popularity of overtypes, especially among brewers, forced the company to put an overtype on the market in 1911; it was a success but, having made its point, Sentinel stopped production in order to concentrate on its undertype. In 1923 the Super-Sentinel was launched, from 1925 fitted with two-speed gears. In 1915 the firm had moved to a large factory in Shrewsbury, and soon became involved with rail-shunters and passenger railcars. By 1928 the rigid-six DG6 model had been launched and become very popular; it was followed by the 15-ton DG8, 29 ft long and the most impressive steam vehicle ever built. The lighter S4 model came out in 1932, with rotating firegrate, automatic stoking, and shaft drive; the boiler was now behind the driver. It was a fast and silent runner, but could not buck the trend to diesel. In 1950 one of a batch of S4s for export was flaunted around the UK, but there was no revival. **RWK**

Hughes and Thomas (1973 and 1987)

The **Servis Recorder**, derived from Service Visible, was a forerunner of the tachograph (q.v.) with two essential differences. The Servis only gave an indication of when the vehicle was stationary or running, with no record of speed or distance. The card was fitted and the clock wound up by the management and locked so the driver could not interfere with the card. The Servis Recorder was in addition to any current legislation such as log sheets (q.v.) or logbooks. Not being a part of the government's legislation it was regarded as the first true 'spy in the cab'. They were first introduced in the UK in the early 1920s and there were other brands such as Autograph recorders. Initially the card only lasted for 24 hours, but by 1930 Servis introduced a 72-hour model which catered for long distance traffic. In 1935, when over 100,000 recorders were claimed to be in use, Servis advertising centred on the theme 'Lost vehicle time is lost money'; by 1949 it had become more conciliatory: 'A good driver is jealous of his reputation.... An unworried driver is a safe driver'.

The fitting of a Servis recorder on a vehicle was interpreted by the driver as a statement that he was not trusted. Every driver whether honest or not regarded it as his duty to stop the recorder. This had to be achieved without causing any external damage to its case. The main method was by ensuring from time to time that the back of the cab received a few heavy knocks while loading. Other drivers covered the recorder with a wet cloth.

Drivers loading out of ICI at Billingham were reputed to have a much more sophisticated method at their disposal. Many hauliers carried large quantities of dry ice carbon dioxide at very low temperature. It was soon found that packing dry ice in a hessian bag around the casing of the Servis reduced the temperature of the instrument so fast that the internal spring shattered. No physical damage was caused to the outside of the recorder but the internal damage was high. This sounds technically unlikely and may be an urban myth. Many employers gave up and removed the recorders, so that by the end of the 1950s few were still in use. One can be seen at Coventry's Museum of British Road Transport.

AMo

Shap. The notorious road over Shap Fell and through Shap village on the main A6 between Kendal and Penrith was probably the best-known of all roads to drivers and operators in the pre-motorway era. It was the only link between England and Scotland on the west side of the country. The road was narrow and steep, with several sharp bends and its exposed nature meant it was often blocked by snow or ice in winter. Snowdrifts sometimes completely covered stranded vehicles. In bad weather hundreds of lorries could be trapped, their drivers accommodated and fed in local homes in the village, the famous Jungle Cafe and on farms. When braking systems were poor accidents were frequent and breakdowns common, the latter mainly due to half-shaft failure. Shap was bypassed by the new M6 motorway in 1970 and today's improved road sees only local traffic and tourists. **JMA**

Gordon Baron and Ron Phillips, *The Shap Story* (Swaftham Prior: Gingerfold, 1998)

Shearman, John (1886–1966), was educated at Westminster School, then apprenticed at the Crewe locomotive works of the LNWR, during which time he also studied at University College, London. He subsequently worked in the LNWR's locomotive department before war service in the Royal Army Service Corps with the British Expeditionary Force. On his return to the LNWR in 1919, his wartime experience of road motor transport won him the job of road motor superintendent, which was then within the locomotive department, yet carried operational as well as technical responsibilities. In 1925, he was appointed the LMSR's road motor engineer, where he remained until his retirement in 1946. He reported at first to the goods manager, but from 1928/9 directly to the company's executive committee.

Now responsible for the country's largest fleet of goods motor vehicles, his particular interest was the development of better vehicles for short-distance collection and delivery work. He is best-known as the originator of the three-wheeled mechanical horse (q.v.) and the automatic coupling (q.v.). In 1938 he placed on record the story of their development in an important paper to the Institution of Automobile Engineers (q.v.) on 'Commercial motor vehicles for short mileage work'. The paper went on to suggest the outlines of a 2½-ton capacity, 4-wheel, short-wheelbase vehicle, with an under-chassis engine allowing a forward-control cab to be set ahead of the front axle. The benefits were a good turning circle, good sightlines for the driver (some 15 years before vehicle manufacturers began to give serious thought to this safety issue), an easy-access cab with a floor height of only 1 ft 0 in. and 82 per cent of the overall vehicle length available for loading. The cab-forward layout had already been seen in the CK and Bantam series of Karrier Motors, with whom Shearman seems to have worked closely over a long period, perhaps dating back to his wartime experience of Karrier lorries. The Second World War intervened and his 'ideal' delivery vehicle concept was not followed up, although the post-war Albion Claymore and Dennis Stork had a cab-forward layout.

Shearman was chairman of the Automobile Research Committee of the IAE, 1941–4, and the penultimate president of the Institution in 1944–5, and was much involved in planning the establishment of the Motor Industry Research Association (q.v.) and the amalgamation of the IAE with the Institution of Mechanical Engineers. His interests included the early history of mechanical road transport and his presidential address to the IAE was primarily an account of the development of steam carriages up to 1840. He was one of the joint authors of the road transport lecture, 'British mechanical road transport vehicles 1851–1951', at the prestigious Joint Engineering Conference organised in 1951 as part of the Festival of Britain.   **RAS/GAB**

Shearman's membership file, Institution of Mechanical Engineers. Shearman's published papers: IAE *Proceedings*, 33 (1938–9), pp. 88–176, and 39 (1944–5), pp. 1–48; ICE, IMechE and IEE, *Proceedings. Joint Engineering Conference* (1951), pp. 311–35

Sheet-racks. Sheet-racks were used from the late 1920s for housing tarpaulins on the cab top and sometimes they incorporated a headboard with the operator's name. They began to disappear in the 1960s when the tilt cab (q.v.) made them less viable and separate sheeting was replaced by curtainsiders (q.v.). They should not be confused with the cab-over platform (q.v.) used to increase carrying capacity for such loads as hay and straw.   **RAS**

Sheet van, see TILT LORRY

Sheeting and roping (Figures 49, 162 and 170). From the cart's day until very recently, two of the most important pieces of any driver's art were sheeting and roping.

Sheets started by being proper tarpaulins, that is heavy canvas coated with tar. Over the years they progressed through lighter weaves of canvas (flax and cotton) eventually to be made of man-made fibres. The waterproofing medium changed from tar and its derivatives, to various wax mixtures. The fly sheet, used on loads vulnerable to wet damage, was generally heavier than the normal sheets and in later years plastic-coated. It went over the top of the normal sheets and ropes and was secured with its own 'strings'. These were often half-inch (12 mm) diameter and very long, while the sheet was reinforced with webbing cross bands to allow it to be dollied down to stop it billowing. Ropes should never be put over it as this damaged the waterproofing, creating weak spots for the water to enter.

Rope, nearly always half inch (12 mm) in diameter, has seen many changes in material over the years. In latter years the use of hemp rope was confined to the large well-known hauliers due to the cost, Sutton & Sons of St Helens being one of the last. The-run-of-the mill haulier used the cheaper sisal rope (also known as grass rope), which was not as flexible or strong (and was hard on the hands in pre-gloves days). The 1970s saw the move to polypropylene or polyethylene, again as a matter of cost. The early plastic ropes were not as good as sisal as they broke down internally due to give and take causing chafing; also if they were pulled over a sharp corner, there was slight movement and the rope melted.

There was a unique rope, which originated in the textile areas. It was made of cotton rags cut into thin strips, which were then spun like any other fibre and laid or wound into rope. They were as good as hemp but the ends had to be spliced or whipped. If they broke or were cut without whipping, the end turned into a bundle of rags that had to be cut off, it could not be remade with fingers in the way that hemp and sisal could. The skilled driver could splice a broken rope or make an eye or back splice or whip an end. These skills were lost with the reduced use of rope and the fact that plastic ropes can be melted to seal the ends or adhesive tape can be used instead of whipping.

With the rope went the 'dolly' (so called because of its shape), known over the years as the Blackwall Hitch, the Glasgow Hitch or the Lorry Man's Knot, in effect the upper half of a sheepshank. This was used to provide a two-to-one multiplication of the driver's pull on the rope. On some soft loads such as baled goods to get a rope really tight, a dolly was used to pull a dolly thus giving a four-to-one advantage. Peculiar to the wool trade was a one-inch (25 mm) rope, fixed at each side of the front of the lorry usually on an over-cab rack (q.v.). This rope was run front to back over the already roped load and tightened with a capstan built in under the back rail of the body.

Corner boards were used to protect loads which could be cut into by the rope, such as cartoned goods. They were originally made of two strips of wood held together with webbing, evenly screwed to form a right angle. These were used on steel with chains. Then fibreboard impregnated with bitumen with a preformed fold became the norm. Just before ropes went out of use for carton goods, which are now carried in curtainsiders, there were some trials with moulded plastic.

With steel and timber, chains and sylvesters (which tightened the chain by a toggle lever action) or bottle screws also called turnbuckles (exploiting left- and right-hand threads in a tube) were in general use. In the late 1970s these were steadily being replaced with the ratchet strap, a nylon webbing strap with a hook or claw on one end, the other threaded through a small ratchet-locked capstan device, on a short length of strap.

The scotch was an essential driver's tool. It was a triangular piece of wood vital when carrying large reels of paper (q.v.) and tubes.

The **Shefflex Motor Co.** was a minor manufacturer, evolved from the Sheffield-Simplex car firm, backed by the coal magnate, Earl Fitzwilliam. During the First World War Sheffield-Simplex had produced ammunition, aero engines, and small Commer lorries under licence. Commer's post-war difficulties left Sheffield-Simplex with a batch of unsold lorries, 41 of which went to the Great Eastern Railway, and the Shefflex name was conceived to distance them both from Commer and, sufficiently, from Sheffield-Simplex. R A Johnstone, a local garage owner, war surplus dealer and haulier, was able to dispose of a batch bought at a very low price and in 1926 he acquired the marque and set up the Shefflex Motor Co. Production was approximately one vehicle a fortnight and sales gradually spread beyond the Sheffield area. A 4-ton 6-wheel lorry was developed, but the effects of the depression and competition reduced production to eighteen vehicles in 1931 and eight in the following year. Shefflex then made a crucial mistake by committing

themselves to the Petter 2-stroke diesel engine, which gave great problems to operators from vibration and over-heating. Shefflex lorry production thus petered out by the end of 1933, but the firm continued as manufacturers under licence of the Faun refuse-compaction system. Vehicles were produced on a variety of chassis, including a few more by Shefflex. To reflect its changed activity, the firm was renamed Shefflex Ltd in 1938; it continued after the war as a municipal vehicle, then general, bodybuilder.

RAS

Nick Baldwin, 'The Shefflex story', *VCVM*, 2 (1984), pp. 28–31; *idem.*, 'Sheffield Simplex', *OM*, 9, 4 and 5 (1975), pp. 295–303 and 358–71

Shelvoke & Drewry was set up in Letchworth by two former employees of Lacre in 1923. They had invented an ingenious transverse-engined, small-wheeled lorry, the Freighter, but Lacre was not interested in the concept. The SD Freighter, with 20-inch wheels and a 1 foot 11 inch loading height, was unique. The driver was seated ahead of the front axle and had two tiller controls, one for steering, the other for operating the vertically-mounted epicyclic gearbox. They were economical vehicles and some flatbed and van bodies were produced, although the chassis with its low loading height became particularly popular for fitting with bodies for refuse collection.

Some of the approximately 4000 Freighters built went to such undertakings as the London Co-operative Society, Shell, Express Dairies and United Dairies, Hovis, J Lyons & Co. Ltd (q.v.), Barclay, Perkins & Co. Ltd, which used a demountable flat body system for crate carriage, and Post Office Telephones, for cable drum transport. The SD Freighter was a design in advance of its time yet surprisingly successful. It had a transverse engine, tiller steering and gear control, and semi-automatic transmission. It was relatively easy for an ex-horseman to learn to drive it, its 20 mph/15 mpg and manoeuvrability were very helpful in urban traffic and its small diameter wheels provided an ergonomic advantage for loading.

In 1946 the conventional control W-type was introduced, it too became popular with municipal refuse departments. In the 1950s and

1960s SD manufactured a heavy-duty fork-lift truck, the Freightlifter, about 50 of which, with 8-ton capacity, were in service with British Railways by 1958. Others were used as kiln-loaders with the London Brick Co. SD continued to produce a heavy-duty internal combustion engine powered fork-lift truck. In 1971 the company became part of the Butterfield-Harvey Group, an engineering firm which also made tankers and diversified into off-road vehicles. In 1984 it merged with the American company, Dempster, and adopted the name Shelvoke-Dempster. In 1990 Shelvoke Dempster was bought by its senior management, but production ceased in 1992. Earlier, in 1991 Trinity Holdings had bought the design rights and stock of Shelvoke Ltd. During the period 1932 to 1939 the company manufactured the French Latil tractor (q.v.) under licence.   **GK**

Stevens-Stratten (1993); Baldwin and Negus (1980); Hinton J Sheryn, *An Illustrated History of Fork-Lift Trucks* (Shepperton: Ian Allan, 2000)

Shirley's Transport commenced operations in 1936 from its Stoke-on-Trent base, with a mixed fleet of three vehicles (a Bedford, Fordson and Dodge), mainly carrying livestock, later expanding into removals. By 1955 it had diversified into general haulage, using Bedford, BMC and Leyland vehicles, gaining a contract with Allied Breweries around 1960 and switching to mainly Albions. The founder's sons, Arthur and James, joined the business in 1961 and 1965 respectively. They operated their first bulk liquids trailer in 1966, with a contract to deliver animal fats. The 1990s trailer fleet comprised about half tanker trailers, much of the non-hazardous traffic was lubricants. The fleet was sixty strong mainly of Scanias and Volvos.
GM

The **Shore Porters' Society**, Aberdeen, has been in existence for over 500 years, with records referring to it in 1467. For centuries, until recently, its purpose was to move cargoes to and from shipping in Aberdeen harbour, the 'members' often carrying (portering) 2-cwt loads. The title Shore Porters' Society became used in 1836, and it remains a partnership today. Earlier titles referred to workmen. Until

about 1850 it was controlled by Aberdeen Council, notably in the rates it could charge. In February 1919 it bought its first motor lorry, a 6-ton Leyland on solid tyres. In December it bought a second. It ran as far as Glasgow, the journey taking about twelve hours one-way as the maximum speed was 12 mph. In July 1928 it bought its first lorry on pneumatic tyres, an Albion. A staple trade from the 1920s until 1939 was carting imported Canadian flour from the dockside Regent Sheds. The work recommenced after the war but faded away in the late 1960s. Until the 1930s the movement of goods included manually-pulled sledges and trollies, with no use of fork-lift trucks or elevators. Nor did the Society hasten to dispense with horses. In 1939 it had only four motors and the last horse was retired in 1957. In 1963 it absorbed another haulier, Frank Hay, with six lorries and by 1969 had thirty motor lorries. The major business now is removals, packing and storage, including much valuable antiques traffic. A branch depot, with 10 vans and warehousing for removals was opened at Richmond, London, in 1992. Of the 50 Mercedes-Benz and Scania vehicles operated, 10 are used for haulage contracts.   **GM**

Gordon (1970)

The **Short Distance Road Hauliers' Alliance,** previously known as the Hauliers' & Aggregate Merchants' Alliance, changed its name in September 1931 to signal that it would recruit any short distance haulier of any commodity. Its moving spirit was Frank F Fowler who specialised in tipping work in south-west London. In April 1932 this alliance merged with the Long Distance Road Haulage Association (q.v.) to form the Road Haulage Association (q.v.)   **JA**

P E Hart, 'The restriction of road haulage', *Scottish Journal of Political Economy,* VI (1959), pp. 119–28; Dunbar (1981), p. 79

Shrapnell-Smith, Edward Shrapnell (1875–1952) was born Edward Shrapnell Smith but in 1912 he compounded by deed poll his mother's maiden name, Shrapnell. He was a pioneer of commercial road motor transport and the leading spokesman for the industry until the early 1930s.

Educated at the Liverpool Royal Institution School and Liverpool University College, he began a career as a research chemist, but became interested in mechanical road transport. He was a founder member of the Liverpool Self-Propelled Traffic Association (q.v.) and served as its honorary secretary and organiser of the Lancashire heavy motor vehicle trials (q.v.) of 1898, 1899 and 1901. He was also a founder member in 1897 of the Automobile Club, later the Royal Automobile Club. Following the disputes which led to the formation of the Automobile Association (q.v.), he was elected to the reconstituted committee of the RAC and remained on it until his death. He was one of the founders and general manager and secretary of the pioneering Road Carrying Co. (q.v.) in 1902–3. In 1903 he helped to establish what became the Commercial Motor Users' Association (q.v.) and held office as honorary treasurer (1903–18), chairman (1918) and president (1920–9). As the first editor of *Commercial Motor* from 1905 to 1917, his influence on the formative period of the industry was considerable.

From 1912 to 1929 he was the first chairman of the Standing Joint Committee of Mechanical Road Transport Associations (q.v.). During the First World War he began to get involved in public work, as commandant of the Motor Transport Column of the City of London National Guard (1915–19), from which he retired as an honorary major, and as chief economy officer and deputy director (unpaid) of HM Petroleum Executive (1917–19), for which he was awarded the CBE in 1918. From this time he also served on various government committees and represented the government at International Road Congresses, culminating in his appointment as a member of the Appeal Tribunal (q.v.), set up under the Road & Rail Traffic Act 1933, which continued until the Tribunal's abolition in 1951. In 1929 and 1931 he stood unsuccessfully as Conservative Parliamentary candidate for East Woolwich, no doubt wishing to represent road transport interests at a time when it was a particularly contentious political issue. He held several directorships in goods transport, bus, motor insurance and industrial companies,

In 1945 he delivered the first Henry Spurrier Memorial Lecture, 'Five decades of commercial road transport with inferences about its future', in which he drew upon his personal involvement in the key events to write the first substantial history of the industry, still a useful reference for historians. **RAS/GAB**

CM, 75th anniversary issue, 15 March 1980; Plowden (1973); Seth-Smith (1975), p. 48; *The Times,* 10 and 28 April 1952; E S Shrapnell-Smith, 'Five decades of commercial road transport with inferences about its future'; *Journal of the Institute of Transport,* 23 (1946), pp. 214–324

Shunter is a railway-derived term, originally referring in road haulage to a, usually pensioned-off, tractor unit used for moving trailers in a depot. The market for purpose-built tractors, shunters or 'dock-spotters' grew from the 1970s with the development of containerisation (q.v.) and ro-ro services (q.v.), combined with the dominance of the semi-trailer. Purpose-built shunters are also to be found in the inland depots of major hauliers and at distribution centres; for example, Asda placed a Terberg shunter in service at its depot in Magna Park, Lutterworth, Leics. in late 1999. During 1998–9 foreign firms such as Kalmar, MAFI, Sisu and Terberg entered the UK shunter market; a new UK entrant in 1999 was Vallely Engineering of Leeds, which attracted a number of key Reliance-Mercury staff on the closure of the Reliance Halifax works in 1998, when production was transferred to Douglas (q.v.). There are rare examples of special, purpose-built vehicles, for example a Dennis/ Reliance-Mercury D-Mount Major, developed in 1996 for handling demountable bodies for Kelloggs.

The word 'shunter' has also been applied since the 1930s to a driver who serviced trunk lorries. The trunk run was often undertaken at night and during the day the shunters unloaded and reloaded the trunk vehicle and did deliveries and collections. Their duties often included roping, sheeting and fuelling the trunk vehicle. See also TRUNK OPERATIONS. **RAS**

CM (23 May 1996), p. 27; (31 October 1996), p. 17; (20 May 1999), p. 14; information kindly supplied by G McBirnie

Silver Roadways, see TATE & LYLE TRANSPORT LTD

Simms, Frederick Richard (1863–1944) was born in Hamburg. From 1885 to 1888 he was an apprentice with A G für Automatischen Verkauf at Hamburg and Berlin. He became their engineer and manager until 1894. He spent much time in London, where in 1890, with a partner, he started Simms & Co. From 1894 he was sole partner in Simms & Co. He was also a director of Daimler Motoren Gesellschaft from 1892 to 1902.

In 1893 he formed the Daimler Motor Syndicate Ltd to take commercial advantage for Great Britain of Daimler's internal combustion engine patents. In 1895 he sold these patents to the British Motor Syndicate. In 1896 he became consulting engineer to the newly-formed Daimler Motor Co. Ltd of Coventry.

Together with Robert Bosch he developed magneto ignition, establishing the Simms Manufacturing Co. in London with a French subsidiary to exploit it. Later a quoted company, titled Simms Motor Units, and manufacturing fuel injection, lighting and starting equipment, the business was acquired by Lucas in 1968. For a short period from 1904 to 1908 Simms was a manufacturer, on a small scale, of Simms-Welbeck cars and commercial vehicles.

Simms was founder and first vice-chairman of what is now the Royal Automobile Club (q.v.) and founder and first president of the Society of Motor Manufacturers and Traders (q.v.). Above all he was an innovator and a tireless advocate of motor transport. **GM/RAS**

St John C Nixon, *The Simms Story* (1955); Bryan Morgan, *Acceleration, The Simms Story from 1891 to 1964* (Newman Neame: 1965); Nockold, (1978), pp. 239–42; *DBB*, vol. 5 (1986); Lord Montagu and D Burgess-Wise, *Daimler Century* (1995); obituary in *Engineer* (26 April 1944)

Singer is more usually associated with cars than commercial vehicles, but vans were produced intermittently in the early years (1905–16) of Singer & Co. Ltd, Coventry. Between 1928 and 1932 they concentrated on mechanically sophisticated, larger commercials of 25- to 45-cwt capacity. Thereafter, light vans were

produced until 1940. A substantial order for Singer vans was received from the Royal Air Force in the mid-1930s. **RAS**

Stevens-Stratten (1988); Kevin Atkinson, *The Singer Story* (Godmanstone: Veloce Publishing, 1996)

Skeletal trailers or, usually, semi-trailers were used for the transport of containers from the 1960s. To save weight they consist of a central spine or two parallel side-members with at intervals outriggers or cross-members extending the full width of the trailer. Twistlocks at the ends of the outriggers or cross-members secure the containers. Modern skeletals are usually designed to accept 20 ft, 30 ft or 40 ft ISO containers or two 20 ft containers. The newest can also carry the growing number of American 45 ft containers now coming into the UK. The need to avoid overloading individual axles when carrying loaded containers led to the development of sliding skeletals, in which the two or three axles are on a separate moveable frame. This can be secured in a small number of fixed positions to ensure correct weight distribution on both skeletal and tractive unit. Initially carriage of containers was normally on flat platform trailers which were fitted with retractable twist-locks so that conventional loads could also be carried. Where container carriage was regular work, there was little point in using a more expensive and heavy platform skeletal and continental skeletals gained in popularity. Development of the skeletal trailer came in the 1960s and was linked to the growing use of containers in international shipping and the acceptance of the ISO criteria of standard lengths and heights. **JMA**

Sling-van was an early form for a covered container, see CONTAINERISATION

The **Slough dump**: The end of the First World War left the military authorities with a huge number of surplus vehicles, most of which were still overseas and included some 42,000 goods vehicles. Most were assembled back in the UK at locations such as Catford, Grove Park and Kempton Park racecourse. A Disposal Board was set up and auction sales begun in London, very high prices being realised initially.

Prompted by the need for Kempton Park to return to its peacetime use, a national repair depot was set-up on a greenfield (and subsequently extremely muddy) site at Cippenham Court Farm near Slough. Surplus vehicles were removed there. Many were in a poor or damaged state, and work began on reconditioning, using the parts from others, with more auctions taking place at the site. After a critical report by a select committee the Slough Trading Company was established to take over and run the depot, the company later becoming Slough Lorries and Components Ltd. Buildings were established on the site and proper repair systems set up. The vehicles handled included not only UK makes (except Leyland) but also many US-built vehicles that had come from the US during the war. Some 3,000 US-made Peerless lorries were ultimately refurbished, increasingly with the use of new components.

Leylands were not repaired, as the maker bought back all 6411 (3227 overseas) that were available, and overhauled and reconditioned to a high standard 2914 of them to protect its reputation. In addition some vehicle dealers and operators themselves recovered many ex-UK military vehicles from overseas, some being sourced from Belgian or French dealers, also for reconditioning. For example, the GWR bought and reconditioned some 130 AECs.

The availability of these vehicles, together with trained drivers and mechanics and gratuities paid to ex-servicemen helped create a growing road haulage industry in the UK. It also depressed the price of a new vehicle, for some years the re-conditioned ones being sold at less than half the price of a similar new vehicle. The Slough site subsequently developed into the huge Slough Trading Estate. **JMA**

B. H. Vanderveen; *Old Motor & Vintage Commercial*, Vol. 3, 2; Cassell (1992)

Smiths of Eccles Ltd began about 1910 when Roy Rouse acquired the business of a haulier George Smith (Eccles) Ltd. Expansion followed in the 1920s, with the first use of motor vehicles. William Rouse took over from his father in 1934, with services being extended to the Birmingham region. Among the work carried out whilst under the RHO (q.v.) was the removal of the first Nylon production plant built by Courtaulds Engineering at their Coventry works. Smiths became a voluntary acquisition by the BTC in 1949. Initially they did dock work and carried textiles and general haulage. Later they were still in dock traffic, carrying engineering goods from Manchester and general haulage.

Rouse re-entered the industry in 1954, successfully tendering for special A-licence units, to operate as Smith's of Eccles Ltd from a new base at Urmston. Depots were opened at Barking, London, Liverpool, Nottingham and West Bromwich. Smiths also regularly employed a number of sub-contractors. Contract vehicles were also operated including for a period the seasonal heating oil deliveries from Stanlow. Rouse sold out to TDG (q.v.) in 1967, remaining a manager until retiring in 1975. Smiths acquired H Evers Ltd Manchester, operating some 27 tipping lorries when taken over in 1972. Evers was founded about 1890, carrying textiles. Following Harry Evers being invalided out of the army in 1916, he took over control of the business and there was a change to tipping work. At the peak some 100 horses were operated, the last horses being sold in 1947. The earliest mechanical transport included steam wagons. Evers was acquired by Settle Speakman about 1970 but were sold to TDG, following a change of policy in 1972.

In 1975 Walter Denton, Hyde, heavy hauliers were taken over. They are believed to have started about 1866, and the first (secondhand) road locomotives were placed in service about 1904. The first diesel tractor was operated in 1938. Three Scammell 4.5-ton low loaders were placed in service about 1943. Walter Denton died in 1940, and his widow continued the business. Use of the last two road locomotives finished by the mid-1950s and six diesel tractors were being operated in 1975. **GM**

The **Society of Motor Manufacturers & Traders** was founded by F R Simms (q.v.) in 1902 to provide a voice for the infant motor industry and trade on matters of public policy. A major stimulus to action was the perceived need to regularise the show (q.v.) situation, to produce a single, regulated showcase for the industry, instead of competing displays. This was achieved by a show covenant entered into by SMMT members, replaced by a bond in 1907. Membership of the SMMT grew from 90 by mid-1903 to 1165 at the end of 1922. In 1923 it represented 70 commercial vehicle manufacturers; these included the makers of steam vehicles, who had a section of their own, as one of the Society's 13 sections, which also included those for petrol commercial vehicle, electric vehicle, pneumatic and solid rubber tyre manufacturers (reminders of the transitional stage which motor transport had reached in the years immediately after the First World War). The Steam Section undertook significant lobbying in the early 1930s in co-operation with the Commercial Motor Users' Association (q.v.) and the Mining Association to protect the position of the steam road vehicle. The SMMT made critical representations to the Minister of Transport on the Salter Report (q.v.) and the Society was one of the founders of the British Road Federation (q.v.); the question of road/rail competition continued to exercise the SMMT throughout the 1930s. Its normal work largely in abeyance during the Second World War, the Society produced in 1944 a major report for the Board of Trade on the capacity, employment and equipment of the motor industry and was involved in the planning of an orderly disposal of government vehicle stocks after the war, to protect the industry and the safety of the public. However, public opinion, activated by the sight of vehicle dumps, put pressure on government, resulting in auction sales of non-guaranteed vehicles. In the second half of the twentieth century the SMMT widened its activities considerably, with involvement of its staff and members on numerous aspects of vehicle design, operation and legislation. As well as special committees covering light commercials, heavy commercials and trailers, other subjects covered included bar-coded transport labels, brakes, crash-worthiness, fuel tanks, mirrors, noise, seatbelts, tyres, stability and weights and dimensions. The SMMT also continued its statistical and publishing activity, of which the *Motor Industry of Great Britain* is probably the best known. **RAS**

St J C Nixon, *The Story of the SMMT 1902–1952* (SMMT, 1952); Jonathan Wood, *The Motor Industry of Britain Centenary Book* (SMMT, 1996); SMMT publications in the Modern Records Centre, University of Warwick Library: MSS.226X/IND

Spans the South was the slogan from 1930 of London & Southern Counties Transport Co. Ltd, which was formed in 1922, when Roger W Sewill became managing director, operating two converted First World War Buick ambulances from premises in the yard of the Swan Hotel in Reigate, Surrey, before acquiring its own base near Reigate gasworks. Initially it collected milk in churns in Surrey, Sussex, and Kent for London dairies, a service much boosted by the General Strike (q.v.). It expanded services to the West Country carrying mainly agricultural products to London and parcels and smalls as a return load. The company established itself as a pioneer in 1927 of hanging carcase meat transport from abattoirs in Devon and Cornwall, destined for the London wholesale markets, utilising Leyland lorries. This was much helped by an embargo on imported veal and pork. It moved into transport of eggs, poultry and rabbits.

In due course, depots were opened at Penryn near Falmouth, Wilton near Salisbury, and Camberwell in south London, where return loads 'down west' consisted mainly of 'smalls traffic'. Early in 1932 Spans the South became overnight front page news, when it inaugurated the Flower Express service bringing fresh spring flowers (shipped from the Scilly Isles) from Penzance to Covent Garden, in record non-stop time, beating the journey-time by the GWR. This was achieved by a change of drivers twice during the 300-mile journey, firstly at Exeter, then at Wilton, and utilising three newly purchased petrol-engined AEC Mandator 7-ton vans, lightly loaded and despite local police forces repeatedly stopping the lorries for speeding.

The company also operated in 1933 a meat carcase service from Aberdeen and occasionally Inverness in the Scottish Highlands to Smithfield meat market in the City of London for a short while using Duramin bodies on Leyland Hippo chassis. Having initially standardised on heavy

Leyland Bull 6- to 7-ton insulated vans, the fleet now had an addition of 10-ton 6-wheel Hippo vans. The ageing Bulls were duly replaced by new Beaver 7 to 8-ton versions. Roger Sewill went on to become the director of Associated Road Operators (q.v.), leaving 'Spans' in 1935, which was eventually absorbed into H Pye Transport of Rotherhithe in the late 1930s to become Pye & Southern Counties Transport Co. See also FLOWER TRAFFIC   **CRS**

Allan (1946), pp. 162–5

Sparshatt, J H, & Sons Ltd of Portsmouth were coachbuilders with a clientele extending beyond the south of England and a national reputation for over half a century, as well as being Dennis, then Leyland, distributors. The business was founded in 1921 by Jack Sparshatt, an experienced body builder, who died in the mid-1940s. Its initial activity was the reconditioning and sale of ex-WD vehicles (an activity repeated after 1946, including a large order for Argentina). By 1969 the firm was producing three vehicles a day, under the direction of the founder's son, his three sons and a great-grandson. Particular specialisms were brewery drays, pantechnicons and temperature-controlled vehicles (from 1962); bus bodies were also built, primarily for the export market, until the firm offered personnel carriers on Leyland 420/550 FG and Terrier chassis from 1971. 1969 was a record year, with over 1000 bodies produced. In 1970 it was reported that Sparshatts had built more than 10,000 pantechnicons since their foundation and in 1971 they delivered their 250th pantechnicon to White & Co. of Botley. Other customers included Watneys Brewery (a 25-year relationship), Harrods Ltd (q.v.), J Lyons (q.v.) (for example, 50 bakery delivery vans in 1970, after orders for refrigerated vehicles), Bishop & Sons Depositories Ltd (q.v.), the NAAFI, and Fine Fare Ltd. By 1971, in addition to their main works at Portsmouth, Sparshatt had commercial vehicle sales and service depots at Aldershot, Ashford, Bexhill, Bexley, Croydon, Horsham, Lancing and Tonbridge. Their tanker division was Fergussons (Motor Engineers) Ltd, also of Portsmouth, which had been founded in 1932 as a vehicle repair company. After a long association, Sparshatts took an interest in the company c. 1958. Sparshatts were innovative body builders: their post-war ribbed aluminium panelled bodies derived from a form of construction devised by the founder in the Second World War for emergency water tanks, based on simple trays formed by folding the edges of flat sheet and fastening the edge folds together, with a sealing strip. They also patented a steel frame for vehicle bodies, made up of tubes joined by Sparshatt coupling blocks. In 1972 a range of swap bodies for smaller lorries was introduced, shortly before Wadham Stringer acquired Sparshatts. Early in 1976 integration replaced Wadham Stringer Sparshatt as the trading name by Wadham Stringer (Commercials) Ltd, producing Victory bodies.

RAS

Cornwell (1963), p. 58; cuttings-books and photographs, mainly late 1960s–1970s, notes made in a 1940 trade diary: BP Library of Motoring, National Motor Museum

SPD Ltd (Figure 172) was the distribution service of the washing products to foodstuffs producer Unilever. SPD was set up after the First World War by Lord Leverhulme and Major-General Sidney Selden Long (q.v.), who had had a distinguished career in military logistics, culminating as Director of Supplies & Transport at the War Office 1914–16. SPD took some time to evolve: it was not incorporated until 4 July 1918 and Leverhulme's concept of centralised transport for his separate companies was in practice restricted to delivery of the product and did not encompass raw material carriage. SPD's title, which stood for 'Speedy, Prompt Delivery', itself suggested the element of speed. Motor and horse vans were transferred from Lever Brothers and others, probably including ex-army vehicles, were acquired. Despite its title, the fleet (Maudslays and Thornycrofts) was heavy, slow and solid-tyred until the late 1920s. Throughout this period SPD's position within Lever Brothers (Unilever from September 1929) was by no means secure. A lengthy dispute with Planters' Margarine produced a clear declaration by Long that associated companies had to give all their traffic to SPD, if they wished to benefit from rebates, in line with the policy of other carriers. Yet associated companies were free to make their own arrangements and, its valuable service during the General Strike (q.v.) notwithstanding, SPD's fleet dropped from 208 to 180 between 1924 and 1928, which suggests that associated companies were making other transport choices, even though an increase in vehicle capacity may have offset the fall in numbers.

Between 1929 and 1935 SPD went through a prolonged crisis, with elements in Unilever hostile to its survival and there were prolonged negotiations for a railway takeover of Unilever's distribution operations. This did not materialise, but regional agreements were reached, which undermined SPD's comprehensiveness. In the event, the effects of the Road & Rail Traffic Act 1933 were crucial to SPD's survival, since the advantage of it being an established carrier, in a position to obtain A licences for the conveyance of Unilever group companies' products, was strikingly obvious. Lighter and faster Commers replaced heavier and slower vehicles in the SPD fleet and the sales value, although unquantifiable, of direct contact with Unilever's customers through SPD's drivers came to be recognised.

From 196 vehicles, 16 depots and 25 buffer depots, SPD's activities expanded on a large scale in the Second World War, particularly through its role in the distribution of margarines and cooking fat for the government producer Marcom and as a result of its operation of the Container Recovery Service, set up to save shipping space for packaging materials. CRS grew to operate 140 lorries on temporary contracts and continued until 1953. Its head, F Sadgrove, devised a cheap pantechnicon body, the Sadgrove Special, for use on CRS vehicles. The number of SPD-serviced depots, including CRS and buffer depots, grew to 284 by mid-1943; in 1945 distribution depots alone amounted to 105, with 372 vehicles.

SPD's post-war traffic developed in various directions: there was a marked increase in the transport of toilet preparations, with a much higher value-to-bulk ratio than washing powders with its depots and vehicles, which had earlier been a part of SPD. There were interesting or margarine. A much greater tonnage increase was a feature of the traffic in products of Batchelors, the canner and dehydrated soup manufacturer, acquired by Unilever in the Second World War. The other major business acquired at that time and developed after the war, Birds Eye Frozen Foods, made more specialised transport demands, in terms of cold store provision and refrigerated vehicles. These were provided by SPD, which began Birds Eye traffic in 1947; refrigerated lorries were run in Birds Eye livery, with a discreet SPD logo.

When nationalisation (q.v.) became an issue after the war, Unilever exchanged its A licences for C, making it clear beyond any doubt that it was a trader's fleet and therefore not liable for nationalisation. Until the change of licensing in 1964, SPD's terms of reference were strictly within Unilever's Transport Division, a post-war creation. Nonetheless an ambitious plan for the building of new depots designed for mechanical handling operations evolved from as early as 1946/7; the first fully palletised (q.v.) depot was opened in 1951 at Stockton and eight were completed by 1955, five with outside finance. However, the growing costs of new depot development contributed to a major internal challenge to SPD in the mid-1950s to produce a greater yield on its capital, which resulted in SPD setting new, more commercial rates. Partly as a result of the changing pattern of retail trade, which meant an increase in direct delivery, from factory to supermarket, the growth of depots proved to have been over-ambitious, creating substantial overcapacity.

By the beginning of the 1980s SPD was making losses and derived less than 50 per cent of its traffic from Unilever companies, so that in late 1984 Unilever reached agreement with the National Freight Consortium to sell SPD. The SPD sale followed others by Unilever designed to rationalise its peripheral businesses such as transport, including the Carryfast (q.v.) management buy-out in 1983 and a reorganisation of other operators as Unispeed, based at Watford. NFC subsequently bought another Unilever distribution operation, the specialist frozen food carrier Birds Eye Walls personal links between NFC and Unilever, in that NFC's chairman at the time of the SPD acquisition, Sir Peter Thompson (q.v.), had begun his career in business transport with SPD and the chairman of NFC at the time of Thompson's appointment as head of BRS in 1972 was Sir Daniel Pettit (q.v.), who had been chairman of SPD a decade before.　　**RAS**

Reader (1969); Thompson (1990)

Speed limits have been imposed on mechanically-propelled vehicles since 1861, primarily to limit the damage that they cause to road surfaces, but also with safety in mind. The detail of vehicle speed limits is complex: already in 1896 there were four different limits for the new light motor vehicles, depending upon their unladen weight and whether they were hauling a trailer. Later, one of the most significant factors was the type of tyre. Vehicles (including trailers) with solid tyres have generally had a lower limit imposed than similar vehicles with pneumatic tyres, because they caused more damage to the road surface; since 1981 they have been restricted to 20 mph. Those with steel tyres have never been allowed to travel faster than 10 mph, reduced to 5 mph since 1922.

Table 13 does not, therefore, present the complete picture; rather it summarises, for each year when the limits were changed, the highest speed limit applicable to each of the main classes of goods vehicle (see VEHICLE TYPES, LEGAL DEFINITION OF). It shows a progressive raising of speeds, made possible by technological advances in road pavements (q.v.), vehicle suspensions and tyres (q.v.), and vehicle braking. However, the higher limits were often only introduced after agitation by the associations representing motor vehicle users; indeed it was the campaign for changes to the 4 mph limit in 1895 that led to the formation of the oldest of these groups, the Self-Propelled Traffic Association (q.v.).

The raising of the limit to 30 mph in 1931 for vehicles under 2½ tons was a spur to the development of lightweight construction, including the use of aluminium alloys. The progressive advances in speed limits during the inter-war period were not resumed until many years after the Second World War, reflecting Britain's long years of post-war austerity. This held back the development of home-produced lorry designs, which generally followed, rather than anticipated, regulatory changes. Thus when the changes did come, the more-advanced Continental lorry designs were well-placed to break into the British market. The regulations discouraged the development of the drawbar combination in this country between 1957 and 1984, because its braking performance was considered to be less reliable than that of the articulated vehicle.

As well as the speed limits for specific vehicle classes, limits were also laid down for roads. From 1861 there was a 5 mph limit for mechanically-propelled vehicles in cities, towns and villages, reduced to 2 mph in 1865. In 1904 the standard limit for urban roads was set at 10 mph, which was raised to 30 mph in 1935. Also 50 and 40 mph limits were introduced on sections of road that were previously unrestricted, either for safety reasons or to increase traffic flow on heavily-used sections, under powers given in the Road Traffic Act 1962. Motorways were at first unrestricted, speeds being quite effectively limited, particularly in the case of lorries, by the under-powered engines of vehicles designed for the pre-motorway era. Superior power-weight ratios soon followed, however, leading to the introduction in 1965 of a 70 mph limit for all vehicles and, from 1971, a 60 mph limit for lorries over 3 tons unladen weight. An emergency 50 mph limit was placed on roads from 8 December 1973 to 28 March 1974 to conserve fuel during the oil crisis following the Arab-Israeli War.

Following the raising of speed limits in 1957 and the opening of the M1 motorway, the Transport & General Workers Union made agreements with several operators, including British Road Services, to maintain former average speeds in order to avoid reductions in employment and earnings. However, exceeding the speed limits in order to gain commercial advantage or for the driver's personal convenience is more typical of the industry's culture. The introduction of the tachograph (q.v.) controlled the wilder excesses, but the speed monitoring statistics that have been published annually since 1991 show that more

Table 13: Speed Limits (mph)

	Motor car (goods)	Heavy motor car (goods)			Motor tractor + trailer	Light locomotive + trailer	Heavy locomotive + trailer
		Rigid	Rigid + trailer	Artic			
1861							10
1865							4
1896	8 [2] 12 [1]	5	5				4
1904	20 [2]	5	5				4
1905	20 [2]	8/12 [6]	5				4
1922	20 [2]	12	5	12			4
1928	20	20	12	12			4
1931	30 [3]	20 Horseboxes 30	16	16	8	8	5
1934	30 [3]	20 Horseboxes 30	20	20	20	12	5
1957	30	30	20	30	20	12	12
1967	70 [m]/40	70 [m]/40	70 [m]/30	70 [m]/40	30	20	20
1971	70 [m]/50 [5] 70 [m]/40 [4]	60 [m]/40	60 [m]/30	60 [m]/40	30	20	20
1984	70 [m]/60 [d]/50	70 [m]/60 [d]/50 [7] 60 [m]/50 [d]/40	60 [m]/50 [d]/50 [7] 60 [m]/50 [d]/40	60 [m]/50 [d]/50 [7] 60 [m]/50 [d]/40	40 [m]/30 [d]/30	40 [m]/30 [d]/30	40 [m]/30 [d]/30

[1] under 1½ tons ULW
[2] under 2 tons ULW
[3] under 2½ tons ULW
[4] under 3 tons ULW
[5] if not exceeding 1½ tons ULW
[6] 12 mph if registered axle load did not exceed 6 tons
[7] if not exceeding 7.5 tonnes GVW
[d] limit on dual-carriageways
[m] limit on motorways

than 5 per cent of 4-, 5- and 6-axle lorries still exceed the 50 mph limit on dual-carriageways by more than 10 mph and 25 per cent exceed the 40 mph limit on single-carriageway A roads by the same margin. However, the compulsory fitting of speed limiters has virtually eliminated disregard of the 60 mph on motorways. They were introduced in 1992 for new lorries over 7.5 tonnes gross weight and subsequently applied retrospectively to those over 12 tonnes that were first registered after 1987. Initially they were required to limit the speed to 60 mph, but for lorries over 12 tonnes this was later reduced in line with EC regulations to 90 km/h (56 mph). **GAB**

Acts of Parliament and Statutory Instruments; *Transport Statistics, Great Britain*, 1992–2000.

The **Speedway Group**, which had its heyday in the 1950s to 1970s, was a loose association of companies concentrating on coal haulage, the founders or directors of several having formerly been speedway stars. The central firm was Oliver Hart & Sons Ltd of Coppull, founded by Oliver Hart, formerly of Bellevue Speedway, and operating some forty vehicles, many of them sturdy hybrids designed to maximise payloads by reducing unladen weight. Hart was succeeded by his sons, Oliver junior and Ron, and also owned Rollon Transport of Derby (its title deriving from the sons' forenames). Associate companies were Blainscough Transport Ltd and Flechart Ltd, later renamed Hart's Bulk Haulage Ltd. Harts had close links with Little Haywood Transport of Burton-on-Trent and Coal Deliveries (East Midlands) Ltd of Mansfield, both founded by another speedway rider, Ron Mason, and with Fletchers of Ibstock. Ron Johnston, a former speedway rider from New Zealand, was managing director of Fletchers, which was absorbed by Little Haywood Transport in the mid-1970s, and another ex-speedway-star, Ron Clarke, was a director of both Coal Deliveries and Rollon Transport. Ron Mason was involved in Transport Vehicles (Warrington) Ltd, to which another coal haulier, S Jones (q.v.) of Aldridge, was linked by shareholding. Little Haywood Transport Ltd was part of the MJ Group of companies, 'industrial coal hauliers', which also included Maurice James & Co. (1959) Ltd and Wild Haulage Ltd. In 1962 it claimed to handle

2 million tons of coal a year and that its King Kole Service was Britain's largest producer of pre-packed fuel. **RAS**

P Davies, 'Affair of the Hart', *CVC,* 3, 8 (April 1998), pp. 16–18; MJ Group advertisement, 1962

Spurrier, Sir Henry III (1898–1964) was in many ways regarded as the architect of the growth of Leyland into Britain's premier producer of commercial vehicles. He was born into a family of engineers and his father was a director of the Lancashire Steam Motor Co., which in 1907 changed its name to Leyland Motors Ltd. Henry went into the family firm as an engineering apprentice and saw war service in the Royal Flying Corps. As a relative junior he experienced the awkward time for Leyland in the 1920s, when the decision to design and build a super-expensive luxury car and to buy back from the government and refurbish ex-RAF Leyland lorries at unremunerative prices brought Leyland to the brink of bankruptcy. This made a lasting impression and Turner claims that under Spurrier, Leyland was 'a parsimonious outfit' and Spurrier a cautious manager, though very ambitious. In 1930 Spurrier was made assistant general manager and in 1942 general manager. In 1949 he became managing director and in 1957 chairman as well. He gave up both positions in 1963 after a serious illness.

His main positive contribution to Leyland's growth came from three directions. Firstly he promoted overseas sales of both lorries and buses. These were successful with large orders from India, South Africa and Russia. In 1932 Leyland claimed to have agents in 54 countries and by 1939 one fifth of its production was exported. Spurrier had good products to promote. The T type chassis, which was the basis of the Bison and Buffalo, was popular with hauliers for its economy, quietness and reliability. Spurrier's second contribution to Leyland's success was after the Second World War when, realising the need for scale economies, he embarked on a cautious acquisition policy, with Albion Motors in 1951, Scammell Lorries in 1955 and Associated Commercial Vehicles, which in turn had acquired Crossley, Maudslay and Thornycroft,

in 1962. This gave Leyland a large share of British-owned heavy goods vehicle production. The third contribution made by Spurrier was to ensure Leyland continued to do much more than assemble, and manufactured most of the components it needed to build its lorries. This gave it greater control and higher added-value. Thus Leyland was vertically integrated and its products were of such good quality that they sold them to other commercial vehicle builders, Dodge and Bedford, for instance, buying engines.

Spurrier made one questionable decision in 1960 when he bought Standard-Triumph in order to get into volume car production. The skills needed for lorry production and sales, and motor car manufacture and sale were totally different and none of Leyland's board had any relevant experience. Also Alick Dick, the chairman of Standard-Triumph, had misled Spurrier about the company's position and Spurrier paid well over the odds. That said, Spurrier had the vision to see Leyland needed to grow and he oversaw that growth; in 1947 Leyland produced about 3,500 commercial vehicles, in 1964 it made 29,000.

He was also one of the first senior people in the transport industry to see merit in preserving representative historic vehicles, building up a modest collection for Leyland. After his illness the collection was allowed to deteriorate before many were disposed of. In 1955 Spurrier was knighted. He died of a brain tumour aged only 66. **JA**

DBB, Vol. 5, (1986), pp. 253–9; Turner (1971)

Spy in the cab, see TACHOGRAPH

The **Square Deal Campaign** took place in 1938–9 when the four railway companies petitioned for greater freedom from regulation over the fixing and publishing of rates for goods carriage. Their complaint was against the unequal treatment of the railways compared to road haulage which they thought allowed the latter to undercut the railway rates. There was some truth in this, though the structural adjustments in the economy and decline in heavy industries also played a part in reducing railway traffic. The immediate cause of the campaign was the 1937 report of the Transport Advisory Council (q.v.) which advocated avoidance of overlapping services but failed to suggest any practical remedies for low railway revenue. Their petition was referred to the Transport Advisory Council which appointed a twenty-person committee under the TAC's chairman, Sir Arthur Griffith-Boscawen (q.v.) to try to come to some agreement. Before any action could be taken the Second World War broke out and the campaign was obscured in the national emergency and the steep rise in railway revenue and government guarantees. In any case, as Walker points out, the problem of low rates being charged by road hauliers was unlikely to be solved by regulation or voluntary arrangements. The structure of the road haulage industry was highly competitive, with over 20,000 firms averaging three lorries per business. Even if the larger operators negotiated with the railways, the small-scale operator was likely to continue to undercut. If large operators and the railways negotiated higher rates it was hardly likely to prove popular with the users of transport.   **JA**

Walker (1942), chap. 10; Savage (1957), pp. 17–19; *OCBRH*, p. 172; E A Gibbins, *Square Deal Denied* (Alsager: Leisure Products, 1998)

The **Standard Motor Co. Ltd**, founded in 1903 by R W Maudslay and taken over by Leyland Motors in 1960, was primarily a car manufacturer. Most of its light commercials were car-derived, with the exception of the Atlas of 1958 and its successors. In 1911 Standard offered a fast delivery van on its 15-hp chassis and supplied some light truck-bodied vehicles in its Delhi Durbar fleet. A 3-cwt van and traveller's sample van were introduced in 1913. In the 1930s 6-, 7- and 10-cwt vans were offered, replaced in 1934 by an Atlas van, but production ceased in 1936. During the Second World War over 10,000 light vans, utilities and ambulances were produced, finding their way into civilian use during the post-war vehicle shortage. In 1948 Standard introduced a van and pick-up version of the Standard Vanguard saloon, which had been launched in 1947. These light commercials were ordered extensively by the RAF and were also used as service vans by Standard and Ferguson tractor dealers. Lighter vans appeared in 1954, with a 6 cwt van and pick-up based on the Standard Ten. In 1958 Standard uncharacteristically entered the forward-control, walk-through van sector, reusing the Atlas model name. Positive features were its turning circle, petrol consumption and servicing accessibility (the engine, gearbox and front suspension could be easily removed as a single unit), but it was initially underpowered, its load-carrying space tempted users to overload, and there were chassis and handbrake problems. A larger engined Major version was introduced in 1960 and in 1962, after the Leyland takeover, the Standard Fifteen and Twenty van and pick-up appeared as an evolution of the Atlas. Scammell, also within Leyland, used Atlas components for its Scarab 4 4-wheel mechanical horse (q.v.). Standard acquired the remains of the Coventry car-producer Triumph in 1944. There had been a few car-based Triumph light vans between 1932 and 1935; then between 1962 and 1965 the 5-cwt Courier van was offered by Standard-Triumph, based on the Herald car chassis. It shared the Herald's useful manoeuvrability, but was uncompetitively priced.   **RAS**

J R Davy, *The Standard Car 1903–1963: an illustrated history* (Coventry, 1967); B Long, *Standard Motor Company Limited: the illustrated history including Standard-Triumph* (Godmanstone, 1993); Stevens-Stratten (1991); records in the Modern Records Centre, University of Warwick Library, MSS. 226/ST

The **Standing Joint Committee of Mechanical Road Transport Associations** was founded in 1912 to confer on legislation and taxation likely to affect motor road transport and to take such steps as might be agreed. Its other objectives included co-operation where this was thought desirable, the collection and circulation of statistics and information and the advising of its members on relevant legislation. One of its early members was Sir Arthur Griffith-Boscawen (q.v.) who was later chair of the 1928–31 Royal Commission on Transport. Its first chairman until 1929 was E S Shrapnell-Smith (q.v.) and its constitution was largely drafted by Frank

Pick, later to be so important in London Transport. Its delegates represented the Commercial Motor Users Association (q.v.), the Mansion House Association (q.v.) and the National Traction Engine Users Association (q.v.) among others. Its honorary secretary was F G Bristow (q.v.). The committee also represented road hauliers at the initial meeting of the Pybus Committee on Road and Rail Co-ordination which determined membership of what became the Salter Conference on Road and Rail Transport (q.v.). The editor of *Commercial Motor* objected that some of the bodies which were members of the Standing Joint Committee were small-scale, had little importance and were not much concerned with road haulage. This may have been a reference to the Automobile Association (q.v.) and Royal Automobile Club, which were members of the SJC, but by then represented motorists rather than hauliers. In the early 1930s the SJC changed its name to the Special Operators Committee and in 1932 joined the British Road Federation (q.v.). **RAS/JA**

E S Shrapnell-Smith, 'Five decades of commercial road transport with inferences about its future', *Journal of the Institute of Transport* (1946), pp. 214–29

Standing Joint Committee of Road Hauliers' National Organisations. Despite the existence of the Liaison Committee on Rates (q.v.), founded in January 1938, the SJC was established by some leading members of the trade associations at a somewhat secretive meeting at Frascati's restaurant, London, on 13 December 1938 to represent 'A' and 'B' licence-holders. According to Dunbar, Pickfords, McNamara and Holdsworth Hanson were certainly involved and possibly Transport Services and, less certainly, A Renwick of Fisher Renwick. R P Bailey of the National Road Transport Employers' Federation (q.v.) was authorised to circularise the relevant associations and the first meeting was held on 26 January 1939, constituting a Standing Joint Committee of eight representatives of Associated Road Operators and six each from Commercial Motor Users' Association (q.v.), National Conference of Express Carriers (q.v.) and National Road Transport Employers' Federation

(q.v.). It was later joined by the National Association of Furniture Warehousemen & Removers (q.v.) and the two Scottish associations. The SJC was seen by Dunbar as 'one of the landmarks in the history of the haulage industry', leading as it did towards the reorganisation of the employers' organisations at the end of the Second World War and the emergence of the present RHA. Dunbar considered that the influence of the NRTEF was responsible for the election of J H Turner as chairman and G W Quick-Smith (q.v.) as secretary. For the latter this represented a significant stage in his successful career in road haulage at the highest policy level. **RAS**

Dunbar (1981); there is a file in the Dunbar papers in the Modern Records Centre, University of Warwick Library, MSS. 347/SJ/1/1

The **Star** engineering firm of Wolverhampton existed in various forms as a vehicle manufacturer between 1904 and 1932. For most of the period it was in the hands of the Lisle family and for the greater part of its existence traded under the name of the Star Engineering Co. Ltd. Like numerous other motor manufacturers, Star progressed from cycle to motor vehicle production. A 6-cwt. van was introduced in 1902 and by 1907 Star commercials had a sufficient reputation for Lever Brothers to operate a fleet of nineteen. In 1913 Star advertised a range of commercials from a 5- to 8-cwt van to a 3- to 4-ton lorry, although in this year Star suffered a reverse when its bodyshop was destroyed by fire. 1914 customers included Pratts Petroleum, owned by the Anglo-American Oil Co. Ltd, as well as Wolverhampton brewers, footwear and provision firms. During the First World War substantial government orders were received for both cars and lorries, including for Russia. 30-cwt, 1½- and 2½-ton vehicles were offered after the war and a low-loading passenger chassis was introduced in 1927, which evolved into the Star Flyer, which was used as the basis of horseboxes, as well as coaches. Star 20/25-cwt capacity vans were popular with several larger London stores, including Selfridges, in the 1920s. In 1928 the Lisle family sold out to Guy Motors (q.v.); Star continued as a separate marque for a few years, in new work at Bushbury, although Guy ended the potential competition from its heavier commercials. Non-existent profit margins on Star cars and Guys' financial difficulties led to Star's receivership in 1932. In its time Star had been significant regionally for its commercial vehicle production and with some national presence.   **RAS**

J Boulton and H Parsons, *Powered Vehicles made in the Black Country* (Kingswinford, 1990); J Boulton, *Black Country Road Transport* (Stroud, 1995); Baldwin and Ingram (1977)

The Star Group, see TRANSPORT SERVICES LTD

Steam Carriage & Wagon Co. Ltd was the first title of Thornycroft's road vehicle building business, changing to Thornycroft Steam Wagon Co. Ltd in 1901.

Steam road tractors and lorries (Figure 53). In 1842 Ransomes of Ipswich produced what was probably the first British traction engine but essentially for agricultural use. Although 70 road vehicles were built between 1801 and 1860, none was for carrying goods. In the latter year Thomas Aveling of Rochester, designed a self-moving threshing engine which could also be used to haul wagons. He was quickly followed by Robey of Lincoln and others; due to repressive legislation, these engines were seldom seen on the road unless hauling threshing gear, or heavy machinery in the docks. The extent of restrictive legislation, both national and local, can be gauged from the fact that a mechanical vehicle could only move in Lewisham, South London, between the hours of 10 pm and 6 am. Fines were imposed in most towns on engines with fewer than three attendants, or moving at over 2 mph.

In 1867 Robert Thomson of Edinburgh devised the 'road steamer', a three-wheeled engine with a vertical boiler and rubber tyres, capable of 10 mph (though this was illegal). Examples were built by several makers but most went overseas.

In the 1880s compounding and four-shaft drive provided more power and flexibility; at the end of the nineteenth century when speed restrictions were eased, light traction engines were made, and adopted for hauling agricultural produce, light engineering output and colourful pantechnicons. Heavy engines continued to be used in farming, especially Fowlers equipped with drums for steam ploughing. Large loads on the roads still required them; Pickfords sometimes used up to three engines to haul heavy machinery.

The steam lorry was first developed in 1896 by Thornycroft of Chiswick, and the Lancashire Steam Motor Co. of Leyland in Lancashire. The Thornycroft had a vertical water tube boiler and drive to the front wheels, steering being by a small rear cart. The Leyland was a light van of conventional design, except for using oil fuel. However, when in 1897 the *Engineer* held a prize competition at the Crystal Palace, the only goods vehicle to appear was a van built by the Liquid Fuel Engineering Co. of East Cowes. Legislation limited tare weight to 3 tons, and John I Thornycroft in a paper before the Royal Society claimed it was impossible to design a satisfactory machine within this limit. The heavy overtype lorry, virtually a light tractor with a lorry body, did not therefore appear until 1901 with the famous Foden. The chief maker of the undertypes (engine below the frame and usually a vertical boiler) was the Sentinel works of Alley & McLellan of Glasgow (later Shrewsbury) and these two took a large part of the market for thirty years.

In the competition between undertype and overtype designs, the latter had the disadvantage of poor visibility with the driver having to peer at the road ahead over escaping steam and flying motion. The under-type, of which there were several different layouts, was more difficult to maintain and the boilers were less reliable than the locomotive type used by the overtypes, which were preferred by users having much waiting time, such as brewers and furniture removers. In 1911 even Sentinel felt the need to offer an overtype, but it was produced only for a year or two, as Sentinel felt that they had made the point that they could build a very good overtype.

By the 1930s the emphasis was on speed, multiple gears and extended body space, and undertypes took what was now a shrinking market. In 1934 taxation changes came down heavily on steam lorries due to their greater tare weight, which was considered detrimental to road surfaces and foundations, road tax rising for six tons unladen weight to £90 (£120 if on solid tyres). Laden weight was limited to 19 tons for six-wheelers, which gave a poor payload for steamers. Their registrations dropped from 168 in 1934 to 30 in 1935.

Sentinel had fought hard with a DG (double geared) series and in 1932 a light version of its popular Super Sentinel, but the convenience of internal combustion vehicles prevailed; the Sentinel DG8 needed to take on board 10 cwt of coal and 120 gallons of water. Foden offered diesel alternatives from 1931.

Though capacious water tanks were provided, drivers of steam tractors and lorries always needed to know of streams or stand-pipes on their routes to pick up water by injector or pump; coal or coke was usually carried in sufficient quantity. Drivers were sometimes fined for taking water illegally from fire hydrants. In Liverpool, with its preponderance of steam lorries travelling to and from the docks, the corporation water works provided roadside hydrants worked through a key and token system. There were even plans for a national hydrant scheme.

Traction engines were becoming rare by 1939, but the war caused some to remain in use; steam lorries vanished more gradually despite lack of spares, fitters, skilled drivers and the need for the boiler to be lit up well before the vehicle was required for service. The need to carry a second man or stoker was a further disadvantage. A road test in the UK in 1950 of a Sentinel S-type tipper for overseas use did not lead to a revival at home.   **RWK**

Kidner (1948)

Steel traffic (Figures 173 and 174). The type of goods vehicle in most common use for steel traffic was the flat-backed lorry with wooden decking. Steel is a demanding product to move. It comes in varying forms and each type of product has its own particular handling requirements. It is a heavy commodity to move in proportion to its volume; sometimes the amount of load space taken up on a goods

vehicle may seem absurdly low, but the observer must appreciate that the maximum axle weight may have been reached, if not the maximum permitted gross vehicle weight.

Lorries which worked regularly on steel traffic, whether on local or long distance journeys, were worked very hard. They were usually loaded to full capacity, with heavy items being lifted on and off at frequent intervals. Such punitive work influenced most operators to choose the heavier and more robust makes of vehicle, such as AEC, Leyland and Scammell, although the lighter models produced by such manufacturers as Bedford and Ford were also used on this type of work. Some specialist variations of the flat-backed vehicle could also be seen. One such was the coil carrier; a semi-trailer which had a large semi-circular channel running longitudinally down its centre. Coils of steel strip were placed snugly into this, which achieved two purposes, firstly the load security was increased and secondly the load's centre of gravity was lowered, increasing the vehicle's stability. Other specialist equipment included frames and gantries to support RSJs and similar fabrications which were too long for normal transport. Some firms based in Sheffield which specialised in steel traffic included J J Shepherd which used ERFs to deliver steel to the Glasgow area from the 1950s to the 1980s, and George Bonsall which operated AECs to deliver steel, mainly in the form of billets throughout the country until about 1980. Syd Harrison of Rotherham ran a substantial fleet of Scammells to carry steel, often with adaptations made in their own workshops.

Steel, especially the bright variety, has a propensity to slip when positioned on or against other steel. For this reason it required packing and bedding for it to be carried safely. Given that it was usually lifted on and off by crane or fork-lift truck, it was not placed directly on the lorry body. Timber battens were placed across the flat body of the lorry, immediately above the chassis bearers, to direct the weight to the points where the vehicle was best equipped to sustain it. The steel was then placed upon them, thus allowing the lifting chains, or the forks of the truck, to be freed, and conversely, to gain access for unloading. For additional security and safety the headboard, which is the bulkhead at the front of the load immediately behind the cab, was often reinforced with steel plate. This prevented the load from sliding forward through the cab if heavy braking was needed.

To counter lateral movement in transit the load was wedged against something solid at the sides of the lorry. For this purpose the lorries used in steel-producing areas had a raised section down either side of the body, known as a choc rail. The chocs or scotches were placed against this, and the load packed against them, by crowbar if necessary. Drivers usually carried a good supply of timbers, scotches and nails on the lorry, but sometimes there was a need for improvisation. In the absence of proper scotches, bricks or any pieces of packing material left lying around were used to good effect.

Where the load did not take up the full width of the platform, lateral movement was prevented by one of two methods. Either scotches or flat pieces of timber were nailed to the battens across the platform, or battens were used which had been drilled out at intervals across their length. Steel pegs were inserted into these holes at the point nearest to the edge of the load. Generally speaking the former method was used for heavier round bars, and the latter for lighter consignments. The expression 'bars', in this context refers to steel items of a wide variety of sizes, shapes and weights, some round, some square and others hexagonal. They also varied from those which are extremely heavy, individually, to others which are comparatively light and are despatched in bundles. Dimensions can vary from taking up the entire length of the vehicle, 40 ft billets, for example, being quite a common load, to measuring only a few inches from end to end. Forgings were a common load, and also varied in size and weight. Sometimes life would be made easier by despatching them in steel containers, or stillages (q.v.), which were filled with the forgings and lifted onto the lorry by crane or fork-lift. When small forgings were loaded loose one of the best ways of securing them was to build a frame of timbers nailed longways and across the platform, inside which they were packed. Larger items were dealt with according to their individuality, employing whatever combination of equipment was most appropriate.

Some consignments required to be sheeted over, while others did not. As a general rule bright steel was covered, while 'black bar' (steel which had yet to be machined) could often be left exposed. To the casual observer it may seem that the traditional use of sheets and ropes was to secure the load, although in reality the main method of security was the loading method described above. The sheet's main purpose was to protect the load from the elements, and the ropes to keep the sheet in place, although it offered a bonus in the event of an accident or a need for emergency braking. However, in the case of small items, such as the forgings referred to above, the sheet was a very effective method of keeping them secure. Chains were also widely used to secure steel products, especially long bars and steel plate. The load itself was secured first, with the chain serving as a safety measure should the load move in transit.

Steel has other characteristics which affect the way in which it is loaded. If there are sharp edges these will cut through sheets and ropes with ease, therefore it was necessary to use packing to avoid direct contact. Again this called for resourcefulness on the driver's part in utilising any pieces of cardboard or plastic which could be found. Chains could present the opposite problem in that they could mark the load itself when tightened, and so packing was used to prevent this.

A lot of internal movement within steelworks, and local deliveries from one works to another, involved the transport of hot steel loaded immediately after a particular process had finished, to the place where the next stage would be undergone. In these circumstances bars were literally red hot. These were loaded onto steel bearers laid across the lorry, as ordinary timber battens would be burned through. The lifting chains were removed with the aid of long iron rods, and repositioned in the same manner at the destination. Even from such a 'safe' distance the heat was very powerful. It was not unknown for a finished consignment to be extremely hot at the time of loading, and it was sometimes wise to defer the sheeting of it until later, at the depot, rather than risk the sheet, and then the lorry itself, catching fire.

The driver who carried steel needed a variety of specialist skills and a modicum of physical strength. As mentioned above, although cranes and fork-lifts brought the load to the vehicle, much of the precision was achieved by physical effort and crowbar. Timbers and other packing sometimes required nailing into position and this is why wooden decking was necessary. The metal decking fitted to lorries built for other traffic could render them unusable when seeking a return load from Sheffield.

Steel traffic was not carried exclusively by road transport operators; the railways also played a role. In terms of steel manufacturing the input stage of the process was often, but not always, where the railways were competing from a position of strength. Raw materials were used in large quantities and therefore moved in bulk, the type of operation where rail is at its most efficient. The output stage is where the road operators competed most avidly for traffic, but certainly not to the exclusion of rail. Movement of finished products could also call for bulk movement, where road hauliers were disadvantaged. Much of this traffic comprised bespoke orders, and comparatively small consignments to a customer base and destination range which was widely distributed.   **MB**

CVC, 7, 8 and 9 (April and May 2002), pp. 36–40, 20–4

The **Stepney Carrier Co. Ltd** marketed the Karivan, a 3-wheel trade carrier with two front wheels under the trade-box and a motor cycle-type rear end, from 1930 to 1936, with an address in High Holborn, WC1. In 1932 a more sophisticated version of the Karivan with enclosed rear cab was introduced. New premises at 94–100 St John Street, Clerkenwell were designed in a modern style by the Milner & Craze partnership in 1935, incorporating fire-proof materials and providing a garage, office and box carrier store and repair area. In the early 1920s, as Renault agents, they had offered 'a complete service with driver' of Renault vans in customers' livery; their works at that time were in Stepney, with office and garage off

Kingsway. By the late 1930s from their Clerkenwell address they advertised for hire a range of Commer, Ford and Morris vans, from 5- to 30-cwt capacity, in customers' livery, with or without driver, on a yearly contract. Strakers, the stationers, and Waterman's Pens were among those using SC vans, which were identified by a large ownership transfer and a circled fleet number. Carrier cycles and tricycles of 56 lb or 2-cwt capacity, were also available. The firm claimed to have been founded in 1824.
RAS

Advertising handbill of Stepney Carrier Co. (1920s); leaflet (1930s); Baldwin and Ingram (1977); *CM 1935–6 Commercial Chassis*; A Forsyth, *Buildings for the Age* (HMSO, 1982), illus. 10–11

Stewart, John, & Co. Ltd of Poplar, London, produced the London steam wagon in 1905. It was an undertype with vertical boiler and compound engine, the crankshaft of which was extended into an enclosed two-speed gearbox attached to the differential gearing. It was a sound design, but failed to attract enough custom. This firm had no connection with D Stewart & Co. of Glasgow which made Thornycroft-type steam lorries.   **RWK**

Stewart & Arden Ltd, of the Vale, Acton, were sole London distributors for Morris and Morris-Commercial (q.v.). Their Cunard coach-building factory at Wembley could produce all classes of bodywork on Morris-Commercial vehicles and Morris light vans. Before acquiring Cunard in 1931, their 'Esanday' bodywork had been produced by Wilson of Kingston-upon-Thames. The Vale depot was reconstructed after its use as an aero-engine factory in the Second World War. Other S&A depots ringed greater London from South Tottenham to Sutton and Staines to Southend.   **RAS**

Walker (1997), pp. 106–7, 189

STGO vehicles, see ABNORMAL OR INDIVISABLE LOADS

Stillages, see PALLETS AND STILLAGES

Stirling was a pioneer marque in the UK, produced by Stirling Motor Carriages Ltd of

Hamilton, from 1897 to 1905, then by Scott-Stirling at Edinburgh and Twickenham. John Stirling was essentially an assembler, buying in chassis frames and engines, but producing the bodywork. Principally bus builders, Stirling also made 2-ton lorries, including two for the War Office. Stirling ceased production in 1908 after the failure of their main bus customer in London the previous year. **RAS**

Grieves (1997)

Stobart, Eddie, Ltd (Figures 54 and 175) was founded in 1970 by the father of Edward Stobart (b. 1954), who was a Cumbrian agricultural contractor. Edward left school at fourteen to work for his father, who operated half a dozen trucks on farm delivery of fertilisers. At eighteen Edward began to find other traffic for the business and at 21 set up a depot in Caldbeck with his own vehicles, which carried his father's name, Eddie Stobart. By the late 1970s fifteen employees and ten trucks operated from a single depot which moved to Carlisle from Caldbeck in 1976. Further relocation, to Kingstown industrial estate near the M6, took place in 1980. By 1984 the workforce had doubled. In early 1997 1800 employees and 600 trucks operated from eighteen depots and 500,000 sq. feet of warehousing was under construction in a new freight terminal at Crick. By 2000 the business, with 1000 vehicles, was the largest privately owned truck operator in the UK and one of the biggest in Europe, the sole shareholders being Edward and his brother, William. This expansion was achieved by Stobart's dedication to intensive work, in a highly centralised concern but a crucial element in the firm's growth, as Davies explains, has been its commitment to property buying and developing judiciously, then selling and leasing back. Edward's father, Eddie, played a significant part in the 1980 Kingstown acquisition. Contracts with the Metal Box Co. from 1976 for the delivery of cans to breweries, which led to delivery of the filled cans, were the basis of expansion, and food and beverage conveyance came to form 90 per cent of Stobart's business. Early policy decisions included the purchase of curtain-sided lorries and trailers, their extra initial cost being offset by speed and ease of loading and unloading, protection of the load and the opportunity to publicise the fleet on the vehicle sides. Apart from some secondhand acquisitions in the late 1970s, company policy was to operate new vehicles, whether purchased outright, on contract hire or leased, with buy-back deals to help monitor and control costs. Drawbar units were once a major feature of the fleet, but were reduced following length-limit changes. The majority of trailers in use were Boalloy-bodied but the fleet also included 12 Montracon bulk-tipping trailers and step-frame trailers to Stobart's design by Don-Bur (q.v.).

A major set-back to the company's development came in 1985, when the recession seriously affected transport, and half the Stobart fleet was laid up, very much as a result of the volume of sub-contracting carried out by Stobart up to that point. Stobart's younger brother William took over the operating side at this juncture, Colin Rutherford, formerly transport manager at Metal Box, took up this post with Stobart and an accountant, Barry Thomas, became commercial director, leaving Edward Stobart free to oversee the firm's development. As a private company, a heavy load of debt was carried to meet its expansionist drive; Stobart aimed for 3 to 5 per cent profit, and in 1996 achieved some £3.5 million pre-tax on a turnover of £68 million. An important part of his policy was that the fleet should make a notable impact by its smart presentation, in a green, white and red livery with gold lettering and with a uniformed staff and individually named vehicles. This aspect of his operations caught the public's imagination and gave rise to a fan club, the financial return from which in 2000 helped to offset the effects of fuel prices on the firm's trading results. In 1998 a Stoke-on-Trent firm, Jenerite with 20 vehicles, was acquired to form the basis of Eddie Stobart International in order to expand into European operation, not as a crude 'flagging-out' (q.v.) operation, but as a move into a new area with potential for growth. The British base was moved to Warrington and a depot established in Belgium near Ghent. A major Naafi contract to service bases in Germany, secured in 1999, consolidated this new venture. In addition to these two divisions, UK and international haulage, Stobart operations included the warehousing division and process management, which involves Stobart staff and mechanical handling equipment working for customers on their sites. At home Stobart has been considering since early 1997 the possible role of rail freight services as part of his operations and the site at the Daventry International Rail Freight Terminal, Crick, would fit into that strategy, if the time came to implement it. Stobart depots are strategically sited, the largest a few miles from a motorway and each about one hundred miles from the next depot, which facilitates depot-to-depot runs. There is a concentration of marques in certain depots, partly related to proximity to the relevant service dealer and partly to facilitate the switching of drivers between similar vehicles. Some Stobart vehicles operated in customers' livery, for example the Mirror Group and United Glass, but with discreet identifying markings; Stobart also operated closely with James Irlam & Sons Ltd (q.v.) on a shared soft drinks contract. **RAS**

Davies (2001); Byron Rogers, 'King of the road', *Daily Telegraph Magazine* (15 February 1997), pp. 32–4, 36; Kevin Eason, 'Trucker with his own fan club', *The Times* (28 December 1996), 'Car Supplement', p. 7; M Brignall, 'New track for Eddie Stobart', *CM* (27 March 1997), p. 11; Anne-Katrin Purkiss, 'Steady Eddie', *Director*, vol. 52, no. 4 (November 1998), pp. 50–4; *CM* (17 December 1998), p. 7; Millar (2000); N Davidson, *Only the Best Will Do* (Belfast: Ambassador Publications, 1998)

Strachans the coachbuilders of London, Hamble and Eastleigh, Hants were mainly producers of passenger vehicle bodies. However, goods vehicles were an important part of their output and problems associated with a major van body project hastened the end of the business. Founded in 1908 at Shepherds Bush by James Marshall Strachan, within a few years expansion to Park Royal and Kensington took place, with wartime aircraft and ambulance production leading to consolidation in larger premises in Kensington. After the war, the business built itself a new factory at Acton, fully

in use by 1922. At about this time the sales side was greatly strengthened by the addition of W E Brown and the business was renamed Strachan & Brown (the dates and details of the Strachan-Brown relationship are given somewhat differently by Walker). Following Brown's departure to Duple in 1928 and the founder's death in 1929, the Strachan family formed a limited company, Strachans (Acton) Ltd. This was restructured as Strachans (Successors) Ltd in 1935, after Strachan's widow had married Sir William Noble. Strachan concentrated on commercial vehicle contracts in the 1930s, some 'very large' and advertisements show a Watneys barrel lorry and a Dennis van for gas appliance delivery. In 1961 the company was sold to the Giltspur Group, which had diverse interests, including packaging, and a former aircraft repair works at Hamble, Hants, to which Strachans were moved, with a change of name to Strachans (Coachbuilders) Ltd. The proximity of this works to Ford's van plant at Southampton facilitated co-operation on a parcel van body for the Transit. In addition a new works was later opened at Eastleigh in connection with a parcel van body for the Ford A-series, introduced in 1973. It proved to be less than the anticipated success, and this, together with Giltspur's own problems, brought Strachans' closure by the end of 1974. After an interval, the integral parcels van was produced by Willenhall Radiator Co., but the model was discontinued by mid-1976.

RAS

G Burrows, 'Coachwork by Strachans', *Classic Bus Yearbook 8* (Hersham: Ian Allan, (2002), pp. 73–87; Walker (1997), pp. 173–4; Cole (1980), pp. 61–2

Straker-Squire. Although largely forgotten today, Sidney Straker, a consulting engineer with manufacturing interests in Bristol, was a sufficiently significant figure in the early years of the motor industry to succeed F R Simms (q.v.) in 1904 as the second president of the Society of Motor Manufacturers & Traders (q.v.). Straker, educated at King's College, was promoter of a number of vehicle-producing firms, which moved from steam to petrol, during the period 1899 to 1926. Details of the seven Straker businesses, at Bristol between 1899 and 1917 and London in 1899 and from

1917 to 1926, will be found in Georgano. Straker was also 'advisor on matters of design' to the Daimler Co., from 1899 to 1901. Straker-Squire buses, based on the German Büssing chassis, were the most prominent make in London c.1908; the German connection ceased in 1909. By 1913 the firm's range included 25- and 35-cwt goods vehicles, ¾-ton chassis and a 5-ton chain-driven lorry. Several hundred 3-ton vehicles were provided for Service use in the First World War. In 1919 the firm moved to a former shell factory at Edmonton; post-war models included the 5-ton A semi-forward-control bus or goods chassis, short-wheelbase tippers and the BW 2½-ton goods chassis from 1922. Production ceased in 1926, following the death of the founder in a riding accident. Civilian customers at different times included Carter Paterson, the GWR for its parcels service, and Peek Frean, the biscuit manufacturer.   **RAS**

Dunbar (1981); Lord Montagu and D Burgess-Wise, *Daimler Century* (Sparkford: Patrick Stephens, 1995)

Straker Steam Vehicle Co. was one of several enterprises of Sidney Straker, a Bristol engineer, whose first connection with transport was the equipping of two Daimler buses for London in 1899. The first steam vehicle, a 3-ton with vertical boiler and all-gear drive, came out in 1902 and caused some interest, including in the War Office. Conventional models for 5 and 7 tons were entered in trials, where their steel wheels showed more lasting power over cobbles than the wooden ones of several rivals. In 1905 the company brought out an overtype with locomotive-type boiler. Admitting that it used more fuel, they claimed it was more suited to unskilled drivers, but it was not a success. Also in 1905 the business was amalgamated with that of Sidney Straker & Squire Ltd, which imported German Bussing bus chassis. This was rapidly expanding and a large new headquarters was built at Nelson Square, Blackfriars; interest in steam lorry production dwindled. A new factory at Fishponds, Bristol was opened at the end of 1906.   **RWK**

The **structure of the industry** can be analysed in various ways. Firstly there is the distinction between public carriers, who offer their transport services 'for hire or reward', and own-account operators or ancillary users (q.v.), who carry their own goods in connection with a trade or business that is not primarily a transport undertaking. The former are also called hauliers, although this term is generally not applied to parcels carriers or local delivery firms. The distinction was formalised by the carriers' licensing system introduced in 1934 (see LICENSING OF GOODS VEHICLE OPERATORS). One of its results was the publication of annual statistics, which help to illuminate the subsequent evolution of the industry.

Even before the Second World War, own-account operation was growing faster than public haulage; indeed the latter seems to have suffered a small decline. Between 1935 and 1938 the number of C-licence vehicles grew by 22 per cent to 372,000, while A- and B-licence vehicles fell by 4 per cent to 149,000. After the war, manufacturers were generally sceptical of the standards of service that nationalised transport would provide and following nationalisation many found that they were paying higher rates. In consequence, own-account operation advanced very rapidly; the number of vehicles it employed grew by 160 per cent between 1945 and 1951, compared with a 17 per cent increase in the public haulage fleet. The numbers of own-account vehicles continued to grow rapidly until 1962, when there were 1,227,000 compared with only 193,000 in public haulage. However, the C-licence vehicles were predominantly light vans, many used by the service industries rather than for carriage of goods. The comparable 1962 figures for heavy goods vehicles over 1½ tons unladen weight were 428,000 and 182,000.

When the licensing system changed in 1970, 121,000 firms were licensed to operate vehicles over 3.5 tonnes gross weight. The easier entry to the industry as a result of the replacement of 'quantity' by 'quality' licensing encouraged many newcomers to start up haulage businesses. By 1975 there were 143,000 licensed operators and the number of heavy goods vehicles had increased from about 490,000 to 563,000. At the same time own-account operators seeking back-loads were allowed to carry other firms' traffics. The market could not sustain this growth in capacity and many smaller firms failed. From 1978 the number of licences fluctuated around 130,000 until 1993, after which it declined to 110,000 in 2000. By this date the number of heavy goods vehicles had fallen to 397,000, although their size had increased (see WEIGHT LIMITS).

Public carriers typically employed larger vehicles and used them much more intensively, so a better measure of the relative importance of public haulage and own-account operation are the figures for goods lifted (tonnes) and goods moved (tonne-km), which are available from 1958. These show that from 1963 the public haulage sector became steadily more competitive and, except during the recession years 1978–84, slowly increased its market share. In 1963 it was responsible for 41 per cent of the tonnes lifted and 51 per cent of the tonne-km, but by the end of the century it was dominating the industry with 65 per cent of the tonnage and 75 per cent of the tonne-km. Much of this was attributable to the growing popularity of contract hire (q.v.).

The rise in the fortunes of the public carriers since the early 1980s coincided with an increase in the average length of haul from 74 km in 1981 to 94 km in 2000. In the last 25 years of the century, as cargo flow patterns (q.v.) changed, the tonnage of goods carried less than 100 km remained broadly constant, whereas longer-distance traffic doubled.

The second distinction is between public and private ownership. Nationalised road transport is dealt with in the articles on nationalisation (q.v.), denationalisation (q.v.), BRS (q.v.), the Transport Holding Company (q.v.), the National Freight Corporation (q.v.) and railway-owned road transport (q.v.). Here it is sufficient to note that, even when the combined fleets of BRS and British Railways reached a peak of 56,000 vehicles in 1951, there were still nearly twice that number of un-nationalised public haulage vehicles. Following the privatisation of Freightliners Ltd (q.v.) in 1996, the Post Office was the only remaining hire-or-reward operator in the public sector at the end of the century.

Thirdly, companies vary considerably in the size of their fleets. In 1938 over 60 per cent of public hauliers operated only one vehicle, over 90 per cent had fewer than five vehicles and there were only some 35 public hauliers, including the railway companies, with fleets of more than a hundred goods vehicles of all types. Some own-account operators who opposed nationalisation built up large fleets during the early post-war period, and the experience of nationalisation also seems to have encouraged more large public hauliers to emerge from the process of denationalisation. From the 1960s through to the end of the century the general pattern remained surprisingly uniform. There were some 300–400 fleets (public and own-account) with more than a hundred heavy goods vehicles. Fewer than one per cent of operators of heavy goods vehicles had fleets of more than 50, between them owning around 25 per cent of all vehicles over 3.5 tonnes gross. At the other end of the scale 86–89 per cent of operators still had fleets of five or less and 53–59 per cent operated only one vehicle, in spite of the disappearance of small manufacturers and traders serving local and regional markets that were their traditional customers.

The survival of many of these small operators, particularly the owner-drivers (q.v.), is linked to the growth of sub-contracting in its various forms. Some of the larger haulage contractors employ sub-contractors to cover workload peaks. Some manufacturing companies' transport departments now sub-contract to small hauliers instead of running their own fleet (see CEMENT TRAFFIC for an example); or they may have retained their trailer fleet and hire-in only the tractors and drivers. In the 1990s a new type of transport provider emerged that may be regarded as a successor to the clearing houses (q.v.): although acting as the customer's main transport contractor, it has neither vehicles nor drivers, but sub-contracts all the haulage work to small hauliers.

A fourth way in which operators can be categorised is by the type of service they provide, for example: general haulage, bulk loads, parcels, local delivery or specialised services for abnormal loads, bulk liquids, livestock or removals. There are no statistics which analyse operators in this way, but the statistics of body types and the commodities carried give some indication. In 1975 flat and sided open bodies predominated for general purpose vehicles over 3.5 tonnes gross weight. By 2000 their numbers had more than halved, while box bodies had increased to become the most prolific type. This was partly because box bodies provided more reliable weather protection and a better image, as well as saving the unproductive time required for sheeting and roping (q.v.). It also reflected changes in the mix of traffics. The bulk traffics – minerals, earths and stones, solid fuel and scrap metal – and traditional general haulage traffics like iron and steel, building materials and fertilisers have failed to grow or have declined, while the tonne-km of food and drink and retail products grew at least two-fold in the last quarter of the century. This period also saw a big increase in insulated and refrigerated vehicles, but a big reduction in the number of liquid tankers. **GAB**

See also CONSORTIA, GROWTH OF ROAD FREIGHT TRANSPORT, OUTSOURCING

Annual Reports of the Licensing Authorities, 1934–8 and 1947–2001; *Highway Statistics*, 1963–1973; *Transport Statistics Great Britain*, 1974–2001; Gwilliam and Mackie (1975)

Studebaker Distributors Ltd of Euston Road, London, sold this American truck in the UK in the 1930s. In the 1920s, before the levy of import duty in 1926, some car-derived vans were bought by prestigious UK customers, such as Bourne & Hollingsworth. The American parent company was never a major contender on the commercial vehicle market, but from 1928, when it merged with Pierce-Arrow, it developed a series of heavier vehicles. At the 1931 Commercial Motor Show models giving greater payloads (2- and 2½-tons) were displayed as Studebaker Pierce-Arrows (q.v.). In 1935 3-ton, 3 to 4- and 4 to 5-ton models were being advertised and in 1937 the distributors had a stand at the Commercial Motor Show, exhibiting 3-, 4- and 5-ton models, each with 'American all-steel cab' and the heavier ones with Hercules engines. One operator was Milex Transport Ltd of Spon Lane, West Bromwich, which operated both articulated and rigid versions of the Studebaker. Fisher Renwick replaced their Peerless lorries by Studebakers in the late 1920s. They were 3- and 4-ton normal-control

chassis with flat, van, and Luton bodies. They had five-speed gearboxes and hydraulic brakes and were described as 'fast and nippy'. During the Second World War 6-wheel Studebaker 2½-ton trucks served in the UK with American forces stationed here. **RAS**

CM (10 November 1931), p. 481, (8 November 1935), advert p. 39; Commercial Motor Transport Exhibition catalogue, November 1937; *CVRTC Newsletter* 10/80 (October 1980), p. 3; Baldwin and Ingram (1977), p. 13

Sub-depots. Long-distance hauliers operating into London often found it convenient to establish a sub-depot for London delivery and collection. The trunker driver handed over to a locally-based day driver, who undertook delivery and return-loading within the capital, handing back to the long distance driver for the return run. Flight Garage at Holloway (Parkhurst Garage of what was once an independent petrol distributor, Flight Petroleum Co. Ltd) was one such location. This privately-owned filling station with extensive garage accommodation was the London base in the 1950s for such firms as Ironfields of Accrington hauling cables and metals, Halls of Bury and Lloyds of Trafford Park, Manchester. Other sub-depots were situated on the fringe of greater London. One such in the 1960s was that of F & F Robinson (Stockton-on-Tees) Ltd, located at Marsh Lane, Ware, Herts, 20 miles north of London on the A10. Alternatively drivers might be changed at a transport café (q.v.) nearer to the midway point of the trunking run, such as Bob's Café at Dunsmore. Although mostly a London phenomenon, some hauliers serving Liverpool and Manchester also established them because of their dock traffic.

In the horse-drawn and early motor van era, London sub-depots operated in the outward direction. For example, Maple & Co. established six sub-depots at a distance of eight miles from their Tottenham Court Road store. These were then serviced each morning from the main store and the previous day's horse-van returned empty. In this way delivery radius was extended from 15 to 23 miles. Subsequently the use of motor vehicles encouraged the setting up of depots beyond greater London, for example at Ware and Guildford, giving a 55-mile delivery radius. **RAS**

J Cooper, 'From the A1 to Route 66', *VRS* 59 (June–August 1999), pp. 104–5; R Storey, 'Some aspects of transport in Ware', *Hertfordshire Past & Present*, 10 (1970), p. 46; information from E Lazarus; Gibson (2001), p. 51

Subsidy schemes were intended to provide a pool of suitable mechanical transport for the military without government incurring the expense of outright purchase. They were first considered in 1902 but abandoned due to insufficient vehicles being available. Reconsidered in 1905, the subvention scheme required two years' planning before instigating. Vehicles qualifying for the scheme were divided into two classes: Class A for traction engines with trailers and Class B for heavy motor cars. Class B was sub-divided into five further classes dependent on size. By registering the vehicle with the War Office, the owner guaranteed to maintain it and to sell or hire it to the War Office in time of war or national danger. Any vehicle that complied with the class groups could be registered subject to War Office inspection. Registration was for two years, extendable annually thereafter. The subsidy paid was £50 towards the purchase cost and £20 per annum towards operating costs. If the lorry was purchased by the War Office it promised to pay market price plus 25 per cent for disruption of trade. The vehicles registered were also to be available for army manoeuvres. If so employed their owners were paid a per diem rate of between £2 and £4 per vehicle, this to cover crew wages. The editor of *Commercial Motor* thought this rather mean.

An additional subsidy scheme was introduced in 1911, applicable to military specification lorries. Operating in parallel with the subvention scheme it was overly complex and equally unpopular. The subsidy paid failed to compensate the owner for the additional costs of operating a military specification vehicle and threats to discontinue the subvention scheme were used to encourage take-up of the subsidy scheme. These threats proved ineffective and there is no record of them being carried out.

With no Treasury funding available to purchase vehicles, the schemes were intended to provide a fleet of readily available lorries. By 1911 only 100 vehicles were registered throughout the country compared with over 600 with the simpler German subsidy scheme. The schemes were successful inasmuch as some 37,000 subsidy model lorries were built during the war years to standards approved beforehand by the War Office. These standards included the pedal layout (from left to right, clutch, brake and accelerator). There was also a subsidy scheme for horses, but this was not continued after the war, whereas that for lorries was, albeit in a different form.

The scheme was continued after the war, finally ending in 1935. In its later years it offered operators annual payments of ten per cent of the cost of the vehicle as well as a contribution towards its initial cost. A vehicle had to be available, if required, at 72 hours' notice, and if taken the owner received market value plus 25 per cent. However by the early 1930s the scheme was losing its appeal to potential users. Non-subsidy models were of simpler design, and cheaper to buy and operate. In addition the rules were changed from time to time, which probably added to potential users' distrust. **RL/JMA**

Sunter Brothers Ltd (Figure 50) of Northallerton, for decades prominent heavy hauliers, had their origins in the Yorkshire Dales in 1923, when Thomas and Joseph Sunter began operations with a Ford T, carrying agricultural produce. Their first move towards specialisation was into timber haulage, operating secondhand vehicles, rigid as well as articulated, their first new vehicle, an ERF, being bought in 1937. Sunters' experience with long timber loads led Robinsons of Stockton to subcontract steel traffic to them in the late 1930s, which prompted Sunters' move to Northallerton, as a more convenient base for Teesside–London running, although their timber work continued. Their first low-loading semi-trailer was acquired in 1943. Following nationalisation in 1947, they kept in motor transport by setting up Broadway Coaches, which was well placed for Catterick Camp traffic. On denationalisation in 1954 Sunters moved into the heavy haulage sector, with a Scammell Mountaineer and Contractor and a Foden 100-ton capacity ballast tractor. Adapted AEC Mammoth Majors, a Guy Invincible and Diamond T tractors were among vehicles joining the fleet, to which a Rotinoff was added for their Bradwell power station contract. These power units were matched by appropriate trailers and bogies, including 200-ton capacity Crane bogies. The business was registered as Sunter Brothers Ltd in 1957, Leonard and Rosa also being part of the family team. Sunters' fleet was enhanced by the acquisition of Crook & Willington Carriers after its founder's death, but Sunters' independent existence came to an end after the deaths of Joseph, followed by Thomas in 1963. In May 1964 Bulwark United Transport purchased Sunters with 40 special-type vehicles, a few months after United had acquired another prominent heavy haulier, Wynns. Sunters maintained their operating identity with Len's son, Peter, as managing director for nearly two decades after this change of ownership. Heavy haulage into Europe commenced in 1967, Volvo and Scania tractive units being acquired in this context. In addition to the Rotinoff, Sunters operated a number of other distinctive vehicles: a German Titan, a custom-built, normal-control six-wheel Atkinson ballast tractor and a Nicolas Tractomas, one of only about 50 built-to-order over twenty years by the French heavy trailer maker, which also supplied Sunters with hydraulic modular trailers. The Tractomas continued to operate for Econofreight Transport Ltd, at the time a joint BET/TDG concern, after it acquired Sunters in 1986. **RAS**

Tuck (1991), ch. 15; idem, (1985); idem., 'The fearless Frenchie', *Truck* (November 2001), pp. 104–5; Eaton (2001)

Sutton & Son (St Helens) Ltd (Figure 177). Alfred (Alf) Sutton joined A B Sutton & Sons, his mother's ailing domestic coal business, in 1923, after a dispute with his foreman at Lea Green colliery. He expanded, carrying to Liverpool. He then purchased a Leyland Hippo six-wheel flat working through Ex-Army Transport. Three years later he added a second-hand Leyland Cub and later a new AEC Mammoth Major diesel rigid eight-wheel lorry. During the war he acquired Mckinnell of Irlam, operating nine vehicles. The end of the war, a Labour government and impending nationalisation (q.v.) caused Alf Sutton to acquire the St Helen's Nuffield dealership, apparently to replace the haulage business. He also purchased Richard Pilkington, whose 33 vehicles included Vulcan tippers. A B Sutton was nationalised as a voluntary acquisition. He then accepted the post of manager of St Helens British Road Services (q.v.) Sherdley Road, becoming highly regarded for his achievements there. At denationalisation he was successful in tendering for 17 Special A-licenced vehicles and a service van. Apart from two Maudslays, the others were Atkinson rigid six-wheel flats. He also had two new Atkinson rigid eight-wheel flats, replacing unserviceable vehicles. He immediately started operating his London night trunk service. To increase carrying capacity he carried out his legendary conversions to rigid eights. He replaced the heavy chassis rails by lighter versions, adding the second steering axle and a trailing axle for the second driving axle. These, and an aluminium body, produced a rigid eight legally able to carry an extra four tons, giving a 16-ton payload. They also pulled a drawbar trailer. His next acquisition was Williams Bros of Peterborough, whose fleet included a Bedford articulated lorry. This eventually led to articulated units replacing the rigids and drawbar trailers. By 1970 the trunk services had expanded to serve Glasgow and the north east. He was also a member of the consortium which formed Transport Vehicles (Warrington) Ltd. Sutton operated five TVW vehicles. Sutton expanded in bulk liquids transport, at first through use of his patent 'Portolite', a rubber container intended to be unrolled to contain liquids in a normal dropside body. It has some use today, but in ISO 20 ft containers. At Alfred Sutton's death in 1987, his son Michael, managing director since 1978, became head of Sutton & Son (St Helens). The bulk liquids business expanded, to include an international ISO bulk liquids container operation. Sutton in 1999 was solely concerned with bulk liquids, recently winning a five year contract for all BP Chemical's bulk liquids distribution, including European deliveries. This required 70 vehicles. Sutton suffered problems and changes. A new chief executive, Andrew Callaghan was appointed in 2000 and began introducing the changes considered necessary to restore Sutton to their former pre-eminent position. The small amount of general haulage and storage was increased by distributing the packaged products produced by their bulk customers. By 2000 they had European bases or offices in Le Havre, Rotterdam and Langenfeld (Germany) and also a working partnership with Bourgey Montreuil, Edison, Houston and Chicago (USA) and Shanghai (China), Kuantan (Malaysia) and Tokyo. **GM**

Tuck (1989)

A **swap body** is a form of container for rail/road inter-modal use. See CONTAINERIS-ATION. The term is also used for convertible or interchangeable bodies (q.v.).

Swift Transport Services, like many other British road haulage businesses, began with one man, the ebullient Harold Swift (1903–80), and a single, worn-out, second-hand Albion lorry which cost him £7 10s in Skegness in 1928.

Harold Swift built up his business on general haulage in and around Lincolnshire. This included haulage for local builders and builder's merchants, the carriage of fresh vegetables from Lincolnshire farms to Covent Garden and other principal regional markets, the collection of milk, the delivery of coal and beer and a furniture removals business. He also established a strong relationship with Billy Butlin, carrying materials for the holiday camps Butlin developed at Skegness and Mablethorpe, ferrying dodgems and rides from one camp to another and transporting the animals Butlin kept in the small zoos he opened at several of his sites.

H & A Swift Ltd was incorporated in 1938 with an issued capital of £2500. By 1939 Harold Swift had a fleet of nine vehicles, nearly all Bedfords, and a turnover of under £8000. Ten years later the Swift fleet had grown to 15 vehicles. Harold Swift resisted nationalisation and his business was acquired by BRS through compulsory purchase. When BRS was broken up in the early 1950s, Harold Swift bought his business back and began trading once more as H & A Swift in 1954. The only lasting change made by BRS was to alter the livery from green to red.

During the 1950s Swift concentrated on purchasing Fords. By 1962 the fleet of 15 consisted of 14 Fords. Harold Swift also began to buy new vehicles – in 1968 19 of Swift's 29 vehicles were two years' old or less. At the same time Harold Swift transformed his business by winning a contract to deliver spare parts for Ford in East Anglia. Swift quickly won additional contracts and Ford soon accounted for 90 per cent of the company's business. In 1968 Swift employed almost 60 people, turned over £136,000 and made profits of £26,000.

Harold Swift's son, Rick, entered the business at his mother's request when his father fell ill in 1968 although Harold remained involved until his death in 1980. Rick's background was as a school teacher and so he felt a need for someone with considerable experience of the industry. Under Dennis Yardy, appointed Swift's first general manager in 1971, Swift began to expand its operations for Ford throughout the Midlands and into Wales. Premises built to cater for this expansion in Northampton in 1975 became the company's headquarters in 1982 and Skegness was closed in 1983. By 1975 the 75-strong fleet consisted of 53 Fords, 10 AECs and 8 Volvos with a handful of pickups and vans.

John Brotherton joined Swift from Ford in 1979 and under Yardy and Brotherton the business mirrored the changing shape of the industry as it moved from a regional to a national distribution business during the 1980s. The decisive moment in this transformation came in 1983 when Swift was awarded the UK parts distribution contract for Peugeot Talbot.

At the same time Swift was increasingly involved in the development of operational computer systems for tracking (q.v.) and logistics (q.v.).

While Swift continued to strengthen ties with Ford, investing heavily to meet Ford's shift to specialist roller-container operation, half of its turnover lay with other industrial distribution contracts for firms such as Rockware, Elida Gibbs, DSM Resins and Nacanco. By 1985, Swift's turnover stood at £14 million, pre-tax profits at nearly £1 million, employees at more than 450 and the fleet at 150 vehicles. Swift was now in the top 200 haulage businesses in the UK.

In 1985 Rick Swift decided to sell the business, as he felt it had grown too large and impersonal for him to continue to enjoy running it, and it became part of the LEP (q.v.) Group whose intention was to use Swift as the springboard for the development of distribution in Europe. LEP-Swift, as the European operation was called, was formed in 1987 and acquired transport companies in Germany, Holland, Belgium and Denmark. In the UK, Swift began the first non-parcels long distance, through-the-night, multiple-user delivery service in 1988 for Ford and Massey-Ferguson.

But LEP's over-ambitious expansion plans led to its collapse and the disintegration of LEP-Swift. At a traumatic time and after tortuous negotiations, Swift's management team negotiated a management buy-out of the business for £26 million in February 1992. Over the next 18 months, Swift continued to grow but lacked access to the capital necessary not only for continued UK growth but also for the European capability it needed. Swift sought tenders from interested parties for the acquisition of the business. When Swift finally relinquished its independence to Christian Salvesen (q.v.) for £85 million in October 1993, Swift Transport Services had a 750-strong fleet, more than 3,000 employees, 22 depots and a turnover in excess of £100 million. **NW**

Watson (1997)

T

The **tachograph** is an instrument mounted in the vehicle's dashboard, which indicates to the driver, time, speed and distance and provides a record of vehicle movements, the speeds at which it travelled and the distance covered. These data are recorded on special wax-coated circular charts against a 24-hour time scale. Tachograph fitment to most goods vehicles over 3.5 tonnes gross weight and certain passenger vehicles is required by law throughout the European Union to control the amount of time that drivers may spend behind the wheel in the interests of public safety.

Tachographs of this analogue type were first produced in Germany in 1927/8 and in the period 1936/7 Daimler-Benz and Krupp became the first vehicle manufacturers to fit the instruments as standard equipment. By 1938 the first instruments fully flush-mounted in the dashboard were in use. Development of the analogue tachograph progressed to the instrument known at the end of the century. In 1972 the first electronic version was produced and 1973 saw the introduction of instruments conforming to the EC specification in Annex 1 to Regulation 1463/70/EEC, which has since been replaced by Regulation 3821/85/EEC.

While tachographs were a legal necessity in Germany from 1953, the statutory requirement for their use in the UK was first specified in the Transport Act 1968. After a long battle with drivers and trade unions over the instrument's 'spy in the cab' image, they were fitted to relevant existing vehicles in 1979–81 and brought into compulsory use in 1982.

Analogue tachographs are driven from the vehicle gearbox via cable or electronic link. Two styluses within the instrument are activated to record speed and distance travelled and a third stylus records driver activity in accordance with the manual selection of activity modes by a switch on the face of the instrument. These recordings are made against time as the chart rotates, being driven from the integral clock.

Drivers have to keep their tachograph charts with them for all of the current week, plus the last chart from the previous week worked, and then hand them in to their employer within 21 days of their use. Where a vehicle is double-manned, it must be fitted with a tachograph capable of recording on two charts simultaneously. Drivers have to enter on the charts their name, date, vehicle registration number, and starting and finishing locations and mileages. Vehicles exempt from the need for a tachograph include postal vehicles and those used for collecting milk from farms.   **DL**

Manufacturers' literature from VDO Kienzle GmBH; David Lowe, *The Tachograph Manual* (2nd edn, Kogan Page, 1989); Foster (1978), p. 66

Tail-lifts (Figure 56), which originated in the USA, revolutionised deliveries to smaller premises, as the driver could now deliver heavy items –– even pallets and roll-cages –– without needing a fork-lift truck or, indeed, assistance of any sort. Following publication of the Manual Handling Operations Regulations 1992, which imposed on employers the duty of preventing lifting injuries, particularly back injuries, the use of tail-lifts increased and they are to be seen on all types of vehicles, including semi-trailers, from 3.5 tonnes upwards.

The two main types of tail-lift are column and cantilever. First in the UK was the column type introduced by Ratcliff Tail Lifts in 1948, while the first cantilever ones were produced by Anthony Hoists. Column lifts, as the name implies, work on a column mounted on each side of the rear opening aperture of a body, while cantilever ones are ram operated with the mechanism mounted on or below the chassis frame at the rear. A disadvantage of both types is that when not in use the platform is stowed in an upright position behind the rear roller shutter, meaning a vehicle cannot be backed up to a loading bank. A development of the cantilever type is the retractable, tuck-away or tuck-under platform which folds into two and is stowed below the chassis at the rear. This variant is popular with rental companies since it can be locked out of use when not required (or paid for), enabling a tail-lift fitted vehicle to be rented out at a lower rate.

Recent design innovations include Ray Smith's Night Owl, which has a sound-deadened electro-hydraulic power unit and a platform coated with a non-slip noise-deadening material, while Ratcliff has a Rear Frame lift which combines the rear frame of the vehicle's body with a rear closure and tail-lift in a single unit.   **JMA/GM**

Target Express was founded in 1982, concentrating on business-to-business parcel delivery in such growth sectors as electronics, information technology and pharmaceuticals. In 2000 when it was operating from 43 depots in the UK and Ireland, it was the subject of a management buyout, supported by 3i. Some of its operations were undertaken by sub-contractors such as Harry Heer Transport.

RAS

MT (24 February 2000); *Evening Standard* (21 February 2000).

Tarpaulins, see LOADING AND UNLOADING; SHEETING AND ROPING

Tartan Arrow Service Ltd was formed by John Chester in 1953 to operate a next-day parcel service between London and Scotland using denationalised BRS units. It became a public company in 1964.

In 1965 the firm contracted to send its goods by rail for the trunk haul, in order to achieve faster transits, and invested in rail-connected depots at Kentish Town and Bridgeton. Its trains, conveying both vans for parcels and smalls and containers, began a nightly service in late 1966. To avoid the operation being caught up in the 'open terminals' dispute with the National Union of Railwaymen (see FREIGHTLINERS LTD), the company was bought by the Transport Holding Co. (q.v.) in 1967-7, becoming part of the Tayforth (q.v.) Group, later passing to the NFC (q.v.). The service ceased in 1976.   **GAB**

T R Gourvish, *British Railways 1948-1973: a Business History* (Cambridge: Cambridge University Press, 1986), p. 546; Alan A Jackson, *The Railway*

Dictionary (Stroud: Alan Sutton, 1996), p. 276; *Modern Railways*

Taskers of Andover (1932) Ltd, trailer manufacturers, originated in the business founded by Robert Tasker, a country blacksmith, which moved in 1813 to Anna Valley, the site of the developing enterprise for over a century and a half. The title Waterloo Ironworks was applied in the 1830s. Taskers' involvement with road transport began with horse-drawn wagon manufacture, but in 1869 the firm's first steam traction engine, 'Hero', took to the road, the result of the initiative of Henry Tasker, the founder's grandson. By 1878 eighteen self-moving engines had been built.

Around 1900, changing legislation opened the way for a light road engine below 5 tons and Taskers produced the Little Giant light road-going steam tractor. The claim was made that it could haul a trailer loaded to 13 tons. The engine could be oil-fired. A wagon version was brought out in 1909.

These steam vehicles were successful, but the firm was not: Henry Tasker had been obliged to buy out the shares of his two predeceased brothers and had selected George Hoare, son of his coachman, to share the running of the limited liability company, W Tasker & Sons Ltd, which he founded in 1896. Possibly as a result of its move into machinery hiring, it went into receivership in 1903, but continued to trade. A new company, under the same name, was registered in 1907, without any Tasker family participation; however, continued involvement in machinery hiring seems to have contributed to another financial crisis. For the duration of the war, government contracts kept the firm going.

Taskers was then in serious financial difficulty with the onset of the post-war depression. An articulated steam wagon was produced in 1922, but remained a prototype. An agreement of 1923 to produce the American single-wheel Autohorse tractor unit produced no results and the firm went into voluntary liquidation in 1926. Now antiquated and run-down, it was sold to a triumvirate of businessmen and professionals, including Lt-

Col D S Kennedy, who brought Indian Army contacts, useful for orders and who developed such mechanical devices as military vehicle chain tracks. The son of one of the new directors, A B Fuller, who was a trained and experienced manufacturing engineer, also joined the firm at this time. Various orders kept Taskers going, but a split arose in 1929, when Kennedy and the works manager left to set up their own engineering business.

Taskers' new management specialised in trailers, obtaining important orders from Chaplins (q.v.), and the War Department. Significant technical developments at this time were the Tasker ball-coupling, later combined with a ramp-coupling design, and an articulated rear bogie low-loading trailer.

There was yet another voluntary liquidation and the foundation of Taskers of Andover (1932) Ltd, with one of the 1927 purchasers, A L Fuller, as chairman and his son, A B Fuller, as managing director. Concentration on semi-trailer production and the installation of new equipment followed, the introduction of electric arc welding in 1936 being a vital innovation. A policy of using relatively few standard components and sourcing as far as possible in-house was adopted, with outside sourcing, for example Bendix servo brakes, where necessary. In addition to heavier semi-trailers, semis for light articulated units of 3 tons unladen weight were produced, sizeable orders being obtained from two Southampton firms: Taggart, Morgan & Coles, and George Baker.

War Office orders increased in significance as re-armament quickened pace, notably a high-loading semi-trailer for carrying aircraft wings to be followed by the firm's most famous product, the Queen Mary (q.v.) semi- trailer for the transport of aircraft fuselages, a total of 3586 being built. Civilian priority trailers brought wartime production to over 19,000 units, requiring works extension and new plant, such as a turn-over jig for the Queen Mary production.

After the war, the Easiload for pantechnicon requirements was developed from the Queen Mary. Four hundred 20-ton trailers were ordered by the Ministry of Supply and 1,250 low-loaders were produced for the transport of

sections of the AIROH aluminium prefabricated house. This provided an important contract for Taskers during the transition to the post-war market. For a few years from 1947 diversification into the production of light car trailers and caravan chassis took place, side-by-side with the manufacture of a variety of heavy commercial trailers. The Air Ministry and the aviation industry continued to be important customers and exports also took a significant amount of Taskers' output. The advent of BRS in 1948 provided a major customer requiring standardisation of units and Taskers reacted positively to this new opportunity. BRS exerted its influence to bring about standardisation of tractor-trailer coupling, by the fifth-wheel (q.v.). Other significant post-war customers included British Railways, the GPO and the Services.

In 1962 new premises were built at Andover, in the following year a second factory, at Cumbernauld, and a third, at Skelmersdale, in 1965. In the mid-1960s spares were kept for all models up to ten years old, older models being catered for by special order. Taskers' product range at this period was large, including straight-frame semi-trailers, drop-frame and step-frame machinery low-loaders, the Easiload chassis, van bodies on semi-trailers, deep-step chassis, tipper and tanker semis, and cable drum and timber pole carriers. Special trailer production included for Freightliners, oilfield and aircraft low-length semis, draw and agricultural trailers. In addition, regular production included bogies for load carriers and converter dollies.

In November 1968 Taskers was acquired by the John Brown & Co. Group, as a wholly-owned subsidiary of Cravens Industries Ltd, in parallel with the Cravens Homalloy (q.v.) group. Cravens Tasker closed the Andover works in 1984.   **RWK/RAS**

Rolt (1969); illustrated product brochure (c.1966): MSS.226X/IND/132 in University of Warwick, Modern Records Centre; some records survive with Hampshire County Council Museums Service, Winchester

Tate & Lyle Transport Ltd (Figure 55). The origins of the business which eventually became Tate & Lyle Transport Ltd pre-date sugar refining by Henry Tate and Abraham Lyle in London, Liverpool and Greenock. Before 1840 Robert Pease was trading in the raw materials of soap and glue and in 1893 acquired premises at Wandle Wharf Wandsworth, which were in continuous use until 1975. In 1912 Tate and Lyle began to use Pease Transport for delivery of their products from Wandle Wharf, while transport in Liverpool and Greenock was owned and operated by the respective refineries. During this period steam wagons, including Leylands and Atkinsons, replaced horse-drawn vehicles and McCurd petrol-engined lorries were operated.

In 1921 Henry Tate & Sons and Abraham Lyle & Sons combined to form Tate & Lyle Ltd. In 1936 Pease & Son, the official name, became a fully owned subsidiary of Tate & Lyle. During the 1930s Foden diesel lorries began to replace the steam wagons and Bedfords, particularly the WTL model, were favoured for the lighter work. Articulation commenced in the form of chain-driven Scammells with both flatbed and box trailers though initially the trailers had no provision for being separated from the units.

Recovery from the Second World War was slow, sugar not being de-rationed until 1953. Pease Transport operated on a C licence with sugar being taken to the outer parts of the sales area in the main by A-licence hauliers for distributors to make the final movement. From 1950 onwards the business began to expand in a number of ways. Depots were acquired or built at Caversham, just outside Reading, Totton near Southampton, Keynsham east of Bristol, Taunton, Tavistock, Daventry, Elmswell and later at Cardiff.

A major development was the movement of dry granulated sugar in bulk. This commenced with the use of aluminium tanks mounted on Bedford O chassis. Discharge was by gravity, deliveries being made to Huntley & Palmers of Reading and Peak Frean of Bermondsey. A packing station was opened at the Keynsham depot with the sugar being transported in 8-wheeled AEC tankers, one of which was depicted on the cheques sent out to suppliers by Pease Transport. The AEC tankers were supplanted by Foden 8-wheeled tankers, one or two of which pulled drawbar trailers.

The next move in bulk sugar delivery was the use of pneumatics. Tate & Lyle was in the forefront in the development of this technique. Liquid sugar tankers in use at that time had the load discharged through electric or power-take-off driven pumps.

The 1968 Transport Act enabled Tate & Lyle Transport to distribute products other than sugar. This development, referred to as multiple distribution, commenced in a small way at Totton depot. This diversification was matched by the engineering function: commercial vehicle sales and servicing through dealerships at new premises for ERF vehicles at Tottenham, Foden at Avonmouth and Mercedes-Benz in Scotland.

The pattern of sugar distribution was now changing rapidly with the introduction initially of cash-and-carry stores and then supermarkets. The small multiple shops were rapidly eliminated and the independents went to cash and carries. T&L's shop delivery fleet was rapidly reduced and closure of Wandsworth depot was followed by Daventry and Elmswell. In each case link services were introduced, this being a far more cost-effective option. The articulated fleet developed to meet the increase in target deliveries, from Bedford S types to Commers, followed by AEC Mercurys, then Leyland Lynxes, and onto the larger Foden S80 and Leyland Buffalo models. Likewise the 8-wheel rigid Foden pneumatic tankers began to be replaced by articulated combinations with both Foden S80 and Leyland Buffalo units.

The mid-1970s saw the introduction of Mercedes-Benz vehicles at a time when British manufacturers were struggling to meet the demand. The continental makes, including Volvo, Scania and Mercedes-Benz, had improved performance and far better driver facilities. The trusty, highly fuel-efficient slow-revving Gardner engine was now outclassed by the turbo-charged continental challengers. The engineering staff, being very loyal to British products, did not look kindly at first upon the

Mercedes-Benz vehicles being introduced in London.

Following the partial denationalisation of road haulage, Tate & Lyle set up an A-licence operation under the name of Silver Roadways, the nucleus being ex-BRS staff and vehicles from the former General Roadways (q.v.). By setting up clearing house offices in locations near the main sugar depots, Silver Roadways vehicles were able to run loaded in both directions, whereas, other than for a very small movement of tinplate and paper materials for packing, all the Tate & Lyle Transport vehicles used on stocking the depots returned empty to the refinery. Silver Roadways made extensive use of sub-contractors in order to ensure that sufficient work was available for the return loads for its own fleet, which peaked at around 65 vehicles.

Whilst originally the vehicles employed tended to reflect those used by Tate & Lyle Transport, Silver Roadways first bought Mercedes-Benz vehicles many years before Tate & Lyle Transport and had some of the earliest post-war Mercedes-Benz vehicles operated in this country. They also operated one of the pre-production Ford Transcontinental articulated units. The 1980s onwards saw a reduction in the Tate & Lyle Transport fleet, the sale of the multiple distribution operation and finally the remainder of the bulk fleet to Hoyer (q.v.).

For many years Pease Transport and Tate & Lyle Transport maintained a tradition of a strong engineering base working closely with manufacturers and suppliers helping to develop easy access covered vehicles, pneumatic handling, air suspension and low deck height vehicles.   **JL**

Unpublished history of Tate & Lyle Transport by Jeff Lemon available at the Tate & Lyle Archive.

Tautliner, see BOALLOY INDUSTRIES LTD

Tayforth Ltd began life in the late 1940s as a public company to look after the warehousing and cold storage activities of the Alexander family which had sold its extensive bus operations in Scotland at nationalisation and invested instead in such services. At denationalisation in 1954 Alexanders bought some of BRS's depots, lorries and licences and set up Road Services (Caledonian) Ltd and Road Services (Forth) Ltd as subsidiaries of Tayforth Ltd. In 1954–6 Coast Lines Ltd, the coastal shipping combine, sold its Scottish road transport feeders to Tayforth, being paid in Tayforth shares. In the late 1950s Tayforth developed its business by acquiring a number of haulage subsidiaries: Bell & Co. (Transport) Ltd, Siddle C Cook Ltd (see ELDDIS TRANSPORT), Hanson Haulage Ltd, D McKinnon (Transport) Ltd and Watsons (Carriers) Ltd. Two contituent companies, Caledonian Bulk Liquids Ltd and Scottish Parcel Carriers Ltd were created from various other Tayforth companies.

Facing increasing competition in a harsh market, Tayforth offered itself for nationalisation in 1965. The Transport Holding Co. (q.v.) bought a 75 per cent share, the remaining 25 per cent continuing to be owned by Coast Lines and Alexanders. This was seen as a radical new approach in forming a partnership between public and private ownership. The THC maintained a Tayforth group within its organisational structure, rather than integrating it into the British Road Services, BRS Parcels and Pickfords groups, and further acquisitions were added to it: Bridges Transport Ltd (q.v.) in 1966, J & E Transport Ltd in 1967 and H S Morgan Transport (Southampton) Ltd in 1968.

When the National Freight Corporation (q.v.) was formed in 1969, Tayforth Ltd and its subsidiaries with a total of some 1600 vehicles were transferred to it, along with the THC's other freight interests. Tayforth's non-transport subsidiaries were disposed of and its transport companies divided between the three divisions into which the NFC now organised itself: general haulage (to which Tayforth contributed 1000 vehicles and 17 depots), parcels (550 vehicles and 11 depots) and special traffics. In 1970 the outstanding 25 per cent holding in the Tayforth companies was acquired by the NFC, but Tayforth Ltd and its general haulage subsidiaries continued to be a separately identified part of the general haulage division until 1980, when the Tayforth name was dropped. **GM/GAB**

Transport Holding Company, *Annual Reports & Accounts,* 1965-8; National Freight Corporation, *Annual Reports & Accounts,* 1969-80

Temperature-controlled transport (Figures 58 and 179). At the beginning of the twentieth century refrigerated transport was used for fish (q.v.) and for longer-distance movements of imported frozen meat (q.v.) by rail to cold stores. Fish were packed directly in ice in fishboxes, but the frozen meat was carried in vans which were insulated by means of an airspace between double wooden walls and refrigerated by built-in ice tanks. The ice was now generally made by mechanical refrigeration plant in ice factories at the ports, which had largely supplanted for this purpose the natural ice imported from Norway. In the 1920s road haulage adopted these methods when it began to carry some of the longer-distance traffic. Cork insulation, dry ice (solid carbon dioxide with brand names such as ICI's Drikold) and refrigerated containers were all introduced in the late 1920s.

At this period other perishable foodstuffs — fresh meat, milk (q.v.) in churns, fruit and vegetables (q.v.) — were carried in vehicles with louvred or slat sides, to allow air to circulate over them during transit. Milk, pre-cooled at the farm, began to travel in insulated road tankers in the mid-1920s. The Union Cold Storage Company's movement of meat to its retail outlets, Dewhursts, was one of the earliest refrigerated road distribution systems, while both SPD Ltd (q.v.), which carried for T. Wall & Sons, and J Lyons & Co. (q.v.) developed methods of distributing ice-cream. The commonest food vehicle seen on the road in the inter-war years was not a mechanically-propelled vehicle but the Wall's Stop-Me-And-Buy-One tricycle.

The frozen food revolution began in 1947/8 when Birds Eye Foods Ltd, set up by Unilever, introduced frozen peas and other vegetables, for which SPD established a network of cold stores and distribution services. The product range was extended as food rationing was withdrawn and, following the introduction of television advertising (1954) and fish fingers (1955), there was an extremely rapid growth in demand for frozen foods, particularly from working married women. SPD developed a fleet of four-axle insulated vehicles capable of carrying up to 14 tons, known as 'Fish Fillet Specials', to distribute frozen fish from the former MacFisheries plant in Grimsby. The growing market led to the introduction of improved refrigeration systems for road vehicles and containers. The British Oxygen Co's Polarstream system, which released controlled amounts of liquid nitrogen, was simpler, but mechanical refrigeration units became universal. With both systems, the temperature could be thermostatically-controlled to the range of temperatures appropriate to the particular type of food. It was this that led to the introduction of the term temperature-controlled transport. Concerns about health risks from incorrectly-handled frozen foods during transport led to the publication of a code of practice by the Royal Society for the Promotion of Health in 1965. This was overtaken by the ATP (q.v.) agreement in 1971.

Multiple retailers followed suit by establishing their own distribution systems. Sainsbury's (q.v.) bought a refrigerated fleet of 12-ton TK Bedford vans in c.1964. This type of vehicle became the workhorse of the industry. Rigid-bodied two-axle 'reefer' vans, frequently equipped with Thermo King refrigeration units, were used by specialist frozen-food firms up to the end of the twentieth century. Sainsbury's acquisition of a large regional distribution depot at Basingstoke in 1962, designed from the outset to handle frozen foods as well as other produce, was a pattern for the future. Larger vehicles and refrigerated trailers began to be used for trunking from the 1970s. The expansion in the range of frozen-food products, particularly ready-prepared meals and commercial cook-freeze catering for airlines and large-scale institutions such as hospitals, generated further market growth in the 1970s and 1980s.

The 1970s also saw supermarket chains begin to employ specialist contractors operating refrigerated trailers. Nevertheless Sainsburys retained a lorry fleet of 425 vehicles in 1981, though numbers had fallen to 386 by 1990. Out-sourcing logistics became a major trend in the 1990s with specialist firms offering to store and transport foodstuffs using a wider range of controlled bands below ambient temperatures, from produce to chilled and frozen. The growing range of products, which now include fresh fruit and vegetables, made the temperature-controlled trailers of firms such as Wincanton (q.v.), Exel (q.v.), Gist (formerly BOC Distribution), Frigoscandia and Christian Salvesen (q.v.) a familiar sight on Britain's motorways. Another development of the 1990s was the big increase in imports of exotic perishable produce as air freight (q.v.). Energy consciousness led to attempts to power refrigeration units by solar panels on the trailer roof. During the 1990s the dependence on large trailer units encouraged some variation in the low-temperature vehicles used. The development of town-centre convenience stores required the use of smaller rigid-bodied vehicles. This was accompanied by the growth of courier firms operating refrigerated vans capable of handling loads from 200 to 300 litres, as smaller refrigeration units (Hubbard, Carrier) became available. By the end of the twentieth century rental firms offered refrigerated vans for hire. Nevertheless, in 2000 the 15 principal retailers operated 3486 temperature-controlled trailers, of which 1495 were owned by Safeway and nearly 1300 by Sainsburys. However, the desire to maximise space utilisation in trailers has led to the development of composite vehicles, capable of operating at different temperatures for different loads. In 2000, there were almost 3000 composite trailers in use, of which Tesco operated 1200.   **DJO**

See also TRANSFRIGOROUTE

Temperature-controlled Food Transport: code of practice on construction, maintenance and operation (Royal Society for the Promotion of Health, 1965); R David, 'The demise of the Anglo-Norwegian ice trade', *Business History*, 37 (1995), p. 66; Elizabeth David, *Harvest of the Cold Months: the social history of ice and ices* (Joseph, 1994); W J Reader, *Birds Eye: the early years* (Walton-on-Thames: Birds Eye Foods, 1963); Bridget Williams, *The Best*

Butter in the World: a history of Sainsbury's (Ebury, 1994), p. 141; J Sainsbury plc, *Annual Review 1998*, p. 24; N Finegan & T Patel (ed), *Retail Logistics 2001*, pp. 30–1

Thames, see FORDSON

The **Thames Ironworks, Shipbuilding & Engineering Co. Ltd,** a remnant of London's shipbuilding industry, was a small and short-lived producer, at Greenwich, of cars, public service vehicles and commercial vehicles from 1905 to liquidation in 1914. Its initial vehicles were steam-powered, but motor vehicles soon predominated. These included light commercials (vans and 3-ton lorries), as well as the lorry chassis, cars and taxis for which it was probably better known. A cache of glass negatives of Thames products survives in the archive of Chivers of Histon, having been transferred by Henry Jones when he moved from Thames Ironworks to Chivers.   **RAS**

R C Haughey, 'Thames Ironworks', *VCV*, 81 (September 1996), p. 23

Thatcham Road Transport Services provides a good example of a road haulage business changing its name, ownership and, to some extent, activities over a period of time. Wilfred Street set up in business in 1919, operating from a public house yard in Thatcham, near Newbury, Berkshire, contracting to work for the local Colthrop Board & Paper Mills. The rates proving uneconomic, Street, together with Sydney Ashman, set up as general hauliers under the title Thatcham Road Transport Services, operationally identified as TRTS. Steam lorries were followed by Albions and then Fodens. The expansion of the business led to the acquisition of a larger depot, which included warehousing, workshops and a filling station. A private limited company had been established in 1936; nationalisation into the Reading Group of BRS occurred in 1949.

The Thatcham depot and its fleet were denationalised in 1953 as the Cropper & Colthrop Transport Co. Ltd, finance coming from Cropper & Co. and the Colthrop Mills (thus taking traffic back to the origins of Street's business). When the Reed paper group shortly after took over the Colthrop Mills, the Thatcham operation became part of Reed Transport Ltd. Over 100 vehicles were operated in the 1960s, more than 70 of them being on A licences. Cropper & Colthrop had established nightly trunking in association with Poplar Motors of Lymm in Cheshire. Reed expanded trunking in various directions, but broke the link with Poplar Motors after acquiring a firm at Wigan. In 1985 the TRTS depot was closed and replaced by a smaller one, operated by SCA Transport since 1987, when Reed sold out to the Swedish conglomerate SCA. The closure of the Colthrop Board Mill was announced in 2000.

SW/RAS

Thomas Nationwide Transport, see TNT

Thompson, Sir Peter (b.1928) was the chairman of National Freight Corporation (q.v.) when it was privatised in 1981 by an employee buyout. Thompson was educated at the Warehousemen, Clerks & Drapers School near Croydon and Bradford Grammar School before national service in the Royal Armoured Corps. He read economics at Leeds University. He joined the Unilever management trainee scheme, specialising in transport, and then went on to GKN for a couple of years before joining the Rank Organisation to head its transport operations for a similar period. In 1966 he was appointed head of the Transport and Shipping Operations of the newly-nationalised British Steel which put most of its road transport through BRS.

In 1972 he was recruited to head BRS when Len Payne moved on to the National Freight Corporation's headquarters organisation where the chairman was Daniel Pettit (q.v.). Thompson was responsible for 9000 vehicles, 11,000 employees and 120 depots. The general haulage business was losing money and Thompson cut the size of the headquarters, devolved many decisions, and tried to build up contract hire and truck rental where profits could be made. In 1973 he clashed with Alan Law (q.v.), the powerful Transport & General Workers Union leader, over a £3 per week premium being demanded for drivers holding a heavy goods vehicle licence. A four-week strike ensued. BRS did not pay the premium. As a result of Thompson's leadership in the 1970s BRS became increasingly profitable.

In 1976 Thompson was recruited as vice-chairman operations for NFC, the parent body. It had lost money, about £30 million in 1975, because the parcels business and European companies were making losses larger than the profits of BRS and Pickfords (q.v.). Thompson took drastic measures, changing nearly all the top management team, closing the European subsidiaries, and making 'massive redundancies' in National Carriers (q.v.) which was making huge losses. New services were introduced, such as Fashionflow for Marks & Spencer, separating and boosting the travel side of Pickfords, and by introducing truck rentals. Slowly the losses were reduced so that by the end of the 1970s NFC was making reasonable returns.

The story of NFC's privatisation under the Thatcher government is covered under the entry on NFC. Thompson's part as the chief executive was crucial. He had a left-wing leaning, hence his willingness to work for nationalised industries, and his views on fairness and the need for unity of purpose between managers and workforce were influential in bringing about an employee buy-out rather than the simpler management buy-out. He devoted much time to touring the depots and persuading the workers of the opportunities available, despite the official opposition of some of the unions involved. The success of NFC after the buy-out until its flotation in 1991 was synonymous with Thompson, who remained chairman until 1991 and was then president until 1993. He broke with the company because he felt the core values of co-operation, participation and consultation were being eroded and a more managerial approach adopted. **JA**

Thompson (1991); *idem, Long Range Planning,* 18 (1985), pp. 19–27

Thornycroft (Figure 88), the bus and lorry manufacturer, had its origins in steam power. The founder, John Isaac Thornycroft (1843–

1928), designed a steam vehicle at the age of 19 but discouraged by the restrictions of the Locomotives Act of 1865, he turned to steam launch design and production. His son, John Edward (1872–1960), and the 1896 Act encouraged him to return to steam road locomotion, with a vertical-boilered 1-ton van. The Steam Carriage & Wagon Co. Ltd was established at Chiswick, expanding to a new site at Basingstoke in 1898. Two larger vans followed in 1898, one a tipper marketed as Stewart-Thornycroft.

Paraffin- and petrol-engined vehicles were introduced in 1902. A petrol chassis with single chain drive was followed in 1905 by a more powerful one with twin-chain transmission used for some lorries including a number for the GWR. A 2-ton lorry and steam gun tractor were produced for the army, beginning a long association of Thornycroft with military vehicle production. Steam vehicle production ceased in 1907, although a licensing agreement with D Stewart (1902) Ltd of Glasgow continued until 1911. With the ending of steam road vehicle manufacture, the motor side became a division of John I Thornycroft & Co. Ltd, which was also involved in marine construction.

The Thornycroft J type 4-ton wagon introduced in 1912 was accepted for the War Office subsidy scheme (q.v.) and wartime production concentrated on this, with an output of 4500. By the time production of the J type ceased in 1927 over 7000 had been made. Inter-war model development included a 30-cwt A1 subsidy-type chassis, a new three-ton lorry and a rigid six. The A1, introduced in 1924, helped to carry the firm through the difficult 1920s trading conditions. From 1933 a plethora of type names appeared, including the Trusty, Handy and Nippy. Between the wars the mainline railway companies were important customers, the GWR operating models ranging from the 30-cwt A1, as parcels vans and flat lorries, to the 10-ton JC 6-wheeler for the Theale & Great Western Sand & Ballast Co. and including chassis for Ransomes & Rapier cranes. In 1929 the GWR ordered 100 4-ton Thornycroft chassis and Thornycroft advertised that the LNER had ordered 69 A1 vehicles in a single year. Second World War production included Bren gun

carriers, the Nubian 4-wheel drive, over 2000 Amazon chassis for Coles EMA [Electric Mobile Aerodrome] cranes for the RAF, and Nippy and Sturdy types for essential civilian users.

In 1948 vehicle production became a wholly owned subsidiary, Transport Equipment (Thornycroft) Ltd. The Sturdy and Nippy continued in production and new six and eight wheelers were added, but manufacture for overseas and specialised markets became increasingly significant, the Mighty Antar 85-ton tractor being introduced in 1950 for oilfield work, but finding additional military and heavy haulage employment. Ford initiated collaboration with Thornycroft in 1960–1 on a heavier weight range. Four prototypes were built, but then Thornycroft's situation changed. The capacity of the Basingstoke works was under-utilised by 1961 and attracted a takeover by ACV. Three generations of the family had been in control from the foundation of the company to its sale in 1961. By the end of 1961 production of goods models ceased, remaining stock being sold to Oswald Tillotson & Co. Ltd. Basingstoke production continued with the Nubian airfield emergency vehicle, and the Antar to which were added the AEC Militant and Dumptruk and Scammell Townsman, and gearboxes after AEC and Leyland merged. After the closure of the Basingstoke works in 1972, production of Thornycroft models continued at Scammells' Watford works. The last Thornycroft spares and equipment were moved from Basingstoke in 1973. **RWK/RAS**

Baldwin (1989); Kelley (1973); Klapper (1973); Marshall and Bishop (1972 and 1979); H J Sheryn, *An Illustrated History of Cranes* (Ian Allan, 1997); Stevens-Stratten, (1988 and 1978); Stevens-Stratten and Aldridge (1987); Townsin (2001); Sir John E Thornycroft, 'Early trials and tribulations', *Motor Transport Supplement* (10 June 1955), p. 7; M Wilson and K Spink, *Coles 100 Years: the growth story of Europe's leading crane manufacturer 1879–1979* (Uxbridge: Coles Cranes, 1978); K C Barnaby, *100 Years of Specialised Shipbuilding and Engineering* (Hutchinson, 1964); handbook of first Thornycroft Society rally, Basingstoke, 23 June 1991; some records survive with the Hampshire County Council Museums Service, Winchester

Three-wheelers, see VANS

Tibbett & Britten. To John Tibbett, who began delivering for London's East End 'rag trade' to the West End shops in the 1950s, goes the credit of developing the technique of carrying clothes on hangers (see GARMENT CARRIAGE). He was joined by Frank Britten and the business was incorporated as Tibbett & Britten Ltd in 1958. It expanded slowly through the 1960s, then in 1969 John Harvey, chairman of SPD Ltd (q.v.), arranged for SPD and the Dutch carrier, Van Gend & Loos, each to buy a 37½ per cent share in order to finance major expansion. Moving its headquarters to Tottenham, it soon established itself as the first nationwide hanging garment carrier. It won its first contract with Marks & Spencer in 1973 and over the next decade took over all hanging garment distribution for M&S and its suppliers.

In 1984, following SPD's decision to sell its transport operations, Harvey led a management buyout of T&B. In 1986 he launched it as a public company, Tibbett & Britten Group plc, in order to finance further expansion in three directions. First was diversification into distribution of consumer goods other than clothing. By 1989 it had contracts with manufacturers, such as Colgate-Palmolive and Black & Decker, and with high street and supermarket chains, Woolworth, Asda and Sainsbury. International expansion began in 1989 through a series of acquisitions, mainly in North America and Europe. Then in 1992 T&B entered the car delivery (q.v.) market through the acquisition of Silcock Express Ltd, followed by Toleman Ltd in 1994. These it consolidated into Axial Ltd, but profits were disappointing and T&B withdrew from this market in 2001 and sold Axial. Between 1985 and 2000. Harvey took T&B from a niche operator with 1500 employees to one of the leading international logistics companies employing 20,000. He was still chairman in 2002. **JMA/GAB**

IDCH, 32 (2000) pp. 449–52; *CM* (21 March 2002)

Tilling, Thomas, Ltd originated in 1847 in Peckham, south-east London as a jobmaster

and horse-bus operator, later taking up the motor-bus and investing in its manufacture. Although best known as bus operators, in the provinces as well as London, Tillings was also a substantial operator of goods vehicles, mostly on contract hire. It was one of the earliest operators of mechanically-propelled vehicles on behalf of the General Post Office, and by 1905 ran a London–Brighton route with three Milnes-Daimlers. By 1921 it offered regular London to Bristol, Birmingham, Liverpool and Manchester haulage services. Contract customers later also included Macfarlane, Lang & Co. Ltd, the biscuit manufacturers, George Vickers Ltd of Brixton, newspaper and magazine distributor and Cadbury Brothers which hired 12 Dennis lorries. In the mid-1930s Tilling took over E W Rudd (q.v.). Tilling's Commercial Motor Department suffered severe damage to vehicles and premises from enemy action on several occasions during the Second World War. The company claimed to be the first to have operated a rigid 8-wheeler with a drawbar trailer when the law was changed in the Second World War. In 1948 Tilling was one of the 'lead' companies which voluntarily sold to the British Transport Commission for £25 million. Tillings' managing director at the time, Sir Frederick Heaton, favoured integration and was prepared to accept nationalisation if that was the only way to bring it about. Some 880 goods vehicles and 120 horses as well as 8200 buses and coaches passed into public ownership and Tillings' modern depot in south-east London became BRS 9A Newington Butts. **RWK/RAS**

Ingram and Mustoe (1999); *DBB*, 3 (1985), pp. 148–51; Anon., *The War that Went on Wheels* (Tilling, 1945; Bradford: Autobus Review, 1978); Tilling (1957)

Tilling-Stevens Ltd of Maidstone, Kent originated as W A Stevens Ltd, electrical engineers, in 1897. Thomas Tilling (q.v.), a major customer, held a substantial shareholding from 1911 to 1930, when the business was reconstituted as T S Motors Ltd. On the acquisition of Vulcan in 1937 the name reverted to Tilling-Stevens Ltd. Although best known for its petrol-electric buses, it also produced some goods chassis and goods vehicle bodies on passenger chassis. Its petrol-electric system, developed in 1906, used the petrol engine to power a generator, which supplied current to an electric motor driving the rear axle. From 1920 to 1924 Dennis Brothers produced for W A Stevens a goods vehicle of his design. Tilling-Stevens itself manufactured a number of chassis for commercial users in the 1920s and early 1930s, some with petrol-electric drive and some with conventional gearboxes. A 4-ton forward control chassis of 1931 was perhaps the most popular. Operators of Tilling-Stevens commercials included Peek Frean, the biscuit makers, British Petroleum and Lewis's, the Birmingham furnishers and removers.

During the Second World War, Tilling-Stevens advertised 2½- and 3-ton battery-electric chassis. The Rootes Group acquired Tilling-Stevens in 1950 and production of vehicles ceased in 1952, although the TS3 three-cylinder, two-stroke diesel engine, from 1954 a significant power unit for Rootes' Commer forward-control lorry series, was built at the Maidstone works. **RAS/GK**

J Bullock, *The Rootes Brothers: story of a motoring empire* (Sparkford: Patrick Stephens, 1993); Stevens-Stratten (1988); B Ritchie, *Portrait in Oil: an illustrated history of BP* (British Petroleum Co, 1995); G N Georgano, *The World's Commercial Vehicles 1830–1964* (Temple Press, 1965); Jenkinson (1977); Hills (1943); Carverhill (2002)

Tillotson, Oswald, Ltd. John Oswald Tillotson started as a carman in Burnley. After his two horses with their car were destroyed in 1909, he re-started with a motor vehicle. By 1911 he had the Leyland agency for Burnley. His lorries were requisitioned in 1914, but business prospered, with government contracts in addition to civilian commercial repairs.

After the war, Tillotson concentrated on Leyland commercial vehicle sales and service, adding a successful bodybuilding division and became an early Morris Commercial dealer. In 1927 the firm began to acquire transport companies: W V Greenwood of Burnley, which specialised in textile traffic, and later Same Day Deliveries, a parcels carrier serving Greater Manchester. Tillotson was supplying all Bouts Brothers trunk vehicles, and, following the end

of his association with Leyland, on gaining the AEC distributorship, Bouts changed to operating AECs with Tillotson bodies for its trunk services. This led to Oswald Tillotson gaining a financial interest in the business.

Oswald Tillotson was affected by the losses incurred by Bouts-Tillotson Transport (q.v.) and was acquired by Holdsworth & Hanson in 1935, but continued to trade under its own name as a successful AEC dealer. **GM**

Interview with Leslie Bouts

A **tilt** is a cover of canvas, tarpaulin or plastic coated sheet, supported over the load-carrying area of a vehicle; hence tilt van, colloquially shortened to tilt, also known as a sheet van. The vehicle itself invariably had fixed sides and in its simplest form, which dates back to at least the fourteenth century, the tilt was supported by removable wooden, or later metal, hoops that fitted into slots on the body sides. The rigid tilt, which was already in use on horse-drawn vehicles by the late nineteenth century, had horizontal planks linking the hoops, over which the tilt was tightly stretched. Although in some cases this was also intended to be removable, it was also the earliest form of fixed body for covered vans. In the late 1920s the GWR put into service a number of lorries equipped with a tilt, approximately two-thirds of which could slide forward on runners to facilitate loading. The device was supplied by the Portsmouth Motor Co. In the 1930s it employed mechanical-horse trailers which had a rigid tilt over the front half and a simple tilt on hoops over the rear half. Although the fixed rigid tilt was superseded by the van body constructed of metal panels early in the twentieth century, horse-drawn examples could still be seen in use into the 1950s. Motor lorries with removable tilts were in common use, but by the 1980s were rare, except for military transport. Loading and unloading was time-consuming and the tilt, like sheeting (q.v.), was largely superseded by curtain-side (q.v.) lorries. However, it continued in use for specialist applications; for example a low permanent tilt, carried on a folding lattice-work frame that could be pushed back on runners, was used on trailers used for carrying steel coils on piggyback (q.v.) trains. **RAS/JMA**

Kelley (1973 and 1982); Twells and Bourne (1983); Stevens-Stratten and Aldridge (1987)

Timber haulage (Figures 59 and 182) is one of the oldest specialist transport operations, with the haulier being responsible from the point where the tree is felled right through to the sawmill. When horses were used it was dangerous, hard on the men and women and harder on their horses. The haulier began by extracting the felled timber from where it had been growing to a suitable site for loading, in some instances moving to an estate yard or, after steam power became available, to a mobile sawmill. Before the log could be moved, its side branches had to be removed, the larger ones sawn into cord wood for charcoal production or firewood. This was taken away on flat vehicles, horse-drawn until steam traction, and later motor transport, took over. Transporting the logs to the loading point, often referred to as 'tushing', employed a chain placed around the bottom end of the butt and hooked to the harness or tractor tow bar. From the late 1920s, and particularly from the 1940s, the tractor or its winch was used, latterly sometimes with a logging arch or sulky. This was the modern successor to a bob or nib, a pair of large cartwheels on a curved axletree from which the heavy end of the log was suspended and dragged out for loading. The modern arch was fabricated from steel, the wheels being mounted on stub axles. The tractor winch cable was used to lift and hold the suspended log.

The logs were positioned for loading alongside and parallel with the pole wagon, carriage, drag, drug or trailer whose rear axle could be moved along the pole to suit the length of the logs. A pair of logs was positioned to form a skid from the ground up to the bolsters. The logs were then pulled up to the skid by a pair of chains secured to the pole wagon and then carried under and back over the logs to a C-hook connected to the horse's harness or to a winch cable. If there was more than one, the first layer was positioned and safely secured, the skids then placed on top of the laid logs and the

process repeated until a full load was made up. In the north, tripods or shear legs were used with pulleys to lift the logs up, allowing the pole wagon to be placed under as required.

In the early days of horse haulage, water transport and later the railways were used when possible for longer journeys. The advent of steam traction made the journey somewhat easier, but travelling through towns had its own difficulties. The length and heights of loads required care to avoid damage or jamming. The First World War, with an insatiable demand for timber for industry and military purposes, created shortage of mature timber. Following the Armistice timber haulage began to use motor vehicles, despite the slump affecting profitability. The Latil four-wheel-driven-and-steered tractor became a popular replacement for steam tractors. Foden used surplus steam engine parts in 1934/5 to produce a chain-driven, diesel-powered timber tractor. It had a Gardner engine mounted transversely behind the cab, but was not a success, steering being a particular problem. Several of the dozen made were rebuilt as conventional vehicles. Unipower also offered specific timber tractors from the late 1930s.

A recovery was just being achieved when the outbreak of war in 1939 meant all available timber was again extracted. This time government agencies hired 500 various vehicles to add to the timber hauliers' overworked and ageing fleets. Horses continued to have a role in 'tushing' to the loading point, particularly in the Forestry Commission plantations, but crawler tractors and other specialist tractors became increasingly used, not least because of the many difficult sites.

After the war the availability of ex-army four-wheel-drive tractors, notably the AEC Matador with its powerful winch, replaced most pre-war tractors. These were fitted with loading jibs, making loading easier and quicker, but still hazardous. Long loads were still the norm, but any exceeding legal weight limits were now more likely to be identified by police or in Ministry checks. From the 1950s developments in mill machinery meant a requirement for shorter butt lengths, enabling the use of rigid vehicles as well as multi-bolstered standard semi-trailers.

From the 1960s the AEC, ERF, Foden and Leyland met competition from the first European and Scandinavian imports. Few mass-produced chassis were successfully used in timber haulage, the arduous duties, particularly when working in the forests, made them uneconomic. The same period saw changes in legislation and the virtual end of the use of drawbar trailers; the overloaded timber vehicles with their lengthy loads disappeared. Foden, Scania and Volvo rigid or articulated vehicles became the most used for timber haulage and were equipped with mounted loading cranes, which with the smaller lighter logs being handled were able to self load.

In the 1960s timber haulage declined with a shortage of suitable trees, and timber merchants closing. Among the distinguished names to disappear were T T Boughton, later TTB (Haulage) Ltd (q.v.) of Amersham Common; S Darke & Sons, Worcester; H P Kitching Ltd, Stratford-upon-Avon; Yorkley Timber Company, Ross-on-Wye. Most plots of mature hardwood timber had been cleared. There were short-lived demands caused by the effects of Dutch Elm Disease and especially the 1987 hurricane. The Forestry Commission, formed after 1918 to ensure supplies of home-grown softwoods, provided work handling pulpwood, some of which was delivered by rail. Pulpwood comes straight from the forest in the round, as a vital raw material for the paper (q.v.) industry. This comprises thinnings or specially grown young trees about 9 in to 1 ft in diameter sawn into 8 ft lengths. These are often carried on a trailer which has a row of upright 6-foot stakes along each side. These trailers are often fitted with an onboard crane for self loading at the edge of the forest. There are a few which will pick up the felled tree and saw off the correct lengths and load automatically. New regulations following investigations into fatal accidents mean that small timber must be loaded parallel with the vehicle and pins and chains used to secure the load.　　　　**GM**

Boughton (1992), chap. 5; *CM* (25 January 1935), pp. 810–13; Sanders (1984, 1987, 1990, 1997, 1999 and 2000)

TIP Trailer Rental opened its first UK depot on a greenfield site at Grays, Essex in 1968. TIP stood for Trailers International Pool and it later became a subsidiary of General Electric Capital of the USA. Typical of its depots was a new one opened at Grays in 1986 with capacity for 150 trailers. In 1995, when it became a member of GE Capital, it claimed to be the largest trailer rental company in the world.　　　　**RAS**

Tippers (Figure 183). Rear-tipping bodies were fitted to 2-wheeled carts used for carrying stone, coal and other minerals, but with 4-wheeled wagons there was a choice of end- or side-tippers. On wagons and more sophisticated carts, tipping was controlled by a hand-operated screw mechanism, but commonly the body of a tip cart was released and controlled only by a wooden bar.

Motor body builders supplied end-tippers from 1898 and side-tippers from 1907, using a variety of manual devices incorporating elevating screws. One system gave both end and side tipping on the same vehicle. Mann provided steam-powered tipping by a chain mechanism on its short Cart in 1906. The first example of power tipping on a petrol vehicle was on a Vulcan in 1915, equipped by Bromilow & Edwards with power take-off from the flywheel rim. Shortly after, a twin-ram system taking off from the propeller shaft was offered by Leyland. After developing the three-way tipper, the Edwards brothers set up in Bolton in 1927 to specialise in tipping gear.

Although there were steel-bodied tippers produced by steam wagon manufacturers before the First World War, timber continued to be used for tipper bodies until after the Second World War. By then they were usually steel lined. Aluminium tipper bodies became popular from the mid-1930s, especially for grain, but steel was preferred for civil engineering applications and other heavy uses. Hard-wearing hi-tensile steel was chosen for some applications towards the end of the twentieth century.
See also EDBRO HOLDINGS　　　　**GAB/RWK**

Tipper, annual supplement to *Truck.*

The **TIR procedure** (Figures 60 and 185) was established under the Customs Convention on the International Transport of Goods by Road 1959 (hence 'TIR', the acronym of the French version of the convention's title). This provided for goods in Customs-sealed vehicles or containers accompanied by a TIR carnet (an internationally recognised Customs document) to cross land frontiers with a minimum of Customs formalities. Within the European Community (subsequently Union) the Community Transit scheme replaced TIR carnets from 1973.   **RAS**

David Lowe, *The Transport and Distribution Manager's Guide to 1992* (Kogan Page, 1989)

TNT Ltd (Figure 61) was founded in Australia in 1946 by Ken W Thomas, a one-man truck operator in Sydney. The firm grew steadily and was incorporated first as a private company in 1951 and then as a public company, Thomas Nationwide Transport Ltd, in 1962. (Its name was abbreviated to TNT Ltd in 1983.) In 1967 it merged with Alltrans, which had been set up in 1950 by Peter Abeles and George Rockey, Hungarian immigrants to Australia. Alltrans brought to TNT some 500 lorries and Abeles, knighted in 1972, became TNT's chief executive.

Having already extended its activities into North America, TNT opened a small office in London in 1972 and started its Kwikasair express delivery service in 1973, originally between London and Paris, then to serve much of Europe. The operation was not meeting targets and Don Dick was sent to deal with the problem; his Australian background led him to think that TNT could offer a better parcels service than was then available from any British carrier. The entry of TNT into Britain's domestic parcels industry in 1978 was to have far-reaching repercussions. It acquired Inter County Express with 600 employees and 300 vehicles, followed by smaller acquisitions, to give a nationwide service.

In 1980 TNT (UK) Ltd became a publicly-quoted company. Alan Jones from Roadline was appointed general manager, with responsibility for nine subsidiaries, employing 4000 people and 1000 vehicles from 39 depots.

It then introduced the Overnite service, the first to offer guaranteed next-morning delivery virtually nationwide via its hub depot at Atherstone, Warwickshire. Further dedicated services were introduced, among them contract services, including TNT Brewery Distribution, TNT Just-in-Time, TNT Automotive and TNT Garment Express. Homefast, which was started in 1982 for mail order traffic, was one of the first franchise operations, but effective tactics from the Post Office resulted in its closure.

In 1979 Abeles had joined with the media tycoon, Richard Murdoch, in the purchase of Ansett Airlines. This relationship resulted in TNT becoming involved in bringing to an end the bitter labour dispute between Richard Murdoch and the Fleet Street printing trade unions in 1986. It established the Newsfast road distribution service to allow Murdoch to circumvent sympathetic action by the rail unions when he moved production of *The Times* to Wapping. Other Fleet Street proprietors quickly followed (see NEWSPAPER TRAFFIC).

To general surprise in 1983 TNT Ltd acquired IPEC (International Parcel Express Company), including its British subsidiary, which was competing with TNT's European services. TNT continued to develop these services, contracting to buy BAe 146 200QT jet freighter aircraft; 24 were used to expand the Overnite service. In 1992 it acquired Federal Express's French Chronoservice express business. Following TNT's acquisition by the Dutch Post Office in 1996, it became part of the TNT Post Group (renamed TPG in 2001), forming two of its three divisions: TNT Express, with Alan Jones as general manager, and TNT Logistics. Both have grown rapidly through worldwide acquisitions and alliances. Within the UK, TNT Logistics expanded in 2000 through the acquisition of Taylor Barnard, with its fleet of 750 units, while TNT Express, noted for its quality of service, can claim to be the UK's leading business-parcel carrier (home deliveries were abandoned in 1999).   **GM**

A Wright, *abc Cargo Airlines* (Shepperton: Ian Allan, 2000); R Milliken, obituary of Sir Peter

Abeles, *Independent* (7 July 1999); *IDCH*, 5 (1992), pp. 523–5

Tracking systems were beginning to gain currency with operators at the end of the twentieth century to optimise the use of their vehicles, although trade press comment suggested that there were limitations to their usefulness at that stage of development. The tracking process utilises the satellite-based global positioning system, to give a locational fix to within 100 metres in the UK or theoretically world-wide. Driver criticism has been experienced by some operators, on the lines of the 'spy in the cab' controversy over the introduction of the tachograph (q.v.), and the non-functioning of systems unless the vehicle ignition is switched on is an obvious drawback.

RAS

CM (9 March 2000), pp.28–37

Traction is the term usually used to describe the provision of a tractive unit or tractor, that is the drawing or powered part of an articulated outfit. Such provision has become a particular role for the owner-driver (q.v.), especially since the growth in containerisation (q.v.). A number of large operators who specialise in container traffic make considerable use of owner drivers, some of whom paint their tractive units in the colours of the fleet operator.

JMA/GAB

Traction engine, see STEAM ROAD TRACTORS AND LORRIES

Tractors (agricultural and industrial) on the road. There were limited applications for steam vehicles on farms because of their weight. The higher power-to-weight ratio of the petrol tractor introduced the possibility of an interchange of agricultural and transport roles. Indeed, some of the earliest motor tractors were devised and marketed with this in mind. There have been two main periods in which the essentially agricultural tractor has been used to any extent on the road: between the wars and at the present time. In the 1920s and 1930s, in an attempt to expand tractor sales, Fordson and International, in particular, promoted the industrial tractor, on solid tyres or high pressure pneumatics, as a

road-going variant of the agricultural tractor, to some extent in competition with the mechanical horse, as contemporary advertising illustrates. At the end of the twentieth century, road-going tractors, notably the JCB Fastrac, aroused considerable opposition from hauliers, who claimed that their users operated them, in effect, as road haulage vehicles, while avoiding the latters' costs. The agricultural rationale for the Fastrac, which can haul 14 tonnes at a speed of 40 mph, is the increasing roadtime of tractors on larger and more widespread farms.

RAS

J Wilkie, *The Illustrated History of Tractors* (Shepperton: Ian Allan, 1999); M Wright, *Tractors since 1889* (Ipswich: Farming Press, 1991); S McQueen, 'Field trips', *CM* (5 December 1996), pp. 36–7

The **trade press** has been an important part of the road haulage industry from its practical beginnings. The first examples were issued as supplements or included among the articles in motoring journals, notably *Autocar*, *Motor* and *Motor Car Journal*. The major newspapers, *The Times* and The *Daily Telegraph* also included supplements or references in their industry pages. *Motor Traction* (*Motor Transport* from 1920) was spun off from the *Autocar* and *Commercial Motor* from *Motor*, and were published by highly competitive rivals. Their coverage included passenger transport. The editorial content was not too different from that to-day. There were accounts of operators, impressions of new vehicles, queries and answers. One feature which disappeared by the mid-1930s was tips from drivers. Each title had its particular features. *CM* was possibly more technical, always interested in farm mechanisation, and had great concern with operating costs and management. *MT* was considered to be better for coverage of steam power until the mid-1920s and was aimed more at the operator and management, although both were well read by drivers. Also highly regarded was *World's Carriers*, which covered business aspects rather than technical topics. It also issued an annual diary, which included details of many operators.

The First World War established these as essential reading; although there was censorship, details of operating conditions on the fighting fronts were published, often by staff writers serving with the forces who had their salaries made up while they were serving. They showed how motor transport had became essential and dependable. The end of the war and the influx of new entrants to the industry strengthened the importance of the trade journals. They were critical of the government's handling of disposal of ex-army vehicles. They gave advice for newcomers, criticised the Ministry of Transport's actions and were critical of the railway's attitude to road haulage. Both were later to be involved in campaigns against nationalisation, and then covered the successful tenderers for the Special A licences at denationalisation.

A weekly newcomer appeared in 1919, *Modern Transport*, dealing with all four forms of transport, road, rail, sea and air. Advertised as *The Times* for transport, it was influential until the 1950s. This was a result of its later editor, Charles Klapper. It also changed the form of road tests under its tester, Captain R Twelvetrees. Its high dependance on rail-oriented advertising led to revenue losses in the wake of the Beeching report. It was bought by Ian Allan, which published it as a monthly magazine for a short time in the early 1960s.

The manufacturers began to produce their own journals, which, although concentrating on their own models and operators of them, were useful for servicing notes, but these were eventually not considered effective publicity and were discontinued. Since the 1960s new monthly titles have appeared. The first to have some influence was *Truck*, and its more popular sister title *Truck & Driver*. These, with *CM* and *MT* are all now published by Reed Business Information. Also monthly is *Trucking*, with a similar format to *Truck*. It has steadily increased its circulation. Some have websites for the most up-to-date information and advertisements. A new weekly appeared in the 1980s for a short time: *Transport Week,* produced by Morgan Grampian. **GM**

'Where do we start', Baldwin, (1980), pp. 30–5

The **Traders Road Transport Association** was formed in 1945 to represent own-account operators following the dissolution of the Commercial Motor Users Association (q.v.). From 1945 to 1963 the TRTA could co-operate with the Road Haulage Association and Passenger Vehicle Operators Association through the National Road Transport Federation (q.v.) which provided secretarial and office services. In the late 1960s it offered members a maintenance check scheme using its own inspectors. It strongly supported the RHA in its opposition to the 1968 Transport Bill. In 1969 it merged with two other organisations to form the Freight Transport Association (q.v.). **JA**

Dickson-Simpson (1969), p. 18; Hamer (1987), p. 14; Birch and Harper (1995) passim

Traffic administration. The administrative overheads of a moderate-sized haulage firm with, say, twenty lorries were quite small. Typically they comprised the owner, a vehicle mechanic, a traffic clerk and a part-time bookkeeper. The traffic clerk, who was often the owner's wife or daughter, was responsible for organising the day-to-day operations. The first stage in the process was a series of telephone calls from customers, giving details of what was to be despatched and where to, which the traffic clerk recorded in a daybook. As the orders were received, it was his/her job to plan how part-loads were to be consolidated into full-loads and to allocate the work to vehicles and drivers in such a way that customers' requirements were met without incurring unnecessary vehicle mileage or infringing the drivers' hours regulations.

Some drivers collected consignments which were brought back to the depot for consolidation onto other vehicles. Sometimes the traffic lent itself to consolidation by the driver for throughout transit on the collecting vehicle. It was, therefore, important that the driver was properly informed before starting the collections, in order that the loading could be planned appropriately. It was not unknown, however, for a late change of plan to be made, which could result in a degree of friction between the traffic clerk and the drivers.

When the collecting drivers handed in the consignment documentation (q.v.) at the depot, the traffic clerk had to scan it carefully and exercise great care to ensure that delivery was effected to the correct place and the correct charges raised for the work undertaken.

Then, when the delivery notes or sheets were handed in by the delivery drivers at the end of the day or on their next visit to the depot, the traffic clerk had to check that every consignment had been signed for. These documents were then securely filed away or returned to the customer, according to the agreed practice, to be available as proof of delivery (POD) in the event of a dispute between the consignor and consignee. If POD could not be produced, relations between haulier and his customer were put under strain, the consignor probably delaying payment until proof could be established or his claim for loss settled. The traffic clerk was therefore a key figure.

If the firm grew, the administration might need to be strengthened. In place of the traffic clerk there might be a traffic office headed by a traffic manager. (The term traffic office has now generally been replaced by terms like distribution or planning office.) Only in large firms with several depots, or offering a wider range of services such as warehousing, was anything much more elaborate required. Parcels firms had the most complex traffic administration, with a range of clerical and handling staff undertaking a variety of jobs. For example, checkers were employed to see that goods brought into the depot for transhipment agreed with the entries on the senders' consignment notes and that outgoing loads were accompanied by the proper documents. They were assisted by a caller-off, who shouted out the details on the package labels. Because of the multiplicity of consignments, clerks were often assigned to specific duties, such as receiving collection orders or dealing with queries.

MB/GAB

Dunbar (1953) and (1981); Lowe (2002)

Traffic Commissioners, see LICENSING AUTHORITY

Trailer Disposals Ltd was set up by the trailer manufacturers at the end of the Second World War to ensure the orderly disposal of war surplus trailers, in order to avoid a repeat of the market flooding experienced after the First World War. A B Fuller, chairman of Taskers, was a director. According to Rolt, it was not particularly successful, although John Crane considered the system worked well. **RAS**

Rolt (1969), pp. 192–3; Crane (1991), p. 81

Tramp operations used to be a traditional part of the work of many smaller hauliers and owner-drivers: its opposite, trunking (q.v.), was the more glamorous and regular side. Typically, in the 1930s and late 1940s a flat-platform vehicle with an A licence set out with a load (or several part loads) of general goods destined for one area or location. Once there and unloaded the driver or his traffic office sourced a further load for some other destination, or a clearing house (q.v.) might be used. That process was probably repeated again, this time hopefully finding work which took driver and vehicle back to its home. The vehicle carried sufficient sheets and ropes to keep the rain or snow off any shape or size of load, and the driver (also known as a roamer) was given a small sum of money to buy further fuel. Triangular runs of this nature were quite common, given suitably resourceful drivers who did not mind loading overnight in a variety of towns and cities. After the dissolution of the Road Haulage Organisation (q.v.) in 1946 Fisher Renwick (q.v.) had up to seven Seddon-Carrimores on such work.

A few drivers had arrangements at factories where they were known and trusted so that they could usually obtain a load if they called. There were also opportunities for the less honest: after dropping a load in Manchester a driver going to Liverpool to pick up another load might, unbeknown to his employer do 'a foreigner', and carry for cash a load from Manchester to Liverpool.

Many of the tramping companies were taken over by BRS, which converted some roaming work into regular directional services; but confined to one route, this was not very successful as many depots tried to keep potential work for themselves.

This type of traffic, or perhaps the availability of drivers able and willing to handle it, diminished and did not resume to any great extent after de-nationalisation. Such traffic is probably now mainly handled by the pallet networks (q.v.), but the practice is not entirely dead. There is a modern equivalent in machinery moving at auctions, where it is not unknown for a vehicle (usually a low-loader) and crew sent to collect for one customer to manage another small job unknown to their employer. **GM/JMA**

Tramways and the transport of parcels and goods. The 1870 Tramways Act envisaged the carriage of merchandise as well as passengers, but only in 1887 did Huddersfield inaugurate a parcels service on its municipal steam tramways. Several steam, cable and some horse tramways introduced services, but significant growth of parcels traffic followed electrification. Dublin United was the model for major schemes in Manchester, Bradford and the company-owned Birmingham & Midland Tramways in 1905.

A legal challenge by Sutton & Company, carriers, brought a 1906 ruling that Manchester Tramways could collect and deliver provided part of the transport was by tram, but excluded general carrier powers. By 1928-9, Manchester was carrying 2,309,021 parcels a year using seven freight tramcars and 46 motor vans as well as passenger tramcars. By then, 66 out of 105 municipal tramways and 34 out of 60 company-owned tramways were carrying parcels and mails with a net revenue (profit) of £76,024. Some only carried on line-of-route, but others had extensive collection and delivery systems, and through rates with main line railways. The Manchester operation eventually became SELNEC Parcels (q.v.).

Despite many efforts to promote freight carrying, particularly from Liverpool via the South Lancashire Tramways, general goods carriage by tramway occurred only in a few places. Notable examples included coal in Huddersfield, sand and fireclay in Leeds, and tin ore between Camborne and Redruth; rail wagons were hauled over tram tracks at

Glasgow and Blackpool. During the First World War Birmingham & Midland's Tramways Parcels Express carried goods and Bradford used a trolley-battery lorry, taking power from tram wires. While parcels traffic grew, goods declined in the 1920s and by 1928-9 only ten tramways returned statistics. Parcels services were generally continued as buses replaced trams. **IAY**

Ministry of Transport tramways statistical returns; *Garcke's Manual of Electrical Undertakings 1919-20*; various articles in *Tramway & Railway World*, *Light Railway & Tramway Journal* and *Bus & Coach*; Annual reports from Manchester and Bradford tramways

Trans-Action, see PROTEST MOVEMENTS

Transfrigoroute Europe was set up by the International Road Transport Union (q.v.) in 1955 at the request of the UN Economic Commission, which wanted an international body to promote the development of temperature-controlled transport of perishable goods. Its membership, originally confined to transport operators, was subsequently widened to include manufacturers of vehicles and equipment. It was renamed Transfrigoroute International in 1983 and is now a federation, with headquarters in Bern, Switzerland, of national groups in 27 countries in Europe and North Africa. Transfrigoroute UK was established in 1984 and in 1999 had 120 member firms. **JMA/RAS**

CM (13 June 2002), p. 37

Transport & General Workers' Union. In its conception and at its formation in 1922, the TGWU was a transport union. The original initiative in 1920 by Bevin (general secretary of the Dockers' Union) was to unite the various dockers' unions that were to be found in Britain's ports, together with the 'general' workers who had been recruited to them at various times (and had sometimes been crucial to their survival). But the discussions were soon extended to the road transport unions and the quick adhesion of the National Union of Vehicle Workers (q.v.) ensured success. The TGWU was born in 1922. It adopted a decentralised government of twelve areas for general administration and six trade groups to deal with collective bargaining, united under a general executive council. This structure gave the union the flexibility to respond to local and sectional pressures and to adapt to new challenges and amalgamations. In particular, the amalgamation with the Workers' Union in 1928 laid the basis for expansion into the Midlands manufacturing industry during the 1930s and after.

The TGWU Road Transport Commercial trade group united the commercial membership of all the amalgamating unions (a number of which were also recent amalgamations): Amalgamated Carters, Lurrymen & Motormen's Union (Bolton), Amalgamated Association of Carters & Motormen (Leeds), Associated Horsemen's Union (Greenock), Dockers' Union (Bristol, south Wales), National Union of Vehicle Workers (London), North of Scotland Horse & Motormen's Association (Dundee), and the United Vehicle Workers. The RTC group's two strongest sections were in Areas 1 and 6. The latter comprised the North of England Commercial Section which was the name taken by the ACLMU in Bolton (a union that had retained a degree of autonomy through a series of previous amalgamations). After a hesitant start, the RTC group grew in strength during the later 1930s and the Second World War, and its position as the drivers' trade union was later consolidated by the amalgamation with the Liverpool & District Carter's & Motormen's Union (q.v.) in 1947 and the Scottish Commercial Motormen's Union (q.v.) in 1972.

The object of the RTC group at its formation in 1922, in conformity with much of British trade unionism, was to obtain a national collective agreement for the sector. There had been a brief and partial success in 1919 when a joint industrial council was formed but this soon collapsed. Thereafter it struggled to persuade companies to support a national agreement but again, in 1936, this ended in failure. The RTC group then joined forces with the leading employers' association to persuade the National government to agree to statutory regulation in the form of a wages board (see INDUSTRIAL RELATIONS).

In the 1950s the TGWU, organisationally sclerotic and obsessed by anti-communism, became dependent upon statutory regulation and proved incapable of initiating any effective campaign to strengthen union organisation in the industry, in spite of the energy of Frank Cousins (q.v.) who by now was RTC group national secretary. Instead this was undertaken at local level, notably in Birmingham, Liverpool, and London. A parallel process was underway in the SCMU in central Scotland. Power was devolved within the RTC group to districts and this provided the basis for local collective bargaining and control over industrial action, in particular during the hire and reward dispute in 1979. Since 1980 the group has been especially hard hit by economic restructuring and restrictive employment law.

PS

Coates and Topham (1991); the records of the TGWU and some of its constituents are at the Modern Records Centre of the University of Warwick Library, Coventry (MSS. 126)

Transport 2000 was established in 1972 as a pressure group. Its aim was and remains to promote the part played by public transport, especially the railways, and to encourage the diminution of road transport both by car and lorry. It was supported and funded by a broad spectrum of interests including railway and other trade unions, environmental and transport user groups such as Friends of the Earth and the Women's Institutes, and various transport industry interests. It was largely the brainchild of Sidney Weighell, general secretary of the National Union of Railwaymen, supported by Ray Buckton, general secretary of the Associated Society of Locomotive Engineers & Firemen and Michael Harris of the Railway Industry Association. During the 1980s the organisation lobbied against road building and against raising the size and weight of lorries allowed on the roads. It also attacked the road lobby which it believed was anti-rail and pro-road construction. It produced a number of influential publications which in the 1980s took a strong anti-lorry stance.

SJ

Philip S Bagwell, *The Railwaymen: the history of the National Union of Railwaymen*, 2 (Allen & Unwin, 1982), pp. 390–3; *OCBRH*, p. 540; Hamer (1987)

The **Transport Advisory Council** was established in 1933 under Part III of the Road & Rail Traffic Act of that year. Its function was to advise the Minister of Transport as and when required, and it was to take cognisance of transport co-ordination, though little was achieved in this direction. Its first report on Services and Rates was not published until 1937. This promoted the idea of transport co-ordination, advocated adequate alternative facilities for traders but the avoidance of unfair competition, and stressed the right of traders to choose the means of transport they wanted. It was chaired by Sir Arthur Griffith-Boscawen, MP, a past president of the National Traction Engine Owners' & Users' Association. Its lack of specific outcomes was in part a function of the economic realities whereby the reductions in operating costs of a fast-changing new industry were passed on to merchants and manufacturers as a result of intense competition between numerous firms. This, at a time of depressed demand and industrial gloom, was only too welcome to transport users.　　**JA**

Walker (1942); Savage (1957)

The **Transport Arbitration Tribunal** was the court of law established by the Transport Act 1947 to settle the compensation that was paid to the previous owners of the railway, canal and road transport undertakings taken into public ownership. It had two functions in the process of road haulage nationalisation: its confirmation was required for every agreement for compensation exceeding £20,000, thereby exercising independent control over the British Transport Commission's negotiators; and it arbitrated on any dispute arising over the terms of compensation. The proceedings of some of its significant arbitration hearings that determined questions of principle were published as *Road Haulage Cases*.　　**GAB**

Road Haulage Cases: Selected Decisions given by the Tribunal for the settlement of questions arising in connection with Compulsory Acquisitions of Road Haulage Undertakings (1950–5). The Tribunal's records for England and Wales are in the Public Record Office (class MT 24), while those for Scotland are in the Scottish Record Office. They provide the only complete listing of the road haulage firms that were nationalised and the compensation they received.

The **Transport Association's** origins lie in the Transport Arrangement, a grouping of 52 haulage companies which maintained working relationships following the end of centralised control during the Second World War. These companies then sold out voluntarily *en bloc* to the British Transport Commission ahead of compulsory nationalisation. Following denationalization a new organisation, the Transport Association, was formed in 1955 by sixteen former Transport Arrangement member companies that had re-purchased their businesses. New members were admitted from 1956 and membership grew to a maximum of 80, but typically 60, businesses.

In 2000 member companies operated 4000 vehicles and were in most cases family-owned, medium-size haulage businesses. The Association was financed through an annual levy on members based on the number of vehicles owned. Election of members was based on principles of (i) professionalism and ethical standards (ii) an even national spread across the UK (iii) the avoidance of direct competitors.

The Association's original objectives were primarily the mutual provision of refuelling, breakdown and return load facilities; bulk buying of fuel and other items was considered but not found cost-effective. Increasing vehicle reliability led to a decline in use of the breakdown facility. Concentration in both road haulage and customer industries in the late 1990s brought an awareness that major customers sought national or international coverage in their distribution contracts and that regional hauliers, who characterised TA membership, may be neglected or excluded. It was therefore envisaged that TA members might in future also collaborate in joint tendering for such contracts. In this regard they acted like consortia (q.v.), based on mutual trust through Association membership.

The TA generally avoids involvement in political lobbying, leaving this to the RHA (q.v.). It lobbied UK truck manufacturers in the 1960s regarding quality standards and in 1999/2000 commented on issues of fuel and vehicle taxation.

The transport journalist John Darker observed: 'Outsiders, envious above all, I suspect, of the decently rated back-loading traffic, would say the TA is a selfish club of fat-cats. Perhaps the fat-cats have qualified for the cream by years of virtuous road haulage operation, giving service with integrity to customers, employees and each other?' The logo of the TA comprises an entwined capital 'T' and 'A' within a red circle. Long serving members included firms such as John Jempson (q.v.) Elddis (q.v.), Taylor Barnard and Baylis Distribution. **DMH**

Ian P Ramsay, *History of the Transport Association*, (private publication, 1992); John Darker, 'Privilege and professionalism', *CM* (16 February 1979); 'Sound off', *CM* (7 October 1999), p.54; 'All for one', *MT* (10 February 2000), p.24; 'Keeping the mid-range contenders in the frame', *Distribution Business* (March 2000), p.7; Peter Acton Associates

Transport cafés were an essential part of the road haulage scene from the 1920s to the 1970s. Whereas horse-drawn carriers used inns as staging posts, the motor lorry equivalent was the transport café, more vernacularly known as a 'caff' or 'greasy spoon'. It appeared in the 1920s, sometimes as a cabin or converted lorry body, when longer-distance lorry traffic was developing. Speeds were low, roads slow and tortuous, lorries noisy, hot in summer and cold in winter, so the chance to stop and have something to eat and drink was welcomed. The job was also quite demanding physically and hence rest and refreshment were needed. Cafés gained a reputation for strong tea, greasy food or at least carbohydrate- and protein-rich meals, which provided comfort as well as nourishment. The transport café was also important for social interaction, especially in the 1960s when mates became less common and then almost unknown, for the job became increasingly lonely and the café more welcome.

Other activities went on at cafés than just feeding and resting. Information relevant to the job was exchanged, of speed traps, firms looking for drivers, return loads, hold ups on the road and so on. Gossip might be swapped and goods traded which had been purloined from loads. Some cafés became famous as change-over points for drivers, such as that on the A45 at Meriden where Fisher Renwick's Manchester to London service swapped drivers. The limitation on drivers' hours meant that sometimes time had to be killed if the driver was making too good a progress. For maximum legal speeds were low, 20 mph till 1957 and 30 mph thereafter for lorries over 3 tons unladen. Many cafes also offered overnight accommodation at rock bottom prices, which allowed a little surplus from the overnight allowance. Some also offered female company for the night for a few shillings extra. Many became legendary, such as The Jungle Café at Shap on the A6, or Three Sisters at Markyate on the A5, and Kate's Kabin on the A1.

Transport cafés began to decline when the motorway system became widespread from the late 1960s. Travellers on motorways could only stop at the designated motorway service areas which were run by large organisations, rather than the small scale, often family-owned cafés. Motorway service areas increasingly provided special facilities for lorry drivers who were reluctant to detour far from the motorway to visit the former cafés. This lack of use was reinforced by much faster speeds, more comfortable lorries reducing the need for overnight stops or providing sleeper cabs with heating, washing and television. Many cafés were bought up by chains such as Little Chef or Happy Eater which switched them to cater for family car drivers, where four eat per small parking-space, compared to one trucker who needed several car bays for his lorry. In any case transport cafés made poor neighbours with their noise, sweeping headlights and visual intrusion, and health inspectors gave them a hard time. By the 1990s they were rare, to some extent replaced by 'stand outside' units in lay-bys and the caravan-style tea waggons. They provided cheap meals of the bacon butty style but no cover or seating. All compare unfavourably with facilities at the truckstops in the United States. **JA**

Dave Young, 'Full English breakfast', *Truck* (October 1999), pp. 82–5; Hollowell (1968); Gordon Baron and Flo Goodall, 'The Jungle Cafe', in Gordon Baron and Ron Phillips (eds), *The Shap Story* (Swaffam Prior: Gingerfold, 1998), pp. 34–6; British Road Federation, *Road Transport Cafes: some observations and recommendations* (BRF, 1948); Murphy (1963); Gibson Cowan, *Loud Report* (Michael Joseph, 1938); Mustoe (1997), pp. 49, 58 and 59; David Lawrence, *Always a Welcome: the Glove Compartment History of the Motorway Service Area* (Between Books, 1991); 'The night café', *CM* (25 October 1935), pp.314–5; C Woodcock, 'Café society', *CVC*, 7, 9 (May 2002), pp. 26–7

The **Transport Development Group** originated as the General Lighterage Co. with a nominal capital of £10,000, formed after the First World War by Colonel Edgar Richard Hatfield DSO, a director of the London & Cologne Shipping Co. The two barges of General Lighterage, operating from a Hay's Wharf office in the Pool of London, provided a lighterage service for the two vessels of London & Cologne Shipping. A young ex-soldier, Philip Henman (1889–1986), who joined General Lighterage as accountant in 1922, became its mainspring, buying out Hatfield's partners and becoming managing director in 1929. Navigation problems on the Rhine and difficulties in the London & Cologne Shipping Co. led Hatfield to sell out to Henman between 1933 and 1939 when Henman became chairman of General Lighterage, and Hatfield left the board in 1942. By 1940 pre-tax profits were almost £40,000.

Meantime Henman was diversifying the business, acquiring wharfage, warehousing, road haulage, and other ancillary services, as well as barges and tugs. When shipping was diverted away from the Port of London during the Second World War, Henman developed the road transport, warehousing, and storage side of his operations. Among his customers were the Ministry of Food and other government departments.

After 1945 the Labour Government's nationalisation programme swept all long-distance road haulage firms into public ownership (under the Transport Act of 1947). In 1948 Henman avoided nationalisation of his road fleet by confining it to short-distance haulage operations. In 1950 he floated on the London Stock Exchange a public holding company, General Lighterage (Holdings) Ltd, to run 16 subsidiaries, mostly operating barges and wharves in the Port of London and road haulage services in metropolitan London. The group offered a 'package' service from ship to inland customer. Troubled labour relations in London's docks plus new methods of conveying commodities from ship to shore (such as pipelines) pointed Henman away from lightering and London, though he was on the way to controlling 1200 of London's 6700 lighters as well as barge fleets in Liverpool and Hull.

Denationalisation of long-distance road services and the construction of a national motorway system provided major opportunities that Henman seized with alacrity. By the time he retired in 1969 his group (renamed the Transport Development Group in 1957, and re-named again as TDG plc in 2000) operated over 4,500 lorries, compared to 150 in 1950. TDG was organised as a classic holding company. Operating subsidiaries were allowed nearly complete independence, to the extent of retaining their own names and liveries; negotiating their own rates and wages; choosing their own equipment; and owning their premises and maintenance facilities. The holding company monitored its subsidiaries through weekly, monthly and half-yearly figures. Stronger operators were encouraged to grow, weaker ones were trimmed or broken up.

By 1969 TDG comprised over 80 operating subsidiaries in Britain, three in South Africa and Rhodesia, three in Australia, and seven in Europe. One of the largest acquisitions was Beck & Pollitzer (q.v.), with assets of £2 million, purchased in 1961 by means of the less usual method (for TDG) of a rights issue. Turnover of the whole group in 1968 stood at £50 million, compared to under £1 million in 1950; net assets at £47 million, compared to £475,000 in 1950; and profit before tax at £6.3 million, compared to £100,000 in 1950. In two decades TDG grew twenty times faster than the national economy.

Henman's strict attention to the selection of targeted acquisitions, and their monitoring once they joined the group, were not the only reasons for this rapid growth. Rationing ended in the 1950s and in the 1960s the protracted expansion of consumption and the retail sector began. In addition Henman had an able and highly-motivated managerial team. At its core from 1947 was a partnership with William Fraser (1908–80), a Glasgow University mathematics graduate and former commercial executive with the Trent Navigation Co. (whose imminent nationalisation drove him out). Fraser's financial skills and outgoing personality complemented Henman's talents and low public profile. Like Henman, Fraser was a son of the manse. James Blair Duncan (1927–), a Scottish chartered accountant who joined in 1953 and became a director in 1960, completed the powerful triumvirate at the head of TDG. From the mid-1950s Fraser was the driving force and he succeeded Henman as chairman. Sir Reginald Wilson (q.v.) followed. However, it was Duncan who pushed the company forwards while he was CEO from 1970 and then chairman from 1975 until 1990.

The TDG formula seemed to work until the mid-1970s. Until then demand for haulage and storage services was greater than supply. Competition chiefly came from the less efficient nationalised BRS (q.v.), which in 1973 had 9000 vehicles and 11,000 employees, compared to TDG's 5150 vehicles and 13,600 employees. Markets drastically changed in the 1970s and 1980s. Britain's accession to the EEC exposed UK haulage firms to European competition. The oil price shocks of 1973 and 1979 ended the economic boom of the 1950s and 1960s. The Conservatives' privatisation measures of the 1980s unleashed a new competitor, the employee-owned NFC, and other strong competitors were TNT, Hays, Exel, Tibbett & Britten and Wincanton. Changes in technology, particularly roll-on-roll-off ferries, containerisation and computerisation, increased the scale of operations and costs. Above all, changes in the structure of the British economy, diminishing manufactures and relatively expanding services, shifted the balance of economic power in the supply chain from manufacturers to giant retailers.

TDG was slow to respond to these new circumstances. Its structure in 1979 of 130 modest-sized semi-autonomous operating subsidiaries, responsible to a dozen non-trading holding companies grouped by region and function, in turn responsible to the main board, was inappropriate for dealing with large national customers like Safeway and Sainsbury, Cadbury, Mars and Nestlé. Furthermore, TDG's favoured measure of performance inhibited expansion. Adequate returns on capital employed was the criterion for expansion, rather than a more entrepreneurial approach to new markets. Managers' commission was related to profits, rather than turnover, as well as return on capital employed. Until the late-1970s there was little investment in information technology. For management trainees, the company had a long-standing preference for young chartered accountants and was slow to recruit graduates.

Corporate structure and culture were big problems. De-centralised autonomous units required welding together in terms of both organisation and identity. The board in 1985 recognised that the old geographical and functional structure no longer met changed market conditions. Some adjustment was made by getting rid of ill-fitting businesses, such as the exhibition side, where Beck & Pollitzer Contracts and other subsidiaries were sold in 1987. The identity issue was tackled with a common livery and a new logo, the juggler, introduced in 1989.

Under Sir James Duncan (knighted in 1981) TDG more than held its own. Profits grew from £7.4 million on a turnover of £129 million (1975) to £39 million on a turnover of £584 million (1991). A fresh team took the helm of TDG in 1990–1 and ran the company for almost a decade. Martin Llowarch (1935–), a chartered accountant by background, was part-time chairman and Alan J Cole (1942–), a lawyer by training, was full-time chief executive officer. Under Cole's influence the company was slimmed again, with overseas subsidiaries in Australia and the USA being sold. The policy failed to solve the company's problem. Turnover declined from £565 million in 1992 to £469 million in 1998 and profits plummeted from £33 million to £4 million. Employment, around 12,000 in the 1970s and 1980s, contracted to 8,000 in the late 1990s. On the other hand, dividends were maintained in the 1990s and disposals allowed a return of capital to shareholders of £110 million in 1998. Llowarch stepped down in 2000, confessing that 'an overall improvement in results has proved elusive because of the lack of a strong customer-oriented, growth culture in the management of the company'.

A new chief executive officer, David Garman (from Allied Bakeries) arrived in 1999 promising to make TDG a provider of 'fully integrated supply chain solutions that deliver competitive advantage to its customers'. His formula aimed at a proactive role for TDG, using logistical expertise to mobilise new technology and subcontracted service firms to meet the changing needs of large customers, not only in storage and distribution but also in new services such as outsourcing and contract packing. In 2000 a new part-time chairman, Charles Mackay (also chairman of EuroTunnel Group and former chief executive officer of Inchape plc) was appointed.   **DJJ**

Australian Transport (June 1986); *Distribution Business* (June 2001), p.18; General Lighterage (Holdings) Ltd, Report and Accounts, 1955, 1956; Interviews with Paul Byrne (4 September 2001), William R Fraser (4 October 2001); Sir James B Duncan, thanksgiving tribute on William Fraser, 24 April 1980; William Fraser (1908–80), profile, 4 June 1969; William R Fraser, thanksgiving tribute on Philip Henman, 18 November 1986; *DBB* vol. 3 (1985), pp. 158–64; *Stock Exchange Official Year Book,* 1968, 1973, 1977, 1983, 1987, 1994; TDG plc, Report and Accounts, 1957, 1977–99; Thompson, (1990); *Who's Who,* 1999; there is a small collection of records of some absorbed companies and TDG Reports and Accounts in the Modern Record Centre of the University of Warwick Library (MSS.272)

The **Transport Holding Company** was set up in 1963 to take over the nationalised road transport and sundry other interests of the British Transport Commission, when it was abolished by the Transport Act 1962. As well as British Road Services (q.v.), these included a half share in David MacBrayne Ltd (q.v.). Following the change of government in 1964, the new Labour minister gave the THC freedom to expand its road businesses through voluntary acquisitions as well as fleet expansion. As a consequence, its combined motor goods vehicle fleet increased from 16,000 to 18,400, representing a 45 per cent increase in tonnage capacity, and the number of employees grew from 35,000 to 38,500. Turnover increased by 35 per cent in real terms, but trading profit declined from 10.3 to 4.0 per cent of turnover.

For the history of the THC's road haulage interests, including details of the acquired companies, see BRITISH ROAD SERVICES, BRS PARCELS, PICKFORDS, LAWTHER & HARVEY LTD, TARTAN ARROW SERVICE LTD and TAYFORTH LTD. See also ULSTER TRANSPORT AUTHORITY for the THC's interest in North Ireland Carriers Ltd. The THC was abolished by the Transport Act 1968 and its road haulage interests transferred to the new National Freight Corporation (q.v.).   **GAB**

Transport Holding Company, *Annual Reports & Accounts* (1963–8); Aldcroft (1975), pp. 91, 95 and 102; Bagwell (1988), pp. 326–7, 339; T R Gourvish, *British Railways 1948–73: a business history,* (Cambridge University Press, 1986), pp. 365 and 546

Transport Research Laboratory Ltd. In 1931 a small experimental station to test concrete for road projects was built for the Ministry of Transport on the Colnbrook bypass near Harmondsworth, Middlesex. The scope of the work soon widened and in 1933 the Road Research Laboratory (RRL) was formally established. Until 1939 its work was limited to research on materials and construction, but by then the increase in road accidents was causing concern. The Select Committee of the House of Lords on the Prevention of Road Accidents recommended setting up a road safety research board but it was not until 1945 that agreement was reached to add research into road traffic and safety to the work of RRL. Research between 1939–1965 expanded steadily to solve the problems created by the rapid growth of road traffic.

The Laboratory moved to Crowthorne, Berkshire in 1967 and in 1972 change its name to the Transport and Road Research Laboratory (TRRL), reflecting the wider nature of its work. It is at this point that research into freight movement and HGVs began in earnest. A research and development programme was set up in collaboration with industry to design a 'quiet' lorry. Its aim was to produce an engine suitable for a heavy lorry with a target noise level of not more than 80 decibels. In 1973 the Heavy Commercial Vehicles Act came into force and during the 1970s TRRL's research covered lorry tyre noise; lorry parks; the management of urban freight movement; injuries to occupants of HGVs and the prediction of HGV fuel consumption.

In the 1980s attention to energy conservation and fuel consumption continued and the TRRL also looked at the environmental disturbance caused by articulated lorries and drawbars. Road pavement (q.v.) wear by HGVs was examined, as well as weighing systems for overloaded vehicles, suspension loads, trends in goods transport, public attitudes to lorry nuisance and the monitoring of lorries contravening lorry bans.

In 1992 the Laboratory became an executive agency of the Department of Transport and was renamed the Transport Research Laboratory (TRL). Becoming an Agency gave greater financial freedom and the opportunity to strengthen links with industry and bid for new business.

As the maximum permitted weights of heavy goods vehicles increased, the TRL conducted surveys to review the impacts of these changes. Emphasis on environmental issues led to research into noise measurement and perception, acceleration smoke tests and emission characteristics of diesel engines. Safety issues included examining HGV accident statistics, underrun guards, anti-lock braking systems and sleepiness in HGV drivers.

The TRL successfully transferred into the private sector in 1996 as the Transport Research Foundation, a non-profit foundation constituted to provide independence and impartiality. TRL currently employs around 400 technical specialists. Research into the safety and environmental impacts of road haulage and logistics continues. TRL maintains its leading edge capability in transport research, complemented by consultancy and advice services. **SB**

Charlesworth (1987)

Transport Services Ltd was formed as a publicly-quoted holding company in 1936 for General Roadways Ltd (q.v.) and Ex-Army Transport Ltd, followed by further acquisitions until 1946. Claud Barrington (q.v.) was the leading force behind TS, with financial backing from Harley Drayton whose city connections made him chairman. CD&T did not itself join TS until 1944 but, as a Scammell agent, influenced many TS companies to operate Scammell lorries. TS was sometimes known as the Star Group, as the only common identity was the fleet number placed within a star emblem on the front scuttle. As it expanded, a start was made on amalgamating the acquisitions into larger regional companies. At nationalisation TS was quickly acquired by the British Transport Commission to take advantage of its management expertise in building up BRS. Much of the BRS operating manual was based on TS practice. The Road Haulage Executive took over the 22 haulage subsidiaries listed below.

A H Barlow (Transport) Ltd, a Manchester haulier operating chiefly between the North West and London, acquired in the late 1930s.

Henry Bayes & Sons Ltd, an old-established local haulier of London EC2 that specialised in market and produce deliveries, using horse-drawn vans as well as motor vehicles.

J Blaney Ltd, of Felling, Gateshead, acquired in the mid-1940s.

W Bradbrook & Sons Ltd of Bethnal Green, general haulier.

CD&T (Contracts) Ltd, the contract-hire subsidiary of Carey, Davis & Thomas Ltd. Whitbread & Co. Ltd and Bulmers Cider were major clients, but Bulmers took over its lorry fleet at the time of nationalisation and Whitbreads not long after.

Davies & Brownlow Ltd, St Helens.

East Anglian Transport Services Ltd, formed from Child & Sons Ltd, formerly Child & Pullen Ltd of Ipswich, which operated services to London, the Midlands and the North, chiefly for agricultural produce.

Gamman & Dicker Ltd of Chatham, cold-store operators and carriers of meat, provisions, parcels and smalls, acquired by TS in the late 1930s, General Roadways Ltd.

Kinders Transport Ltd, formerly Kinders Garage & Haulage Co. of Blaby, with its mainly Leyland Octopus fleet, was acquired in 1941, Alice Walker (q.v.) then being its sole director. It was renamed in 1944 when the Loughborough Transport Co. was acquired by TS and merged with it.

Kneller & Chandler Ltd, general haulier of London E1, with services to Bristol and Birmingham, acquired in 1936. Its largely Sentinel steam waggon fleet had been replaced mainly with Scammell and Foden flats. C Durston Ltd of Stratford E15 was absorbed when acquired by TS in 1942.

S J Mengis Ltd, a local haulier of London SE1.

North Western Transport Services Ltd, was the name adopted in 1942 for Ex-Army Transport Ltd of Salford, a general haulier, originally set up as a clearing house/operator for ex-service men, with services extending as far as Glasgow, Gateshead, Bristol and London. It included owner-drivers operating vehicles in its livery. Samuel Royle, its driving force, became a director of TS. Its Hull depot was operated by NWTS Ltd (Hull) Ltd.

Northumbrian Transport Services Ltd, a regional subsidiary formed by TS from Northumbrian Transport Ltd of Newcastle, which had origins similar to Ex-Army Transport Ltd and ran services to Manchester and Liverpool. It joined TS in 1936 and subsequently absorbed Orrell & Brewster of Gateshead, Atkinson Transport Ltd of Newcastle, Joynson Loughton & Co. and County Transport of Glasgow.

Quinceys Ltd, a Leicester-based parcels and smalls carrier serving London and Leeds, acquired in the mid 1940s.

South Eastern Roadways Ltd, Cheriton, Folkestone.

Southern Transport Co. Ltd, Brighton, was a late acquisition in 1946. It operated locally, with a London trunk service. It also had a contract-hire operation, Brighton Co-operative Society being its major customer.

West Midlands Roadways Ltd, formed by TS in 1945 by an amalgamation of Henry Hawker of Burton, H & S Hawker Ltd of Nuneaton and A G Andow & Co. Ltd of Walsall, all mainly tipper operators.

West Wales Roadways Ltd, formed by the merger of two Pembrokeshire acquisitions, John Ford (Pembroke) Ltd and Fred Rees (Nayland) Ltd.

Bert Whiting & Son Ltd of Dalston E8, a local carrier of meat, parcels and smalls, which joined TS soon after the war. Its depot was also used by other TS Companies. Donaldson

Wright Ltd, which grew out of the Nottingham Chamber of Commerce clearing house, operated a parcels and smalls service between Nottingham and London. Its new depot opened at Lenton in 1940 also served NWTS.

The group's body-building subsidiary, Star Bodies Ltd at Salford, was also taken over and continued to build bodies for BRS and NFC until c.1988. The TS subsidiary RPC Transport Ltd, which provided contract-hire vehicles for the Rugby Portland Cement Co., was acquired by the cement company prior to nationalisation.

GM

Dunbar (1981); Ingram and Mustoe (1999)

Transport Tribunal, see APPEAL TRIBUNALS

Transport Unit Finance Ltd was a finance company set up by the Road Haulage Association (q.v.) with the United Dominions Trust Ltd in 1953, to provide financial facilities for RHA members wishing to buy Road Haulage Executive (q.v.) assets. Some directors were appointed by the RHA, which also made arrangements to collect information from members and former members about their requirements and recommendations in connection with RHE disposals. **RAS**

Birch and Harper (1995)

Transport Vehicles (Warrington) Ltd was established by a consortium including Tom Ward of North Cheshire Motors and Ron Mason of R E Mason group, long distance coal hauliers, major Sentinel operator and a member of the Speedway group (q.v.), which acquired the manufacturing rights of the Sentinel Road Vehicle Division when Rolls-Royce Ltd purchased the Sentinel concern in 1956. From 1957 TVW lorries were assembled in a factory at Winwick Street, Warrington, to Sentinel designs, the early ones utilising actual Sentinel parts. A few had Sentinel engines, though most had proprietary ones. When production ceased in 1961, some one hundred TVW lorries had been built; the factory had also rebuilt, re-engined, re-configured, and re-cabbed a quantity of existing Sentinels.   **RAS**

Matlock (1987); E J Muckley, 'The story of Ernest B Ward/TVW', *Vintage Roadscene*, 15, 57, pp. 12–17

Transports Gefco was founded in 1950 as Groupages express de Franche-Comté. It merged in 1956 with Transauto, which specialised in the transport of Peugeot vehicles by rail and road. In 1969 the Bellier concern of Grenoble was acquired. When Peugeot took control of Citroen in 1978 Transports Stur (Société des Transports Urbains et Ruraux) came under Gefco control. It now provided commercial vehicle rental services. Transport Gefco's UK operations in particular centre on Peugeot's plants in Coventry. Worldwide it employs 5500 at 150 sites, transporting 2 million cars and vans and 6.5 million tonnes of goods per annum. In 1999 the Swiss firm Kühne & Nagel joined Gefco in a new organisation, Gefco-KN, in which Gefco had a majority holding.   **RAS**

Charge Utile, 73 (January 1999), pp. 22–3; *transporte mundial,* 147 (September 1999), p.44

Trials, see LANCASHIRE HEAVY MOTOR VEHICLE TRIALS; ROAD TESTS; WAR OFFICE TRIALS

Trojan cars and light vans were designed in 1913 by L H Hounsfield and produced by Leyland in its factory at Kingston-on-Thames, Surrey, from 1922 to 1928, during which time 11,000 cars and 6700 vans were made, and

afterwards at Hounsfield's own factory in Croydon. The first 5-cwt model had solid tyres, chain drive, a two-speed epicyclic gearbox with the footbrake operating on the rear wheels and the handbrake on the transmission. The engine was a two-stroke with only seven moving parts and was rated at 10 hp. A 7-cwt model which could be fitted with pneumatic tyres was introduced in 1926 and was replaced in 1933 by an improved model taking a 10-cwt load. Solid tyres were available on Trojan vans into the 1930s. Hounsfield contended that the Trojan's long cantilever spring suspension made pneumatic tyres unnecessary, thereby significantly reducing operating costs. The vans were popular as tradesman's delivery vehicles and were extensively used by the Brooke Bond Tea Company which ordered nearly 2000 between 1924 and 1929. Other well-known customers included the Post Office and Marley Tiles.

In 1937 the 12-cwt Senior was introduced with the original features except that Bendix brakes were now fitted. In 1947 a completely new 15-cwt van was introduced, still with a two-stroke engine, but an alternative Perkins engine was now offered. The last model in 1958 was the forward-control 25-cwt with a Perkins 3-cylinder diesel engine. It was not a commercial success and the company merged with Lambretta Concessionaires Ltd in 1959. Thereafter scooters were its major concern, although vans continued until 1965, including a few Heinkel bubble cars badged Trojan and available as parcel carriers.   **GK**

P Collins and M Stratton, *British Car Factories from 1896* (Godmanstone: Veloce Publishing, 1993); Stevens-Stratten (1993); Brian Culpan, 'Trojan Service', *Classic Van and Pick-up,* 1, 1 (2000), pp. 12–13; Lord Montagu, *Lost Causes of Motoring* (Cassell, 1960), chap. 10; Nick Baldwin, 'The Leyland Cub', *OM,* 9, 3 (1975), p. 212; Eric Rance and Don Williams, *Can you afford to walk?: the history of the Hounsfield Trojan motor car* (Minster Lovell: Book-Marque, 1999)

Truck. Although the word was used from the eighteenth century for various forms of wheeled vehicle used to assist the manual movement of heavy loads, its twentieth-century meaning of a motor goods vehicle originated in the USA. It was incorporated into British military usage during the First World War and was used in UK advertising by American manufacturers between the wars. It was not much used in a civilian context until the 1970s, when it became associated with the new 'macho' image of the haulage industry and largely replaced the older word lorry (q.v.). The success of the new magazine *Truck*, launched in 1974, probably helped to consolidate the term in the UK. **GAB**

CM Show Issue (8 November 1935); *Economist* (1976)

The **Truck of the Year Award** was conceived by Pat Kennett, founding editor of *Truck* and first presented in 1977 by an all-British selection panel. For the following year the panel comprised an international team of journalists from Belgium, Denmark, Holland and Germany, with Kennett as chairman. Representatives from more European countries have since been added. From 1992 the panel has also nominated a separate International Van of the Year Award.

The Truck of the Year winners were

1977	Seddon Atkinson SA 200		
1978	MAN 280	1991	Renault Magnum AE
1979	Volvo F7	1992	Iveco Ford EuroCargo
1980	MAN 321	1993	Iveco Ford EuroTech
1981	Leyland T45 Roadtrain	1994	Volvo FH range
1982	Ford Cargo	1995	MAN F2000
1983	Renault G260/290	1996	Scania R range
1984	Volvo F10	1997	Mercedes-Benz Actros
1985	Mercedes LN2	1998	DAF 95XF
1986	Volvo FL range	1999	Mercedes-Benz Atego
1987	MAN F90	2000	Volvo FH range
1988	DAF 95	2001	MAN TG-A
1989	Scania 3 series	2002	DAF LF
1990	Mercedes-Benz SK		**GM**

Truckfests have been a regular feature of the road haulage scene since 1982. They are as much a social as a commercial phenomenon, although manufacturers normally have a presence, as well as operators and clubs. The principal Truckfest takes place at the East of England Showground, Peterborough, in association with EuroShell, but there are others at Driffield, Shepton Mallet and Edinburgh. Sponsors include manufacturers of vehicles, components and models, Eddie Stobart Ltd, the RHA and TGWU.   **RAS**

Truck racing had been a popular spectacle on the Continent for many years, but was not introduced into the UK until 1984, when a first event at Donington Park, Leics, race circuit attracted a crowd of over 100,000. It was supported openly or discreetly by a number of truck manufacturers, but by 2002 spectator interest was running at rather lower levels. **JMA**

Trunk operations (Figure 77) are regular long-distance services (compared to tramping (q.v.)). The first such services were those operated by McNamara & Co. Ltd (q.v.) for GPO parcel post before the First World War, but the first to operate trunk services in connection with a general haulage business was Fisher Renwick (q.v.). By 1922 it was running a daily service in each direction between its Manchester and London depots. Even with two drivers, the 186-mile journey took 28 hours at this period. By the late 1930s the second driver was no longer necessary; following the raising of the speed limit (q.v.) to 20 mph, improvements to the trunk roads and opening a new London depot at Muswell Hill, which cut out the journey across London to the previous depot at Shadwell, the journey could now be completed within a driver's permitted 11-hours driving time. Originally the drivers had worked right through to the vehicle's destination, but now it was normal practice for the London and Manchester drivers to exchange vehicles at the Meriden transport café (q.v.) on the A45 and return to their home depot, thus eliminating the costs and inconveniences of lodging-out. The trunk journey could now be undertaken overnight, carrying consignments collected during the afternoon for delivery next morning. This followed the pattern developed from the 1880s by the railways' express goods services, which was geared particularly to the needs of the meat, fish, fruit and vegetable markets. The trunk vehicle was 'double-shifted', the day driver participating in the delivery and collection work and loading the vehicle ready for the next trunk journey. In some firms the day driver was paid at a lower rate, but the two drivers allocated to each Fisher Renwick trunk vehicle were of equal status and worked 'week about'.

This pre-war Fisher Renwick operation was the archetypal road trunk service, however, there were variations on this pattern. All were designed to optimise the productivity of both drivers and vehicles, while meeting the demands of the customer. For example, as journey times improved, the trunk driver might also be engaged on collections or deliveries to make up a full working day. Lodging-out continued to be economic in some circumstances: it was a good way of establishing a new route without having to set up a depot at the destination; it might also be used to avoid setting up a depot in an area with high wage costs or labour shortages. At places without a depot, a shunter (q.v.) might be employed for the collection and delivery work, or an arrangement made for this to be undertaken by a local haulier. This working relationship could lead to joint operation of the route by the two hauliers.

By 1939 there were several firms whose trunk networks provided almost national coverage, at least between main centres, but it was BRS, after nationalisation, that built up the first truly national general haulage trunking network. The last quarter of the century saw major changes. Trunking for the large logistics contracts become a round-the clock operation; warehouses were built where there were no planning restrictions on delivery times and up to three trailers were employed for each tractor unit, so that the tractors could be kept in almost continuous use, except for maintenance requirements. The large express carriers developed hub-and-spoke operations, with the trunk services all radiating from a single midlands sorting depot. When BRS pulled out of general haulage in the 1980s, the trunking networks for mixed loads of general traffic disappeared. **MB/GAB**

Mustoe (1997), pp. 27–9, 58–9, 100; Ingram and Mustoe (1999)

Turn That Lorry Round campaign was launched in October 1962 by the Road Haulage Association (q.v.) and joined by BRS (q.v.) in an attempt to get the maximum utilisation of road haulage fleets. The background to the campaign included complaints about delays at the major docks. A cab-side logo incorporating a curved arrow was used in the year-long campaign. **RAS**

CM (23 December 1999), p.39; Baldwin (1982), p. 62

Turners (Soham) Ltd was established by Wallace Turner (d. 2000) and his brothers in 1931. From a farming family, their business was initially closely related to agriculture. Rapid expansion followed the partial denationalisation of the early 1950s: several small depots in Fenland were acquired and the large ex-BRS depot at Fordham, which remained the company's headquarters until 1993. 250 lorries were operated by the mid-1960s, rising to 700 lorries and 1000 trailers at the end of the century. Headquarters were moved to a new depot at Newmarket in 1993, which had cold store and chilled load consolidation facilities and workshops. Acquisitions in the 1990s included Hargrave International and Lowes of Paddock Wood and among major contracts were those for J Sainsbury and British Sugar, the latter retaining the company's historic links with agricultural products. **RAS**

G Edge, *CVC*, 6, 1 (September 2000), p.12

Twin-steer, see CHINESE SIX

Tyrer Transport Services came into being in 1973 but had a much longer history. Henry Tyrer started his own shipping agency and cargo handling firm in 1879 at Liverpool docks, mostly in the West African trades. A transport department was established in the 1930s as a means of extending its stevedoring role. Initially much was put out to independent owner-drivers (q.v.) but any intention to build up its own fleet ended with nationalisation.

In the mid-1960s Tyrer needed to move imported timber quickly from Canada Docks, Liverpool, when bulk carriers were introduced bringing much greater quantities than previously in one load. The firm tried unsuccessfully to interest the Transport Development Group (q.v.)

to undertake the road transport. Eventually the Liverpool depot of BRS took it on reluctantly, but it never provided adequate numbers of vehicles so Tyrer found itself introducing contract-hire vehicles regularly. To deal with this problem, at a time when diversification was seen as a sensible strategy, Speed Haulage was set up in 1970 as a wholly-owned subsidiary of Henry Tyrer Ltd. It learnt the business by having a tie with a long-established haulier, D R Pass & Co. of Southport, which undertook many of the services for Speed Haulage, which bought a few tractors and trailers.

Henry Tyrer was drawn deeper into road transport at the end of 1971 when BRS closed its loss-making Liverpool depot and withdrew from timber haulage. No other company was keen to take on the traffic. In 1973 Speed Haulage changed its name to Tyrer Transport Services and by 1975 was operating six tractors and an equal number of trailers. By 1978 this had increased to fifteen tractors, mostly Atkinsons and sixteen trailers. In addition a road haulage depot was acquired in Bootle and all activities were carried out in-house, the services of D R Pass being no longer necessary. **JA**

Peter N Davies, *Henry Tyrer: a Liverpool shipping agent and his enterprise, 1879–1979* (Croom Helm, 1979)

Tyres. In 1839 Charles Goodyear in the USA discovered the vulcanisation of rubber, enabling compounds for solid tyres to be developed. By 1881 solids had superseded iron tyres as the standard fitment on London's hansom cabs.

In 1888 the pneumatic tyre was re-invented by John Boyd Dunlop, who developed it for bicycles. At the turn of the century, the Michelin brothers pioneered pneumatics for the emergent car industry, but commercial motor vehicles were restricted to solids, and it was two decades before suitable pneumatics could be developed for commercials. The solid tyre was puncture-proof, but had a fundamental flaw. Under normal loads it overheated and then disintegrated at speeds much over 15 mph. The subsequent increase in the speed limit to 20 mph offered no practical benefit to solid-tyred vehicles. Solids also placed restrictions on vehicle design. Vehicles had to be very heavily built, because solids offered so little cushioning from road shocks.

Early pneumatic tyres also overheated, particularly with increases in speed and load. The problem was that the tyre casing was canvas, the warp and weft rubbing together as the tyre flexed and generating excessive heat. Part of the solution was to reduce flexing by running at higher tyre pressures, but the real solution came with the widespread adoption of cord (weftless) fabric as a casing material. This allowed the transport of heavier loads at higher speeds, since it could flex much more than canvas casings without overheating. In 1916 'Giant' pneumatic tyres for commercial vehicles became a reality and such tyres were offered in 1921 price-lists.

The Finance Act of 1928 allowed hackneys and commercials a 20 per cent rebate on road tax, if fitted with pneumatics. By 1930 almost all but the heaviest commercials were produced with pneumatics fitted. Soon solids were found, and still are, only on vehicles for specialised uses. The tubed cross-ply tyre, fitted on a multi-piece wheel (q.v.), thus became the standard.

From the early 1930s to the early 1950s, tyre developments, for example the use of rayon and nylon casings, met the increasing demands of both truck manufacturers and operators. However a radical development had taken place. Michelin had pioneered the concept of the radial ply tyre. This, at first, was adopted by the car industry, and rendered the cross ply, in spite of enormous improvements, obsolete. The benefits of radial ply construction were immediately recognised by operators, and their spread, as a tubed tyre on a multi-piece rim, was rapid. In the mid-1960s the tubeless radial fitted to a one-piece drop-centre rim arrived. This unit is lighter, more reliable, cooler running, more fuel-efficient, and must be capable of being remoulded at least once. This is the position today, though constant improvements and developments, e.g. super singles and low profile units, continue. **JB**

U

The **Ulster Transport Authority** (1948–67) was the successor to the Northern Ireland Road Transport Board (q.v.). The UTA took over the Board's goods and passenger vehicle fleets, which included pre-war Leyland lorries, purchasing only 66 new goods vehicles between its foundation and 1955. In 1950–1 the Board decided to increase the proportion of articulated units in the fleet, as experience with those already in service showed them to be more efficient and economical than rigids. This is evident in the vehicle purchases of the second half of the 1950s, although rigid vehicle purchases predominated thereafter.

UTA traffic, with appropriate vehicle types, included removals and livestock haulage, for which distinctive tilt-covered lorries, trailers and containers were employed; bulk cement work included tank vehicles and covered tippers. A heavy haulage and machinery transport division operated a number of Scammell tractor units. Privatisation demands were resisted in 1956; following the government decision in 1964 to break up the UTA, a successor road haulage undertaking, Northern Ireland Carriers Ltd, was established in conjunction with the Transport Holding Co. The UTA freight department closed in mid-1965, although some contract hire agreements were continued to their expiry date; the Lobitos contract inherited from the Board had ended c.1951. By the end of 1965 the new undertaking had a fleet of 700 vehicles, which had risen to 800 by the time it joined the National Freight Corporation (q.v.) in 1969.

RAS

Boyle (2000); Baldwin (1982), p.122

Unipower 4×4 timber tractors, for use on- as well as off-road, were introduced in 1937 by Universal Power Drives Ltd of Perivale, Middlesex, which already had an established business as a four- to six-wheel converter. Government home timber production policy in the Second World War ensured good demand for the Forester 4×4. In 1968 Unipower changed the direction of its output, introducing the

Invader, a forward-control 4×4 for recovery work and subsequently with an aircraft crash tender variant. In 1977 AC Cars bought Unipower and moved production to its Thames Ditton works. When the BLMC decided to dispose of Scammell Motors in 1988 (but without the marque name or the Watford factory), Unipower's experience made it a suitable purchaser. Employing largely ex-Scammell staff, Unipower set up on a smaller scale on another site in Watford, initially deriving most of its income from agreed Scammell parts manufacture, but developing the Scammell S24 and Nubian models and introducing a new 8-wheel military forward-control vehicle, the M series, which was adapted for various roles. Unipower's military vehicle potential resulted in its acquisition by Alvis plc in 1994.

RAS

Georgano (1997)

United Carriers Ltd was created in 1963 by the decision of Geoffrey Willis of Frank Willis & Son Ltd of Wellingborough and Rex Kearsley of K & D Transport Ltd of Earls Barton, to merge their two parcels businesses, with 91 vehicles serving Northamptonshire and Leicestershire and depots at Bradford, Bristol, London and Glasgow. They intended to develop a national parcels service using its own depots, by acquiring suitable businesses. To achieve this United Carriers became a publicly quoted company on the London Stock Exchange in 1963 enabling its shares to be used in payment.

By 1964 acquisitions had extended services into the north-west and the east, and then into West Yorkshire, the north-east and central Scotland. By 1966 some 300 vehicles were operated from 16 depots. In 1967 Collins Express Parcels Service Ltd, which covered the west midlands with 100 vehicles from two depots, merged with United and shortly after East Anglian Carriers was acquired to give full coverage of East Anglia and most of London. The 1968 Transport Act allowed organic growth as well as strategic acquisitions, as operators could no longer object to additional vehicles. In 1970 S E Thomas Ltd was acquired, giving coverage to the south east.

United had achieved its objective. The constituent companies became divisions of United and traded as United Carriers with standardisation of the primrose yellow and blue livery of the original United Carriers fleet. New or extended depots were opened and the fleet standardised on the Bedford TK range and ERF tractor units. A Sovereign Distribution Service offering a next-day service was introduced for selected customers at first from depots at Risley and Hitchin, then expanded to serve major conurbations.

Diversification into related areas took place; the first in 1978 was leasing vehicles, trailers and specialised equipment through United Carriers Leasing Ltd. In 1979 Abel Demountable Services Ltd was acquired, followed by the establishment of United Bodybuilders Ltd to build or refurbish bodies for the group and outside customers. The recession of the early 1980s was an opportunity for further selective expansion with the acquisition of a southern Irish carrier, a south-eastern-based carrier and Parcels Express, formerly SELNEC (q.v.). National Cover was formed, intended to give regions the ability to offer national coverage using United Group's depots and service.

In 1982 the group changed its title to United Parcels plc. Three further acquisitions were made, Scorpio International, a subsidiary of Coats Paton Textile Group, gave United its hanging garment service, the others strengthened United's English and Northern and Southern Irish services. In 1983 Graham Millard, chairman, and Keith Willis, the last founder director, retired. James White, managing director of Bunzl, joined the group to become non-executive chairman. Economic conditions caused a merging of parcels divisions and closing of depots.

York, Ward & Rowlatt, Bedford and Vauxhall dealers, who had previously supplied many United vehicles and bodies were acquired. Insurmountable financial problems caused the shock rescue of Atlas Express (q.v.) in 1984, adding some £200 million turnover, 1500 employees and 600 vehicles. This was followed in 1985, by the acquisition of York Trailer (q.v.). Bunzl made a successful offer to United

shareholders, and United became the fifth Bunzl division, Bunzl Transportation. The parcels business was renamed United Parcels and an overnight next-day service, Multifreight, was introduced. The division rapidly expanded, with a number of acquisitions including Ripponden & District Motors, a regional carrier serving the north west. The division did not prosper as part of Bunzl and became an independent company in 1989 following a management buy-out. The new group comprised four divisions: parcels, distribution and warehousing, textile distribution and transport engineering but continued to make losses. There were closures and disposals of the engineering division and the former distribution, now logistics, businesses. New acquisitions included Carpet Express and Manspeed, providing transport service to Vauxhall and General Motors' European operation. United Carriers again became a quoted company in 1994. Altogether there were 34 depots and 3100 vehicles, trailers and demountable swap bodies. New management did not enable the Group to achieve its former eminence and profitability and in 1999 it was acquired by Geodis (France) and closed in 2002, still being unprofitable. **GM**

United Parcel Service was the name adopted in 1919 for what began in Seattle in 1907 as a cycle messenger and delivery service, organised by Jim Casey. Motor-van delivery for retail stores soon became its main activity and expansion into other US cities began. Because increasing car ownership was eroding its delivery business, UPS changed in the early 1950s into a long-distance common carrier of parcels, in direct competition with the US postal service, using air for its premium service, with a weight limit of 50 lbs and a combined size limit (length plus width) of 108 inches. By 1975 it covered all 48 contiguous US states and parts of Canada. A unique feature of its operations was insistence on clean-shaven drivers. Moustaches or beards were not allowed. In 1976 it embarked on its first venture in Europe, a domestic service within Germany. At first this had operating problems caused by cultural differences, particularly the German dislike of working overtime.

In 1988 UPS launched an international carrier service with its own airline. At the end of the year this extended to 41 countries, including the UK where it acquired Ark Star/Atlasair and IML Couriers. By 1992 it was serving 200 countries and claimed to be the world's largest express carrier and package delivery company but it was not until the late 1990s that these international operations became profitable.

Seeking to expand its British operation, it had unsuccessful talks with United Parcels, formerly United Carriers (q.v.), but then in 1992 acquired Carryfast Ltd (q.v.) together with its Haulfast subsidiary. Carryfast was successfully transformed into UPS's UK arm and by 2001 had 3600 employees and a delivery fleet of over 900 in the now familiar Pullman railroad brown livery first adopted between the wars. It served the East Midlands, Edinburgh and Stansted airports which were linked to UPS's European air hub at Cologne/Bonn airport. The UK head office at Feltham, Middlesex, reported to the headquarters of UPS Europe in Brussels, which in turn reported to the company HQ, which moved to Atlanta in 1991. The Haulfast subsidiary, still trading under its own name, includes trunk services for UPS. In the early 1990s UPS was the first to issue its drivers with hand-held computers, linked to the company's parcel tracking system, to scan the label barcodes of delivered parcels and capture proof-of-delivery signatures.

An unusual feature of UPS operation was its use of vans (termed package cars) built since 1988 to its own designs for at least a 12-year life. It introduced the first of these to the UK in 1994, by which time over 4000 left-hand drive versions were already in use in France and Germany. They were built in four sizes, the smallest being the P36 (with 360 cu. ft loadspace) and the largest the P80. Bodywork is mainly in aluminium, but with some glass fibre. The main features of the vans are their height, the unobstructed cab area and sliding doors. Driveline components came from several sources, including Citroen, Mercedes-Benz and VW, with construction undertaken by German bodybuilders. **GM**

IDCH, 5 (1992), pp. 433–5; *IDCH*, 17 (1997), pp. 503–6; A J Wright, *abc Cargo Airlines* (Shepperton: Ian Allan, 2000), pp. 201–4; UPS public relations factsheets

United Parcels Ltd, see UNITED CARRIERS LTD

The **United Road Transport Union,** the last remaining road transport union outside the Transport & General Workers Union (q.v.), formed in 1890 in Manchester as the United Carters' Association (leaving the Mersey Quay & Railway Carters Union). The union underwent a series of name changes to become finally the URTU in 1964. It has frequently pursued a policy distinct from other transport unions. Thus during the General Strike (q.v.) of 1926 it avoided calling out its members by the liberal issue of emergency transport permits. It has frequently been at odds with the TGWU RTC group and there were a number of clashes as the latter grew in strength during the 1960s. Manchester remains its centre, especially in own-account distribution, although it has retained pockets of support elsewhere, including in the hire and reward sector. **PS**

United Service Transport Co., one of London's largest independent contract hire specialists, was formed in the early 1900s by Walter Flexman French who had started business in the 1880s as a bicycle manufacturer in Balham, London. After experimenting with De Dion motor chassis, he diversified into coach operation before setting up a goods service, which was engaged primarily on contract hire, aimed at giving employment to ex-servicemen.

It held many large contracts, for example, with breweries, but its most notable operation in later years was newspaper delivery for the *Evening Standard*. For this a fleet of specialist high-power vans was employed. In the 1950s the Austin FX3 taxi chassis was favoured, primarily for its tight turning circle and ample engine power. A notable feature of UST vehicles was that all radiator cowls displayed a 'UNITED' badge, the only reference to the operator's name, with no other sign-writing on the usual two-tone green livery, unless the hirer's own colour scheme was used.

The organisation avoided nationalisation in 1948 as all operations were within a twenty-five mile radius of its Wandsworth base garage. The building featured a façade incorporating mosaic stonework displaying the company name, a practice also adopted at its sub-depots in Euston, Blackfriars and Balham. UST finally ceased in the late 1960s, when it was absorbed into the Hertz organisation before becoming part of the Godfrey Davis Group. **CS**

The **United Vehicle Workers' Union** was created in 1919 through the amalgamation of the London and Provincial Union of Licensed Vehicle Workers (the 'red button' union) and the Amalgamated Association of Tramway and Vehicle Workers (the 'blue button' union). The former, formed in 1913 from an amalgamation of the London Cabmen's Trade Union (established 1894) and the London Bus, Tram and Motor Workers' Union (about which little is known), was imbued with a syndicalist ethos. It had a small commercial haulage membership. The AATVW had been established in 1889 and had expanded throughout England in the tram sector. Its ethos of responsible trade unionism was quite different from the LPULVW. In 1893 it amalgamated with the Manchester and Salford Carters' Union and it later strengthened its organisation in commercial haulage through adhesion of the Belfast Carters' Union and the Huddersfield Carters' Union.

The goal of the UVWU was an industrial union for all road transport workers. In 1919 the Amalgamated Carters, Lurrymen and Motormen's Union joined as the North of England Commercial Section, followed in 1920 by the National Union of Carriers (a London-based union that recruited in Carter Paterson Ltd) as an autonomous section, and the Stoke Horsemen's Union. The UVWU proved unable to overcome the sharp differences between the LPULVW and the AATVW, and after the stalling of negotiations with the National Union of Vehicle Workers, it became a founding constituent of the Transport & General Workers Union (q.v.). The UVWU made an important contribution to both the TGWU as a whole and the RTC group at the union's formation in 1922. **PS**

Utility International is an American trailer manufacturer, established in 1914 by E and H Bennett, the sons of a British immigrant. Still a family business, it has seven factories in the USA (where it holds the rights to the Tautliner). In 1998 it set up in the UK in the former York (q.v.) factory at Northallerton, on the basis of equally-shared ownership with Wordsworth Holdings, a conglomerate. Its UK product range comprised refrigerated and curtain-sided trailers and rigid bodywork, produced at the former Glasgow branch of Grahams of Gildersome. In 2002 the UK operation was put into voluntary liquidation. Poor sales and market reluctance to buy refrigerated bodywork with external rivets were the main reasons for the failure. **RAS**

CM (18 November 1999), pp. 12–13; *MT* (25 July 2002)

V

Van (Figures 109, 144, 146, 180 and 188) shortened from caravan came into use in the early nineteenth century for light 4-wheeled, or occasionally 2-wheeled usually single-horse, vehicles with elliptical springs, used chiefly for parcels and tradesmen's deliveries. They were open, with sides, headboard and drop-down tailboard, or covered, the cover developing from a tilt (q.v.), through a more permanent canvas-covered structure, to a panelled body. Horse-drawn vans usually had tarpaulin curtains above a drop tailboard at the back and an open or partially-covered front, with the driver sitting under the protection of the cover. The fully-enclosed body, or box van, did not generally appear until the motor era.

Typically a motor van had a pair of doors at the rear, but large vans might also have a door at the front of one or both sides to provide better access to mixed loads. Roller-shutters (q.v.) became available as an alternative form of van door from the 1920s and the tailboard began to be superseded by the tail-lift (q.v.) from the 1950s. Side-access designs, sometimes with sliding doors, were often preferred for street deliveries to premises without rear access. Special-purpose van types include bullion or security vans (q.v.), gown vans (q.v.) and temperature-controlled (q.v.) vehicles.

Vans were seen as a significant use of the motor vehicle's potential from the earliest days of the industry. For example, the somewhat optimistic prospectus of H J Lawson's Great Horseless Carriage Co. of 1896 included motor express vans and parcels delivery among the specified uses of the new motor vehicle. In the following year an order for 100 Daimler chassis at the rate of two, then three, per week was placed by the London Motor Van & Waggon Co. Daimler lost on the deal, as the clients complained that the vans needed constant repair and Daimler had to second a staff member to the company.

These early vans set the trend for car-derived vehicles, especially in the 5-cwt to 10-cwt payload sector, for many years, until the post-1945 period was marked by such distinctive models as the Morris-Commercial PV (parcels van) and J series, the Austin K8 Three-way van and later the Bedford CA and Ford Transit. When the CA series was replaced by the CF in 1970, 370,000 CA vans had been produced in its 17 year run; this sliding-door model had proved its usefulness and popularity. Its successor had to contend with the appeal of the Ford Transit, produced in 1965, from Southampton and Ghent, Belgium.

The Transit was designed as a joint European venture as the result of a decision taken in 1961, five years before Ford of Europe was initiated. The brief was to produce a medium-sized, capacious and economical commercial vehicle of extreme versatility. The original model line-up included 78 variations, from bare chassis to 15-seat bus; 2 million Transits were produced in its first twenty years. The second generation Transit was launched in 1986. Superimposition of the body profiles of marks one and two showed their close relationship, although the second generation was more aerodynamic, with a lower drag coefficient, achieved by an angled front and vertically extended rear. The development of the third generation Transit, launched in 2000, was largely a Detroit exercise, although with British engineers involved and a close study of the European market. The launch by Iveco in mid-1999 of its new Daily City Truck illustrated the global nature of van production and marketing at the end of the twentieth century. In addition to two European plants, at Suzzara (Italy) and Valladolid (Spain), it was produced in Brazil and China (as a market penetrator). Iveco's acquisition of the major European contract hire firm Fraikin provided further potential penetration for the new van, the appeal of which was enhanced by the variety of volume, load length, load height and payload offered by nine standard models on three different wheelbases.

For van manufacturers, large fleet orders, above all from the Post Office (q.v.) were of considerable importance; for a small manufacturer such as Trojan the loyalty of a single customer (in Trojan's case, the Brooke Bond Tea Co.) provided a reliable demand. In their heyday, co-operative societies (q.v.) were cumulatively large operators of vans, as are such contemporary enterprises as Securicor Omega Express and GUS White Arrow Express Ltd, which in 1986 operated an exclusively Transit van fleet of 2000 vehicles. On a smaller scale, in the same year Harold Cross of west London had a self-drive tipper rental fleet which included some 75 Transits.

The conventional van occupies a place towards the end of the delivery chain, but even lighter, three-wheel vans had their advocates, especially in the first three decades of the twentieth century, on the grounds of low cost of purchase and operation (including lower road tax) and manoeuvrability. Fitness of purpose was also argued; not using a larger vehicle when a smaller one would carry a small load. Meyrick-Jones and Wyatt, writing in 1913 identified 'tricars' and 'light carriers' as light vehicle types which should be considered by business purchasers, the tricar, if below 7-cwt unladen weight, had the advantage that it could be driven by a 14 year old boy, thereby avoiding a man's wage. There were at that time two basic configurations, the driver behind the load-box, as with the Autocarrier, Omnium and Warrick, and in front, which included the Girling and the Wall. Of these marques, Autocarrier was the best known, its customers including the GWR and the London & South Western Railway, newspaper and biscuit firms, Freeman, Hardy & Willis and Boots. Meyrick-Jones forecast the replacement of the tricar by the light, four-wheel van when this evolved.

In the event, the conventional light vans of the inter-war period, such as the Austin Seven, Ford and Morris (such as the 5-cwt of 1930), provided the necessary substitute for the three-wheel van, most marques of which expired between 1914 and 1925. Exceptions were the James (1929–39) and the Raleigh (1929–35), the latter leading to the Reliant (q.v.), and the Fleet (1932–6).

Even further down the delivery chain than tricars were motor cycle combinations (q.v.), which were advocated by the motor cycle industry between the wars. Special requirements for vans were posed by newspaper traffic (q.v.). There was some penetration of the UK van market in the 1920s by foreign firms, such as

Fiat and Unic (which already had a foothold in the related taxi-cab sector), but the growth of UK production tended to outprice such competition. An unusual variation was the conversion of Delaunay-Belleville car chassis into vans by its London concessionaires. The advertising potential of the panel van was appreciated by users and promoted by manufacturers such as Ford, resulting in distinctive liveries, with illustrations as well as lettering.

In recent years, a variety of businesses, including Harrods (q.v.) have recognised the publicity value of replica vintage vans for local delivery. They have the advantage of modern running gear and the robust Ford Transit chassis was a suitable basis for such vehicles, produced, for example, by Anthony Stevens of Warwick, the Asquith Motor Carriage Co. and the Fleur de Lys group. The ultimate publicity machine might be a Rolls-Royce-based van, of which various examples have appeared over the years, including a Cunard-bodied van in 1937, operated by H Pye & Sons Ltd for Seager's Gin, and a 1977 Silver Shadow converted to carry Krug champagne; Johnson Matthey, the metal refiners, used Rolls-Royce vans in the 1950s, but, for security reasons, without identification. Retail delivery of foodstuffs to individual homes, taken for granted in many areas until the spread of car ownership and the supermarket from the 1950s, made a comeback at the century's end, with home delivery (q.v.) pioneered in 1998 by Iceland and Somerfields. Other supermarkets followed using vans with special bodywork incorporating ambient, chilled and frozen food compartments. **RAS/GAB**

Lord Montagu and D Burgess-Wise, *Daimler Century* (Yeovil: Patrick Stephens, 1995); Baldwin and Ingram (1977); N Baldwin, *Old Delivery Vans* (Princes Risborough: Shire, 1987); Stevens-Stratten, (1991); P Llewellin and D Burgess-Wise, *Tranny: the Ford Transit's first 20 Years* (Ford Motor Co., 1986); *CM* supplement, *Transit: the second chapter* (1986); Meyrick-Jones and Wyatt (1913); Cole (1980); Ford Transit advertisement, *CM* (18 October 1986); T Clark, 'Rebirth for the mighty Transit', *CM*, (13 January 2000), pp 16–19; *Iveco Daily: the city truck*: supplement to *Truck* (February 2000); Thompson (1980); Smith (1994); Twells and Bourne (1983)

Van boys (Figure 186) were a recognised feature of urban distribution in the nineteenth century and their alternative designation, van guard, indicates one of their roles, that of protecting a tilt van with no other means of security, while deliveries were being made. They also ensured the horse was not left unattended and speeded up deliveries. By the 1920s those with professional interests in the welfare of young people were concerned that some categories of van-boy employment were unprotected by legislation, especially in terms of hours worked, which the spread of the motor lorry had tended to increase, by raising the radius of delivery travel. Parents might be indifferent to the long hours worked by their children (there were some van girls, at least in Liverpool), but the more responsible employers were conscious of abuses and of the blind alley nature of the job, it not being generally possible to re-employ and redeploy every van boy on reaching the age of 18. Although protection by law or negotiated agreement covered many such juvenile workers (for example, in the retail trade and railway van boys), there was sufficient problem for Liverpool Corporation to attempt to address it by local legislation. The papers of (Sir) Joseph Hallsworth of the National Union of Distributive & Allied Workers provide good coverage of the subject in 1930. After the Second World War, with full employment, higher wages and greater educational opportunities, van boys began to disappear, to be replaced in some cases by dogs travelling in the van to provide security. **RAS**

Hallsworth Papers (MSS.70/3/4) in the Modern Records Centre, University of Warwick Library; David Fowler, *The First Teenagers: the lifestyle of young wage-earners in interwar Britain* (Woburn Press, 1995), ch. 1

Van salesmen are a long-established feature of the transport scene, though their vehicles may sometimes more correctly be described as lorries. Such salesmen with their vehicles make regular calls on corner shops, cafés, restaurants and licensed premises, usually with perishable products such as food and drink. Bread and cakes, pork pies and crisps are typical items sold and delivered in this fashion.

In the 1920s and 1930s, when product distribution was not as well organised, selling in this fashion to retailers was more common. London biscuit maker Meredith & Drew began with ten salesmen with Ford vans in 1919 'to sell to small retailers for immediate delivery against cash'. Ten years later more than 150 1½-ton Morris or Dennis vans were employed, working from 23 depots. Access to the loadspace was through rear double doors or a central sliding door beside the driver's seat.

Vehicles used by van salesmen more recently have been conventional delivery vehicles with shelving and racking inside, but without any facilities for viewing. An example of a large van-salesman operation is that of Cadbury Cakes. In 1971 it operated 16 artics (with 28 semi-trailers), seven rigid trucks and 284 salesvans, almost all being on contract hire. Ford Transits formed the largest part of the fleet and the interior layout included a small desk at the rear. Household deliveries of soft drinks still survive today in parts of Scotland.

Van salesmen call at specific retail premises, whereas mobile shops (q.v.) usually carry a wider range of goods but normally park at certain locations and wait for customers to come to them. **JMA**

Vauxhall, see BEDFORD

Vehicle manufacturing industry. From the earliest days UK lorry-builders had considerable success in export markets, though some of this was the result of protectionism, in that most British colonies ultimately imposed punitive tariffs on products sourced from outside the Empire. The flood of US-built vehicles was stemmed in the 1920s by a protective tariff, a move which contributed to the decision by General Motors to set up a UK truck-builder. Bedford not only sold successfully in the UK but was able to build up numerous markets in the British colonies. British builders such as AEC, Albion, Guy, Leyland, Thornycroft developed big overseas markets, in the Empire and elsewhere. In the 1920s and 1930s vehicle builders were going bankrupt or being taken-over. Such closures suggest an over-crowded industry from the outset, with too many small firms, unable to benefit from economies of scale.

The UK's truck-making industry declined dramatically during the last three decades of the twentieth century. That decline was preceded by take-overs and mergers from the 1950s, when the post-war building boom was over and most fleets had re-equipped.

It has become almost a tradition to bemoan take-overs and blame the winning suitor, but most were the result of declining sales, perhaps because design and development of improvements or new models had fallen behind, probably because of lack of sufficient investment. That in turn was usually because profits were low, because sales were too low or dividends to shareholders too high.

From the 1960s multi-national manufacturers have gained size and influence and have tended to regard Western Europe as almost a single entity, so that closure of a factory in a particular country is of relatively minor importance to them, in a much greater scenario. The decision to stop building Bedford trucks followed several years of under-investment and hence declining sales: parent General Motors was spending its resources on its car plants, pending development of a new world truck design. When it came to decision time, it was judged that catching up would be just too costly.

The other principal reason for the modern decline in the number of manufacturers, a situation repeated in most Western European countries, is the high level of reliability and low servicing requirements of the modern truck. It may not be kept for as long as previously but, aided by the higher speed limits, the mileage it runs is far higher. Add to that double- or even treble-shifting of a vehicle, and the truck population as a whole is bound to fall. The rises in weight limits (q.v.) and maximum dimensions also reduced the total number of trucks. There is only so much to be moved at a given time and even a small increase in weight, say from 38 to 40 tons, reduced the number of trucks required to do the same amount of work.

Increases in gross weights in the UK have generally been much slower than elsewhere in Western Europe, and that has been a considerable handicap to UK builders. The most noteworthy example of this was in the 1960s when an expected increase in maximum weights from 24 to 32 tons was long hinted at, but slow in coming. Indeed some makers put into production new models of greater strength and more power to handle the increase, only to find that the government again dithered and they were left in the short term trying to sell vehicles which weighed more and therefore had a lower payload than the models they replaced. The appreciably lower maxima that then applied in the UK also deprived makers of much practical experience in designing and running heavier vehicles and undoubtedly gave Swedish and German makers an advantage when they began selling in the UK. Lack of practical 'at home' experience of higher weights probably also had an adverse effect on exports. The lorries made by foreign firms were also often better appointed.

UK truck exports once ran at high levels: combined, Leyland, Albion and Scammell were exporting to over 100 countries by the early 1960s. Governments want their country to develop its own industries, including truck-building. Any successful importer then has to invest considerable sums in building a local assembly plant, or face the prospect of ultimately being forced out by high tariffs on imports. It is easy to bemoan the demise of the UK's home truck industry, but most other European countries in 2000 also now have only one or two home-based makers and trucks are still built in relative quantity in the UK: Land-Rover, Dennis and LDV are made in the Midlands, Vauxhall and Renault vans in Luton, the Transit at Southampton and DAF and Foden in Leyland.   **JMA**

Vehicle types, legal definition of. The legal terms are not synonymous with those in common usage. The word 'locomotive' was first used, in the context of road transport, to mean a steam-powered vehicle, but in the Locomotives Act 1861 (the first Public General Act to regulate their use on public highways) it was defined as meaning a road vehicle with any form of mechanical propulsion.

The distinctive character of the new motor vehicles that started to appear in the 1890s, whose light-weight construction had more in common with horse-drawn carriages than with heavy steam locomotives, was recognised by the Locomotives on Highways Act 1896, which created a separate legal class of mechanically-propelled vehicles at first known as 'light locomotives'. This term was soon replaced by 'motor cars', brought into legal usage by the Motor Car Act 1903.

For the purpose of the Construction & Use Regulations (q.v.) the Heavy Motor Car Order 1904 divided the motor car class into two, defining a 'heavy motor car' as one with an unladen weight of more than 2 tons. At the same time the maximum weight was increased to encompass the new motor lorries and motor buses that were now emerging. In the 1920s the heavy motor car class was further extended to embrace the new 6- and 8-wheel rigid and articulated lorry types.

The Road Traffic Act 1930 re-defined the classification of mechanically-propelled vehicles; goods vehicles were now divided into five classes, which remain unchanged except that the defining weights were metricated in 1981. Those vehicles that carry goods (and may also haul a trailer) are either *motor cars* or, if the unladen weight exceeds 2½ tons (2540 kg), *heavy motor cars*. Those that only haul trailers are *motor tractors* (unladen weight not exceeding 7¼ tons (7370 kg)), *light locomotives* (unladen weight greater than 7¼, but not exceeding 11½ tons (11690 kg)) or *heavy locomotives* (unladen weight greater than 11½ tons). **GAB**

Vincents of Reading, coachbuilders, was a pioneer horse-box producer from 1912, when it first built one on a Dennis chassis at the request of a well-known trainer. Vincents produced other commercial vehicle bodies, changing to field kitchens during the First World War. It was also agents for a wide range of makes, including, in 1920, the Hupmobile and the Robey steam wagon.

After the war, Vincents' patent horse-box led in its niche market; features included a flush-set, coiled spring device, which permitted the vehicle loading ramp to be operated single-handed. The ramp was held in place by Vincents' patent fastening system; fittings and partitions were adjustable or removable for flexible use of the vehicle. In time its range of large and fast horse-boxes was extended by production on smaller and cheaper chassis for horse-owners who were their own drivers. General livestock bodies, including double-deck (q.v.) and articulated trailer livestock carriers, were also produced, as well as less specialised goods bodywork. Although bodies were of traditional timber-framing and panelling until the 1960s, Vincents developed a faired-in cab and body roof as a distinctive feature. By the late 1930s it had built over 900 horse-boxes, supplying among others the royal family, Indian princes, the India Office, the War Department and railway companies.

During the Second World War bodybuilding continued, including on at least 2000 AEC Matadors, as well as war-work. Horse-box production was resumed after 1945, but trailer boxes became increasingly popular with private owners and Lambourn (q.v.) was a rival. In the 1970s the Penta Group acquired Vincents, moved production to a new factory at Frome, concentrating on car sales in Reading, and then decided after ten years to cease horse-box production. **RAS**

N Baldwin, 'Vincents of Reading', *VCVM*, 57 (July 1994), pp. 44, 66–9; copy of Vincents' publicity, late 1930s: BP Library of Motoring, National Motor Museum

Viney, H, & Co. Ltd (Figure 187) of Preston was a Lancashire haulier associated for most of its existence with the Leyland marque. It was founded in 1906 with the intention of producing steam wagons, but instead began haulage with Coulthard wagons, changing to Leyland after the demise of Coulthard. C M le Gosselin (q.v.) purchased the business in 1908, having joined as manager. At the peak of its employment of Leyland steam wagons it operated some 25, the last being withdrawn in 1933. Textiles, timber and engineering products provided regular traffic, including trams from the Dick, Kerr works; drawbar trailers were used for these, the tram trucks being carried on the lorry. Aircraft sections were carried in the First World War, using an articulated van conversion. In 1926 a separate fuel distribution operation was established as a subsidiary, Lancashire Petrol Deliveries, to carry industrial alcohols, benzole and coal tar derivatives. By 1949 Viney was operating over 80 vehicles, mainly Leylands, while LPD had over 50 tankers. Nationalisation by voluntary acquisition that year saw the LPD operation absorbed by Pickfords. **RAS**

Volvo Truck Corporation (Figures 10, 41, 54, 62, 67, 79, 83, 156 and 175). The parent AB Volvo began car manufacture in 1927 and light commercial vehicle production soon evolved from this, with heavier commercials appearing in the 1930s. Acquisitions over the years added to Volvo's range and strength. By 1961 some 13,000 commercials were being produced annually. The introduction of the F85, 86 and 88 series in 1965 was the prelude to serious penetration of the UK market, through Ailsa Trucks (q.v.), after testing the UK market between 1956 and 1958 through Scottorn Ltd (q.v.). In 1971 Volvo opened a shipping terminal at South Killingholme, Lincolnshire, to handle both incoming vehicles and parts and the movement of British components to overseas Volvo assembly plants. DAF cars was acquired in 1975 and Volvo/ DAF collaborated with Saviem (France) and Magirus-Deutz (q.v.) (Germany) in the so-called Club of Four scheme for a rationalised middle-weight truck with shared features. From 1993 Volvo went through a complicated sequence of merger and takeover plans and offers, which finally resulted in its acquisition of Renault VI in 2000. Volvo moved into the lorry rental business in 1998 by acquiring BRS (q.v.) truck rental from National Freight Corporation (q.v.). Volvo Contract Services and its UK sales, marketing and finance operations were merged two years later to further its policy of 'looking beyond truck ownership'. **RAS**

CM (23 March 2000), p.14

Vulcan (Figure 63). For much of its existence (1902–53) Vulcan was a struggling vehicle manufacturer in Southport, producing initially cars and from 1907 light vans and continuing with car production until 1928. For a short period from 1919 Vulcan was part of Harper Bean Ltd, a hopelessly over-optimistic consortium, which benefited none of the firms or individuals involved. Medium-sized lorries, including low-height municipal vehicles and some War Department subsidy (q.v.) types, were the post-1918 mainstay of Vulcan Motor & Engineering (1906) Ltd, accompanied by public service vehicles in the 1920s and early 1930s. Financial difficulties through the 1920s resulted in receivership in 1931, followed by purchase by the trailer maker J Brockhouse (q.v.), for the sake of the Vulcan site. Tilling-Stevens (q.v.) in 1937 acquired production rights and manufacture was transferred to its works at Maidstone in 1938. A new model, the 6VF (6-ton Vulcan forward-control), was designed in 1939. Authority was given in 1940 for its production for civilian use and Vulcan appears to have been allowed to concentrate on the home market during the post-war 'export or die' period. This may well account for the number of Vulcans in service with BRS, some as tippers or articulated tractors (some of these were converted from tippers). The Rootes Group took over Tilling-Stevens in 1950 and Vulcan gave way to Rootes' other commercials within a few years. **RAS**

See also LOW HEIGHT VEHICLES.

Stevens-Stratten (1988); Baldwin (1982); Wood (2001); file on Vulcan in Rubery Owen Holdings archive, Modern Records Centre, University of Warwick; Carverhill (2002)

W

W & G du Cros Ltd of Acton, vehicle manufacturers, succeeded W&G Express Carriers (q.v.), with the latter's close association with Napier. Du Cros began vehicle production in the First World War with a 30-cwt lorry similar to a Napier, moving to 2- and 2½-ton lorries after the war, powered by Dorman engines. Customers included Carter Paterson & Co. (q.v.), Pickfords (q.v.), J Lyons & Co. Ltd (q.v.), the Anglo-American Oil Co. Ltd and the Army & Navy Stores. The L drop-frame bus chassis, which continued into the 1930s, was also suitable for quality horse transporters.

The firm moved into low-height, small-wheel vehicles for municipal use from 1929, but that year was its last Commercial Motor Show although production of some kind continued until 1935. Perhaps as a consequence of the death of William Harvey du Cros in 1918, W&G in 1920 became part of the Sunbeam-Talbot-Darracq combine, STD Motors, although this was not made evident, for example, through their advertising. **RAS**

T Gaffney, 'The W & G legend', *Vintage Lorry Annual* (1979)

W & G Express Carriers was an offshoot of the large taxi firm set up as W & G du Cros Ltd in July 1908 by William and George du Cros, two of the six sons of William Harvey du Cros, founder of the Dunlop Pneumatic Tyre Co., whose financial support was behind the ambitious new concern. Premises were erected in Acton Vale, close to the works of D Napier & Son Ltd (q.v.), whose substantial new cabs were operated by the du Cros brothers. When the demonstration transport of a military battalion from London to Hastings was staged in 1910, W&G supplied twenty Napiers, which it had rebodied as lorries; this proved to be a portent of things to come.

A long strike of taxi drivers in the first half of 1913 led to a suggestion by the du Cros manager, W A T Turpin, that the firm should diversify into parcels and van hire work. Accordingly a hundred 15-hp Napiers were rebodied as 1-ton vans on Dunlop pneumatic tyres (and featured in an advertisement for Napier 'Business Vehicles'). A City depot was established in Watling Street and a large central depot in Clerkenwell. Heavier Napiers, Albions, a Milnes-Daimler and Panhard operated a feeder service between Acton and the City. The speed and manoeuvrability of the Napier delivery vans in the distinctive green and yellow W&G livery contributed to a successful operation, several hundred vans operating in Greater London from Egham to Watford and Romford to Redhill.

A van hire service was set up in Westminister in early 1914, using similar Napier vans with W&G drivers. W H Smith, Nevill's Bread and national newspapers were among those signing contracts. The First World War brought a major change of activity. All W&G Napiers were requisitioned for war service, Carter Paterson took over the Clerkenwell depot and, in 1915, the whole parcels business, which it closed down. The du Cros Acton Vale works were devoted to war production. By the end of the war W & G du Cros Ltd (q.v.) had become vehicle manufacturers, ironically supplying Carter Paterson, its former competitors. **RAS**

T Gaffney, 'The W & G legend', *Vintage Lorry Annual* (1979); C H Wilson and W J Reader, *Men and Machine: a history of D Napier & Son, Engineers Ltd, 1808–1958* (Weidenfeld & Nicolson, 1958), p. 94; *DBB*, vol 3, p. 191; Turnbull (1979), pp. 157–8

Wagon or waggon was adapted from the Dutch *wagen* when this heavy 4-wheeled vehicle was introduced from the Netherlands in the sixteenth century. By the later nineteenth century its meaning was more specific: a large, horse-drawn, 4-wheeled goods vehicle fitted with sides to contain the load (cf. dray; lorry). Wagons were commonly fitted with a draught pole for haulage by a pair of horses, one on each side. For heavy loads more horses could be attached in front, hauling on draught chains. When empty, a pair of shafts might be fitted for a single horse.

By 1900 the word wagon was applied to steam vehicles and then petrol-driven vehicles with the equivalent style of body, but already the words lorry/lurry and wagon/waggon were being used interchangeably for any large mechanised goods vehicle. **GAB**

OED; John Vince, *Discovering Carts and Wagons* (3rd edn, 1987)

The **Waldorf Group** was founded in 1936 as a loose association of about a dozen of the largest operators in the parcels and smalls business. Members included both railway-owned firms and major independents: Pickfords, Carter Paterson, Bouts-Tillotson, Fisher Renwick, Holdsworth-Hanson and McNamara. Its aim was to reach agreement on rates. Its 'manifesto' claimed that only by such agreements could the 'smaller and respectable contractor' find his place in the better development of the industry and at the same time protect his capital investment. It was reasonably successful in fixing rates, using predatory services to ensure smaller firms did not undercut them. It was a secretive organisation, issuing no minutes of its meetings. This probably explains why the Labour Research Department got it confused with the Transport Arrangement (q.v.) believing the Waldorf Group comprised fifty large haulage firms. In 1941 the Group made an offer to the Ministry to run the wartime haulage organisation which was not accepted. It faded away in the formal co-operation imposed in the Second World War. **RAS**

Labour Research Department, *Why Haulage must be Nationalised* (1946); *MT* (28 November 1942)

Walker, Alice M, began her career in road transport before 1914, working for Harold Kinder of Blaby, Leicester, in his garage and driving Daimler hire cars and later a lorry on a munitions contract. After the war she canvassed the neighbouring Leicestershire area to establish a parcels and smalls service. She then moved to a new job in Coventry but was asked to return to help Kinder in the now struggling business. This she did by changing direction, obtaining a contract to move a factory full of machinery from Bradford to Leicester. Miss Walker chose to train her own drivers, considering this more helpful for unemployed ex-servicemen.

In 1922 the business which was then operating five lorries, including an FWD and Maudslay,

became Kinder's Garage & Haulage Ltd. Her seven fellow, male, directors were reluctant to invest in new vehicles so in 1930 she bought them out and bought new vehicles, eight Leyland lorries, two of which were convertible to charabancs at weekends. By 1938 Kinder was operating 20 Leyland Octopus lorries and a 6-wheel Cub. The parcels and smalls business had been sold as it was considered too labour-intensive. The main traffic was machinery and engineering products, constructional steelwork and pre-cast concrete products, mostly for specific contracts. There was no spot hire or tramping work. It also had the contract for storing and distributing Tate & Lyle sugar throughout Leicestershire. In 1941 Kinder was acquired by Transport Services Ltd (q.v.), Miss Walker continuing as managing director and in 1944 after TS's acquisition of Loughborough Transport, heavy haulage specialist, this also came under her management.

At nationalisation Kinder became an early acquisition as part of TS as Unit A12. It became the lead undertaking to form 41E South Leicester Group of BRS, Miss Walker being appointed group manager. Loughborough Transport became part of 40E North Leicester Group, the heavy haulage operations were merged into Pickfords. Miss Walker's abilities and standards were favourably commented upon by Major General Russell (q.v.) when he visited Blaby on a fact-finding tour. She presented the Alice Walker Cup awarded annually for the unit with the best kept fleet.

At denationalisation in 1954 she successfully tendered for ten Special-A-licenced vehicles, now operated under her own name as A M Walker Ltd. Again concentrating on contracted traffic, the business grew, partly by the acquisition of Arnold's Transport Ltd and J A Smith (Enderby) Ltd, to 45 vehicles. In 1966 it was acquired by Transport Development Group Ltd. Miss Walker was famed for her driving skills and her ability to service her vehicles, being able to carry out any job that she expected of her employees. Noted for adhering to the regulations on driving hours, weight limits and the mechanical condition of her vehicles, she was also considered a disciplinarian reinforced by judicious use of her umbrella, yet highly regarded as an employer. Miss Walker married a long-standing friend, Lord Hall. She also had a successful role in local government. **GM**

CM (27 December 1974), pp. 31–3

Walker Bros Ltd, see PAGEFIELD

Walkers of Wakefield Ltd originated in 1958 when Charlie Walker set up as an owner-driver with a secondhand Austin, moving coal at screening plants. He was used to such work from his previous employment hauling coal from colliery to power station for Hargreaves of Rothwell, where he had become a union representative. Walker's Austin was followed by other vehicles past their prime, which he regularly worked over-loaded. He is quite frank, but repentant, in his memoirs about other dishonest practices he resorted to in order to make his way in the world of transport: the theft of diesel fuel from contractors' plant, the use of a mixture of burning oil and engine oil as fuel, the bribing of weighbridge operators to increase his apparent productivity, the use of false number plates and licences, drawing sick pay and insurance benefit whilst working, and driving beyond the limits of fatigue. Walker managed to buy a new Thames Trader tipper and then hit upon a recipe for growth, the purchase of a new chassis/cab, which he extended and fitted with a secondhand body. In this way he built up his fleet, Charles Transport, to four vehicles, operating on a limited B licence.

In 1964 when his father died, Charlie sold up his own business and took over his father's trading name, W Walker & Son, with a single removal lorry. He developed the business, by becoming main contractor for a variety of furnishing stores within the Great Universal Stores Group, as well as undertaking household removals. Personal contact gave Walker work for another local firm, Rawsons, and enabled him to pre-arrange return loads from the businesses to which he had delivered, irrespective of the customers' own transport fleets. Traffic built up to 14–20 pantechnicons (q.v.) working every day for Electrolux, and 10–14 for the British Mail Order Corporation,

but with other work subcontracted, eventually reaching up to 90 per cent of the total.

Walker obtained a depot and built up a sizeable fleet, at one time buying two dozen secondhand Penman (q.v.) demountable pantechnicon bodies for use with Bedford chassis. Under pressure from the local authority Walker was obliged to move his depot to an industrial estate. As his business grew he came to feel that it was moving beyond his managerial competence and control, to such an extent that he put it on the market in the late 1970s. However, on reflection he decided to retain the business, introducing more systematic controls over its operation and to concentrate on national haulage, rather than distribution. He also began a separate garage and recovery business, for his own fleet and customers, Walkers Garages Wakefield Ltd.

Then at 55 years of age he decided to opt for retirement and in 1987 negotiated the sale of the business, remaining involved in its direction until the end of 1988, increasingly critical of its new policy of buying into other haulage contractors, whereas it had been Walker's policy to make profit from subcontracting to them. **RAS**

Walker (2000)

Wallis & Steevens of Basingstoke were making single-cylinder traction engines in the early 1880s and introduced compounding about 1900. At that time they made a small tractor for their own use and a one for a Reading miller. With minor modifications, the tractor could be brought below the 3-ton weight limit and they claimed to have been the first to produce such a machine, useful for light loads such as market produce or furniture, and later made by other engine firms. They brought out an overtype steam lorry, but it proved less popular than the tractor. Relatively few were produced, the largest single customer being Pickfords (q.v.) which ran a fleet of about 40. The company also made road rollers. **RWK**

R A Whitehead, 'Wallis & Steevens', *OM*, 9, 3 (1975), pp. 175–81; Whitehead (1983)

The **War Office trials** were first held in December 1901 around Aldershot by the newly-formed War Office Committee on Mechanical Transport to evaluate whether mechanically-propelled vehicles were sufficiently efficient to make them viable for army use. They were inspired in part by the Lancashire heavy motor vehicle trials (q.v.) of 1898, held around Liverpool, at which military officers observed. The trial notice specified 'lorries', meaning vehicles carrying goods on their own back, which ruled out steam tractors towing a trailer. Hence many steam engine makers were excluded. The dates chosen ensured wet, muddy and slippery conditions. Eleven vehicles were entered, some the result of amateur endeavours, but also competing were two Thornycrofts, a Foden, a Straker and a Milnes. All were steamers except for the Milnes which was petrol-engined. About thirty miles were covered each day and time taken and fuel consumption noted. Courses were chosen to give varied conditions including hill climbs. Each lorry carried three tons and pulled a trailer with a two-ton load, so that all- up weight was between 10 and 12 tons. After seven days of tests the Thornycroft was judged the winner and awarded the £500 prize. The Foden came in second, though it had been the fastest, averaging about 6½ mph, and the most economical in terms of fuel. The trials were extensively covered in the national press, bringing home to merchants, manufacturers and the general public the reliability, speed and economy of steam lorries. Compared with horse transport (q.v.) they were faster and carried larger loads.

The War Office held another trial in 1903, this time for tractors weighing a maximum of 12½ tons. They had to maintain 8 mph over a measured mile, climb a 1 in 6 gradient and travel a set distance without replenishing either fuel or water. This provoked a disappointing response. Only one vehicle arrived at the start line, a Hornsby traction engine. It was awarded the first prize of £1000.

The 1909 trials took place in early March in very poor weather with snow and sleet to complicate hill climbing. The rules required that the tractor weigh no more than seven tons gross and be capable of carrying an eight-ton load. It had to be able to travel 100 miles without refuelling or taking on any water. This largely ruled out steamers. Only three entrants arrived at the start line, a Thornycroft, a Broom & Wade, and a Stewart, the last steam-powered. Eight days of tests followed which included speed trials, where a minimum of 5 mph was required, hill climbing up a 1 in 7 gradient, braking and manoeuvrability. The Thornycroft was declared the winner and awarded the £750 prize. Partially as a result of these trials, by 1910 the army had largely ruled out steam engines.

In 1912 the War Office conducted another set of trials, this time to determine which makes of petrol-driven vehicle should qualify for the subsidy scheme (q.v.). There were two classes, 30-cwt and 3-ton. Leyland entered a vehicle in each class and were the only ones to be awarded a certificate. This was important, as purchasers of this type of vehicle could obtain a purchase subsidy of £50 per vehicle, and £20 per year for three years. The condition was that in an emergency the War Department could purchase the vehicle at its market value plus 25 per cent. Other trials were held in 1913 and 1914 for the same purpose.

These trials and their relatively generous prizes acted as an incentive to manufacturers to improve their vehicles. The well-publicised results helped to convince traders, as well as the army, that the motor lorry was an efficient and economical means of transport. **RL/JA**

Kennett (1978), pp. 40–6; Seth-Smith (1975), pp. 28–30 and 80–1; *Vintage Roadscene*, 56 (1998) and 57 (1999)

Waste disposal, SEE REFUSE COLLECTION

Watson, Henry, & Sons, SEE BERNA

Weight limits. Three different weights are used to define the size of a lorry: unladen weight, gross vehicle weight and capacity or payload.

Until 1937 the Construction & Use Regulations (q.v.) included maximum permissible unladen weights. The government used unladen weight as the basis for classifying vehicles (see VEHICLE TYPES, LEGAL DEFINITION OF) and, from 1921 to 1982, for charging vehicle excise duty on goods vehicles. Until 1982, therefore, unladen weight was the

Table 14: Weight Limits

Year	Rigid			Rigid + trailer			Articulated				Locomotive [1]		
	2 axles	3 axles	4 axles	4 axles	5 axles	6 axles	3 axles	4 axles	5 axles	6 axles	2 axles	3 axles	4 axles
	maximum unladen weight (upper figure), maximum gross weight (lower figure in brackets) (tons)												
1861											12		
1865											14		
1905	5 / 12			6½ / 20							14		
1921	7¼ [2] / 12			9¾ [2] / 20							14		
1922	7¼ / 12			9¾ / 22			18½				14		
1925	7¼ / 12			9¾ / 22			18½				20½		
1927	7¼ / 12	10 / 19		9¾ / 22			18½				20½		
1930	7¼ / 12	10 / 19	11 / 22	9¾ / 22			18½				20½		
1931	7¼ / 12	10 / 19	11 / 22	9¾ / 22			19	22			20½		
	maximum gross weight (tons)												
1937	12	19	22	22			19	22			20½		
1947	12	19	22	32			19	22			20½		
1955	14	20	24	32			20	24			22	26	30
1964	16	22	28	32			22	32			22	26	30
1966	16	22	28	32			24	32			22	26	30
	maximum gross weight (tonnes) (1 ton = 1.016 tonnes)												
1973	16.26	24.39	30.49	32.52			24.39	32.52			22.36	26.42	30.49
1983	16.26	24.39	30.49	32.52			24.39	32.52	38		22.36	26.42	30.49
1988	17	24.39	30.49	32.52			24.39	32.52	38		22.36	26.42	30.49
1993	17	26	32	35			26	35	38		22.36	26.42	30.49
1994	17	26	32	35	38	38 / 44 [3]	26	35	38	38 / 44 [3]	22.36	26.42	30.49
1999	18	26	32	36	40	41 [4] / 44 [3]	26	38	40 / 44 [5]	41 [4] / 44 [3]	22.36	26.42	30.49
2001	18	26	32	36	40	44	26	38	40 / 44 [5]	44	22.36	26.42	30.49

[1]   From 1931 the combined weight of trailers drawn by a locomotive was limited to 40 tons (40.65 tonnes from 1973). This was increased to 44 tonnes in 1999.

[2]   These increases were not designed to increase actual permissible weights, but to legalise existing practice following the definition in the Roads Act 1920 of the components and equipment that were to be included in the unladen weight.

[3]   44 tonnes allowed for road/rail combined transport movements of containers, swap bodies and rail-road bi-modal vehicles within the UK. In 1997 this was extended to piggyback semi-trailers.

[4]   Limit applicable only to movements within the UK.

[5]   Limit applicable only to a 3+2 axle articulated vehicle carrying a 40 ft ISO container to/from a railhead before/after an international rail movement via the Channel Tunnel.

measure normally used in government statistics and publications. Vehicle manufacturers, on the other hand, normally quoted a vehicle's maximum payload, this being a figure of more relevance to users. The trade press also generally followed this practice. In 1982 the government changed to gross vehicle weight as the basis for charging vehicle excise duty and, since then, this has become the weight normally quoted in both government and trade literature.

Weight limits are imposed in conjunction with speed limits (q.v.), for three main reasons: to ensure that the vehicle brakes are not overloaded, to avoid damage to bridges (q.v.)

and to limit the wear and tear on the road pavement (q.v.). As regards the first, vehicles hauling trailers were the main concern, but the progressive improvements in brake system technology effectively resolved the problem. From the beginning, the Construction & Use Regulations have specified limits for both gross vehicle weights (imposed on bridges) and axle loads (imposed on the road pavement).

Table 14 demonstrates the progressive advances in permissible unladen weight and gross weight for each of the main classes of goods vehicle, which have come from a combination of developments in road and vehicle technology and campaigning by the road haulage industry. The figures quoted are the highest permissible in each year that the limits were changed and were often subject to the vehicle meeting various requirements in regard to tyres, suspension, brakes and plating. When limits were increased, they might be accompanied by new safety or road-friendliness requirements that only new vehicles were expected to meet; the previous limits continued to apply to older vehicles.

Damage to the road pavement increases very rapidly if axle loads are increased — in proportion to the fourth power of the axle load. If an axle is overloaded by 10 per cent, damage is increased by almost 50 per cent. In consequence, maximum permissible axle loads have increased relatively little over the past century and then chiefly because of improvements in wheels and suspensions. The 8-ton maximum axle load set for lorries in 1904 was increased to 9 tons in 1955 after solid tyres had virtually disappeared, to 10 tons in 1966 for wheels with twin or wide tyres, to 11 tons in 1983 for 4-wheeled axles (see FOUR-IN-LINE) and to 11.5 tonnes under the EC Regulations introduced in 1999 for vehicles with only one driving axle. The big increase in gross vehicle weights has been achieved mainly by increasing the number of axles.

The introduction of plating (q.v.) in 1964 allowed regulations of greater complexity to take account of the latest research. The first step was to relate gross weight limits to the distance between the front and rear axles; longer lorries, which spread their weight better

on bridges, were allowed higher gross weights. Then in 1972 further new regulations related axle-load limits to the spacing between adjacent axles; permissible axle loads were reduced for closely-spaced axles in order to limit their combined effect on the lower levels of the road pavement and the sub-grade.

Following representations from manufacturers and operators, 2-axle steam lorries were eventually allowed 2 extra tons on their gross weight to compensate for the higher weight of their water and fuel, provided they did not exceed 12 mph (3-axle lorries were only allowed one ton extra), but this did not come about until 1937 when it was too late for the steam lorry to regain its competitive position. From 1940 gas-powered lorries were similarly allowed ¾ or 1 ton extra.

Developments since the 1980s have mainly been driven by Brussels. EC Directive 85/3 introduced harmonised standards for vehicles used for international transport within the EC. They were effective from 1986 for 5- and 6-axle vehicles and from 1993 for 2-, 3- and 4-axle vehicles, but the UK and Eire were given a derogation until the end of 1998 to allow time for major bridge strengthening programmes. Directive 96/53 extended the application of these standards to domestic transport. The UK duly introduced them on 1 January 1999 through the Authorised Weight Regulations 1998, which, for the time being, stand alongside the weight limits in the C&U Regulations which are still applicable to older vehicles.

The 44-tonne 6-axle vehicles, which the road haulage industry had long campaigned for, eventually came into general use in 2001, although it had been allowed since 1994 for specified forms of combined transport (q.v.) as part of a policy of encouraging diversion of goods traffic to the railways.   **GAB**

Welch's Transport Ltd of Stapleford, Cambs, was founded by brothers Gordon and Jim Welch in 1934. it had 40 vehicles by 1947. Before the war it carried agricultural products and did some removals work. Nationalised, then denationalised, it had grown to 200 vehicles by the early 1970s, including approximately 100 Bedford TK lorries. The firm later switched to Atkinsons, but maintained a mixed fleet, which by 1977 included 23 Bedford TMs. The business grew with mixed traffic and some contracts, including tanker work for Shell Mex & BP from its Royston fuel terminal, for which three Scammell artic eights were acquired. One of the tractor units was bought back by the firm in 1998 and was restored in Welch's blue livery.

RAS

Supertruck, 1977; G Edge, 'Special birthday present', *CVC* (November 1999), pp.8–9

Wheels. The first wheels used on motor vehicles were wooden spoked wheels with a metal rim; very little different from those used on horse-drawn wagons. However, it was obvious that the potential of sustained speeds and higher loads made it essential to develop something better. Wheels of self-propelled vehicles also had the added requirement of transmitting torque. Light vehicles used wooden, artillery-type wheels with a metal hub plate; British lorries of over *c.*1 ton used cast metal wheels with an integral hub; traction engines, because of their size and weight, used wheels fabricated from cast sections.

The 'hammer' effect caused by the awful road surfaces was transmitted to every part of the vehicle. The fitting of solid rubber tyres was a considerable improvement. The rubber was vulcanised to a metal band, which was then pressed onto the wheel rim. Solids did not puncture, so there was no need to change wheels at the roadside, no spares, or inter-changeability. There was little standardisation, wheels of differing diameters and widths being used on front and rear axles, and the desirability of a common wheel was not considered very important.

The spoked cast metal wheel fitted with a solid rubber tyre, with all its limitations, was the practical solution until the advent of the giant pneumatic tyre in the late 1920s.

The giant pneumatic tyre (cover, tube and flap) was a lot larger than the solid of similar load capacity. The well-base, car-type rim was not suitable so the rim adapted was one with a rolled steel, flat-base rim, having a fixed flange as part of the rolling, and a variety of loose flanges and lock rings to secure the tyre. A dished pressed steel plate nave was riveted or welded to the rim.

The commercial vehicle wheel was an item dictated by function, unlike the car wheel which from earliest development was influenced by 'style'. The production volumes of a given car model could justify the production of a wheel specific to that model range. Industry standards were established for commercial vehicle wheels, for offsets (depth of dish of nave), bore (size of hole in nave centre), number of stud holes, their dimensions and pitch (PCD). This enabled a common wheel to be used as singles or twins and be interchangeable between different makes and models of vehicles. There were, of course, many special non-standard wheels produced with offset and drilling variations, two-piece split rims for large giant tyres, and an early tubeless tyre used a flat base rim with modified lock rings and an O-ring as the seal. Alternative stud and spigot fixings developed. On the continent the Trilex wheel was widely used. It consisted of a detachable rim, rolled in three sections, and when assembled with the tyre, bolted to the hub with a spider or lugs.

The rapid and widespread adoption of radial truck tyres made use of this wheel, until the advent of the tubeless truck tyre in the late 1960s. This called for a new type of truck wheel; essentially a very large car wheel, a one-piece, drop-centre rim with a 15° bead seat taper. This concept, with variations e.g. super singles, is the current state of the art. **JB**

White van man entered into the mythology of road transport in the 1990s. By virtue of its unlettered anonymity the white van (usually envisaged as a vehicle of Ford Transit size and type) became associated with careless or aggressive driving and with illegal activity. This might range from the use of the van as a bomb-carrier to the wholesale infringement of customs regulations by the illegal import of alcohol and cigarettes. The white van's ubiquity as the work-horse of jobbing builders and similar tradesmen, worsening urban traffic and parking congestion, has further added to the myth. The white van is not a feature particularly associated with orthodox road haulage, since parcels and home delivery services are normally executed by distinctively liveried vans. **RAS**

Metro (11 August 2000), p.8; *Daily Mail* (11 August 2000), p.39; *Oxford Compact English Dictionary* (2000); P Silverton, 'In praise of white-van man', *Observer Magazine* (20 August 2000), p.8

The **Wilkinson Transport Group Ltd** began at denationalisation in 1954. Edwin Wilkinson's original business, which had been nationalised, had specialised in dock and export traffic for the Lancashire textile industry. Noting the profitability of BRS Parcels, he built up a national parcels service, largely by acquiring 12, mainly smaller, local carriers, some being in decline, with elderly vehicles and poor depots, Bee's Transport (Hinckley) Ltd, a quoted company being an exception. Although a private company, Wilkinson was able to finance acquisitions and invest in new depots and vehicles by issuing shares. It ran a very mixed fleet.

Wilkinson became quoted on the London Stock Exchange in 1971, increasing the value of the shares. The group was acquired by Lex Holdings in 1972, valued at £5.6 million. A later acquisition was Townsend's Carriers Ltd of Rushden. This had been previously acquired by W H Smith Transport Ltd, which had long been involved in newspaper delivery and held a variety of licences since 1934. WHST hoped to integrate Townsend with its newspaper distribution operation but found this was not practical, and Townsend was acquired by Lex to become Lex-Wilkinson.

It was the first British carrier to build and operate an automated central hub, at Nuneaton in 1981. Lex found its investment unprofitable and, failing to acquire United Carriers (q.v.), sold out to Federal Express (q.v.), for whom they had been acting as delivery agent. They too were unable to operate profitably and closed the business. The Nuneaton hub was sold to Lynx (q.v.) in 1987, the vehicles sold, and the Systemline management system was acquired by Ryder. **GM**

Wilson, Sir Reginald H, (1905–1999) took a B Com at London University and then qualified as a Scottish chartered accountant and became a partner in Whinney Murray & Co from 1937 to 1940 before joining successively the Treasury, Ministry of Shipping, and Ministry of Transport. He returned to the City at the end of the Second World War, but remained an unpaid financial adviser to the Ministry of Transport. In 1947 he was made financial comptroller of the British Transport Commission and for the next two decades had a distinguished career in public service, concentrating on the financial aspects of transport operations. He was knighted in 1951 for those services. From 1953 to 1962 he was a member of the BTC and in 1962 became deputy chairman of the Transport Holding Company and in 1967 chairman at the time of the Tartan Arrow (q.v.) purchase. He was the first chairman of the National Freight Corporation (q.v.) from 1968 to 1971, and chairman of Thomas Cook from 1967 to 1976, which included the period when it was purchased by Midland Bank and much rationalised. In 1970 he joined the board of TDG (q.v.) and became chairman from 1971 to 1975. He was president of the CIT in 1957-8.

Wilson had great financial expertise, and was good at rationalising and standardising the financial systems of the disparate entities which were nationalised. His accounts for the BTC annual reports were claimed to be a tour de force in clarity. He was committed to the idea of integrated transport and to the decentralisation of management in the large organisations in which he was involved. **JA**

Bonavia (1987); *Who's Who* (1997), p.2117; Piers Brendon, *Thomas Cook. 150 years of Popular Tourism* (1991), pp.296-9; T R Gourvish, *British Railways 1948–73. A Business History* (1986), pp.32 and 106.

Wilson Double Deck Trailers Ltd, of Craigavon, County Armagh, originated with the need of the F G Wilson (Engineering) Ltd group to make urgent overseas deliveries by overland trailer of the diesel power-generating sets, which it began manufacturing in 1973. The inability of existing trailers to load to maximum weight capacity led Fred Wilson to devise a double deck trailer, which first went into production in 1986 after five years' development and an investment of £2 million. The design, which eliminated the need for a chassis in the area of the axles, allowed for full standing height on both floors of the trailer, within the height of a conventional semi-trailer. The tail-lift formed the door of the upper floor. The former Goodyear tyre factory at Perivale was acquired, and went into production in 1987. Early orders came from Royal Mail Parcels, Argos and Initial Services; major customers by 1995 included Parcelforce, Tesco and Business Post. In 2002 the firm was bought by Ross & Bonnyman, tail-lifts makers (q.v.). **RAS**

Advertisements in *CM* (18 October 1986 and 28 September 1995)

Willys Overland Crossley Ltd, see MANCHESTER LORRY

Wincanton Logistics Ltd (Figure 64) was created as Wincanton Transport in 1925 as the transport subsidiary of Cow & Gate by the Gaunt family, which had started a local dairy business at Guildford in 1885. They began in 1904 making baby food, which was marketed as Cow & Gate. Its success led to the dairy business, by then expanded to become a regional operation, being renamed Cow & Gate in 1929. Wincanton was created to provide transport and mechanical services to the processing businesses. At first the transport side collected almost all the milk processed, and distributed Cow & Gate's products. After the creation of the Milk Marketing Board in 1933 it became the major customer. Wincanton also gained contracts for bulk milk deliveries and expanded into bulk liquid transport. United Dairies (UD) acquired Cow & Gate in 1959, to form Unigate. UD had no outside transport operations and following a consultant's report into the possible scope for Wincanton decided to develop Wincanton into a specialised road transport contractor. This led to Unigate acquiring its milk collection contractors, Meirs Transport of Wolverhampton, transferring the operations to Wincanton. Wincanton was a large AEC user and was service agent for much of the south

west in the late 1950s. Wincanton developed its vehicle dealerships with Unigate's acquisition of Arlington Holdings. At its largest it had some 34 branches including bodybuilders, tipper manufacturing and chassis conversions. It offered vehicle hire and rental and motor auctions. The acquisition of Giltspur Bullens by Unigate and its transfer to Wincanton provided expansion into business and commercial removals and computer removals and installation. Wincanton Transport was renamed Wincanton Distribution Services in 1987 as it developed its food distribution business, building new chilled and ambient stores and distribution centres, and moving into temperature-controlled transport. The acquisition of Glass Glover in 1994, originally produce and fruit distributors but then involved in food warehousing and distribution, was followed by Wincanton opening their first automated grocery warehouse in 1994. Unigate demerged Wincanton, to become Wincanton Logistics in 2001, the former Unigate foods business being renamed Uniq. Wincanton Logistics held then the contract for delivering Texaco fuels. Other major contracts were for Argos, B&Q, Heinz and the major supermarkets. **GM**

IDCH, 2 (1990), pp. 586–7; 28 (1999), pp. 488–91

Wolseley Motors Ltd of Birmingham was founded as the Wolseley Tool & Motor Car Co. Ltd in 1901. The name changed in 1914. It manufactured a variety of commercial vehicles from 1901 to 1921, when it concentrated on car production. A 10-cwt delivery van was followed by heavier vehicles. By 1906 the commercial range included a 2-cwt parcelcar and a forward-control 2-ton lorry. Customers included the GWR. In 1905 J D Siddeley took over from Herbert Austin as general manager, remaining until 1912. Lorry production ceased between 1908 and 1912, but revived under his successor, A A Remington, to include six commercial models by 1914, the largest with a 5-ton capacity. The 30-cwt and 4-ton lorries were War Office-approved types and continued in production during the First World War; Wolseley's final commercial was a 7-cwt van on a light car chassis in 1921. **RAS**

St J Nixon, *Wolseley: a saga of the motor industry* (Foulis, 1949); N Baldwin, 'The submerging of Wolseley', *VCVM* (March/April 1989), pp. 166–9

Women in the road haulage industry. The undoubted culture (q.v.) of machismo of road haulage at the drivers' level should not obscure the part played by women in the industry, especially in administration and management, since the time of BRS (q.v.) and earlier. The Women's Road Traffic Club was set up in 1936 for women in senior positions, or owners, in road haulage, partly because other organisations refused to accept women or treated them as second class members. The WTC encouraged professional development and the exchange of views.

For decades it has been accepted practice in small firms for the proprietor's wife or daughter to keep the books, while husbands and sons were on the road. The Hanson (q.v.) business was begun by Mrs Mary Hanson in 1830 and Langdons (q.v.) originated with Mrs Bessie Langdon's egg and poultry transport needs. On occasion a widow took over a haulage firm after the death of her husband, as did Mrs Hilda Mary Borrowdale, managing director of H Borrowdale & Co. Ltd of Leeds, which she took over and expanded in the late 1940s after her husband's death. At that time there were also examples of women group managers in BRS: Amy M Alexander of Chiswick and Alice M Walker (q.v.) of Leicester.

In the early 1950s *Motor Transport* ran a series of profiles on 'Women in transport'. In the mid-1970s women began to compete for the Lorry Driver of the Year awards, with Lesley Smith in 1975 becoming the first Lady Trucker of the Year, but there were still relatively few women drivers. In the late 1990s, both Sheila McCabe, past president of the Irish Road Haulage Association, and Anne Preston, chair of Prestons of Potto (q.v.), created outstanding careers through their ability and commitment and were active beyond the confines of the firm. Women began to occupy key posts and prominent positions in road-haulage-related industries and organisations, examples being Nikki King, managing director of Isuzu Truck (UK) Ltd, whose working week was profiled in the trade press, and Mary Williams, founder of Brake (q.v.), who was awarded the OBE in 2000 for her work.

At the driving level, a survey indicated only slow progress during the second half of the 1990s, the highest percentage of women drivers amounting to only 1 per cent, in firms with five to ten vehicles. A Lady Truckers Club, originally founded for the mutual provision of overnight facilities when these were not available for women at truck-stops, continued in being with more of a general social role. In 2000 Iveco created a new group 'Women in Transport', with Lisa Fuller as the UK national officer. It was intended to change the public perception of the road haulage industry and emphasise its importance to everyday life. The group covered technical developments, legislation, and political issues. The British group, chaired by Pauline Edwards, joined groups in six EC countries, with others to follow. Members were operators, fleet or logistics directors, or had other key roles in the industry.   **RAS/GM**

World's Carriers (15 January 1949); BRS, *National Gazetteer* (March 1951); *CM* (16 April 1976), p. 14, (31 December 1998), p. 42, (2 March 2000), pp. 38–44; *MT* (13 January 2000) p. 22; *Trucking International* (September 1998), pp. 45–8; *MT* (8 May 1948), p. 9

Wordie & Co. There was a Wordie of Stirling in cartage in the mid-eighteenth century and John Wordie carried by road between Stirling and Glasgow in the early nineteenth. He was not over-successful and died financially embarrassed in 1830. His son William restored the business, paying off creditors and improving the Stirling–Glasgow service. His real achievement was to provide the new railways with the collection and delivery services they needed.

His first contract was in 1842 with the newly-opened Edinburgh & Glasgow Railway. From that date he never looked back, although it was work for the rival Caledonian Railway that ensured success. By 1866 it controlled the route from Carlisle to Glasgow and on to Edinburgh, Perth and Aberdeen, with William Wordie as cartage agent for the companies involved. From the mid-1850s he also established links with the

English carriers, Pickfords, forwarding goods to English cities and receiving for Scottish destinations.

From the Caledonian, Wordie progressed to act as carting contractor for the Highland Railway (1868) and the Great North of Scotland Railway (1869), so by 1870 he had a chain of stables from the Glasgow headquarters to Thurso. He died in 1874, the business passing to his sons John and Peter. They continued the forward policy, establishing links with shipping companies serving Belfast, Londonderry and other Irish ports, France, and from Aberdeen to the Orkneys and Shetlands. Shipping agency work to Ulster was followed by cartage in Belfast for the Great Northern Railway of Ireland in 1892, later extended to the whole GNR system, while in 1896 a depot was opened in Newcastle upon Tyne, followed by a contract with the North Eastern Railway. By 1905 Wordies owned nearly three thousand horses and in 1905/6 bought its first petrol-engined lorries for work in Glasgow and Aberdeen. It had steam lorries too and a growing warehousing business.

John Wordie died in 1910 and Peter in 1913, but family management continued with John's son William and nephew Archie Watson. The 1923 railway grouping left Wordies in the LMSR camp, except for its work for the GNSR, now part of the LNER. For the latter a separate company, Wordie's (North Eastern) Ltd, was created. By the end of the 1920s Wordie & Co., like many others, was in poor financial shape, but it was rescued in 1932 by the LMSR, which acquired a 51 per cent stake with representation on the board of the new Wordie & Co. Ltd. The GNSR and Irish businesses, the latter now hampered by a customs barrier, remained outside LMSR control, although the Irish work expanded to include cartage for the LMSR in Northern Ireland.

LMSR control of the Scottish mainland business led to expansion of motor transport, for from 1928 the railways were granted wider powers by Parliament to undertake road trunk services as distinct from feeders to rail. So Wordies, acting under LMSR authority, developed operations from Glasgow to Manchester and London, from Inverness to Glasgow and Wick, from Newcastle to the West Riding, plus more local work.

This was achieved with a range of vehicles, Albions, Leylands and ERFs. By 1938 Wordie & Co. and its associates had 824 horses, 257 motors and 104 trailers, with 260 horses, 19 motors and 9 trailers remaining in the family-run business. Associates is the key word, for under the LMSR Wordies pursued from the late 1930s an acquisitive policy, buying up hauliers in Inverness, Edinburgh, West Calder near Bathgate and several in south-west Scotland. A notable acquisition came in 1937 with Road Engines & Kerr of Glasgow and its six traction engines and a fleet of trailers on heavy-haulage work, notably locomotives from the North British Locomotive Company to the docks. For railway work mechanical horses (q.v.) were introduced; the LMSR employed Karrier Cobs from the early 1930s and in 1936 acquired the Karrier Bantams, Wordies following suit.

Nationalisation submerged Wordie & Co. Ltd in BRS, the Wordie family selling its 49 per cent stake to the LMSR some months beforehand. It had sold Wordie (North Eastern) in 1946 and the Dublin subsidiary at about the same time, but the business in Northern Ireland remained as Wordie & Co. (Ulster) Ltd until sold in 1970. Today the Wordie name is kept alive by a property company founded in 1903 to look after the stables and warehouses and now with interests mainly in business premises, some on the sites of former stables. **EWPT**

Paget-Tomlinson (1990); McTaggart (1989), pp. 102–3

Works trucks came into widespread use during the First World War, as part of the process of increasing efficiency for production. Early on some were licensed for roadwork between nearby sites. When the load-bearing tray of a works truck was made to lift a stillage (q.v.) then transport and lower it elsewhere, the principle of the fork-lift truck (q.v.) had been in part realised.

The introduction of the Lister Auto Truck in 1926, which was petrol-engined and highly manoeuvrable, was a major step forward in the evolution and spread of the works truck. Other firms followed suit with similar designs, for example the Brush battery electric industrial truck, which also offered a 90 degree lock.

RAS

D E Evans, *Listers: the first hundred years* (Gloucester: Alan Sutton, 1979), ch. 8; B Johnson, *Classic Plant Machinery* (Boxtree, 1998), ch. 4; *Modern Internal Transport* (Loughborough, Brush Coachwork, undated); H Pynegar (ed), *Mechanical Handling Yearbook and Manual* (Paul Elek, 1943); L Hoefkens, *Material Handling in Works Stores* (Iliffe, 1952)

Wreckers, see RECOVERY SERVICES

Wynn, Robert, & Sons Ltd (Figures 29 and 190) dates back to 1863, when Thomas Wynn was working for the GWR at Newport, Monmouthshire, and saw the potential for a carrying service linking the South Wales valleys with the Newport railhead. Thomas died in 1878, to be succeeded by his eldest son, Robert (1863–1923) who had the assistance of his elder sister Emma. In 1884, Robert acquired the round timber haulage business of the late Robert Small. Wynn remained in timber haulage until the business was sold to its foreman in 1964. Robert expanded and hauled for the growing steel and associated heavy industry then being developed in South Wales. This required the movement of abnormal loads (q.v.) and Robert obtained a 40-ton boiler trolley, requiring up to 48 horses to pull it.

Five of Robert's sons joined the business which grew to employ 200 horses. The first steam tractors, Fowlers and Garretts, and road locomotives were operated in the late 1890s. The first steam road locomotive was acquired in 1903, and the first steam lorries, Fodens and Sentinels, in 1908. In 1910 the first motor lorry was bought. Robert did not end his association with the GWR and Wynn acted as a cartage agent for them until nationalisation. Wynn was also contracted to deliver a considerable tonnage of groceries and flour. The business expanded during the First World War, despite having some steam tractors requisitioned early on. The needs of the steel and associated heavy industries for arms and the demand for timber caused their heavy horses to be exempt from requisitioning.

1923 saw Wynn become a limited company, trading as Robert Wynn & Sons Ltd, he and his wife being the shareholders. At Robert's death, later in 1923, his holding was split between his three eldest sons. The steam tractors and road locomotives were phased out by the mid-1920s, being replaced by petrol lorries and Foden and Sentinel steam wagons. The first Scammell low-loader was placed in service in 1927.

The next expansion in 1928 was the introduction of a Newport–London trunk service for parcels and smalls, although tinplate was a major traffic to London. Initially it used steam vehicles, but these were soon replaced by Scammell chain-drive and then later rigid-six and rigid-eight vehicles. In 1930 a depot was opened at Enid Street, London SE16 with Gordon Wynn as manager. At nationalisation some 40 vehicles operated nightly on this trunk service.

Wynns had long provided a leading local contractor, Mabley Parker, with tipping carts for its Newport area contracts. When Mabley opened a branch in Cardiff Wynns opened a depot there. Contracts to supply Cardiff Corporation with tipping vehicles continued until Wynn ceased to operate tipper lorries in the mid-1960s.

The Second World War again found Wynns heavily involved in moving abnormal loads. A Foden 100-ton tractor was allocated to them in 1942 and used to pull various low-loading trailers built in Wynn's workshop. A further diversification took place following the nationalisation of the coal industry in 1947. The National Coal Board chose to sell the former Powell Duffryn Sentinel tar tankers to Wynns who replaced them with Scammell and other articulated and rigid tankers and continued to work for the NCB for 20 years.

Apart from the loss of the Newport–London service Wynn was able to keep most of its business, as more than 50 per cent had been in heavy haulage, round timber, bulk liquids and deliveries within 25 miles radius of its bases. In fact Wynns benefited from the fact that many of their competitors were nationalised and then merged into Pickfords. Wynns was now the alternative to Pickfords for heavy haulage and customers were quick to support them. They purchased their first ex-Army Diamond T 980 transporter tractors in 1949, eventually operating some 30 and six Pacific tractors, which were rebuilt to act as their biggest heavy haulage tractors, the first going into service in 1950. These allowed them to move up to 150-ton loads, after obtaining the first 16-wheeled pneumatic-tyred 150-ton low-loading trailer to be built by Crane. Following Pickfords placing a similar one in service, Wynn specified and ordered larger trailers, eventually employing a 300-ton 48-wheeled version. Its customers encouraged expansion to serve the Sheffield area and north east England and were always willing to support applications for licences for increased tonnage.

Denationalisation saw successful tenders for some 15 heavy haulage tractors and low-loading trailers from Pickfords and the opening of a former heavy haulage depot at Moss Side, Manchester. This was managed by Eddie Clark, previously deputy manager at Pickfords Manchester depot. A useful diversification in the mid-1960s was Crindau Garages, which became the Guy distributors for South Wales. This followed Wynn's satisfaction with its own Invincible chassis.

Wynn celebrated its centenary in 1963, marked by a procession through Newport town centre, headed by a horse-drawn tipper-cart, with a trace horse and finishing with their new 300-ton low-loading trailer pulled by a Scammell tractor. The Diamond Ts were gradually replaced by Scammell Contractors, the first entering service in 1964. The Wynn brothers sold the business to United Transport in 1964, a major factor in the decision being their distress over the Hixon disaster (q.v.). In addition all five brothers were reaching retirement age. Wynns continued as a separate entity as United Transport's heavy haulage division, being joined by Sunter Brothers (q.v.) of Northallerton and Wrekin Roadways. The demand for heavy haulage in Britain began declining in the 1970s. Changes in electrical generating, affecting both suppliers and producers, together with a continuing decline in steel production and heavy engineering saw the merger in 1986 of Wynn, Sunter, Wrekin and Econofreight to become Econofreight United Transport. Econofreight was then part of Transport Development Group (q.v.), it having expanded into heavy haulage. Wynns was closed after a final move to one depot at Stafford. Its bulk liquids business had been merged into United Tankers. United Transport was acquired by the British Electric Traction Ltd which in turn was acquired by Rentokil. Peter Wynn, a great-great-grandson of Thomas Wynn formed Wynn's Ltd to act as consultants for heavy transport and abnormal load movements. **GM**

Wynn (1995); Allan (1946), pp. 159–162

Y

The **York Trailer Co. Ltd** was founded at Burnley in 1957 by Fred Davies, formerly of the Canadian Trailmobile concern. His brother had founded the Davies Magnet fifth-wheel (q.v.) firm. Davies was assured of support by Lewis Morgan, chief engineer of BRS, and he in turn greatly encouraged John Pierce of Rubery Owen (q.v.). Davies has been described as 'the prime motivator in the UK articulation revolution', which was stimulated by the introduction of the 32-ton weight limit (q.v.) in 1964.

York flourished, offering in the mid-1960s a complete range of standard frameless trailer vans (the York Freightliner). In 1976 it bought Anthony Carrimore, the tipping gear producer, and in 1979, in conjunction with Roy Bowles Transport, York developed trailers to accommodate the 8x8-foot air-freight 'igloo' pallet. York Trailer International was established in 1974 as an autonomous group to sell York products overseas.

York enjoyed a record year in 1977; however, the loss of the Iran market and UK recession brought York to near-bankruptcy in the 1980s and led to two takeovers in quick succession. In 1985 United Carriers (q.v.) took over York; relations between Fred Davies and his son, Jim, were strained and the founder resigned. Three months later the Bunzl Group acquired United Carriers and in 1988 a management buyout, led by Jim Davies, restored York's independence. It did not last long. The York Group (as it had become) collapsed in 1991. Subsequently York Thermostar, which built refrigerated trailers at Harelaw, Co. Durham, was sold to a subsidiary of the German company Schmitz-Anhänger; tipper builder Neville Charrold went to Lycett Industries; Abel Demountable Systems to W H Davis; and the assets (but not property) of TEC Transport Equipment & Components, York

Trailer Co. and Transport (UK) to Aveling Barford (Machines); while French company Titan Remorques was closed down. Fred Davies died in 1997, aged 90. The American trailer manufacturer, Utility International (q.v.), began production at the Northallerton site in 1998, but called in receivers in 2002.   **RAS**

MT supplements: 'York Trailer', (10 May 1984), 'Rubery Owen Rockwell' (20 April 1988); *Observer* (3 July 1988); obituary *Daily Telegraph* (16 September 1997); Crane (1991)

The **Yorkshire Patent Steam Wagon Co. Ltd** was a subsidiary of Deighton's Patent Flue & Tube Co. Ltd of Vulcan Works, Hunslet, Leeds. A six-ton tipper lorry was produced in 1905. It was unusual in that the boiler was double-ended, with the firebox in the centre, and placed transversely in front of the driver. The make became very popular in the north and there was no substantial change in design until 1930, when a 12-ton rigid-six appeared, still with transverse boiler but sheathed to give a tidier appearance. Four-speed gears and a fully-enclosed cab gave this model, which also had a four-wheeled version, parity with the larger companies, but nevertheless the company had to leave the market.

Customers included general hauliers, British Petroleum, and local authorities. The last steam vehicle produced, in 1937, went to Sheffield Corporation's electricity department. Between 1933/4 and 1938 a small number of diesel lorries was produced, using bought-in components and proprietary engines (Dorman and Gardner). At the 1935 Commercial Motor Show a 7- to 8-ton 4-wheel tipping lorry and a 15-ton rigid eight-wheeler were displayed, the latter for the first time, and some major operators, such as the Cement Marketing Co., placed orders. However, the construction methods resulted in high prices and in 1938 the company gave up lorry production in favour of specialised municipal vehicles.   **RWK/RAS**

CM (8 November 1935), pp. 487, 499

Bibliography of Books and Pamphlets

The aim has been to include all works that deal specifically with the history of goods road transport (but not military transport) in the twentieth century. Histories of road transport or transport generally are included only if their coverage of goods road transport is particularly useful. Contemporaneous works on goods road transport are likewise included only selectively. Magazine supplements are excluded.

The place of publication is London unless shown otherwise.

Adams, Paul and Milligan, Roy, *Albion of Scotstoun: a century of cars, trucks & buses* (Paisley: Albion Vehicle Preservation Trust, 1999)

Aldcroft, Derek H, *British Transport since 1914: an economic history* (Newton Abbot: David & Charles, 1975)

Aldridge, Bill, *The London Brick Company* (Appleby: Trans-Pennine, 1998)

—— *Mechanical Horses* (Appleby: Trans-Pennine, 2000)

Aldridge, Bill and Earnshaw, Alan, *Great Western Railway Road Vehicles* (Appleby: Trans-Pennine, 2000)

Allan, Robert, *The Royal Road* (Pitman, 1946)

Allen, Michael and Geary, Les, *The Illustrated History of Ford Vans, Trucks & PSVs* (Sparkford: Haynes, 1988)

Allen, Thomas, Ltd, *The First One Hundred Years of Thomas Allen Ltd* (Globe, 1954)

Anon, *The Modern Diesel* (various editions, later editions edited by G G Smith and then Donald H Smith; Iliffe, 1932–59)

'Apple Jack' [pseud. F. Gibbons?], *The Driver's Tales* (North Walsham?: author?, 1984?)

Atkinson Vehicles Ltd, *Atkinson: a Short History of Atkinson Vehicles Limited: the company and its vehicles from 1907 to 1967* (Preston, 1967)

Backhouse, Gerry, *Old Trade Handcarts* (Princes Risborough: Shire, 1982)

Bagwell, Philip S., *The Transport Revolution 1770–1985* (2nd edn, Routledge, 1988)

Baldwin, Nick (comp), *The Observer's Book of Commercial Vehicles* (Frederick Warne, [3rd] edn [1974]; [4th] edn 1978; [5th] edn 1981)

—— (ed), *Vintage Lorry Annual* [no. 1] (Marshall, Harris & Baldwin, 1979); *Vintage Lorry Album* [no. 2] (Marshall, Harris & Baldwin, 1980); *Vintage Lorry Album* [no. 3] (Warne, 1983)

—— *A Pictorial History of BRS: 35 years of trucking* (Warne, 1982)

—— *The Illustrated History of Leyland Trucks* (Sparkford: Haynes, 1986)

—— *Old Delivery Vans* (Princes Risborough: Shire, 1987)

—— *The Illustrated History of Dennis Buses and Trucks* (Sparkford: Haynes, [c.1987])

—— *The Illustrated History of Albion Vehicles* (Sparkford: Haynes, 1988)

—— *The Illustrated History of Thornycroft Trucks and Buses* (Sparkford: Haynes, 1989)

—— *The Illustrated History of Seddon Atkinson Trucks & Buses* (Sparkford: Haynes, 1990)

—— *Proprietary Engines for Vehicles* (Princes Risborough: Shire, 2001)

Baldwin, Nick and Ingram, Arthur, *Light Vans and Trucks, 1919–1939* (Almark Publng, 1977)

Baldwin, Nick and Negus, William, *Kaleidoscope of Shelvoke & Drewry* (Marshall, Harris & Baldwin, 1980)

Barker, Theo, *The Transport Contractors of Rye: John Jempson & Son: a chapter in the history of British road haulage* (Athlone, 1982)

Barker, Theo and Gerhold, Dorian, *The Rise and Rise of Road Transport, 1700–1990* (Basingstoke: Macmillan, 1993)

Barker, Theo C and Savage, C I, *An Economic History of Transport in Britain* (3rd edn, Hutchinson, 1974)

Beaumont, Anthony, *Ransomes Steam Engines: an illustrated history* (Newton Abbot: David & Charles, 1972)

Billings, Tony, *Scammell: 45 years of rigid-eights: a Scammell engineering history* (Watford: Leyland Vehicles Ltd, 1982)

Birch, Clive and Harper, Len, *On the Move: the Road Haulage Association 1945–1994* (Whittlebury: Baron Birch, 1995)

Bishop's Move Group, *On the Move for Over 125 Years* (1979)

Bonavia, Michael R, *The Nationalisation of British Transport: the early history of the British Transport Commission, 1948–53* (Basingstoke: Macmillan / London School of Economics, 1987) [ch. 7, 'The creation of British Road Services']

Boughton, John H, *Steam in the Veins, being an account of memories of the Boughton family business and related happenings in the Chiltern hills* (Little Chalfont: author, 1990)

—— *Triumphs of Transport: being an account of the involvement of the Boughton family and their contemporaries in road transport and equipment related to it from the late 1800s to date* (Little Chalfont: author, c.1992)

Boyle, B C, *The Northern Ireland Road Transport Board 1935–1948* (Newtownards: Colourpoint, 1999)

—— *The Ulster Transport Authority 1948–1967* (Newtownards: Colourpoint, 2000)

Bridges, Harold, *As I Remember: 90 years in the 1900s, 1900–1990; 47 years in road transport, 1921–1968* (Burrow: author, 1992)

Broatch, Stuart Fergus and (vol. 2 only) Townsin, Alan, *Bedford* (2 vols, Glossop: Venture, 1995–6).

Brown, Stewart J, *Dennis: 100 years of innovation* (Ian Allan, 1995)

Brummer, Alex and Cowe, Roger, *Hanson: a biography* (Fourth Estate, 1994); pprbk edn, *Hanson: the rise and rise of Britain's most buccaneering businessman* (1995)

Brunner, Christopher T, *The Problem of Motor Transport: an economic analysis* (Benn, 1928); simplified version, *Road versus Rail: the case for motor transport* (1929)

Buchan, Keith, *The Development of Lorry Routeing in England & Wales* (Freight Transport Information Service, 1978)

Butler, Herbert James, *Motor Bodywork: the design and construction of private, commercial and passenger types* (Howell, 1924)

Card, Peter W, *Early Vehicle Lighting* (Princes Risborough: Shire, 1987)

Carverhill, Geoff, *The Commer Story* (Ramsbury: Crowood Press, 2002)

Cassell, Michael, *Long Lease! The story of Slough Estates, 1920-1991* (Pencorp, 1991)

Charlesworth, George, *A History of British Motorways* (Thomas Telford, 1984)

—— *A History of the Transport and Road Research Laboratory 1933–1983* (Aldershot: Gower / Avebury, 1987)

Chivers, Keith, *The Shire Horse: a history of the breed, the Society and the men* (J. A. Allen, 1976)

Clark, Edward N, *The Cart Horse on the Quay: the story of the Liverpool cart horses* (Garstang: Countryside, 1989)

Clark, Ronald H, *Steam-engine Builders of Suffolk, Essex and Cambridgeshire* (Norwich: Augustine Steward, 1950)

—— *Chronicles of a Country Works: being a history of Messrs Charles Burrell & Sons of Thetford, the famous traction engine builders* (Percival Marshall, 1952)

—— *Steam-engine Builders of Lincolnshire* (Norwich: Goose, 1955)

—— *The Development of the English Traction Engine* (Norwich: Goose, 1960)

—— *The Development of the English Steam Wagon* (Norwich: Goose, 1963)

—— *Steam-engine Builders of Norfolk* (Norwich: Augustine Steward Press, 1948; Sparkford: Haynes, 1988)

Coates, Ken and Topham, Tony, *The History of the Transport and General Workers' Union, vol. 1: The making of the Transport and General Workers' Union: the emergence of the labour movement* (Oxford: Blackwell, 1991); paperback edn, *The Making of the Labour Movement: the formation of the Transport & General Workers' Union 1870–1922* (Nottingham: Spokesman, 1994)

Coates, Robert, *Pulling Pints: brewery vehicles, past, present, future* (Croydon: Fitzjames, 1993)

Cole, Len, *Ford Panel Vans* (Hornchurch: Henry, 1980)

Collins, Michael J, *Freightliner* (Sparkford: Oxford Publishing, 1991)

Conradi, Charles Guthrie, *Mechanical Road Transport* (Macdonald & Evans, 1923)

Corfield, Tony, *The Rule of Law: a study in trade union organisation and method* (Birmingham: Brierly, 1982)

Cornwell, Edward L, *Commercial Road Vehicles* (Batsford, 1960)

—— *Commercial Vehicles* (Ian Allan, 1963)

Coster, Graham, *A Thousand Miles from Nowhere: trucking on two continents* (Viking, 1995)

Crane, John L B, *We Made Trailers: the history of Cranes (Dereham) Ltd to 1960* (Oswestry: Nelson, 1991)

Dampier, A J, *Kingdom of the Workhorse* (Brinscall: Countryside, 1987) [Manchester]

Daunton, Martin J, *Royal Mail: the Post Office since 1840* (Athlone, 1985)

Davies, Hunter, *The Eddie Stobart story* (HarperCollins Entertainment, 2001)

Davies, Peter J, *The Rigid Eight: a brief pictorial history 1934–1984* (Bedford: author, c.1985)

—— *British Trucks at Work in the 'sixties: a pictorial review of road haulage* (Nynehead: Roundoak, 1988)

—— *British Lorries of the 40s and 50s* (Nynehead: Roundoak, 1989)

—— *British Lorries of the Sixties* (Nynehead: Roundoak, 1991)

—— *Drawbar Outfits* [*Trucks in Britain* series] (Nynehead: Roundoak, 1992)

—— *'The World's Best Oil Engined Lorry': ERF: 60 years of truck building* (Nynehead: Roundoak, 1994)

—— *Eight Wheelers in Colour* (Nynehead: Roundoak, 1995)

—— *Atkinson* (Nynehead: Roundoak, 2000)

—— *The World Encyclopedia of Trucks: an illustrated guide to classic and contemporary trucks around the world* (Lorenz, 2000; also reduced size edn, Hermes House, 2002)

De Boer, Roger F, *Birmingham's Electric Dustcarts* (Birmingham: Birmingham & Midland Motor Omnibus Trust, 1990)

Dickson-Simpson, John M, *Era of Articulation* (Transport Press Services, 1968)

Dobsons of Edinburgh, *One Hundred Years: a history of Dobsons, 1879–1979* (Edinburgh, 1979)

Downs, Bill, *The Antediluvian Lorryman: an autobiography by the driver Bill Downs* (Ipswich: East Anglian Magazine, 1983)

Dunbar, Charles S, *Goods Vehicle Operation: principles and practice for students and executives* (2 edns, Iliffe, 1949 & 1953)

—— *Road Haulage* [*ABC* series] (Ian Allan, 1959)

—— *The Rise of Road Transport 1919–1939* (Ian Allan, 1981)

Dyos, H J and Aldcroft, Derek H, *British Transport: an economic survey from the seventeenth century to the twentieth* (Leicester Univ. Press, 1969)

Earle, J B F, *A Century of Road Materials: the history of the Roadstone Division of Tarmac Ltd.* (Oxford: Blackwell, 1971)

—— *Black Top: a history of the British flexible roads industry* (Oxford: Blackwell, 1974)

Earnshaw, Alan and Aldridge, Bill, *British Railways Road Vehicles 1948–1968* (Penryn: Atlantic Transport / Appleby: Trans Pennine Publng, 1997)

—— *LMS Railway Road Vehicles* (Appleby: Trans-Pennine, 2001)

Earnshaw, Alan and Berry, R W, *Bedford Light Commercials of the 1950s & '60s* (Appleby: Trans-Pennine, 2001)

Eaton, A E, *Sunters: high — wide & mighty* (Northallerton: ReCall Publns, 2001)

Edge, Graham, *AEC Lorries in the Post-war Years 1945–1979* (Nynehead: Roundoak, 1994)

440

—— *The AEC Mandator V8* (Swaffham Prior: Gingerfold, 1997)

—— *A Century of Petroleum Transport* (Nynehead: Roundoak, 1998)

—— *The Leyland Comet* (Swaffham Prior: Gingerfold, 1998)

—— *Spiers of Melksham* (Swaffham Prior: Gingerfold, 1998)

—— *AEC Mammoth Major Mk III* (Swaffham Prior: Gingerfold, 1999)

—— *The Leyland Beaver* (Swaffham Prior: Gingerfold, 2000)

—— *The AEC Mercury* (Swaffham Prior: Gingerfold, 2001)

—— *The AEC Mustang and Marshal* (Swaffham Prior: Gingerfold, 2002)

—— *L Gardner and Sons Limited: legendary engineering excellence* (Swaffham Prior: Gingerfold, 2002)

Edwards, Harry, *Morris Commercial Vehicles* (Stroud: Sutton, 1992)

Evans, Penny (ed), *Where Motor-car is Master: how the Department of Transport became bewitched by roads* (Council for the Protection of Rural England, 1992)

Farnsworth, Bert, *From Lorry Wheels to Tank Tracks* (Darwen: Hoad, 1996) [driver's memoirs]

Fenelon, K G, *Transport Co-ordination: a study of present-day transport problems* (King, 1929)

Ferodo Ltd, *The Ferodo Story: sixty years of safety, 1897–1957* (Chapel-en-le-Frith, 1957)

Freathy, Les and Pearson, Robin, *Diamond T Type 980/981* (Nynehead: Roundoak, 2001)

Friends of the Earth, *Heavy Lorries* (1985)

Gammons, Walter, *Forty Years in Transport* (Industrial Transport Publications, 1931)

Gardner, L, & Sons, *Gardners of Patricroft, 1868–1968*, written by David Whitehead (Newman Neame, 1968)

Geary, Les, *Commercial Vehicles in Great Britain* (Isleworth: Transport Bookman, 1979

—— *Railway Road Vehicles* (Romford: Henry, 1987)

—— *Bedford: the commercial vehicle for all purposes* (Romford: Henry, 1991)

—— *Rootes Commercial Vehicles* (Romford: Henry, 1993)

Geary, Les, Thomas, Alan, Bladon, Stuart and Burgess-Wise, David, *Task Force: a history of Ford commercial vehicles* (IPC Transport Press, 1976)

Georgano, G. Nick (ed), *The Complete Encyclopedia of Commercial Vehicles* (Osceola, Wisconsin: Motorbooks International, 1979)

—— *World Truck Handbook* (Jane's, 1983 & 1986)

—— *Electric Vehicles* (Princes Risborough: Shire, 1996)

—— *Scammell: the load movers from Watford* (Nynehead: Roundoak, 1997)

Georgano, G N and Demand, Carlo, *Trucks: an illustrated history 1896–1920* (Macdonald & Jane's, 1979)

Gibbard, Stuart, *County: a pictorial review* (Ipswich: Farming Press, 1997) [County Commercial Cars Ltd]

Gibson, Thomas, *Road Haulage by Motor in Britain: the first forty years* (Aldershot: Ashgate, 2001)

Gilbert, G F A, *Burrell: Burrell style 1900–1932* (Road Locomotive Soc., 1994)

Gilbert, G F A *Traction Engine Design & Construction 1900–1930* (Woodwalton: author, 2001)

Gillford, F H, *The Traction Engine* (South Godstone: Oakwood, 1952)

Glasgow, George, *General Strikes and Road Transport: being an account of the road transport organisation prepared by the British government to meet national emergencies, with a detailed description of its use in the emergency of May 1926* (Bles, 1926)

Goodman, Geoffrey, *The Awkward Warrior: Frank Cousins, his life and times* (2 edns: Davis-Poynter, 1979; Nottingham: Spokesman, 1984)

Goodyear Tyre & Rubber Co., *The Story of the Tyre: a record of a modern industrial achievement* (Wolverhampton, c.1950)

Gordon, George, *The Shore Porters' Society of Aberdeen, 1498–1969* (Aberdeen: Reid, [1969])

Grieves, Robert, *Truckin' Round Scotland* (Ratho: Southern, 1997)

—— *Albion Album 1899–1999* (Newbridge, Midlothian: Arthur Southern, 1999)

Guy, Anthony E, *The Illustrated History of Guy Trucks and Buses* (Sparkford: Haynes, 1989)

Gwilliam, K M and Mackie, P J, *Economics and transport policy* (Allen & Unwin, 1975) [ch 13, Road haulage]

Hall, H Scott, *Commercial Motors: their maintenance, repair, and general management* (3 vols, Virtue, 1935)

Hamer, Mick, *Wheels Within Wheels: a study of the road lobby* (Routledge & Kegan Paul, 1987)

Hampshire, Jack, *I Worked with Traction Engines* (Falmouth: Lake, 1967) [in family's Sussex haulage firm]

Hannay, Robin and Broatch, Stuart Fergus, *80 years of Guy Motors 1914–1994* (Glossop: Venture, 1994)

Hanson, John, *Leyland Lorries and Vans* (Leeds: Malvern House, 1996)

Hartley, William P, *The ABC of British Road Services* (Ian Allan, 6 edns, 1951, 1952, 1953, 1957, 1961, 1963)

Harvey, Russell, *Morris Minor light commercials* (Brimscombe Port: Tempus, 2000)

Hay's Wharf Cartage Co., *Transport Saga, 1646–1947* (1947)

Hazell, Ernest Clifford, *The Gentle Giants: an illustrated history of a family of Bristol timber hauliers, 1880–1935*, ed. Ken Griffiths and Roy Gallop (Bristol: Fiducia Press, 1997)

Heaton, Paul, *L C Lewis: heavy haulage* (Abergavenny: Heaton, 1996)

Hills, Stanley M, *Battery-Electric Vehicles* (Newnes, 1943)

Hilton, Ralph, 'Hilton Transport Services' *in* Lynn, Richard (ed), *The Entrepreneur: eight case studies* (Allen & Unwin, 1974)

Hoad, L, *One Hundred Years of Bituminous Road Binder Development* (Preston: Lanfina Bitumen, c.1998)

Holden, Bryan, *The Long Haul: the life and times of the railway horse* (F A Allen, 1985)

—— *Birmingham's Working Horses: a century of horse power on road, rail & canal* (Birmingham: Barbryn, 1989)

Holloway, J S, *Road Transport Methods and Costs in relation to Retail Co-operative Societies* (Manchester: Co-operative Union, 1931)

Hollowell, Peter G, *The Lorry Driver* (Routledge & Kegan Paul, 1968) [a study in occupational sociology]

Hooker, Charles E, *My Seventy Years with Traction Engines* (Lingfield: Oakwood, 1973)

Hoole, K, *North Eastern Railway Buses, Lorries & Autocars* (Knaresborough: Nidd Valley Narrow Gauge Rlys, 1969)

Holder, Robert W, *Taunton Cider and Langdons: a West Somerset story of industrial development* (Chichester: Phillimore, 2000)

Hudson, A, *Post Office Motor Transport* (Post Office, 1936)

Hudson, Kenneth, *The History of English China Clays: fifty years of pioneering and growth* (Newton Abbot: David & Charles, 1969)

Hughes, W J and Thomas, Joseph L, *'The Sentinel': a history of Alley & MacLellan and the Sentinel Waggon Works, vol. 1: 1875–1930* (Newton Abbot: David & Charles, 1973); Anthony R Thomas and Joseph L Thomas, *vol. 2, 1930–1980* (Worcester: Woodpecker, 1987)

Hume, John R and Moss, Michael S, *Beardmore: the history of a Scottish industrial giant.* (Heinemann, 1979)

Ignarski, Sam (ed), *The Box: an anthology celebrating 25 years of containerisation and the TT Club* (EMAP Business Communications, for TT Club, 1996)

Ingram, Arthur, *Lorries, Trucks and Vans, 1927–1973* (Poole: Blandford, 1975)

—— *London's Lorries: a pictorial review of road transport in the capital during the '50s & '60s* (Nynehead: Roundoak, 1990)

—— *Brewery Transport* [*Trucks in Britain* series] (Nynehead: Roundoak, 1991)

—— *Whitbread: 250 years of brewery transport* (Nynehead: Roundoak, 1992)

—— *The Story of Pickfords* (Nynehead: Roundoak, 1993)

Ingram, Arthur and Mustoe, Gordon, *BRS: the early years, 1948–1953* (Nynehead: Roundoak, 1999)

Institution of Mechanical Engineers, *Commercial vehicles: engineering and operation* (IMechE, 1967)

Jack, Doug, *The Volvo Truck and Bus Irvine Factory* (Nuneaton: Condie, 2000)

Janes, Allen and Sposito, Phil, *Bristol Goods Vehicles* (Bristol: authors, 1989)

Jeffreys, Rees, *The King's Highway: an historical and autobiographical record of the developments of the past sixty years* (Batchworth Press, 1949)

Jenkinson, Keith A, *Preserved Lorries* (Ian Allan, 1977)

Junner, G. Mackenzie, *The Road Transport Engineer* (Temple Press, 1957)

Kahn-Freund, Otto, *Law of Carriage by Inland Transport* (4 edns, Stevens, 1939–65)

Karrier Motors Ltd, *A Brief History of Karrier Motors Ltd* (Huddersfield, c.1963)

Kelley, Philip J, *Road Vehicles of the Great Western Railway* (Oxford: Oxford Publishing, 1973); *Great Western Road Vehicles Appendix* (1982)

Kelly, Maurice A, *The Overtype Steam Road Waggon* (Norwich: Goose, 1971)

—— *The Undertype Steam Road Waggon* (Cambridge: Goose, 1975)

Kennett, Pat, *The Foden Story* (Cambridge: Patrick Stephens, 1978)

—— *World Truck* series: 1, *ERF*; 3, *Seddon-Atkinson*; 6, *Dennis*; 8, *Scammell*; 10, *AEC*; 12, *Berliet*; 14, *Leyland* (Cambridge: Patrick Stephens, 1978–83)

Keogh, Michael, *This Haulage Life: an anthology of awful truths* (Bexley: C. S. Enterprises, 1974)

Kidner, R W, *The Steam Lorry* (2nd edn. Lingfield: Oakwood, 1956)

Klapper, C F, *British Lorries 1900–1945* (Ian Allan, 1973)

Kuipers, J F J, *A History of Commercial Vehicles of the World* (Lingfield: Oakwood, 1972)

Lane, Michael R, *The Story of the Steam Plough Works: Fowlers of Leeds* (Northgate, 1980)

—— *The Story of the Britannia Iron Works: William Marshall Sons & Co, Gainsborough, 1848–1992* (Quiller, 1993)

—— *The Story of the St Nicholas Works: a history of Charles Burrell & Sons Ltd* (Stowmarket: Unicorn, 1994)

—— *The story of the Wellington Foundry, Lincoln: a history of William Foster & Co Ltd* (Unicorn Press, 1997)

Lee, David, *Heavy Haulage and Abnormal Loads: a pictorial review* (3 vols, Nynehead: Roundoak, 1992, 1994, 1997)

Leeming, D J and Hartley, R, *Heavy Vehicle Technology* (Hutchinson, 1976 & 1981)

Leyland 90th Anniversary Committee, *Official History 1896–1986*, (Leyland, 1986)

Lowe, David, *The Dictionary of Transport and Logistics* (*Kogan Page*, 2002)

McBirnie, Glen, *Rugby Portland Cement Transport: a story of vehicles and their drivers* (Rugby: Neil Terry, 2002)

Mackie, Peter J, Simon, David and Whiteing, Anthony E, *The British Transport Industry and the European Community: a study of regulation and modal split in the long distance and international freight market* (Aldershot: Gower, 1987)

McKinstry, Sam, *Sure as the Sunrise: a history of Albion Motors* (Edinburgh: Donald, 1997)

McLachlan, Sandy, *The National Freight Buy-out* (Macmillan, 1983)

McMillan, James, *The Dunlop Story* (Weidenfeld & Nicolson, 1989)

McNamara & Co., *A Historical Review of McNamara's* (1937)

McTaggart, Tom, *Pioneers of Heavy Haulage* (Ayr: Alloway, 1985)

—— *The Big Box: England's era of steam haulage* (Ayr: Alloway, 1986)

—— *The Iron Men of the Road* (Ayr: Alloway, 1989)

Mance, Sir H. Osborne, *The Road and Rail Transport Problem* (Pitman, 1940)

Manwaring, L A (ed), *The Observer's Book of Commercial Vehicles* (Frederick Warne, [1966]); [2nd] edn, Olyslager Organisation (comp) (1971); [3rd, 4th & 5th] edns, Baldwin, Nick (comp), ([1974], 1978, 1981)

Marshall, Prince and Bishop, Denis, *Lorries, Trucks and Vans, 1897–1927* (Blandford, 1972)

Martin, Colin (comp), *Gloucestershire Goods & Service Vehicles* (Brimscombe Port: Tempus, 2000)

Matlock, Neil A, *Sentinel Diesel Lorries: a pictorial record* (Burton-on-Trent: Trent Valley, 1987)

McKinstry, S, *Sure as the Sunrise: a history of Albion Motors* (Edinburgh: John Donald, 1997)

Meadows, Tom, *Pagefield Motor Vehicles* (Wistaston: author, 1997)

Meyrick-Jones, L M and Wyatt, Horace, *Motor Traction for Business Purposes: a guide to the selection, cost of running & maintenance of commercial and public service motor vehicles* (Iliffe, 1913)

—— *Commercial Motor Road Transport* (Pitman, 1933)

Middlemiss, John L and Sawford, Eric, *William Allchin, Globe Works, Northampton* (Nuneaton: Condie, 1990)

Millar, Alan, *Truck Recognition* (Ian Allan, 1986; 2nd edn, 1997)

—— *Eddie Stobart* [*ABC* series] (Hersham: Ian Allan, 2001)

Miller, Denis, *The Illustrated Encyclopedia of Trucks and Buses* (*Quarto*, 1982; repr. Quantum, 2002)

Moye, Eric C, *Milestones along my Memory Road, 1925 to 1990s* (Chelmsford: Avalon, 1996) [driver's memoirs]

Murphy, Ted, *The Big Load: the story of a long distance heavy lorry and continental coach driver* (Foulis, 1963)

Mustoe, Gordon, *Fisher Renwick: a transport saga 1874–1972* (Nynehead: Roundoak, 1997)

Mustoe, Gordon and Ingram, Arthur, *BRS Parcels* (Nynehead: Roundoak, 2002)

Nancollis, Harold, *Foden: my life with the company* (Glossop: Venture, 1995)

Nixon, St John C, *Daimler, 1896–1946: a record of fifty years of the Daimler Company* (Foulis, c.1946)

Noble, Dudley and Junner, G. Mackenzie, *Vital to the Life of the Nation: a historical survey of the progress of Britain's motor industry from 1896 to 1946* (Society of Motor Manufacturers & Traders, 1946)

Nockolds, Harold, *Lucas: the first 100 years*: 1, *The king of the road*; 2, *The successors* (Newton Abbot: David & Charles, 1976–8)

Ó Riain, Mícheál, *On The Move: Córas Iompair Éireann 1945–1995* (Dublin: Gill & Macmillan, 1995)

Paget-Tomlinson, Edward, *The Railway Carriers: the history of Wordie & Co.* (Lavenham: Dalton, 1990)

Paterson, James, *The History and Development of Road Transport* (Pitman, 1927)

Phillimore, John, *Motor Road Transport for Commercial Purposes (liquid fuel, steam, electricity)* (Pitman, [1920]); 2nd edn, *Up-to-date Motor Road Transport....* ([1923])

Phillips, Ron and Baron, Gordon, *100 years of transport: the history of Bassetts of Tittensor 1897–1997* (Tittensor: Bassett, 1997)

Plowden, William, *The Motor Car and Politics, 1896–1970* (Bodley Head, 1971); paperback edn, *The Motor-car and Politics in Britain* (Harmondsworth: Penguin, 1973)

Post Office Vehicle Club, *Royal Mail* [*Trucks in Britain* series] (Nynehead: Roundoak, 1995)

Prescott, David, *JF&S: John Fishwick & Sons 1907–1997* (Glossop: Senior Publns, 1997)

Preston, J M, *Aveling & Porter, Ltd., Rochester* (Rochester: North Kent Books, 1987)

Pryke, Richard, *The Nationalised Industries: policies and performance since 1968* (Oxford: Robertson, 1981) [ch 7, 'The National Freight Corporation']

Rance, Eric and Williams, Don, *Can You Afford to Walk?: the history of the Hounsfield Trojan motor car* (Minster Lovell & New Yatt, Oxon: Bookmarque, 1999)

Reader, William J, *Hard Roads and Highways: SPD Limited, 1918–1968: a study in distribution* (Batsford, 1969)

Reid, Graham L and Allen, Kevin, *Nationalized Industries* (Harmondsworth: Penguin, 1970) [ch. 6 on road haulage]

Rolt, L T C, *Waterloo Ironworks: a history of Taskers of Andover, 1809–1968* (Newton Abbot: David & Charles, 1969)

Rowlands, Don, *British Railways Wagons: the first million* (Newton Abbot: David & Charles, 1985) [ch. 12, containers]

Russell, Janet, *Great Western Horse Power* (Sparkford: Oxford Publishing, 1995)

Sanders, Maurice H, *Stories of Round Timber Haulage* (Luton: Cortney, 1984)

—— *Men, Mud and Machines: more achievements in round timber haulage* (Luton: Cortney, 1987)

—— *Characters of Wood, Wurlitzer & Wesley: Maurice Sanders looks back* (Baldock: Cortney, 1990)

—— *Giants of Timber and Transport: they don't make them like that any more* (Baldock: Cortney, 1997)

—— *Earth and Tree Moving in War and Peace: 60 golden years* (2 vols, Baldock: Cortney, 1999–2000)

Sanguineti, Raffaele and Salazar, Carlo, *Iveco Story: the world of transport* (St Gallen: Norden, 1994)

Savage, Christopher I, *Inland Transport* [*History of the Second World War* series] (HMSO, 1957)

Sedgwick, Michael, *Bedford: G.M.'s British commercial* (Dalton: Watson, 1980)

Seth-Smith, Michael, *The Long Haul: a social history of the British commercial vehicle industry* (Hutchinson Benham, 1975)

Seymour, Peter J, *The Development of 8 & 10 cwt Morris Light Vans 1924–1934, with 70 & 105 cu ft Royal Mail vans* (Battle: P & B Publng, 1999)

Sharp, Clifford, *Living with the Lorry: a study of the goods vehicle in the environment* (Mansfield: Road Haulage Association and Freight Transport Association, 1973)

Sheryn, Hinton J, *An Illustrated History of Road Tankers* (Hersham: Ian Allan, 2001)

Shirley, Dick and Reid, Keith, *MIRA 1946–1996: fifty years of excellence* (Atalink Projects, for the Motor Industry Research Association, 1996)

Short, Jack, *Aspects of Freight Transport in Ireland* (Dublin: Economic & Social Research Institute, 1985)

Sibley, Brian and Sandra, *Past Glimpses of Nursling and Rownhams* (Rownhams: E J Sibley Ltd, 1988) [History of E J Sibley Ltd, fuel merchants and hauliers]

Skinner, P, *On the Move: a history of transport in Northamptonshire* (Rotary Club of Rushden Chichele, 1999

Smith, Donald J M, *A Dictionary of Horse-Drawn Vehicles* (J. A. Allen, 1988)

—— *Discovering Horse-Drawn Vehicles* (Princes Risborough: Shire, 1994)

Smith, Paul, 'The road haulage industry, 1945–79: from statutory regulation to contested terrain', *in* Wrigley, Chris (ed), *A History of British Industrial Relations, 1939–1979* (Cheltenham: Elgar, 1996)

—— *Unionization and Union Leadership: the road haulage industry* (Continuum, 2001)

Sprake, Derek, *Put Out the Flag: the story of Isle of Wight carriers 1860–1960* (Newport, IoW: Cross, 1993)

Stevens-Stratten, Seymour W, *British Lorries 1945–83* (2nd edn. Ian Allan, 1978)

—— *British Lorries 1900–1945* (Ian Allan, 1988)

—— *Light Commercial Vehicles* (Ian Allan, 1991)

—— *British Lorries 1900–1992* (Ian Allan, 1992); new edn, revised by Alan Millar, *British Lorries since 1900* (Hersham: Ian Allan, 2001)

Stevens-Stratten, Seymour W and Aldridge, W J, *Railway-owned Commercial Vehicles* (Ian Allan, 1987)

Stobart, Eddie and Nora with Davidson, Noel, *Only the Best Will Do: the Eddie Stobart story* (Belfast: Ambassador, 1998)

Storey, Richard A, *Road Haulage History Sources* (Coventry: Modern Records Centre, Univ. of Warwick, 1996)

Tate & Lyle Transport Ltd, *Pease Progress: the story of Tate & Lyle road transport* (Croydon, c.1974)

Thackray, Brian, *The A.E.C. Story*, pt 1 (Glossop: Venture, 2001)

Thomas, Alan, *Leyland Heritage* (Feltham: Temple, 1984)

—— *Wreck and Recovery: vehicles, emergency equipment, rescue techniques* (Wellingborough: Patrick Stephens, 1987)

Thomas, Alan and Aldridge, John, *Licensed to Carry: Leyland's 80 years in commercial transport* (IPC Transport Press, 1976)

Thomas, Joseph L and Thomas, Anthony R, *An Album of 'Sentinel' Works Photographs, 1: Standards & Supers* (Worcester: Woodpecker, 1992)

Thompson, F M L, *Victorian England: the horse-drawn society* (Bedford College, 1970)

Thompson, John, *Horse-drawn Trade Vehicles: a source book* (2nd edn, Fleet: author, 1980)

—— *Horse-drawn Heavy Goods Vehicles: a source book* (2nd edn, Fleet: author, 1980)

Thompson, Peter, *Sharing the Success: the story of NFC* (Collins, 1990)

Tilling, John, *Kings of the Highway* (Hutchinson, 1957) [Thomas Tilling Ltd, 1847–1930]

Tomkins, Eric, *The History of the Pneumatic Tyre* (Eastland, for Dunlop Archive Project, 1981)

Townsin, Alan, *AEC* (Shepperton: Ian Allan, 1998)

—— *Thornycroft* (Hersham: Ian Allan, 2001)

Townsin, Alan and Goulding, Brian, *80 years of AEC* (Glossop: Senior, 1992)

Tritton, Paul, *Wincheap Memories: a pictorial history of a corner of Canterbury* (Canterbury: Brett, 1996) [Robert Brett & Sons Ltd, haulage contractors and aggregate suppliers]

Tuck, Bob, *Mammoth Trucks: modern day heavy, heavy haulage* (Osprey, 1985)

—— *Hauling Heavyweights: moving extra-large loads by road* (Wellingborough: Stephens, 1986)

—— *Move it!: an illustrated history of heavy haulage vehicles at work* (Wellingborough: Stephens, 1987)

—— *Carrying Cargo: an illustrated history of road haulage* (Wellingborough: Stephens, 1989)

—— *Classic Hauliers* (2 vols, Croydon: Fitzjames, 1989–91) [short histories of 30 haulage companies]

—— *Robson's: the history of the famous name in distribution* (Nynehead: Roundoak, 1990)

—— *The Golden Days of Heavy Haulage* (Nynehead: author/Roundoak, 1992)

—— *A Road Transport Heritage* (3 vols, Yarm: author, 1993–5) [pictorial histories of 127 haulage fleets]

—— *100 years of Heavy Haulage* (Yarm: author, 1996)

—— *King of the Road: a personal selection of classic lorries of yesterday and super trucks of today* (Yarm: author, 1999)

Tuckett, Angela, *The Scottish Carter: the history of the Scottish Horse and Motormen's Association 1898–1964* (Allen & Unwin, 1967)

Turnbull, Gerard L, *Traffic and Transport: an economic history of Pickfords* (Allen & Unwin, 1979)

Turner, Graham, *The Leyland Papers* (Eyre & Spotiswoode, 1971)

Twells, H N and Bourne, T W, *A Pictorial Record of LMS Road Vehicles* (Poole: Oxford Publishing, 1983)

Twelvetrees, Richard and Squire, Pepys, *Why Dennis — and how* (Guildford: Dennis Bros, 1945)

Van den Burg, G, *Containerisation and Other Unit Transport* (Hutchinson Benham, 1975)

Vanderveen, Bart H (ed), *Scammell Vehicles* (Warne, 1971; repr. Nynehead: Roundoak, 1990)

Vauxhall Motors Ltd, *You See Them Everywhere: a history of Bedford commercial vehicles since 1931* (Luton, 1978)

Waite, Mick, *Recovery Vehicles* (Nynehead: Roundoak, 1998)

Walker, Charlie G, *Welcome to my World* [Pen Press, 2000] [founder of the haulage firm, Walkers of Wakefield]

Walker, Gilbert, *Road and Rail: an enquiry into the economics of competition and state control* (2 edns, Allen & Unwin, 1942, 1947)

Walker, Gilbert and Savage, C I, 'Inland carriage by road and rail' *in* Burn, Duncan (ed), *The Structure of British Industry* (Cambridge Univ. Press, 1958)

Walker, N, *A–Z of British Coachbuilders, 1919–1960* (Bideford: Bay View Books, 1997)

Wallis-Taylor, A J, *Motor Vehicles for Business Purposes: a practical handbook for those interested in the transport of passengers and goods* (Crosby Lockwood, 1905)

Warburton, David J, *ABC of Commercial Vehicles* (Ian Allan, 1953; repr. 2001)

—— *ABC of British Lorries* (Ian Allan, 3 edns, 1954, 1955, 1956 (by E J Smith))

Wardroper, John, *Juggernaut* (Temple Smith, 1981) [the case of the anti-road lobbyists]

Watson, Nigel, *Excellence by Caring: the continuing story of Silcock Express* (James & James, 1991)

—— *The Story of Christian Salvesen, 1846–1996* (James & James, 1996)

—— *Swift: the story of a transport business* (James & James, 1997)

Weatherley, Brian (ed), *The ERF story* (Commercial Motor, c.1992

Wentworth, Felix R L (ed), *Physical Distribution Management* (Gower Press, 1970); 2nd edn, *Handbook of Physical Distribution Management* (1976)

Wheeler, C, *The Development of Mechanical Transport in the GPO* (Watford: Bushey Artists & Craftsmen Assocn, 1934)

White, L G, *Road Transport in War-time: an explanation of the emergency organisation of road transport* (Jordan, 1939)

Whitehead, R A, *Wallis & Steevens: a history* (Farnham: Road Locomotive Society, 1983)

—— *Jesse Ellis and the Maidstone Wagons: an account of a pioneer builder of steam road wagons* (Tonbridge: author, 1992)

—— *Garrett Wagons*: 1, *Pioneers & overtypes*; 2, *Undertypes*; 3, *Electrics & motors* (Tonbridge: author, 1994–6)

—— *Garrett Traction & Ploughing Engines* (Tonbridge: author, 1997)

—— *Garrett Steam Tractors & Rollers* (Tonbridge: author, 1999)

Wood, J, *The Bean* (Princes Risborough: Shire, 2001)

Woodhams, John, *Old Lorries* (Princes Risborough: Shire, 1985)

Wooding, Harry, *Liverpool's Working Horses* (Liverpool: Print Origination, 1991)

Wright, Colin, *Trucks in Britain, 1: The Eight Wheelers* (Skipton: Wyvern, 1983)

—— *Trucks in Britain, 5: Tankers* (Skipton: Wyvern, 1986)

—— *Trucks in Britain, 6: Post Office stores and telephone vehicles* (Skipton: Wyvern, 1987)

—— *Trucks in Britain: Articulated Lorries* (Skipton: Wyvern, 1989)

—— *Trucks of the Eighties* (Clevedon: Channel View Publns, 1994)

Wyatt, Horace, *Motor Transports in War* (Hodder & Stoughton, 1914)

Wynn, John, *Wynns: the first 100 years* (Abergavenny: Heaton, 1995)

—— *Wynns: the last 20 years* (Abergavenny: Heaton, 1996)

Government Publications (in date order)

Local Government Board, Departmental Committee on Motor Cars, *Report...* (2 vols, HMSO, 1904, Cd 2069–70)

Royal Commission on Motor Cars, *Report of the Royal Commission on Motor Cars* (2 vols, HMSO, 1906, Cd 3080–81)

Select Committee on Motor Traffic, *Report...* (5 vols, HMSO, 1913)

Ministry of Transport, Departmental Committee on Taxation and Regulation of Road Vehicles in Great Britain and Ireland, *Interim Report*; *Second Interim Report*; and *Third Interim Report* (HMSO, 1920, 1922, 1924)

Ministry of Transport, *Reports of the Committee on Road Conveyance of Goods by Railway Companies* (HMSO, 1921, Cmd 1228)

Ministry of Transport, *Draft Road Traffic Bill* (HMSO, 1927) [what was later called a White Paper]

Royal Commission on Transport, *Final Report: the co-ordination and development of transport* (HMSO, 1931, Cmd 3751)

Ministry of Transport, *Royal Commission on Transport: communications received from certain organisations in response to the Ministry of Transport's request for their observations on the conclusions and recommendations of the final report of the Royal Commission on Transport* (HMSO, 1932)

Ministry of Transport, *Report of the Conference on Rail and Road Transport, 29th July, 1932* (HMSO, 1932) [Salter Conference]

Ministry of Labour and Ministry of Transport, *Report of the Committee on the Regulation of Wages and Conditions of Service in the Road Motor Transport Industry (Goods)* (HMSO, 1937, Cmd 5440)

Ministry of Transport, Transport Advisory Council, *Report on Service and Rates* (HMSO, 1937)

Ministry of Transport, *Organisation of Road Transport for a Defence Emergency: goods vehicles* (HMSO, 1939)

Transport Arbitration Tribunal, *Transport Act, 1947: Road Haulage Cases* (HMSO, 1950–5)

Ministry of Transport, *Transport Policy* (HMSO, 1952, Cmd 8538) [White Paper on de-nationalisation of road haulage]

Ministry of Transport, *Reorganisation of the Nationalised Transport Undertakings* (HMSO, 1960, Cmnd 1248) [White Paper]

Ministry of Transport, *Carriers' Licensing* (HMSO, 1965) [Geddes report]

Ministry of Transport, *Transport Policy* (HMSO, 1966, Cmnd 3057) [White Paper]

Ministry of Transport, *The Transport of Freight* (HMSO, 1967, Cmnd 3470) [White Paper]

National Freight Corporation, *Report on Organisation* (HMSO, 1969)

Bayliss, B T and Edwards, S L, *Industrial Demand for Transport* (HMSO for Ministry of Transport, 1970)

Edwards, S L and Bayliss, B T, *Operating Costs in Road Freight Transport: a study of the costs of operating road goods vehicle fleets and of the performance and costs of running vehicles of different types and sizes* (Dept of Environment, c.1971)

Freight Integration Council, *First Report* and *Second Report* (HMSO, 1970, 1973)

Bayliss, Brian T, *The Small Firm in the Road Haulage Industry* (HMSO for Committee of Inquiry on Small Firms, 1971)

Department of the Environment, *Report of the Working Party on Parking of Lorries.* (HMSO, 1971)

Edwards, S L and Bayliss, B T, *Operating Costs in Road Freight Transport: a study of the costs of operating road goods vehicle fleets and of the performance and costs of running vehicles of different types and sizes* (Dept of Environment, 1971)

National Board for Prices & Incomes, *Costs, Charges and Productivity of the National Freight Corporation* (HMSO, 1971)

Bayliss, Brian T, *The Road Haulage Industry since 1968* (HMSO for Department of the Environment, 1973)

D E A Pettit, *Lorries and the World we Live In* (HMSO for Department of the Environment, 1973)

Department of the Environment, *Transport Policy: a consultation document* (HMSO, 1976)

Department of Transport, *Transport Policy* (HMSO, 1977, Cmnd 6836) [White Paper]

Department of Transport, *Road Haulage Operators' Licensing: report of the independent committee of inquiry. Chairman: Professor Christopher Foster* (HMSO, 1978)

Department of Transport and Department of Prices & Consumer Protection, *Report of the Committee of Inquiry into Motorway Service Areas* (HMSO, 1978)

Price Commission, *The Road Haulage Industry* (HMSO, 1978)

Armitage, Arthur, *Inquiry into Lorries, People and the Environment* (HMSO, 1980)

Department of Transport, *Heavier Lorries for Combined Road/Rail Transport: a consultation document* (1993)

Department of Transport, *Transport — the way forward: the Government's response to the transport debate* (HMSO, 1996, CM 3234)

Department of the Environment, Transport & the Regions, *A New Deal for Transport: better for everyone* (HMSO, 1998, Cm 3950) [White paper]

Trade and Professional Journals

Automobile Commercial Vehicle Review (1903–5); *Industrial Motor Review* (1905–8)

Carriage Builders' Journal (1898–1902); *Automobile & Carriage Builders' Journal* (1902–49); *Motor Body* (1950–63); *Automotive Body Engineering* (1963–5); *Motor Body* (1965–7)

Commercial Motor (1905–)

CMUA Journal (1927–40); *Commercial Vehicle Users' Journal* (1941–55); *Commercial Vehicles* (1955–73)

Distribution (1988–)

The Electric Vehicle (1914–29); *Electric Vehicles & Batteries* (1930–6); *Electric Vehicles* (1936–52)

Focus (1982–7); *Focus on Logistics & Distribution Management* (1987–93); *Logistics Focus* (1993–9); *Logistics and Transport Focus* (1999–)

Freight (1969–) [Freight Transport Association]

Freight Management (1966–83); *Freight Management & Distribution Today* (1986–91); *Freight Management International* (1991–2000)

Headlight (1946–99)

Industrial Road Transport (1966–8) [Traders Road Transport Association]

Modern Transport (1919–80)

Motor Traction (1905–20) [previously the 'Industrial Vehicle Section' of *Autocar*]; *Motor Transport* (1921–)

Roadway (1944–) [Road Haulage Association]

Traffic Administrator (1974–9); *Transport Management* (1979–) [Institute of Traffic/Transport Administration]

Transport Journal / Transport Managers Journal (1953–) [Institute of Transport Management from 1977]

Transport Management (1927–68)

Truck (1974–)

Truck & Driver (1984–)

Trucking International (1983–)

World's Carriers & Contractors' Review (1904–63)

Vehicle Manufacturers' House Journals

ADC / AEC / ACV / AEC Gazette (1926–68)

BMC User (1965–9)

Challenge [Ford trucks]

Chassis: the Journal of ERF Limited (1962–63)

Chevrolet Magazine (1930–1); *Chevrolet & Bedford Magazine* (1931–2); *Bedford Transport Magazine* (1932–77)

Foden News (–1977)

Inside Lane (1999?–) [Volvo Truck & Bus Ltd]

Karrier Gazette (1926–34)

LDV Magazine

Leyland News (1964–69); *Leyland Truck & Bus Times* (1969–72)

Leyland Journal (1935–39, 1946–70)

Payload: Austin Commercial Vehicle Magazine (1958–64)

Rangeability (1963–6); *The Atkinson* (1966–71); *The Seddon Atkinson Magazine* (1971–2)

Sentinel News (1916–21); *Sentinel Transport News* (1921–34)

Sidelights (1956–68) [BMC Drivers' Club]

Transport Efficiency (1934–67) [Morris Commercial Cars]

Vauxhall Bedford News (1932–58)

Transport Operators' House Journals

British Road Services Magazine (1950–68); *Hotline* (1969–71); *Freightway* (1970–73)

The Driving Mirror (1946–49) [Hay's Wharf Cartage]

The Window Card (1927–46) [Carter Paterson]

Historical, Enthusiast and Preservation Journals

Classic & Vintage Commercials (1995–)

Classic Van & Pick-up (2000–)

CVRTC News (1966–) [Commercial Vehicle & Road Transport Club]

Historic Commercial News (1985–) [Historic Commercial Vehicle Society]

Leyland Society Journal (1999–)

Leyland Torque (1999–) [Leyland Society]

Post Horn (1967–) [Post Office Vehicle Club]

Roads & Road Transport History Conference/Association Newsletter (1991–)

Sentinel Drivers Club Newsletter (1987–93); *Sentinel Transport News* (1994–)

Vintage Commercial (1962); *Old Motor* (1963); *Old Motor & Vintage Commercial* (1963–6); *Old Motor* (1966–79)

Vintage Commercial Vehicle Magazine (1984–96); *Vintage Commercial Vehicles* (1996–2001); *Heritage Commercials* (2002–)

Vintage Roadscene (1984–)